NATIVE AMERICAN
FOLKLORE, 1879-1979

NATIVE AMERICAN FOLKLORE, 1879-1979

An Annotated Bibliography

Compiled by

William M. Clements   Frances M. Malpezzi

SWALLOW PRESS
• Athens Ohio • London • Chicago •

Swallow Press books are published by
Ohio University Press, Athens, Ohio 45701

Library of Congress Cataloging in Publication Data

Clements, William M., 1945-
   Native American folklore, 1879-1979.
   Includes indexes.
   1. Indians of North America—-Folklore—Bibliography.
2. Folklore—North America—bibliography.   I. Malpezzi,
Frances M., 1946-   . II. Title.
Z1209.C57   1984   016.398'08997073   83-6672
[E98.F6]
ISBN 0-8040-0831-0

To

J. T. Clements

1907–1981

CONTENTS

IV. MIDWEST

V. PLAINS

INTRODUCTION

The year 1879 marks the nativity of Native American studies. Although many serious students of Native American cultures had pursued their interests both in the field and in the library throughout the nineteenth century and even earlier, 1879 saw two events that focused such interests in an organized, scientific direction. One event was the founding of the Bureau of Ethnology of the Smithsonian Institution (BAE) under the directorship of John Wesley Powell, an agency delegated to sponsor archeological and ethnological researches in the Americas. The other event in 1879 was Frank Hamilton Cushing's arrival at Zuni Pueblo in New Mexico. Sponsored in part by the BAE, Cushing's visit laid the foundation for the participant observation method of field research which has been so productive for ethnologists studying Native Americans. (See item 3866 in the bibliography for Cushing's account of his experiences at Zuni.)

The interests of the early researchers for the BAE and of their contemporaries in the private sector were varied, but among the most important was a concern with the rich traditions of oral literature which characterized most Native American cultures. This interest paralleled similar research emphases among British and Continental students of what William J. Thomas had denominated "folklore" some thirty years before the BAE was organized. By 1900 the Americanists had collected a great deal of Native American oral literature to add to the material that had been more casually collected earlier during the eighteenth and nineteenth centuries. This interest in Native American folklore continued into the twentieth century as anthropologists were joined by historians, musicologists, literary critics, folklorists, popularizers, and other enthusiasts in the collection, publication, and analysis of the myths, legends, folktales, songs, and other folklore forms of Native Americans. By 1979, a century after the birth of Native American studies, the mass of published material was staggering. It was also relatively inaccessible to the general student, since much of it appeared in out-of-the-way places and was of uneven quality. A clear need for a guide to published sources in Native American folklore was evident. The purpose of this work is to serve as that guide.

Scope of the Bibliography

Defining "folklore" is a thorny problem, as the many attempts to do so demonstrate. The twenty-one distinct definitions of the term in the *Funk and Wagnalls Standard Dictionary of Folklore, Mythology and Legend* (42; vol. 1, pp. 398–403) have served as a useful reminder of the complexity of folklore and of the varied emphases which its students have placed upon it. For the purposes of this bibliography, we have combined the widely accepted anthropological definition of the term, particularly in reference to nonliterate cultures, with its current usage in behavioral folkloristics. Thus, we view "folklore" as verbal art and endorse William Bascom's idea that the term covers "myths, legends, tales, proverbs, riddles, the texts of ballads and songs, and other forms of lesser importance" (378; p. 284). We also view "folklore" as the performance of verbal art, following the lead articulated by Dan Ben-Amos and other contemporary folklorists (for example, see Ben-Amos' definition of the term in 149; pp. 3–15). Our view of folklore as the "texts and performances of verbal art" has required us to include material that some students of Native American cultures would not see as "folklore." For instance, some might argue that the esoteric songs and chants of dance societies are more "elite" than "folk," since only a few specialists know and perform them. And some might suggest that oration texts lack the traditional content that for some students is the essence of folklore. We have taken the position that although such materials lack qualities which are often characteristic of folklore, their status as oral literature makes them of interest to folklorists. Moreover, we have included material on the settings for folklore performance such as studies of the music of Native American songs and descriptions of ceremonial contexts for verbal art. The result is that this bibliography includes books and articles which treat oral narratives, songs, chants, prayers, formulas, orations, proverbs, riddles, word play, music, dances, games, and ceremonials. Our policy has been one of liberality: To include materials which might appear irrelevant seems preferable to excluding something that is possibly relevant.

Our concern is with the verbal art of all Native Americans who have traditionally resided north of Mexico. We have attempted a thorough coverage of books and articles in English published during the century following the organization of the BAE. We have also included many pre-1879 works, but do not pretend that our coverage of that early literature is anywhere near complete. We have omitted three major categories of publications: highly ephemeral sources such as newspaper articles, books and articles aimed at children, and reviews. Some children's works, though, may appear in the bibliography if they are written by an important figure in Native American studies or if the intended audience seems to include more than children. Again, we have tried to be inclusive when dealing with doubtful works and realize that in doing so we may occasionally have entered children's material and ephemeral documents in our listings.

Organization of the Bibliography

For the most part, articles and books are organized according to tribal groups, which in turn are organized according to culture areas. Usually our authority for tribal designations (and spellings) and for culture areas has been the *Ethnographic Bibliography of North America* (49). In several cases, though, the nature of the literature has dictated departures from that model. For instance, we use the term "Sioux" as a tribal name instead of employing the more specific and accurate designations Santee, Teton, and Yankton. Most of the authors represented in the Sioux section (2511–2663) did not distinguish precisely which groups of specific Siouans they were treating. Where possible the specific names have been incorporated into the Subject Index for the bibliography. We have followed a similar generalizing procedure in treating the Apache as a single group (instead of providing separate sections for the Chiricahua, Jicarilla, Lipan, and Mescalero) and in putting together all Eskimo material into the general Arctic culture area section.

To introduce the culture area and tribal sections, we begin with a general section of entries which includes works that survey a broad scope of Native American folklore or those which treat the folklore of several tribal groups. We have also handled works which treat several groups by cross-listing their index numbers. Our general section, which includes collections of folklore as well as theoretical and reference works, is arranged primarily according to genre of folklore treated.

Each listing in the bibliography begins with an index number. We then provide the name of the author(s), the title of the book or article, and publication information. Periodical and serial titles are abbreviated, and a key to those abbreviations has been provided. We have tried to adhere as closely as possible to the bibliography format prescribed by *The MLA Handbook*.

Our annotations, though primarily descriptive, sometimes imply evaluative judgments. For folklore collections, for instance, we provide inventories of the collected material (number and genres of folklore texts) and the date of collection, when available. We also list the critical apparati accompanying the texts and point out when none has been provided in the work. We believe that at a bare minimum a collection of folklore should contain verbatim texts and some explanatory and comparative notes. When our annotation indicates that a work does not contain such material, we are passing judgment on the work. In treating theoretical and descriptive works, our annotations seldom evaluate. Space limitations have simply not allowed us first to summarize an author's argument and then to criticize it.

The indexes to the bibliography allow the location of items by author (or editor or translator) and by subject. Topics listed in the Subject Index, though, are not meant to be exhaustive. For example, the listings for "Peyotism" do not include every reference to peyote use in the books and articles, but cover every book and article in the bibliography in which the verbal art associated with peyote use is a major topic. The general organization and the indexes allow any book or article in the bibliography to be located in three ways: by culture area and tribal group, by author or editor or translator, and by subject.

Conclusions

Although this work, as a research tool designed for use by serious students of Native American culture, is not meant to theorize, several conclusions about Native American folklore studies have emerged from our research. One is that in terms of volume the study of Native American folklore has accomplished a great deal. The almost 5500 items listed here suggest substantial interest in the material, an interest that shows no signs of abating in the last quarter of the twentieth century. Another conclusion is that this interest has come from a variety of sources. It has not been confined to anthropologists and folklorists, but has been touched on by students in most disciplines in the social sciences and humanities as well as by the purveyors of popular culture. A glance through the titles of the c. 390 periodicals and serials in our List of Abbreviations reveals the diverse nature of the sources in which Native American folklore has been published. We can also conclude that certain aspects of Native American folklore and its contexts have particularly attracted the imaginations of researchers at various time periods. For example, interest in Native American oratory was pronounced in the nineteenth century, concern with especially "exotic" rituals such as the Hopi Snake Dance marked early work in this century, and studies of the Native American Trickster have been particularly popular in recent decades. An interesting research question would be to ask why certain interests predominated at certain times. A final conclusion is that though much has been done in Native American folklore studies, much remains to be done. The relative lack of theoretical work is amazing, especially in light of the vast amount of collected material available. We hope that researchers who use this bibliography will spot some of the theoretical gaps and direct their efforts toward filling them.

Acknowledgments

We have incurred many debts in the eighteen months spent collecting material for this bibliography. We are most obliged to the staffs of the ten libraries at which we worked: Dean B. Ellis Library, Arkansas State University; Arkansas State University Museum Library; John Wesley Powell Library of Anthropology, Smithsonian Institution; West Virginia University Library; Doheny Library, University of Southern California; Southwest Museum Library; Texas Tech University Library; Perry-Castaneda Library, The University of Texas at Austin; Brister Library, Memphis State University; and Shelby County (Tennessee) Public Library. We also wish to thank the following individuals who provided us with intellectual and physical comfort during our research: T. J. and Dorothy Clements, Leah Johnson, Timothy and Julia Johnson, and Albina Malpezzi. Finally, we acknowledge financial support from the Arkansas State University Faculty Research Committee, which provided us with funds to offset some travel expenses.

ABBREVIATIONS

The following abbreviations are used for periodicals and serials.
Also, "Native American" is abbreviated as NA and "Euro-American"
as EA in the annotations.

A	*Anthropos*
AA	*American Anthropologist*
A&A	*Art and Archaeology*
AAA	*Annals of Archeology and Anthropology*
AAAPSS	*Annals of the American Academy of Political and Social Science*
AABN	*American Architect and Building News*
AAn	*American Antiquity*
AAOJ	*American Antiquarian and Oriental Journal*
AAr	*American Artist*
AArc	*Acta Arctica*
Aca	*Acadiensis*
ACQR	*American Catholic Quarterly Review*
AE	*American Ethnologist*
AEPPM	*Archaeological and Ethnological Papers of the Peabody Museum*
Aff	*Affword*
AFFL	*American Forests and Forest Life*
AFSBSS	*American Folklore Society Bibliographic and Special Series*
AG	*Alaska Geographic*
AH	*American Heritage*
AHQ	*Arkansas Historical Quarterly*
AHR	*Alberta Historical Review*
AI	*American Imago*
AiA	*Art in America*
AIAM	*American Indian Art Magazine*
AICRJ	*American Indian Culture and Research Journal*
AIFA	*Archives of the International Folk-Lore Association*
AIn	*American Indian*
AIQ	*American Indian Quarterly*
AJ	*Appalachian Journal*
AJP	*American Journal of Psychology*
AJS	*American Journal of Sociology*
AJT	*American Journal of Theology*
AL	*American Libraries*
AM	*American Mercury*
Ame	*America*
AMJ	*American Museum Journal*
AmN	*American Naturalist*
Ams	*Americas*
An	*Anthropologica*
AnI	*Annals of Iowa*
AnL	*Anthropological Linguistics*
AnQ	*Anthropological Quarterly*
Ant	*Anthropology*
AP	*Anthropological Papers (Bureau of American Ethnology)*

APAMNH	*Anthropological Papers of the American Museum of Natural History*
ApJ	*Appleton's Journal*
APUAK	*Anthropological Papers of the University of Alaska*
APUAZ	*Anthropological Papers of the University of Arizona*
APUNM	*Anthropological Papers of the University of New Mexico*
APUPM	*Anthropological Papers of the University of Pennsylvania Museum* \
APUU	*Anthropological Papers of the University of Utah*
AQ	*American Quarterly*
ArA	*Arctic Anthropology*
ARBAE	*Annual Report of the Bureau of American Ethnology*
Arc	*Arctic*
ArQ	*Arizona Quarterly*
ARR	*American Review of Reviews*
ARSI	*Annual Report of the Smithsonian Institution*
AS	*American Speech*
Asia	*Asia and the Americas*
ASR	*American-Scandinavian Review*
ASTCB	*Arizona State Teachers College Bulletin*
AtM	*Atlantic Monthly*
Au	*Audubon*
AW	*American West*
AWR	*American Whig Review*
B	*Beaver*
BAEB	*Bureau of American Ethnology Bulletin*
BAMNH	*Bulletin of the American Museum of Natural History*
Be	*The Bellman*
Bl	*Blackwood's*
BMNA	*Bulletin of the Museum of Northern Arizona*
BMNCA	*Bulletin of the Museum of Navajo Ceremonial Art*
Bo	*The Bookman*
BPBMB	*Bernice P. Bishop Museum Bulletin*
BPMCM	*Bulletin of the Public Museum of the City of Milwaukee*
BRH	*Bulletin of Research in the Humanities*
BSHS	*Bulletin of the Spokane Historical Society*
BUK-HS	*Bulletin of the University of Kansas, Humanistic Studies*
BZSSD	*Bulletin of the Zoological Society of San Diego*
C	*Collier's*
CA	*Current Anthropology*
Cal	*The Californian*
CaM	*Canadian Magazine*
CC	*Cross Currents*
CCC	*College Composition and Communication*
CCP-LS	*Colorado College Publications, Language Series*
CE	*College English*
Cent	*Century Illustrated Monthly Magazine*
CF	*Canadian Forum*
CFQ	*California Folklore Quarterly*
CGJ	*Canadian Geographical Journal*
CGSMB	*Canadian Geological Survey Museum Bulletin*
Ch	*The Chautauquan*
ChJ	*Chambers's Journal*
ChrC	*Christian Century*
CI	*The Canadian Indian*
CJ	*Classical Journal*

CJL	Canadian Journal of Linguistics
CM	Cornhill Magazine
CMAI	Contributions from the Museum of the American Indian, Heye Foundation
CMHS	Collections of the Minnesota Historical Society
CNAE	Contributions to North American Ethnology
CO	Chronicles of Oklahoma
Con	Conservationist
Cos	The Cosmopolitan
CQ	Colorado Quarterly
Cr	The Craftsman
CRAS	Canadian Review of American Studies
CSHSND	Collections of the State Historical Society of North Dakota
CSHSSD	Collections of the State Historical Society of South Dakota
CUAAS	Catholic University of America Anthropology Series
CUB	Catholic University Bulletin
CUCA	Columbia University Contributions to Anthropology
CuH	Current History
CW	Catholic World
D	Diogenes
DaR	Dalhousie Review
Dd	Daedalus
De	The Delineator
Di	The Dial
DJA	Davidson Journal of Anthropology
DM	Dance Magazine
DR	The Drama Review
DWM	DeLestry's Western Magazine
E	Ethos
Eh	Ethnohistory
EJ	English Journal
Em	Ethnomusicology
En	Ethnos
EP	El Palacio
ErJ	Eranos-Jahrbuch
Esk	The Eskimo
Eth	Ethnology
Etu	The Etude
Ev	Everybody's Magazine
F	Folklore (Great Britain)
FA	Folklore Annual (University of Texas)
FFBSS	Folklore Forum Bibliographic and Special Series
FFC	Folklore Fellows Communications
FL	The Folk-Lorist
FLR	Folk-Lore Record
FMNH-DAL	Field Museum of Natural History, Department of Anthropology Leaflet
Fo	The Forum
FR	Fortnightly Review
G	Genre
Gal	Galaxy
GBM	Golden Book Magazine
GH	Good Housekeeping
GR	Georgia Review
GS	The Great Southwest
H	Harper's (Monthly)

HB	House Beautiful
HF	Hoosier Folklore
HM&NQ	Historical Magazine & Notes and Queries
Ho	Horizon
HR	History of Religions
HT	History Today
HTR	Harvard Theological Review
HuR	Hudson Review
HW	Harper's Weekly
Hy	Hygeia
IA&VE	Industrial Arts and Vocational Education
IAE	Internationales Archiv Für Ethnographie
ICA	International Congress of Americanists
IH	Indian Historian
IHS-PRS	Indiana Historical Society Prehistory Research Series
IJAL	International Journal of American Linguistics
IJAL-NATS	International Journal of American Linguistics, Native American Texts Series
IN	Indian Notes
IN&M	Indian Notes and Monographs
Ind	The Independent
Int	Intellect
IQ	International Quarterly
IUPAL	Indiana University Publications in Anthropology and Linguistics
IW	Indians at Work
JAEA	Journal of American Ethnology and Archaeology
JAF	Journal of American Folklore
JAIGBI	Journal of the Anthropological Institute of Great Britain and Ireland
JAMS	Journal of the American Musicological Society
JAR	Journal of Anthropological Research
JCS	Journal of Cherokee Studies
JES	Journal of Ethnic Studies
JFI	Journal of the Folklore Institute
JHUSHPS	Johns Hopkins University Studies in Historical and Political Science
JIFMC	Journal of the International Folk Musical Council
JPC	Journal of Popular Culture
JR	Journal of Reading
JSA	Journal de la Societe des Americanistes
JW	Journal of the West
JWAS	Journal of the Washington Academy of Sciences
JWIRI	Journal of the Wisconsin Indian Research Institute
K	Knickerbocker
KF	Keystone Folklore
KFR	Kentucky Folklore Record
Ki	The Kiva
L	Life
La	Language
LAg	Living Age
LD	Literary Digest
LH	Leisure Hour
Lin	Linguistics
LJ	Library Journal
LM	Lippincott's Monthly
Lo	Look
LS	Land of Sunshine

M	*Masterkey*
MA	*Michigan Academician*
MAAA	*Memoirs of the American Anthropological Association*
Mac	*Macleans*
MAES	*Memoirs of the American Ethnological Society*
MAFS	*Memoirs of the American Folklore Society*
MAH	*Magazine of American History*
MAMNH	*Memoirs of the American Museum of Natural History*
Man	*Man*
MAPS	*Memoirs of the American Philosophical Society*
Me	*The Mentor*
MF	*Mexican Folkways*
MFR	*Mississippi Folklore Register*
MH	*Magazine of History*
MHM	*Michigan History Magazine*
MIJAL	*Memoirs of the International Journal of American Linguistics*
MiQ	*Midwest Quarterly*
MnH	*Minnesota History*
MNMNA	*Museum Notes, Museum of Northern Arizona*
MNMRR	*Museum of New Mexico Research Records*
Mo	*The Month*
MonAES	*Monographs of the American Ethnological Society*
MPMB	*Milwaukee Public Museum Bulletin*
MQ	*Musical Quarterly*
MRW	*Missionary Review of the World*
Mu	*Music*
MuA	*Musical America*
Mus	*The Musician*
MWF	*Midwest Folklore*
MWH	*Magazine of Western History*
N	*The Nation*
Na	*Nature*
Nam	*Names*
NAR	*North American Review*
NC	*Nineteenth Century and After*
NCF	*North Carolina Folklore Journal*
NCW	*New Catholic World*
NEM	*New England Magazine*
NEQ	*New England Quarterly*
NF	*Northeast Folklore*
NG	*National Geographic*
NH	*Natural History*
NLH	*New Literary History*
NM	*Nature Magazine*
NMA	*New Mexico Anthropologist*
NMCB	*National Museums of Canada Bulletin*
NMFR	*New Mexico Folklore Record*
NMHR	*New Mexico Historical Review*
NMMCPE	*National Museum of Man of Canada Publications in Ethnology*
NMQ	*New Mexico Quarterly*
NOQ	*Northwest Ohio Quarterly*
NR	*National Republic*
NRep	*New Republic*
NW	*National Wildlife*

NWR	Northwest Review
NWS	Northwest Science
NY	The New Yorker
NYFQ	New York Folklore Quarterly
NYH	New York History
NYSEDB	New York State Educational Department Bulletin
NYSMB	New York State Museum Bulletin
NYTM	New York Times Magazine
O	Outlook
OC	The Open Court
OCMAUM	Occasional Contributions from the Museum of Anthropology of the University of Michigan
OHQ	Oregon Historical Quarterly
OM	Overland Monthly
OSF	Old Santa Fe
OT	The Olden Time
Ou	Outing
OW	Out West
P	Parabola
PA	Pioneer America
PAAS	Proceedings of the American Antiquarian Society
PAES	Publications of the American Ethnological Society
PAHA	Publications of the Arkansas Historical Association
Pal	Palimpsest
PAPS	Proceedings of the American Philosophical Society
PDCIS	Proceedings of the Delaware County Institute of Science
PFCM-AS	Publications of the Field Columbian Museum, Anthropological Series
PFF	Publications of the Folklore Foundation (Vassar College)
PIAS	Proceedings of the Indiana Academy of Science
PL	Poet-Lore
PlA	Plains Anthropologist
Plat	Plateau
PM	Primitive Man
PMASAL	Publications of the Michigan Academy of Sciences, Arts, and Letters
PMHB	Pennsylvania Magazine of History and Biography
PMLA	Publications of the Modern Language Association
Po	Poetry
PPAS	Publications of the Philadelphia Anthropological Society
PPM	Papers of the Peabody Museum
PQ	Philological Quarterly
PS	Prairie Schooner
PSM	Popular Science Monthly
PSWE	Papers of the Southwest Expedition (Philips Academy)
PT	Psychology Today
PTFS	Publications of the Texas Folklore Society
PTRSC	Proceedings and Transactions of the Royal Society of Canada
Pu	Putnam's Monthly and the Reader
QJS	Quarterly Journal of Speech
QQ	Queen's Quarterly
Ram	Ramparts
RCAP	Report of the Canadian Arctic Expedition, 1913–18
Rec	Recreation
Rep	The Reporter
RR	Romanic Review

RS	Research Studies (Washington State University)
RUSNM	Report of the United States National Museum
S	Science
SAM	School Arts Magazine
SAQ	South Atlantic Quarterly
ScA	Scientific American
SCK	Smithsonian Contributions to Knowledge
ScM	Scientific Monthly
Scr	Scribners
ScT	Scholastic Teacher
SD	Science Digest
SDSCB	South Dakota State College Bulletin
SE	Social Education
SEP	Saturday Evening Post
SeR	Sewanee Review
SFQ	Southern Folklore Quarterly
SIS	Southern Indian Studies
SJA	Southwestern Journal of Anthropology
SLM	Southern Literary Messenger
Sm	Smithsonian Magazine
SMC	Smithsonian Miscellaneous Collections
SmCA	Smithsonian Contributions to Anthropology
SNL	Science News Letter
SR	Saturday Review
SS	Studia Septentrionalia
ST	Sun Tracks
Su	The Survey
Sun	Sunset
SWF	Southwest Folklore
SWL	Southwestern Lore
SWML	Southwest Museum Leaflets
SWR	Southwest Review
T	Travel
TA	Tennessee Archaeologist
TAES	Transactions of the American Ethnological Society
TAM	Theatre Arts Monthly
TAPS	Transactions of the American Philosophical Society
TCCSR	Twentieth Century Classics and School Readings
TFSB	Tennessee Folklore Society Bulletin
Ti	Time
TKAS	Transactions of the Kansas Academy of Science
To	Tomorrow. Quarterly Review of Psychical Research
TR	Texas Review
TRSL	Transactions of the Royal Society of Literature
TT	Twin Territories
UAB	University of Arizona Bulletin
UASAL	Utah Academy of Sciences, Arts, and Letters
UCPAAE	University of California Publications in American Archaeology and Ethnology
UCP-AR	University of California Publications, Anthropological Records
UCPL	University of California Publications in Linguistics
UCS	University of Colorado Studies
UHR	Utah Humanities Review
UNCMA-OP-AS	University of Northern Colorado Museum of Anthropology, Occasional Publications, Anthropological Series

UNMB-AS	*University of New Mexico Bulletin, Anthropological Series*
UNMB-BS	*University of New Mexico Bulletin, Biological Series*
UNS	*University of Nebraska Studies*
UOMA	*University of Oregon Monographs in Anthropology*
USCM&MR	*United States Catholic Magazine and Monthly Review*
USGS	*United States Geological Survey*
USLG	*United States Literary Gazette*
UTN	*University of Tennessee Newsletter*
UWPA	*University of Washington Publications in Anthropology*
VFPA	*Viking Fund Publications in Anthropology*
VH	*Vermont History*
WA	*Wisconsin Archaeologist*
WAL	*Western American Literature*
WE	*Western Explorer*
WF	*Western Folklore*
WHQ	*Washington Historical Quarterly*
WHR	*Western Humanities Review*
WMQ	*William and Mary Quarterly*
WO	*World Outlook*
WR&MM	*Western Review and Miscellaneous Magazine (Lexington, Kentucky)*
WVM	*Wiener Völkerkundliche Mitteilungen*
WW	*The World's Work*
WWS	*Western Writers Series (Boise State University)*
YR	*Yale Review*
YUPA	*Yale University Publications in Anthropology*

I GENERAL WORKS

A. Bibliographies and Other Reference Works

1. Aarne, Antti, and Stith Thompson. *The Types of the Folktale. A Classification and Bibliography.* 2nd revision. Helsinki: Suomalainen Tiedeakatemia, 1964 (FFC No. 184).

Standard catalogue of EA folktales. Relevant to NA folklore studies in showing influence and diffusion of EA materials.

2. Benedict, Ruth. "A Matter for the Field Worker in Folk-Lore." *JAF,* 36 (1923), 104.

Argues that the fieldworker should note discrepancies between folklore and cultural behavior. Uses illustrations from various NA groups.

3. Boas, Franz, ed. *Handbook of American Indian Languages.* 2 volumes. Washington: GPO, 1911 (BAEB No. 40).

General editorial introduction to various linguistic analytical methods and categories followed by in-depth treatments of several NA languages: Tlingit and Haida (by John R. Swanton); Tsimshian, Kwakiutl, and Chinook (by Boas); Maidu (by Roland B. Dixon); Fox (by William Jones and Truman Michelson); Dakota (by Boas and Swanton); Eskimo (by William Thalbitzer); Takelma (by Edward Sapir); Coos (by Leo J. Frachtenberg); and Siuslawan (by Frachtenberg). Several of the analyses of particular languages have oral narrative texts with free and literal translations.

4. Bradley, Ian L. "Revised Bibliography of Indian Musical Culture in Canada." *IH,* 10, No. 4 (Fall 1977), 28–32.

Unannotated list of books and articles. Alphabetized by author.

5. Brandon, William. "American Indian Literature." *IH,* 4, No. 2 (Summer 1971), 53–55.

Bibliographic guide to sources for NA oral literature.

6. Briscoe, Virginia Wolf. "Ruth Benedict, Anthropological Folklorist." *JAF,* 92 (1979), 445–76.

Study of the folklore contributions of a major student of NA cultures during the first half of the twentieth century.

7. Cashman, Marc, and Barry Klein. *Bibliography of American Ethnology.* Rye, N.Y.: Todd, 1976.

Error-filled, cursory list of books dealing with ethnology and ethnic relations. Brief sections on NA folklore and mythology.

8. Center for the Study of Man (Smithsonian Institution). "Current North American Indian Periodicals." *SE,* 36 (1972), 494–500.

List of magazines and newspapers by, for, and about NAs. With brief annotations.

9. Chamberlain, Alexander F. "Mythology of Indian Stocks North of Mexico." *JAF,* 18 (1905), 111–12.

Bibliographic survey of published texts of NA mythology.

10. ———. "Work Accomplished in the Study of American Indian Folk-Lore." *JAF,* 15 (1902), 127–29.

Survey of published materials on NA folklore, tabulated by culture group.

11. Chambers, Keith S. "The Indefatigable Elsie Clews Parsons—Folklorist." *WF,* 32 (1973), 180–98.

An assessment of Parsons' career, much of which was devoted to the study of NA folklore.

12. Davidson, Levette J. *A Guide to American Folklore.* Denver: Univ. of Denver Press, 1951.

Brief introductory definitions of folklore concepts with accompanying bibliographies. Some NA material included.

13. Densmore, Frances. "The Study of Indian Music in the Nineteenth Century." *AA,* 29 (1927), 77–86.

Essentially a bibliographical article, this piece summarizes work on NA music done from 1880 to 1900.

14. Dillingham, Peter. "The Literature of the American Indian." *EJ,* 62 (1973), 37–41.

Bibliographical survey of recently published NA literature (oral and written) with focus on its pedagogical potential for high school.

15. Dockstader, Frederick J., comp. *The American Indian in Graduate Studies. A Bibliography of Theses and Dissertations.* 2nd edition. CMAI, 25, Part 1, 1973.

List of 3659 graduate papers alphabetized by authors. No annotation. Covers from 1890 to 1955.

16. ———, and Alice W. Dockstader, comps. *The American Indian in Graduate Studies. A Bibliography of Theses and Dissertations.* CMAI, 25, Part 2, 1974.

List of 3786 graduate papers written between 1955 and 1970. Includes subject index for Parts I (No. 15) and II with headings for "Dance," "Ceremony," "Religion," "Folklore; mythology; legends," and "Music."

17. Dorsey, J. Owen. "Modern Additions to Indian Myths, and Indian Thunder Superstitions." *JAF,* 6 (1893), 232–33.

Comments on papers delivered at AFS annual meeting in 1892 deal with variation in NA mythology and with cross-cultural thunder beliefs.

18. Downie, Robert Angus, ed. *Anthologia Anthropologica. The Native Races of America: A Copious Selection of Passages for the Study of Social Anthropology, from the Manuscript Notebooks of Sir James George Frazer.* London: P. Lund, Humphries, 1939.

Extracts and summaries of published and unpublished sources on NAs. Includes data on ceremonialism and mythology.

19. Duff, Wilson. "Contributions of Marius Barbeau to West Coast Ethnology." *An,* n. s. 6 (1964), 63–96.

Examination of Barbeau's work, especially his interpretations of mythology and totem pole art.

20. Dundes, Alan. *Folklore Theses and Dissertations in the United States.* Austin: Univ. of Texas Press, 1976.

Unannotated chronological listing of academic papers, 1860–1968. Subject index includes general heading "Indian, American," with several subheadings.

21. ———. "North American Indian Folklore Studies." *JSA,* 56, No. 1 (1967), 53–79.

Bibliographic survey and history of research.

22. Farrer, Claire. "Fieldwork Ethics," in 136, pp. 59–63.

Surveys proper field techniques for collecting folklore from NAs. Draws upon experiences among Mescalero Apaches.

23. Fenton, William N., L. H. Butterfield, and Wilcomb E. Washburn. *American Indian and White Relations to 1830: Needs and Opportunities for Study.* Chapel Hill: Univ. of North Carolina Press, 1957.

Extensive bibliography includes section on "Literature, Songs, and Art."

24. Fewkes, J. Walter. "On the Use of the Phonograph in the Study of the Languages of American Indians." *S,* 15 (2 May 1890), 267–69.

Suggests possibilities for recording songs and rituals. Includes one Hopi song text (words and music).

25. Flanagan, John T. "A Pioneer in Indian Folklore: James Athearn Jones." *NEQ,* 12 (1939), 443–53.

Biography and evaluation of work of early-nineteenth century writer (1791–1854) who published several volumes of NA oral narratives.

26. Freeman, John F. *A Guide to Manuscripts Relating to the American Indian in the Library of the American Philosophical Society.* Philadelphia: APS, 1966.

Annotated list of 3995 mss. arranged for the most part by tribal group. Index has headings for "Myth" and other folklore-related topics.

27. Frost, John, ed. *The Book of the Indians of North America: Illustrating Their Manners, Customs, and Present State.* Hartford: W. J. Hamersley, 1844.

A handbook approach with sections on religion, games, dances, ceremonialism, and oratory.

28. Gaines, Ruth. *Books on Indian Arts North of Mexico.* New York: Exposition of Indian Tribal Arts, 1931.

Brief bibliographical pamphlet includes sections on ceremonialism, storytelling, and singing.

29. Garfield, Viola E. "Contemporary Problems of Folklore Collecting and Study." *APUAK,* 1 (1953), 25–36.

Outlines responsibilities of collector and editor of folklore with special reference to materials from NW Coast and Arctic groups.

30. Guédon, Marie-Françoise. "Canadian Indian Ethnomusicology: Selected Bibliography and Discography." *Em,* 16 (1972), 465–78.

Unannotated listing divided into following culture areas: Eastern Woodlands-Great Lakes, Plains, Yukon-Mackenzie Basins, Plateau, NW Coast.

31. Haines, Elijah M. *The American Indian (Uh-nish-in-na-ba): The Whole Subject Complete in One Volume.* Chicago: Massin-na'-gan, 1888.

Encyclopedic treatment with chapters on oral tradition, dance, religion, ceremonialism, belief systems, oratory, and music. Contains song and music texts, myth and legend summaries.

32. Haslam, Gerald. "American Oral Literature: Our Forgotten Heritage." *EJ,* 60 (1971), 709–23.

Surveys oral literature from various ethnic groups in U.S. and argues for its inclusion in the English curriculum. Includes some NA illustrations.

33. Haywood, Charles. *A Bibliography of North American Folklore and Folksong: Volume Two; The American Indians North of Mexico, Including the Eskimos.* 2nd revised edition. New York: Dover, 1961.

Very extensive work. Mostly unannotated, arranged by tribal group, and indexed by author and subject. Marred by inaccuracies and a much too broad concept of "folklore" (almost a synonym for "culture").

34. Hirschfelder, Arlene B., comp. *American Indian Authors: A Representative Bibliography.* New York: Association on American Indian Affairs, 1970.

Annotated list of books and articles by NA writers. Some folklore works.

35. ———. "Bibliography of Sources and Materials for Teaching About American Indians." *SE,* 36 (1972), 488–93.

Designed for social studies teachers. Includes recordings of traditional music as well as several books dealing with oral literature.

36. Hodge, Frederick Webb, ed. *Handbook of American Indians North of Mexico.* 2 volumes. Washington: GPO, 1907 (BAEB No. 30).

Encyclopedic reference work with entries for tribal names, significant individuals, place names, objects of material culture, and other cultural features. Of folklore interest are long articles on mythology (by J. N. B. Hewitt), the god "Nanabozho" (also by Hewitt), music and musical instruments (by Alice C. Fletcher), and oratory (also by Fletcher). Handy, though dated, compendium of information.

37. *Indians of the Americas: A Bibliography.* Regina, Saskatchewan: Bibliographic Services Division, Provincial Library, 1973.

Annotated list of books in Provincial Library of Saskatchewan. Includes sections on "Culture and Religion," "Myths and Legends," and "Language and Literature."

38. Jacobs, Melville. "Folklore," in 119, pp. 119–38.

Survey of Franz Boas' collecting of and theoretical work on NA folklore.

39. Kallmann, Helmut. "Toward a Bibliography of Canadian Folk Music." *Em,* 16 (1972), 499–503.

Brief discussion of a bibliographic project undertaken by the Canadian Folk Music Society.

40. Klein, Barry T., ed. *Reference Encyclopedia of the American Indian.* 3rd edition. 2 volumes. Rye, N.Y.: Todd, 1978.

Guide to various resources on NAs. Classified bibliography has sections on "Folklore," "Legends," "Mythology," "Poetry," and other areas relevant to folklore study. Entries are unannotated, and coverage is very sketchy. 1st edition = 1967; 2nd edition = 1973.

41. Knor, Russell L. *American Indian Index.* River Grove, Ill.: NP, 1953–1968.

Periodically published subject index to books about NAs. Includes a number of relevant subject headings.

42. Leach, Maria, and Jerome Fried, ed. *Funk and Wagnalls Standard Dictionary of Folklore, Mythology and Legend.* 2 volumes. New York: Funk & Wagnalls, 1949–50.

Contains a number of brief articles relevant to NA folklore. Subject index provides access to these articles by tribal group. A one-volume, slightly revised edition appeared in 1972.

43. Leitch, Barbara A. *A Concise Dictionary of Indian Tribes of North America.* Algonac, Mich.: Reference Publications, 1979.

Entries occasionally summarize religious concepts and ceremonialism.

44. Ludewig, Hermann (with additions and corrections by Wm. W. Turner). *The Literature of American Aboriginal Languages.* Ed. Nicolas Trübner. London: Trübner, 1858.

Early bibliographic work concentrates on linguistics, but includes a number of works relevant to folklore studies. Arranged by tribal groups (North and South America).

45. Marken, Jack W. *The American Indian: Language and Literature.* Arlington Heights, Ill.: AHM, 1978.

Unannotated list of 3695 books and articles on NA language, oral literature, and written literature. Arranged by culture area and tribal group. Author-subject index.

46. Marquis, Arnold. *A Guide to America's Indians. Ceremonials, Reservations and Museums.* Norman: Univ. of Oklahoma Press, 1974.

Includes calendars of events, list of reservations, directory of campgrounds on NA lands, list of museums, directory of NA associations, and a brief bibliography. Most material is arranged according to culture region.

47. Mason, Otis T. *Ethnological Directions Relative to the Indian Tribes of the United States.* Washington: GPO, 1875.

Finding list of ethnological topics includes sections on music, religion (myths and rituals), and games and pastimes.

48. May, Jill P. "Modern Interpretations of Native American Legend." *SWF*, 3, No. 4 (Fall 1979), 16–22.

Essentially a review essay of children's books which portray NA religious traditions. Also examines EA stereotypes of NA folklore.

49. Murdock, George Peter, and Timothy J. O'Leary. *Ethnographic Bibliography of North America.* 4th edition. 5 volumes. New Haven: Human Relations Area Files Press, 1975.

Unannotated bibliography of books and articles treating NA culture. Arranged by culture area and tribal group. Volume I includes material on culture areas; volumes II–V contain material on tribal groups. Folklore material included throughout. 1st edition = 1941 (*YUPA* No. 1); 2nd edition = 1953; 3rd edition = 1960.

50. Naumer, Janet Noll. "American Indians: A Bibliography of Sources." *AL*, 1 (1970), 861–64.

Brief overview of material which could be used to enhance the NA collection of a library.

51. Nichols, Frances S. *Index to Schoolcraft's "Indian Tribes of the United States."* Washington: GPO, 1954 (BAEB No. 152).

Subject index to the Schoolcraft work (see 58) includes following folklore entries: names of mythological characters, "Legends," "Origin Traditions," "Songs," "Prayer," "Oratory," and names of ceremonies.

52. Nida, Eugene. "Field Techniques in Descriptive Linguistics." *IJAL*, 13 (1947), 138–46.

The final stage in linguistic fieldwork is the collection of texts, either traditional stories or descriptions of customs. Illustrated with NA material.

53. Opler, Morris Edward. "New Approaches to North American Indian Traditions." *JAF*, 72 (1959), 95–96.

Introduction to a special issue of *JAF* dealing with NA folklore.

54. Powell, John Wesley. *Introduction to the Study of Indian Languages with Word Phrases and Sentences to Be Collected.* 2nd edition. Washington: GPO, 1880.

Finding list for linguistic fieldworkers includes sections on religion and mortuary customs.

55. Price, John A. *Native Studies: American and Canadian Indians.* Toronto: McGraw-Hill Ryerson, 1978.

Examines NA studies in U.S. and Canada with chapters which deal with ceremonialism, storytelling, music, and dance.

56. Prucha, Francis Paul. *A Bibliographical Guide to the History of Indian-White Relations in the United States.* Chicago: Univ. of Chicago Press, 1977.

List of 9705 items, some with brief annotations. Although the focus is on contact history, some sections (e.g., "Ghost Dance," "peyote") are relevant to folklore study.

57. Roberts, Warren E. "Collections and Indexes: A Brief Review." *JAF*, 70 (1957), 49–52.

Part of a symposium on the folktale, the bibliographical essay includes coverage of some NA materials.

58. Schoolcraft, Henry R. *Historical and Statistical Information, Respecting the History, Condition and Prospects of the Indian Tribes of the United States: Collected and Prepared Under the Direction of the Bureau of Indian Affairs per Act of Congress of March 3d, 1847.* 6 volumes. Philadelphia: Lippincott, Grambo (later J. P. Lippincott), 1851–1857.

Massive collection of data on NA culture, including mythology and ceremonialism. Includes myth and song texts from various groups and extensive discussion of NA oral literature. Appendix to volume 5 includes some essays by observers other than Schoolcraft. An index to the series has been prepared by Frances S. Nichols (see 51).

59. ———. *Inquiries, Respecting the History, Present Condition, and Future Prospects, of the Indian Tribes of the United States.* Philadelphia: Lippincott, Grambo, 1851.

Questionnaire written for the Bureau of Indian Affairs on general history and ethnography. Contains 348 inquiries on such topics as dancing, ceremonialism, religion, and mythology.

60. ———. "Plan for American Ethnological Investigation." *ARSI for 1885*, pp. 907–14.

Posthumously published outline of topics to be a part of the ethnological study of NAs. Includes "Music and Poetry," "Oral Tales and Legends," and "Mythology."

61. Sherwood, John. "Life with Cushing: Farewell to Desks." *Sm*, 10, No. 5 (Aug. 1979), 96–113.

Biographical essay and survey of the fieldwork of Frank Hamilton Cushing, especially among the Zuni.

62. Smith, Dwight L., and John C. Ewers. *Indians of the United States and Canada: A Bibliography.* Santa Barbara: ABC-Clio, 1974.

Annotated list of 1687 articles arranged by culture area and tribe. Index includes folklore headings. Entries come from data bank of *America: History and Life* and cover the period from 1954 through 1972.

63. Smith, William F., Jr. "American Indian Literature." *EJ*, 63 (1974), 68–72.

Bibliographical essay which evaluates pedagogical value of publications in NA literature, oral and written.

64. Spofford, Ainsworth R. "Rare Books Relating to the American Indians." *AA*, 3 (1901), 270–85.

Bibliographic survey of books and pamphlets relating to NAs. Concerned with accounts of early explorers, missionary narratives, captivity narratives, and other early publications. Sparse annotations.

65. Stensland, Anna Lee. "American Indian Culture and the Reading Program." *JR*, 15 (1971), 22–26.

Recommends books that could be included in a public school library. Several oral literature anthologies included.

66. ———, and Aune M. Fadum. *Literature by and About the American Indian. An Annotated Bibliography.* 2nd edition. Urbana, Ill.: National Council of Teachers of English, 1979.

Pedagogically oriented bibliography includes selected books (c. 675). Each book is summarized and critical comments are quoted from authoritative sources. Books are graded by educational level and arranged under subject headings (e.g., "Myth, Legend, Oratory, and Poetry" and "Music, Arts, and Crafts"). Has title and author indexes and an introductory essay on teaching about NAs. 1st edition = 1973.

67. Stevenson, Robert. "English Sources for Indian Music Until 1882." *Em,* 17 (1973), 399–442.

Bibliographical survey of pre-twentieth century treatments of NA music.

68. ———. "Written Sources for Indian Music Until 1882." *Em,* 17 (1973), 1–40.

A bibliographical survey of materials, mostly non-English, dealing with NA music, published before Theodore Baker's *Uber die Musik der Nordamerikanischen Wilden* (1882).

69. Stoutenburgh, John L., Jr. *Dictionary of the American Indian.* New York: Philosophical Library, 1960.

Entries are a melange of tribal names, clan names, and rituals. Definitions are very sketchy. No apparent logic behind inclusions.

70. Thompson, Stith. *Motif-Index of Folk-Literature. A Classification of Narrative Elements in Folktales, Ballads, Myths, Fables, Medieval Romances, Exempla, Fabliaux, Jest-Books and Local Legends.* 2nd edition. 6 volumes. Bloomington: Indiana Univ. Press, 1955–1958.

Catalogue of characters, incidents, and objects found in international folk literature. With bibliographical references for most entries. 1st edition = 1932–1936.

71. Thorsen, Timothy H. H. "Folkloristics in A. L. Kroeber's Early Theory of Culture." *JFI,* 10 (1973), 41–55.

Kroeber saw folklore as an expression of the particular genius of a group. Also as a clear definer of intercultural boundaries.

72. Trout, Lawanna. "Experimental Approaches to Oral Tradition Literature." *EJ,* 64 (1975), 94–97.

Discussion of pedagogical approaches to oral literature. Draws upon NA examples.

73. Ullom, Judith C., comp. *Folklore of the North American Indians. An Annotated Bibliography.* Washington: Library of Congress, 1969.

Well annotated list of 152 books. Emphasis is on value of collections of folklore for children.

74. Voegelin, Erminie W. "North American Indian Folklore," in 42, pp. 798–802.

Brief, but thorough, survey of the nature of NA oral tradition.

75. ———. "North American Native Literature," in *Encyclopedia of Literature.* Ed. Joseph T. Shipley. New York: Philosophical Library, 1946, Vol. 2, 706–21.

Survey of NA oral literature, arranged for the most part by culture area.

76. Wolf, Carolyn E., and Karen R. Folk. *Indians of North and South America: A Bibliography Based on the Collection at the Willard E. Yager Library-Museum, Hartwick College, Oneonta, N. Y.* Metuchen, N. J.: Scarecrow, 1977.

Unannoated list of 4204 items alphabetized by author. Also includes annotated list of 181 packets of newspaper clippings in the Yager collection. Subject index for bibliography includes headings for folklore and music.

77. Wright, Muriel H. *A Guide to the Indian Tribes of Oklahoma.* Norman: Univ. of Oklahoma Press, 1951.

Tribe-by-tribe treatment of NAs residing in Oklahoma in twentieth century. Each tribal description includes some information on ceremonials and public dramas.

See also 196, 227, 235, 241, 251, 609, 618, 619, 664, 754, 785, 839, 856, 861, 870, 872, 900, 942, 1305, 1382, 1385, 1514, 1634, 1742, 1765, 1849, 2018, 2034, 2075, 2570, 2672, 2676, 2695, 2791, 3024, 4139, 4140, 4171, 4200, 4556, 4596, 4863, 4983, 5092, 5104, 5270, 5345.

B. Essay Anthologies

78. Abernethy, Francis Edward, ed. *The Folklore of Texan Cultures.* PTFS No. 38 (1974).
Contains 1304, 1556, 3816.

79. Bassett, Helen Wheeler, and Frederick Starr, eds. *The International Folk-Lore Congress of the World's Columbian Exposition. Vol. I.* Chicago: Charles H. Sergel, 1898.
Contains 507, 2547, 3090, 3658, 4520.

80. Basso, Keith H., and Morris E. Opler, eds. *Apachean Culture History and Ethnology.* Tucson: Univ. of Arizona Press, 1971.
Contains 2745.

81. Bataille, Gretchen M., David M. Gradwohl, and Charles L. P. Silet, eds. *The Worlds Between Two Rivers. Perspectives on American Indians in Iowa.* Ames: Iowa State Univ. Press, 1978.
Contains 2044.

82. Bauman, Richard, and Joel Sherzer, eds. *Explorations in the Ethnography of Speaking.* London: Cambridge Univ. Press, 1974.
Contains 1041, 5162.

83. Beach, W. W., ed. *The Indian Miscellany; Containing Papers on the History, Antiquities, Arts, Languages, Religions, Traditions and Superstitions of the American Aborigines; with Descriptions of Their Domestic Life, Manners, Customs, Traits, Amusements and Exploits; Travels and Adventures in the Indian Country; Incidents of Border Warfare; Missionary Relations; etc.* Albany: J. Munsell, 1877.
Contains 934, 1012, 1756, 2137, 2564.

84. Ben-Amos, Dan, ed. *Folklore Genres.* Austin: Univ. of Texas Press, 1976.
Contains 3170.

85. Bingham, Edwin R., and Glen A. Love, eds. *Northwest Perspectives. Essays on the Culture of the Pacific Northwest.* Seattle: Univ. of Washington Press, 1979.
Contains 4606.

86. Blackburn, Thomas C., ed. *Flowers of the Wind. Papers on Ritual, Myth and Symbolism in California and the Southwest.* Socorro, N.M.: Ballena Press, 1977 (Anthropological Papers No. 8).
Contains 3274, 4116, 4165, 4212, 4248, 4271.

87. Boas, Franz, ed. *Handbook of American Indian Languages. Part 3.* NP: J. J. Augustin, 1933–1938.
Contains 1559, 1578, 4806, 5000.

88. ———. *Race, Language, and Culture.* New York: Macmillan, 1940.

Contains 386, 551, 552, 555, 557, 4504, 5090, 5256.

89. Boatright, Mody C., ed. *Mexican Border Ballads and Other Lore.* PTFS No. 21 (1946).

Contains 1336.

90. ———, ed. *The Sky Is My Tipi.* PTFS No. 22 (1949).

Contains 2379, 2764.

91. ———, and Donald Day, eds. *Backwoods to Border.* PTFS No. 18 (1943).

Contains 2272.

92. ———, and Donald Day, eds. *From Hell to Breakfast.* PTFS No. 19 (1944).

Contains 1674, 1885.

93. ———, Wilson M. Hudson, and Allen Maxwell, eds. *And Horns on the Toads.* PTFS No. 29 (1959).

Contains 2165.

94. ———, Wilson M. Hudson, and Allen Maxwell, eds. *Texas Folk and Folklore.* PTFS No. 26 (1954).

Contains 1335, 2380.

95. Brinton, Daniel G. *Essays of an Americanist.* Philadelphia: Porter & Coates, 1890.

Includes "Native American Poetry" (not previously published), which surveys NA poetic performances with texts from various groups. Also contains 829.

96. Capps, Walter H., and Ernst F. Tonsing, eds. *Seeing with a Native Eye. Essays on Native American Religion.* New York: Harper, 1976.

Contains 392, 520, 2971, 3648.

97. Chapman, Abraham, ed. *Literature of the American Indians: Views and Interpretations. A Gathering of Indian Memories, Symbolic Contexts, and Literary Criticism.* New York: New American Library, 1975.

Contains 373, 386, 472, 695. With excerpts from 174, 323, 390, 806, 1013, 1745, 1964, 2260, 2548, 2554.

98. Crumrine, N. Ross, ed. *Ritual Symbolism and Ceremonialism in the Americas. Studies in Symbolic Anthropology.* UNC-MA-OP-AS No. 33 (1979).

Contains 3569, 4963.

99. Darnell, Regna, ed. *Linguistic Diversity in Canadian Society.* Edmonton: Linguistic Research, 1971.

Contains 1040.

100. d'Azevedo, Warren L., ed. *The Washo Indians of California and Nevada.* APUU No. 67 (1963).

Contains 4101, 4102, 4112.

101. Dégh, Linda, Henry Glassie, and Felix J. Oinas. *Folklore Today. A Festschrift for Richard M. Dorson.* Bloomington: Indiana Univ. Research Center for Language and Semiotic Studies, 1976.

Contains 3590.

102. Diamond, Stanley, ed. *Culture in History. Essays in Honor of Paul Radin.* New York: Columbia Univ. Press, 1960.
Contains 398, 1767, 1949, 3040, 3431, 4056, 4660.

103. Dobie, J. Frank, ed. *Coffee in the Gourd.* PTFS No. 2 (1923).

Contains 2731a.

104. ———, ed. *Legends of Texas.* PTFS No. 3 (1924).
Contains 2278, 2715.

105. ———, ed. *Rainbow in the Morning.* PTFS No. 5 (1926).

Contains 1982.

106. ———, ed. *Southwestern Lore.* PTFS No. 9 (1931).
Contains 1555.

107. ———, ed. *Texas and Southwestern Lore.* PTFS No. 6 (1927).

Contains 1557.

108. ———, and Mody C. Boatright, eds. *Straight Texas.* PTFS No. 13 (1937).

Contains 1331, 1332, 1333.

109. ———, Mody C. Boatright, and Harry H. Ransom. *Coyote Wisdom.* PTFS No. 14 (1938).

Contains 546, 2938, 3330.

110. ———, Mody C. Boatright, and Harry H. Ransom. *In the Shadow of History.* PTFS No. 15 (1939).

Contains 3231.

111. ———, Mody C. Boatright, and Harry H. Ransom. *Mustangs and Cow Horses.* PTFS No. 16 (1940).

Contains 2170.

112. Du Bois, Cora, ed. *Lowie's Selected Papers in Anthropology.* Berkeley: Univ. of California Press, 1960.

Contains 323, 458, 2302, 2308 ("Some Cases of Repeated Reproduction").

113. Dundes, Alan, ed. *Every Man His Way. Readings in Cultural Anthropology.* Englewood Cliffs, N.J.: Prentice-Hall, 1968.

Contains 3664, 4191 (excerpt), 5158.

114. ———, ed. *The Study of Folklore.* Englewood Cliffs, N.J.: Prentice-Hall, 1964.

Contains 378, 379, 578, 607, 671, 779, 2308 ("Some Cases of Repeated Reproduction").

115. Fenton, William N., ed. *Symposium on Local Diversity in Iroquois Culture.* BAEB No. 149 (1951).

Contains 1017, 1038, 1084.

116. ———, and John Gulich, eds. *Symposium on Cherokee and Iroquois Culture.* BAEB No. 180 (1961).

Contains 1026, 1159, 1384, 1422, 1458.

117. Georges, Robert A., ed. *Studies on Mythology.* Homewood, Ill.: Dorsey, 1968.

Contains 606, 615 (excerpt), 3853 (excerpt), 4504.

118. Ghosh, Samir K. *Man, Language, and Society. Contributions to the Sociology of Language.* The Hague: Mouton, 1972.

Contains 3054.

119. Goldschmidt, Walter, ed. *The Anthropology of Franz Boas. Essays on the Centennial of His Birth.* MAAA No. 89 (1959).

Contains 38.

120. Graburn, Nelson H. H., ed. *Ethnic and Tourist Arts. Cultural Expressions from the Fourth World.* Berkeley: Univ. of California Press, 1976.

Contains 4708.

121. Greenway, John, ed. *Folklore of the Great West. Selections from Eighty-Three Years of the Journal of American Folklore.* Palo Alto, Cal.: American West, 1969.

Contains twenty-three selections from articles about NA folklore published in *JAF.* Most of the material is texts.

122. Hand, Wayland D., ed. *American Folk Legend. A Symposium.* Berkeley: Univ. of California Press, 1971.

Contains 3169.

123. ———, ed. *American Folk Medicine. A Symposium.* Berkeley: Univ. of California Press, 1976.

Contains 677, 3814, 4119.

124. Heizer, Robert F., and M. A. Whipple, eds. *The California Indians. A Source Book.* 2nd edition. Los Angeles: Univ. of California Press, 1971.

Contains 2885, 4145, 4463, 4557. 1st edition = 1951.

125. Helm, June, ed. *Essays on Verbal and Visual Arts. Proceedings of the 1966 Annual Spring Meeting of the American*

Ethnological Society. Seattle: American Ethnological Society, 1967.
Contains 3460.

126. Hill, Carole E., ed. *Symbols and Society. Essays on Belief Systems in Action.* Athens, Ga.: Southern Anthropological Society, 1975 (Proceedings No. 9).
Contains 1154, 5174.

127. Hymes, Dell, ed. *Language in Culture and Society. A Reader in Linguistics and Anthropology.* New York: Harper & Row, 1964.
Contains 4064, 4451.

128. ———, and William E. Bittle, eds. *Studies in Southwestern Ethnolinguistics. Meaning and History in the Language of the American Southwest.* The Hague: Mouton, 1967.
Contains 2892, 3459, 3502.

129. *Indian Voices. The First Convocation of American Indian Scholars.* San Francisco: Indian Historian Press, 1970.
Contains 472, 477.

130. Kersting, Rudolf, ed. *The White World. Life and Adventures Within the Arctic Circle Portrayed by Famous Living Explorers.* New York: Lewis, Sinclair, 1902.
Contains 5421, 5429.

131. Kroeber, A. L., and T. T. Waterman, eds. *Source Book in Anthropology.* New York: Harcourt, Brace, 1931.
Contains 3082, 4251, 4315.

132. Lantis, Margaret. *Ethnohistory in Southwestern Alaska and the Southern Yukon. Method and Content.* Lexington: Univ. of Kentucky Press, 1970.
Contains 4599.

133. Leach, Edmund, ed. *The Structural Study of Myth and Totemism.* London: Tavistock, 1967.
Contains 574, 4967.

134. Leacock, Eleanor Burke, and Nancy Oestreich Lurie, eds. *North American Indians in Historical Perspective.* New York: Random House, 1971.
Contains 1029, 4085, 4893.

135. Mahon, John K., ed. *Indians of the Lower South: Past and Present.* Proceedings of the Gulf Coast History and Humanities Conference No. 5 (1975).
Contains 1518.

136. Mannenbach, Stephen, ed. *Trends and New Vistas in Contemporary Native American Folklore.* FFBSS No. 15 (1976).
Contains 22, 1042, 2532, 2602, 4585, 4861, 4900, 5447.

137. Maranda, Pierre, and Elli Köngäs-Maranda, eds. *Structural Analysis of Oral Tradition.* Philadelphia: Univ. of Pennsylvania Press, 1971.
Contains 4656.

138. McGee, Harold F., Jr., Stephen A. Davis, and Michael Taft, comps. *Three Atlantic Bibliographies.* Halifax: St. Mary's Univ. Department of Anthropology, 1975.
Contains 856.

139. Mead, Margaret, and Ruth L. Bunzel, eds. *The Golden Age of American Anthropology.* New York: George Braziller, 1960.
Contains 1878, 1953, 2078, 2465, 3082, 3523, 3908, 4720. With excerpts from 1101, 2045, 2236, 2290, 2433, 5250.

140. Mereness, Newton D., ed. *Travels in the American Colonies.* New York: Macmillan, 1916.
Contains 1371, 1494, 1517, 1520, 1876.

141. Middleton, John M., ed. *Magic, Witchcraft, and Curing.* Garden City, N.Y.: Natural History Press, 1967.
Contains 1162, 5242.

142. ———, ed. *Myth and Cosmos. Readings in Mythology and Symbolism.* Garden City, N.Y.: Natural History Press, 1967.
Contains 1949.

143. Muensterberger, Warner, and Sidney Axelrad, eds. *The Psychoanalytic Study of Society.* 2 volumes. New York: International Universities Press, 1962.
Contains 3890.

144. Needham, Rodney, ed. *Right and Left. Essays on Dual Symbolic Classification.* Chicago: Univ. of Chicago Press, 1973.
Contains 1882.

145. *Opportunities in Arizona Folklore. UAB* No. 9 (1945).
Contains 3965.

146. Orrick, Allan H., ed. *Nordica et Anglica. Studies in Honor of Stefán Einarsson.* The Hague: Mouton, 1968.
Includes 910.

147. Ortiz, Alfonso, ed. *New Perspectives on the Pueblos.* Albuquerque: Univ. of New Mexico Press, 1972.
Contains 3357, 3384, 3408, 3883, 3942.

148. Owen, Roger C., James J. F. Deetz, and Anthony D. Fisher. *The North American Indians. A Sourcebook.* New York: Macmillan, 1967.
Includes 524, 2013, 2063, 2381, 4040, 4827, 5364. With excerpts from 1766, 2078, 5083, 5250.

149. Paredes, Americo, and Richard Bauman, eds. *Toward New Perspectives on Folklore.* Austin: Univ. of Texas Press, 1971.
Contains 3941, 5070.

150. Ray, Verne F., ed. *Proceedings of the 1960 Annual Spring Meeting of the American Ethnological Society.* Seattle: American Ethnological Society, 1960.
Contains 5123.

151. Rice, Stuart A., ed. *Methods in Social Science. A Case Book.* Chicago: Univ. of Chicago Press, 1931.
Contains 4972.

152. Richmond, W. Edson, ed. *Studies in Folklore. In Honor of Distinguished Service Professor Stith Thompson.* Bloomington: Indiana Univ. Press, 1957.
Contains 676, 1933.

153. Sawyer, Jesse, ed. *Studies in American Indian Languages. UCPL* No. 65 (1971).
Includes 1184, 4444.

154. Sebeok, Thomas A., ed. *Current Trends in Linguistics. Volume 10. Linguistics in North America.* The Hague: Mouton, 1973.
Series of essays of current NA language studies with bibliographies.

155. ———, ed. *Myth. A Symposium. AFSBSS* No. 5 (1955).
Contains 3500, 3897.

156. Singer, André, and Brian V. Street, eds. *Zande Themes. Essays Presented to Sir Edward Evans-Pritchard.* Oxford: Basil Blackwell, 1972.
Contains 1970.

157. Slater, Peter, ed. *Religion and Culture in Canada.* NP: Canadian Corporation for Studies in Religion, 1977.
Contains 4548.

158. Smith, M. Estellie, ed. *Studies in Linguistics in Honor of George L. Trager.* The Hague: Mouton, 1972.
Contains 5585.

159. Smith, Marian W., ed. *Indians of the Urban Northwest. CUCA* No. 36 (1949).
Contains 4564, 4607, 4833, 4847, 4882.

160. Spicer, Edward H., ed. *Ethnic Medicine in the Southwest.* Tucson: Univ. of Arizona Press, 1977.

Contains 3977.

161. Spier, Leslie, A. Irving Hallowell, and Stanley S. Newman. *Language, Culture, and Personality. Essays in Memory of Edward Sapir.* Menasha, Wis.: Sapir Memorial Publication Fund, 1941.

Contains 3488, 4005, 4989.

162. Tax, Sol, ed. *Indian Tribes of Aboriginal America. Selected Papers of the XXIXth International Congress of Americanists.* Chicago: Univ. of Chicago Press, 1952.

Contains 545, 570, 650, 1085, 5020.

163. Tedlock, Dennis, and Barbara Tedlock, eds. *Teachings from the American Earth. Indian Religion and Philosophy.* New York: Liveright, 1975.

Contains 351, 1767, 2063, 3835, 3937, 5129. With excerpts from 2045, 2078, 2522, 3266, 4490.

164. Thompson, Stith, ed. *Round the Levee. PTFS* No. 1 (1916).

Contains 1556, 2670.

165. Wallace, Anthony F. C., ed. *Men and Cultures. Selected Papers of the Fifth International Congress of Anthropological and Ethnological Sciences. Philadelphia, September 1–9, 1956.* Philadelphia: Univ. of Pennsylvania Press, 1960.

Contains 788, 2789, 3302, 4664.

166. Waugh, Earle H., and K. Dad Prithipaul, eds. *Native Religious Traditions.* NP: Canadian Corporation for Studies in Religion, 1979.

Contains 301, 559, 597, 2159, 2973, 3067, 5171.

167. *World of the American Indian, The.* Washington: National Geographic Society, 1974.

Contains 4138, 5277.

C. General Collections

168. Astrov, Margot. *The Winged Serpent: An Anthology of American Indian Prose and Poetry.* New York: John Day, 1946.

Texts of stories, songs, and orations reprinted from various sources with brief notes on contexts and functions. Introduction surveys the role of oral literature in NA life and the effects of Christianity on traditional cultures.

169. Barbeau, Marius, and Grace Melvin. *The Indian Speaks.* Caldwell, Idaho: Caxton, 1943.

Rewritten and excerpted myths and songs from various groups. Illustrated with woodcuts. Sources identified.

170. Brotherston, Gordon. *Image of the New World. The American Continent Portrayed in Native Texts.* London: Thames and Hudson, 1979.

Song, myth, prayer, oratory, and legend texts from NAs in North and South America. Used to create a portrait of traditional NA life as well as reponses to EA contact. All previously published, but with some new translations.

171. Coffin, Tristram P., and Hennig Cohen, eds. *Folklore in America: Tales, Songs, Superstitions, Proverbs, Riddles, Games, Folk Drama and Folk Festivals.* Garden City, N.Y.: Doubleday, 1966.

Anthology of folklore texts previously published in *JAF.* NA materials are two stories, one song, and one game.

172. Curtis, Edward S. *The North American Indian. Being a Series of Volumes Picturing and Describing the Indians of the United States and Alaska.* Ed. Frederick Webb Hodge. 20 volumes. Seattle: E. S. Curtis, 1907–1930.

Curtis' famous photographs illustrate brief ethnographic descriptions of groups in Southwest, Plains, Plateau, Northwest Coast, California, Great Basin, Sub-Arctic, and Arctic. Work presents myth, folktale, and song texts and descriptions of ceremonialism from various groups. Selections from this work have been frequently reprinted; for example, see Barry Gifford, ed., *Selected Writings of Edward S. Curtis, Excerpts from Volumes I-XX of The North American Indian* (Berkeley: Creative Arts, 1976) and 198.

173. Curtis, Natalie. *The Indians' Book. An Offering by the American Indians of Indian Lore, Musical and Narrative, to Form a Record of the Songs and Legends of Their Race.* 2nd edition. New York: Harper, 1923.

Anthology of stories, songs, prayers, and chants. Song texts are in original languages with interlinear translations and music. Organized by culture area and tribe.

174. Fletcher, Alice C. *Indian Story and Song from North America.* Boston: Small Maynard, 1900.

Texts of myths and songs (words and music) from various groups. Sometimes placed in context. Work generalizes about the relationship between NA story and song and about the nature of song performance.

175. Greenway, John, ed. *The Primitive Reader: An Anthology of Myths, Tales, Songs, Riddles and Proverbs of Aboriginal Peoples Around the World.* Hatboro, Penn.: Folklore Associates, 1965.

All materials taken from previously published sources. NAs are represented by various groups.

176. Hamilton, Charles, ed. *Cry of the Thunderbird. The American Indian's Own Story.* New York: Macmillan, 1950.

Short excerpts from writings by NAs which deal with both everyday life and significant historical occurrences. Some of the pieces bear directly on folklore and its contexts. Biographical notes for the NA authors. Re-issued in 1972 by the Univ. of Oklahoma Press.

177. Henry, Jeannette, ed. *The American Indian Reader: Literature.* San Francisco: Indian Historian Press, 1973.

Anthology of NA oral and written literature including traditional song and story texts. No commentary with individual texts.

178. Katz, Jane B., ed. *I Am the Fire of Time: The Voices of Native American Women.* New York: E. P. Dutton, 1977.

Anthology of very brief selections of traditional and contemporary NA literature written or performed by women. No context commentary for selections.

179. Levitas, Gloria, Frank Robert Vivelo, and Jacqueline J. Vivelo, eds. *American Indian Prose and Poetry: We Wait in the Darkness.* New York: Putnam, 1974.

Anthology of oral literature with a brief section on contemporary NA writing. Texts of myths, songs, chants, and oratory (all previously published) arranged into two sections—pre-contact and post-contact—and then by culture area and tribe. General introduction, but little commentary on specific texts.

180. Moquin, Wayne, and Charles Van Doren, eds. *Great Documents in American Indian History.* New York: Praeger, 1973.

Attempts to survey NA life and history in the words of NAs. Includes creation myths, oratory, personal reminiscences, and oral history (all previously published). Various groups represented.

181. Nabokov, Peter, ed. *Native American Testimony: An Anthology of Indian and White Relations, First Encounter to Dispossession.* Preface by Vine Deloria, Jr. New York: Thomas Y. Crowell, 1978.

Anthology of short pieces which present the NA perspective on contact history with EAs. Includes life histories, oratory, oral history, and oral narratives.

182. Parker, Arthur C. *The Indian How Book.* New York: George H. Doran, 1927.

Generalized description of how NAs performed such activities as joking, dancing, singing, and performing various rituals. With story, song, and oratory texts from various groups.

183. Sanders, Thomas E., and Walter W. Peek. *Literature of the American Indian.* Beverly Hills: Glencoe, 1973.

Anthology of oral and written literature from various NA groups. Includes myths, songs, oratory, and life histories. With a general introduction and an introduction to each section.

184. [Schoolcraft, Henry Rowe]. *Western Scenes and Reminiscences. Together with Thrilling Legends and Traditions of the Red Men of the Forest. To Which Is Added Several Narratives of Adventures Among the Indians.* Buffalo: Derby, Orton, & Mulligan, 1853.

Anthology of descriptions of NA life, captivity narratives, song texts, myths, and historical legends. Folklore material identified by group, but no indication of sources for materials.

185. Turner, Frederick W., III, ed. *The Portable North American Indian Reader.* New York: Viking, 1973.

Includes writings by and about NAs as well as an extensive section on oral literature with texts of myths, songs, and oratory. Each text has a brief headnote providing data on cultural background.

186. Velie, Alan R., ed. *American Indian Literature. An Anthology.* Norman: Univ. of Oklahoma Press, 1979.

Collection of oral and written literature from various groups. Includes stories, songs, life histories, and oratory. Texts are accompanied by explanatory notes.

187. Vogel, Virgil J. *This Country Was Ours. A Documentary History of the American Indian.* New York: Harper and Row, 1972.

Selection of documents dealing with NA history. Oral literature is represented by an Arapaho creation myth and samples of oratory. Contains an extensive bibliography.

188. Witt, Shirley Hill, and Stan Steiner. *The Way. An Anthology of American Indian Literature.* New York: Knopf, 1974.

Includes songs, stories, oratory, and jokes, as well as contemporary writing. Focus is on literary expressions that respond to contact with EAs. Brief commentary with each selection.

D. Story Collections

189. Appleton, LeRoy H. *Indian Art of the Americas.* New York: Scribners, 1950.

Various art forms are put into cultural perspective through the presentation of oral narratives and ritual descriptions from previously published sources (mostly BAE papers). Re-issued as *American Indian Design and Decoration* (New York: Dover, 1971).

190. Armour, R. C. *North American Indian Fairy Tales. Folklore and Legends.* London: Gibbings, 1905.

Thirty-two rewritten myth and folktale texts. No annotations or commentary. Tribal groups not specified.

191. Bierhorst, John, ed. *The Red Swan. Myths and Tales of the American Indians.* New York: Farrar, Straus & Giroux, 1976.

Sixty-four myth and folktale texts and excerpts. Notes for each selection provide as much information on collecting situation as is possible. General introduction on the concept of myth. Stories are arranged thematically.

192. Bright, William, ed. *Coyote Stories.* Chicago: Univ. of Chicago Press, 1978 (IJAL-NATS No. 1).

Twenty myth texts with free and literal translations from various groups in Northwest Coast, Plateau, California, and Southwest culture areas. Brief introduction to each text emphasizes linguistic significance.

193. Brown, Dee. *Tepee Tales of the American Indian Retold for Our Time.* New York: Holt, Rinehart, and Winston, 1979.

Rewritten stories from various NA groups. Sources identified.

194. Carr, William H. "Indian Beaver Legends." *NH,* 31 (1931), 81–92.

Summaries from various NA groups of myths involving beavers.

195. Coffer, William E. *Spirits of the Sacred Mountains. Creation Stories of the American Indian.* New York: Van Nostrand Reinhold, 1978.

Rewritten texts of cosmogonic myths from various NA groups. Introduced by scientific and pseudoscientific theories of creation and by various explanations of the settling of the New World. Brings a NA perspective to theories of the origin of life.

196. Coffin, Tristram P. *Indian Tales of North America. An Anthology for the Adult Reader.* Philadelphia: American Folklore Society, 1961 (AFSBSS No. 13).

Forty-five story texts, all originally published in *JAF.* Introduction addresses literary significance of material. Purpose of volume is to fill gap between children's versions of NA folklore, on one hand, and inaccessible scholarly collections, on the other. Also includes an index to NA folklore published in *JAF* and other AFS books and periodicals.

197. Cunningham, Caroline. *The Talking Stone. Being Early American Stories Told Before the White Man's Day on This Continent by the Indians and Eskimos.* New York: Knopf, 1939.

Five rewritten myth texts. Sources identified.

198. Curtis, Edward S. *The Girl Who Married a Ghost and Other Tales from the North American Indian.* Ed. John Bierhorst. New York: Four Winds, 1978.

Nine myth and folktale texts selected from *The North American Indian* (172). No annotations. Bierhorst's foreword briefly summarizes Curtis' career.

199. Davidson, Levette J. "White Versions of Indian Myths and Legends." *WF,* 7 (1948), 115–28.

Thirteen examples of reports of NA myths and legends by nineteenth-century EA observers. Concludes that they are romanticized versions of the originals.

200. Dorsey, J. O., A. S. Gatschet, and S. R. Riggs. "Illustration of the Method of Recording Indian Languages." *ARBAE,* 1 (1879–1880), 579–589.

Five texts with literal and free translations and linguistic commentary: Omaha myth, three Klamath ethnographic descriptions, Dakota myth.

201. Flanagan, John T., and Arthur Palmer Hudson, eds. *Folklore in American Literature.* Westport, Conn.: Greenwood, 1958.

Anthology of literary works in which folklore is utilized. NA section includes three folktales retold by Schoolcraft.

202. Fleming, R. M. *Stories from the Early World.* New York: Thomas Seltzer, 1923.

International collection of folktales includes several NA texts (Tlingit, Zuni, and Eskimo).

203. Gridley, Marion E. *Indian Legends of American Scenes.* Chicago: M. A. Donohue, 1939.

Forty-seven rewritten NA myths and legends associated with American landmarks.

204. Hartman, Carl. "Traditional Belief Concerning the Generation of the Opossum." *JAF,* 34 (1921), 321–23.

Includes some NA accounts of how the marsupial is born.

205. Haslam, Gerald W. *Forgotten Pages of American Literature.* New York: Houghton Mifflin, 1970.

Anthology focuses on written literatures of various ethnic minorities, but includes three NA oral narratives. Introductory essay treats NA verbal art in general.

206. Hungry Wolf, Adolf. *Legends from the Old People.* Invermere, British Columbia: Good Medicine, 1972.

Twenty-two rewritten myth texts from various NA groups. No annotations. Sources not identified.

207. *Indian Legends by Pupils of Haskell Institute, United States Indian Training School.* Lawrence, Kan.: Haskell Printing Department, 1914.

Myth and legend texts and descriptions of customs written by representatives of various NA groups.

208. Insley, Bernice. *Indian Folklore Tales.* New York: Exposition, 1952.

Twenty unannotated, rewritten myth and folktale texts from various groups. No commentary.

209. Johnson, Elizabeth Bishop. *Animal Stories the Indians Told.* New York: Knopf, 1927.

Previously published texts from various NA groups. No commentary or annotation.

210. Jones, James Athearn. *Traditions of the North American Indians: Being a Second and Revised Edition of "Tales of an Indian Camp."* 3 volumes. London: Henry Colburn and Richard Bentley, 1830.

Collection of myths, folktales, and legends from various groups. Includes explanatory notes and attempts at comparative commentary. Materials from first-hand collection and previous publications. Reasonably good for such an early work.

211. Jones, Louis Thomas. *So Say the Indians.* San Antonio: Naylor, 1970.

Collection of myths and legends taken from previously published sources. Emphasis on cross-cultural similarities of narratives.

212. Judd, Mary Catherine. *Wigwam Stories Told by North American Indians.* Boston: Ginn, 1901.

Rewritten myth and legend texts and short sketches describing NA customs. Sources of material are identified. May be for children?

213. Lesueur, J. W. *Indian Legends.* Independence, Mo.: Zion, 1928.

Narrative texts (some previously published) and ceremonial descriptions designed to show NA-Hebrew parallels.

214. "Lively Legends of the Indians, The." *L,* 47 (2 November 1959), 66–77.

Rewritten myth and folktale texts from various groups. No annotations or commentary.

215. Lopez, Barry Holstun. *Giving Birth to Thunder, Sleeping with His Daughter. Coyote Builds North America.* Foreword by Barre Toelken. Kansas City: Sheed Andrews and McMeel, 1977.

Retellings of Coyote stories from various groups. No commentary or annotations. Toelken's foreword briefly comments on the role of Coyote in NA folklore.

216. Macfarlan, Allan A. *Fireside Book of North American Indian Folktales.* Harrisburg, Penn.: Stackpole, 1974.

Unannotated texts of myths and folktales from various NA groups. Some very general data on cultural background. Texts are rewritten.

217. Marriott, Alice L., and Carol K. Rachlin. *American Indian Mythology.* New York: Thomas Y. Crowell, 1968.

Myth and legend texts, mostly from first-hand collection. Contains data on cultural background. Texts arranged thematically.

218. Mason, Bernard S. *Dances and Stories of the American Indian.* New York: A. S. Barnes, 1944.

Primarily designed for recreation directors. Includes instructions for dances from various groups and some retellings of associated myth texts.

219. Matson, Emerson N. *Legends of the Great Chiefs.* Nashville: Thomas Nelson, 1972.

Myth and legend texts collected from various groups by the author or from mss. and previously published sources. No commentary or annotations.

220. Morris, Cora. *Stories from Mythology: North American.* Boston: Marshall Jones, 1924.

Rewritten texts from various culture groups. No commentary or annotations.

221. Skinner, Charles M. *American Myths & Legends. Vol. I.* Philadelphia: Lippincott, 1903.

Rewritten legend and folktale texts without commentary or annotations. Some of the material apparently derives from NA sources.

222. Spence, Lewis. *The Myths of the North American Indians.* London: George G. Harrap, 1914.

Provides a general overview of NA religion and ceremonialism. Some rewritten myth texts from various groups.

223. Squier, Emma-Lindsay. *Children of the Twilight. Folk-Tales of Indian Tribes.* New York: Cosmopolitan, 1926.

Rewritten myth, legend, and folktale texts placed in performance contexts. No commentary or annotation.

224. Sun Bear. *Buffalo Hearts. A Native American's View of Indian Culture, Religion and History.* Healdsburg, Cal.: Naturegraph, 1970.

Miscellany of pieces about NA life and history. Includes a chapter which contains several myth texts from various groups. Also, some data on ceremonialism.

225. Taylor, Dorothy Bright. "Indian Medicinal Herbs and the White Man's Medicine." *NYFQ,* 23 (1967), 274–82.

Survey of NA medicinal plantlore introduced by a myth text from an unidentified group.

226. Thompson, Stith. "Sunday School Stories Among Savages." *TR,* 3 (1917–1918), 109–16.
Treats NA versions of Old and New Testament narratives learned from missionaries.

227. ———. *Tales of the North American Indians.* Cambridge: Harvard Univ. Press, 1929.
Ninety-six stories taken, for the most part, from ethnological monographs. Very thorough comparative annotations make this a landmark volume. Introduction comments on the history of collecting folklore from NAs and the problems of devising categories for NA oral narratives. Contains an extensive bibliography. Re-issued in 1966 by the Indiana Univ. Press.

228. "Visit to the Dead, The, An Indian Legend." *OM,* n. s. 52 (1908), 276–77.
Rewritten Orpheus myth from an unidentified NA group. No commentary or annotation.

229. Williams, Mentor L. *Schoolcraft's Indian Legends.* East Lansing: Michigan State Univ. Press, 1956.
Selections from the 1839 edition of *Algic Researches.*

230. Wood, Charles Erskine Scott. *A Book of Tales. Being Some Myths of the North American Indians.* New York: Vanguard, 1929.
Twenty rewritten myth and folktale texts. Some data on storytelling contexts.

E. Song and Poem Collections

231. Austin, Mary. *The American Rhythm. Studies and Reëxpressions of Amerindian Songs.* Revised edition. Boston: Houghton Mifflin, 1930.
Song texts (words only) from various groups. Extensive introduction on style, poetics, and function of NA verse. 1st edition = 1923.

232. Barnes, Nellie. *American Indian Love Lyrics and Other Verse.* Foreword by Mary Austin. New York: Macmillan, 1925.
Anthology of song texts (words only) from various groups. No context data. An appendix surveys NA poetics.

233. Bierhorst, John. *A Cry from the Earth: Music of the North American Indians.* New York: Four Winds, 1979.
Anthology of song texts (words and music) from various groups. Some data on ritual and other contexts accompany the texts.

234. ———, ed. *In the Trail of the Wind. American Indian Poems and Ritual Orations.* New York: Farrar, Straus and Giroux, 1971.
Translated texts from a variety of groups. Some commentary in endnotes and in a brief general introduction. Major positive feature is Bierhorst's avoidance of tampering with translations made by ethnologists.

235. Brandon, William. *The Magic World: American Indian Songs and Poems.* New York: William Morrow, 1971.
Reworkings of previously translated material. The only commentary is a brief bibliographical essay. Texts identified by group, but no contextual data.

236. Cronyn, George W., ed. *The Path of the Rainbow. An Anthology of Songs and Chants from the Indians of North America.* Foreword by Mary Austin. Afterword by Constance Lindsay Skinner. New York: Boni and Liveright, 1918.

Anthology of songs (words only) from various groups. Translated by various hands. Groups identified, but no other annotation. Also, a section of "Interpretations," poems on NA themes.

237. Curtis, Natalie. "American Indian Cradle-Songs." *MQ,* 7 (1921), 549–58.
Seven lullaby texts (words and music) with brief cultural commentaries for each.

238. Day, A. Grove. *The Sky Clears: Poetry of the American Indians.* New York: Macmillan, 1951.
Texts of NA songs arranged by culture area. Running commentary places material in ritual contexts and reports on poetic value.

239. Densmore, Frances. "The Songs of Indian Soldiers During the World War." *MQ,* 20 (1934), 419–25.
Three song texts (words and music) sung by NAs during service in World War I.

240. Finnegan, Ruth. *A World Treasury of Oral Poetry.* Bloomington: Indiana Univ. Press, 1978.
Cross-cultural anthology includes song texts from Pueblo and Arctic groups.

241. Highwater, Jamake. *Ritual of the Wind. North American Indian Ceremonies, Music, and Dances.* New York: Viking, 1977.
Presents ceremonials with prayer, ritual formula, and song texts from various NA groups. Includes discography of NA music.

242. Rothenberg, Jerome. *Shaking the Pumpkin: Traditional Poetry of the Indian North Americas.* Garden City, N.Y.: Doubleday, 1972.
Attempts to capture oral performance of songs and chants of various NA groups through "total translation." Most of the material is not new translations, but reworkings of earlier translations by ethnologists. Sparse context data for the texts.

243. ———. *Technicians of the Sacred: A Range of Poetries from Africa, America, Asia & Oceania.* Garden City, N.Y.: Doubleday, 1968.
Precursor of 242. NA material comes from a variety of groups. General introduction identifies Rothenberg's poetic principles. Short commentaries accompany each text.

244. Thompson, Denys. *Distant Voices: Poetry of the Preliterate.* Totowa, N.J.: Rowman & Littlefield, 1978.
International anthology includes some sparsely annotated texts from NA groups.

245. Trask, Willard R., ed. *The Unwritten Song: Poetry of the Primitive and Traditional Peoples of the World.* 2 volumes. New York: Macmillan, 1966–1967.
International collection of song texts (words only) with no annotation or context commentary. Sections on the Arctic and on North America.

246. Van Stone, Mary R. "Songs of the Indians." *EP,* 48 (1941), 149–154.
Texts (words and music) of four songs from various groups. Brief informant commentaries on songs.

247. Warren, David. "In Beauty I Walk." *NW,* 12, No. 1 (December–January 1974), 4–11.
Seven song texts (words only) from various groups. Supposed to illustrate NA communion with nature.

248. Yeadon, David. *When the Earth was Young. Songs of the American Indian.* Garden City, N.Y.: Doubleday, 1978.
Song texts (words only) from BAE publications. Some very general comments on the nature of NA song.

F. Collections of Oratory and Miscellaneous Genres

249. Armstrong, Virginia Irving, ed. *I Have Spoken. American History Through the Voices of the Indians.* Introduction by Frederick W. Turner III. Chicago: Swallow, 1971.

Collection of NA oratory from seventeenth through twentieth centuries. Texts are placed in historical contexts. Turner comments on historical value of material.

250. Drake, Samuel G. *The Book of the Indians of North America: Comprising Details in the Lives of About Five Hundred Chiefs and Others, the Most Distinguished Among Them. Also, a History of Their Wars; Their Manners and Customs; Speeches of Orators, &c., from Their First Being Known to Europeans to the Present Time. Exhibiting Also an Analysis of the Most Distinguished Authors Who Have Written Upon the Great Question of the First Peopling of America.* Boston: Josiah Drake, 1833.

Drake's narrative is primarily historical and focuses on groups in the Northeast and Southeast. Some accounts of oratorical performances are interspersed in the narrative. The volume went through a number of editions during the nineteenth century.

251. ———. *Indian Biography, Containing the Lives of More Than Two Hundred Indian Chiefs: Also Such Others of That Race as Have Rendered Their Names Conspicuous in the History of North America from Its First Being Known to Europeans to the Present Period. Giving at Large Their Most Celebrated Speeches, Memorable Sayings, Numerous Anecdotes; and a History of Their Wars. Much of Which Is Taken from Manuscripts Never before Published.* Boston: Josiah Drake, 1832.

Biographical dictionary of famous NAs, including some oration texts.

252. Dundes, Alan, and C. Fayne Porter. "American Indian Student Slang." *AS,* 38 (1963), 270–77.

Survey of vocabulary usages among students at Haskell Institute in 1962.

253. *Events in Indian History Beginning with an Account of the Origin of the American Indians, and Early Settlements in North America, and Embracing Concise Biographies of the Principal Chiefs and Head-Sachems of the Different Indian Tribes, with Narratives and Captivities, Including. . . . Also an Appendix, Containing the Statistics of the Population of the U. States, and an Indian Vocabulary.* Lancaster: G. Hills, 1842.

Contact history with some oration texts.

254. [Goodrich, S. G.]. *Celebrated American Indians.* Boston: Taggard and Thompson, 1864.

Brief biographies. Some oration texts included.

255. Humphrey, Norman B. "The Mock Battle Greeting." *JAF,* 54 (1941), 186–90.

Descriptions of sham battles among various NA groups, which were in fact expressions of friendship. Accounts include depictions of body decorations and war cries.

256. Humphrey, Seth K. *The Indian Dispossessed.* Revised edition. New York: Young People's Missionary Movement, 1905.

Discussion of federal mistreatment of NAs includes excerpts from speeches delivered by representatives of various groups.

257. "Indian Proverbs." *JAF,* 19 (1906), 173–74.

Reprint of an editorial from the *Boston Herald* for 12 March 1906. Contains a list of proverbs attributed to NAs.

258. Jackson, Helen Hunt. *A Century of Dishonor. A Sketch of the United States Government's Dealings with Some of the Indian Tribes.* Boston: Roberts, 1886.

Indictment of federal Indian policy. Includes some oration texts taken from published sources.

259. Lamb, E. Wendell, and Laurence W. Shultz. *Indian Lore.* Winona Lake, Ind.: Light and Life Press, 1964.

Hodgepodge of popularized, romanticized images of NA culture. Contains texts of two speeches (Miami, Seneca).

260. Muntsch, Albert. "American Indian Riddles." *JAF,* 54 (1941), 85.

Reports two accounts of NA riddling.

261. Princess Red Wing. "Indian Communications." *CCC,* 23 (1972), 350–56.

Survey of NA contributions to world literary culture includes texts of prayers and songs.

262. Vanderwith, W. C. *Indian Oratory: Famous Speeches by Noted Indian Chiefs.* Foreword by William R. Carmack. Norman: Univ. of Oklahoma Press, 1971.

Anthology includes texts of speeches delivered between 1758 and 1910. For each text, a note provides biographical data on the orator and some historical context. Carmack's foreword comments briefly on the importance of oratory in NA life.

263. Washburn, Wilcomb E. *The Indian and the White Man.* New York: New York Univ. Press, 1964.

Anthology of documents which relate NAs to American history. Includes several oration texts.

G. Ceremonial and Other Contexts for Folklore Performance

264. Amsden, Charles. "The Changing Indian: The Intertribal Ceremonial at Gallup." *M,* 4 (1930), 101–09.

Description of the ceremonial in 1930. One song text.

265. Andrews, Ralph W. *Curtis' Western Indians.* Seattle: Superior, 1962.

Sketchy biography of the photographer-ethnologist with selected photographs. Commentary for latter includes some material on ceremonialism.

266. Azbill, Henry. "Native Dances: A Basic Part of Culture, Tradition, Religion." *IH,* 1, No. 1 (December 1967), 16–17, 20.

Cross-cultural survey of the importance of dance in NA life.

267. Benedict, Ruth Fulton. *The Concept of the Guardian Spirit in North America.* MAAA No. 29 (1923).

Cross-cultural survey of the guardian spirit concept with attention to its relationship with cultural features such as shamanism.

268. ———. "Religion," in *General Anthropology.* Ed. Franz Boas. Boston: D. C. Heath, 1938, pp. 627–65.

International survey of religious and ceremonial practices includes NA examples.

269. Bergquist, Laura. "Peyote: The Strange Church of Cactus Eaters." *Lo,* 21 (10 December 1957), 36–41.

Survey of belief system and ritual procedure of the NA Church.

270. Blumensohn, Jules. "The Fast Among North American Indians." *AA,* 35 (1933), 451–69.

Concerned with ritual aspects of fasting, with mythic accounts of its origin, and with fasting as an accompaniment for sacred narration.

271. Boas, Franz. "The Ethnological Significance of Esoteric Doctrines." *S,* n. s. 16 (28 November 1902), 872–874.

Describes work that has been done on complex NA ceremonialism and suggests that equal attention should be paid to less elite activities by ethnologists.

272. Boyd, James P. *Recent Indian Wars, Under the Lead of Sitting Bull, and Other Chiefs; with a Full Account of the Messiah Craze, and Ghost Dances.* NP: Publishers Union, 1891.

History of NA-EA conflicts from 1840s through Wounded Knee Massacre 1890. One chapter focuses on the Ghost Dance. Useful for contemporary response.

273. Boyd, Susan H. "This Indian Is Not an Indian: Labelling Play in Powwowdom," in *Play: Anthropological Perspectives.* Ed. Michael A. Salter. West Point, N.Y.: Leisure Press, 1978, pp. 213–26.

Cross-cultural survey of ways in which NAs express "Indianness" and of the dynamics of pan-Indian ceremonials.

274. Carter, William Harry. *Medical Practices and Burial Customs of the North American Indians.* London, Ontario: Namind, 1973.

Pamphlet includes a miscellany of data from newspapers and other periodicals. Some descriptions of ceremonials.

275. Charles, Lucile Hoerr. "Drama in First-Naming Ceremonies." *JAF,* 64 (1951), 11–35.

International survey of rituals wherein the first name is bestowed on a newborn child. With several NA examples. Chanting and singing may accompany such rituals.

276. ———. "Drama in Shaman Exorcism." *JAF,* 66 (1953), 95–122.

International survey of dramatic elements in shamanic rituals includes some NA examples. Some treatment of songs and chants.

277. ———. "Drama in War." *JAF,* 68 (1955), 253–81.

International survey of the psychological significance of dramatic elements in the warfare of nonliterate peoples. With several NA examples. Some attention to battle cries, songs, and dialogues.

278. ———. "Growing Up Through Drama." *JAF,* 59 (1946), 247–62.

International survey of dramatic elements in puberty rituals uses examples from various NA groups. Discusses chanting and singing.

279. ———. "Regeneration Through Drama at Death." *JAF,* 61 (1948), 151–74.

International survey of dramatic elements occurring during mortuary rituals. Some examples come from NA groups.

280. Collins, John J. *Primitive Religion.* Totowa, N.J.: Littlefield, Adams, 1978.

Overview of the anthropology of religion focuses on ceremonialism with many NA examples.

281. Culin, Stewart. "American Indian Games (1902)." *AA,* 5 (1903), 58–64.

Classifies NA games into two types: those of chance, those of dexterity. Most of the games have ceremonial associations.

282. ———. "Games of the North American Indians." *ARBAE,* 24 (1902–1903), 3–809.

General typological catalogue of NA games. Data on mythic references to and mythic sources for some games as well as musical accompaniment for games. Information is drawn from previously published sources.

283. Dall, William Healey. "On Masks, Labrets, and Certain Aboriginal Customs, with an Inquiry into the Bearing of Their Geographical Distribution." *ARBAE,* 3 (1881–1882), 67–203.

Survey of ceremonial masking throughout the western hemisphere. Treats NA groups from Southwest, Northwest Coast, Arctic, and Northeast (Iroquois).

284. Darnell, Regna. "Hallowell's 'Bear Ceremonialism' and the Emergence of Boasian Anthropology." *E,* 5 (1977), 13–30.

Study of the effects of A. Irving Hallowell's essay on bear ceremonialism (294) as a transition between distributional studies and the study of cultural integration.

285. Davis, H. L. "An American Apostle." *AM,* 30 (October 1933), 219–27.

Very negative treatment of the development of the Ghost Dance.

286. Dixon, Roland B. "Some Aspects of the American Shaman." *JAF,* 21 (1908), 1–12.

Enumeration of common features of NA shamans with emphasis on lack of dependence on deities and reliance on natural forces.

287. Eastman, John. "Powwow." *NH,* 70 (November 1970), 24–27.

Description of a pan-Indian festival held in Michigan.

288. Eaton, Evelyn. "Towards Initiation." *P,* 1, No. 3 (Spring 1976), 42–46.

General description of procedures and philosophy of NA initiation rituals.

289. Elliott, Henry W. "Wild Babies." *H,* 57 (1878), 829–38.

Cross-cultural survey of NA socialization practices includes description of a shamanistic curing ritual.

290. Ellis, Havelock. "Mescal: A Study of a Divine Plant." *PSM,* 61, No. 1 (May 1902), 52–71.

Primary concern is with psychosomatic effects of mescaline usage, but some attention to ceremonial uses by NAs.

291. Farb, Peter. "Ghost Dance and Cargo Cult." *Ho,* 11 (Spring 1969), 58–65.

General consideration of revitalization movements, primarily among NAs. Data on Longhouse Religion and Ghost Dance.

292. Fletcher, Alice C. "Some Ethnological Aspects of the Problem." *AA,* 14 (1912), 37–39.

Part of a symposium on the origin and distribution of NA groups. Points out ceremonial similarities among various groups.

293. Gaddis, Vincent H. "The Cult of the Sacred Cactus." *T,* 92 (November 1948), 16–17, 33.

Brief survey of history and ritual procedures of the NA Church.

294. Hallowell, A. Irving. "Bear Ceremonialism in the Northern Hemisphere." *AA,* 28 (1926), 1–175.

Thorough survey of the place of the bear in religious systems throughout North America and Eurasia. Verbal performances which are mentioned include hunters' songs, post-hunting prayers and songs, and other ceremonial texts. See 284 for an evaluation of the effects of this study.

295. Hartley, Marsden. "Red Man Ceremonials. An American Plea for American Esthetics." *A&A,* 9 (January 1920), 7–14.

Argues that NA ceremonialism can provide the basis for a national esthetic consciousness.

296. Hewett, Edgar L. "Native American Artists." *A&A,* 13 (March 1922), 103–12.

Description of contemporary NA painters includes discussion of their ceremonial subjects. Includes an Omaha song text.

297. Highwater, Jamake. *Song from the Earth: American Indian Painting.* Boston: New York Graphic Society, 1976.

Historical survey and description of work of several contemporary NA painters. Carefully relates specific paintings to ceremonialism.

298. Hobday, José. "Forced Assimilation and the Native American Dance." *CC,* 26 (1976), 189–94.

Treats effects of acculturation on ceremonialism.

299. Hofmann, Charles. "American Indian Music in Wisconsin, Summer 1946." *JAF,* 60 (1947), 289–93.

Description of pan-Indian festival.

300. Howard, James H. "Pan-Indian Culture of Oklahoma." *ScM,* 81 (November 1955), 215–20.

Shows effects of amalgamation of tribal groups in Oklahoma on ceremonalism and other aspects of culture.

301. Hultkrantz, Åke. "Ritual in Native North American Religions," in 166, pp. 135–47.

Survey of types and functions of NA ceremonialism. Response from Joseph Epes Brown (pp. 147–49).

302. Hurdy, John Major. *American Indian Religions.* Los Angeles: Sherbourne, 1970.

Poorly written, nonscholarly treatment of ways in which NA religions provide alternatives to addiction to wealth and power.

303. Jaeger, Ellsworth. "The Way of the False Face." *SAM,* 43 (November 1943), 92–93.

Cross-cultural survey of ceremonial masks among NAs. Halloween feature.

304. Jarvis, Samuel Farmer. *A Discourse on the Religion of the Indian Tribes of North America, Delivered Before the New-York Historical Society, December 20, 1819.* New York: C. Wiley, 1820.

General survey of NA religious practices, compared unfavorably with Christianity.

305. Jenkins, Linda Walsh, and Ed Wapp, Jr. "Native American Performance." *DR,* 20, No. 2 (June 1976), 5–12.

Cross-cultural treatment of NA ceremonials as drama. With song texts (words only).

306. Jones, Louis Thomas. *Love—Indian Style.* San Antonio: Naylor, 1973.

Survey of NA courtship and marriage customs and ceremonies.

307. Kellar, H. "Magic Among the Red Men." *NAR,* 157 (1893), 591–600.

Discusses the magical practices of various NA groups. Emphasizes the deep seriousness of the practices.

308. Kinney, J. P. *Facing Indian Facts.* Laurens, New York: Press of the Village Printer, 1973.

Defense of federal policies toward NAs. Reprints letters written by Charles H. Burke, Commissioner of the Office of Indian Affairs, condemning NA dances.

309. Kurath, Gertrude. "Masked Clowns." *To,* 4, No. 3 (Spring 1956), 108–12.

Explores function of ritual clowns in various NA cultures.

310. ———. "Pan-Indianism in Great Lakes Tribal Festivals." *JAF,* 70 (1957), 179–82.

Description of "powwows," occurring in the Great Lakes area, which bring together representatives of various NA groups for song and dance performances.

311. ———. "Summertime Is Powwow Time." *DM,* 40, No. 5 (May 1966), 40–41, 85–86.

Description of pan-Indian ceremonial performances.

312. La Barre, Weston. "The 'Diabolic Root.'" *NYTM,* 1 November 1964, pp. 96–98.

Brief description of peyote ritual. Major focus is on legal status of NA Church.

313. ———. *The Ghost Dance: Origins of Religion.* Garden City, N.Y.: Doubleday, 1970.

Study in the anthropology and psychology of religion with focus on the Plains Ghost Dance. Elements of the Ghost Dance are discussed in comparative perspective.

314. ———. "Native American Beers." *AA,* 40 (1938), 224–34.

Though primarily concerned with surveying alcoholic drink among NAs, La Barre cites folklore about such beverages. In oral narratives and descriptions of ceremonialism includes references to beers.

315. ———. *The Peyote Cult.* YUPA No. 19 (1938).

Survey of aspects of peyotism based on fieldwork with various groups in 1930s. Some data on ritual procedure.

316. ———, David P. McAllester, J. S. Slotkin, Omer C. Stewart, and Sol Tax. "Statement on Peyote." *S,* n. s. 114 (30 November 1951), 582–83.

Argues legitimacy of NA Church by analyzing the belief system.

317. La Farge, Oliver. *A Pictorial History of the American Indian.* New York: Crown, 1956.

Profusely illustrated survey includes references to mythology and ceremonialism. Chapters on the Ghost Dance and peyotism.

318. Laubin, Reginald and Gladys. *Indian Dances of North America. Their Importance to Indian Life.* Norman: Univ. of Oklahoma Press, 1977.

Describes the dances, costumes, body decorations, and musical accompaniment. Occasional allusions to myths associated with dances, but the volume misses the opportunity to explore the relationship between verbal art and dance.

319. Leh, Leonard L. "The Shaman in Aboriginal North American Society." *UCS,* 21 (1934), 199–263.

Cross-cultural survey of NA shamanism. Includes descriptions of rituals and accounts of shamanistic activities.

320. Levine, Stuart. "Our Indian Minority." *CQ,* 16, No. 3 (Winter 1968), 297–320.

Treatment of status of contemporary NAs deals with modern ceremonialism, including peyotism, and joking. Focuses on generalizations made about NAs.

321. Loeb, Edwin M. "Tribal Initiations and Secret Societies." *UCPAAE,* 25 (1929), 249–88.

International survey of initiation rituals includes NA examples.

322. Lowie, Robert H. "American Indian Cultures." *AM,* 20 (July 1930), 362–66.

Argues that NA cultures are diverse. With some attention to ceremonialism.

323. ———. "Ceremonialism in North America." *AA*, 16 (1914), 602–31.

Enumeration of important ceremonies from several NA culture areas and discussion of problems arising from ceremonial data. The relationship between myth and ritual is explored.

324. ———. "Prestige Among Indians." *AM*, 12 (December 1927), 446–48.

Treats role of ceremonialism in securing and maintaining prestige.

325. MacLeod, William Christie. *The American Indian Frontier*. New York: Knopf, 1928.

Contact history includes chapter on revitalization movements and their ceremonies (Ghost Dance, peyotism).

326. Maddox, John Lee. *The Medicine Man. A Sociological Study of the Character and Evolution of Shamanism*. New York: Macmillan, 1923.

Cross-cultural survey of ritual procedures of tribal healers. Some NA illustrations.

327. Makarius, Laura. "Ritual Clowns and Symbolic Behaviour." *D*, 69 (1970), 44–73.

Discusses the ceremonial role of the clown, especially among the Zuni.

328. Matthews, Washington. "The Study of Ceremony." *JAF*, 10 (1897), 257–63.

Survey of methodologies for proper study of ceremony ("ceremoniology") with NA examples.

329. Millspaugh, Charles F. "Indian Corn." *Ch*, 31 (July 1900), 338–43.

Written by a botanist, but some attention to NA ceremonialism associated with corn.

330. Mooney, James. "The Indian Navel Cord." *JAF*, 17 (1904), 197.

Brief overview of customary treatments, among various NA groups, of umbilical cord.

331. Newberne, Robert E. L. *Peyote: An Abridged Compilation from the Files of the Bureau of Indian Affairs*. 3rd edition. Lawrence, Kan.: Haskell Institute, ND [1925?].

Pamphlet designed to warn NAs of the dangers of peyote. Includes some data on peyotism and its rituals.

332. Oaks, Orville A. "Poplar, the People's Tree." *IA&VE*, 46 (June 1957), 185–87.

Surveys ceremonial uses of the poplar by various NA groups.

333. ———. "Red Cedar or Miskáwak." *IA&VE*, 48 (February 1959), 56–58, 26A.

Lists NA groups for whom cedar is sacred. Some data on ceremonialism.

334. Peet, Stephen D. "Secret Societies and Sacred Mysteries." *AAOJ*, 27 (1905), 81–96.

Survey of esoteric religious organizations and their ceremonialism. Includes NA examples.

335. *The Peyote Ritual. Visions and Descriptions of Monroe Tsa Toke*. San Francisco: Grabhorn, 1957.

Paintings of peyote symbols with explanations of their ritual significance.

336. Pierson, Mrs. Delavan L. "American Indian Peyote Worship." *MRW*, 38 (March 1915), 201–6.

Hostile treatment of belief system and practices of NA Church. With ceremonial description.

337. Radin, Paul. "Religion of the North American Indians." *JAF*, 27 (1914), 335–73.

Cross-cultural survey of NA religious beliefs and practices. Includes discussion of theology, supernaturalism, and ceremonialism.

338. Rister, Carl Coke. *Baptist Missions Among the American Indians*. Atlanta: Home Mission Board, Southern Baptist Convention, 1944.

General data on religion and ceremonialism.

339. Rukeyser, Muriel. "Indian Fiesta Huge Success." *N*, 144 (29 May 1937), 616–18.

Sardonic description of a highly staged pan-Indian festival in Palm Springs, California.

340. Safford, William E. "Daturas of the Old World and New: An Account of Their Narcotic Properties and Their Use in Oracular and Initiatory Ceremonies." *ARSI for 1920*, pp. 537–67.

Includes descriptions of ceremonies among Zuni, Luiseño, and Algonquins.

341. Seig, Louis. *Tobacco, Peacepipes, and Indians*. Palmer Lake, Col.: Filter, 1971.

Pamphlet surveys ritual usages of tobacco among various NA groups.

342. Seymour, Gertrude. "Peyote Worship. An Indian Cult and a Powerful Drug." *Su*, 36 (13 May 1916), 181–84.

Historical survey of peyote use in North America and thorough description of ritual procedure of NA Church.

343. Snow, Dean R. "Rock Art and the Power of Shamans." *NH*, 77 (February 1977), 42–49.

Argues for a connection between NA pictographs and petroglyphs and shamanism. Cites ceremonialism and mythology from various groups.

344. Stewart, Kenneth M. "Spirit Possession." *To*, 4, No. 3 (Spring 1956), 41–49.

Discusses shamanism among various NA groups.

345. ———. "Spirit Possession in Native America." *SJA*, 2 (1946), 323–39.

Cross-cultural survey of shamanistic spirit possession.

346. Stirling, Matthew W. *Indians of the Americas*. Washington: National Geographic Society, 1955.

Popular survey of NA groups arranged by culture area. Contains extensive data on ceremonial behavior.

347. Stockwell, G. Archie. "Indian Medicine." *PSM*, 29 (1886), 649–60.

Cross-cultural survey of shamanistic ceremonialism.

348. Stone, Eric. *Medicine Among the American Indians*. New York: Paul B. Hoeber, 1932.

Survey of NA medical practices includes chapters on supernatural and ceremonial therapeutics.

349. Swanson, Guy E. "The Search for a Guardian Spirit: A Process of Empowerment in Simpler Societies." *Eth*, 12 (1973), 359–78.

Cross-cultural survey of the guardian spirit complex throughout North America. Some ceremonial descriptions.

350. Tait, W. McD. "Indian Dances." *OM*, n. s. 65 (1915), 88–91.

Surveys ceremonial singing and dancing among various groups.

351. Tedlock, Barbara. "The Clown's Way," in 163, pp. 105–18.

Discusses the role of the sacred clown among various NA groups.

352. Townsend, James G. "Disease and the Indian." *ScM*, 47 (December 1938), 479–95.

Surveys shamanistic healing ceremonies and contrasts them with modern hospital care.

353. Underhill, Ruth M. *Red Man's Religion. Beliefs and Practices of the Indians North of Mexico.* Chicago: Univ. of Chicago Press, 1965.

Broad, popularly oriented survey of religious beliefs and practices among NAs. Includes extensive data on ceremonialism.

354. Van De Water, Marjorie. "Old Indian Custom—Boo." *SNL,* 60 (27 October 1951), 262–63.

Cross-cultural survey of NA ceremonial masking. Halloween feature.

355. Van Gennep, Arnold. *The Rites of Passage.* Trans. Monika B. Vizedom and Gabrielle L. Caffee. Chicago: Univ. of Chicago Press, 1960.

International survey of life crisis ceremonies includes NA adoption and initiation rituals.

356. Vogel, Virgil J. *American Indian Medicine.* Norman: Univ. of Oklahoma Press, 1970.

Emphasis is on NA medicinal plantlore. Some attention to ceremonialism.

357. von Schmidt-Pauli, Edgar. *We Indians. The Passing of a Great Race. Being the Recollections of the Last of the Great Indian Chiefs, Big Chief White Horse Eagle.* Trans. Christopher Turner. New York: E. P. Dutton, 1931.

Weirdly romantic work which surveys the cultures of various groups including their ceremonials. Allegedly from the oral testimony of an Osage.

358. Webster, Hutton. *Primitive Secret Societies. A Study in Early Politics and Religion.* New York: Macmillan, 1908.

International survey of functions and rituals of secret societies. With some NA examples.

359. Willoughby, Charles C. *Indian Masks.* New York: Exposition of Indian Tribal Arts, 1931.

Pamphlet discusses masks, their mythological associations, and their ritual uses.

360. Willoya, William, and Vinson Brown. *Warriors of the Rainbow. Strange and Prophetic Indian Dreams.* Healdsburg, Cal.: Naturegraph, 1962.

Surveys NA visionary experiences. Among the topics covered are the Ghost Dance and peyotism.

361. Wilson, Eddie W. "The Gourd in Magic." *WF,* 13 (1954), 113–24.

International survey includes data on NA use of gourds as ceremonial rattles.

362. Wissler, Clark. "The Indian and the Supernatural." *NH,* 42 (1938), 121–26, 154.

Random notes on supernaturalism in an unidentified group includes descriptions of ceremonials.

363. ———. "The Lore of the Demon Mask." *NH,* 28 (1928), 339–52.

International survey of ceremonial masking. Several NA groups are cited. Some masks represent mythical beings.

364. Work, Hubert. "The Indian Medicine Man." *ARR,* 70 (1924), 516–20.

Surveys shamanism among various NA groups.

365. Worsley, Israel. *A View of the American Indians. Their General Character, Customs, Language, Public Festivals, Religious Rites, and Traditions: Shewing* [sic] *Them to Be the Descendants of the Ten Tribes of Israel. The Language of Prophecy Concerning Them, and the Course by Which They Travelled from Media into America.* London: by the Author, 1828.

Argument based, in part, on parallels between NA and Hebrew religious systems and ceremonialism.

366. Wright, Robert C. *Indian Masonry.* Ann Arbor, Mich.: Tyler, 1907.

Describes several NA secret societies and their ceremonies. Connects them with Freemasonry.

367. Yarrow, H. C. "A Further Contribution to the Study of the Mortuary Customs of the North American Indians." *ARBAE,* 1 (1879–1880), 87–203.

Broad survey of funerary practices includes discussions of ceremonies from various groups.

H. Theory and Commentary: General

368. Aitken, Barbara. "Temperament in Native American Religion." *JAIGBI,* 60 (1930), 363–87.

Identifies two types of NA religion: personalized (exemplified by Winnebago) and social (e.g., Pueblo). Contains summaries of myths and descriptions of ceremonialism.

369. Alexander, Hartley Burr. "The Great Spirit." *NMQ,* 1 (1931), 3–15.

Survey of the concept of a high god among various NA groups.

370. ———. "Philosophic Imagination in Indian America." *NMQ,* 1 (1931), 239–46.

Discussion of the "savage mind" among NAs. With comparisons to western thought.

371. ———. "The Religious Spirit of the American Indian as Shown in the Development of His Religious Rites and Customs." *OC,* 24 (1910), 45–54, 74–109.

Cross-cultural survey includes descriptions of ceremonials. With ritual and song texts.

372. ———. *The World's Rim: Great Mysteries of the North American Indians.* Foreword by Clyde Kluckhohn. Lincoln: Univ. of Nebraska Press, 1953.

Attempts to capture the NA world view through an examination of rituals, chants, songs, prayers, and myths. Contains texts and excerpts from a number of forms. With descriptions of Calumet Ritual, Corn Dance, Hako, Sun Dance, and others. Technique is description and cross-cultural comparison.

373. Allen, Paula Gunn. "The Sacred Hoop: A Contemporary Indian Perspective on American Indian Literature." *CC,* 26 (1976), 144–63.

Urges scholars to view NA oral literature from an NA perspective. Published in slightly different form in 97 (pp. 111–35).

374. ———. "Symbol and Structure in Native American Literature: Some Basic Considerations." *CCC,* 24 (1973), 267–70.

Warns against applying EA concepts to NA oral literature. NA material embodies such ideas as the unity and symbolic potential of all creation.

375. Astrov, Margot. "The Indian and the Word." *NMFR,* 6 (1951–1952), 7–10.

Surveys the importance of oral tradition in NA cultures.

376. Austin, Mary. "Aboriginal American Literature," in *American Writers on American Literature.* Ed. John Macy. New York: Tudor, 1934, pp. 426–41.

General survey of NA oral literature and of some of its students.

377. Barrett, S. M. *Sociology of the American Indians.* Kansas City, Mo.: Burton, 1946.

Attempt at a general delineation of NA society. Chapters on dance, music, and religion. Several rewritten myth texts.

378. Bascom, William R. "Folklore and Anthropology." *JAF,* 66 (1953), 283–90.

Presents an anthropological definition of "folklore" and cites anthropological concerns in the study of folklore. Cites NA materials for illustrations. Reprinted in 114 (pp. 25–33).

379. ———. "Four Functions of Folklore." *JAF,* 67 (1954), 333–49.

Suggests that folklore generally operates toward the maintenance of social and cultural cohesion. Several illustrations drawn from NA traditions. Reprinted in 114 (pp. 279–98).

380. Benedict, Ruth. "Configurations of Culture in North America." *AA,* 34 (1932), 1–27.

Characterization of the ethoi of various NA groups using Nietzsche's Apollonian/Dionysian distinction. Views folklore as a key to the ethos of a culture. Includes song and prayer texts.

381. Bierhorst, John. "American Indian Verbal Art and the Role of the Literary Critic." *JAF,* 88 (1975), 401–8.

Because of esoteric, allusive quality of much NA oral literature, its student must often serve as literary critic and explain pervasive themes, metaphors, and motifs.

382. ———. "The Concept of Childhood in American Indian Lore." *BRH,* 81 (1978), 395–405.

Refers to children in myth, song, and ceremonialism.

383. Bischoff, Robert. "The Peyote Cult." *WA,* n. s. 29 (1948), 28–37.

History of peyotism includes legend text and ceremonial description.

384. Boas, Franz. "Evolution or Diffusion?" *AA,* 26 (1924), 340–44.

Primary concern is with similar social systems among Northwest Coast and Southwest groups. Also shows how studies of NA folklore have revealed the importance of diffusion in accounting for cross-cultural similarities.

385. ———. "The Origin of Totemism." *JAF,* 23 (1910), 392–93.

Reaffirms the idea that totemism grew out of belief in personal guardian spirits. Cites Northwest Coast mythology and ceremonialism.

386. ———. "Stylistic Aspects of Primitive Literature." *JAF,* 38 (1925), 329–39.

International survey of primitive literature, much of it from NA groups, demonstrates a consistent emphasis on rhythmic form.

387. Bourke, John G. "Remarks [Folk-Lore Concerning Arrows]." *AA,* o. s. 4 (1891), 71-74.

Response to a symposium on "Arrows and Arrowmakers" includes data on arrows in the folklore of various NA groups.

388. Bradford, Alexander W. *American Antiquities and Researches into the Origin and History of the Red Race.* New York: Dayton and Saxton, 1841.

Attempts to reconstruct NA prehistory through archeological and ethnological investigations. Examines NA mythology and ceremonialism as compared to Old World traditions.

389. Brandon, William. *The Last Americans: The Indian in American Culture.* New York: McGraw-Hill, 1974.

Revised edition of the text for *The American Heritage Book of Indians.* Focuses on history of NAs, especially in contact situations. Contains "A Portfolio of American Indian Poetry," translated oral texts. References to mythology and ceremonialism occur throughout the volume.

390. Brinton, Daniel G. *Aboriginal American Authors and Their Productions; Especially Those in the Native Languages. A Chapter in the History of Literature.* Philadelphia: NP, 1883.

Survey of literary productions, primarily oral, of NAs. Includes narrative, didactic, oratorical, poetical, and dramatic literature. Examines both literary and ethnological values.

391. Brown, Joseph Epes. "Contemplation Through Actions: North American Indians," in *Contemplation and Action in Western Religions.* Ed. Yusuf Ibish and Ileana Marculescu. Houston: Rothko Chapel, 1978, pp. 243–53.

Argues that inability to find doctrinal structures in NA religions arises from the interrelationship of those religions with all of life.

392. ———. "The Roots of Renewal," in 96, pp. 25–34.

Suggests that NA religion and oral tradition continue to provide a well-rooted approach to existence.

393. Brownell, Charles de Wolf. *The Indian Races of North and South America; Comprising an Account of the Principal Aboriginal Races; A Description of Their National Customs, Mythology, and Religious Ceremonies; the History of Their Most Powerful Tribes, and of Their Most Celebrated Chiefs and Warriors; Their Intercourse and Wars with the European Settlers; and a Great Variety of Anecdote and Description, Illustrative of Personal and National Character.* New York: H. E. & S. S. Scranton, 1854.

Survey of contact history, but does include data on ceremonialism and summaries of myths and historical legends from Northeast, Southeast, Midwest, and Plains groups.

394. Buchanan, James. *Sketches of the History, Manners, and Customs, of the North American Indians, with a Plan for Their Melioration.* 2 volumes. New York: William Borradaile, 1824.

Historical work includes a Delaware legend about arrival of Dutch at Manhattan and several oration texts from various groups.

395. Bunge, Robert P. "The American Indian: A Natural Philosopher." *Int,* 106 (June 1978), 493–98.

Emphasizes joy of life in the philosophy of NAs.

396. Burton, Jimalee. *Indian Heritage, Indian Pride: Stories That Touched My Life.* Foreword by W. W. Keeler. Norman: Univ. of Oklahoma Press, 1974.

Paintings and narrative recount author's Cherokee childhood. Brief chapters on ceremonialism, music, and dance generalize about various NA groups.

397. Campbell, John. "The Ancient Literature of America." *PTRSC,* 2nd series, 2, section 2 (1896), 41–66.

Surveys NA aptitude for verbal art. Includes song and story excerpts.

398. Campbell, Joseph. "Primitive Man as Metaphysician," in 102, pp. 380–92.

International survey, including many NA examples, of philosophical concepts among nonliterate groups.

399. Cardenal, Ernesto. "Indian Heavens." *Ams,* 16, No. 1 (January 1964), 23–27.

Cross-cultural treatment of NA concepts of paradise. Includes references to myths and texts of Ghost Dance songs.

400. Carter, E. Russell. *The Gift Is Rich.* New York: Friendship Press, 1955.

Romantic overview of NA life by former religious work director of Haskell Institute. Includes some traditional verbal art and some Christian songs, prayers, and poems attributed to NA sources.

401. "Church and the Cactus, The" *Ti,* 64 (9 August 1954), 49–50.

Description of ritual of NA Church. With excerpt from origin myth.

402. Conrad, Laetitia Moon. "The Idea of God Held by North American Indians." *AJT,* 7 (1903), 635–46.

Characterization of NA theology with prayer texts and excerpts from myths.

403. Cook, Elizabeth. "Propulsives in Native American Literature." *CCC,* 24 (1973), 271–74.

EA fears of the death of NA culture are unfounded, as shown by preservation of cultural values and recognition of necessity of culture change in NA literature, oral and written.

404. Corlett, William Thomas. *The Medicine-Man of the American Indian and His Cultural Background.* Springfield, Ill.: Charles C. Thomas, 1935.

Cross-cultural survey of healers in North and South America. Includes references to myths and descriptions of ceremonies.

405. Currier, Charles Warren. "Indian Traits." *LM,* 94 (September 1914), 324–33.

Covers religion, folklore, and metaphorical language.

406. Curtis, Natalie. "The Perpetuating of Indian Art." *O,* 105 (22 November 1913), 623–31.

Cites need to preserve NA artistic achievements in music and painting. One song text (words and music) from Zuni.

407. Cushman, H. B. *History of the Choctaw, Chickasaw, and Natchez Indians.* Greenville, Tex.: Headlight Printing House, 1899.

Historical focus is on Southeast groups, but general introduction to NA culture includes references to folklore materials.

408. Dam, Cornelia H. "Tobacco Among the Indians." *AM,* 16 (January 1929), 74–76.

Survey of the role of tobacco in various cultures. Contains a Winnebago myth text.

409. Day, Gordon M. "Oral Tradition as Complement." *Eh,* 19 (1972), 99–108.

Demonstrates historical value of some NA oral traditions by citing Abnaki accounts of an event that occurred in 1759.

410. Deloria, Vine, Jr. *God Is Red.* New York: Grosset & Dunlap, 1973.

General survey of contemporary status of NA religions —traditional and Christian—with emphasis on theological comparisons between them.

411. ———. "Religion and the Modern Indian." *CuH,* 67 (December 1974), 250–53.

Surveys traditional and contemporary NA religious ideas with attention to modern pan-Indianism.

412. Densmore, Frances. "Notes on the Indians' Belief in the Friendliness of Nature." *SJA,* 4 (1948), 94–97.

Treats references to nature in some NA myths and songs.

413. Dial, Adolph L. "Death in the Life of Native Americans." *IH,* 11, No. 3 (September 1978), 32–37.

Cross-cultural survey of symbolic role of death in mythology, ceremonialism, and general world view.

414. Dobie, J. Frank. "Coyote: Hero-God and Trickster." *SWR,* 32 (1947), 336–44.

Overview of the image of Coyote in NA folklore.

415. Dorman, Rushton M. *The Origin of Primitive Superstitions and Their Development into the Worship of Spirits and the Doctrine of Spiritual Agency Among the Aborigines of America.* Philadelphia: Lippincott, 1881.

Discusses relevance of "doctrine of spirits" to NA culture. Includes references to mythology and ceremonialism.

416. Dorris, Michael. "Native American Literature in an Ethnohistorical Context." *CE,* 41, No. 2 (October 1979), 147–62.

Argues that courses in NA folklore and literature must recognize the multi-cultural nature of NA life. Analyzes a Tanaina story to show necessity of having background knowledge of culture.

417. Dorsey, J. Owen. "Indian Doctrine of Souls." *JAF,* 6 (1893), 298.

Cross-cultural parallels to concepts among the Chinook discussed by Boas (4647).

418. Dorson, Richard M. "Ethnohistory and Ethnic Folklore." *Eh,* 8 (1961), 12–30.

Survey of scholars' attitudes toward the historicity of oral tradition and of ways in which history and folklore can relate. Some NA examples.

419. Dundes, Alan. "Oral Literature," in *Introduction to Cultural Anthropology. Essays in the Scope and Methods of the Science of Man.* Ed. James A. Clifton. Boston: Houghton Mifflin, 1968, pp. 117–29.

Treats the nature of oral literature and its study with special reference to NA traditions.

420. Eastman, Charles A. "Education Without Books." *Cr,* 21, No. 4 (January 1912), 372–77.

Characterizes NA socialization, including the role of traditional narratives.

421. ———. "The Indian and the Moral Code." *O,* 97 (7 January 1911), 30–34.

General survey of NA morality.

422. Eastman, Elaine Goodale. "The American Indian and His Religion." *MRW,* 60 (March 1937), 128–30.

Argues that the decline of traditional NA cultures and harmful features of some NA religions make missionizing urgent.

423. Eastman, Mrs. Mary H. *The American Aboriginal Portfolio.* Philadelphia: Lippincott, Grambo, 1853.

Collections of vignettes of NA life (various groups). Includes song/prayer texts and descriptions of ceremonialism.

424. ———. *Chicóra and Other Regions of the Conquerors and the Conquered.* Philadelphia: Lippincott, Grambo, 1854.

Similar to 423. Includes retellings of myths and legends, song texts, and descriptions of ceremonialism.

425. Embree, Edwin R. *Indians of the Americas. Historical Pageant.* Boston: Houghton Mifflin, 1939.

Popular survey treats ceremonialism among Plains and Pueblo groups and Iroquois. Summaries of myths included.

426. Farwell, Arthur. "The Artistic Possibilities of Indian Myth." *PL*, 15 (1904), 46–61.

Surveys the literary potential of NA folklore and of works based thereon. Includes text of Pawnee Hako song.

427. Fiske, John. *The Discovery of America with Some Account of Ancient America and the Spanish Conquest.* 2 volumes. Boston: Houghton Mifflin, 1901.

Chapter I, "Ancient America," treats NA cultures in Southeast, Northeast, and Southwest. Some data on ceremonialism. References to mythology.

428. Fletcher, Alice C. "Glimpses of Indian Child Life." *O*, 53 (16 May 1896), 891–92.

Description of socialization processes includes a myth text in storytelling context.

429. Foreman, Carolyn Thomas. *Indians Abroad, 1493–1938.* Norman: Univ. of Oklahoma Press, 1943.

Discussion of exhibitions of NAs in Europe with descriptions of song and dance performances.

430. Frost, John. *The Indian: on the Battle-Field and in the Wigwam.* Boston: Wentworth, Hewes, 1859.

Collection of sketches of NA life includes descriptions of ceremonies and oration texts.

431. Gatschet, Albert S. "Water-Monsters of American Aborigines." *JAF*, 12 (1899), 255–60.

Survey of beliefs and narratives regarding water monsters from various groups.

432. Goddard, Pliny Earle. "The Relation of Folk-Lore to Anthropology." *JAF*, 28 (1915), 18–23.

Sees folklore as valuable in preserving history of nonliterate peoples and in reflecting their lifeways. Cites NA examples.

433. Goldenweiser, A. A. "Totemism, An Analytical Study." *JAF*, 23 (1910), 179–293.

Emphasizes the emotional rather than the religious elements of totemism. Includes myth texts and ceremonial descriptions from various Northwest Coast groups. See 457.

434. Grinnell, George Bird. "Shall Indian Lore Be Saved?" *AMJ*, 13 (1913), 135–37.

Urges ethnographic and folklore fieldwork before knowledge of traditional life disappears.

435. ———. "Tenure of Land Among the Indians." *AA*, 9 (1907), 1–11.

NA concept of private property did not extend to land ownership, but included possession of rights to sacred songs and particular stories.

436. ———. "The Wild Indian." *AM*, 83 (1899), 20–29.

Attempts to counteract stereotypes of NAs. Includes summary of a Blackfoot myth which illustrates the importance of family affection in NA life.

437. Hallowell, A. Irving. "The Impact of the American Indian on American Culture." *AA*, 59 (1957), 201–17.

Examination of the interest in NA verbal art and music, among other topics. Primary concern is with the transformation of NA folklore in art and literature.

438. Hamm, Victor H. "Greeks and Indians: A Study in Mythic Syncretism." *Th*, 50 (1975), 351–66.

Points out similarities between Hellenic and NA myths and ceremonials, but differences in their influences: Hellenic has affected art; NA has shaped anthropology.

439. Hertzberg, Hazel W. *The Search for an American Indian Identity: Modern Pan-Indian Movements.* Syracuse, N.Y.: Syracuse Univ. Press, 1971.

Includes discussions of peyotism and the NA Church. Some attention to mythological system and ceremonialism, but major focus is on political organization.

440. Hewett, Edgar L. "Religion in Ancient America." *EP*, 34 (1933), 157–63.

Brief survey of NA religious concepts and practices. Includes an Omaha song text.

441. Hewitt, J. N. B. "Serpent Symbolism." *AA*, o. s. 2 (1889), 179–80.

Surveys symbolic significance of serpents in various NA cultures, especially Northeast and Plains groups.

442. Highwater, Jamake. *Many Smokes, Many Moons: A Chronology of American Indian History Through Indian Art.* Philadelphia: Lippincott, 1978.

Begins with an origin myth (source unspecified) and continues through 1973. Paintings by NA artists accompany many of the cited incidents.

443. Hill-Tout, Charles. "Totemism: A Consideration of Its Origin and Import." *PTRSC*, 2nd series, 9, section 2 (1903), 61–99.

Argues that totemism arises from dependence on natural environment. Cites a NA clan origin myth (group unidentified).

444. Holmes, William H. "Art in Shell of the Ancient Americans." *ARBAE*, 2 (1880–1881), 179–305.

Discussion of shell art is primarily archeological, but treatment of designs used in engraving shells introduces concepts from myths of various NA cultures.

445. Hultkrantz, Åke. *Conceptions of the Soul Among North American Indians. A Study in Religious Ethnology.* Stockholm: Ethnographical Museum of Sweden, 1953 (Monograph Series No. 1).

Cross-cultural survey of beliefs about the nature of the soul from throughout North America. Some ideas derived from mythology.

446. ———. *The Religions of the American Indians.* Trans. Monica Setterwall. Berkeley: Univ. of California Press, 1979.

Deals with major aspects of religion on a cross-cultural basis: theology, cosmogony, supernaturalism, totemism, shamanism, ceremonialism, and eschatology.

447. James, E. O. "The Concept of the Soul in North America." *F*, 38 (1927), 338–57.

Cross-cultural survey of varying concepts of the soul among NAs.

448. James, George Wharton. *Indian Basketry.* 2nd edition. New York: Henry Mollsan, 1902.

Includes chapters on the place of basketry in myth, legend, and ceremonialism.

449. Jenness, Diamond. "The Indian's Interpretation of Man and Nature." *PTRSC*, 3rd series, 24, section 2 (1930), 57–62.

Surveys mythic concepts regarding the nature of man and his environment.

450. Kleber, Louis C. "Religion Among the American Indians." *HT*, 28 (February 1978), 81–87.

Survey of NA religious ideas. With song texts (words only).

451. La Flesche, Francis. "Who Was the Medicine Man?" *JAF*, 18 (1905), 269–75.

Brief overview of the nature and role of the sacred individual in NA cultures. Includes a song text.

452. Lang, Andrew. "The Red Indian Imagination." *Ind*, 52 (18 January 1900), 163–65.

Discusses literary capabilities of NAs as evidenced by oral literature.

453. Lemos, Pedro J. "Our First American Artists." *SAM,* 33 (September 1933), 10–36.

Survey of various NA art forms includes data on ceremonialism and a Navajo chant text.

454. Lévi-Strauss, Claude. *The Savage Mind.* Chicago: Univ. of Chicago Press, 1962.

Cross-cultural description of the fundamental processes of human thought as manifested especially in myth and ceremonial. Cites NA examples.

455. ———. *Structural Anthropology.* Trans. Claire Jacobson and Brooke Grundfest Schoepf. New York: Basic Books, 1963.

Collection of essays—including a revision of "The Structural Study of Myth" (3897)—which present a structuralist approach to language, social structure, mythology, art, and ceremonialism. Includes many NA examples.

456. Lommel, Andreas. *Masks: Their Meaning and Function.* Trans. Nadia Fowler. New York: McGraw-Hill, 1972.

Section on NAs includes some data on ceremonialism and song texts (words only).

457. Lowie, Robert H. "A New Conception of Totemism." *AA,* 13 (1911), 189–207.

Positive critique of Goldenweiser's essay on totemism (433). Goldenweiser responded in *AA,* 13 (1911), 589-97.

458. ———. "Oral Tradition and History." *JAF,* 30 (1917), 161–67.

Argues against historicity of oral tradition. Illustrates by citing Nez Perce materials.

459. ———. "Supernormal Experiences of American Indians." *To,* 4, No. 3 (Spring 1956), 9–16.

Cross-cultural survey of NA psychic experiences.

460. Mallery, Garrick. "Israelite and Indian: A Parallel in Planes of Culture." *PSM,* 36 (1889), 52–76, 193–213.

Considers various correspondences between NA and Hebrew cultures, including myths and ceremonialism.

461. ———. "Pictographs of the North American Indians. A Preliminary Paper." *ARBAE,* 4 (1882–1883), 3–256.

Survey of NA graphic art includes catalogue of mythological figures and other allusions to verbal performance represented in pictographs.

462. ———. "Picture-Writing of the American Indians." *ARBAE,* 10 (1888–1889), 3–807.

Continuation of study of NA graphic art explores petroglyphs and pictographs. Several items discussed refer to mythic figures or other aspects of verbal art. Pictorial equivalents of chants, myths, and legends are presented.

463. *Manners, Customs, and Antiquities of the Indians of North and South America, The.* Boston: Geo. C. Rand, 1852.

General cultural survey includes descriptions of ceremonialism and belief systems. Texts of songs, myths, and oratory. By "the Author of Peter Parley's Tales."

464. Marriott, Alice, and Carol K. Rachlin. *American Epic. The Story of the American Indian.* New York: G. P. Putnam's Sons, 1969.

Historical survey which emphasizes cultural interrelationships. Presented from a NA perspective. Many references to mythology and ceremonialism.

465. Martin, William B. "Religious Ideas of the American Indians." *CUB,* 10 (1904), 35–68, 225–45.

Survey of NA religious concepts especially in relation to missionary work.

466. McLean, John. *The Indians. Their Manners and Customs.* Toronto: William Briggs, 1889.

Cross-cultural survey focusing on Canadian groups but including myth texts from throughout North America. Some descriptions of ceremonialism, including the potlatch of the Northwest Coast.

467. McLoughlin, William G. "Red Indians, Black Slavery, and White Racism: America's Slaveholding Indians." *AQ,* 26 (1974), 367–85.

Study of racial interrelationships. Contains examples of NA oratory and a racial origin myth.

468. McNickle, D'Arcy. "The Healing Vision." *To,* 4, No. 3 (Spring 1956), 25–31.

Discusses relationship between health and religious wholeness among various NA groups.

469. Mead, Margaret. *The Changing Culture of an Indian Tribe. CUCA,* 15 (1932).

Acculturation study of an unidentified group contains some life history texts.

470. Miles, Charles. *Indian and Eskimo Artifacts of North America.* Foreword by Frederick J. Dockstader. New York: Bonanza, 1963.

Picture book illustrates arts and crafts of various groups. Includes chapters on ceremonialism and music.

471. Moffett, Thomas C. *The American Indian on the New Trail: The Red Man of the United States and the Christian Gospel.* New York: Missionary Education Movement of the United States and Canada, 1914.

Historical survey of missionary work includes some general background. Data on poetic performances and text of Logan's speech.

472. Momaday, N. Scott. "The Man Made of Words," in 129, pp. 49–84.

Argues for the importance of oral literature as a way of preserving NA identity.

473. Morse, Rev. Jedidiah. *A Report to the Secretary of War of the United States, on Indian Affairs, Comprising a Narrative of a Tour Performed in the Summer of 1820, Under a Commission from the President of the United States, for the Purpose of Ascertaining for the Use of the Government, the Actual State of the Indian Tribes in Our Country.* New Haven: Howe & Spalding, 1822.

Includes texts of orations and descriptions of religious attitudes and ceremonialism from various groups.

474. Mueller, Theodore. "The Social Significance of Our Legends and Folklore." *WA,* n. s. 25 (1944), 136–38.

Not available for examination.

475. Niethammer, Carolyn. *Daughters of the Earth. The Lives and Legends of American Indian Women.* New York: Macmillan, 1977.

Generalized chronology of the life of a NA woman. Includes myth and folktale texts and descriptions of ceremonialism from various groups.

476. "On the Field and Work of a Journal of American Folk-Lore." *JAF,* 1 (1888), 3–7.

Statement of editorial policy emphasizes NA traditions as one area of concern.

477. Ortiz, Alfonso. "American Indian Philosophy: Its Relation to the Modern World," in 129, pp. 9–47.

Suggests that traditional NA world view offers a viable perspective on contemporary life.

478. Parker, W. Thornton. "The Religious Character of the North American Indians." *OC,* 15 (1901), 46–56.

Emphasizes positive nature of NA religion. With several song texts (words only).

479. Parsons, Elsie Clews. "Links Between Religion and Morality in Early Culture." *AA,* 17 (1915), 41–57.

Challenges the assumption that religion becomes linked with morality only as a late cultural development. Cites ceremonials and narratives from Southwest and Plains groups in support.

480. Peet, Stephen D. "Ethnographic Religions and Ancestor Worship." *AAOJ,* 15 (1893), 230–45.

International survey uses NA examples to treat shamanism, totemism, sun worship, sky worship, and anthropomorphism. Uses evolutionary scheme.

481. ———. "The Growth of Symbolism." *AAOJ,* 7 (1885), 321–349.

Traces the development of symbolism in graphic art, mythology, and ceremonialism.

482. ———. "Mythologic Totems." *AAOJ,* 19 (1897), 190–210.

Examination of totemism and related mythology among various NA groups.

483. ———. *Myths and Symbols or Aboriginal Religions in America.* Chicago: Office of the American Antiquarian, 1905.

Survey of religion, mythology, and symbolism among NA groups with special attention to animal and solar symbolism.

484. ———. "Personal Divinities and Nature Powers in America." *AAOJ,* 26 (1904), 281–96.

Cross-cultural survey of mythology and ceremonialism relating to sun, moon, stars as objects of worship.

485. ———. "Races and Religions in America." *AAOJ,* 26 (1904), 345–60.

Describes religious systems prevalent among NA groups from an evolutionary stance.

486. ———. "Sabaeanism or Sky Worship in America." *AAOJ,* 16 (1894), 217–37.

Cross-cultural survey of evidences of sky worship in NA art, architecture, mythology, and ceremonialism.

487. ———. "The Serpent Symbol." *AAOJ,* 9 (1887), 133–63.

Describes representations of serpents in NA art and architecture. Some attention to myth and ceremonialism.

488. ———. "The Serpent Symbol in America." *AAOJ,* 8 (1886), 197–221.

Cross-cultural survey of graphic, mythic, and ritual uses of the serpent figure.

489. ———. "Water Cult and the Deluge Myth." *AAOJ,* 13 (1891), 352–60.

Interprets NA ceremonialism and art in terms of Old World flood myths.

490. Powell, John Wesley. "The Lessons of Folklore." *AA,* 2 (1900), 1–36.

Defines folklore as the science of "vestigial opinions no longer held as valid." Some illustrations in this international survey come from NA groups.

491. ———. *Outlines of the Philosophy of the North American Indians.* New York: Douglas Taylor, 1877.

Pamphlet discusses general theology and cosmology. Includes excerpts from two myths.

492. Radin, Paul. "The Basic Myth of the North American Indians." *ErJ,* 17 (1950), 359–416.

Not available for examination.

493. ———. *Primitive Man as Philosopher.* New York: D. Appleton, 1927.

Argues for the existence of intellectual activity and of a thinking class in primitive societies. Cross-cultural study with a number of references to and texts of NA oral literature, especially songs.

494. Ramsey, Jarold. "The Teacher of Modern American Indian Writing as Ethnographer and Critic." *CE,* 41, No. 2 (October 1979), 163–69.

Tries to balance the reader's need for ethnographic knowledge and critical judgment when dealing with contemporary NA written literature. Applies ideas to oral literature as well.

495. Reade, John. "The Literary Faculty of the Native Races of America." *PTRSC,* 1st series, 2, section 2 (1884), 17–30.

Surveys aptitude for verbal art among NAs.

496. Ricketts, Mac Linscott. "The North American Indian Trickster." *HR,* 5, No. 2 (Winter 1966), 327–50.

Views Trickster as a "humanist" who tries to deal with life without supernatural aid.

497. Saler, Benson. "Supernatural as a Western Category." *E,* 5 (1977), 31–43.

Historical survey of ideas about the supernatural in western culture. Treats briefly the applicability of the concept to NA culture.

498. Sanders, Thomas E. "Tribal Literature: Individual Identity and the Collective Unconscious." *CCC,* 24 (1973), 256–66.

Argues that NA oral literature expresses a collective conscious which is absent from EA literature. Includes a number of song texts.

499. Sanford, Rev. D. A. *Indian Topics or, Experiences in Indian Missions with Selections from Various Sources.* New York: Broadway, 1911.

Includes Arapaho and Cheyenne song texts and data of Apache ceremonialism.

500. Schmidt, W. *High Gods in North America. Upton Lectures in Religion, Manchester College, Oxford, 1932.* Oxford: Clarendon Press, 1933.

Argues that various NA groups worshiped "high gods" —the mark of true religion. Uses mythology and ritual as well as comparative method to argue for existence of NA high gods.

501. Seton, Ernest Thompson, and Julia M. Seton. *The Gospel of the Red Man: An Indian Bible.* New York: Doubleday, Doran, 1939.

Attempt to synthesize NA religious and ethical beliefs and practices. Includes prayer, song, and myth texts.

502. Smith, DeCost. *Indian Experiences.* Caldwell, Ida.: Caxton, 1943.

Impressionistic work dealing with several aspects of NA culture: the Omaha Pipe Dance, Iroquois and Sioux mythology, and the Ghost Dance.

503. Smith, Henry Goodwin. "The Beliefs of the American Indians." *AJT,* 6 (1902), 89–100.

Survey of NA religious systems with comparative emphasis.

504. Snyder, Gary. "The Incredible Survival of Coyote." *WAL,* 9, No. 4 (Winter 1975), 254–72.

Surveys presence of Coyote in NA story and song. Primary concern is with use of NA folklore in contemporary literature, but some attention to the folklore itself.

505. "Some Remarks and Annotations Concerning the Traditions, Customs, Languages, &c., of the Indians in

North America, from the Memoirs of the Rev. David Zeisberger and Other Missionaries of the United States." *OT*, 1 (1846), 271–81.

Very general description of NA religious beliefs and ceremonials.

506. Spencer, Robert F., Jesse D. Jennings, and others. *The Native Americans: Prehistory and Ethnology of the North American Indians.* New York: Harper and Row, 1965.

Survey of NA cultures by culture area includes data on ceremonialism and mythology.

507. Stanberry, Katherine S. "The Antiquity of the Folk-Lore of the American Indians," in 79, pp. 278–79.

Suggests that most NA folklore is a recent inheritance from EAs. Abstract of the full presentation.

508. Steiger, Brad. *Medicine Power. The American Indian's Revival of His Spiritual Heritage and Its Relevance for Modern Man.* Garden City, N.Y.: Doubleday, 1974.

Argues that ideas inherent in traditional NA religious systems have value for contemporary life.

509. ———. *Medicine Talk. A Guide to Walking in Balance and Surviving on the Earth Mother.* Garden City, N.Y.: Doubleday, 1975.

Uses religious ideas collected from Seneca, Sioux, and Ojibwa informants to develop a lifeway for dealing with contemporary problems.

510. Steiner, Stan. *The New Indians.* New York: Harper and Row, 1968.

Discussion of social protest among NAs includes some song texts and descriptions of ceremonialism.

511. Stensland, Anna Lee. "The Indian Presence in American Literature." *EJ*, 66, No. 3 (March 1977), 37–41.

Concerned with influence of NA materials on EA writers, but contains some discussion of actual NA myths and songs.

512. Strong, James C. *Wah-Kee-Nah and Her People. The Curious Customs, Traditions, and Legends of the North American Indians.* New York: Putnam, 1893.

General survey of NA history and culture with special emphasis on Northwest Coast groups. Data on oratory, ceremonialism, and religious concepts.

513. Strong, William Duncan. "Indian Religion in the Modern World," in *The Changing Indian.* Ed. Oliver La Farge. Norman: Univ. of Oklahoma Press, 1942, pp. 158–62.

Discusses the role that traditional NA religion can play in modern American culture. Considers the beauty of sacred narratives and songs.

514. Swanton, John R., and Roland B. Dixon. "Primitive American History." *AA*, 16 (1914), 376–412.

The authors assume that oral traditions have some historical value when confirmed by other data and apply their position to various NA groups. Discussion of the historicity of NA oral tradition in response came from Robert H. Lowie, *AA*, 17 (1915), 597–99; Dixon, *AA*, 17 (1915), 599–600; Swanton, 17 (1915), 600; and A. A. Goldenweiser, *AA*, 17 (1915), 763–64.

515. Szasz, Margaret C., and Ferenc M. Szasz. "The American Indian and the Classical Past." *MiQ*, 17, No. 1 (October 1975), 58–70.

Compares pre-contact NA culture with Greek and Roman culture. Some attention to ceremonialism and verbal art.

516. Terrell, John Upton. *American Indian Almanac.* New York: World, 1971.

Popular historical treatment divided into ten culture areas. Each area's prehistory and early contact history are covered.Occasional references to myths and other folklore.

517. ———, and Donna M. Terrell. *Indian Women of the Western Morning. Their Life in Early America.* New York: Dial, 1974.

Cross-cultural survey of status and roles of pre-contact NA women. Includes some summaries of myths and ritual descriptions.

518. Thatcher, B. B. *Indian Traits: Being Sketches of the Manners, Customs, and Character of the North American Natives.* New York: J. and J. Harper, 1833.

Anecdotal attempt to characterize NA culture. Includes data on games, ceremonialism, song texts, and religious attitudes.

519. Toelken, J. Barre. *The Dynamics of Folklore.* Boston: Houghton Mifflin, 1979.

Textbook emphasizing the processes of transformation which characterize folklore. Also focuses on folklore performance. Includes examples from such NA groups as the Hopi, Navajo, and Coos.

520. ———. "Seeing with a Native Eye: How Many Sheep Will It Hold?," in 96, pp. 9–24.

Points out different ways of perceiving developed by different cultures. Illustrates with examples of Navajo attitudes and art.

521. Tooker, Elisabeth. "Clans and Moieties in North America." *CA*, 12 (1971), 357–76.

Survey of social structure includes data on mythological origins of clans and moieties and their ceremonial roles. With twelve brief responses.

522. Turner, G. *Traits of Indian Character; as Generally Applicable to the Aborigines of North America.* 2 volumes. Philadelphia: Key & Biddle, 1836.

Random sampling of NA culture elements supposed to reveal general NA character. Includes songs, myths, legends, toasts, and ceremonialism.

523. Underhill, Ruth Murray. *Red Man's America. A History of Indians in the United States.* Chicago: Univ. of Chicago Press, 1953.

Balances pre-contact and post-contact history of various groups. Includes references to mythology, descriptions of ceremonialism, and excerpts from song texts.

524. ———. "Religion Among American Indians." *AAAPSS*, 311 (May 1957), 127–36.

Describes NA traditional religious forms as they affect acculturation. Special attention to peyotism.

525. Vestal, Stanley. "Amerindian Traits." *SWR*, 28, No. 1 (Autumn 1942), 53–62.

Cross-cultural survey of NA character traits, with special emphasis on "face."

526. Wake, C. Staniland. "Asiatic Ideas Among the American Indians." *AAOJ*, 27 (1905), 153–62, 189–97.

Comparative study, emphasizing parallels between NA and Near Eastern religions and mythologies.

527. Wilson, Daniel. "The Artistic Faculty in Aboriginal Races." *PTRSC*, 1st series, 3, section 2 (1885), 67–117.

Surveys NA aptitude for verbal, graphic, and plastic arts.

528. ———. *Prehistoric Man: Researches into the Origin of Civilisation in the Old and the New World.* 2 volumes. Cambridge: Macmillan, 1862.

Contains some data on NA mythology and ceremonialism.

529. Wilson, Eddie W. "American Indian Concept of Saliva." *MWF,* 1 (1951), 229–32.
Includes data on role of saliva in cosmogonic myth and in ceremonialism.
530. ———. "The Gourd in Folk Symbolism." *WF,* 10 (1951), 162–64.
Cross-cultural survey of use of gourd as symbol in literature, art, and folklore with some NA examples.
531. ———. "The Moon and the American Indian." *WF,* 24 (1965), 87–100.
Cross-cultural survey of NA folklore relating to the moon. Includes texts of prayers and songs and descriptions of ceremonials.
532. ———. "The Owl and the American Indian." *JAF,* 63 (1950), 336–44.
Sees owl as a portentously sacred bird in various NA traditions. Regarded both as benefactor and as malevolent influence.
533. ———. "The Shell and the American Indian." *SFQ,* 16 (1952), 192–200.
Includes symbolic significance and ceremonial usages of shells. With song texts.
534. ———. "The Spider and the American Indian." *WF,* 10 (1951), 290–97.
Cross-cultural survey of the role of the spider in creation and other myths as well as in magic, medicine, and art.
535. Wissler, Clark. *The American Indian. An Introduction to the Anthropology of the New World.* 3rd edition. Gloucester, Mass.: Peter Smith, 1957.
Cross-cultural survey of NA groups includes chapters on "The Fine Arts," "Ritualistic Observances," and "Mythology."
536. Zolla, Elémire. *The Writer and the Shaman: A Morphology of the American Indian.* Trans. Raymond Rosenthal. New York: Harcourt Brace Jovanovich, 1973.
Consideration of the image of NAs in various literary traditions. Some treatment of NA song and life history.

I. Theory and Commentary: Story

537. Alexander, Hartley Burr. "Giver of Life." *NMQ,* 20 (1950), 315–21.
Surveys imagery of light in NA mythology.
538. ———. *The Mythology of All Races: North American.* Boston: Marshall Jones, 1916.
Treats cosmogonic and cosmological ideas of NAs from all culture areas. Includes summaries of myth texts and extensive notes on their sources.
539. ———. "The Rain Cloud in Indian Myth." *EP,* 21 (1926), 314–19.
Cross-cultural survey of symbolic significance of clouds in NA mythology.
540. ———. "The Sense of Antiquity in Indian Mythology." *M,* 7 (1933), 132–40.
Overview of historical sense manifested in NA myths.
541. "American Mythology Compared with Oriental." *AAOJ,* 29 (1907), 354–55.
Brief treatment of cross-cultural parallels.
542. Appleton, LeRoy H. *Indian Art of the Americas.* New York: Scribners, 1950.

Considers storytelling to be an art and includes story and prayer texts in survey of NA art forms, arranged by culture area. Reprinted by Dover in 1971.
543. Austin, Mary. "The Folk Story in America." *SAQ,* 33 (1934), 10–19.
General survey of NA storytelling. Draws a dichotomy between myths and "realistic stories."
544. Ball, Sydney. "The Mining of Gems and Ornamental Stones by American Indians." BAEB No. 128 (AP No. 13), 1941.
Primarily a survey of technology, but with some summaries of etiological myths about particular stones.
545. Barbeau, Marius. "The Old-World Dragon in America," in 162, pp. 115–22.
Cross-cultural survey of dragon-like figures in NA mythology.
546. Barclay, Lillian Elizabeth. "The Coyote: Animal and Folk-Character," in 109, pp. 36–103.
Survey of Coyote's appearance in various narrative traditions including NA. Special focus on the Southwest.
547. Barr, Margaretta. "Indian School Library Collections." *LJ,* 60 (1935), 702–03.
Suggests that library work and storytelling are related. NAs should be encouraged to develop libraries of their oral literature.
548. Bascom, William. "The Forms of Folklore: Prose Narratives." *JAF,* 78 (1965), 3–20.
Attempts to define myth, legend, and folktale. Presents schemes for classifying narratives developed in several NA cultures.
549. Beauchamp, W. M. "Indian Corn Stories and Customs." *JAF,* 11 (1898), 195–202.
Cross-cultural survey of myths about origin of corn and ceremonials regarding corn.
550. Beck, Horace P. "The Animal That Cannot Lie Down." *JWAS,* 39 (1939), 294–301.
Treats NA oral narratives which seem to preserve memories of the mammoth.
551. Boas, Franz. "The Development of Folk-Tales and Myths." *ScM,* 3 (October 1916), 335–43.
Emphasizes diffusionist approach to folktale distribution and idea that myths arise from observation of natural phenomena.
552. ———. "Dissemination of Tales Among the Natives of North America." *JAF,* 4 (1891), 13–20.
Surveys the diffusion process among various NA groups.
553. ———. "The Mythologies of the Indians." *IQ,* 11 (July 1905), 327–42; 12 (October 1905), 157–73.
Discusses historical background of various NA mythologies and contrasts them with classical mythology.
554. ———. "Mythology and Folklore," in *General Anthropology.* Ed. Franz Boas. Boston: D.C. Heath, 1938, pp. 609–26.
Cross-cultural survey of religious oral narrative includes NA examples.
555. ———. "Mythology and Folk-Tales of the North American Indians." *JAF,* 27 (1914), 374–410.
Treats problems of distinguishing between myth and folktale as well as matters of diffusion and history of NA oral narratives.
556. ———. "The Origin of Death." *JAF,* 30 (1917), 486–91.

Cross-cultural survey of NA myths about the origin of death.

557. ———. "Romance Folk-Lore Among American Indians." *RR*, 16 (1925), 199–207.

Treats NA traditions, the sources of which seem to be French, Spanish, and Portuguese folklore.

558. Brinton, Daniel G. *The Myths of the New World. A Treatise on the Symbolism and Mythology of the Red Race of America.* New York: Leypoldt & Holt, 1868.

Interpretative work which explains NA myths as nature allegories. Follows the "comparative mythology" approach of Max Müller.

559. Brown, Joseph Epes. "The Immediacy of Mythological Message: Native American Traditions," in 166, pp. 101–16.

Treats concept of time in NA mythology—a time outside of ordinary time.

560. Buchanan, Charles Milton. "The Indian: His Origin and Legendary Lore." *OM*, n. s. 36 (1900), 114–22.

Considers various origin theories and surveys the mythologies of various groups.

561. Burland, Cottie. *North American Indian Mythology.* New York: Tudor, 1965.

Profusely illustrated volume which surveys mythic systems of various NA groups. No texts. Appendix identifies "Chief Gods and Spirits of North America."

562. Campbell, Joseph. *The Masks of God: Primitive Mythology.* New York: Viking, 1959.

Eclectic approach to myth interpretation which involves Jungian psychology, ethnology, and diffusionism. This volume, the first in a tetralogy, explores NA materials as well as myths of other nonliterate cultures.

563. Carroll, Michael P. "A New Look at Freud on Myth: Analyzing the Star-Husband Tale." *E*, 7 (1979), 189–205.

Psychoanalytic interpretation of the widely collected NA myth.

564. Carter, W. H. *North American Indian Games.* London, Ontario: Namind, 1974.

General survey of play activities includes a brief discussion of storytelling.

565. Chamberlain, Alexander F. "American Indian Legends and Beliefs About the Squirrel and the Chipmunk." *JAF*, 9 (1896), 48–50.

Cross-cultural survey of narrative folklore, from various NA groups, concerning the two creatures.

566. ———. "The Mythology and Folk-Lore of Invention." *JAF*, 10 (1897), 89–100.

Overview of mythic figures supposed to have given man objects or skills. Some NA examples.

567. ———. "Taboos of Tale-Telling." *JAF*, 13 (1900), 146–47.

Discussion of seasonal and temporal restrictions on storytelling among NAs.

568. Colby, B. N., George A. Collier, and Susan K. Postal. "Comparison of Themes in Folktales by the General Inquirer System." *JAF*, 76 (1963), 318–23.

Description of a computer system for counting and comparing folktale themes. Among the five cultures sampled are Kwakiutl and Eskimo.

569. Corkran, David H. "The Serpent and the Turtle." *SIS*, 14 (October 1962), 19–26.

Comparative study of symbolic figures which appear in NA mythology.

570. Count, Earl W. "The Earth-Diver and the Rival Twins: A Clue to Time Correlation in North-Eurasiatic and North American Mythology," in 162, pp. 55–62.

Comparative treatment of NA creation myths with Slavic analogues.

571. Dawson, Principal. "American Myths: as Related to Primitive Ideas of Religion." *LH*, 1876, pp. 421–24, 523–27, 616–19, 698–99.

Extracts religious ideas from NA mythology, focusing on the idea of a god and belief in immortality.

572. Dixon, Roland B. "Mythology." *AA*, 14 (1912), 57–59.

Part of a symposium on the origin and distribution of NA groups. Assesses the role of mythology in tracing routes of cultural diffusion.

573. [Dooling, D. M.] "The Wisdom of the Contrary: A Conversation with Joseph Epes Brown." *P*, 4, No. 1 (February 1979), 54–65.

Discussion of the ritual clown figure, especially the Contrary of the Sioux, as a manifestation of the same principle as the mythic Trickster. Some data on Black Elk.

574. Douglas, Mary. "The Meaning of Myth with Special Reference to 'La Geste d'Asdiwal,' " in 133, pp. 49–69.

Criticizes Lévi-Strauss' method because it ignores cultural time concepts and takes no account of myths, the order of which is irreversible. See 4967.

575. Dundes, Alan. "African Tales Among the North American Indians." *SFQ*, 29 (1965), 207–19.

Survey of Black American influences on NA storytelling traditions.

576. ———. "Earth-Diver: Creation of the Mythopoeic Male." *AA*, 64 (1962), 1032–51.

Psychoanalytical study of widespread NA creation myth. Interprets Earth-Diver myth as an account of anal creativity.

577. ———. *The Morphology of North American Indian Folktales.* Helsinki: Suomalainen Tiedeakatemia, 1964 (FFC No. 195).

Formalistic study of NA folk narratives reveals four structural patterns as basis for longer stories. Proves that NA folktales are not random, haphazard constructions.

578. ———. "Structural Typology in North American Indian Folktales." *SJA*, 19 (1963), 121–30.

Summarizes ideas developed in 577. Reprinted in 114 (pp. 206–215).

579. Eiseley, Loren C. "Indian Mythology and Extinct Fossil Vertebrates." *AA*, 47 (1945), 318–20.

Brief survey of possible references to prehistoric mammals in NA myths.

580. ———. "Myth and Mammoth in Archaeology." *AAn*, 11 (1945), 84–87.

Considers evidence regarding the mammoth in NA oral traditions and New World archeology.

581. Emerson, Ellen Russell. *Indian Myths or Legends, Traditions, and Symbols of the Aborigines of America Compared with Those of Other Countries Including Hindustan, Egypt, Persia, Assyria, and China.* Boston: James R. Osgood, 1884.

Consideration of NA myths and myth themes as they compare with Eurasian traditions. Meant to demonstrate man's psychic unity.

582. Espinosa, Aurelio M. "Western Hemisphere Versions of Aarne-Thompson 301." *JAF*, 65 (1952), 187.

Cites nine different texts of the folktale collected from NAs. See 592.

583. Farrand, Livingston. "The Significance of Mythology and Tradition." *JAF*, 17 (1904), 14–22.

Argues that mythology and "tradition" express earlier beliefs and customs and are thus important to psychology and ethnology. Cites NA examples.

584. Fiske, John. "Myths of the Barbaric World." *AtM*, 29 (1872), 61–76.

Application of "comparative mythology" approach to NA and other tribal materials. Sees myths as nature allegories.

585. Gayton, A. H. "English Ballads and Indian Myths." *JAF*, 55 (1942), 121–25.

Argues that the study of EA and NA traditions involves parallel endeavors. In both, the student is concerned with history of the folklore material, similarities and differences in comparison to other materials, and distribution.

586. ———. "The Orpheus Myth in North America." *JAF*, 48 (1935), 263–93.

Historic-geographic study of Orpheus-like narratives among NAs. Finds a fairly stable plot line to be widespread.

587. Gest, J. Henry. "Our Indian Mythology." *PSM*, 23 (August 1883), 527–30.

Takes evolutionary approach to culture development and assumes NA myths shed light on primitive religion in general.

588. Gibbon, William B. "Asiatic Parallels in North American Star Lore: Milky Way, Pleiades, Orion." *JAF*, 85 (1972), 236–47.

Points out similarities between NA and Asiatic names for three constellations.

589. ———. "Asiatic Parallels in North American Star Lore: Ursa Major." *JAF*, 77 (1964), 236–50.

Shows correspondences between NA and Asiatic names for the constellation.

590. Gillette, J. M. "Introduction to Indian Mythology." *CSHSND*, 2 (1908), 493–94.

Brief comments on the nature of NA sacred stories.

591. Green, James. "Indian Traditions." *O*, 86 (27 July 1907), 676–80.

Black writer's recollections of his father's relation of folktales from an unspecified NA source. Includes summaries of texts.

592. Hallowell, A. Irving. " 'John the Bear' in the New World." *JAF*, 65 (1952), 418.

Bibliographic note on NA texts of AT 301. See 582.

593. Hancock, Cecily. "The 'Me All Face' Story: European Literary Background of an American Comic Indian Anecdote." *JAF*, 76 (1963), 340–42.

A story, attributed to NAs primarily in nineteenth-century sources, is shown to have European analogues as old as the second century A.D.

594. Harshberger, John W. *Maize: A Botanical and Economic Study.* Philadelphia: Univ. of Pennsylvania Press, 1893 (Contributions from the Botanical Laboratory of the Univ. of Pennsylvania, 1, No. 2).

Primarily deals with botanical matters, but contains a section of cross-cultural discussion of NA myths about maize.

595. Hatt, Gudmund. "The Corn Mother in America and in Indonesia." *A*, 46 (1951), 853–914.

Cross-cultural survey of myths about a female deity who gives maize to mankind.

596. Hinsdale, Wilbert B. "Spirit Stones." *PMASAL*, 14 (1930), 103–12.

Considers sacred stones from various NA groups. Summaries of myth texts.

597. Hultkrantz, Åke. "Myth in Native North American Religions," in 166, pp. 77–97.

Survey article treats types and functions of NA mythology and traces history of its study. Response by J. W. E. Newberry (pp. 97–99).

598. ———. *The North American Indian Orpheus Tradition. A Contribution to Comparative Religion.* Stockholm: Ethnographical Museum of Sweden, 1957 (Monograph Series No. 2).

Cross-cultural survey of Orpheus myth in NA cultures. Sees a connection between the myth and shamanism.

599. Jablow, Alta. "The Many Faces of Trickster." *Ant*, 3 (1979), 59–71.

International survey of the mythic figure, including references to NA mythologies. Discusses various interpretations proposed by mythographers.

600. Jackson, Bruce. "*Vagina Dentata* and Cystic Teratoma." *JAF*, 84 (1971), 341–42.

Suggests the *vagina dentata* motif (F547.1.1) in NA tradition is corroborated physically by dermoid cysts.

601. James, Edwin Oliver. "Cremation and the Preservation of the Dead in North America." *AA*, 30 (1928), 214–42.

Cross-cultural treatment of funerary rituals. Some are related to eschatological mythology.

602. Jenks, Albert Ernest. "Faith as a Factor in the Economic Life of the Amerind." *AA*, 2 (1900), 676–89.

Points out mythic beliefs related to various economic activities among NAs. Sees mythic faith as a stumbling block to progress.

603. Johnson, Ludwell H., III. "Men and Elephants in America." *ScM*, 75 (October 1952), 215–21.

Considers NA oral traditions about mammoths in light of paleontological findings.

604. Klapp, Orrin E. "The Clever Hero." *JAF*, 67 (1954), 21–34.

Cross-cultural synthesis of the traits of the clever hero is illustrated by reference to the NA characters of Coyote and Raven.

605. ———. "The Folk Hero." *JAF*, 62 (1949), 17–25.

Survey of mythic and legendary hero patterns draws several examples from NA traditions.

606. Kluckhohn, Clyde. "Myths and Rituals: A General Theory." *HTR*, 35 (1942), 45–79.

Argues that no simple theory of precedence of myth or ritual is possible. Cites NA examples.

607. ———. "Recurrent Themes in Myths and Mythmaking." *Dd*, 88 (1959), 268–79.

Generalizes about cross-cultural (including NA) distribution of myth themes, particularly the Oedipus Myth and the Myth of the Hero. Reprinted in 114 (pp. 158–68).

608. Köngäs, Elli Kaija. "The Earth-Diver (Th.A. 812)." *Eh*, 7 (1960), 151–80.

Offers a shamanistic explanation for the widespread creation myth.

609. Kroeber, A. L. "Catch-Words in American Mythology." *JAF*, 21 (1908), 222–27.

Application of Lowie's concept of recurrent elements in myths to NA narratives, especially those of California groups. See 618–19.

610. Kurath, Gertrude P. "Dance and Mythology in North America." *MWF,* 10 (1960–1961), 207–12.

Shows associations of dance with myths in NA cultures: in dance origin myths, in dramatizations of myths through dance.

611. "Legendary Lore of the Indians." *AAOJ,* 31 (1909), 233–39.

Survey of characteristics of NA oral narratives.

612. Lester, David. "The Relation Between Discipline Experiences and the Expression of Aggression." *AA,* 69 (1967), 734–37.

Among groups studied are NAs. Aggression portrayed in folktales is one measure utilized to show correspondence between physical discipline and tendency toward outward display of aggression.

613. Lévi-Strauss, Claude. *From Honey to Ashes. Introduction to a Science of Mythology: 2.* Trans. John and Doreen Weightman. New York: Harper and Row, 1973.

Continuation of 615: an attempt to capture the logic of mythic thought. Most examples are South American, but uses some NA materials for comparative purposes.

614. ———. *The Origin of Table Manners. Introduction to a Science of Mythology: 3.* Trans. John and Doreen Weightman. New York: Harper and Row, 1978.

See 613. This volume of explorations in mythic logic draws more heavily on NA materials than the previously issued volumes.

615. ———. *The Raw and the Cooked. Introduction to a Science of Mythology: 1.* Trans. John and Doreen Weightman. New York: Harper and Row, 1969.

See 613 and 614. This volume focuses on South American mythologies, but includes some NA material for comparison.

616. Little, Ralph B. "Oral Aggression in Spider Legends." *AI,* 23 (1966), 169–79.

Analysis of oral narratives which involve spiders, emphasizing oral aggression and male/female conflict themes. Some references to NA material.

617. Lowie, Robert H. "Aboriginal Education in America." *AM,* 15 (1928), 192–96.

One pedagogical device is storytelling.

618. ———. "Additional Catch-Words." *JAF,* 22 (1909), 332–33.

Sequel to 619. See also 609.

619. ———. "Catch-Words for Mythological Motives." *JAF,* 21 (1908), 24–27.

List of recurrent elements in myths from various cultures. Some of the catch-words are keyed to NA materials. See 609 and 618.

620. ———. "The Hero-Trickster Discussion." *JAF,* 22 (1909), 431–33.

Considers the relationship between Trickster and the culture hero, especially in NA mythology.

621. ———. "Queries." *AA,* 35 (1933), 288–96.

Deals with a hodgepodge of ethnological concerns, including parallels between North American and South American myths.

622. ———. "The Test-Theme in North American Mythology." *JAF,* 21 (1908), 97–148.

Cross-cultural survey of occurrence of a motif in various NA mythologies. Rejects allegorical theories to

view the mythic hero as a human figure.

623. Luomala, Katharine. *Oceanic, American Indian, and African Myths of Snaring the Sun.* BPBMB No. 168 (1940).

Historic-geographic study includes twenty-six NA texts of myth based on Motif A728. Sun Caught in Snare.

624. Mason, Otis Tufton. "Aboriginal American Zootechny." *AA,* 1 (1899), 45–81.

Cross-cultural survey of industries connected with the animal world. Brief consideration of myths with chart listing animal totems for various NA groups.

625. ———. *Indian Basketry. Studies in a Textile Art Without Machinery.* 2 volumes. London: William Heinemann, 1905.

Material culture survey. Chapter on symbolism relates designs to mythology.

626. Matthews, Washington. "Myths of Gestation and Parturition." *AA,* 4 (1902), 737–42.

Cross-cultural survey of emergence myths, focusing particularly on their occurrence among NAs.

627. ———. "The Study of Ethics Among the Lower Races." *JAF,* 12 (1899), 1–9.

Discussion of moralistic aspects of mythology. Most illustrations come from NA groups in the Southwest.

628. McCartney, Eugene S. "Folk Tales Which Explain How the Races of Mankind Acquired Their Colors." *PMASAL,* 23 (1937), 37–61.

International survey includes some NA texts.

629. McCullen, J. T., Jr. "Indian Myths Concerning the Origin of Tobacco." *NYFQ,* 23 (1967), 264–73.

Cross-cultural survey of etiological myths.

630. Minor, W. H. *The American Indians North of Mexico.* Cambridge: Univ. Press, 1917.

General introduction especially to Plains and Southwest groups. Includes a chapter on mythology which makes cross-cultural comparisons.

631. Moore, Sally Falk. "Descent and Symbolic Filiation." *AA,* 66 (1964), 1308–20.

Treats cultures which have brother and sister as symbolic parents in their descent etiologies. Cites several NA myths involving brother-sister incest.

632. N[ewell], W. W. "The Necessity of Collecting the Traditions of the Native Races." *JAF,* 1 (1888), 162–63.

Argues that a complete record of NA mythology is needed in order to understand NA psychology.

633. Palmer, Rose A. *The North American Indians. An Account of the American Indians North of Mexico, Compiled from the Original Sources.* Washington: Smithsonian Institution, 1929 (Smithsonian Scientific Series Vol. 4).

General coverage of NA cultures. Chapter "Myths and Legends" consists of items reprinted from previously published collections.

634. Peet, Stephen D. "The Borrowed Myths of America." *AAOJ,* 14 (1892), 336–43.

Comparative study of Old World and NA myths.

635. ———. "Indian Myths and Effigy Mounds." *AAOJ,* 11 (1889), 32–61.

Cross-cultural survey of relationship between prehistoric mounds in North America and NA mythology.

636. ———. "Personal Divinities and Culture Heroes of the Uncivilized Races." *AAOJ,* 15 (1893), 348–72.

Cross-cultural survey of NA gods and heroes.

637. ———. "The Story of the Creation Among the American Aborigines a[s] Proof of Prehistoric Contact." *AAOJ,* 17 (1895), 127–50.

Compares NA creation myths to those of Asiatic groups.

638. ———. "The Story of the Deluge." *AAOJ*, 27 (1905), 201–16.

Comparative study of flood myths, including NA texts.

639. ———. "Transformation Myths." *AAOJ*, 16 (1894), 275–98.

Survey of myths, many from NA groups, about shape-shifting.

640. Pettitt, George A. "Primitive Education in North America." *UCPAAE*, 43 (1946), 1–182.

Cross-cultural study of socialization processes includes data on ceremonialism. Also material on training for shamans. One chapter deals with storytelling as a didactic method.

641. Pope, Polly. "Toward a Structural Analysis of North American Trickster Tales." *SFQ*, 31 (1967), 274–86.

Approaches analysis of NA folktales from the perspective of plot contour. Applies idea to texts of "The Bungling Host."

642. Powell, John Wesley. "Esthetology, or the Science of Activities Designed to Give Pleasure." *AA*, 1 (1899), 1–40.

Myth is included in the discussion of fine arts in this survey. Some NA examples.

643. ———. "On Limitations to the Use of Some Anthropologic Data." *ARBAE*, 1 (1879–1880), 71–86.

General discussion of the resources available to the student of NA cultures. Includes a short section on mythology.

644. ———. "Sophiology, or the Science of Activities Designed to Give Instruction." *AA*, 3 (1901), 51–79.

General survey of epistemological systems and educational methods. Includes a section on mythology, with references to NA materials.

645. Radin, Paul. *Literary Aspects of North American Mythology.* CGSMB No. 16 (Anthropological Series No. 6), 1915.

Uses NA mythology to counteract Ehrenreich's theory of an original, correct version of every myth. Takes into account each storyteller's psychology as a means of shaping his performance of a myth.

646. Ramsey, Jarold. "The Bible in Western Indian Mythology." *JAF*, 90 (1977), 442–54.

Examines evidence of the impact of Christian evangelism on NA narrative folklore. Cites parallels in ceremonialism, such as the NA Church.

647. Rayfield, J. R. "What Is a Story?" *AA*, 74 (1972), 1085–1106.

Attempts to discover criteria which characterize a verbal text as a story. Suggests that these criteria relate more to the structure of a text than to its content. Uses NA illustrations.

648. Reichard, Gladys A. "Literary Types and Dissemination of Myths." *JAF*, 34 (1921), 269–307.

Discusses problems in the study of myths, especially their unresponsiveness to standard literary analysis and their diffusion. Uses NA illustrations.

649. Rich, George W. "Rethinking the 'Star Husbands.'" *JAF*, 84 (1971), 436–41.

Argues that Dundes' treatment of the "Star Husband Tale" in *The Morphology of North American Indian Folktales* (577) is better suited to handling variations in the tale than Thompson's historic-geographic approach (671).

650. Róheim, Géza. "Culture Hero and Trickster in

North American Mythology," in 162, pp. 190–94.

Psychological study of mythic figures.

651. Rooth, Anna Birgitta. "The Creation Myths of the North American Indians." *A*, 52 (1957), 497–508.

Develops an eight-part typology of cosmogonies based on content.

652. Rydjord, John. *Indian Place-Names. Their Origin, Evolution, and Meanings, Collected in Kansas from the Siouan, Algonquian, Shoshonean, Caddoan, Iroquoian, and Other Tongues.* Norman: Univ. of Oklahoma Press, 1968.

Primarily an interpretation of place names of NA origin, but includes summaries of and references to myths and legends from various groups.

653. S., H. F. "Spider Myths of the American Indians." *NH*, 21 (1921), 382–85.

Cross-cultural survey of spider characters in NA mythology.

654. Schmerler, Henrietta. "Trickster Marries His Daughter." *JAF*, 44 (1931), 196–207.

Historic-geographic study of an incest myth. Based on thirty-three texts from twenty-seven groups.

655. Schwarz, Herbert F. "Eclipses as Interpreted by the American Aborigines." *NH*, 25 (1925), 162–65.

Cross-cultural survey of NA myths about solar eclipses.

656. Shook, Charles A. *Cumorah Revisited or "The Book of Mormon" and the Claims of the Mormons Re-examined from the Viewpoint of American Archaeology and Ethnology.* Cincinnati: Standard, 1910.

Attacks idea that NA oral narratives parallel Hebrew history. One basis of a general argument against the validity of the Book of Mormon.

657. Sinclair, A. T. "Tattooing of the North American Indians." *AA*, 11 (1909), 362–400.

Survey of the art throughout North America. In some groups, designs represented figures from mythology.

658. Smith, William F., Jr. "American Indian Autobiographies." *AIQ*, 2, No. 3 (Autumn 1975), 237–45.

Discusses several NA life histories, oral and written.

659. Speck, Frank G., and John Witthoft. "Some Notable Life-Histories in Zoological Folklore." *JAF*, 60 (1947), 345–49.

Presents accounts from the natural history of several NA groups which describe the metamorphosis of one creature into another. Suggests that early EA naturalists accepted the factuality of these accounts.

660. Spinden, Herbert J. "Sun Worship," in *ARSI for 1939*, pp. 447–69.

General treatment of subject includes some NA examples of myths involving the sun.

661. Squier, E. G. *The Serpent Symbol, and the Worship of Reciprocal Principles of Nature in America.* New York: Putnam, 1851.

General survey of religious significance of the serpent among NAs. Includes references to the occurrences of serpents in myths.

662. Strong, W. D. "North American Indian Traditions Suggesting a Knowledge of the Mammoth." *AA*, 36 (1934), 81–88.

Discusses NA historical traditions which seem to suggest recollections of prehistoric animals. Focuses especially on accounts from the Naskapi and the Chitimacha. Responses came from Frank G. Speck, who reported a Montaignais-Naskapi myth in *AA*, 37 (1935), 159–63; Truman Michelson in *AA*, 38 (1936), 141–43; and F. T. Siebert, Jr., who reported a Penobscot text in *AA*, 39 (1937), 721–25.

663. Swanson, Guy E. "Orpheus and Star Husband: Meaning and the Structure of Myths." *Eth*, 15 (1976), 115–33.

Interpretation of the two widely occurring myths shows correlation between their occurrence in a culture and the nature of the social organization. Emphasizes how myths relate to corporate decision-making.

664. Swanton, John R. "A Concordance of American Myths." *JAF*, 20 (1907), 220–22.

Proposes development of a reference work to facilitate comparative study of NA mythology.

665. ———. "Some Practical Aspects of the Study of Myths." *JAF*, 23 (1910), 1–7.

Addresses such issues as transmission, accretion, ritualization, and ultimate origin. Cites NA examples.

666. Thomas, Arthur Caton. "Mythology—A Short Presentation on the Subject." *AAOJ*, 23 (1901), 316–19.

Introduction to the concept of myth. With some NA examples.

667. Thompson, Laura. "Attitudes and Acculturation." *AA*, 50 (1948), 200–15.

Reports results of systematic testing of NA children's belief in immanent justice. Groups whose deities and other mythic personages figured in the responses were Sioux, Ojibwa, Navajo, Papago, and Hopi.

668. Thompson, Stith. "Analogues and Borrowings in North and South American Indian Tales," in *Languages and Cultures of Western North America. Essays in Honor of Sven S. Liljeblad*. Ed. Earl H. Swanson, Jr. Pocatello: Idaho State Univ. Press, 1970, pp. 277–88.

Lists and discusses some NA narrative motifs found in folklore repertoires of other continents.

669. ———. "European Tales Among the North American Indians: A Study in the Migration of Folk- Tales." *CCP-LS*, 2, No. 34 (April–May 1919), 319–471.

Type-by-type comparative analysis of twenty-seven NA and European narratives and story categories. Attempts to show how NAs transformed the folklore they acquired from EA sources.

670. ———. *The Folktale*. New York: Dryden Press, 1946.

Major theoretical work on the history and form of the folktale. One section deals with the folktale among NAs. Essentially an examination of distribution of types and motifs cross-culturally.

671. ———. "The Star Husband Tale." *SS*, 4 (1953), 93–163.

Most important historic-geographic study of NA folklore. Analyzes eighty-six texts of a NA myth in order to determine original form, point and time of origin, and nature of major variations from the original. Reprinted in 114 (pp. 414–74). See also 649.

672. Trotter, Spencer. "The Indian Fairy Book." *PSM*, 76 (June 1910), 565–69.

Reminiscence about encounter with NA folktales as a child. Compares NA and EA traditions.

673. Utley, Francis Lee. "The Migration of Folktales: Four Channels to the Americas." *CA*, 15 (1974), 5–27.

Attempts to gather evidence of dissemination of Old World folktales to New World. Considerable attention to diffusion to NA groups. Includes brief responses by fourteen scholars.

674. Vallette, Marc F. "American Mythology as Related to Asiatic and Hebrew Tradition." *ACQR*, 40 (1915), 584–601.

Comparison of NA myths and ceremonials to those of Oceania and the Near East.

675. Voegelin, C. F. "A Modern Method for Field Work Treatment of Previously Collected Texts." *JAF*, 67 (1954), 15–20.

Discusses a technique for eliciting performance features from NAs: by reading a previously collected text to them with no variations in tone and stress, then asking them to repeat the text with appropriate emphases.

676. Voegelin, Erminie W., and Remedios W. Moore. "The Emergence Myth in Native North America," in 152, pp. 66–91.

Cross-cultural survey of emergence myth types among NAs with some attention to their function.

677. Vogel, Virgil J. "American Indian Foods Used as Medicine," in 123, pp. 125–41.

Survey of plants used by NAs for both food and medicine includes references to and excerpts from validating mythology.

678. Volney, C. F. *A View of the Soil and Climate of America: with Supplementary Remarks upon Florida; on the French Colonies on the Mississippi and Ohio, and in Canada; and on the Aboriginal Tribes of America*. Trans. C. B. Brown. Philadelphia: J. Conrad, 1804.

Based on tour of America in 1790s. Includes an outline of the mythology of an unspecified NA group.

679. Wake, C. Staniland. "Legends of the American Indians." *AAOJ*, 26 (1904), 23–28.

Overview of NA narrative traditions, especially their value as mirrors of culture.

680. Waterman, T. T. "The Explanatory Element in the Folk-Tales of the North-American Indians." *JAF*, 27 (1914), 1–54.

Argues that etiological elements have become attached to oral narratives of NAs. They do not generate the narratives.

681. Wissler, Clark. *Star Legends Among the American Indians*. New York: American Museum of Natural History, 1936 (Guide Leaflet Series No. 91).

Cross-cultural survey with text summaries of NA mythology involving celestial bodies.

682. Witthoft, John. *The American Indian as Hunter*. Harrisburg: Pennsylvania Historical and Museum Commission, 1967.

Reconstruction of the mind and manners of NA hunters, primarily from Northeast and Southeast groups. Includes myth summaries.

683. Young, Frank W. "A Fifth Analysis of the Star Husband Tale." *Eth*, 9 (1970), 389–413.

Emphasizes the social symbolism of the myth. Evaluates previous analyses by Dundes (577), Lévi-Strauss, and Thompson (671).

684. ———. "Folktales and Social Structure: A Comparison of Three Analyses of the Star-Husband Tale." *JAF*, 91 (1978), 691–99.

Compares attempts to relate the Star Husband Tale to social institutions: that of Swanson (663), that of Lévi-Strauss, and his own. See 683.

J. Theory and Commentary: Song

685. Adams, Charles. "Melodic Contour Typology." *Em,* 20 (1976), 179–215.

Reviews the approaches to melodic contour description and typology and constructs a formal definition of the concept. Uses NA examples.

686. Alexander, Hartley Burr. "The American Indian: Poet and Pragmatist." *N,* 126 (6 June 1928), 641–43.

Identifies pragmatic nature of NA philosophy as revealed in poetry.

687. ———. "Indian Songs and English Verse." *AS,* 1 (1925–1926), 571–74.

Examines problems in translating NA oral poetry into English.

688. Astrov, Margot. "Death the Life Maker." *SWR,* 38, No. 2 (Spring 1953), 115–23.

Cross-cultural survey of NA mortuary ceremonies, especially those which reaffirm life. Cites song texts (words only).

689. ———. "The Word Is Sacred." *Asia,* 46 (1946), 406–11.

Surveys the power and role of language in NA cultures. Poem texts from various groups.

690. Austin, Mary. *Indian Poetry.* New York: Exposition of Indian Tribal Arts, 1931.

Pamphlet surveys NA poetry in relation to other arts.

691. ———. "The Road to the Spring." *N,* 123 (13 October 1926), 360–61.

Surveys esthetics of NA poetry.

692. Barnes, Nellie. "American Indian Verse. Characteristics of Style." *BUK-HS,* 2, No. 4 (1 December 1921), 1–64.

Cross-cultural survey of shaping forces and stylistic features of NA verse. With texts.

693. ———. "Indian Choral Songs." *SWR,* 13, No. 4 (July 1928), 481–90.

General survey of NA religious singing with texts (words only) from various groups.

694. ———. "On the Age of American Indian Songs." *SWR,* 18, No. 2 (January 1933), 186–89.

Shows how comparison of modern field notes with early explorers' accounts reveals age of songs.

695. Bevis, William. "American Indian Verse Translations." *CE,* 35, No. 6 (March 1974), 693–703.

Negative response to contemporary translations of NA oral poetry, especially *The Magic World* by William Brandon (235) and *Technicians of the Sacred* (243) and *Shaking the Pumpkin* (242) by Jerome Rothenberg.

696. Boas, Franz. "Literature, Music, and Dance," in *General Anthropology.* Ed. Franz Boas. Boston: D. C. Heath, 1938, pp. 589–608.

Cross-cultural survey of song literature of non-literate groups includes examples from NAs.

697. Brinton, Daniel G. "Primitive American Poetry." *PL,* 4 (1892), 329–31.

Generalizes about NA song texts with examples from the Delaware and Pawnee.

698. Brisbin, James S. "The Poetry of Indians." *H,* 57 (1878), 104–08.

Survey of NA song with texts, both in original and in translation.

699. Buttree, Julia M. *The Rhythm of the Redman in Song,* *Dance, and Decoration.* New York: A. S. Barnes, 1930.

Contains sections on singing (with texts and context data) and ceremonialism. Mostly devoted to dance instructions. Seventy song texts (words and music).

700. Cadzow, Donald A. "The Vanishing American Indian Medicine-Man." *ScA,* 140 (1929), 418–20.

Cross-cultural survey of NA shamanism, including treatment of song and chant performances.

701. Chamberlain, Alexander F. "Primitive Woman as Poet." *JAF,* 16 (1903), 205–21.

Cross-cultural survey of poems and songs associated with women in non-literate cultures. Includes some NA examples.

702. Charles, Lucile Hoerr. "The Clown's Function." *JAF,* 58 (1945), 25–34.

International survey of clowning in non-literate cultures. Discusses NA singing and chanting.

703. Crane, Edward. "She Collects War Whoops." *Etu,* 59 (October 1941), 672, 718, 720.

Account of the career of Frances Densmore.

704. Curtis, Natalie. "Folk Music of America: Four Types of Folk-Song in the United States Alone." *Cr,* 21, No. 4 (January 1912), 414–20.

One type is NA, which is sketchily characterized.

705. ———. "The Song of the Indian Mother." *Cr,* 15, No. 1 (October 1908), 57–63.

Cross-cultural discussion of NA lullabies. With one Hopi text (words and music).

706. Day, A. Grove. "The Indian as Poet." *AIn,* 6, No. 3 (Spring 1952), 13–21.

Surveys nature of NA poetry and includes texts from several groups.

707. Densmore, Frances. "American Indian Poetry." *AA,* 28 (1926), 447–49.

Argues that NA poetry and music are closely interrelated and that the former can be effectively translated into English blank verse.

708. ———. *The American Indians and Their Music.* New York: Woman's Press, 1926.

Cross-cultural survey of instrumentation, types, function, and style of NA music. With some general cultural background.

709. ———. "The Belief of the Indian in a Connection Between Song and the Supernatural." BAEB No. 151 (AP No. 37), 1953.

Brief consideration of the "dream song" in NA cultures. Such songs are considered a manifestation of supernatural power.

710. ———. "Communication with the Dead as Practised by the American Indians." *Man,* 50 (1950), 40–41.

Examples of songs by which the living and dead interrelate among various NA groups.

711. ———. "Folk-Songs of the American Indians." *M,* 24 (1950), 14–18.

Survey of singing traditions, emphasizing song content.

712. ———. "Imitative Dances Among the American Indians." *JAF,* 60 (1947), 73–78.

Cross-cultural survey of NA dances imitative of animals and birds. Tunes of six songs are transcribed.

713. ———. "The Importance of Recordings of Indian Songs." *AA,* 47 (1945), 637–39.

Argues the need for acoustical recording of NA music.

714. ———. "Importance of Rhythm in Songs for the Treatment of the Sick by American Indians." *ScM,* 79 (August 1954), 109–12.

Emphasizes meter of music as a factor in the success of healing rituals. Three musical texts.

715. ———. "Indian Music." *EP,* 10 (1921), 3–9.

Survey of issues in NA musical performance.

716. ———. "The Influence of Hymns on the Form of Indian Songs." *AA,* 40 (1938), 175–77.

Treats influence of Christian hymnody on the songs of the NA Church and the Ghost Dance.

717. ———. "The Melodic Formation of Indian Songs." *JWAS,* 18 (1928), 16–24.

Musicological analysis of melodic contour and structure.

718. ———. "The Music of the American Indian." *SFQ,* 18 (1954), 153–56.

General survey of NA musical performances.

719. ———. "The Music of the American Indians." *OM,* n. s. 45 (1905), 230–34.

Emphasizes performance contexts of the music.

720. ———. "Music of the American Indians at Public Gatherings." *MQ,* 17 (1931), 464–79.

General treatment of ceremonial singing includes ten texts with some commentary on performance contexts.

721. ———. "Music of the Indians in Our Western States." *JAF,* 70 (1957), 176–78.

Brief survey of musical styles among NAs in California, Northwest Coast, Southwest, and Great Basin culture areas.

722. ———. "New Aspects of American Indian Music." *Etu,* 48 (January 1930), 11–12.

Survey of aspects of NA music. Adapted from 708.

723. ———. "On 'Expression' in Indian Singing." *AA,* 36 (1934), 487–88.

Excerpts an unpublished paper by Alice C. Fletcher on NA singing style.

724. ———. "Peculiarities in the Singing of the American Indians." *AA,* 32 (1930), 651–60.

Cites aspects of NA singing which are foreign to EA listeners: use of separate tones without words, uneven accents, absence of rests, pulsing of the voice on prolonged tones.

725. ———. "Scale Formation in Primitive Music." *AA,* 11 (1909), 1–12.

Suggests that music of non-literate groups represents formative stages of simple scales such as the pentatonic. Examples from NA groups.

726. ———. "Some Results of the Study of American Indian Music." *JWAS,* 18 (1928), 395–408.

Presents results of functional and musicological analysis of over 1000 NA songs. Also considers problems in using EA musical notation to study NA music. Also published in *Praktika de l'Académie d'Athènes,* 3 (1928), 347–60.

727. ———. "The Songs of the Indians." *AM,* 7, No. 25 (January 1926), 65–68.

Survey of NA singing with emphasis on the importance of context for appreciating the songs.

728. ———. "The Study of Indian Music." *MQ,* 1 (1915), 187–97.

Outlines justification and methods for examining NA music.

729. ———. "The Study of Indian Music." *ARSI for 1942,* pp. 527–50.

Survey of history and problems in the collection and editing of NA music.

730. ———. "Technique in the Music of the American Indian." *BAEB* No. 151 (AP No. 36), 1953.

Brief survey of musicological issues, including tone production, tempo, pitch levels, and variations in words and tunes.

731. ———. "Traces of Foreign Influences in the Music of the American Indians." *AA,* 46 (1944), 106–12.

Asserts that words exhibit more stability than tunes in NA music. Finds a number of outside accretions—especially Hispanic and Black American—in words of NA songs.

732. ———. "The Use of Meaningless Syllables in Indian Songs." *AA,* 45 (1943), 160–62.

Concerned with how "meaningless" syllables in NA music contrast with EA song texts. Suggests that NA songs must be approached from a NA esthetic.

733. ———. "The Use of Music in the Treatment of the Sick by American Indians." *MQ,* 13 (1927), 555–65.

Describes NA healing rituals which involve singing. Includes seven texts (words and music) from various groups. A later version of this paper appeared in *ARSI for 1952* (pp. 439–54).

734. ———. "What Intervals Do Indians Sing?" *AA,* 31 (1929), 271–76.

Deals with the small gradations in pitch which characterize NA music. Suggests that they reflect a more complex musical system than that of EAs.

735. ———. "The Words of Indian Songs as Unwritten Literature." *JAF,* 63 (1950), 450–58.

Emphasizes literary qualities of NA songs, especially poetry, humor, and historical allusions.

736. Dobkins de Rios, Marlene, and Fred Katz. "Some Relationships Between Music and Hallucinogenic Ritual: The 'Jungle Gym' in Consciousness." *E,* 3 (1975), 64–76.

International study of the use of music in ceremonialism involving narcotics. Some NA examples.

737. Eames, Henry Purmort. "The Gamut of Expression in Indian Music." *TAM,* 17 (August 1933), 611–15.

General discussion of vocal performances of NAs. Pitch and rhythm emphasized.

738. Elson, Louis C. *The History of American Music.* Revised edition. New York: Macmillan, 1915.

Brief section on NA music presents several texts (words and music) and a typology of music categories.

739. Everett, Katharine Kennedy. "The Poetry of the North American Indian." *IW,* 3, No. 5 (15 October 1935), 17–19.

Argues that understanding NA poetry affords insight into heart of cultures.

740. Fillmore, John Comfort. "The Harmonic Structure of Indian Music." *Mu,* 16 (1899), 453–72.

Musicological treatment of songs of various NA groups. With music texts. Also published in *AA,* 1 (1899), 297–318.

741. ———. "Scale and Harmonies of Indian Songs." *Mu,* 4 (1893), 478–89.

Discusses various musicological issues. With texts (words and music).

742. ———. "The Scientific Importance of the Folk-Music of Our Aborigines." *LS,* 7, No. 1 (June 1897), 22–25.

Argues that music provides insight into a group's world view.

743. ———. "A Study of Indian Music." *Cent,* n. s. 25 (1893–1894), 616–23.

Musicological analysis of NA music, based on Omaha material.

744. ———. "What Do Indians Mean to Do When They Sing, and How Far Do They Succeed?" *JAF,* 8 (1895), 138–42.

Discusses problems in transcribing NA music. Argues that depicting individual performance variables misrepresents the text.

745. Finnegan, Ruth. *Oral Poetry: Its Nature, Significance and Social Context.* Cambridge: Cambridge Univ. Press, 1977.

General survey of principles of and theories about oral poetry. Examples from NA as well as other traditions are cited and reproduced.

746. Fletcher, Alice C. *Indian Games and Dances with Native Songs Arranged from American Indian Ceremonials and Sports.* Boston: C. C. Birchard, 1915.

Adaptations of song and dance performances from NA ceremonies and games. Several song texts included. Dedicated to "The Youth of America."

747. ———."Indian Music." *Mu,* 6 (1894), 188–99.
Survey of NA musical performances and of techniques used to collect the music.

748. ———. "Indian Songs and Music." *JAF,* 11 (1898), 85–104.

Survey of aspects of NA music with several Omaha texts (music only). Concerned with taxonomy, singing style, rhythm, form, and contexts of performance.

749. ———. "Music as Found in Certain North American Indian Tribes." *Mu,* 4 (1893), 457–67.
Cross-cultural survey of NA musical performances.

750. Gundlach, Ralph H. "A Quantitative Analysis of Indian Music." *AJP,* 44 (1932), 133–45.

Reports an experiment to determine whether objective factors in a piece of music relate directly to the mood it arouses. Factors such as rhythm, range, and melodic intervals are compared from several NA singing traditions.

751. Hamilton, Anna Heuermann. "The Music of the North American Indians." *Etu,* 63 (July 1945), 376, 414–15.
Primarily an account of Frances Densmore's career.

752. Haslam, Gerald. "American Indians: Poets of the Cosmos." *WAL,* 5, No. 1 (Spring 1970), 15–29.
Argues for the poetic genius of NAs, arising out of their recognition of the magical power of language. Uses contemporary as well as traditional oral poetry.

753. Hofmann, Charles. *American Indians Sing.* New York: John Day, 1967.
Survey covers functions, musical instruments, and contexts of NA singing. A random sampling of song texts and contexts is included.

754. ———, ed. *Frances Densmore and American Indian Music. A Memorial Volume. CMAI,* 23 (1968).
Survey of Densmore's life and work, using extracts from her autobiographical writings and essays on NA music. Includes bibliography of works by and about Densmore.

755. ———. "Frances Densmore and the Music of the American Indian." *JAF,* 59 (1946), 45–50.
Assesses Densmore's career, viewing her as both analyst and preserver of NA musical traditions.

756. Howard, Helen Addison. *American Indian Poetry.* Boston: Twayne, 1979.
Survey of the styles of NA poetry with evaluations of the work of translators (Mary Austin, Natalie Curtis, Frances Densmore, Alice Fletcher) and of some interpreters.

757. ———. "Literary Translators and Interpreters of Indian Songs." *JW,* 12, No. 2 (April 1973), 212–28.
Evaluates the work of Alice Fletcher, Frances Densmore, Mary Austin, Natalie Curtis, Alice Henderson, Eda Lou Walton, and Ruth Underhill.

758. Ish-Ti-Opi (as told to L. Wielich). "Art and Life in Indian Music." *Etu,* 59 (March 1941), 161–62, 194.
Suggests that music and art are central to NA life. Author is one-half Choctaw.

759. Kurath, Gertrude P. "Native Choreographic Areas of North America." *AA,* 55 (1953), 60–73.
Distinguishes regional dance patterns of NAs. Discusses ground plans, style of steps, body movements, and cultural implications.

760. Lee, Sylvia. "Indian Music and Dances." *Rec,* 35 (October 1941), 433–34, 473.
Summary of ideas of students of NA music and dance with intent of informing recreation workers about their playground potential.

761. Lieurance, Thurlow. "The Musical Soul of the American Indian." *Etu,* 38 (October 1920), 655–56.
Composer who draws upon NA materials discusses contexts of song performances and provides one legend text (Arapaho).

762. Lincoln, Kenneth. "(Native) American Poetries." *SWR,* 63 (1978), 367–84.
Compares NA poetry, oral and written, with EA. Treats imagery, style, and poet's cultural role.

763. ———. "Native American Tribal Poetics." *SWR,* 60 (1975), 101–16.
NAs share a poetic esthetic which recognizes kinship among man, nature, and the supernatural.

764. Lomax, Alan. "Folk Song Style." *AA,* 61 (1959), 927–54.
Suggests an approach to describing musical styles cross-culturally on the basis of eight variables. Illustrates methodology with some NA examples.

765. ———. *Folk Song Style and Culture.* Washington: American Association for the Advancement of Science, 1968.
Discussion of cantometrics, a method for relating the musical style of a culture to other cultural factors. NA materials are used extensively, and cantometric profiles for several NA groups are constructed.

766. Lounsbury, Floyd G. "Stray Number Systems Among Certain Indian Tribes." *AA,* 48 (1946), 672–75.
Surveys counting systems used primarily as linguistic play among various NA groups. Some of the systems involve chanting or singing.

767. Lueders, Edward. "Color Symbolism in the Songs of the American Indians." *WHR,* 12 (1958), 115–20.
Discusses lack of significant color imagery in NA songs except for established symbolic colors.

768. Mays, John B. "The Flying Serpent: Contemporary Imaginations of the American Indian." *CRAS,* 4 (1973), 32–47.
Primarily concerned with fashions in the translation of NA oral poetry.

769. McAllester, David P. "The Astonished Ethno-Muse." *Em,* 23 (1979), 179–89.

Reflections on the development of the discipline and subject matter of ethnomusicology include some illustrations from NA songs.

770. McAllister, H. S. " 'The Language of Shamans': Jerome Rothenberg's Contribution to American Indian Literature." *WAL,* 10, No. 4 (Winter 1976), 293–309.

Assessment of *Shaking the Pumpkin* (242). Argues that the translations of the NA poetry therein capture their non-European nature.

771. Mead, Charles W. "Indian Music." *NH,* 20 (1920), 209–11.

Brief, general survey of NA singing style.

772. Nettl, Bruno. *Folk and Traditional Music of the Western Continents.* Englewood Cliffs, N.J.: Prentice-Hall, 1965.

Ethnomusicological survey includes one chapter on NA music. Deals with cultural role of music, musical styles, and functions of music. Several song texts.

773. ———. "Historical Aspects of Ethnomusicology." *AA,* 60 (1958), 518–32.

Summarizes some of the historical concerns of ethnomusicology, including problems of origin and change. Uses some NA examples.

774. ———. *An Introduction to Folk Music in the United States.* Detroit: Wayne State Univ. Press, 1960.

Ethnomusicological survey includes one chapter on NA music. With song texts.

775. ———. *Music in Primitive Culture.* Cambridge: Harvard Univ. Press, 1956.

Introductory survey of ethnomusicology includes one chapter on NA music. Emphasizes musical variation among culture areas.

776. ———. "Musical Cartography and the Distribution of Song." *SJA,* 16 (1960), 338–47.

Treats methods for mapping NA musical styles.

777. ———. *North American Indian Musical Styles.* Philadelphia: AFS, 1954 (MAFS No. 45).

Survey of musical styles by culture area. Appends 28 texts (music only) from various NA groups. Also published in *JAF,* 67 (1954), 44–56, 297–307, 351–68.

778. ———. "Notes on Musical Composition in Primitive Culture." *AnQ,* 27 (1954), 81–90.

Describes several types of primitive musical composition with some NA examples.

779. ———. "Unifying Factors in Folk and Primitive Music." *JAMS,* 9 (1956), 196–201.

Brief analysis of such devices as isorhythm, contour, and tonality which unify musical performances of traditional singers. Uses NA examples. Reprinted in 114 (pp. 175–81).

780. "North American Indians." *SLM,* 6 (1840), 190–92.

General description of NA "society" includes a brief section on music and poetry.

781. Ortiz, Simon J. "Song/Poetry and Language." *ST,* 3, No. 2 (Spring 1977), 9–12.

Celebration of song as a language act basic to all vocal expression.

782. Podolsky, Edward. "The Use of Music as a Healing Agent Among the Indians." *Etu,* 52 (July 1934), 434.

Brief note on use of songs in healing rituals of various NA groups.

783. Pound, Louise. "The Beginnings of Poetry." *PMLA,* 32 (1917), 201–32.

Argues against communal composition theory of poetic origins, in part by citing NA examples of individual ownership of songs.

784. Powers, William K. *Here Is Your Hobby: Indian Dancing and Costumes.* New York: Putnam, 1966.

Contains instructions for performing dances from various groups. Some data on singing. With song texts (words and music).

785. ———. "The Study of Native American Music." *KF,* 20 (1975), 39–56.

Survey of state of NA music study with good bibliographical and discographical sections.

786. Reade, John. "Aboriginal American Poetry." *PTRSC,* 1st series, 5, section 2 (1887), 9–34.

Surveys nature of NA oral poetry and criticizes theoretical perspectives of a number of contemporaries. Includes text excerpts.

787. Rhodes, Willard. "American Indian Music." *To,* 4, No. 3 (Spring 1956), 97–102.

Survey of ritual function of NA singing.

788. ———. "The Christian Hymnology of the North American Indians," in 165, pp. 324–31.

Survey of hymn-singing among various NA groups includes four music texts.

789. Roberts, Helen H. "Melodic Composition and Scale Foundations in Primitive Music." *AA,* 34 (1932), 79–107.

Challenges applicability of EA concepts of musicology to primitive music. Cites NA examples. George Herzog responded in *AA,* 34 (1932), 546–48.

790. ———. *Musical Areas in Aboriginal North America.* *YUPA,* 12 (1936).

Distributional study of types of vocal and instrumental music.

791. ———. "New Phases in the Study of Primitive Music." *AA,* 24 (1922), 144–60.

Emphasizes the need for stylistic and structural analyses of primitive music. Illustrates with Pawnee songs.

792. Rothenberg, Jerome. "Reality at White Heat." *N,* 209 (27 October 1969), 444–46.

Discusses problems in translating NA oral poetry. Reprinted as introduction to *Shaking the Pumpkin* (242).

793. Sandburg, Carl. "Aboriginal Poetry." *Po,* 19, No. 5 (February 1917), 251–55.

Discusses the poetic potential of NA folklore, especially oral poetry.

794. Skilton, Charles Sanford. "Indian Music at Home." *Mus,* 23 (July 1918), 459.

Describes performance of NA music by students at Haskell Institute.

795. Spinden, Herbert J. "American Indian Poetry." *NH,* 19 (1919), 301–07.

Cross-cultural survey of NA song with several texts in original and free translations.

796. Stensland, Anna Lee. "Traditional Poetry of the American Indian." *EJ,* 64, No. 6 (September 1975), 41–47.

Survey of NA poetry with emphasis on its relationship to cultural context. Sees poetry as mirror of culture.

797. Walton, Eda Lou, and T. T. Waterman. "American Indian Poetry." *AA,* 27 (1925), 25–52.

Explores the nature of NA poetry in general and with special reference to Navajo, Pima, and Pueblo groups.

Emphasis on stylistics and transcription problems.
798.   Wead, Charles K. "The Study of Primitive Music." *AA*, 2 (1900), 75–79.
Suggestions for musicological investigation. Draws upon NA materials.
799.   "Whoop Collector." *Ti*, 32 (7 November 1938), 25.
Sketch of the career of Frances Densmore.
800.   Yeager, Lyn Allison. "A Kaleidoscope of Folk Music Colors." *PA*, 5, No. 2 (July 1973), 48–57; 6, No. 1 (January 1974), 1–13.
Amateurish survey of various North American folk music traditions includes sections on "Indian Music" and "Eskimo Music." With texts (words and music).

K. Theory and Commentary: Oratory and Miscellaneous Genres

801.   Aumann, F. R. "Indian Oratory." *Pal*, 46 (1965), 251–56.
Brief survey of NA oratorical performances with texts.
802.   Barbeau, Marius. "Indian Eloquence." *QQ*, 39 (1932), 451–64.
Survey of the art of oratory among various NA groups.
803.   Bernard, Jessie. "Political Leadership Among North American Indians." *AJS*, 34 (1928), 296–315.
Argues that oratory was one method by which political leaders attained and held power.
804.   Chamberlain, Alexander F. "Further Notes on Indian Child Language." *AA*, o. s. 6 (1893), 321–22.
List of baby talk from various groups.
805.   ———. "The Poetry of American Aboriginal Speech." *JAF*, 9 (1896), 43–47.
Cross-cultural survey of figurative language in the speech of various NA groups.
806.   Deloria, Vine, Jr. *Custer Died for Your Sins. An Indian Manifesto.* New York: Macmillan, 1969.
Chapter on "Indian Humor" treats contemporary NA oral literary forms.
807.   Dorsey, J. Owen. "Indian Personal Names." *AA*, o. s. 3 (1890), 263–68.
Classified list of NA names meant to be the beginning of a larger project on the subject.
808.   Edmunds, R. David. "Indian Humor: Can the Red Man Laugh?," in *Red Men and Hat-Wearers, Viewpoints in Indian History. Papers from the Colorado State University Conference on Indian History, August 1974.* Ed. Daniel Tyler. NP: Pruett, 1976, pp. 141–53.
Survey of practical joking and verbal and visual jokes among NAs.
809.   Fletcher, Alice C. "Prayers Voiced in Ancient America." *A&A*, 9 (February 1920), 73–75.

Describes function and style of NA prayers. With illustrative texts.
810.   "Indian Eloquence." *K*, 7 (April 1836), 385–90.
General comments on NA oratorical skills.
811.   Jones, Louis Thomas. *Aboriginal American Oratory. The Tradition of Eloquence Among the Indians of the United States.* Los Angeles: Southwest Museum, 1965.
Historical treatment of oratorical traditions with numerous texts.
812.   ———. "Indian Speech Arts." *M*, 37 (1963), 91–97.
Historical survey of NA oratory.
813.   Mallery, Garrick. "Sign Language Among North American Indians Compared with That Among Other Peoples and Deaf-Mutes." *ARBAE*, 1 (1879–1880), 263–552.
Cross-cultural survey of NA gestural communication. Includes three narratives (Paiute, Ojibwa, Mescalero Apache) and two orations (Wichita, Hidatsa) delivered through gestures. Some data on other NA nonverbal communication such as smoke signals.
814.   Murphy, Marjorie N. "Silence, the Word, and Indian Rhetoric." *CCC*, 21 (1970), 356–63.
Examines language used in NA speeches about social and political injustice within the context of cultural values.
815.   Roberts, John M. "Oaths, Autonomic Ordeals, and Power." *AA*, 67 (1965), 186–212.
Presents a cross-cultural survey of appeals to supernatural power in legal contexts. Cites NA traditional oaths.
816.   Sheehan, Bernard W. "Paradise and the Noble Savage in Jeffersonian Thought." *WMQ*, 3rd series, 26 (1969), 327–59.
One aspect of NA behavior that impressed Jeffersonians was speaking ability. Data on perceptions of NA oratory.
817.   Sorber, Edna C. "Indian Eloquence as American Public Address." *IH*, 5, No. 3 (Fall 1972), 40–46.
Argues that nineteenth-century NA oratory should be studied for literary and historical reasons.
818.   ———. "The Noble Eloquent Savage." *Eh*, 19 (1972), 227–36.
Survey of conventional view of NAs as particularly skilled in oratory.
819.   Taylor, Archer. "American Indian Riddles." *JAF*, 57 (1944), 1–15.
Challenges scholarly commonplace that NAs had no riddles. Argues that if riddling were not indigenous to NAs, many groups readily adopted EA riddles.
820.   Tracy, William. "Indian Eloquence." *ApJ*, 6 (11 November 1871), 543–45.
Brief survey of NA oratorical skills.
821.   Waddell, William. *The Red-Man or the Destruction of a Race.* St. Louis: Perrin & Smith, 1909.
Discusses the waning of NA cultures. With a chapter on oratory.

II NORTHEAST

A. General Works

822. "Autobiography of David Meade." *WMQ,* 1st series, 13 (1904–1905), 41–45, 73–102.

Life of an eighteenth-century Virginia gentleman. Contains account of NA oratorical performance style as witnessed on a trip to Montreal.

823. Axtell, James. "The White Indians of Colonial America." *WMQ,* 3rd series, 32 (1975), 55–88.

Examines attractions of NA life for EA colonists. One appeal was the dancing and singing of some groups.

824. Barber, John Warner. *The History and Antiquities of New England, New York, New Jersey, and Pennsylvania. Embracing the Following Subjects, viz: Discoveries and Settlements—Indian History—Indian, French, and Revolutionary Wars—Religious History—Biographical Sketches—Anecdotes, Traditions, Remarkable and Unaccountable Occurrences—with a Great Variety of Curious and Interesting Relics of Antiquity.* Hartford: Allen S. Stillman, 1844.

Includes descriptions of religious beliefs and ceremonies and a legend text relating first NA contact with the Dutch.

825. Beck, Horace P. *Gluskap the Liar and Other Indian Tales.* Freeport, Maine: Bond Wheelwright, 1966.

Rewritten myth and folktale texts from various NA groups in Maine—especially the Penobscot, Passamaquoddy, Micmac, and Malecite.

826. Beck, Jane C. "The Giant Beaver: A Prehistoric Memory?" *Eh,* 19 (1972), 109–22.

Views oral traditions about a giant beaver among various NA groups in the Northeast as a fossil memory of an extinct Pleistocene creature.

827. Benson, Adolph, ed. *The America of 1750: Peter Kalm's Travels in North America, The English Version of 1770.* 2 volumes. New York: Wilson-Erickson, 1937.

Kalm was primarily interested in zoology and botany, but provides a fairly thorough description of a dance (including song texts) performed by some NAs in Canada.

828. Boyle, David. *Notes on Primitive Man in Ontario.* Toronto: Warwick Bros. & Rutter, 1895.

Includes some data on religion, mythology, and ceremonialism among various NA groups.

829. Brinton, Daniel G. "The Chief God of the Algonkins, in His Character as a Cheat and Liar." *AAOJ,* 7 (1885), 137–39.

Note on the nature of the high god among various Northeast and Sub-Arctic groups.

830. Bushnell, David I., Jr. *Native Cemeteries and Forms of Burial East of the Mississippi.* BAEB No. 71 (1920).

Primarily an archeological study, but describes some mortuary customs (Huron in 1636 and 1675, Seneca in 1731). Also some data on beliefs in an afterlife.

831. Chamberlain, Alexander F. "The Maple Amongst the Algonkian Tribes." *AA,* o. s. 4 (1891), 39–43.

Particularly concerned with the significance of the maple in the mythologies of groups in the Northeast and Midwest.

832. Clark, J. V. H. *Lights and Lines of Indian Character, and Scenes of Pioneer Life.* Syracuse: E. H. Babcock, 1854.

Collection of sketches of life on the frontier includes some rewritten myth and legend texts from Northeast and Midwest groups.

833. Davis, Rose M. "How Indian Is Hiawatha?" *MWF,* 7, No. 1 (Spring 1957), 5–25.

Studies Longfellow's sources to determine the degree to which his epic hero corresponds to NA original.

834. DeForest, John W. *History of the Indians of Connecticut from the Earliest Known Period to 1850.* Hartford: Wm. Jas. Hamersley, 1853.

Early chapters include data on religious beliefs, ceremonials, and singing.

835. "Deities of the Early New England Indians, The" *JAF,* 12 (1899), 211–12.

Discussion of terms for and attitudes toward deities among various Northeast groups. From seventeenth-century sources.

836. Dewey, Edward H. "Football and the American Indians." *NEQ,* 3 (1930), 736–40.

Excerpts from accounts of colonial travelers about NA ball games. Some data on ritual associations of game.

837. Drake, Samuel Adams. *A Book of New England Legends and Folk Lore in Prose and Poetry.* Boston: Roberts, 1884.

Most of the material is EA, but several of the texts—rewritten by Drake or in verse by someone else—appear to be of NA origin.

838. Eggleston, Edward. "The Aborigines and the Colonists." *Cent,* 26 (May 1883), 96–114.

Brief historical survey of NA-EA relations in pre-nineteenth century America. Among "obstacles" to civilizing NAs were mythic and magical systems as preserved in stories and ceremonials.

839. Fenton, William N. "The Present Status of Anthropology in Northeastern North America: A Review Article." *AA,* 50 (1948), 494–515.

Focuses on the Iroquois in this survey of available knowledge of Northeast groups. Suggests that tribal mythologies may exhibit distinctive regional styles.

840. Goddard, Ives. "Some Early Examples of American Indian Pidgin English from New England." *IJAL,* 43 (1977), 37–41.

Presents texts of pidgin English reported by seventeenth and eighteenth-century observers of NA culture. One text purports to be that of an oration by King Philip.

841. Hagar, Stansbury. "The Celestial Bear." *JAF,* 13 (1900), 92–103.

Cross-cultural survey of NA attitudes toward Ursa Major. With one myth text. Focuses on Northeast groups.

842.   Hale, Horatio. " 'Above' and 'Below.' A Mythological Disease of Language." *JAF,* 3 (1890), 177–90.

Illustrates the validity of Max Müller's "disease of language" concept by citing myths from various Northeast groups.

843.   Hamilton, James Cleland. "The Algonquin Manabozho and Hiawatha." *JAF,* 16 (1903), 229–33.

Discusses source material for Longfellow's *Song of Hiawatha.*

844.   Heckewelder, John. *History, Manners, and Customs of the Indian Nations Who Once Inhabited Pennsylvania and the Neighbouring States.* Philadelphia: Publication Fund of the Historical Society of Pennsylvania, 1876 (Memoirs of the Historical Society of Pennsylvania, No. 12.)

Historical and cultural survey with data on oratory, ceremonialism, singing, and mythology of various Northeast groups.

845.   Hemmeon, Ethel. "Glooscap. A Synopsis of His Life; The Marked Stones He Left." *CF,* 12 (February 1932), 180–81.

Summary of the culture hero's career from myths of various Northeast groups.

846.   Hicks, George L, and David I. Kertzer. "Making a Middle Way: Problems of Monhegan Identity." *SJA,* 28 (1972), 1–24.

Investigation of a racially mixed group, pseudonymously called "Monhegan," who assert their NA identity by attendance at ceremonials.

847.   Hoffman, Charles Fenno. "The Flying Head: A Legend of Sacondaga Lake." *MH,* 4 (November 1906), 282–88.

Rewritten folktale text from an unidentified Northeast group. No annotation or commentary.

848.   Hooke, Hilda Mary. *Thunder in the Mountains: Legends of Canada.* London: Oxford Univ. Press, 1947.

Rewritten and excerpted myths and legends. Sources not identified. Apparently from Northeast and Sub-Arctic groups.

849.   J. "Indian Traditions. The Creation of the Island of Nantucket." *USLG,* 4, Nos. 9 and 10 (August 1826), 357–61.

Rewritten myth text. Some comments on collection situation.

850.   Jiskogo. "The Story Bag." *M,* 5 (1931–1932), 147–52, 179–83.

Romanticized ethnographic descriptions include some data on storytelling and a myth text. From various Northeast groups.

851.   Judson, Katharine Berry, ed. *Myths and Legends of British North America.* Chicago: A. C. McClurg, 1917.

Myth and legend texts from Canadian NAs (Northeast, Midwest, Northwest Coast, Sub-Arctic, and Arctic culture areas). Identified by tribe, but sources not cited.

852.   Kenton, Edna, ed. *The Indians of North America.* 2 volumes. New York: Harcourt, Brace, 1927.

Selections from 68 documents written by Jesuit missionaries in 1600s and 1700s. Included are accounts of ceremonials, mythology, and religious attitudes of various groups in the Northeast and Midwest.

853.   Lanman, Charles. *Haw-Ho-Noo; or, Records of a Tourist.* Philadelphia: Lippincott, Grambo, 1850.

Collection of essays. Appended are texts of several NA

myths and legends, some of which are identified by source. Groups from Northeast, Southeast, and Midwest are represented.

854.   Leland, Charles G. "The Mythology, Legends, and Folk-Lore of the Algonkins." *TRSL,* 14, Part 1 (1887), 68–91.

Survey of the material as it compares to Old World mythology.

855.   Matthews, Cornelius. *The Enchanted Moccasins and Other Legends of the American Indians.* New York: G. P. Putnam, 1877.

Twenty-six myth and folktale texts rewritten from Schoolcraft's originals. No annotations or commentary. First published as *The Indian Fairy Book* in 1867.

856.   McGee, Harold Franklin, Jr. "Ethnographic Bibliography of Northeastern North America," in 138, pp. 1–69.

Unannotated list of 380 books and articles arranged alphabetically by author.

857.   Mélançon, Claude. *Indian Legends of Canada.* Trans. David Ellis. Toronto: Gage, 1974.

Thirty-four myth and folktale texts adapted from previously published sources. No annotations, but brief headnotes on cultural backgrounds introduce each culture area section (Northeast, Midwest, Northwest Coast, Sub-Arctic).

858.   Moore, William V. *Indian Wars of the United States from the Discovery to the Present Time from the Best Authorities.* Philadelphia: R. W. Pomeroy, 1840.

Historical survey begins with general account of NA culture, including data on ceremonialism, supernaturalism, and oratory. Two speech texts (by Logan, by a Pawnee orator). Focus on Northeast and Southeast groups.

859.   *Observations on the Inhabitants, Climate, Soil, Rivers, Productions, Animals, and Other Matters Worthy of Notice. Made by Mr. John Bartram, in His Travels from Pennsylvania to Onondago, Oswego and the Lake Ontario, in Canada. To Which Is Annex'd, a Curious Account of the Cataracts at Niagara. By Mr. Peter Kalm, a Swedish Gentleman Who Travelled There.* London: J. Whiston & B. White, 1751.

Contains some descriptions of NA ceremonialism and singing.

860.   Porter, Frank W., III. *Indians in Maryland and Delaware. A Critical Bibliography.* Bloomington: Indiana Univ. Press, 1979.

Unannotated list of 230 books and articles, primarily about Nanticokes, Piscataways, Susquehannocks, and Choptunks. Introductory essay has no section clearly relevant to folklore.

861.   Ronda, James P. " 'We Are Well as We Are': An Indian Critique of Seventeenth-Century Christian Missions." *WMQ,* 3rd series, 34 (1977), 66–82.

Summary of responses to missionary work from several Northeast groups. Includes references to NA ceremonialism and supernaturalism.

862.   S., F. W. ["Peter Cram" His Historian]. "The Old Indians of Long-Island." *K,* 32 (September 1848), 237–43.

Survey of several Long Island groups. Includes sketchy data on religion and ceremonialism.

863.   Salisbury, Neal. "Red Puritans: The 'Praying Indians' of Massachusetts Bay and John Eliot." *WMQ,* 3rd series, 31 (1974), 27–54.

Consideration of Eliot's missionary attempts includes distinction between Christian world view and that evident in NA mythologies. Also some attention to role of oral tradition in spread of Christian ideas.

864. Sears, Clara Endicott. *The Great Powwow. The Story of the Nashaway Valley in King Philip's War.* Boston: Houghton Mifflin, 1934.

Historical work includes sections on NA culture, including song and prayer texts and descriptions of ceremonialism.

865. Skinner, Charles M. *Myths & Legends Beyond Our Borders.* Philadelphia: J. B. Lippincott, 1899.

Rewritten texts of myths, legends, and folktales from various NA groups in Canada (Northeast, Northwest Coast, Sub-Arctic). No annotation or commentary. (Half of the volume deals with Mexico.)

866. Smith, G. Hubert. "Legend of the Origin of Nantucket Island." *JAF*, 54 (1941), 83.

Reprint of an etiological narrative, attributed to NAs, which first appeared in *The Columbian Magazine* in 1787.

867. Speck, Frank G. "The Eastern Algonkian Wabanaki Confederacy." *AA*, 17 (1915), 492–508.

Discusses the confederacy composed of the Penobscot, Passamaquoddy, Malecite, and Micmac. Focuses on ceremonial wampum belts associated with confederacy and on the orations which related to the belts.

868. ———. "The Family Hunting Band as the Basis of Algonkian Social Organization." *AA*, 17 (1915), 289–305.

Survey of the role of hunting band in Northeast cultures, especially the Penobscot and Micmac. Includes partial text of an oration from an Ojibwa chief (for comparative purposes) and references to various mythic beings.

869. ———. "Reptile Lore of the Northern Indians." *JAF*, 36 (1923), 273–80.

Consideration of beliefs and oral narratives involving reptiles, among various Northeast groups.

870. Tooker, Elisabeth. *The Indians of the Northeast. A Critical Bibliography.* Bloomington: Indiana Univ. Press, 1978.

Unannotated list of 270 books and articles. Introductory essay is arranged by culture group.

871. ———, ed. *Native North American Spirituality of the Eastern Woodlands: Sacred Myths, Dreams, Visions, Speeches, Healing Formulas, Rituals and Ceremonials.* New York: Paulist, 1979 (Classics of Western Spirituality).

Myth texts and ritual descriptions taken from previously published sources and treating various groups from the Northeast and Midwest. Editor's commentary places the material in context.

872. Trigger, Bruce G., ed. *Handbook of North American Indians. Volume 15. Northeast.* Washington: Smithsonian Institution, 1978.

Massive reference work with separate essays on various tribal groups and subgroups. No specific essays deal with folklore, but many of the essays describe the mythologies and ceremonials of the groups, and related matters.

873. Turner, O. *History of the Pioneer Settlement of Phelps and Gorham's Purchase, and Morris' Reserve; Embracing the Counties of Monroe, Ontario, Livingston, Yates, Steuben, Most of Wayne and Allegany, and Parts of Orleans, Genesee and Wyoming. To Which Is Added, a Supplement, or Extension of the Pioneer History of Monroe County.* Rochester: William Alling, 1851.

Includes oration texts.

874. Wallace, Paul A. W. *Indians in Pennsylvania.* Harrisburg: Pennsylvania Historical and Museum Commission, 1961.

Historical and ethnographic introductions to several groups native to the state (especially the Iroquois and Delaware). Contains paraphrases of some myths and descriptions of ceremonialism.

875. Weslager, C. A. *Magic Medicines of the Indians.* Somerset, N. J.: Middle Atlantic Press, 1973.

Contains some descriptions of ceremonies, but major concern is with medicinal usages of plants by Northeast and Southeast cultures.

876. Witthoft, John. *Green Corn Ceremonialism in the Eastern Woodlands. OCMAUM* No. 13 (1949).

Cross-cultural survey of ceremonialism among Northeast and Southeast groups. Includes a discussion of corn origin myths.

See also 30, 250, 393, 427, 441, 682, 1596, 1598, 1604, 1607, 1610, 1614, 1617, 1624, 1627, 1631, 1841, 4501, 5038, 5092, 5099, 5113, 5116, 5123.

B. Abnaki

877. "Abenaki Witchcraft Story." *JAF*, 15 (1902), 62–63.

Unannotated folktale text. No commentary.

878. Baxter, James P. "The Abnakis." *NEM*, n. s. 3 (September 1890), 42–51.

Culture survey includes some data on religious ideas.

879. Brown, Mrs. W. Wallace. "Wa-Ba-Ba-Nal, or Northern Lights. A Wabanaki Legend." *JAF*, 3 (1890), 213–14.

Two unannotated myth texts. Brief comment on collecting situation.

880. Chamberlain, Montagu. "The Primitive Life of the Wapanaki Women." *Aca*, 2 (1902), 75–86.

Discusses role of Abnaki women including ceremonial participation and folklore performances.

881. Day, Gordon M. "The Western Abenaki Transformer." *JFI*, 13 (1976), 75–89.

Trickster figures in Abnaki myths fall into two categories: well-known culture heroes such as Gluskap and a stratum of older heroes.

882. Frost, Helen Keith. "Two Abnaki Legends." *JAF*, 25 (1912), 188–90.

Myth texts with some commentary on content. No annotations.

883. Gaynor, W. C. "When the Whippoorwill Sang Among the Abenaki." *CW*, 87 (September 1908), 794–802.

Unannotated legend text in storytelling context. No commentary.

884. Harrington, M. Raymond. "An Abenaki 'Witch-Story.'" *JAF*, 14 (1901), 160.

Unannotated legend text with brief data on the informant.

885. Laurent, Stephen. "The Abenakis: Aborigines of Vermont—Part II." *VH*, 24, No. 1 (January 1956), 3–11.

Includes two historical legends in original language with interlinear translations.

886. Leland, Charles G. "The Edda Among the Algonquin Indians." *AtM*, 54 (1884), 222–34.

Compares Abnaki mythology to that of Norse as preserved in the Edda.

887.   Le Sueur, Jacques. "History of the Calumet and of the Dance." *CMAI,* 12, No. 5 (1952), 3–22.

Not much on the actual ceremonial. Primarily concerned with whether it is compatible with Christianity. Originally published in French in 1864.

888.   Mallery, Garrick. "The Fight with the Giant Witch." *AA,* o. s. 3 (1890), 65–70.

Text of a myth with some comparative commentary.

889.   Masta, Henry Lorne. *Abenaki Indian Legends, Grammar and Place Names.* Victoriaville, P. Q.: La Voix des Bois-Francs, 1932.

Linguistic work contains several traditional stories in original with free translations.

890.   Nicolar, Joseph. *The Life and Traditions of the Red Man.* Bangor, Me.: C. H. Glass, 1893.

Focuses on material culture, but includes some data on world view and religion of Abnakis. Written by a Christianized NA.

891.   Reade, John. "Some Wabanaki Songs." *PTRSC,* 1st series, 5, section 2 (1887), 1–8.

Two song texts (words only) with free translations. Introduced by good discussion of cultural background.

892.   Speck, Frank G. "Abnaki Text." *IJAL,* 11 (1940), 45–46.

Historical legend text recorded in 1932.

893.   ———. "Wawenock Myth Texts from Maine." *ARBAE,* 43 (1925–1926), 165–97.

Texts of three myths and one drinking song with interlinear and free translations. Short introduction to cultural background.

894.   Vetromile, Eugene. *The Abnakis and Their History. Or Historical Notices on the Aborigines of Acadia.* New York: James B. Kirker, 1866.

Chapter on "Religion and Superstition" contains rewritten myth about Mt. Katahdin. General religious attitude discussed.

See also 409, 1257.

C. Algonkin

895.   Beck, Horace P. "Algonquin Folklore from Maniwaki." *JAF,* 60 (1947), 259–64.

Potpourri of material collected in Quebec in 1943. Included are myths, folktales, and beliefs.

896.   Brinton, Daniel G. "The Myths of Manibozho and Ioskeha." *HM&NQ,* n. s. 2 (1867), 3–6.

Solar interpretation of the culture hero.

897.   Carr, Lloyd G., and Carlos Westez. "Surviving Folktales and Herbal Lore Among the Shinnecock Indians of Long Island." *JAF,* 58 (1945), 113–23.

Twelve anecdotes, mostly about supernatural encounters, are presented with miscellaneous plantlore collected on the Shinnecock Reservation.

898.   Chamberlain, Alexander F. "Some Items of Algonkian Folk-Lore." *JAF,* 13 (1900), 271–77.

List of terms dealing with supernaturalism and oral performance taken from Abbé Cuoq's dictionary of the Nipissing dialect.

899.   Davidson, D. S. "Folk Tales from Grand Lake Victoria, Quebec." *JAF,* 41 (1928), 275–82.

Nine myth and legend texts, several dealing with the culture hero. Collected in 1926. General remarks about cultural background. No annotations.

900.   Flannery, Regina. "Algonquian Indian Folklore." *JAF,* 60 (1947), 397–401.

Report of folklore studies among the Algonkin, which was part of a general report prepared by the AFS Committee on Research in Folklore.

901.   Kirtley, Bacil F. "On the Origin of the Maine-Maritimes Legend of the Plucked Gorbey." *JAF,* 87 (1974), 364–65.

Suggests that a legend circulating among Maine lumbermen may have been associated with Algonkin weather magic.

902.   Morrison, Kenneth M. "Towards a History of Intimate Encounters: Algonkian Folklore, Jesuit Missionaries, and Kiwakwe, the Cannibal Giant." *AICRJ,* 3, No. 4 (1979), 51–80.

Argues that Algonkin folklore, especially Windigo stories, reveals NA responses to culture change wrought by white contact.

903.   Orcutt, Samuel. *The Indians of the Housatonic and Naugatuck Valleys.* Hartford: Case, Lockwood & Brainard, 1882.

Primarily a history of land tenure and mission work, but includes some legend texts and paraphrases.

904.   Schoolcraft, Henry R. "Mental Character of the Aborigines." *SLM,* 28 (1859), 466–67.

Assumes that oral narratives and songs reflect mental traits of Algonkins.

905.   ———. "Mental Traits of the Aborigines: Mondamin; or, The Origin of Indian Corn." *SLM,* 29 (1859), 12–13.

Rewritten myth text.

906.   Skinner, Alanson. "The Algonkin and the Thunderbird." *AMJ,* 14 (1914), 71–72.

Brief description of perception of a mythical being.

907.   Speck, Frank G. *Family Hunting Territories and Social Life of Various Algonkian Bands of the Ottawa Valley. CGSMB,* Anthropological Series No. 8 (1915).

Ethnographic survey done in 1913 includes some data on ceremonial dancing and singing.

908.   ———. *Myths and Folk-Lore of the Timiskaming Algonquin and Timagami Ojibwa. CGSMB,* Anthropological Series No. 9 (1915).

Nine Algonkin myths, sixteen legends and beliefs; fourteen Ojibwa myths, thirty-three legends and beliefs. Two folktales collected by Neil C. Fergusson. Most of the material appears in free translation only. All collection done in 1913. No commentary or annotation.

909.   ———. "River Desert Indians of Quebec." *IN,* 4, No. 3 (July 1927), 240–52.

General ethnographic notes contain data on mythology.

910.   Thompson, Stith. "Icelandic Parallels Among the Northeastern Algonquians: A Reconsideration," in 146, pp. 133–39.

Examines Leland's study of Algonkin oral narratives (854) and decides that apparent Icelandic parallels evaporate upon close examination.

911.   Wake, C. Staniland. "Migrations of the Algonkins." *AAOJ,* 16 (1894), 127–39.

History of tribal movements, based in part on oral literature.

See also 340.

D. Delaware

912.   Adams, Richard C. *The Adoption of Mew-Seu-Qua, Tecumseh's Father, and the Philosophy of the Delaware Indians with Unpolished Gems.* Washington: Crane, 1917.
Texts of orations, rituals, and narratives spliced together to relate the adoption of a Shawnee into the Delaware nation.

913.   ———. *Legends of the Delaware Indians and Picture Writing.* Washington: NP, 1905.
Rewritten folktale texts and descriptions of customs. No commentary or annotations.

914.   Brinton, Daniel G. *The Lenâpé and Their Legends; with the Complete Text and Symbols of the Walam Olum, a New Translation, and an Inquiry into Its Authenticity.* Philadelphia: D. G. Brinton, 1885 (Library of Aboriginal Literature, No. 5).
Text and translation of the Walam Olum. Introduced by a survey of Delaware culture, particularly oral literature. One chapter summarizes various myths and legends.

915.   ———. "Lenâpé Conversations." *JAF,* 1 (1888), 37–43.
Rambling account of data learned from a Delaware informant includes some data on mythology.

916.   Errett, Russell. "Legend as to the Origin of the Delawares." *MWH,* 9, No. 2 (December 1888), 107–15.
Criticizes the historicity of tribal origin myth as recorded by Heckewelder (921).

917.   Godfrey, Carlos E. *The Lenape Indians: Their Origin and Migrations to the Delaware.* Trenton, N. J.: Trenton Historical Society, 1919.
Pamphlet presents migration history as preserved in the Walam Olum.

918.   Harrington, M. R. "A Preliminary Sketch of Lenápe Culture." *AA,* 15 (1913), 208–35.
Ethnographic data on Delawares living in Oklahoma collected in 1908. Includes information on ceremonialism, the cosmology, and music.

919.   ———. *Religion and Ceremonies of the Lenape. IN&M,* Miscellaneous Series No. 19 (1921).
Descriptions of ceremonials with song texts and ritual origin myths.

920.   ———. "Vestiges of Material Culture Among the Canadian Delawares." *AA,* 10 (1908), 408–18.
Description of ceremonial objects with attention to ceremonial contexts for oral song performances.

921.   Heckewelder, John. *A Narrative of the United Brethren Among the Delaware and Mohegan Indians, from Its Commencement, in the Year 1740, to the Close of the Year 1808. Comprising All the Remarkable Incidents Which Took Place at Their Missionary Stations During That Period Interspersed with Anecdotes, Historical Facts, Speeches of the Indians, and Other Interesting Matter.* Philadelphia: McCarty & Davis, 1820.
Historical work contains numerous oration texts, narrative summaries, and descriptions of ceremonialism.

922.   Howard, James H. "The Nanticoke-Delaware Skeleton Dance." *AIQ,* 2, No. 1 (Spring 1975), 1–13.
Ceremonial description with two song texts (words and music).

923.   Hunter, Charles E. "The Delaware Nativist Revival of the Mid-Eighteenth Century." *Eh,* 18 (1971), 39–49.
Examination of a religious response to cultural disintegration.

924.   Kinietz, Vernon. "European Civilization as a Determinant of Native Indian Customs." *AA,* 42 (1940), 116–21.
Focuses on the Delaware Big House Ceremony to show how NAs consciously revived moribund cultural forms when EA influences challenged them.

925.   Mercer, H. C. *The Lenape Stone or The Indian and the Mammoth.* New York: Putnam, 1885.
Describes pictograph depicting NAs in combat with a mammoth. Cites historical song chronicles of various groups, especially the Delaware, as evidence for authenticity.

926.   "Migrations of the Lenni Lenape or Delawares." *AAOJ,* 19 (1897), 73–81.
Treats traditional records of migrations such as the Walam Olum.

927.   Petrullo, Vincenzo. *The Diabolic Root: A Study of Peyotism, the New Indian Religion, Among the Delawares.* Philadelphia: Univ. of Pennsylvania Press, 1934.
Historical and ethnographic account of Delaware peyotism. Includes several oral literature texts: origin legends of peyotism, descriptions of rituals, narratives of peyote experiences.

928.   Prince, J. Dyneley. "A Modern Delaware Tale." *PAPS,* 41 (1902), 20–34.
Witchcraft story with free translation and linguistic commentary.

929.   Skinner, Alanson. "The Lenapé Indians of Staten Island." *APAMNH,* 3 (1909), 3–62.
Archeological survey and an attempt to reconstruct culture include text of a creation myth recorded in 1679 by Dankers and Sluyter.

930.   Speck, Frank G. "The Boy-Bear (The Bear Abductor)." *A,* 35–36 (1940–1941), 973–74.
Unannotated myth text. No commentary.

931.   ———. *Oklahoma Delaware Ceremonies, Feasts and Dances. MAPS* No. 7 (1937).
Ceremonial descriptions with texts of ritual origin myths, prayers, and orations. With interlinear translations. Collected between 1928 and 1932.

932.   ———. *A Study of the Delaware Indian Big House Ceremony.* Harrisburg: Publications of the Pennsylvania Historical Commission, 1931.
Text of the ritual in original and free translation preceded by extensive commentary on the history and religious significance of the ceremony. Collected in 1928.

933.   ———, and Jesse Moses. *The Celestial Bear Comes Down to Earth. The Bear Sacrifice Ceremony of the Munsee-Mahican in Canada as Related by Nekatcit.* Reading, Penn.: Public Museum and Art Gallery, 1945 (Scientific Publication No. 7).
Thorough description of the ceremonial based on data collected during 1930s. Includes texts of related myths and recitatives.

934.   Squier, E. G. "Historical and Mythological Traditions of the Algonquins; with a Translation of the 'Walum-olum,' or Bark Record of the Linni-Lenape." *AWR,* February 1849, pp. 173–93.
Six song texts (words only)—two in original with interlinear translations and discussions of mythic

allusions. All taken from the Walam Olum. Reprinted in 83.

935. Tantaquidgeon, Gladys. *A Study of Delaware Indian Medicine Practice and Folk Beliefs.* Harrisburg: Pennsylvania Historical Commission, 1942.

Primarily concerned with medicinal plants, but includes texts of three myths.

936. Voegelin, C. F. "Delaware Texts." *IJAL,* 11 (1940), 105–19.

Texts with interlinear translations. Recorded in 1939. No commentary.

937. Voegelin, Erminie W. "Cultural Parallels to the Delaware Walam Olum." *PIAS,* 49 (1939), 28–31.

Points out cross-cultural analogues to major elements of the Walam Olum (pictographs, genealogies, deluge motifs).

938. Wake, C. Staniland. "The Migrations of the Lenape." *AAOJ,* 30 (1908), 221–23.

Consideration of oral traditions about tribal movements.

939. Wallace, Anthony F. C. *King of the Delawares: Teedyuscung 1700–1763.* Philadelphia: Univ. of Pennsylvania Press, 1949.

Biography includes many excerpts from the orations of the subject.

940. *Walum Olum or Red Score. The Migration Legend of the Lenni Lenape or Delaware Indians. A New Translation, Interpreted by Linguistic, Historical, Archaeological, Ethnological, and Physical Anthropological Studies.* Indianapolis: Indiana Historical Society, 1954.

Thorough treatment of the document. Includes translation by C. F. Voegelin with commentaries by Eli Lilly (historical validity), Erminie W. Voegelin (cultural background), Paul Weer (history of the ms.), Glenn A. Black (archeological background), and Georg K. Neumann (relevance to physical anthropology of society).

941. Weslager, C. A. *The Delaware Indian Westward Migration with the Texts of Two Manuscripts (1821–22) Responding to General Lewis Cass's Inquiries About Lenape Culture and Language.* Wallingford, Penn.: Middle Atlantic Press, 1978.

Responses to a questionnaire distributed by Cass in the 1820s include data on religion, musical and narrative performances, and ceremonialism.

942. ———. *The Delawares. A Critical Bibliography.* Bloomington: Indiana Univ. Press, 1978.

Bibliographical essay precedes an unannotated list of 224 books and articles.

943. ———. "Name-Giving Among the Delaware Indians." *Nam,* 19 (1971), 268–83.

Fairly thorough description of ceremonialism.

944. "Willie's Tales." *Ti,* 34 (7 August 1939), 45.

Description of Linguistic Institute of America focuses on a Delaware storyteller.

945. Witthoft, John. "The 'Grasshopper War' Folktale." *JAF,* 66 (1953), 295–301.

Discusses a narrative about how the Shawnee and Delaware became separate groups. Told no longer by NA storytellers, but still recounted by EA raconteurs.

See also 394, 699, 874, 1001, 1440, 1457, 2458.

E. Huron

946. Barbeau, C. Marius. *Huron and Wyandot Mythology. CGSMB,* Anthropological Series No. 11 (1915).

Texts of forty myths, thirty-four folktales, and twenty legends collected in 1911 and 1912. Appendix includes forty-nine narrative texts previously published by other collectors. Good introduction on context, content, and style of the narratives. Some explanatory and comparative annotations.

947. ———. *Huron-Wyandot Narratives in Translations and Native Texts.* Ottawa: Canada Department of Northern Affairs and Natural Resources, 1960.

Forty myth and folktale texts with free and literal translations. Collected in 1911 and 1912 from informants in Oklahoma.

948. ———. "Supernatural Beings of the Huron and Wyandot." *AA,* 16 (1914), 288–313.

Discusses the cosmogonic deities and sky gods of the two groups. Includes summaries of myths.

949. Cranston, J. Herbert. *Etienne Brûlé, Immortal Scoundrel.* Toronto: Ryerson, 1949.

Biography of an early explorer of New France. Some data on Huron culture: oration texts, sketchy account of religious system.

950. de Brebeuf, Jean. "Burial Ceremonies of the Hurons." Trans. Nora Thomas. *ARBAE,* 5 (1883–1884), 110–19.

Descriptions of funeral customs and the Feast of the Dead. Translated from *Relations des Jésuites* (1636).

951. Hale, Horatio. "Huron Folklore." *JAF,* 1 (1888), 177–83.

Text of cosmogonic myth with explanatory notes and data on collecting situation and cultural background.

952. ———. "Huron Folk-Lore." *JAF,* 2 (1889), 249–54.

Unannotated myth text with description of collecting situation and cultural background.

953. ———. "Huron Folk-Lore." *JAF,* 4 (1891), 290–94.

Myth text with extensive commentary on cultural background.

954. ———. "A Huron Historical Legend." *MAH,* 10 (1883), 475–83.

Legend text with commentary on historical background.

955. Heriot, George. *Travels Through the Canadas, Containing a Description of the Picturesque Scenery on Some of the Rivers and Lakes; with an Account of the Productions, Commerce, and Inhabitants of Those Provinces. To Which Is Subjoined a Comparative View of the Manners and Customs of Several of the Indian Nations of North and South America.* London: Richard Phillips, 1807.

Travel account includes brief description of Huron dancing. Some data on other NA ceremonials.

956. Herman, Mary W. "The Social Aspect of Huron Property." *AA,* 58 (1956), 1044–58.

Describes gift-giving at Huron ceremonials. Some discussion of oratory.

957. McIlwraith, T. F. "The Feast of the Dead: Historical Background." *An,* 6 (1958), 83–86.

Treats suppression of the Feast in 1649 and its revival in 1956.

958. Sagard, Father Gabriel. *The Long Journey to the Country of the Hurons.* Ed. George M. Wrong. Trans. H. H. Langton. Toronto: Champlain Society, 1939.
Travel account first published in 1632. Contains a great deal on Huron culture: song texts, myth summaries, outline of religious attitudes, descriptions of ceremonialism.

959. Sargent, Margaret. "Seven Songs from Lorette." *JAF,* 63 (1950), 175–80.
Description of an extensive collection of Huron songs recorded in 1911. Presents seven texts.

960. Tooker, Elisabeth. *An Ethnography of the Huron Indians, 1615–1649.* BAEB No. 190 (1964).
Based on the works of French explorers and missionaries. Includes data on ceremonials, myth summaries, discussion of singing.

961. Wilson, Daniel. "The Huron-Iroquois of Canada, A Typical Race of American Aborigines." *PTRSC,* 1st series, 2, section 2 (1884), 55–106.
Cultural and linguistic survey includes data on ceremonialism and summaries of myths.

See also 830, 989, 1050, 1606, 1931.

F. Iroquois (Cayuga, Mohawk, Oneida, Onondaga, Seneca)

962. Akweks, Aren. "A Mohawk Adoption." *NYFQ,* 6 (1950), 44–46.
Description of ceremony performed for Paul A. W. Wallace. Includes oration text.

963. Allen, Hope Emily. "An Oneida Tale." *JAF,* 57 (1944), 280–81.
Text of a folktale collected in 1917.

964. Barbeau, Marius. "The Dragon Myths and Ritual Songs of the Iroquoians." *JIFMC,* 3 (1951), 81–85.
Discusses presence of "Old World" dragon figure in myths and songs.

965. Bearskin, James and Amanda. "Green Corn Feast." *IW,* 3, No. 23 (15 July 1936), 23–24.
Description of a ceremony.

966. Beauchamp, William M. "Civil, Religious, and Mourning Councils and Ceremonies of Adoption of the New York Indians." *NYSMB,* 113 (1907), 341–451.
Ceremonial descriptions with song texts.

967. ———. "The Early Religion of the Iroquois." *AAOJ,* 14 (1892), 344–49.
Characterizes Iroquois religion on the basis of seventeenth-century documents.

968. ———. "The Good Hunter and the Iroquois Medicine." *JAF,* 14 (1901), 153–59.
Two myth texts which explain the origins of hunting rituals. Brief comments on cultural background. No annotations.

969. ———. "The Great Mosquito." *JAF,* 2 (1889), 284.
Legend text reprinted from Cusick's *History of the Six Nations* (1015).

970. ———. "Hi-a-wat-ha." *JAF,* 4 (1891), 295–306.
Survey of the oral traditions and history associated with the Iroquois leader.

971. ———. "An Iroquois Condolence." *JAF,* 8 (1895), 313–16.
Brief description of a ceremony. With fragmentary song texts.

972. ———. *Iroquois Folk Lore Gathered from the Six Nations of New York.* Syracuse: Dehler Press, 1922.
Random collection from various sources of myth and legend texts, descriptions of ceremonials and of religious attitudes. Includes Tuscarora material.

973. ———. "Iroquois Notes." *JAF,* 4 (1891), 39–46.
Description of a ceremony associated with the installation of chiefs. Observed in 1889.

974. ———. "Iroquois Notes." *JAF,* 5 (1892), 223–29.
Discusses belief in witches, giants, and other supernatural beings. Some story texts.

975. ———. *The Iroquois Trail, or Foot-Prints of the Six Nations, in Customs, Traditions, and History, in Which Are Included David Cusick's Sketches of Ancient History of the Six Nations.* Fayetteville, N. Y.: H. C. Beauchamp, 1892.
To Cusick's work (1015), Beauchamp appends a lengthy commentary which includes summaries of narrative traditions and references to mythic personages and ceremonies.

976. ———. "The Iroquois White Dog Feast." *AAOJ,* 7 (1885), 235–39.
Compares past and present observances of the ceremony.

977. ———. "Mohawk Notes." *JAF,* 8 (1895), 217–21.
Survey of ceremonials. With fragmentary song and chant texts.

978. ———. "The New Religion of the Iroquois." *JAF,* 10 (1897), 169–80.
Survey of the Longhouse Religion: origin, beliefs, and ceremonials.

979. ———. "Notes on Onondaga Dances." *JAF,* 6 (1893), 181–84.
Brief description of ceremonials with translated song texts.

980. ———. "Onondaga Customs." *JAF,* 1 (1888), 195–203.
Miscellany includes data on ceremonialism and mythology.

981. ———. "Onondaga Folk-Lore." *S,* 16 (12 December 1890), 332.
Potpourri of material includes myth and legend summaries and descriptions of ceremonies.

982. ———. "Onondaga Notes." *JAF,* 8 (1895), 209–16.
Description of the White Dog Feast as observed in 1894. With some song and chant fragments. Miscellaneous data about other ceremonials and games.

983. ———. "Onondaga Tale of the Pleiades." *JAF,* 13 (1900), 281–82.
Rewritten myth text with some data on cultural background.

984. ———. "Onondaga Tales." *JAF,* 1 (1888), 44–48.
Two unannotated folktale texts. No commentary.

985. ———. "Onondaga Tales." *JAF,* 2 (1889), 261–70.

Unannotated myth text with some data on cultural background.

986. ———. "Onondaga Tales." *JAF,* 6 (1893), 173–80.

Two folktale texts. Unannotated, but with some data on collecting situation. Also includes some summaries of narratives involving bears.

987. Beck, Horace P. "Jesse Cornplanter's Tall Tales." *NYFQ,* 4 (1948), 268–78.

Ten unannotated folktale texts with commentary on cultural background. Collected in 1947.

988. Bierhorst, John, ed. *Four Masterworks of American Indian Literature: Quezalcoatl/The Ritual of Condolence/Cuceb/ The Night Chant.* New York: Farrar, Straus and Giroux, 1974.

The Iroquois Ritual of Condolence appears in translations by Horatio Hale, J. N. B. Hewitt, and William N. Fenton. The Navajo Night Chant is Washington Matthews' translation. Extensive contextual commentary by Bierhorst.

989. Blau, Harold. "Dream Guessing: A Comparative Analysis." *Eh,* 10 (1963), 233–49.

Description of Onondaga ceremony involving riddles. Compared to similar rituals among the Huron.

990. ———. "Function and the False Faces: A Classification of Onondaga Masked Rituals and Themes." *JAF,* 77 (1966), 564–80.

Describes False Face Ceremony. Some attention to ritual origin myths, narratives about supernatural encounters, and accounts of dreams.

991. ———. "The Iroquois White Dog Sacrifice: Its Evolution and Symbolism." *Eh,* 11 (1964), 97–119.

Thorough description of the ritual includes some of the verbal formulas used.

992. ———. "Mythology, Prestige and Politics: A Case for Onondaga Cultural Persistence." *NYFQ,* 23 (1967), 45–51.

Suggests that prestige acquired through mythologically ascribed status accounts for Onondaga cultural stabiliy.

993. ———. "Onondaga False Face Rituals." *NYFQ,* 23 (1967), 253–64.

Ritual description with text of a dream narrative (in original and translation).

994. Bloomfield, J. K. *The Oneidas.* New York: Alden Brothers, 1907.

Primary concern is with history of missions, but includes some data on mythology, religious beliefs, and ceremonialism.

995. Boyle, David. "On the Paganism of the Civilised Iroquois of Ontario." *JAIGBI,* 30 (1900), 263–73.

Surveys mythic beliefs and ceremonialism.

996. Brant-Sero, J. O. "O-Nō-Dah." *JAF,* 24 (1911), 251.

Description of a medicinal herb used in Iroquois ceremonialism.

997. Brinton, Daniel G. *American Hero-Myths, A Study in the Native Religions of the Western Continent.* Philadelphia: H. C. Watts, 1882.

Comparative mythological approach (following Müller) of mythic heroes throughout North and Central America. Focuses especially on Iroquois and other Northeast groups. Emphasis on the mythic hero as solar hero.

998. Brush, Edward Hale. "An Ancient Iroquois Rite." *ScA,* 86 (7 June 1902), 401.

Description of Thanksgiving Ceremony.

999. Canfield, William W. *The Legends of the Iroquois Told by "The Cornplanter."* New York: A. Wessels, 1902.

Myth and legend texts based on outlines preserved from narration of the Cornplanter in the 1830s and fleshed out from other sources. No comparative notes, but interpretative commentary for each text.

1000. Carter, W. H., and G. B. Fenstermaker. *Seneca Indians: "Guardians" of the "Western Door" of the League of the Iroquois Long House. Their Home, Life and Culture.* London, Ontario: Namind, 1974.

Collection of data contributed by Seneca informants. Includes descriptions of games and ceremonies and some myth and legend texts.

1001. Cassell, Abraham, ed. "Notes on the Iroquois and Delaware Indians. Communications from Conrad Weiser to Christopher Saur." Trans. Helen Bell. *PMHB,* 1 (1877), 163–67, 319–23.

Letters written in 1740s. Some contain data on religion and ceremonialism.

1002. Chadwick, Edward Marion. *The People of the Longhouse.* Toronto: Church of England Publishing Company, 1897.

Sketchy historical survey includes text (words and music) of a dance song.

1003. Chafe, Wallace L. *Seneca Thanksgiving Rituals.* BAEB 183 (1961).

Presents two ceremonial texts in Seneca with free translations and linguistic commentary. Includes music for songs. Discusses context of the rituals in the Longhouse Religion.

1004. Chamberlain, Alexander F. "Mohawk Folk-Lore." *S,* 16 (21 November 1890), 289.

Miscellany includes folktale and legend texts and descriptions of ceremonialism.

1005. ———. "A Mohawk Legend of Adam and Eve." *JAF,* 2 (1889), 228, 311.

Retelling of the Genesis myth, collected in 1888. No annotation or commentary.

1006. Clark, Joshua V. H. *Onondaga; or Reminiscences of Earlier and Later Times; Being a Series of Historical Sketches Relative to Onondaga; with Notes on the Several Towns in the County, and Oswego.* 2 volumes. Syracuse: Stoddard and Babcock, 1849.

Historical work. One chapter summarizes Onondaga myths and legends; another describes ceremonials and compares them to classical religious rituals.

1007. Congdon, Charles E. "The Good News of Handsome Lake." *NYFQ,* 23 (1967), 290–97.

Reproduces Henry Simmons' account of Handsome Lake's first vision. Some comments on contemporary significance of the Longhouse Religion.

1008. Conklin, Harold C., and William C. Sturtevant. "Seneca Indian Singing Tools at Coldspring Longhouse: Musical Instruments of the Modern Iroquois." *PAPS,* 97 (1953), 262–90.

Description of musical instruments with attention to their ceremonial uses.

1009. Converse, Harriet Maxwell. *Myths and Legends of the New York State Iroquois.* Ed. Arthur Caswell Parker. *NYSMB* No. 125 (1908).

Myth, legend, and song texts. No comparative notes, but some attention to cultural background. Parker's introduction describes collecting situation. Data on ceremonialism appended.

1010. ———. "The Seneca New-Year Ceremony and Other Customs." *IN,* 7 (1930), 69–89.

Ritual descriptions.

1011. Cornplanter, Jesse J. *Legends of the Longhouse.* Philadelphia: Lippincott, 1938.

Collection of seventeen letters written in 1930s to Mrs. Walter A. Henricks. Each letter contains a story or some ethnographic data.

1012. Crowell, Samuel. "The Dog Sacrifice of the Senecas," in 83, pp. 323–32.

Ceremonial description as observed in 1830. Originally published in the *Cincinnati Miscellany* for February 1845.

1013. Curtin, Jeremiah. *Seneca Indian Myths.* New York: E. P. Dutton, 1922.

Texts of c. ninety myths collected in 1880s and presented in free translations. No annotations or commentary.

1014. ———, and J. N. B. Hewitt. "Seneca Fiction, Legends, and Myths." *ARBAE,* 32 (1910–1911), 37–813.

Texts of 107 narratives collected by Curtin in the 1880s and of 30 narratives collected by Hewitt in 1896. One text is presented in Seneca with interlinear translation. Hewitt characterizes Seneca mythology and evaluates Curtin's work in the foreword.

1015. Cusick, David. *Sketches of Ancient History of the Six Nations, Comprising—First—A Tale of the Foundation of the Great Island (Now North America), the Two Infants Born, and the Creation of the Universe. Second—A Real Account of the Early Settlers of North America, and Their Dissensions. Third—Origin of the Kingdom of the Five Nations, Which Was Called a Long House: The Wars, Fierce Animals, &c.* Lockport, N.Y.: Turner & McCollum, 1848.

Lengthy myth and legend texts, including the cosmogony. Important early work.

1016. Darlington, William M. *Christopher Gist's Journals with Historical, Geographical and Ethnological Notes and Biographies of His Contemporaries.* Pittsburgh: J. R. Weldin, 1893.

Edition of a journal kept during travels in 1750s. Contains a Seneca oration text.

1017. Deardorff, Merle H. "The Religion of Handsome Lake: Its Origin and Development," in 115, pp. 77–107.

Describes Handsome Lake's visionary experiences, their relationship to traditional ceremonialism, and their effects in creating a new religion. Some descriptions of the oral transmission of Handsome Lake's message.

1018. Dodge, Ernest S. "A Cayuga Bear Society Curing Rite." *PM,* 22 (1949), 65–71.

Description of a ceremony observed in 1944.

1019. Donohoe, Thomas. *The Iroquois and the Jesuits: The Story of the Labors of Catholic Missionaries Among These Indians.* Buffalo: Buffalo Catholic Publication Company, 1895.

Includes some data on pre-contact Iroquois culture. Brief chapter outlines religious beliefs and ceremonies.

1020. Dunning, R. Wm. "Iroquois Feast of the Dead: New Style." *An,* 6 (1958), 87–118.

Thorough description of a ceremony conducted in 1956. Contains oration text.

1021. Eggen, Doris. "Indian Tales of Western New York." *NYFQ,* 6 (1950), 240–45.

Three unannotated folktale texts collected on the Cattaraugus Reservation. Brief comments on cultural background.

1022. Elm, Lloyd M., Sr. "The Founding of the League of the Iroquois." *Con,* 30, No. 4 (January-February 1976), 4–5.

Retelling of ritual origin myth. Some comments on cultural background.

1023. "False Faces." *JAF,* 17 (1904), 210.

Brief description of ceremony reprinted from the *Worcester Spy* for 24 October 1902.

1024. Fenton, William N., ed. "Another Eagle Dance for Gahéhdagowa (F. G. S.)." *PM,* 22 (1949), 60–64.

Description of a ritual performed for Frank G. Speck. Written by NA performers. Fenton provides context data.

1025. ———. "Contacts Between Iroquois Herbalism and Colonial Medicine." *ARSI for 1941,* pp. 503–26.

Some consideration of Iroquois healing ritual which included singing.

1026. ———. "Iroquoian Culture History: A General Evaluation," in 116, pp. 253–77.

Survey of the status of Iroquois and Cherokee culture takes into account role of mythology and ceremonialism in studies of the culture.

1027. ———. *The Iroquois Eagle Dance: An Offshoot of the Calumet Dance. BAEB* No. 156 (1953).

Thorough description of the ritual with myth texts and song texts (words only) as observed in 1930s. Appendix by Gertrude P. Kurath, "An Analysis of the Iroquois Eagle Dance and Songs," provides ethnomusicological commentary on material collected in late 1940s.

1028. ———. "Iroquois Indian Folklore." *JAF,* 60 (1947), 383–97.

Discusses status of folklore research among the Iroquois. Part of a general report prepared by the AFS Committee on Research in Folklore.

1029. ———. "The Iroquois in History," in 134, pp. 129–68.

Survey of Iroquois history from pre-contact to contemporary period includes brief analysis of narrative traditions and ceremonial oration texts.

1030. ———. "The Lore of the Longhouse: Myth, Ritual, and Red Power." *AnQ,* 48 (1975), 131–47.

Compares two variants of the origin myth of the Iroquois Confederacy, collected from the same informant in 1899 and 1912. Emphasizes revitalization aspect.

1031. ———. "Masked Medicine Societies of the Iroquois." *ARSI for 1940,* pp. 397–429.

Includes descriptions of ceremonies and texts of songs and prayers.

1032. ———. *An Outline of Seneca Ceremonies at Coldspring Longhouse. YUPA* No. 9 (1936).

Survey of ceremonial types and functions.

1033. ———, ed. *Parker on the Iroquois: Iroquois Uses of Maize and Other Food Plants; The Code of Handsome Lake, the Seneca Prophet; The Constitution of the Five Nations.* Syracuse: Syracuse Univ. Press, 1968.

Survey of Parker's career introduces reprints of *The Code of Handsome Lake, The Seneca Prophet* (1107) and *Iroquois Uses of Maize and Other Plant Foods* (1109).

1034. ———. "The Seneca Society of Faces." *ScM,* 44 (March 1937), 215–38.

Description of False Face Society includes some data on ceremonialism and some abridged myth texts.

1035. ———. "Seth Newhouse's Traditional History and Constitution of the Iroquois Confederacy." *PAPS,* 93 (1949), 141–58.

Description of a ms. written in 1885 which presents the mythic history and ritual procedure of the Confederacy.

1036. ———. " 'This Island, The World on the Turtle's Back.' " *JAF,* 75 (1962), 283–300.

Examines the Iroquois cosmogonic myth and its relationship to the rest of the culture.

1037. ———. "Tonawanda Longhouse Ceremonies: Ninety Years After Lewis Henry Morgan." *BAEB* No. 128 (AP No. 15), 1941.

Describes ceremonial cycle of the Longhouse Religion. Some comparisons to Morgan's observations in the 1840s.

1038. ———, and Gertrude P. Kurath. "The Feast of the Dead, or Ghost Dance at Six Nations Reserve, Canada," in 115, pp. 139–65.

Description of the ceremony as it occurred in 1945 and 1949. Includes song texts (words and music) and two legend texts.

1039. Fleming, John Winters. "Indians and Conservation." *NM,* 36 (October 1943), 427–29.

Retelling of a Seneca folktale, which illustrates that NAs did not wantonly destroy nature.

1040. Foster, Michael K. "Speaking in the Longhouse at Six Nations Reserve," in 99, pp. 129–54.

Treats speaking roles of ritual participants in the Longhouse Religion.

1041. ———. "When Words Become Deeds: An Analysis of Three Iroquois Longhouse Speech Events," in 82, pp. 354–67.

Analyses of Thanksgiving oration and two Tobacco invocations.

1042. Frisch, Jack A. "Folklore, History, and the Iroquois Condolence Cane," in 136, pp. 19–25.

Treats role of the cane as a mnemonic device in ceremonial oral performances.

1043. "Great Iroquois Gathering." *MWH,* 1 (December 1884), 134–39.

Description of Red Jacket's funeral.

1044. Hale, Horatio. *The Iroquois Book of Rites.* Philadelphia: D. G. Brinton, 1883 (Library of Aboriginal Literature No. 2).

Text and translations of mss. used during 1800s by Iroquois. Includes an extensive introduction placing the mss. in context, and thorough explanatory notes to the text.

1045. ———. "The Iroquois Sacrifice of the White Dog." *AAOJ,* 7 (1885), 7–14.

Description of ritual. With song text.

1046. Hall, Charles H. *The Dutch and the Iroquois. Suggestions as to the Importance of Their Friendship in the Great Struggle of the Eighteenth Century for the Possession of This Continent.* New York: Francis Hart, 1882.

Noteworthy for Hall's vociferous condemnation of Iroquois religion and ceremonialism, which he characterizes as a "religion of hate." Some attention to deities and other mythological beings.

1047. Harrington, M. R. "Da-Ra-Sá-Kwa—A Caughnawaga Legend." *JAF,* 19 (1906), 127–29.

Unannotated myth text with brief commentary on cultural background.

1048. ———. "The Dark Dance of Ji-Gé-Onh. A Seneca Adventure." *M,* 7 (1933), 76–79.

Description of a ritual.

1049. ———. "Some Unusual Iroquois Specimens." *AA,* 11 (1909), 85–91.

Describes several ceremonial artifacts, including figures thought to represent dwarfs which appear in Iroquois myths.

1050. Harris, Dean [W. R.] *The Catholic Church in the Niagara Peninsula, 1626–1895.* Toronto: William Briggs, 1895.

Early chapter in this historical work deals with ceremonialism of Iroquois and Hurons.

1051. Helms, Randel. " 'The Code of Handsome Lake': A Literary Study of Prophecy." *G,* 4 (1971), 18–38.

Tries to establish the "prophetic book" as a literary genre. Uses Handsome Lake's message as a test case.

1052. Hendry, Jean. *Iroquois Masks and Maskmaking at Onondaga. BAEB* No. 191 (1964).

Discusses maskmaking techniques. With description of False Face Society, its origin myth, and its ceremonial procedures.

1053. Henry, Thomas R. *Wilderness Messiah: The Story of Hiawatha and the Iroquois.* New York: William Sloane, 1955.

Historical work dealing with establishment of the League of the Iroquois. Discusses ceremonialism and religion. Some summaries of myths.

1054. Hewitt, J. N. B. "A Constitutional League of Peace in the Stone Age of America: The League of the Iroquois and Its Constitution." *ARSI for 1918,* pp. 527–45.

Includes an account of the League's origin myth and descriptions of its ceremonials.

1055. ———. "The Iroquoian Concept of the Soul." *JAF,* 8 (1895), 107–16.

Survey of theology, eschatology, and ceremonialism relating to the soul.

1056. ———. "Iroquoian Cosmology. First Part." *ARBAE,* 21 (1899–1900), 127–339.

Texts of creation myths presented in original with interlinear and free translations.

1057. ———. "Iroquoian Cosmology. Second Part. With Introduction and Notes." *ARBAE,* 43 (1925–1926), 449–819.

Myth texts collected in 1899 and 1900. Some presented in original with interlinear and free translations.

1058. ———. "Legend of the Founding of the Iroquois League." *AA,* o. s. 5 (1892), 131–48.

Text of myth with brief commentary on cultural background.

1059. ———. "New Fire Among the Iroquois." *AA,* o. s. 2 (1889), 319.

Description of ceremonial purification following a plague or epidemic.

1060. ———. "Raising and Falling of the Sky in Iroquois Legends." *AA,* o. s. 5 (1892), 344.

Very brief note on a motif in Iroquois folklore explained as a response to astronomical phenomena.

1061. ———. "Sacred Numbers Among the Iroquois." *AA,* o. s. 2 (1889), 165–66.

List and discussion of ceremonial significance of special numbers.

1062. ———. "A Sun-Myth and the Tree of Language of the Iroquois." *AA,* o. s. 5 (1892), 61–62.

Myth text with brief content commentary.

1063. ———. "The Term Háii-Háii of Iroquoian Mourning and Condolence Songs." *AA,* o. s. 11 (1898), 286–87.

Etymological discussion of a term in Iroquoian ritual songs.

1064. Hickerson, Harold, Glen D. Turner, and Nancy P. Hickerson. "Testing Procedures for Estimating Transfer of Information Among Iroquois Dialects and Languages." *IJAL,* 18 (1952), 1–8.

Report of an experiment to test intelligibility of various Iroquois languages (including Cherokee and Tuscarora). Speakers recorded verbal texts to be played back to representatives of other groups.

1065. Hough, Walter. "Games of Seneca Indians." *AA,* o. s. 1 (1888), 134.

Brief description of a play activity.

1066. Houghton, Frederick. "The Traditional Origin and Naming of the Seneca Nation." *AA,* 24 (1922), 31–43.

Presents several tribal origin myths. With a discussion of their historicity.

1067. "How an Old Indian Revealed a 'New' Resurrection Myth." *LD,* 93 (7 May 1927), 44–46.

Myth text reprinted from the Philadelphia *Public Ledger.*

1068. Howard, Helen Addison. "Hiawatha: Co-Founder of an Indian United Nations." *JW,* 10 (1971), 428–38.

Historical treatment which draws upon mythic materials.

1069. Howard, James H. "Cultural Persistence and Cultural Change as Reflected in Oklahoma Seneca-Cayuga Ceremonialism." *PlA,* 6, No. 11 (February 1961), 21–30.

Persistence of the Green Corn Festival as the central feature of tribal life is attributed to strength of the culture.

1070. Hubbard, J. Niles. *An Account of Sa-Go-Ye-Wat-Ha or Red Jacket and His People, 1750–1830.* Albany: Joel Munsell's Sons, 1886.

Biographical work with material on oratory.

1071. Huguenin, Charles A. "The Sacred Stone of the Oneidas." *NYFQ,* 13 (1957), 16–22.

Describes mythological origin and ceremonial significance of stone.

1072. Johnson, Elias. *Legends, Traditions and Laws, of the Iroquois, or Six Nations, and History of the Tuscarora Indians.* Lockport, N.Y.: Union Printing, 1881.

Random historical and cultural observations. Includes lengthy text of Tuscarora creation myth and descriptions of monstrous beings from oral tradition. Author was a "Tuscarora Chief."

1073. Johnson, Pauline. "The Iroquois of the Grand River." *HW,* 38 (23 June 1894), 587–89.

Brief culture survey contains some data on religion and ceremonialism.

1074. Judkins, Russell A. "An Iroquois Death Messenger Vision." *NYFQ,* 30 (1974), 153–56.

Account of the effects of a death image on the contemporary Iroquois.

1075. Kemeys, Edward. "The Legend of Little Panther. A Tradition of the Seneca Indians." *Ou,* 37 (January 1901), 458–60.

Rewritten myth text. No commentary or annotations.

1076. Keppler, Joseph (Gyantwaka). *Comments on Certain Iroquois Masks. CMAI,* 12, No. 4 (1941).

Describes masks and mask types, their ritual usage and

their relationship to mythology.

1077. ———. "Some Seneca Stories." *IN,* 6 (1929), 372–76.

Six unannotated myth and legend texts. No commentary.

1078. Ketchum, William. *An Authentic and Comprehensive History of Buffalo, with Some Account of Its Early Inhabitants, Both Savage and Civilized, Comprising Historic Notices of the Six Nations or Iroquois Indians, Including a Sketch of the Life of Sir William Johnson, and of Other Prominent White Men, Long Resident Among the Senecas.* 2 volumes. Buffalo: Rockwell, Baker & Hill, 1865.

Describes ceremonials and games. With oration texts.

1079. Kimm, S. C. *The Iroquois: A History of the Six Nations of New York.* Middleburgh, N.Y.: Pierre W. Danforth, 1900.

Brief historical work contains texts of myths and legends, including tribal origin narrative and Lovers' Leap.

1080. Kolinski, Mieczyslav. "An Apache Rabbit Dance Song Cycle as Sung by the Iroquois." *Em,* 16 (1972), 415–64.

Presents and analyzes a social dance song collected in Ontario in 1967. Adopted by the Iroquois from the Apache in the early 1960s.

1081. Kurath, Gertrude Prokosch. *Dance and Song Rituals of Six Nations Reserve, Ontario. NMCB* No. 220 (1968).

Song texts (words and music) placed in the context of dance movements and ceremonial calendar.

1082. ———. *Iroquois Music and Dance: Ceremonial Arts of Two Seneca Longhouses. BAEB* No. 187 (1964).

164 song texts (words and music) collected by William N. Fenton and Martha Champion Huot between 1933 and 1951. Placed in ceremonial context of the Longhouse Religion. Includes choreographic analysis of related dances.

1083. ———. "The Iroquois Ohgiwe Death Feast." *JAF,* 63 (1950), 361–62.

Describes the Feast of Dead, with emphasis on women's role.

1084. ———. "Local Diversity in Iroquois Music and Dance," in 115, pp. 109–37.

Illustrates stability and change in musical performance in various Iroquois communities by describing ceremonials and analyzing song texts (words and music).

1085. ———. "Matriarchal Dances of the Iroquois," in 162, pp. 123–30.

Ceremonial descriptions with song texts (words and music).

1086. ———. "A New Method of Choreographic Notation." *AA,* 52 (1950), 120–23.

Describes a method for recording dance. The method involves ground plan, steps, and music. Illustrates with the Warriors' Standing Quiver Dance of the Iroquois.

1087. ———. "Onondaga Ritual Parodies." *JAF,* 67 (1954), 404–06.

Describes parodies of sacred rituals observed in 1952. Included were mock oratory and songs.

1088. Laing, Mary E. *The Hero of the Longhouse.* Yonkers-on-Hudson, N.Y.: World, 1920.

Biography of Hiawatha synthesized from oral traditions.

1089. Lanman, Charles. "Indian Stories." *SLM,* 15 (1849), 413–14.

Texts of two myths (Seneca and Choctaw). No commentary.

1090. ———. "The Peace-Maker." *MH,* 3 (February 1906), 115–16.

Unannotated myth text. No commentary.

1091. ———. "The Shooting Meteors." *MH,* 2 (September 1905), 210–12.

Unannotated myth text. No commentary.

1092. Lape, Jane M. "Ticonderoga's Indian Festival." *NYFQ,* 1 (1945), 167.

Description of the Green Corn Festival.

1093. "Logan's Speech." *OT,* 2 (1848), 49–67.

Presents documents relating to the famous oration and associated warfare.

1094. Lone Dog, Louise. *Strange Journey: The Vision Life of a Psychic Indian Woman.* Ed. Vinson Brown. Healdsburg, Cal.: Naturegraph, 1964.

Life history emphasizes subject's spiritual development. Treats traditional and Christian supernaturalism.

1095. Lounsbury, Floyd G. *Oneida Verb Morphology.* *YUPA* No. 48 (1953).

Contains a folktale text collected in 1939. With free translation and linguistic commentary.

1096. Mackenzie, J. B. *The Six-Nations Indians in Canada.* Toronto: Hunter, Rose, 1896.

General overview of reservation culture. With chapters on oratory and religion.

1097. Marshe, Witham. *Journal of the Treaty at Lancaster in 1744, with the Six Nations.* Lancaster, Penn.: New Era, 1884.

Marshe, a Maryland commissioner at the treaty negotiations, describes Iroquois dancing and oratory.

1098. Mathews, Zena Pearlstone. *The Relation of Seneca False Face Masks to Seneca and Ontario Archeology.* New York: Garland, 1978.

Discusses the iconography of ritual masks and pipes with some attention to ceremonial uses.

1099. Mathur, Mary E. Fleming. "Death, Burial, Mourning, Among Western Iroquois." *IH,* 4, No. 3 (Fall 1971), 37–40, 43.

Description of ceremonialism.

1100. ———. "The Iroquois in Ethnography." *IH,* 2, No. 3 (Fall 1969), 12–18.

Compares treatments of the League of the Iroquois by various ethnographers.

1101. Morgan, Lewis Henry. *League of the Ho-dé-no-sau-nee, or Iroquois.* Rochester: Sage and Brother, 1851.

Classic work on history and culture of the Iroquois. Material of folkloric interest appears in chapter "Spirit of the League": belief system, ceremonialism, narrative traditions, oratory, and prayers. Some treatment of Longhouse Religion.

1102. Myers, Albert Cook. *The Boy George Washington, Aged 16, His Own Account of an Iroquois Indian Dance 1748.* Philadelphia: by the Author, 1932.

On 28 March 1728 Washington entered into his journal a brief description of an Iroquois dance. This volume puts the brief passage into context.

1103. Myrtle, Minnie. *The Iroquois; or, The Bright Side of Indian Character.* New York: Appleton, 1855.

Ethnographic notes in praise of the Iroquois. Includes song, myth, legend, and oration texts as well as descriptions of ceremonialism.

1104. Newton, Hilah Foote. "Schoolcraft on the Iroquois." *NYFQ,* 10 (1954), 127–32, 176–88.

Biographical sketch and evaluation of Schoolcraft's career.

1105. O'Donnell, James H., III. "Logan's Oration: A Case Study in Ethnographic Authentication." *QJS,* 65 (1979), 150–56.

Considers ethnographic evidence for the authenticity of the famous speech.

1106. Parker, Arthur C. "Certain Iroquois Tree Myths and Symbols." *AA,* 14 (1912), 608–20.

Survey of references to sacred and symbolic trees in Iroquois folklore. Includes summaries of and excerpts from myth texts.

1107. ———. *The Code of Handsome Lake, the Seneca Prophet.* *NYSEDB* No. 530 (1913); or *NYSMB* No. 163 (1912).

Translation of written text of the code which had circulated orally for four generations. Also includes some description of ceremonialism. Reprinted in 1033.

1108. ———. "Iroquois Sun Myths." *JAF,* 23 (1910), 473–78.

Study of vestiges of sun worship among the group. With myth texts and descriptions of ceremonials.

1109. ———. *Iroquois Uses of Maize and Other Food Plants.* *NYSMB* No. 144 (1910).

Briefly treats references to corn in Iroquois mythology and describes ceremonial associations of corn. Reprinted in 1033.

1110. ———. "Secret Medicine Societies of the Seneca." *AA,* 11 (1909), 161–85.

Briefly outlines medicine societies based on fieldwork done in 1902–1906. Includes descriptions of ceremonials and a text of the opening ritual for the Pygmy Society.

1111. ———. *Seneca Myths and Folk Tales.* Buffalo: Historical Society, 1923 (Publications Series No. 27).

Seventy-six myth and folktale texts with explanatory notes. Introduction describes storytelling customs and collecting methods. Texts identified by informant.

1112. ———. *Skunny Wundy Seneca Indian Tales.* Chicago: Albert Whitman, 1970.

Twenty-eight unannotated myth and folktale texts with no commentary. May be for children. First published in 1926.

1113. ———. "Who Was Hiawatha?" *NYFQ,* 10 (1954), 285–88.

Discusses Iroquois myth on which Longfellow's epic hero is apparently based.

1114. Parker, Chief Everett, and Oleodoska. *The Secret of No Face (An Ireokwa Epic).* Healdsburg, Cal.: Native American Publishing Company, 1972.

Continuous narrative constructed from Seneca myths and legends and embodying the morality of the Code of Handsome Lake.

1115. Peterson, George W. *The Iroquoian Story of the Beginning of the World and Living Things.* Torrington, Conn.: Torrington Printing, 1937.

Retelling of creation myth. Based on material in BAE reports. No commentary or annotations.

1116. Potts, William John. "Iroquois Dog-Sacrifice." *JAF,* 3 (1890), 70–71.

Brief description of the ceremony from the journal of Henry Dearborn (1779).

1117. Preston, W. D. "Six Seneca Jokes." *JAF,* 62 (1949), 426–27.

Texts of riddle-jokes collected in 1946.

1118. ———, and C. F. Voegelin. "Seneca I." *IJAL,* 15 (1949), 23–44.

First in a series of papers on the language. Includes a myth text with interlinear and sectional translations and linguistic analysis.

1119. Randle, Martha Champion. "Psychological Types from Iroquois Folktales." *JAF,* 65 (1952), 13–21.

Iroquois narratives evince cultural and psychological tensions: interactions among relatives, pervasive power of the old, and wish-fulfillment fantasies.

1120. ———. "The Waugh Collection of Iroquois Folktales." *PAPS,* 97 (1953), 611–33.

Thorough description of the ms. collection made by F. W. Waugh between 1910 and 1920. With comparative notes.

1121. Ritzenthaler, Robert. *Iroquois False-Face Masks.* Milwaukee: Public Museum, 1969 (Publications in Primitive Art No. 3).

Presents and discusses the collection of ceremonial masks in the Milwaukee Public Museum. Describes mythological origins and ritual procedures of the False Face Society.

1122. Rutsch, Edward S. *Smoking Technology of the Aborigines of the Iroquois Area of New York State.* Rutherford, N. J.: Fairleigh Dickinson Univ. Press, 1973.

Primarily a material culture study, but includes brief data on the role of tobacco in Iroquois mythology.

1123. Sandefur, Ray H. "Logan's Oration—How Authentic?" *QJS,* 46 (1960), 289–96.

Shows how documentary evidence supports the authenticity of the speech.

1124. Schoolcraft, Henry Rowe. *Census of the Iroquois and Supplementary Report: Antiquities—History—Ethnology.* Albany: E. Mack, 1846 (Documents of the Senate of the State of New York, Sixty-Ninth Session, No. 24).

Culture survey includes presentation of cosmogony, tribal origin myth, and historical legends.

1125. ———. *Notes on the Iroquois; or Contributions to American History, Antiquities, and General Ethnology.* Albany: Erastus H. Pease, 1847.

Historical, ethnological, archeological, and linguistic observations include myth and legend texts and discussion of supernaturalism.

1126. Scofield, Mrs. Glenni W. *Legends and Historical Sketches of the Iroquois Indians, with a Biographical Notice of Cornplanter, a Chief of the Seneca Nation.* NP: Gibson Brothers, 1887.

Myth and legend texts extracted from Cusick's *Ancient History* (1015).

1127. Scott, Duncan C. "Traditional History of the Confederacy of the Six Nations." *PTRSC,* 3rd series, 5, section 2 (1911), 195–246.

Origin myth and ritual description with song texts (words only). Recorded in 1900. No annotations, but some comments on collecting situation.

1128. Seeber, Edward D. "Critical Views on Logan's Speech." *JAF,* 60 (1947) 130–46.

Examines nineteenth-century attitudes toward the oration. It was perceived as a classic of spontaneous eloquence.

1129. *Seneca Indians: Home Life and Culture.* York, Penn.: Conservation Society of York County, 1944.

Survey of Seneca culture includes some myth and legend texts and discussion of religious attitudes. Fairly

extensive coverage of ceremonial calendar.

1130. "Seneca White Dog Feast." *JAF,* 18 (1905), 317–19.

Description of the ceremony reprinted from the *Washington Post* for 1 March 1905.

1131. Shimony, Annemarie Anrod. *Conservatism Among the Iroquois at the Six Nations Reserve.* YUPA No. 65 (1961).

Emphasizes retention of traditional culture among NAs studied in 1950. Includes lengthy survey of ceremonialism and of the conservative influence of the Longhouse Religion.

1132. Shoemaker, Henry W. *Indian Folk-Songs of Pennsylvania.* Ardmore, Penn.: Newman F. McGirr, 1927.

Pamphlet describes NA singing based on testimony of informants from the Cornplanter Reservation. Only texts are poems based on NA songs.

1133. Skenandoah. "Letters on the Iroquois." *AWR,* 5 (1847), 177–90, 242–57, 447–61.

Primarily focuses on the League with attention to ceremonial performances. Also treats oratory and theology.

1134. Skinner, Alanson. "Some Seneca Masks and Their Uses." *IN,* 2 (1925), 191–207.

Treats ceremonialism.

1135. ———. "Some Seneca Tobacco Customs." *IN,* 2 (1925), 127–30.

Includes some ceremonial songs.

1136. Smith, DeCost. "Additional Notes on Onondaga Witchcraft and Hoⁿ-Dó-Ĭ." *JAF,* 2 (1889), 277–81.

Includes data on ceremonialism.

1137. ———. "Witchcraft and Demonism of the Modern Iroquois." *JAF,* 1 (1888), 184–93.

Includes descriptions of ceremonialism with song excerpts (words only).

1138. Smith, Erminie A. "Myths of the Iroquois." *ARBAE,* 2 (1880–1881), 47–116.

Texts of more than fifty narratives and ethnographic descriptions. Some general commentary on Iroquois cosmology and theology.

1139. ———. "Myths of the Iroquois." *AAOJ,* 4 (1881), 31–39.

Survey of the group's mythology with text summaries.

1140. Snowden, James Ross. *An Historical Sketch of Gy-ant-wa-chia—The Cornplanter and of the Six Nations of Indians.* Harrisburg, Penn.: Singerly & Myers, 1867.

Biography of the Seneca chief includes excerpts from some of his orations.

1141. Snyderman, George S. "The Case of Daniel P.: An Example of Seneca Healing." *JWAS,* 39 (1949), 217–20.

Case study based on an informant's account of a healing witnessed during childhood.

1142. ———. "Some Ideological Aspects of Present Day Seneca Folklore." *PM,* 24 (1951), 37–46.

Three folktale texts with commentary on their didactic role in the culture.

1143. Speck, Frank G. "The Banished Wife and Maid Without Hands." *NYFQ,* 3 (1947), 312–19.

Text of an EA folktale collected from a Mohawk informant. Some informant data and comparative commentary.

1144. ———. "How the Dew Eagle Society of the Allegany Seneca Cured Gahéhdagowa (F. G. S.)." *PM,* 22 (1949), 39–59.

Posthumously published account of a healing ritual performed for the author.

1145. ———. *The Iroquois: A Study in Cultural Evolution.* Bloomfield Hills, Mich.: Cranbrook Institute of Science, 1945 (Bulletin No. 23).

Study of culture change. Takes development of ceremonialism into account.

1146. ———, and H. P. Beck. "Old World Tales Among the Mohawks." *JAF,* 63 (1950), 285–308.

Nine folktale texts with comparative data showing European analogues.

1147. ———, and Ernest S. Dodge. "Amphibian and Reptile Lore of the Six Nations Cayuga." *JAF,* 58 (1945), 306–09.

A study of Cayuga ethnozoology includes mostly natural history, but several mythic creatures are mentioned.

1148. ———, and Alexander General. *Midwinter Rites of the Cayuga Long House.* Philadelphia: Univ. of Pennsylvania Press, 1949.

Thorough description of preparations, history, function, and ritual procedure. Includes several myth texts and some discussion of singing.

1149. Stites, Sara Henry. *Economics of the Iroquois.* Lancaster, Penn.: New Era, 1905 (Bryn Mawr College Monographs, Vol. 1, No. 3).

Ethnographic survey focuses on economic life. Contains descriptions of ceremonialism.

1150. Stone, William L. *Life of Joseph Brant—Thayendanegea: Including the Border Wars of the American Revolution, and Sketches of the Indian Campaigns of Generals Harman, St. Clair, and Wayne. And Other Matters Connected with the Indian Relations of the United States and Great Britain, from the Peace of 1783 to the Indian Peace of 1795.* 2 volumes. New York: George Dearborn, 1838.

Biography includes numerous oration texts and some descriptions of ceremonies among the Six Nations.

1151. ———. *The Life and Times of Sa-Go-Ye-Wat-Ha or Red Jacket: Being the Sequel to the History of the Six Nations.* New York: Wiley & Putnam, 1841.

Biographical work. Includes Seneca origin myth and several speeches by Red Jacket.

1152. Tanner, Helen Hornbeck. "Coocoochee: Mohawk Medicine Woman." *AICRJ,* 3, No. 3 (1979), 23–41.

Biography of an eighteenth-century figure with some descriptions of ceremonials.

1153. Taxay, Don. *Money of the American Indians and Other Primitive Currencies of the Americas.* New York: Nummus Press, 1970.

Primarily a survey of material culture, but contains description of performances of wampum-readers among the Iroquois.

1154. Tooker, Elisabeth. "Ethnometaphysics of Iroquois Ritual," in 126, pp. 103–16.

Analysis of the cognitive structure underlying Iroquois ceremonialism.

1155. ———. *The Iroquois Ceremonial of Midwinter.* Syracuse: Syracuse Univ. Press, 1970.

Detailed examination of the ceremony includes prefatory comments on Iroquois ritualism, accounts of the ceremony as observed at six longhouses, and historical perspective on the ceremonial.

1156. ———. "The Iroquois White Dog Sacrifice in the Latter Part of the Eighteenth Century." *Eh,* 12 (1965), 129–40.

Reconstruction of the ceremonial based on historical documents.

1157. ———. "On the New Religion of Handsome Lake." *AnQ,* 41 (1968), 187–200.

Argues that the development of the Longhouse Religion involved more than an attempt to curb social decay.

1158. Voget, Fred. "Acculturation at Caughnawaga: A Note on the Native-Modified Group." *AA,* 53 (1951), 220–31.

Discusses the degree of acculturation on an Iroquois Reserve. Contains a description of the Longhouse Religion.

1159. Wallace, Anthony F. C. "Cultural Composition of the Handsome Lake Religion," in 116, pp. 139–51.

Analyzes the source of the belief system in the Longhouse Religion: in Seneca myth and ritual and in Christianity. Response by Wallace L. Chafe (pp. 153–57).

1160. ———. *The Death and Rebirth of the Seneca.* New York: Knopf, 1970.

Primarily a historical account of the cultural context which led to the development of Handsome Lake's prophecies and the Longhouse Religion. Describes traditional Longhouse ceremonialism.

1161. ———. "The Dekanawideh Myth Analyzed as the Record of a Revitalization Movement." *Eh,* 5 (1958), 118–30.

Views the myth of the founding of the League of the Iroquois as an account of a revitalization movement which occurred several centuries before the earliest text.

1162. ———. "Dreams and the Wishes of the Soul: A Type of Psychoanalytic Theory Among the Seventeenth-Century Iroquois." *AA,* 60 (1958), 234–48.

The group developed a theory and practice in regard to dreams that bears a strong resemblance to Freudian psychoanalysis. Some of the dreams, reported by Jesuit missionaries, involved culture heroes and other figures from narrative folklore.

1163. ———. "Handsome Lake and the Great Revival in the West." *AQ,* 4 (1952), 149–65.

Describes the Iroquois prophet's visions, gospel, and preaching to frontier evangelism which flourished in the early 1800s in the Ohio Valley.

1164. Wallace, Paul A. W. "People of the Longhouse." *AH,* 6, No. 2 (February 1955), 26–31.

General description of the Iroquois. Includes summary of hero myth.

1165. ———. *The White Roots of Peace.* Philadelphia: Univ. of Pennsylvania Press, 1946.

Synthesis of texts of the legendary account of the founding of the League of the Iroquois. Compared to founding of United Nations.

1166. Waugh, F. W. *Iroquois Foods and Food Preparation.* CGSMB No. 86, Anthropological Series No. 12 (1916).

Material culture study. Includes some brief descriptions of agricultural ceremonies.

1167. Weitlaner, R. J. "Seneca Tales and Beliefs." *JAF,* 28 (1915), 309–10.

Five folktale and legend texts and some miscellaneous beliefs collected in 1914. No commentary or annotations.

1168. Wilkes, Florence E. "Indian Thanksgiving Ceremonies." *TT,* 4, No. 11 (November 1902), 313–15.

Brief description of the Green Corn Dance.

1169.   Wilson, Charles B., Jr. "Green Corn—Seneca's Thanksgiving." *IW,* 11, No. 4 (November–December 1943), 6–7.

Description of a ceremony. Reprinted from the Miami, Oklahoma, *Daily News-Record.*

1170.   Wilson, Edmund. *Apologies to the Iroquois.* New York: Farrar, Straus and Cudahy, 1960.

Stimulated by his ignorance of his NA neighbors in upstate New York, Wilson prepared an account of their culture and history. Includes descriptions of ceremonialism, especially that of the Longhouse Religion. Also included is "The Mohawks in High Steel" by Joseph Mitchell. All originally appeared in *NY.*

1171.   Witthoft, John. "Cayuga Midwinter Festival." *NYFQ* 2 (1946), 24–39.

Description of a ceremony observed in 1945.

1172.   Woodworth, Ellis. *The Godly Seer. A True Story of Hi-A-Wat-Ha.* Syracuse: Iroquois Press, 1900.

Pamphlet contains myth text created by collating material from various sources. No commentary or annotations.

1173.   Wulff, Roger L. "Lacrosse Among the Seneca." *IH,* 10, No. 2 (Spring 1977), 16–22.

Surveys the role of the ball game in Seneca society. Excerpts from myth texts which refer to lacrosse are included.

1174.   Yawger, Rose N. *The Indian and the Pioneer. An Historical Study.* 2 volumes. Syracuse: C. W. Bardeen, 1893.

Early chapters treat the pre-contact culture of the Iroquois and describe ceremonialism. Two chapters are devoted to oratory.

See also 259, 283, 425, 502, 509, 830, 839, 874, 933, 961, 1364, 1381, 1394, 1422, 1430, 1468, 1502, 1566–1571, 1816, 5106.

G. Malecite

1175.   [Barratt, Joseph]. *The Indian of New-England, and the North-Eastern Provinces; A Sketch of the Life of an Indian Hunter, Ancient Traditions Relating to the Etchemin Tribe, Their Modes of Life, Fishing, Hunting &c: with Vocabularies in the Indian and English, Giving the Names of the Animals, Birds, and Fish: The Most Complete That Has Been Given for New-England, in the Languages of the Etchemin and Micmacs.* Middletown, Conn.: Charles H. Pelton, 1851.

Contains summaries of Malecite and Passamaquoddy myths.

1176.   Ives, Edward D., ed. "Malecite and Passamaquoddy Tales." *NF,* 6 (1964), 1–81.

Eighteen Malecite myths and legends and ten Passamaquoddy myths and legends. Extensive comparative notes and data on informants. Introductory essay on "Stories and the Art of Storytelling" by E. Tappan Adney.

1177.   Jack, Edward. "Maliseet Legends." *JAF,* 8 (1895), 193–208.

Several myth texts about Gluskap and one legend text. Unannotated, but with some data on cultural background.

1178.   Mechling, W. H. *Malecite Tales.* CGSMB, Anthropological Series No. 4 (1914).

Forty-two myths, legends, and folktales collected

between 1910 and 1912. No commentary.

1179.   ———. "Maliseet Tales." *JAF,* 26 (1913), 219–58.

Seven folktale texts collected in 1912. No commentary. Occasional comparative notes.

1180.   Smith, Nicholas. "Notes on the Malecite of Woodstock, New Brunswick." *An,* 5 (1957), 1–39.

Ethnographic notes with data on mortuary customs, social dancing, Christian festivals, games, storytelling, and supernaturalism.

1181.   Speck, Frank G. "Malecite Tales." *JAF,* 30 (1917), 479–85.

Eight myth and folktale texts with comparative notes. Brief commentary on cultural background.

1182.   ———, and Wendell S. Hadlock. "A Report on the Tribal Boundaries and Hunting Areas of the Malecite Indians of New Brunswick." *AA,* 48 (1946), 355–74.

Uses myths and legends about territorial conflict and family history to outline boundaries among the group. Data collected in 1917–1920 and in 1940s.

1183.   Stamp, Harley. "A Malecite Tale: Adventures of Bukschinskwesk." *JAF,* 28 (1915), 243–48.

Myth text with some comparative notes.

1184.   Teeter, Karl V. "The Main Features of the Malecite-Passamaquoddy Grammar," in 153, pp. 191–249.

Includes linguistic analysis of a legend presented with free translation.

1185.   Wallis, Wilson D., and Ruth Sawtell Wallis. *The Malecite Indians of New Brunswick.* NMCB No. 148 (1957).

Brief ethnographic survey with data on ceremonials, supernaturalism, and storytelling. Based on fieldwork in 1953.

1186.   Watson, Lawrence W. "The Origin of the Melicites." *JAF,* 20 (1907), 160–62.

Myth text previously published in *Prince Edward Island Magazine.* No commentary or annotations.

See also 825, 867.

H. Micmac

1187.   Austin, Mary. "The Canoe That the Partridge Made. A One-Smoke Story." *GBM,* 20 (October 1934), 417–18.

Folktale in storytelling context. Meant to satirize New Deal. May be original creation, but attributed to Micmac source.

1188.   Bock, Philip K. *The Micmac Indians of Restigouche: History and Contemporary Description.* NMCB No. 213 (1966).

Ethnography based on fieldwork done in 1961. Includes data on religion, music, and storytelling.

1189.   Browne, G. Waldo. "Indian Legends of Acadia." *Aca,* 2 (1902), 54–64.

Two myth texts, rewritten in dialect. Probably from Micmac informants.

1190.   Chamberlain, Montague. "Indians in New Brunswick in Champlain's Time." *Aca,* 4 (1904), 280–95.

Description of Micmac culture with data on religious attitudes, ceremonialism, and mythology.

1191.   Clark, Jeremiah S. *Rand and the Micmacs.* Charlottetown: Examiner, 1899.

History of Silas Rand's missionary work among the group. Chapter on mythology summarizes theological and cosmological ideas.

1192. Elder, William. "The Aborigines of Nova Scotia." *NAR*, 112 (January 1871), 1–30.

Culture survey includes data on storytelling, mythology, and ceremonialism. With song and myth texts.

1193. Erskine, J. S. "A Religion of the Golden Age." *DaR*, 51 (1971), 361–65.

Reconstruction of Micmac religion based on collection of myths.

1194. Fauset, Arthur Huff. "Folklore from the Half-Breeds in Nova Scotia." *JAF*, 38 (1925), 300–15.

Sixteen folktale and legend texts collected in 1923 from Micmacs living near a Black community. No commentary or annotations.

1195. Hager, Stansbury. "Micmac Customs and Traditions." *AA*, o. s. 8 (1895), 31–42.

Ethnographic notes taken from two informants include data on games and ceremonialism and one myth text.

1196. ———. "Micmac Magic and Medicine." *JAF*, 9 (1896), 170–77.

Miscellany of data on ceremonials, legends, and beliefs.

1197. ———. "Weather and the Seasons in Micmac Mythology." *JAF*, 10 (1897), 101–05.

Discusses role of Gluskap in creating weather.

1198. Johnson, Frederick. "Notes on Micmac Shamanism." *PM*, 16 (1943), 53–80.

Surveys shamanistic ceremonialism and its mythological sanctions.

1199. Le Clerq, Father Chrestien. *New Relations of Gaspesia, with the Customs and Religion of the Gaspesian Indians.* Ed. and trans. William F. Ganong. Toronto: Champlain Society, 1910.

Edition of a work published in French in 1691. Includes descriptions of Micmac theology, supernaturalism, and ceremonialism.

1200. Leighton, Alexander H. "The Twilight of the Indian Porpoise Hunters." *NH*, 40 (1937), 410–16, 458.

Describes Micmac porpoise hunting. With references to myths about the origin of the activity.

1201. Leland, Charles G. *The Algonquin Legends of New England or Myths and Folk Lore of the Micmac, Passamaquoddy, and Penobscot Tribes.* Boston: Houghton Mifflin, 1884.

Collection of myths and legends based on fieldwork begun in 1882. Includes explanatory notes and informant data. Thorough presentation of the Gluskap cycle.

1202. Martin, Calvin. "The European Impact on the Culture of a Northeastern Algonquian Tribe." *WMQ*, 3rd series, 31 (1974), 3–26.

Primarily concerned with economic impact, but includes some data on ceremonialism.

1203. Michelson, Truman. "Micmac Tales." *JAF*, 38 (1925), 33–54.

Five unannotated myth texts, three of which were written out by an informant in 1910. No commentary.

1204. Parsons, Elsie Clews. "Micmac Folklore." *JAF*, 38 (1925), 55–133.

Collection of forty-seven myths, folktales, legends, and jokes. Collected in 1923. Some comparative annotation. Riddle texts of EA origin are appended.

1205. ———. "Micmac Notes: St. Ann's Mission on Chapel Island, Bras d'Or Lakes, Cape Breton Island." *JAF*, 39 (1926), 460–85.

Narrative account of a field trip includes general ethnographic data on ceremonialism, words of songs, and descriptions of places associated with myths.

1206. Partridge, Emelyn Newcomb. *Glooscap the Great Chief and Other Stories. Legends of the Micmacs.* New York: Sturgis & Walton, 1913.

Thirty-nine myth and legend texts adapted for the most part from Rand's *Legends of the Micmacs* (1213). No annotations. Brief introduction presents Rand's ideas about Micmac folklore.

1207. Prince, J. Dyneley, ed. "A Micmac Manuscript." *ICA*, 15, No. 1 (1906), 87–124.

Ms. includes nine myths and folktales and one song (words only) collected by Peter Googoo, Jr. Presented with interlinear translation and explanatory notes.

1208. Rand, Silas. "The Beautiful Bride Whose Face Was White as Snow, Her Cheeks as Red as Blood, and Her Hair as Black and Glossy as a Raven's Plume." *AAOJ*, 12 (1890), 156–59.

Unannotated folktale text. No commentary.

1209. ———. "The Coming of the White Man Revealed. Dream of the White Robe and Floating Island." *AAOJ*, 12 (1890), 155–56.

Unannotated legend text collected in 1869. No commentary.

1210. ———. "A Giant Story—A-cookwés." *AAOJ*, 13 (1891), 41–42.

Unannotated folktale text. Brief comparative commentary.

1211. ———. "Glooscap, Cuhkw and Coolpurjot." *AAOJ*, 12 (1890), 282–86.

Description of Micmac trinity.

1212. ———. "The Legends of the Micmacs." *AAOJ*, 12 (1890), 3–14.

Summaries with discussion of cultural significance of narratives collected over a forty-year period.

1213. ———. *Legends of the Micmacs.* New York: Longmans, Green, 1894.

Eighty-seven myth and legend texts. Introductory commentary by Helen L. Webster surveys Rand's life and discusses Micmac oral literature.

1214. ———. "The Story of the Moosewood Man." *AAOJ*, 13 (1891), 168–70.

Unannotated folktale text. No commentary.

1215. Speck, Frank G. *Beothuk and Micmac.* *IN&M*, Miscellaneous Series No. 22 (1922).

Data on extinct culture of the Beothuk collected from Micmac informants in 1914. Includes some myth texts and summaries.

1216. ———. "Some Micmac Tales from Cape Breton Island." *JAF*, 28 (1915), 59–69.

Six myth and folktale texts with some explanatory notes. No comparative annotation or commentary.

1217. Wallis, Wilson D., and Ruth Sawtell Wallis. *The Micmac Indians of Eastern Canada.* Minneapolis: Univ. of Minnesota Press, 1955.

Ethnography based on fieldwork done in 1911–1912 and in 1950–1953. Includes data on religion, ceremonialism, and supernaturalism as well as several song texts. Myth, legend, and folktale texts (144) with some explanatory notes.

See also 825, 867, 868, 1175, 1256.

I. Mohegan

1218. Peale, Arthur L. *Uncas and the Mohegan-Pequot.* Boston: Meador, 1939.

Forty-five unannotated myth and legend texts collected by Frank G. Speck. Introduced by several chapters of historical survey.

1219. Prince, J. Dyneley. "A Tale in the Hudson River Indian Language." *AA,* 7 (1905), 74–84.

Text, translation, and linguistic analysis of a Mohegan narrative.

1220. Speck. Frank G. "Native Tribes and Dialects of Connecticut: A Mohegan-Pequot Diary." *ARBAE,* 43 (1925–1926), 199–287.

Edited text of the diary (1902–1905) of Fidelia A. H. Fielding, last native speaker of Mohegan, with free translation. Speck's introduction emphasizes folklore. He appends seven folk narrative texts.

1221. ———. "Notes on the Mohegan and Niantic Indians." *APAMNH,* 3 (1909), 181–210.

Based primarily on historical records and interviews with one informant. Includes three myth texts and some legend summaries.

1222. ———. "Some Mohegan-Pequot Legends." *JAF,* 17 (1904), 183–84.

Three unannotated folktale texts. Brief data on storytelling contexts.

1223. Winship, George Parker. "A Maine Indian Ceremony in 1605." *AA,* 3 (1901), 387–88.

Account of a ritual reprinted from Rosier's account of George Waymouth's voyage to the Maine coast.

See also 921, 1267, 1269, 1270.

J. Montagnais-Naskapi

1224. Blake, Edith. "The Beothuks of Newfoundland." *NC,* 24 (December 1888), 899–918.

Culture survey contains some data on religion and ceremonialism.

1225. Burgesse, J. Allan. "The Spirit Wigwam as Described by Tommie Moar, Pointe Bleue." *PM,* 17 (1944), 50–53.

Ritual description.

1226. Desbarats, Peter, ed. *What They Used to Tell About. Indian Legends from Labrador.* Toronto: McClelland and Stewart, 1969.

Twenty-seven myth and legend texts. Collected by "the Department of Anthropology of the University of Montreal" in 1960s as part of a culture survey associated with dam construction. No annotations, but some data on cultural background.

1227. Farnham, C. H. "The Montagnais." *H,* 77 (1888), 378–94.

General view of the culture includes description of ceremonial dancing and some references to supernaturalism.

1228. Flannery, Regina. "The Shaking-Tent Rite Among the Montagnais of James Bay." *PM,* 12 (1939), 11–16.

Description of the ceremony as observed in 1938.

1229. Garigue, Philip. "The Social Organization of the Montagnais-Naskapi." *An,* 4 (1957), 107–35.

Section on religious organization treats Native concept of deity and ceremonialism.

1230. Honigmann, John J. *Social Networks in Great Whale River: Notes on an Eskimo, Montagnais-Naskapi, and Euro-Canadian Community.* NMCB No. 178 (1962).

Ethnography based on fieldwork done in 1949–1950. Includes data on religious attitudes and ceremonialism.

1231. McGee, John T. *Cultural Stability and Change Among the Montagnais Indians of the Lake Melville Region of Labrador.* CUAAS No. 19 (1961).

Acculturation study based on fieldwork done in 1942–1943 and 1951–1953. Includes data on religion and ceremonialism.

1232. Speck, Frank G. "Ethical Attributes of the Labrador Indians." *AA,* 35 (1933), 559–94.

Analyzes cultural categories of ethical behavior. Bases findings on personal observation and the folklore of the culture.

1233. ———. "Montagnais and Naskapi Tales from the Labrador Peninsula." *JAF,* 38 (1925), 1–32.

Myth, folktale, and legend texts with some explanatory notes and general survey of cultural background.

1234. ———. "Montagnais Art in Birch-Bark, A Circumpolar Trait." *IN&M,* 11, No. 2 (1937), 45–125.

Survey of art includes its origin myth.

1235. ———. *Naskapi. The Savage Hunters of Labrador Peninsula.* Norman: Univ. of Oklahoma Press, 1935.

Ethnography focuses on spiritual life. Contains several myth texts with commentary on cultural background.

1236. ———. "Some Naskapi Myths from Little Whale River." *JAF,* 28 (1915), 70–77.

Four Naskapi myth and folktale texts and one Cree folktale text collected in 1913. No commentary or annotation.

1237. Strong, William Duncan. "Cross-Cousin Marriage and the Culture of the Northeastern Algonkian." *AA,* 31 (1929), 277–88.

Uses the Naskapi to explore the nature of cross-cousin marriage. Includes references to mythology.

1238. Tantaquidgeon, Gladys. "How the Summer Season Was Brought North." *JAF,* 54 (1941), 203–04.

Abstract of a Montagnais etiological narrative collected in 1931.

1239. Turner, Lucien M. "On the Indians and Eskimos of Ungava District, Labrador." *PTRSC,* 1st series, 5, section 2 (1887), 99–119.

Cultural survey includes data on Eskimo and Naskapi religion and ceremonialism and three Naskapi myth texts.

See also 662, 1259, 5186, 5435.

K. Montauk

1240. Dyson, Verne. *Heather Flower and Other Indian Stories of Long Island.* Port Washington, N.Y.: Ira J. Friedman, 1967 (Empire State Historical Publications Series No. 52).

Ten rewritten folktale and legend texts. No annotations. Brief comments on cultural background. Some of the material is about, not by, NAs.

L. Nanticoke

1241.   Speck, Frank G. *The Nanticoke and Conoy Indians with a Review of Linguistic Material from Manuscript and Living Sources: An Historical Study.* Wilmington: Historical Society of Delaware, 1927.
Historical data come in part from oral sources. Sketchy data on ceremonialism.
1242.   ———. *The Nanticoke Community of Delaware. CMAI,* 2, No. 4 (1915), 1–43.
Ethnography based on fieldwork begun in 1911. Includes descriptions of games and ceremonials. Texts of six folktales.

See also 860, 922.

M. Narragansett

1243.   Boissevain, Ethel. *The Narragansett People.* Phoenix: Indian Tribal Series, 1975.
Historical survey includes a description of the Narragansett Pow-Wow, a Pan-Indian ceremony involving song, dance, and oratory.
1244.   Simmons, William Scranton. *Cautantowwit's House: An Indian Burial Ground on the Island of Conanicut in Narragansett Bay.* Providence: Brown Univ. Press, 1970.
Narragansett burial customs, including related mythology and supernaturalism, are reconstructed on the basis of an archeological excavation.

N. Passamaquoddy

1245.   Brown, Mrs. W. Wallace. " 'Chief-Making' Among the Passamaquoddy Indians." *JAF,* 5 (1892), 57–59.
Description of a ceremonial. With one song text.
1246.   Eckstorm, Fannie Hardy. "The Attack on Norridgewock, 1724." *NEQ,* 7 (1934), 541–78.
Excerpts from a number of contemporary documents as well as a historical legend.
1247.   Fewkes, J. Walter. "A Contribution to Passamaquoddy Folk-Lore." *JAF,* 3 (1890), 257–80.
Survey of oral literature includes songs (words and music), myths, and ceremonial descriptions. Contrasts material with Southwest folklore.
1248.   Prince, J. Dyneley. "A Passamaquoddy Aviator." *AA,* 11 (1909), 628–50.
Folktale text written out by a Passamaquoddy informant in 1902. With interlinear translation and linguistic commentary.
1249.   ———. *Passamaquoddy Texts. PAES* No. 10 (1921).
Ten Trickster myths, three miscellaneous myth and legend texts, and four song texts with free translations. Collected for the most part by Lewis Mitchell. Some commentary on status of original text. No annotations.
1250.   ———. "A Passamaquoddy Tobacco Famine." *IJAL,* 1, No. 1 (1917), 58–63.

Folktale text with interlinear translation and linguistic analysis.
1251.   ———. "The Passamaquoddy Wampum Records." *PAPS,* 36 (1897), 479–95.
Discussion of mnemonic method for enhancing knowledge of traditional history. Includes text with free translation of one wampum record.
1252.   ———. "Some Passamaquoddy Witchcraft Tales." *PAPS,* 38 (1899), 181–89.
Six brief legend texts with free translations and linguistic analysis.
See also 825, 867, 1175, 1176, 1184, 1201, 1256.

O. Penobscot

1253.   Beck, Horace P. "The Acculturation of Old World Tales by the American Indian." *MWF,* 8 (1958), 205–16.
Text of a "Jack" tale related by a Penobscot storyteller with discussion of why EA folktales have eclipsed traditional lore.
1254.   "Creation, The. A Penobscot Indian Myth Told by One of the Tribe to Abby L. Alger." *PSM,* 44 (December 1893), 195–96.
Unannotated myth text with some description of the informant.
1255.   Eckstorm, Fannie Hardy. *Old John Neptune and Other Maine Indian Shamans.* Portland, Maine: Southworth-Anthoensen, 1945.
Biography of a family known for shamanism. Some data on tribal culture in general, especially magical practice and traditions of water monsters.
1256.   *In Indian Tents: Stories Told by Penobscot, Passamaquoddy and Micmac Indians to Abby L. Alger.* Boston: Roberts, 1897.
Twenty-three rewritten myth and legend texts. No annotations or commentary.
1257.   Prince, J. Dyneley. "The Differentiation Between the Penobscot and the Canadian Abenaki Dialects." *AA,* 4 (1902), 17–32.
Linguistic survey includes texts, translation, and analysis of a story in both Penobscot and Abnaki.
1258.   ———. "The Penobscot Language of Maine." *AA,* 12 (1910), 183–208.
Primarily a glossary of Penobscot words and phrases. Contains texts of four stories with translations.
1259.   Speck, Frank G. "Dogs of the Labrador Indians." *NH,* 25 (1925), 58–64.
Role of the dog in Montagnais-Naskapi culture. With a summary of a Penobscot myth about how dogs became companions for men.
1260.   ———. "European Folk-Tales Among the Penobscot." *JAF,* 26 (1913), 81–84.
Two folktale texts. No commentary or annotations.
1261.   ———. "Penobscot Shamanism." *MAAA,* 6 (1919), 239–88.
Survey of shamanistic practices with four legends with free and interlinear translations and two legends in English only. Some explanatory notes.
1262.   ———. "Penobscot Tales." *JAF,* 28 (1915), 52–58.

Four folktale texts. No annotations or commentary.

1263. ———. "Penobscot Tales and Religious Beliefs." *JAF,* 48 (1935), 1–107.

Eighty-nine myth and folktale texts, including a number of Trickster stories. No comparative annotations, but an extensive discussion of the group's theology and supernaturalism.

1264. ———, and Newell Lion. "Penobscot Transformer Tales." *IJAL,* 1, No. 3 (1918), 187–244.

Twenty-one story texts collected from Lion by Speck. With interlinear and free translations. All but five of the texts deal with Gluskap.

1265. Stamp, Harley. "The Water-Fairies." *JAF,* 28 (1915), 310–16.

Unannotated legend text with some data on collecting situation.

1266. Warren, John C. "Pomola, the Spirit of Mt. Katahdin." *NEM,* 52 (April 1915), 276–77.

Retelling of myths and legends associated with the Maine landmark.

See also 662, 825, 867, 868, 1201.

P. Pequot

1267. Prince, J. Dyneley. "The Name 'Chahnameed.' " *JAF,* 16 (1903), 107.

Etymology of the name of a hero in a folktale published by Frank G. Speck (1270).

1268. ———, and Frank G. Speck. "The Modern Pequots and Their Language." *AA,* 5 (1903), 193–212.

Texts and translations of a sermon, the Lord's Prayer, and a death song (with music). With linguistic analysis.

1269. Speck, Frank G. "A Modern Mohegan-Pequot Text." *AA,* 6 (1904), 469–76.

Text, translation, and linguistic analysis of a witch story.

1270. ———. "A Pequot-Mohegan Witchcraft Tale." *JAF,* 16 (1903), 104–6.

Unannotated myth text with brief comment on cultural background. See 1267.

See also 1218, 1220, 1222.

Q. Powhatan

1271. Gilliam, Charles Edgar. "Sacred Stone and Bird." *NM,* 43 (August-September 1950), 337.

Retelling of a folktale. No annotation or commentary.

1272. Hendren, Samuel Rivers. "Government and Religion of the Virginia Indians." *JHUSHPS,* 13, Nos. 11–12 (1895), 543–96.

Contains data on religion, mythology, and ceremonialism.

1273. Rowell, Mary K. "Pamunkey Indian Games and Amusements." *JAF,* 56 (1943), 203–07.

Describes toys and games as well as verse texts which accompany games.

1274. Speck, Frank G., Royal B. Hassrick, and Edmund S. Carpenter. "Rappahannock Herbals, Folk-Lore and Science of Cures." *PDCIS,* 10, No. 1 (1 November 1942), 3–47.

Contains some sketchy data on ceremonials and religious associations with plantlore.

See also 1320, 1459.

R. Susquehannock

1275. Weslager, C. A. "Susquehannock Indian Religion from an Old Document." *JWAS,* 36 (1946), 302–05.

The document was written by Tobias Biorck in 1731. Contains data on theology and ceremonialism.

See also 860.

S. Tête de Boule

1276. Davidson, D. S. "Some Tête de Boule Tales." *JAF,* 41 (1928), 262–74.

Myth and legend texts collected in 1925. Some introductory description of cultural background. No annotations.

1277. Guinard, Joseph E. "Witiko Among the Tete-de-Boule." *PM,* 3 (1930), 69–71.

Description of the cannibalistic giant of the folklore of the group.

1278. Jenkins, William H. *Notes on the Hunting Economy of the Abitibi Indians. CUAAS* No. 9 (1939).

Based on fieldwork done in 1937. Contains data on ceremonialism.

1279. Webber, Alika. "Wigwamatew: Old Birch Bark Containers." *AIAM,* November 1978, pp. 56–61.

Considers the mythology of the birch tree.

T. Wampanoag

1280. Howland, Llewellyn. "Creamy Eyes." *AtM,* 169 (1942), 707–12.

Reminiscence of scallop-fishing includes a rewritten legend attributed to a Gay Head NA.

1281. Knight, Mabel Frances. "Wampanoag Tales." *JAF,* 38 (1925), 134–37.

Six unannotated legend texts. No commentary.

1282. Simmons, William S. "Conversion from Indian to Puritan." *NEQ,* 52 (1979), 197–218.

Discusses establishment of a Christian congregation among NAs on Martha's Vineyard in 1640s and 1650s. Some data on NA ceremonialism and belief system.

1283. Tantaquidgeon, Gladys. "Notes on the Gay Head Indians of Massachusetts." *IN,* 7 (1930), 1–26.

Ethnographic sketch includes some summaries of myths.

U. Wyandot

1284. Barbeau, C. M. "Wyandot Tales, Including Foreign Elements." *JAF,* 28 (1915), 83–95.

Three folktale texts collected in 1912–1913. Some explanatory and comparative notes.

1285. Belden, H. M. "Heine's *Sonnenuntergang* and an American Moon-Myth." *MLN,* 20 (1905), 205–06.

Compares a story used by the German poet with a Wyandot myth, the text of which is presented.

1286. [Clarke, Peter]. *Origin and Traditional History of the Wyandotts, and Sketches of Other Indian Tribes of North America. True Traditional Stories of Tecumseh and His League, in the Years 1811 and 1812.* Toronto: Hunter, Ross, 1870.

Some attention to oral history of Wyandots. Description of ceremonial singing and dancing.

1287. Connelley, William E. "Notes on the Folk-Lore of the Wyandots." *JAF,* 12 (1899), 116–25.

Survey of Wyandot mythology includes texts, an outline of the system, and a theological discussion. No comparative notes.

1288. ———. "Wyandot Folk-Lore." *TCCSR,* 1, No. 3 (November 1899), 6–117.

Twenty-five myth and legend texts introduced by general ethnographic commentary. Thorough informant descriptions. No comparative notes.

1289. Elliott, Charles. *Indian Missionary Reminiscences, Principally of the Wyandot Nation. In Which Is Exhibited the Efficacy of the Gospel in Elevating Ignorant and Savage Men.* New York: Lane & Scott, 1850.

Collection of pieces originally published in a Methodist periodical. Some accounts of Christian religious exercises and texts of orations.

1290. Feer, Michael. " 'The Skunk and the Smallpox': Mythology and Historical Reality." *PlA,* 18 (1973), 33–39.

Comparison of a myth about the origin of the disease, with historical data on the group's experience with smallpox.

1291. Finley, James B. *History of the Wyandott Mission, at Upper Sandusky, Ohio, Under the Direction of the Methodist Episcopal Church.* Cincinnati: J. F. Wright & L. Swormstedt, 1840.

Historical work includes chapter on various aspects of Wyandot culture: ceremonies, supernaturalism, games, oration texts, Christian worship exercises.

See also 946, 947, 948, 2458.

III SOUTHEAST

A. General Works

1292. Allsopp, Fred W. *Folklore of Romantic Arkansas.* 2 volumes. NP: Grolier Society, 1931.

Material on NA customs and some rewritten myth and legend texts. Includes Osage as well as various Southeast groups.

1293. Berlandier, Jean Louis. *The Indians of Texas in 1830.* Ed. John C. Ewers. Trans. Patricia Reading Leclerq. Washington: Smithsonian Institution Press, 1969.

Ms., probably completed in 1834, includes description of NA singing, dancing, and ceremonialism.

1294. Brinton, Daniel G. *Notes on the Floridian Peninsula, Its Literary History, Indian Tribes and Antiquities.* Philadelphia: Joseph Sabin, 1859.

Primarily an archeological study, but includes some general comments on religion and mythology of Southeast groups in sixteenth century.

1295. Buel, J. W. *Legends of the Ozarks.* St. Louis: W. S. Bryan, 1880.

Romanticized stories purportedly of NA origin, which deal with vicinity of Hot Springs, Arkansas. No tribal identification of sources.

1296. Burt, Jesse, and Robert B. Ferguson. *Indians of the Southeast: Then and Now.* Nashville: Abingdon, 1973.

Popularized survey of Southeast cultures. Includes references to myths, descriptions of ceremonies, and texts of songs (words and music).

1297. Daggett, Pierre M., and Dale R. Henning. "The Jaguar in North America." *AAn,* 39 (1974), 465–69.

Attributes occurrence of jaguar in Southeast myths to animal's presence in North America and the influence of Mesoamerican cultures.

1298. Densmore, Frances. "A Study of Indian Music in the Gulf States." *AA,* 36 (1934), 386–88.

Brief summary of fieldwork in 1932–1933 among the Alabama, Chitimacha, Choctaw, and Seminole.

1299. Eno, Clara B. "Legends of Arkansas." *AHQ,* 2 (1943), 32–38.

Summaries of several NA narratives involving Hernando de Soto.

1300. *Five Civilized Tribes in Indian Territory, The: The Cherokee, Chickasaw, Choctaw, Creek, and Seminole Nations.* Washington: U.S. Census Printing Office, 1894.

Supplement to Census of 1890 includes descriptions of NA cultures written by Bureau of Indian Affairs agents. Some data on dances and ceremonials.

1301. Foreman, Grant, ed. *A Traveler in Indian Territory:*

The Journal of Ethan Allen Hitchcock, Late Major-General in the United States Army. Cedar Rapids, Iowa: Torch Press, 1930.

Account of several months' travel in Indian Territory in 1841 and 1842. Contains data on traditional and Christian ceremonialism among displaced Southeast and Plains groups.

1302. Fundaburk, Emma Lila. *Southeastern Indians. Life Portraits. A Catalogue of Pictures. 1564–1860.* Laverne, Ala.: by the Author, 1958.

Reproduces paintings, engravings, and other illustrations of various aspects of Southeast cultures. Commentary includes descriptions of ceremonialism.

1303. ———, and Mary Douglass Fundaburk Foreman. *Sun Circles and Human Hands. The Southeastern Indians. Art and Industries.* Laverne, Ala.: by the Author, 1957.

Focuses primarily on material culture, but includes some data on ceremonialism and symbolism.

1304. Gaston, Edwin W., Jr. "Early Texas Indian Songs and Tales," in 78, pp. 7–11.

Random notes on style and content of NA song and story, using illustrations from various Southeast and Southwest groups.

1305. Haas, Mary R. "Southeastern Indian Folklore." *JAF,* 60 (1947), 403–6.

Survey of folklore studies among Southeast groups. Part of a general report prepared by the AFS Committee on Research in Folklore.

1306. Harkness, David James. "Legends of Southern Indians." *UTN,* 40, No. 2 (April 1961), 1–9.

Sixteen unannotated myth and legend texts. No commentary.

1307. Hudson, Charles. *The Southeastern Indians.* Knoxville: Univ. of Tennessee Press, 1976.

Broad survey of cultures of Southeast groups includes data on religion, music, and ceremonialism.

1308. "'Indian' Song, An." *JAF,* 20 (1907), 236.
Unannotated text, apparently from a Southeast group.

1309. Jahoda, Gloria. *The Trail of Tears.* New York: Holt, Rinehart and Winston, 1975.

Historical account of the removal of Southeast groups to Indian Territory. Includes references to myths, excerpts from prayers and orations, and song texts.

1310. James, John. *My Experience with Indians.* Austin: Gammel's Book Store, 1925.

Account of contact with NAs in Texas and Oklahoma beginning in 1869. Discusses Christianity among the Choctaw (one hymn text) and oratory among various groups (texts of speeches by Logan, Red Jacket, Pushamataha, and Black Hawk).

1311. Lewis, Thomas M. N., and Madeline Kneberg. *Tribes That Slumber. Indians of the Tennessee Region.* Knoxville: Univ. of Tennessee Press, 1958.

Primarily an archeological study, but includes some data on mythology and storytelling of Cherokee, Creek, and Yuchi.

1312. McLoughlin, William G. "A Note on African Sources of American Indian Racial Myths." *JAF,* 89 (1976), 331–35.

Shows African source for myth which ranks NAs, EAs, and Blacks. Apparently current among various Southeast groups.

1313. Milling, Chapman J. "Is the Serpent Tale an Indian Survival?" *SFQ*, 1, No. 1 (March 1937), 43–55.

Cites accounts of fabulous snakes among Southeast folk narratives as sources for similar accounts among Blacks.

1314. ———. *Red Carolinians.* Chapel Hill: Univ. of North Carolina Press, 1940.

Historical survey of various Southeast groups, emphasizing conflict with EA culture. Some data on mythology and ceremonialism.

1315. Mook, Maurice A. "Virginia Ethnology from an Early Relation." *WMQ*, 2nd series, 23 (1943), 101–29.

Interprets ethnological data found in documents from colonial Virginia. Some data from various NA groups on singing, dancing, and ceremonialism.

1316. Mooney, James. *The Siouan Tribes of the East. BAEB* No. 22 (1894).

Brief historical and cultural descriptions of eastern Siouan-speaking groups. Draws upon traditional history and describes some ceremonies.

1317. "Original Accounts of De Soto's Journey Through Arkansas and of Marquette's Entertainment by Arkansas Indians." *PAHA*, 1 (1906), 466–502.

Extracts from first-person accounts of explorers' expeditions. Contain elaborated texts of NA oratory and descriptions of ceremonialism.

1318. Pargellis, Stanley. "An Account of the Indians in Virginia." *WMQ*, 3rd series, 16 (1959), 228–43.

Reprints document originally published in 1689, which surveys NA culture with sections on religion, ceremonialism, and the myth of the deluge.

1319. Rights, Douglas L. *The American Indian in North Carolina.* Durham, N.C.: Duke Univ. Press, 1947.

Survey of several Southeast groups includes folklore material: Catawba stories and Cherokee formulas and myths.

1320. Speck, Frank G. "The Ethnic Position of the Southeastern Algonkian." *AA*, 26 (1924), 184–200.

Attempts to relate various Carolina groups to neighboring cultures. Argues that folklore is irrelevant since NA traditions have been supplanted by EA and Black folklore. Also considers the Powhatan.

1321. ———. *Gourds of the Southeastern Indians: A Prolegomenon on the Lagenaria Gourd in the Culture of the Southeastern Indians.* Boston: New England Gourd Society, 1941.

Discusses uses of gourds in the material cultures of Southeast groups. Some data on ceremonialism.

1322. ———. "Some Outlines of Aboriginal Culture in the Southeastern States." *AA*, 9 (1907), 287–95.

Ethnographic notes with some descriptions of ceremonial singing and prayers.

1323. Swanton, John R. "Aboriginal Culture of the Southeast." *ARBAE*, 42 (1924–1925), 673–726.

Surveys common elements throughout region. Includes music, dancing, and ceremonialism.

1324. ———. "Animal Stories from the Indians of the Muskhogean Stock." *JAF*, 26 (1913), 193–218.

Twenty-six folktale texts (fourteen Natchez, six Alabama, three Hitchiti, one Creek) with some comparative notes. Commentary on collecting situation.

1325. ———. *Early History of the Creek Indians and Their Neighbors. BAEB* No. 73 (1922).

Historical sketches of groups comprising the Creek Confederacy contain some data on ceremonialism.

1326. ———. *Indian Tribes of the Lower Mississippi Valley and Adjacent Coast of the Gulf of Mexico. BAEB* No. 43 (1911).

Ethnographic survey of Southeast cultures. Includes some data on ceremonialism and myth texts.

1327. ———. *The Indians of the Southeastern United States. BAEB* No. 137 (1946).

Handbook includes sections on religious and ceremonial elements in the cultures.

1328. ———. "Mythology of the Indians of Louisiana and the Texas Coast." *JAF*, 20 (1907), 285–89.

Cross-cultural survey of common myths among various groups along the Gulf of Mexico.

1329. ———. *Myths and Tales of the Southeastern Indians. BAEB* No. 88 (1929).

Stories collected between 1908 and 1914: ninety-one from Creek, ninety-two from Hitchiti, sixty-four from Alabama, sixty-five from Koasati, forty-three from Natchez. Brief comparative commentary appended.

1330. ———. "Sun Worship in the Southeast." *AA*, 30 (1928), 206–13.

Discusses worship of a solar deity among various Southeast groups.

See also 393, 407, 427, 682, 830, 836, 838, 853, 858, 1499, 1612, 2002, 2052.

B. Alabama

1331. Bludworth, G. T. "How the Alabamas Came Southward," in 108, pp. 298–99.

Rewritten version of tribal migration legend.

1332. Densmore, Frances. "The Alabama Indians and Their Music," in 108, pp. 270–93.

Thorough presentation of musical traditions and contexts. Contains one myth text and twenty song texts (music only).

1333. Heard, Elma. "Two Tales from the Alabamas," in 108, pp. 294–97.

Rewritten folktale texts with no commentary.

1334. Malone, Prairie View. *Sam Houston's Indians: The Alabama-Coushatti.* San Antonio: Naylor, 1960.

Includes two myth texts.

1335. Martin, Howard N. "Alabama-Coushatta Tales," in 94, pp. 12–18.

Five myth texts with no annotation or commentary.

1336. ———. "Folktales of the Alabama-Coushatta Indians," in 89, pp. 65–80.

Nine narrative texts with no annotations or commentary.

1337. ———. *Folktales of the Alabama-Coushatta Indians.* NP: NP, 1946.

Thirty-nine narrative texts with no annotations or commentary.

1338. ———. *Myths and Folktales of the Alabama-Coushatta Indians of Texas.* Austin: Encino, 1977.

Forty-six story texts collected in 1930s. Includes introduction on tribal history and storytelling traditions, index of motifs, and glossary.

See also 1298, 1324, 1329.

C. Atakapa

1339. Gatschet, Albert S., and John R. Swanton. *A Dictionary of the Atakapa Language Accompanied by Text Material.* BAEB No. 108 (1932).
Nine texts in Atakapa with interlinear and free translations. Mostly ethnographic descriptions with a few historical legends.
1340. Swanton, John R. "A Sketch of the Atakapa Language." *IJAL,* 5 (1929), 121–49.
Linguistic survey of the extinct language. Includes text of a legend with interlinear and free translations and grammatical notes.

D. Biloxi

1341. Dorsey, J. Owen. "Two Biloxi Tales." *JAF,* 6 (1893), 48–50.
Folktale texts with some comparative comments.
1342. ———, and John R. Swanton. *A Dictionary of the Biloxi and Ofo Languages, Accompanied with Thirty-One Biloxi Texts and Numerous Biloxi Phrases.* BAEB No. 47 (1912).
Myth texts, collected by Dorsey, are presented in Biloxi with interlinear and free translations and linguistic commentary.
1343. Porter, Kenneth W. "A Legend of the Biloxi." *JAF,* 59 (1946), 168–73.
Account of a mass drowning, narrated in 1943 by a Black informant, who claimed to be a descendant of the Biloxi.

E. Caddo

1344. Dorsey, George A. "Caddo Customs of Childhood." *JAF,* 18 (1905), 226–28.
Surveys ceremonialism associated with socialization. Includes prayer text.
1345. ———. *Traditions of the Caddo.* Washington: Carnegie Institution, 1905.
Seventy myth texts with abstracts. Collected 1903–1905. No commentary or annotation.
1346. Lyon, Owen. "The Trail of the Caddo." *AHQ,* 11 (1952), 124–30.
Historical survey begins with summary of tribal origin myth.
1347. Parsons, Elsie Clews. *Notes on the Caddo.* MAAA No. 57 (1941).
Data collected in 1921–1922 from one informant. Includes ceremonial descriptions (traditional and peyotist) and five folktale texts with explanatory and comparative notes.
1348. Sjoberg, Andrée F. "The Bidai Indians of Southeastern Texas." *SJA,* 7 (1951), 391–400.
Ethnographic overview of a little-known Caddoan group includes data on ceremonialism.
1349. Swanton, John R. *Source Material in the History and Ethnology of the Caddo Indians.* BAEB No. 132 (1942).

Ethnographic notes based on sources dating from as early as 1691. Sections on creation myths, ceremonialism, and religion.

See also 2045.

F. Catawba

1350. Harrington, M. R. "Catawba Potters and Their Work." *AA,* 10 (1908), 399–407.
Describes process of pottery-making. Contains a myth text collected in 1908.
1351. Hudson, Charles M. *The Catawba Nation.* Athens: Univ. of Georgia Press, 1970.
Reconstruction of Catawba history based partially on "folk history." Contains some data on ceremonialism.
1352. Matthews, G. Hubert, and Red Thunder Cloud. "Catawba Texts." *IJAL,* 33 (1967), 7–24.
Three descriptions of customs with free and interlinear translations and linguistic commentary. Thorough description of the informant.
1353. Speck, Frank G. "Catawba Herbals and Curative Practices." *JAF,* 57 (1944), 37–50.
Lists a number of medical beliefs and reports narrative material associated with them.
1354. ———. "Catawba Religious Beliefs, Mortuary Customs, and Dances." *PM,* 12 (1939), 21–57.
Covers supernaturalism, ceremonialism, and the effects of Mormon influence on traditional practices.
1355. ———. "Catawba Text." *IJAL,* 12 (1946), 64–65.
Personal experience narrative with interlinear and free translations. Collected in 1944. Fairly extensive data on informant.
1356. ———. "Catawba Texts." *CUCA,* 24 (1934), 1–91.
Myths, folktales, legends, charms, prayers, songs, and descriptions of customs (117). With free and interlinear translations. Some explanatory notes and data on collecting situation.
1357. ———. "Ethnoherpetology of the Catawba and Cherokee Indians." *JWAS,* 36 (1946), 355–60.
Some attention to the role of reptiles in folklore.
1358. ———. "Some Catawba Texts and Folk-Lore." *JAF,* 26 (1913), 319–30.
Four folktale and legend texts with free and interlinear translations and linguistic notes.
1359. ———, and L. G. Carr. "Catawba Folk Tales from Chief Sam Blue." *JAF,* 60 (1947), 79–84.
Nine narrative texts collected in 1946 from tribal leader. Although the storyteller was one of the few Catawba still to use the native language, he was also a convert to Mormonism.

See also 1319.

G. Cherokee

1360. *Antiquities of the Cherokee Indians Compiled from the Collection of Rev. Daniel Sabin Buttrick.* Vinita, Okla.: Indian Chieftain, 1884.

Myths, legends, and fragments of Cherokee philosophy originally published in the periodical *Indian Chieftain.*

1361. Atalie, Princess. *The Earth Speaks.* New York: Fleming H. Revell, 1940.

Romanticized retellings of Cherokee myths and legends. Based on personal knowledge, some fieldwork, and published materials.

1362. Ballenger, T. L. *Around Tahlequah Council Fires.* Oklahoma City: Cherokee Publishing Company, 1945.

Anecdotal history of the Cherokee in eastern Oklahoma contains a chapter of anecdotes, some of which were apparently related by NA storytellers.

1363. Bender, Ernest. "Cherokee II." *IJAL,* 15 (1949), 223–28.

Three narratives collected in 1945. With interlinear and free translations and linguistic notes.

1364. Berry, M. H. "Indian Wildflower Legends." *NM,* 48 (October 1955), 422–24.

Retellings of etiological myths from Cherokee (six texts), Choctaw (one), Iroquois (one), Creek (one), and Seminole (one). No commentary or annotations.

1365. Boozer, Jack D. "The Legend of Yalloo Falls." *TA,* 11, No. 2 (Autumn 1955), 66–67.

Rewritten, unannotated myth text with some data on cultural background.

1366. Brown, John P. *Old Frontiers: The Story of the Cherokee Indians from Earliest Times to the Date of Their Removal to the West, 1838.* Kingsport, Tenn.: Southern, 1938.

Popular history includes paraphrases of myths and oratory and descriptions of ceremonials.

1367. Carter, Forrest. *The Education of Little Tree.* New York: Delacorte, 1976.

Autobiography relates experiences of growing up with Cherokee grandparents in 1930s. Contains song text.

1368. Carter, Samuel, III. *Cherokee Sunset: A Nation Betrayed. A Narrative of Travail and Triumph, Persecution and Exile.* Garden City, N.Y.: Doubleday, 1976.

Popular history with data on ceremonialism, storytelling, and singing.

1369. "Cherokee 'Deer Lore' Recalled." *IW,* 3, No. 20 (1 June 1936), 47.

Overview of place of the deer in Cherokee mythology. Reprinted from the *Daily Oklahoman.*

1370. Clarke, Mary Whatley. *Chief Bowles and the Texas Cherokees.* Norman: Univ. of Oklahoma Press, 1971.

Biography of Chief Bowles in the context of Cherokee relations with Mexican and Texas Republican governments. Work begins with a summary of tribal origin myth.

1371. "Colonel Chicken's Journal to the Cherokees, 1725," in 140, pp. 95–172.

Includes description of oratory and ceremonialism.

1372. Corkran, D. H. "A Cherokee Migration Fragment." *SIS,* 4 (October 1952), 27–28.

Text of a migration legend told to Alexander Longe in 1717.

1373. ———. "Cherokee Sun and Fire Observances." *SIS,* 7 (October 1955), 33–38.

Survey of ritualism.

1374. ———. "The Nature of the Cherokee Supreme Being." *SIS,* 8 (October 1956), 27–35.

Description of the high god concept. With cross-cultural comparisons.

1375. ———. "The Sacred Fire of the Cherokees." *SIS,* 5 (October 1953), 21–26.

Examination of the symbolism of fire and its ritual songs.

1376. Culbertson, Anne Virginia. *At the Big House Where Aunt Nancy and Aunt 'Phrony Held Forth on the Animal Folks.* Indianapolis: Bobbs-Merrill, 1904.

Unannotated animal tales collected from Black and Cherokee sources. Rewritten in eye dialect. No commentary.

1377. Davis, John B. "Some Cherokee Stories." *AAA,* 3 (1910), 26–49.

Twenty-two unannotated myth and folktale texts. No commentary.

1378. de Baillou, Clemens. "A Contribution to the Mythology and Conceptual World of the Cherokee Indians." *Eh,* 8 (1961), 93-102.

Accounts of Cherokee life, including ceremonials, as written by Moravian missionaries in the early 1800s.

1379 Ethridge, Robbie F. "Tobacco Among the Cherokees." *JCS,* 3, No. 2 (Spring 1978), 76–86.

Discussion of tribal usage of tobacco. Includes an etiological myth.

1380. Evans, J. P. "Sketches of Cherokee Characteristics." *JCS,* 4, No. 1 (Winter 1979), 10–20.

Ms. written about 1835 includes extensive descriptions of Cherokee ceremonialism.

1381. Fenton, William N. "Cherokee and Iroquois Connections Revisited." *JCS,* 3, No. 4 (Fall 1979), 239–49.

Comparison of the cultures with emphasis on supernaturalism and ceremonialism.

1382. Fogelson, Raymond D. *The Cherokees. A Critical Bibliography.* Bloomington: Indiana Univ. Press, 1978.

Unannotated list of 347 books and articles. Introductory essay includes section on "World View, Religion, and Medicine."

1383. ———. "The Cherokee Ballgame Cycle: An Ethnographer's View." *Em,* 15 (1971), 327–38.

Describes the ballgame and associated ceremonialism. Analysis includes perspectives of social structure, cultural background, and psychology.

1384. ———, and Paul Kutsche. "Cherokee Economic Cooperatives: The Gadug," in 116, pp. 83–123.

Ethnographic and historical study of an economic institution includes data on oratory.

1385. Foster, George E. *Literature of the Cherokees. Also Bibliography and the Story of Their Genesis.* Ithaca, N.Y.: Office of the Democrat, 1889.

Commentary on oral and written literature. Includes mythology, prayers, oratory, and songs. Text of creation myth appended.

1386. ———. *Se-Quo-Yah, The American Cadmus and Modern Moses. A Complete Biography of the Greatest of Redmen, Around Whose Wonderful Life Has [sic] Been Woven the Manners, Customs and Beliefs of the Early Cherokees, Together with a Recital of Their Wrongs and Wonderful Progress Toward Civilization.* Philadelphia: Indian Rights Association, 1885.

Biography includes descriptions of Cherokee customs such as the ballgame, Green Corn and other dances, song texts, storytelling. With texts of Piasa myth and others.

1387.   Gabriel, Ralph Henry. *Elias Boudinot, Cherokee, and His America.* Norman: Univ. of Oklahoma Press, 1941.

Biography includes some material on mythology and ceremonialism.

1388.   Gilbert, William H., Jr. "The Cherokees of North Carolina: Living Memorials of the Past," in *ARSI for 1956,* pp. 529–55.

Survey of culture of eastern Cherokee contains data on formulas, mythology, and dances.

1389.   ———. "The Eastern Cherokees." *BAEB* No. 133 (*AP* No. 23), 1943.

Ethnographic notes based on fieldwork done in 1932 contrasted with data on group from 1800s. Contains formula texts (with free translations) and data on mythology.

1390.   Gillespie, John D. "Some Eastern Cherokee Dances Today." *SIS,* 13 (October 1961), 29–43.

Descriptions of ceremonials.

1391.   Hamilton, Gail. "Sunday in Cherokee Land." *NAR,* 146 (1888), 194–202.

Describes Christian worship services among the Cherokee. With some data on hymn-singing.

1392.   Hedges, James S. "Attributive Mutation in Cherokee Natural History Myth." *NCF,* 21 (1973), 147–54.

Surveys myths in which an animal is transformed into its present condition.

1393.   Herndon, Marcia. "The Cherokee Ballgame Cycle: An Ethnomusicologist's View." *Em,* 15 (1971), 339–52.

Uses the music of the all-night dance preceding the ballgame to show how a musical occasion can encapsule the values and structure of a culture.

1394.   Heth, Charlotte. "Stylistic Similarities in Cherokee and Iroquois Music." *JCS,* 4, No. 3 (Summer 1979), 128–62.

Twelve song texts (words and music) with attention to formalistic parallels between the groups.

1395.   Hitchcock, I. B. "Why the Wild-Cat Is Spotted." *TT,* 4 (April 1902), 110–11.

Unannotated folktale text. No commentary.

1396.   Holman, Harriet R. "Cherokee Dancing Remembered: Why the Eastern Band Abjured the Old Eagle Dance." *NCF,* 24 (1976), 101–6.

Reminiscences of a Cherokee recorded in 1973 afford data on tribal dance traditions. Recalls catastrophic storm which accompanied last performance of the Eagle Dance in 1899.

1397.   Howard, James H. "The Yamasee: A Supposedly Extinct Southeastern Tribe Rediscovered." *AA,* 62 (1960), 681–83.

Suggests that the Altamaha Cherokee are, in fact, the Yamasee, who had allegedly been destroyed in the late 1700s. Based on folklore materials.

1398.   ———, Stewart R. Shaffer, and James Shaffer. "Altamaha Cherokee Folklore and Customs." *JAF,* 72 (1959), 134–38.

Surveys traditional culture of the little-known band of Cherokee.

1399.   Hudson, Charles. "Uktena: A Cherokee Anomalous Monster." *JCS,* 3, No. 2 (Spring 1978), 62–75.

Description of rattlesnake-like being who figures in decorative art, formulas, and supernaturalism.

1400.   Irvine, Mrs. Alicia. "How the Turkey Got His Beard: A Cherokee Myth." *SWL,* 16 (1950), 35–36.

Unannotated animal tale. No commentary.

1401.   Johnson, F. Roy, ed. *Stories of the Old Cherokees Based on Reports and Collections of James Mooney and Others.* Murfreesboro, N.C.: by the Author, 1975.

Unannotated myth and folktale texts from previously published sources. Brief introduction on cultural background.

1402.   Kilpatrick, Jack Frederick. "The Buckskin Curtain." *SWR,* 52 (1967), 83–87.

Discusses cultural prejudice leveled at Cherokee. Suggests open-minded study of NA oral literature and religion.

1403.   ———. "Cherokee Love Incantations." *SWR,* 50 (1965), 169–78.

Texts of several formulas with commentary on language and ritual contexts.

1404.   ———. "The Friends of Thunder." *SWR,* 49 (1964), 97–101.

Random observations on contemporary Cherokee culture, including love of music.

1405.   ———, and Anna Gritts Kilpatrick. "A Cherokee Conjuration to Cure a Horse." *SFQ,* 28 (1964), 216–18.

Text and free translation of a healing charm. No commentary or annotation.

1406.   ———, and Anna Gritts Kilpatrick. "Cherokee Rituals Pertaining to Medicinal Roots." *SIS,* 16 (October 1964), 24–28.

Formulas with free translations relating to collecting roots.

1407.   ———, and Anna Gritts Kilpatrick. "Eastern Cherokee Folktales: Reconstructed from the Field Notes of Frans M. Olbrechts." *BAEB* No. 196 (*AP* No. 80), 1967.

Eighty narrative texts collected by Olbrechts in 1927. With some commentary.

1408.   ———, and Anna Gritts Kilpatrick. " 'The Foundation of Life': The Cherokee National Ritual." *AA,* 66 (1964), 1386–91.

Description of a ritual used only in the most serious tribal emergencies. Reported only after Cherokee removal to Oklahoma. Text of ritual in Cherokee with interlinear and free translations.

1409.   ———, and Anna Gritts Kilpatrick. *Friends of Thunder: Folktales of the Oklahoma Cherokees.* Dallas: Southern Methodist Univ. Press, 1964.

Texts of animal stories, myths, and legends collected in 1961. With some informant data.

1410.   ———, and Anna Gritts Kilpatrick. *Muskogean Charm Songs Among the Oklahoma Cherokees. SmCA,* Vol. 2, No. 3 (1967).

Ten song texts (words and music) with contextual commentary. Words preserved in a syllabary ms.; tunes and context data collected in 1964. Original language of words is Muskogean (from a source of Natchez descent).

1411.   ———, and Anna Gritts Kilpatrick. *Notebook of a Cherokee Shaman. SmCA,* Vol. 2, No. 6 (1970).

Fifty charm texts from a syllabary ms. kept by a Cherokee shaman (1896–1938). Each text is presented in phonetic Cherokee with free and interlinear translations and a discussion of the role of the charm in the medical system.

1412.   ———, and Anna Gritts Kilpatrick. "A Note on Cherokee Wind-Controlling Magic." *SFQ,* 29 (1965), 204–06.

Brief note on magical practice. With one translated charm text.

1413. ———, and Anna Gritts Kilpatrick. *Run Toward the Nightland: Magic of the Oklahoma Cherokees.* Dallas: Southern Methodist Univ. Press, 1967.

Presents magical formulas preserved in a syllabary ms. With some discussion of the place of the formulas in the magical system.

1414. ———, and Anna Gritts Kilpatrick, trans. and eds. *The Shadow of Sequoyah: Social Documents of the Cherokees, 1862–1964.* Norman: Univ. of Oklahoma Press, 1965.

Translations of materials written in the syllabary. With several song and myth texts.

1415. ———, and Anna Gritts Kilpatrick. *Walk in Your Soul: Love Incantations of the Oklahoma Cherokees.* Dallas: Southern Methodist Univ. Press, 1965.

Erotic formulas translated freely from syllabary mss. With contextual and explanatory notes.

1416. King, Duane H., and Laura H. King. "The Mythico-Religious Origin of the Cherokees." *AJ,* 2, No. 4 (Summer 1975), 259–64.

Text of Cherokee creation myth with syllabary text. Fairly thorough discussion of cultural significance and comparison with other cosmogonies.

1417. King, Laura H. "The Cherokee Story-Teller: The Deer's Blunt Teeth." *JCS,* 3, No. 1 (Winter 1978), 45–48.

Myth text in syllabary, phonetic Cherokee, literal and free translations. Brief explanatory commentary.

1418. ———. "The Cherokee Story-Teller: The Giant Inchworm." *JCS,* 1, No. 1 (Summer 1976), 55–58.

Myth text in syllabary, phonetic Cherokee, literal and free translations. Brief explanatory commentary.

1419. ———. "The Cherokee Story-Teller: The Raven Mocker." *JCS,* 2, No. 1 (Winter 1977), 190–94.

Legend text in syllabary, phonetic Cherokee, literal and free translations. Brief explanatory commentary.

1420. ———. "The Cherokee Story-Teller: The Red and Green Crayfish." *JCS,* 2, No. 2 (Spring 1977), 246–49.

Myth text in syllabary, phonetic Cherokee, literal and free translations. Brief explanatory commentary.

1421. ———. "The Cherokee Story-Teller: The Trickster Turtle." *JCS,* 1, No. 2 (Fall 1976), 110–12.

Folktale text in syllabary, phonetic Cherokee, literal and free translations. Brief explanatory commentary.

1422. Kurath, Gertrude P. "Effects of Environment on Cherokee-Iroquois Ceremonialism, Music, and Dance," in 116, pp. 173–95.

Explores parallels and divergences between Cherokee and Iroquois musical performances. Comments by William C. Sturtevant follow the essay (pp. 197–204).

1423. Kutsche, Paul. "The Tsali Legend: Culture Heroes and Historiography." *Eh,* 10 (1963), 329–57.

Four texts of a hero legend are analyzed in terms of their correspondence with cultural values.

1424. Lanman, Charles. "A Chapter on Rattlesnakes." *SLM,* 16 (1850), 27–29.

Includes summary of Cherokee myth of origin of rattlesnakes.

1425. ———. *Letters from the Alleghany Mountains.* New York: Putnam, 1849.

Three of the letters report aspects of Cherokee culture: a Christian worship service with sermon text, the ballgame and associated ceremonies, the importance of oratory.

1426. Longe, Alexander. "A Small Postscript on the Ways and Manners of the Indians Called Cherokees." Ed. D. H. Corkran. *SIS,* 21 (October 1969), 6–49.

Modernized and original versions of a work written in 1725. Emphasizes tribal spiritual life with attention to ceremonialism and mythology.

1427. Lusk, Leila Fearn. *Chatu-Huchi or The Painted Rock and Other Alabama Legends.* Dallas: Kaleidograph, 1940.

Four stories: one is apparently original; two are highly romanticized renderings of Cherokee legends; and one is a similar treatment of Creek material.

1428. Mason, Robert Lindsay. "Cherokee Plant Lore of the Smokies." *NM,* 19 (June 1932), 343–47.

Includes summaries of myths and folktales and descriptions of ceremonials.

1429. ———. "Tree Myths of the Cherokees." *AFFL,* 35 (May 1929), 259–62, 300.

Retellings of several myths about trees.

1430. Mooney, James. "Cherokee and Iroquois Parallels." *JAF,* 2 (1889), 67.

Discussion of similarities in the folklore of the cultures.

1431. ———. "The Cherokee Ball Play." *AA,* o. s. 3 (1890), 105–32.

Thorough description of the game with its origin myth and two song texts (words and music).

1432. ———. "Cherokee Plant Lore." *AA,* o. s. 2 (1889), 223–24.

Brief miscellany of myths involving plants.

1433. ———. "The Cherokee River Cult." *JAF,* 13 (1900), 1–10.

Survey of beliefs and rituals associated with concept among the Cherokee of the sacred river. Includes texts of prayers and formulas.

1434. ———. "Cherokee Theory and Practice of Medicine." *JAF,* 3 (1890), 44–50.

Some attention to mythic basis of medical beliefs and descriptions of ceremonialism.

1435. ———. "Myths of the Cherokees." *JAF,* 1 (1888), 97–108.

Two myth texts with explanatory notes and general comments on cultural background. Collected in 1887.

1436. ———. "Myths of the Cherokee." *ARBAE,* 19 (1897–1898), 3–575.

Myth and legend texts (126) collected in 1887–1890. Preceded by sketch of Cherokee history and an essay on oral literature which contains informant data. With comparative and explanatory notes.

1437. ———. "The Sacred Formulas of the Cherokees." *ARBAE,* 7 (1885–1886), 301–97.

Texts of prayers and other incantations from syllabary ms. Each is presented in phonetic Cherokee with translation and explanation. General description of medical system is included.

1438. ———, and Frans M. Olbrechts. *The Swimmer Manuscript: Cherokee Sacred Formulas and Medicinal Prescriptions. BAEB* No. 99 (1932).

Ninety-six formulas from a syllabary ms. kept by Mooney's principal informant. Presented in phonetic Cherokee with interlinear and free translations. Introduction treats the tribal medical system.

1439. Neugin, Rebecca (recorded by Grant Foreman). "Memories of the Trail." *JCS,* 3, No. 3 (Summer 1978), 176.

Personal narrative about the Trail of Tears, recorded in 1932.

1440. Newcomb, W. W., Jr. "A Note on Cherokee-Delaware Pan-Indianism." *AA,* 57 (1955), 1041–45.

Discusses the peyote cult as a factor contributing to pan-Indianism. With descriptions of pan-Indian ceremonials.

1441. Olbrechts, Frans M. "Two Cherokee Texts." *IJAL,* 6 (1931), 179–84.

Texts of a myth and an oration with interlinear and free translations. Myth text is also presented in the syllabary.

1442. "Original Specimens of Eloquence: Speeches Given at the Treaty of Hopewill, 1785." *JCS,* 4, No. 2 (Spring 1979), 54–55.

Oration texts originally published in 1789.

1443. [Owen, Narcissa.] *Memoirs of Narcissa Owen 1831 . . . 1907.* NP: NP, 1907.

Owen, a part-Cherokee, presents some historical legends, but her major focus is on family history as it related to developments in tribal life.

1444. Park, Hugh. *Reminiscences of the Indians by Cephas Washburn.* Van Buren, Ark.: Press-Argus, 1955.

Re-issue of Washburn's work (first published in 1869) with a biography of the author. Several of Washburn's letters about missionary work among the Oklahoma Cherokee include descriptions of tribal cosmological and witch beliefs.

1445. Payne, John Howard. *Indian Justice: A Cherokee Murder Trial at Tahlequah in 1840.* Ed. Grant Foreman. Muskogee, Okla.: Star, 1962.

Edition of Payne's account for the *New York Journal of Commerce* in 1841. Contains trial dialogue, oaths, and prayers.

1446. Perry, Samuel D. "Religious Festivals in Cherokee Life." *IH,* 12, No. 1 (Winter 1979), 20–22, 28.

Treats religious ceremonialism as reaffirmation of harmony with nature and the supernatural.

1447 Reid, John Phillip. *A Law of Blood. The Primitive Law of the Cherokee Nation.* New York: New York Univ. Press, 1970.

Analysis of Cherokee legal system at period of earliest contact with EA culture. Sees myths as sources and validators for certain laws.

1448. Sass, Herbert Ravenel. "Ahowhe of the Overhills. A Cherokee Legend of the Enchanted Deer No Hunter Can Harm." *GH,* 82 (March 1926), 74–75, 104–10.

Rewritten myth text.

1449. ———. *Hear Me My Chiefs!* New York: William Morrow, 1940.

Episodic history of NA defense of land from EA encroachment. Includes a chapter on Cherokee mythology.

1450. Siler, Margaret R. *Cherokee Indian Lore and Smoky Mountains Stories.* Bryson City, N.C.: Bryson City Times, 1939.

Pamphlet includes a miscellany of Cherokee folklore: rewritten myth and legend texts, descriptions of ceremonies, prayer texts. Most from author's newspaper stories.

1451. Speck, Frank G. "Some Eastern Cherokee Texts." *IJAL,* 4 (1927), 111–13.

Four narrative texts with interlinear and free translations. Collected in 1922.

1452. ———, Leonard Broom, and Will West Long.

Cherokee Dance and Drama. Berkeley: Univ. of California Press, 1951.

Inventory and descriptions of dances of eastern Cherokee. Includes texts of songs, formulas, and ritual origin myths.

1453. Starkey, Marion L. *The Cherokee Nation.* New York: Knopf, 1946.

Popular history includes discussion of ceremonialism and mythic concepts.

1454. Starr, Emmet. *History of the Cherokee Indians and Their Legends and Folk Lore.* Oklahoma City: Warden, 1922.

Historical account beginning with pre-contact culture and continuing into 1900s. Some information on mythology and ceremonialism, but not enough to justify title.

1455. ten Kate, H. "Legends of the Cherokees." *JAF,* 2 (1889), 53–55.

Two myth texts collected in 1883. Some data on performance context.

1456. Terrell, James W. "The Demon of Consumption. A Legend of Cherokees in North Carolina." *JAF,* 5 (1892), 125–26.

Unannotated myth text. No commentary.

1457. Thomas, Cyrus. "The Cherokees in Pre-Columbian Times." *S,* 15 (16 May 1890), 295–300; (30 May 1890), 323–28, 330–32; (6 June 1890), 338–42; (20 June 1890), 365–70, 372–73; (27 June 1890), 379–84.

Historical survey includes some data on ceremonialism. Also finds ethnohistorical information about the Cherokee in the Walam Olum.

1458. Thomas, Robert K. "The Redbird Smith Movement," in 116, pp. 159–66.

Brief treatment of a nativistic movement in the 1890s with some attention to ceremonialism. Comments by Fred W. Voget follow the essay (pp. 167–71).

1459. Tooker, William Wallace. "The Problem of the Rechahecrian Indians of Virginia." *AA,* o. s. 11 (1898), 261–70.

Discusses problem in identifying exactly who the Rechahecrians were. Uses oral narratives to support idea of their affiliation with both Cherokee and Powhatan groups.

1460. Tsianina. *Where Trails Have Led Me.* Burbank, Cal.: by the Author, 1968.

Autobiography of a Cherokee woman who became a professional singer. Contains some references to stories and ceremonials from her early life.

1461. Vance, Zebulon Baird. "Indian Legend." *NCF,* 21 (1973), 51–52.

Unannotated myth text. Reprinted from the *North Carolina University Magazine* for March 1852.

1462. Wade, Forrest C. *Cry of the Eagle: History and Legends of the Cherokee Indians and Their Buried Treasures.* Cumming, Ga.: by the Author, 1969.

Most of the "legends" are either historical anecdotes or stories by EAs about Cherokee buried treasure. Some highly rewritten Cherokee material.

1463. Walker, Robert Sparks. *Torchlights to the Cherokees: The Brainerd Mission.* New York: Macmillan, 1931.

History of a mission founded in North Carolina in 1816. Includes folklore data in a section on "Cherokee Customs." Also includes the text of a sermon preached by a Cherokee.

1464. Wilburn, Hiram C. "Judaculla Place-Names and the Judaculla Tales." *SIS,* 4 (October 1952), 23–26.

Discusses geographical references in an ogre story.

1465. Witthoft, John. "The Cherokee Green Corn Medicine and the Green Corn Festival." *JWAS,* 36 (1946), 213–19.

Ceremonial description with two texts of the corn origin myth.

1466. ———. "Notes on a Cherokee Migration Story." *JWAS,* 37 (1947), 304–05.

Finds no evidence of a migration tradition reported by early commentators on the culture.

1467. ———. "Some Eastern Cherokee Bird Stories." *JWAS,* 36 (1946), 177–80.

Six folktale texts collected in 1944–1945. With comparative notes and some data on cultural background.

1468. ———, and Wendell S. Hadlock. "Cherokee-Iroquois Little People." *JAF,* 59 (1946), 413–22.

Surveys traditions about dwarves among the groups.

1469. Woodward, Grace Steele. *The Cherokees.* Norman: Univ. of Oklahoma, 1963.

Historical work contains some data on ceremonialism and a text of the Tsali legend.

1470. Wright, Muriel H. *Springplace: Moravian Mission and the Ward Family of the Cherokee Nation.* Guthrie, Okla.: Co-operative, 1940.

History of a Moravian mission established in Georgia and moved to Oklahoma with the Cherokee exodus. Some data on Cherokee narrative traditions.

See also 396, 1026, 1064, 1311, 1319, 1357, 1503, 4043.

H. Chickasaw

1471. Baird, W. David. *The Chickasaw People.* Phoenix: Indian Tribal Series, 1974.

Historical survey begins with tribal origin myth and descriptions of pre-contact ceremonial life.

1472. Blackwood, Catherine. "Chickasaw Legend." *IW,* 3, No. 10 (1 January 1936), 14.

Myth text. Reprinted from the *Indian School Journal.*

1473. " 'Calumet' Dance." *TFSB,* 13 (1947), 80.

Description of a ceremonial observed by a missionary in 1673.

1474. Malone, James H. *The Chickasaw Nation. A Short Sketch of a Noble People.* Louisville, Ky.: John P. Morton, 1922.

Historical and cultural survey includes some material on mythology and ceremonialism.

1475. Speck, Frank G. "European Tales Among the Chickasaw Indians." *JAF,* 26 (1913), 292.

Unannotated folktale text with brief commentary on content.

1476. ———. "Notes on Chickasaw Ethnology and Folk-Lore." *JAF,* 20 (1907), 50–58.

Ethnographic notes include descriptions of ceremonialism.

1477. Swanton, John R. "Social and Religious Beliefs and Usages of the Chickasaw Indians." *ARBAE,* 44 (1926–1927), 169–273.

General ethnography with some data on dances, ceremonials, and other occasions for verbal performance.

I. Chitimacha

1478. Densmore, Frances. "A Search for Songs Among the Chitimacha Indians in Louisiana." *BAEB* No. 133 (*AP* No. 19), 1943.

Results of fieldwork done in 1933 include miscellaneous reminiscences and four myth texts, all from the same informant.

1479. Hoover, Herbert T. *The Chitimacha People.* Phoenix: Indian Tribal Series, 1975.

Historical survey begins with tribal origin myth and texts of other myths. Some data on ceremonialism.

1480. Swanton, John R. "Some Chitimacha Myths and Beliefs." *JAF,* 30 (1917), 474–78.

Five myth texts and some miscellaneous beliefs with comparative notes and commentary on cultural backgrounds.

See also 662, 1298, 1533.

J. Choctaw

1481. Baird, W. David. *The Choctaw People.* Phoenix: Indian Tribal Series, 1973.

Historical survey begins with tribal origin myth. Some data on ceremonialism.

1482. Benson, Henry C. *Life Among the Choctaw Indians and Sketches of the South-West.* Cincinnati: L. Swormstedt & A. Poe, 1860.

Written by a Methodist minister. Includes descriptions of the ball game and of Christian religious exercises among the Choctaw.

1483. Bounds, Thelma V. *Children of Nanih Waiya.* San Antonio: Naylor, 1964.

Describes ceremonialism and singing among Mississippi Choctaw.

1484. Bushnell, David I., Jr. *The Choctaw of Bayou Lacomb, St. Tammany Parish, Louisiana. BAEB* No. 48 (1909).

Ethnography based on fieldwork done in 1908–1909. Includes data on religious and ceremonial life, several song texts (words and music), and eleven myth and legend texts (in free translation only).

1485. ———. "Myths of the Louisiana Choctaw." *AA,* 12 (1910), 526–35.

Eleven narrative texts collected from a female informant in 1910. Sparse comparative commentary.

1486. Campbell, T. N. "The Choctaw Afterworld." *JAF,* 72 (1959), 146–54.

Prints an account of the group's afterworld obtained in the 1820s and compares it with other accounts to present a composite view of tribal eschatology.

1487. Conklin, Paul. *Choctaw Boy.* New York: Dodd, Mead, 1975.

Presents life of a contemporary Choctaw boy in Mississippi. Some attention to singing and dancing.

1488. Copeland, C. C. "A Choctaw Tradition." *TAES,* 3, Part 1 (1853), 167–71.

Text of a myth about the sun.

1489. Densmore, Frances. "Choctaw Music." *BAEB* No. 136 (*AP* No. 28), 1943.

Six song texts (all with music, some with words) collected in 1933. Includes musicological and contextual analyses which emphasize cross-cultural comparisons.

1490. Dundes, Alan. "A Choctaw Tongue-Twister and Two Examples of Creek Word Play." *IJAL,* 30 (1964), 194–96.

Analysis of verbal play collected from students at Haskell Institute in 1962.

1491. Glassie, Henry. "A Choctaw 'Me All Face' Story." *JAF,* 77 (1964), 258.

Reports an occurrence of a NA comic anecdote among Choctaw in Mississippi in 1812–1813.

1492. Halbert, H. S. "A Choctaw Migration Legend." *AAOJ,* 16 (1894), 215–16.

Legend summary with discussion of historical background.

1493. ———. "The Choctaw Robin Goodfellow." *AAOJ,* 17 (1895), 157.

Note on a fairy-like figure.

1494. "Journal of de Beauchamps' Journey to the Choctaws, 1746," in 140, pp. 259–97.

Includes description of a Choctaw oration.

1495. Lanman, Charles. "The Origin of the Choctaws." *MH,* 3 (January 1906), 40–41.

Unannotated myth text. No commentary.

1496. ———. "Peter Pitchlynn, Chief of the Choctaws." *AtM,* 25 (1870), 486–97.

Biography of Pitchlynn includes texts of several myths which Pitchlynn related to the author.

1497. Swanton, John R. "An Early Account of the Choctaw Indians." *MAAA,* 5 (1918), 53–72.

Presentation of an early eighteenth-century French account of Choctaw life. Includes descriptions of religious attitudes and ceremonialism.

1498. ———. *Source Material for the Social and Ceremonial Life of the Choctaw Indians.* BAEB No. 103 (1931).

Ethnography contains texts of creation myth, other myths, oration text, and descriptions of ceremonialism.

1499. Tubbee, Laah Ceil Manatoi Elaah. *A Sketch of the Life of Okah Tubbee, Alias, William Chubbee, Son of the Head Chief, Mosholeh Tubbee, of the Choctaw Nation of Indians.* Springfield, Mass.: H. S. Taylor, 1848.

Autobiographical narrative, recounted orally by a Choctaw raised in EA culture. Contains prayer texts and descriptions of ceremonialism among the Choctaw and other Southeast groups.

1500. Vickers, Ovid S. "Pacaritambo, Nanih Waiya and That Learning Pole." *MFR,* 7 (1973), 1–6.

Comparative treatment of creation and migration myths of the Choctaw with those of the Inca.

1501. Watkins, John A. "Legend of Cumberland Mountain." *AAOJ,* 15 (1893), 203–06.

Summary of myth with some data on historical background.

See also 758, 1298, 1310, 1364.

K. Creek

1502. Ata, Te. "Native American Thanksgiving." *NH,* 40 (1937), 677–79, 682.

Cross-cultural survey of NA harvest festivals focuses on Creek ceremonies, but includes text of a thanksgiving proclamation from the Iroquois Longhouse Religion.

1503. Bartram, William. "Observations on the Creek and Cherokee Indians." Ed. E. G. Squier. *TAES,* 3, Part 1 (1853), 1–81.

Edition of a ms. apparently written in 1789. Contains some data on Creek religious attitudes. Squier's notes add ceremonial descriptions.

1504. *Brief Account of the Establishment of the Colony of Georgia, Under Gen. James Oglethorpe, A, February 1, 1733.* Washington: Peter Force, 1835.

Contains text of an oration delivered by a Creek leader.

1505. Brinton, Daniel G. *The National Legend of the Chata-Muskokee Tribes.* Morrisania, N.Y.: NP, 1870.

Text of migration legend narrated in 1735. With extensive explanatory notes. Originally published in *The Historical Magazine* for February 1870.

1506. "Ceremony of the Creeks." *IW,* 3, No. 9 (15 December 1935), 46.

Description of the Green Corn Dance. Reprinted from the *Indian School Journal.*

1507. "Chat-ta-hoo-chee River Alabama." *TT,* 5, No. 3 (March 1903), 112–14.

Place-name legend.

1508. Corkran, David H. *The Creek Frontier 1540–1783.* Norman: Univ. of Oklahoma Press, 1967.

Historical account includes some data on ceremonialism and religion.

1509. "Creek Fable Writer." *TT,* 5, No. 7 (July 1903), 255–57.

Biographical sketch of Charles Gibson with a text of an animal fable rewritten by him.

1510. de Milford, Louis LeClerc. *Memoir, or A Cursory Glance at My Different Travels & My Sojourn in the Creek Nation.* Ed. John Francis McDermott. Trans. Geraldine de Courcy. Chicago: R. R. Donnelley, 1956.

Author recounts his travels in late eighteenth century and his service as a mercenary for the Creeks. Includes some description of ceremonialism.

1511. Gatschet, Albert S. *A Migration Legend of the Creek Indians, with a Linguistic, Historic and Ethnographic Introduction.* 2 volumes. Philadelphia: D. G. Brinton, 1884 (Library of Aboriginal American Literature No. 4).

Text and translation of a legend narrated in 1735 and preserved in pamphlet publication. Introduced by lengthy discussion of Creek culture, religion, mythology, and history.

1512. Gibson, Charles. "A Creek Indian Fable." *TT,* 4 (March 1902), 63–65.

Text of an animal tale.

1513. ———. "Why the Lion Eats His Meat Raw." *TT,* 5, No. 2 (February 1903), 61–62.

Text of an animal tale.

1514. Green, Michael D. *The Creeks. A Critical Bibliography.* Bloomington: Indiana Univ. Press, 1979.

Unannotated list of 216 books and articles. Introductory essay focuses on historiography, but has one section on ethnography.

1515. Hatfield, Dorothy Blackmon, and Eugene Current-Garcia. "William Orrie Tuggle and the Creek Indian Folk Tales." *SFQ,* 25 (1961), 238–55.

Evaluates the work of a little-known collector of Creek folklore.

1516. Hewitt, J. N. B. "Notes on the Creek Indians." Ed. John R. Swanton. *BAEB* No. 123 (*AP* No. 10), 1939.

Ethnographic notes recorded by Hewitt in 1880s. Includes data on religion and ceremonialism and two myth texts.

1517. "Journal of David Taitt's Travels from Pensacola, West Florida, to and Through the Country of the Upper and the Lower Creeks, 1772," in 140, pp. 493–565.

Includes brief description of Creek singing and dancing.

1518. Paredes, J. Anthony. "The Folk Culture of the Eastern Creek Indians: Synthesis and Change," in 135, pp. 93–111.

Reports the findings of an oral history project begun among the Creeks in 1971. Included are descriptions of social activities and singing.

1519. Piomingo, A Headman and Warrior of the Muscolgee Nation [John Robinson]. *The Savage.* Philadelphia: Thomas S. Manning, 1810.

Series of letters on philosophical and theological topics. Some very general remarks on NA theological concepts.

1520. "Pole Cat, or Shell Dance, The." *SLM,* 3 (1837), 390–91.

Describes ceremonial dance held by Creeks and Seminoles during westward exodus.

1521. Rands, Robert L. "Horned Serpent Stories." *JAF,* 67 (1954), 79–81.

Points out similarities between a Creek folktale collected by Swanton and a narrative from Nicaragua.

1522. "Ranger's Report of Travels with General Oglethorpe, A, 1739–1742," in 140, pp, 215–36.

Includes description of Creek ceremonial singing and dancing.

1523. Speck, Frank G. *Ceremonial Songs of the Creek and Yuchi Indians. APUPM,* 1, No. 2 (1911).

Forty-two Creek and seven Yuchi song texts (words and music). Includes musicological and contextual commentary.

1524. ———. "The Creek Indians of Taskigi Town." *MAAA,* 2 (1907–1915), 99–164.

Ethnography based on fieldwork done in 1904–1905. Contains data on shamanism and ceremonialism and seventeen myth and folktale texts with annotations.

1525. Swanton, John R. "Indian Recognition of Return Discharge in Lightning." *JAF,* 69 (1956), 46.

Note on a Creek informant's mythic explanation for lightning.

1526. ———. "Religious Beliefs and Medical Practices of the Creek Indians." *ARBAE,* 42 (1924–1925), 473–672.

Summarizes cosmology, supernaturalism, eschatology, and ceremonial observances. Includes texts of oratory and medicine songs in Creek with interlinear and free translations.

1527. ———. "Social Organization and Social Usages of the Indians of the Creek Confederacy." *ARBAE,* 42 (1924–1925), 23–472.

General ethnography includes summaries and paraphrases of creation myths and historical legends. Some context descriptions.

1528. Woodward, Thomas S. *Woodward's Reminiscences of the Creek, or Muscogee Indians, Contained in Letters to Friends in Georgia and Alabama.* Montgomery, Ala.: Barrett & Wimbish, 1859.

Series of letters written in 1857 and 1858 includes descriptions of Creek culture with some attention to oral performances such as oratory.

See also 1311, 1324, 1325, 1329, 1364, 1427, 1490.

L. Karankawa

1529. Gatschet, Albert S. "The Karankawa Indians, the Coast People of Texas." *AEPPM,* 1, No. 2 (1891), 1–167.

Historical and ethnographic work with sketchy data on religious attitudes and some song texts.

1530. Schaedel, Richard P. "The Karankawa of the Texas Gulf Coast." *SJA,* 5 (1949), 117–37.

Ethnography based on historical documents. Contains some data on music and ceremonialism.

M. Lumbee

1531. Barton, Lew. "Me-Told Tales Among the Lumbee." *NCF,* 19 (1971), 173–76.

Rewritten legend texts placed in fictionalized storytelling context.

N. Natchez

1532. Brinton, Daniel G. "The Taensa Grammar and Dictionary." *AAOJ,* 7 (1885), 108–13.

Corrections in translation of a song text which appeared in a Taensa grammar published in France.

1533. Haas, Mary R. "Natchez and Chitimacha Clans and Kinship Terminology." *AA,* 41 (1939), 597–610.

Includes references to clan origin myths and texts of Chitimacha legends about guardian spirits.

1534. Swanton, John R. "The Muskhogean Connection of the Natchez Language." *IJAL,* 3, No. 1 (1924–1925), 46–75.

Comparison of Natchez with Koasati begins with juxtaposition of texts of the same folktale in the two languages.

See also 1324, 1329, 1410.

O. Seminole

1535. Alvord, Benjamin. "The Morning Star—An Indian Superstition." *H,* 66 (1882–1883), 606–8.

Recounts 1841 incident in which a Seminole became ill because of malignant magic. Explanation of ailment involved star mythology.

1536. Capron, Louis. "Florida's 'Wild' Indians, the Seminole." *NG,* 110, No. 6 (December 1956), 819–40.

Cultural survey includes data on ceremonialism.

1537. ———. "The Medicine Bundles of the Florida Seminole and the Green Corn Dance." *BAEB* No. 151 (*AP* No. 35), 1953.

Describes ceremonies observed in 1950. With song texts (original and translations), myth texts, and data on prayers.

1538. Coe, Charles H. *Red Patriots. The Story of the Seminoles.* Cincinnati: Editor, 1898.

Historical work deals extensively with Osceola. Contains oration texts.

1539. Densmore, Frances. *Seminole Music. BAEB* No. 161 (1956).

243 song texts (most with music only), each with musicological and contextual analysis. Some general data on cultural background and musical comparisions with traditions of other NA groups. Eight myth texts appended. Collected in 1931–1934.

1540. ———. "Three Parallels Between the Seminole Indians and the Ancient Greeks." *M,* 25 (1951), 76–78.

The parallels are ecstatic dancing, using music to treat the sick, and a song text used to treat a sick infant.

1541. Dundes, Alan. "Washington Irving's Version of the Seminole Origin of Races." *Eh,* 9 (1962), 257–64.

Comparison of Irving's text (1840) with three others shows the Irving text to be distinctive and probably rewritten.

1542. Fairbanks, Charles H. *The Florida Seminole People.* Phoenix: Indian Tribal Series, 1973.

Historical survey includes some information on ceremonialism, especially dances.

1543. Freeman, Ethel Cutter. "Our Unique Indians, the Seminoles of Florida." *AIn,* 2, No. 2 (Winter 1944–1945), 14–28.

Cultural survey with data on ceremonialism.

1544. "Green Corn Dance Makes Start of New Year for Florida Seminole." *IW,* 7, No. 2 (October 1939), 26.

Description of a ceremony.

1545. Greenlee, Robert F. "Eventful Happenings Among the Modern Florida Seminoles." *SFQ,* 9 (1945), 145–52.

Brief survey of ceremonialism.

1546. ———. "Folktales of the Florida Seminole." *JAF,* 58 (1945), 138–44.

Texts and some commentary on materials collected in 1939.

1547. ———. "Medicine and Curing Practices of the Modern Florida Seminoles." *AA,* 46 (1944), 317–28.

Includes descriptions of curing rituals, texts of chants, and texts of etiological myths about specific illnesses.

1548. McCauley, Clay. "The Seminole Indians of Florida." *ARBAE,* 5 (1883–1884), 469–531.

Ethnographic survey includes data on music and ceremonialism.

1549. Miller, Winifred. "Seminoles of the Everglades." *SAM,* 48 (January 1949), 165–69, 10a.

Cultural survey with some data on singing and storytelling.

1550. Moore-Willson, Minnie. *The Seminoles of Florida.* Philadelphia: American Printing House, 1896.

Historical and cultural survey with sketchy data on music, ceremonialism, and religion.

1551. Munroe, Kirk. "A Forgotten Remnant." *Scr,* 7 (March 1890), 303–17.

Surveys Seminole culture. With some data on ceremonialism.

1552. Neill, Wilfred T. *The Story of Florida's Seminole Indians.* 2nd edition. St. Petersburg, Fla.: Great Outdoors, 1976.

Pamphlet covers various aspects of Seminole history and culture. With a chapter on songs and ceremonies.

1553. Peithmann, Irvin M. *The Unconquered Seminole Indians. Pictorial History of the Seminole Indians.* St. Petersburg, Fla.: Great Outdoors, 1957.

Potpourri of photographs and anecdotal narratives associated with Seminole culture and history. Includes sections on mythology, legends, and songs.

1554. Sturtevant, William C. "Seminole Myths of the Origin of the Races." *Eh,* 10 (1963), 80–86.

Adds some documentary data to Dundes' essay on the subject (1541).

See also 1298, 1364, 1520.

P. Tejas

1555. Castañeda, C. E. "Myths and Customs of the Tejas Indians," in 106, pp. 167–74.

Sketchy ethnographic survey based on seventeenth-century sources. Contains data on ceremonialism, but nothing on mythology.

1556. de Zavala, Adina. "Religious Beliefs of the Tejas or Hasanias Indians," in 164, pp. 39–43.

Survey of supernaturalism and ceremonialism taken from description of an eighteenth-century missionary. Reprinted in 78 (pp. 11–16).

1557. Hatcher, Mattie Austin. "Myths of the Tejas Indians," in 107, pp. 107–118.

Discusses myths, religious concepts, and ceremonialism. Based on missionaries' accounts from 1691 and 1720.

1558. Hilder, F. F. "A Texas Indian Myth." *AA,* 1 (1899), 592–94.

Text of a narrative translated from an unpublished ms. written by a Franciscan friar c. 1780.

Q. Tonkawa

1559. Hoijer, Harry. "Tonkawa, An Indian Language of Texas," in 87, pp. 1–148.

Contains myth text with free and interlinear translations and linguistic analysis.

1560. ———. *Tonkawa Texts. UCPL* No. 73 (1972).

Twenty-seven myth and folktale texts collected between 1928 and 1931. With literal translations and explanatory notes.

1561. Mooney, James. "Our Last Cannibal Tribe." *H,* 103 (1901), 550–55.

Discusses Tonkawa cannibalism, with some attention to ceremonial singing. Some treatment of stories about the Tonkawa in other NA cultures.

1562. Opler, Morris Edward. "A Description of a Tonkawa Peyote Meeting Held in 1902." *AA,* 41 (1939), 433–39.

Ritual description taken from the life history of a Chiricahua Apache. Collected in 1930s.

R. Tunica

1563.   Haas, Mary R. "The Solar Deity of the Tunica." *PMASAL,* 28 (1942), 531–35.
Presents and analyzes myth about the sun.
1564.   ———. "Tunica Texts." *UCPL,* 6, No. 1 (1950), 1–174.
Texts of myths, folktales, legends, personal narratives, and ethnographic descriptions collected 1933–1938. Presented with free translations, linguistic notes, and commentary on collecting situations and cultural background.
1565.   Swanton, John R. "The Tunica Language." *IJAL,* 2, Nos. 1 and 2 (1921–1923), 1–39.
Analysis of the language based on research done in 1880s and confirmed in early 1900s. Includes a legend text with interlinear and free translations and linguistic commentary.

S. Tuscarora

1566.   Graymont, Barbara. "The Tuscarora New Year Festival." *NYH,* 50 (1969), 143–63.
Historical and descriptive treatment of the ceremony.
1567.   Hewitt, J. N. B. "Iroquoian Mythologic Notes." *AA,* o. s. 3 (1890), 290–91.
Discussion of etymologies of names of myth heroes
1568.   Johnson, F. Roy. *The Tuscaroras: Mythology—Medicine—Culture.* Murfreesboro, N.C.: Johnson Publishing Company, 1967.
Contains several rewritten myth and folktale texts from previously published sources. Some data on cultural background.
1569.   Jones, Elma. "From the Tuscarora Reservation." *NYFQ,* 5 (1949), 133–45.
Five legend and folktale texts and two proverbs. Unannotated, but with some data on collecting situation.
1570.   Wallace, Anthony F. C. *The Modal Personality Structure of the Tuscarora Indians as Revealed by the Rorschach Test. BAEB* No. 150 (1952).
Determination of the group's Basic Personality Structure through psychological testing. Introductory ethnographic notes contain some data on mythological concepts as they existed in 1949.
1571.   ———, and William D. Reyburn. "Crossing the Ice: A Migration Legend of the Tuscarora Indians." *IJAL,* 17 (1951), 42–47.
Historical narrative collected in 1948 and 1950 from the same informant. Commentary places texts in historical and narrative traditions of the group. Includes interlinear translation of the 1950 version.

See also 972, 975, 1015, 1064, 1072, 1078, 1079, 1096, 1101, 1127, 1131, 1150.

T. Tutelo

1572.   Frachtenberg, Leo J. "Contributions to a Tutelo Vocabulary." *AA,* 15 (1913), 477–79.
Linguistic material collected in 1907 includes an untranslated song text.
1573.   Kurath, Gertrude P. "The Tutelo Fourth Night Release Singing." *MWF,* 4 (1954), 87–105.
Description of ceremonial as observed in 1952. With two song texts (untranslated words and music) and musicological analysis.
1574.   ———. "The Tutelo Harvest Rites: A Musical and Choreographic Analysis." *ScM,* 76 (March 1953), 153–62.
Thorough treatment of music and dance steps of the ritual.
1575.   Speck, Frank G., and George Herzog. *The Tutelo Spirit Adoption Ceremony.* Harrisburg: Pennsylvania Historical Commission, 1942.
Contains two essays: Speck's "The Tutelo Reclothing and Spirit Adoption Ceremony" describes the ritual as it occurred in 1938–1939; Herzog's "Transcriptions and Analysis of Tutelo Music" includes twenty-seven texts (music only) with musicological analysis.

U. Yuchi

1576.   Gatschet, Albert S. "Some Mythic Stories of the Yuchi Indians." *AA,* o. s. 6 (1893), 279–82.
Four unannotated myth texts. Some content commentary.
1577.   Speck, Frank G. *Ethnology of the Yuchi Indians. APUPM,* 1, No. 1 (1909).
Based on fieldwork done in 1904, 1905, and 1908. Contains data on ceremonialism and sixteen translated myth texts.
1578.   Wagner, Günter. "Yuchi," in 87, pp. 289–384.
Contains creation myth text with free and interlinear translations and linguistic analysis.
1579.   ———. *Yuchi Tales. PAES* No. 13 (1931).
Texts of myths, legends, folktales, and a life history collected in 1928–1929. With free and literal translations and linguistic analyses.
1580.   Wolff, Hans. "Yuchi Text with Analysis." *IJAL,* 17 (1951), 48–53.
Legend text collected in 1947. With free translation and linguistic analysis.

See also 1311, 1523.

IV MIDWEST

A. General Works

1581. Atkeson, Mary Meeks. *A Study of the Local Literature of the Upper Ohio Valley, with Especial Reference to the Early Pioneer and Indian Tales, 1820–1840.* Columbus: Ohio State Univ., 1921 (Contributions in English No. 2).
Contains some NA folktales and legends as reported by EA settlers on the Ohio Valley frontier.

1582. Atwater, Caleb. "Eloquence of the North American Indians." *MAH,* 5 (1880), 211–14.
Discusses oratorical abilities of speakers from various NA groups in Midwest. Written in 1846 and "communicated" to MAH by John Russell Bartlett.

1583. Beckwith, Hiram W., ed. *The Fort-Wayne Manuscript: An Old Writing (Lately Found) Containing Indian Speeches and a Treatise on the Western Indians.* Chicago: Fergus, 1883.
Contains texts of orations delivered in 1811. Also some data on religious ideas and ceremonialism.

1584. ———. *The Illinois and Indiana Indians.* Chicago: Fergus, 1884.
Brief descriptions of Illinois, Miami, Kickapoo, Winnebago, Fox, Sauk, and Potawatomi. Primarily historical, but includes some data on ceremonialism.

1585. Brown, Charles E. "Myths, Legends, and Superstitions About Copper." *WA,* n. s. 20, No. 2 (1939), 35–40.
Not available for examination.

1586. Brown, Dorothy M. "Fire Myths and Legends." *WA,* n. s. 19, No. 4 (1939), 84–90.
Not available for examination.

1587. ———. "Indian Lover's Leap in Wisconsin." *WA,* n. s. 17, No. 4 (1937), 84–87.
Not available for examination.

1588. ———. "Indian Tree Myths and Legends." *WA,* n. s. 19, No. 2 (1938), 30–36.
Not available for examination.

1589. ———. "Indian Winter Legends." *WA,* n. s. 22, No. 4 (1941), 49–53.
Not available for examination.

1590. ———. "Legends of the Wisconsin Hills." *WA,* n. s. 18, No. 1 (1937), 17–24.
Not available for examination.

1591. ———. "Rain Legends and Beliefs." *WA,* n. s. 24, No. 2 (1943), 27–31.
Not available for examination.

1592. ———. "Wisconsin Indian Cave Legends." *WA,* n. s. 18, No. 2 (1938), 59–62.
Not available for examination.

1593. Bubbert, Walter. "Some Indian Myths About Iron." *WA,* n. s. 22, No. 2 (1941), 9–11.
Not available for examination.

1594. Bushnell, David I., Jr. *Burials of the Algonquian, Siouan, and Caddoan Tribes West of the Mississippi. BAEB* No. 83 (1927).
Tribe-by-tribe survey of funeral customs of Midwest and Plains groups.

1595. Chamberlain, Alexander F. "Nanibozhu Amongst the Otchipwe, Mississagas, and Other Algonkian Tribes." *JAF,* 4 (1891), 193–213.
Survey of myth cycles about the culture hero among various Midwest groups.

1596. ———. "The Thunder-Bird Amongst the Algonkins." *AA,* o.s. 3 (1890), 51–54.
Surveys mythic beliefs about the Thunderbird among groups in the Midwest, Northeast, Northwest Coast, and Sub-Arctic.

1597. Colton, C. *Tour of the American Lakes, and Among the Indians of the North-West Territory, in 1830: Disclosing the Character and Prospects of the Indian Race.* 2 volumes. London: Frederick Westley and A. H. Davis, 1833.
Travel account of a trip to the Great Lakes region includes descriptions of ceremonialism and oration texts from several Midwest groups.

1598. Dixon, Roland B. "The Mythology of the Central and Eastern Algonkins." *JAF,* 22 (1909), 1–9.
Cross-cultural survey of common elements in the mythologies of linguistically-related groups in the Midwest and Northeast.

1599. English, Tom. "The Piasa Petroglyph: The Devourer from the Bluffs." *A&A,* 14 (September 1922), 151–56.
Surveys Midwest oral traditions about a monstrous bird.

1600. Faben, Walter W. "Listen for the Thunderers." *NOQ,* 35, No. 4 (Autumn 1963), 164–71; 36, No. 2 (Spring 1964), 99–112.
Historical work on Maumee River Valley. Includes some data on NA inhabitants: ceremonialism, religion, the Thunderbird concept, and oral traditions.

1601. Finley, James B. *Life Among the Indians; or, Personal Reminiscences and Historical Incidents . . . . . . Illustrative of Indian Life and Character.* Cincinnati: Curtis & Jennings, ND.
Contains texts of orations by Tecumseh.

1602. Frazier, Paul. "An Indian Love Ritual of Southeast Missouri." *MWF,* 7, No. 1 (Spring 1957), 25–26.
Unannotated legend text from an unspecified Midwest group about NA courtship.

1603. Fulton, A. R. *The Red Men of Iowa: Being a History of the Various Aboriginal Tribes Whose Homes Were in Iowa; Sketches of Chiefs, Traditions, Indian Hostilities, Incidents and Reminiscences with a General Account of the Indians and Indian Wars of the Northwest; and Also an Appendix Relating to the Pontiac War.* Des Moines: Mills, 1882.
Historical work contains data on religious beliefs, ceremonialism, and oratory among the Iowa, Winnebago, Sauk, Fox, Potawatomi, and Sioux.

1604. Hall, Robert L. "Ghosts, Water Barriers, Corn, and Sacred Enclosures in the Eastern Woodlands." *AAn,* 41 (1976), 360–64.

Interprets prehistoric enclosures in eastern United States as having supernatural significance. View based, in part, on mythology from Midwest and Northeast groups.

1605. Helbig, Alethea K. "Manabozho: Trickster, Guide, and *Alter Ego.*" *MA,* 7 (1975), 357–71.

Survey of the nature of the culture hero and trickster of various Midwest groups.

1606. Hickerson, Harold. "The Feast of the Dead Among the Seventeenth Century Algonkians of the Upper Great Lakes." *AA,* 62 (1960), 81–107.

Describes ceremonial and its history. Traces adoption from Huron into various Midwest cultures, especially Ojibwa. Response by Victor Barnouw in *AA,* 63 (1961), 1006–13.

1607. Houghton, Louise Seymour. *Our Debt to the Red Man: The French-Indians in the Development of the United States.* Boston: Stratford, 1918.

Considers the work of NAs from Midwest and Northeast groups in collecting oral literature and studying ethnography.

1608. Hultkrantz, Åke. *Prairie and Plains Indians.* Leiden: E. J. Brill, 1973 (Iconography of Religions, 10, No. 2).

Presents photographs and drawings of ceremonial behavior with lengthy introduction treating major rituals such as the Sun Dance.

1609. "Indian Folktales." *WA,* n. s. 7 (1928), 223–30.

Five unannotated folktale and myth texts from various Midwest groups: Winnebago (two), Potawatomi, Ojibwa (two).

1610. Jenks, Abert Ernest. "The Wild Rice Gatherers of the Upper Lakes: A Study in American Primitive Economics." *ARBAE,* 19 (1897–1898), 1013–1137.

Economic study of rice-harvesting among Midwest and some Northeast groups includes some data on references to rice in myths.

1611. Jones, William. "The Algonkin Manitou." *JAF,* 18 (1905), 183–90.

Discusses beliefs and rituals associated with the high god among the Fox, Sauk, and Kickapoo.

1612. Judson, Katharine Berry, ed. *Myths and Legends of the Mississippi Valley and the Great Lakes.* Chicago: A. C. McClurg, 1914.

Rewritten texts of narratives from Midwest and Southeast groups. No commentary or annotation.

1613. Kane, Grace Franks. *Myths and Legends of the Mackinacs and the Lake Region.* Cincinnati: Editor, 1897.

Twenty-two rewritten myth and legend texts and two descriptions of ceremonials. From various Midwest groups. No commentary or annotation.

1614. Kubiak, William J. *Great Lakes Indians. A Pictorial Guide.* New York: Bonanza, 1970.

General discussion of Midwest and Northeast groups, followed by tribe-by-tribe treatment. Some data on ceremonialism and oral traditions.

1615. Kurath, Gertrude Prokosch. *Michigan Indian Festivals.* Ann Arbor: Ann Arbor Publishers, 1966.

Surveys festival behavior among various NA groups in Michigan. Includes descriptions of traditional and contemporary religious systems and song texts (words and music).

1616. Makarius, Laura. "The Crime of Manabozo." *AA,* 75 (1973), 663–75.

Sees Trickster as the projection of the magical

violation of taboos. Also connects the figure as relating to traditions of ritual murder.

1617. McClintock, Walter. "The Thunderbird Myth." *M,* 15 (1941), 164–68, 224–27; 16 (1942), 16–18.

Text excerpts and ritual descriptions relating to the Thunderbird figure among Midwest and Northeast groups.

1618. Michelson, Truman. "On the Origin of the So-Called Dream Dance of the Central Algonkians." *AA,* 25 (1923), 277–78.

Argues that the origin myth of the ritual is verifiable history. Resulted in an interchange with Alanson Skinner: Skinner in *AA* 25, (1923), 427–28; Michelson in *AA,* 26 (1924), 293–94; Skinner in *AA,* 27 (1925), 340–43; and Michelson in *AA,* 28 (1926), 566–70.

1619. Peithmann, Irvin M. *Echoes of the Red Man: An Archaeological and Cultural Survey of the Indians of Southern Illinois.* New York: Exposition, 1955.

Poorly conceived attempt at a cultural survey includes sections on mythology, legends, and religion.

1620. Pierce, Joe B. "Dialect Distance Testing in Algonquian." *IJAL,* 18 (1952), 203–10.

Tests intelligibility among linguistically-related dialects (Shawnee, Kickapoo, Ojibwa, and Sauk-Fox) by having informants record and listen to narratives.

1621. Pruitt, O. J. "Some Iowa Indian Tales." *AnI,* 3rd series, 32, No. 3 (January 1954), 203–16.

Miscellany of anecdotes, mostly about various Midwest groups. Some seem to be of NA origin.

1622. Quimby, George Irving. *Indian Life in the Upper Great Lakes, 11,000 B.C. to A.D. 1800.* Chicago: Univ. of Chicago Press, 1960.

Primarily archeological, but sections on specific tribes include data on supernaturalism and ceremonialism.

1623. Ritzenthaler, Robert E. "Woodland Sculpture." *AIAM,* 1 August 1976, pp. 34–41.

Survey of woodworking in the Midwest includes sections on ceremonial uses of wooden objects. Some data on supernaturalism.

1624. Schoolcraft, Henry R. *The Indian in His Wigwam, or Characteristics of the Red Race of America.* Buffalo: Derby & Hewson, 1848.

Miscellany of Schoolcraft's writings includes discussions of mythology and singing. Includes texts from Midwest and Northeast groups.

1625. ———. *Narrative Journal of Travels from Detroit Northwest Through the Great Chain of American Lakes to the Sources of the Mississippi River in the Year 1820.* Albany: E & E. Hosford, 1821.

Includes some descriptions of the ceremonies of various Midwest groups.

1626. ———. *Narrative of an Expedition Through the Upper Mississippi to Itasca Lake, the Actual Source of This River; Embracing an Exploratory Trip Through the St. Croix and Burntwood (or Broule) Rivers: In 1832.* New York: Harper, 1834.

Describes religious beliefs and oratory of Midwest groups. One myth text included.

1627. ———. *Oneóta, or Characteristics of the Red Race of America.* New York: Wiley & Putnam, 1845.

Texts of myths, legends, and songs interspersed with essays treating various aspects of the cultures of Midwest and Northeast groups.

1628. ———. *Personal Memoirs of a Residence of Thirty Years with the Indian Tribes of the American Frontiers: with Brief Notices of Passing Events, Facts, and Opinions, A.D. 1812 to A.D. 1842.* Philadelphia: Lippincott, Grambo, 1851.

Journalistic treatment of experiences in the Old Northwest. Includes discussions of oral narratives, oratory, and ceremonialism among various Midwest groups (especially the Ojibwa, Winnebago, Sauk, and Fox).

1629. Skinner, Alanson. *Medicine Ceremony of the Menomini, Iowa, and Wahpeton Dakota, with Notes on the Ceremony Among the Ponca, Bungi Ojibwa, and Potawatomi. IN&M* No. 4 (1920).

Includes ceremonial description for each group with texts of ritual origin myths and songs.

1630. "Some Aspects of the Folk-Lore of the Central Algonkin." *JAF,* 27 (1914), 97–100.

List and brief discussion of recurrent elements in folklore of linguistically-related groups in the Midwest and Sub-Arctic.

1631. Stevens, Sylvester K., Donald H. Kent, and Emma Edith Woods, eds. *Travels in New France by J. C. B.* Harrisburg: Pennsylvania Historical Commission, 1941.

Travel book originally published in French in 1887 and based on a ms. describing a visit to New France from 1751 to 1761. Includes descriptions of ceremonialism and oratory from groups in the Midwest, Northeast, and Plains.

1632. Swanton, John R. "Siouan Tribes and the Ohio Valley." *AA,* 45 (1943), 49–66.

Surveys evidence for Siouan habitation of Ohio Valley. Considers legends and other verbal traditions of Midwest groups.

1633. Swift, Ivan. "Indian Legend of the Deluge." *MHM,* 23 (1939), 217–19.

Unannotated myth text from an unspecified group. No commentary.

1634. Unrau, William E. *The Emigrant Indians of Kansas. A Critical Bibliography.* Bloomington: Indiana Univ. Press, 1979.

Unannotated list of 187 books and articles dealing with transplanted Midwest and Northeast groups. Introductory essay focuses on historiography.

1635. Walker, Louise J. "Indian Camp Meeting at Greensky Hill." *JAF,* 63 (1950), 96–97.

Describes religious exercises held by Christianized NAs near Charlevoix, Michigan.

1636. ———. "Indian Feast of the Dead." *JAF,* 62 (1949), 428.

Describes NA observance of All Saints' and All Souls' days in Michigan.

1637. Whiteford, Andrew Hunter. "Fiber Bags of the Great Lakes Indians." *AIAM,* 1 May 1977, pp. 52–63.

Discusses use of two mythical beings, Thunderbird and Panther, as designs.

1638. Willoughby, Charles C. "Michabo the Great Hare: A Patron of the Hopewell Mound Settlement." *AA,* 37 (1935), 280–86.

Reports occurrences of reproductions of the culture hero in an archeological site in Ohio.

See also 30, 393, 831, 832, 843, 851, 852, 853, 855, 857, 971, 1988, 1990, 1996, 2002, 2022, 2046, 2063, 5092, 5099, 5102, 5113, 5116, 5119, 5123.

B. Fox

1639. Fugle, Eugene. "Mesquakie Witchcraft Lore." *PIA,* 6, No. 11 (February 1961), 31–39.

Suggests that witchlore functions as covert aggression.

1640. Gearing, Frederick O. *The Face of the Fox.* Chicago: Aldine, 1970.

Ethnographic treatment of one Fox community contains data on ceremonialism.

1641. Harrington, Mark Raymond. *Sacred Bundles of the Sac and Fox Indians. APUPM,* 4, No. 1 (1914).

Contains ritual origin myths and ceremonial descriptions.

1642. Jones, William. "Episodes in the Culture-Hero Myth of the Sauks and Foxes." *JAF,* 14 (1901), 225–39.

Multi-episodic text of a hero myth. With some explanatory notes and data on the storytelling situation.

1643. ———. *Ethnography of the Fox Indians.* Ed. Margaret Welpley Fisher. *BAEB* No. 125 (1939).

Ethnographic notes based on Jones's work at the turn of the century. Includes descriptions of ceremonialism and nine myth texts with comparative notes.

1644. ———. "Fox Indian Manitous." *WA,* n. s. 20, No. 3 (1939), 57–61.

Not available for examination.

1645. ———. *Fox Texts. PAES* No. 1 (1907).

140 legend texts, twenty-nine myth texts, twelve parable texts, four prayer texts. All presented with free translations. Collected in 1901–1902. No annotation or commentary.

1646. ———. "Notes on the Fox Indians." *JAF,* 24 (1911), 209–37.

Ethnographic survey includes myth and legend texts and descriptions of ceremonials. No annotations.

1647. Kurath, Gertrude P. "Meskwaki Powwow." *Ams,* 8, No. 5 (May 1956), 28–31.

Describes assimilation by the Fox of ceremonialism from other groups as revealed at an annual intertribal festival held in Iowa.

1648. Lasley, Mary (Bee-Wah-Thee-Wah). "Sac and Fox Tales." *JAF,* 15 (1902), 170–78.

Seven unannotated myth and folktale texts. No commentary.

1649. Lomax, Alan. "Song Structure and Social Structure." *Eth,* 1 (1962), 425–51.

Cross-cultural demonstration of the cantometric system for relating singing style to other cultural factors includes the Fox as a sample group.

1650. Michelson, Truman. "The Autobiography of a Fox Indian Woman." *ARBAE,* 40 (1918–1919), 291–349.

Life history originally written in the syllabary is presented in phonetic Fox and free translation. Some data on social contexts for verbal performances. With ethnographic and linguistic notes.

1651. ———. *Contributions to Fox Ethnology. BAEB* No. 85 (1927).

Four sections: "Notes on the Ceremonial Runners of the Fox Indians"; "A Sauk and Fox Sacred Pack"; "A Sacred Pack Called A'penäwänä'a Belonging to the Thunder Gens of the Fox Indians"; and "A Sacred Pack Called Sāgimā'kwäwa Belonging to the Bear Gens of the Fox Indians." All material originally written in the syllabary. First two pieces presented in phonetic Fox with translations; last two are in translations only. Ceremonial descriptions include some song texts.

1652. ———. *Contributions to Fox Ethnology—II. BAEB* No. 95 (1930).

Two sections: "A Sketch of the Buffalo Dance of the Bear Gens of the Fox Indians" and "Notes on the Great Sacred Pack of the Thunder Gens of the Fox Indians." Both originally recorded in the syllabary and presented in phonetic Fox and free translation. Contains myth and song texts and ceremonial descriptions. Some linguistic commentary.

1653. ———. *Fox Miscellany. BAEB* No. 114 (1937).

General data on various aspects of Fox ethnography include ritual descriptions, myth texts, and song texts. Most material written in the syllabary and presented in phonetic Fox with free translations. Some commentary on informants and linguistics.

1654. ———. "The Mythical Origin of the White Buffalo Dance of the Fox Indians Together with Texts of Four Minor Sacred Packs Appertaining to This Ceremony." *ARBAE,* 40 (1918–1919), 23–289.

Texts written in syllabary and presented in phonetic Fox and free translations. Includes myth and song texts and descriptions of ceremonials. Some commentary on cultural significance of the material and linguistics.

1655. ———. "Notes on Fox Mortuary Customs and Beliefs." *ARBAE,* 40 (1918–1919), 351–496.

Narrative texts and ethnographic data written in the syllabary and presented in phonetic Fox and free translations. Introduction presents ethnographic data on funeral customs. Appendix includes linguistic analysis.

1656. ———. *Notes on the Buffalo-Head Dance of the Thunder Gens of the Fox Indians. BAEB* No. 87 (1928).

Contains ceremonial description and ritual origin myth texts in Fox and free translation. With ethnographic and linguistic commentary. All material originally recorded in the syllabary.

1657. ———. "Notes on the Fox Society Known as Those Who Worship the Little Spotted Buffalo." *ARBAE,* 40 (1918–1919), 497–539.

Myth and ceremonial description originally recorded in the syllabary and presented in phonetic Fox and free translations.

1658. ———. *Notes on the Fox Wâpanŏwiweni. BAEB* No. 105 (1932).

Four versions of a ritual, each written in the syllabary and presented in phonetic Fox and free translations. With linguistic commentary and numerous song texts.

1659. ———. *Observations on the Thunder Dance of the Bear Gens of the Fox Indians. BAEB* No. 89 (1929).

Two accounts of the ceremony recorded in the syllabary and presented in phonetic Fox and free translations. With ritual origin myth, songs, and orations. Includes linguistic commentary.

1660. ———. *The Owl Sacred Pack of the Fox Indians. BAEB* No. 72 (1921).

Ritual description written in the syllabary and presented in phonetic Fox and free translation. Includes song texts. Sparse commentary.

1661. ———. "Ritualistic Origin Myths of the Fox Indians." *JWAS,* 6 (1916), 209–11.

Brief summaries of ritual origin myths.

1662. ———. "The Traditional Origin of the Fox Soci-

ety Known as 'The Singing Around Rite.' " *ARBAE,* 40 (1918–1919), 541–615.

Ritual origin myth originally written in the syllabary and presented in phonetic Fox and free translation.

1663. ———. "What Happened to Green Bear Who Was Blessed with a Sacred Pack." *BAEB* No. 119 (*AP* No. 4), 1938.

Ritual origin myth freely translated from syllabary text.

1664. Miller, Walter B. "Two Concepts of Authority." *AA,* 57 (1955), 271–89.

Examines concepts of power in Fox and other Midwest folklore. Explains NA resistance to vertical system of authority imposed by EA missionaries.

1665. Owen, Mary Alicia. *Folk-Lore of the Musquakie Indians of North America and Catalogue of Musquakie Beadwork and Other Objects in the Collection of the Folk-Lore Society.* London: David Nutt, 1904 (Publications of the Folk-Lore Society No. 51).

Collection includes creation myth, legendary history, and a number of folktale texts. All material highly embellished. Also, some data on ceremonialism.

1666. ———. "Tree Stories." *FL,* 1 (1893), 101–5.

Three folktales collected from a Black storyteller of Fox ancestry.

1667. Steward, John F. *Lost Maramech and Earliest Chicago: A History of the Foxes and of Their Downfall near the Great Village of Maramech. Original Investigations and Discoveries.* Chicago: Fleming H. Revell, 1903.

Historical work includes a rewritten myth text.

1668. Zielinski, John M. *Mesquakie and Proud of It.* Kalona, Iowa: Photo-Art, 1976.

Surveys contemporary and traditional cultures, emphasizing the persistence of the latter. Includes some data on ceremonials, song texts, oratory, and prayers.

See also 3, 1584, 1603, 1611, 1620, 1628, 2276.

C. Illinois

1669. Armstrong, P. A. *The Piasa, or, The Devil Among the Indians.* Morris, Ill.: E. B. Fletcher, 1887.

Pamphlet connects accounts of a monster depicted in Upper Mississippi Valley rock art with Biblical depictions of Satan. Includes Illinois and Miami oral traditions of the monster.

1670. McAdams, Wm. *Records of Ancient Races in the Mississippi Valley; Being an Account of Some of the Pictographs, Sculptured Hieroglyphs, Symbolic Devices, Emblems and Traditions of the Prehistoric Races of America, with Some Suggestions as to Their Origin.* St. Louis: C. R. Barns, 1887.

Considers traditions of the Piasa among the Illinois. Discounts value of oral traditions in clarifying archaeological data.

1671. Strong, William Duncan. *The Indian Tribes of the Chicago Region with Special Reference to the Illinois and the Potawatomi. FMNH-DAL* No. 24 (1926).

Brief surveys of Illinois, Potawatomi, and Miami cultures with some attention to ceremonialism.

See also 1584, 1912.

D. Kickapoo

1672. Hoad, Louise Green. *Kickapoo Indian Trails.* Caldwell, Ida.: Caxton, 1944.

Record of mother's experience as a missionary to the Kickapoo, beginning in 1858. Contains descriptions of mortuary customs and corn ceremonialism.

1673. Jones, William. *Kickapoo Tales.* Ed. Truman Michelson. *PAES* No. 9 (1915).

Eleven myth and folktale texts collected in 1903 and presented in free translations. Some linguistic and comparative commentary.

1674. Marriott, Alice L. "Dancing Makes Rain," in 92, pp. 88–93.

Description of a Rain Dance held in 1933.

1675. Nielsen, George R. *The Kickapoo Tribe.* Phoenix: Indian Tribal Series, 1975.

Tribal history includes data on ceremonialism.

1676. Peterson, Frederick A., and Robert E. Ritzenthaler. "The Kickapoos Are Still Kicking." *NH,* 64 (1955), 200–206, 224.

Description of contemporary Kickapoo living in Mexico. Includes data on belief system and ceremonial cycle.

1677. Wallace, Ben J. "The Oklahoma Kickapoo: An Ethnographic Reconstruction." *WA,* n. s. 45 (1964), 1–69.

Ethnographic survey includes data on religious beliefs, theology, ceremonialism, and shamanism.

See also 1584, 1611, 1620.

E. Menomini

1678. Atanoqken, Inaqtik, Johan G. R. Baner, and John I. Bellaire. *Medicine-Water: Menominee and Chippeway Indian Legends and Myths.* NP: NP, 1933.

Pamphlet contains a miscellany of materials on the two cultures. With myth and legend texts.

1679. Bloomfield, Leonard. *Menomini Texts. PAES* No. 12 (1928).

Texts of myths, folktales, prayers, and songs (122). Collected in 1920–1921 and presented with free translations. No commentary or annotations.

1680. Curtis, Martha E. "The Black Bear and White-Tailed Deer as Potent Factors in the Folklore of the Menomini Indians." *MWF,* 2 (1952), 177–90.

Thorough survey of the animals' roles in myths and ceremonials.

1681. ———. "Folklore of Feast and Famine Among the Menomini." *PMASAL,* 39 (1954), 407–19.

Analysis of oral narratives for references to food and eating.

1682. Densmore, Frances. *Menominee Music. BAEB* No. 102 (1932).

Song texts (140 – words and music) collected in 1925, 1928, and 1929. Each text accompanied by musicological and contextual analyses. Introduction provides culture background and compares music with that of other NA groups. Some myth texts appear in contextual analyses of particular songs.

1683. Hoffman, Walter James. "The Menomini Indians." *ARBAE,* 14 (1892–1893), 3–328.

Ethnography based on fieldwork done in 1890. Includes descriptions of ceremonials, games, and dances and twenty-six oral narrative texts.

1684. ———. "Mythology of the Menomoni Indians." *AA,* o. s. 3 (1890), 243–58.

Seven unannotated myth texts. Includes discussion of tribal totemic system.

1685. Keesing, Felix M. "The Menomini Indians of Wisconsin: A Study of Three Centuries of Cultural Contact and Change." *MAPS,* 10 (1939), 1–261.

Study of culture change includes references to mythology and ceremonialism drawn from historical records.

1686. Kurath, Gertrude P. "Menomini Indian Dance Songs in a Changing Culture." *MWF,* 9, No. 1 (Spring 1959), 31–38.

Treats developments in musical traditions in response to acculturation.

1687. Michelson, Truman. "Menominee Tales." *AA,* 13 (1911), 68–88.

Three narrative texts collected in 1910. Some explanatory notes.

1688. ———. "The Menomini Hairy Serpent and the Hairy Fish." *JAF,* 48 (1935), 197–99.

Examination of the etymology of the name of the group's water monster.

1689. "Mythology of the Menominees." *AAOJ,* 31 (1909), 10–14.

Summary of mythological system.

1690. Skinner, Alanson. "Associations and Ceremonies of the Menomini Indians." *APAMNH,* 13 (1915), 167–215.

Description of ceremonial organizations and rituals. Includes some oration and song texts.

1691. ———. "A Comparative Sketch of the Menomini." *AA,* 13 (1911), 551–65.

Devotes sections to religion (with ceremonialism) and folklore in a treatment of the group's relation to adjacent cultures.

1692. ———. "European Folk-Tales Collected Among the Menominee Indians." *JAF,* 26 (1913), 64–80.

Three unannotated texts. No commentary.

1693. ———. *Material Culture of the Menomini. IN&M,* Miscellaneous Series No. 20 (1921).

Ethnographic survey with emphasis on material aspects of culture. Includes summaries of myths and descriptions of ceremonials.

1694. ———. "The Menomini Game of Lacrosse." *AMJ,* 11 (1911), 138–41.

Description of ceremonial game observed in 1910. Includes text of Thunderbird myth.

1695. ———. "The Menomini Word 'Häwätûk.'" *JAF,* 28 (1915), 258–61.

Discusses word associated with supernatural power. Illustrates with materials from mythology.

1696. ———. "Social Life and Ceremonial Bundles of the Menomini Indians." *APAMNH,* 13 (1915), 1–165.

Ethnographic data include descriptions of games and ceremonialism with related song texts. Some attention to tribal cosmology.

1697. ———. "Songs of the Menomini Medicine Ceremony." *AA,* 27 (1925), 290–314.

Context description of songs of the Midewin Ceremony as observed in 1919. Includes forty-four song texts with translations.

1698. ———. "War Customs of the Menomini Indians." *AA,* 13 (1911), 299–312.

Includes text of myth which validates war customs and several song texts.

1699. ———, and John V. Satterlee. "Folklore of the Menomini Indians." *APAMNH,* 13 (1915), 217–557.

English texts and abstracts of 134 myths, folktales, and legends collected in 1910–1914. Introduction treats content, function, and performance of the narratives. Comparative notes accompany the abstracts.

1700. Slotkin, J. S. "An Intertribal Dancing Contest." *JAF,* 68 (1955), 224–28.

Describes contest conducted by the Menomini in 1954. Treats adaptations of dance songs among various groups.

1701. ———. "Menomini Peyotism. A Study of Individual Variation in a Primary Group with a Homogeneous Culture." *TAPS,* n. s. 42, Part 4 (1952), 567–700.

History of peyotism with some attention to ritual procedure and dogma. Appendix by David P. McAllester contains transcriptions of twenty-four songs (words and music).

1702. Spindler, Louise S. "Witchcraft in Menomini Acculturation." *AA,* 54 (1952), 593–602.

Reports legends and personal narratives in a survey of the interrelationship between witchcraft and the degree of acculturation among sub-groups of the Menomini.

See also 1629, 1723, 1755, 1906.

F. Miami

1703. Baker, Jessie E. "Piankishaw Tales." *JAF,* 44 (1931), 182–90.

Seven unannotated myth texts. No commentary.

1704. Kinietz, Vernon, ed. *Meẽarmeear Traditions by C. C. Trowbridge. OCMAUM* No. 7 (1938).

Presents a ms. written 1824–1825 which includes myth and folktale texts and descriptions of ceremonialism. Data apparently gathered through questionnaires.

1705. Schorer, C. E. "Indian Tales of C. C. Trowbridge: The Bad Man." *SFQ,* 36 (1972), 160–75.

Text of an Orpheus-like narrative collected by Trowbridge in 1820s. Introduction deals with content explication and comparative matters.

1706. ———. "Indian Tales of C. C. Trowbridge: The Fisherman." *SFQ,* 38 (1974), 63–71.

Text of a revenge story collected by Trowbridge in 1820s. Comparative and explanatory notes in introduction.

1707. ———. "Indian Tales of C. C. Trowbridge: The Gambler." *MWF,* 13, No. 4 (Winter 1963–1964), 229–35.

Narrative text collected by Trowbridge in Detroit in 1820s. Presented with thorough comparative discussion.

1708. ———. "Indian Tales of C. C. Trowbridge: The Giants." *SFQ,* 31 (1967), 236–43.

Text of a narrative concerning the picaresque adventures of a youthful hero. Collected by Trowbridge in 1820s. With introductory commentary.

1709. ———. "Indian Tales of C. C. Trowbridge: The Man Eater Spirit." *SFQ,* 29 (1965), 309–18.

Text with comparative notes of a folktale collected in the 1820s by Trowbridge.

1710. ———. "Indian Tales of C. C. Trowbridge: The Ornamented Head." *SFQ,* 33 (1969), 317–32.

Text of a maturation narrative collected by Trowbridge in the 1820s. With comparative discussion.

1711. ———. "Indian Tales of C. C. Trowbridge: The Red Head." *MWF,* 10, No. 2 (Summer 1960), 86–95.

Folktale text collected by Trowbridge in 1820s. With comparative discussion.

1712. ———. "Indian Tales of C. C. Trowbridge: The Star Woman." *MWF,* 12, No. 1 (Spring 1962), 17–24.

Folktale text collected by Trowbridge in 1820s. With comparative discussion.

1713. ———. "Indian Tales of C. C. Trowbridge: A Story." *SFQ,* 38 (1974), 233–41.

Text of a tale of love and rejection collected by Trowbridge in 1820s. With comparative discussion.

1714. ———. "Indian Tales of C. C. Trowbridge: Thrown Away." *SFQ,* 34 (1970), 341–52.

Text collected by Trowbridge in 1820s of a narrative about an abandoned youth who returns to his people. With comparative discussion.

1715. ———. "Indian Tales of C. C. Trowbridge: The Toadstool Man." *MWF,* 9, No. 3 (Fall 1959), 139–44.

Folktale text collected in 1820s by Trowbridge. With comparative discussion.

1716. Smith, G. Hubert. "Three Miami Tales." *JAF,* 52 (1939), 194–208.

Texts of stories collected by John Dunne and originally published in the *Transactions of the Royal Irish Academy* for 1803.

1717. Wells, William. "Indian Manners and Customs." *WR&MM,* 2 (1820), 45–49, 110–12, 160–93.

Cultural description includes data on ceremonialism.

See also 259, 1584, 1669, 1671, 1912.

G. Ojibwa (Chippewa)

1718. Baldwin, William W. "Social Problems of the Ojibwa Indians in the Collins Area in Northwestern Ontario." *An,* 5 (1957), 51–123.

Study of acculturation with some attention to its effects on ceremonialism.

1719. Barnouw, Victor. "A Chippewa Mide Priest's Description of the Medicine Dance." *WA,* n. s. 41 (1960), 77–97.

Ritual description collected orally in 1944.

1720. ———. "A Psychological Interpretation of a Chippewa Origin Legend." *JAF,* 68 (1955), 73–85, 211–23, 341–55.

Examines tribal origin myth from a psychoanalytic perspective. Considers themes, qualities, and symbols.

1721. ———. "Reminiscences of a Chippewa Mide Priest." *WA,* n. s. 35 (1954), 83–112.

Life history of Tom Badger, recorded in 1944. Includes some data on ceremonialism.

1722. ———. *Wisconsin Chippewa Myths & Tales and Their Relation to Chippewa Life.* Madison: Univ. of Wisconsin Press, 1977.

Myth and folktale texts collected in 1941–1944. Extensive annotations and commentary emphasizing the cultural background.

1723. Barrett, Samuel Alfred. "The Dream Dance of the Chippewa and Menominee Indians of Northern Wisconsin." *BPMCM,* 1 (November 1911), 252–371.

Describes ceremonial conducted in 1910 which is considered to be a survival of the Ghost Dance. Describes dancing, oratory, and music and presents several vision texts.

1724. Bernard, Sister M. "Religion and Magic Among Cass Lake Ojibwa." *PM,* 2 (1929), 52–55.

Surveys supernaturalism and ceremonialism.

1725. Blackwood, Beatrice. "Tales of the Chippewa Indians." *F,* 40 (1929), 315–44.

Nine myth texts collected in 1925–1926. With comparative notes.

1726. Blakeslef, A. D. *The Religious Customs of the Ojibway Indians.* NP: NP, 1890.

Pamphlet treats religious attitudes and describes ceremonials.

1727. Bloomfield, Leonard. *Eastern Ojibwa. Grammatical Sketch, Texts and Word List.* Ann Arbor: Univ. of Michigan Press, ND.

Thirty-eight myth and personal narrative texts collected in 1938.

1728. Brill, Charles. *Indian and Free: A Contemporary Portrait of Life on a Chippewa Reservation.* Minneapolis: Univ. of Minnesota Press, 1974.

Photograph album with accompanying captions. Includes general data on Midewiwin ceremonialism, mythology, and storytelling.

1729. Brown, Paula. "Changes in Ojibwa Social Control." *AA,* 54 (1952), 57–70.

Compares traditional devices for social control (such as joking and tales of magical power) with the formal methods of acculturated life.

1730. Burnham, William H., Jr. *The Legend of O-Na-Wut-A-Qut-O. From North American Indian Folk-Lore and Legends.* Orange, Cal.: Sucasa Press, 1903.

Pamphlet includes rewritten myth text. No commentary or annotations.

1731. Burton, Frederick R. *American Primitive Music with Especial Attention to the Songs of the Ojibways.* New York: Moffat, Yard, 1909.

Treats NA songs in terms of structure, scale, rhythm, and function. Includes thirty-seven Ojibwa song texts (music only) and twenty-eight harmonized versions of Ojibwa songs. Also, some texts of stories associated with the songs.

1732. ———. "Music from the Ojibway's Point of View: Art an Unknown Word to These Primitive People, and Song a Part of Everyday Living." *Cr,* 12, No. 4 (July 1907), 375–81.

Treats nature and role of traditional singing. With song texts (words and music).

1733. Bushnell, David I., Jr. "An Ojibway Ceremony." *AA,* 7 (1905), 69–73.

Describes what was apparently a clan reunion observed in 1899. Considers songs and orations.

1734. Carson, Wm. "Ojibwa Tales." *JAF,* 30 (1917), 491–93.

Abstracts of a myth and of six episodes from the Trickster cycle. No annotations or commentary.

1735. Casagrande, Joseph B. "John Mink, Ojibwa Informant." *WA,* n. s. 36 (1955), 106–28.

Characterizes shaman and storyteller using life history recollections.

1736. ———. "The Ojibwa's Psychic Universe." *To,* 4, No. 3 (Spring 1956), 33–40.

Brief overview of tribal supernaturalism.

1737. Chamberlain, Alexander F. "A Mississaga Legend of Nä'nïbōjū'." *JAF,* 5 (1892), 291–92.

Unannotated myth text with some data on the informant.

1738. ———. "Notes on the History, Customs, and Beliefs of the Mississagua Indians." *JAF,* 1 (1888), 150–160.

Miscellany of data on religion, ceremonialism and singing.

1739. ———. "Tales of the Mississaguas." *JAF,* 2 (1889), 141–47.

Ten myth and folktale texts collected in 1888. Some presented in the original with free and interlinear translations. Extensive explanatory notes.

1740. ———. "Tales of the Mississaguas. II." *JAF,* 3 (1890), 149-54.

Myth and song texts with free and interlinear translations. Some data on cultural background.

1741. Champney, Stella M. "Michigan Indian Trails: Legends of Nena-Boo-Shoo, the Trickster." *MHM,* 19 (1935), 215–29.

Rewritten myth texts. No commentary or annotations.

1742. *Chippewa and Dakota Indians: A Subject Catalog of Books, Pamphlets, Periodical Articles, and Manuscripts in the Minnesota Historical Society.* St. Paul: Minnesota Historical Society, 1969.

Copy of relevant sections of the Card Catalog-Subject Index from the collection.

1743. Coleman, Sister Bernard. "The Religion of the Ojibwa of Northern Minnesota." *PM,* 10 (1937), 33–57.

Survey of religious beliefs and practices and their bases in mythology.

1744. ———, Ellen Frogner, and Estelle Eich. *Ojibwa Myths and Legends.* Minneapolis: Ross and Haines, 1961.

Narrative texts with general discussion of storytelling traditions and specific commentaries with each story. Includes some twentieth-century Trickster tales, data on the Thunderbird, and discussion of magical practices and the Mide Society.

1745. Copway, George [Kah-Ge-Gah-Bowh, Chief of the Ojibway Nation]. *The Traditional History and Characteristic Sketches of the Ojibway Nation.* Boston: Benjamin B. Mussey, 1851.

General survey of Ojibwa culture includes myth texts and descriptions of ceremonials.

1746. Danziger, Edmund Jefferson, Jr. *The Chippewas of Lake Superior.* Norman: Univ. of Oklahoma Press, 1978.

Cultural and historical survey includes data on ceremonialism and storytelling.

1747. Davidson, John F. "Ojibwa Songs." *JAF,* 58 (1945), 303–5.

Texts of six songs (words and music) collected in Ontario in 1936–1937. Also included are two song texts (words only) from the informants' memory culture.

1748. Densmore, Frances. *Chippewa Customs. BAEB* No. 86 (1929).

Ethnographic notes based on fieldwork done between 1905 and 1925. Contains material on religion and ceremonial life as well as folklore texts (five myths and two dream narratives).

1749. ———. *Chippewa Music. BAEB* No. 45 (1910).

Song texts (200 – words, music accompanying birchbark drawings) with musicological commentaries. Includes description of Mide Society and its ceremonials, the origin myth of the Society, and general ethnomusicological concerns.

1750. ———. *Chippewa Music—II. BAEB* No. 53 (1913).

Song texts (180 – words and music), each with musicological and contextual analysis. General introduction addresses musicological concerns.

1751. ———"An Explanation of a Trick Performed by Indian Jugglers." *AA,* 34 (1932), 310–14.

Description of a curing ritual observed among the Ojibwa in 1930. Treats singing and chanting.

1752. ———. "An Ojibwa Prayer Ceremony." *AA,* 9 (1907), 443–44.

Description of a ceremonial observed in 1905 with some technical data about singing.

1753. ———. "Use of Plants by the Chippewa Indians." *ARBAE,* 44 (1926–1927), 275–397.

Ethnobotanical survey with two myth texts involving the culture hero Manabozho.

1754. Dewdney, Selwyn. *The Sacred Scrolls of the Southern Ojibway.* Toronto: Univ. of Toronto Press, 1975.

Description of birchbark scrolls on which are recorded mythology, traditional tribal history, and ritual procedures.

1755. Dorson, Richard M. *Bloodstoppers and Bearwalkers. Folk Traditions of the Upper Peninsula.* Cambridge: Harvard Univ. Press, 1952.

Fieldwork in 1946 yielded folklore from various ethnic enclaves in Michigan's Upper Peninsula including NA groups: Ojibwa, Sioux, Menomini. Includes myth and legend texts with some attention to interview situations and performance styles.

1756. Ducatel, Professor. "A Fortnight Amongst the Chippewas." *USCM&MR,* 5 (1846), 24–28, 92–97.

Includes descriptions of ceremonialism and oratory. Reprinted in 83.

1757. Dunning, R. W. "Some Problems of Reserve Indian Communities: A Case Study." *An,* n. s. 6 (1964), 3–38.

Considers problems of Pine Tree Ojibwa in adjusting to EA culture. Brief ethnography contains data on supernaturalism.

1758. Eifert, Virginia S. "Place of the Golden-Breasted Woodpecker." *NM,* 45 (May 1952), 237–40.

Description of Lake Superior includes summaries of Ojibwa myths.

1759. Ellis, Kenneth M. "Ojibwe's Magic Music." *Scr,* 86 (July 1929), 88–91.

Brief survey of musical performances with texts of five "Poems from the Ojibwe."

1760. Emerson, Ellen Russell. "The Book of the Dead and Rain Ceremonials." *AA,* o. s. 7 (1894), 233–59.

Comparison of contents of Egyptian document with ceremonies conducted by the Ojibwa Mide Society and various Apache and Pueblo groups.

1761. Flannery, Regina. "The Cultural Position of the Spanish River Indians." *PM,* 13 (1940), 1–25.

Considers group's affinities with neighbors in terms of ceremonialism and other culture features.

1762. Gale, Edward C. "The Legend of Lake Itasca." *MnH,* 12 (1931), 215–25.

Retelling of a place legend. Attempts to establish its authenticity as an Ojibwa narrative.

1763. Gilfillan, J. A. "Some Ojibway Legends." *CSHSND,* 3 (1910), 708–24.

Summaries and texts of myths. No annotations or commentary.

1764. Grisdale, Alex (as told to Nan Shipley). "Black Stone's Wife. A Saulteaux Indian Tale." *QQ,* 75 (Winter 1968), 592–95.

Unannotated folktale text. No commentary.

1765. Hallowell, A. Irving. "Concordance of Ojibwa Narratives in the Published Works of Henry R. Schoolcraft." *JAF,* 59 (1946), 136–53.

Lists fifty-eight narratives, variant names assigned to them in Schoolcraft's publications, titles of the books in which they appear, relevant page numbers, and publication dates.

1766. ———. "Ojibwa Ontology, Behavior, and World View," in 102, pp. 19–52.

Attempts to characterize basic ideas of Ojibwa culture by drawing upon mythology. Reprinted in 163 (pp. 141–78).

1767. ———. "The Passing of the Midewiwin in the Lake Winnipeg Region." *AA,* 38 (1936), 32–51.

Correlates oral material with historical documentation to trace decline of ceremonial complex.

1768. ———. *The Role of Conjuring in Saulteaux Society. PPAS* No. 2 (1942).

Contains descriptions of ceremonials.

1769. ———. "Some Empirical Aspects of Northern Saulteaux Religion." *AA,* 36 (1934), 389–404.

Survey of religious system includes discussion of comsogony and cosmology. Shows how views of universe are reinforced by daily experience, dreams, and conjuring. Discusses and presents some religious oral narratives.

1769a. ———. "Some European Folktales of the Berens River Saulteaux." *JAF,* 52 (1939), 155–79.

Collection of narratives, apparently of EA derivation, told by NAs in English.

1770. ———. "The Spirits of the Dead in Saulteaux Life and Thought." *JAIGBI,* 70 (1940), 29–51.

Treats mythic basis for beliefs and ceremonials. With legend and personal narrative texts.

1771. ———. "Temporal Orientation in Western Civilization and in a Preliterate Society." *AA,* 39 (1937), 647–70.

Examines time concepts of Berens River Saulteaux with reference to myths.

1772. Hay, Thomas H. "The Development of Some Aspects of the Ojibwa Self and Its Behavioral Environment." *E,* 5 (1977), 71–89.

Discusses relationship of Ojibwa personality to culture change including adjustments in ceremonialism.

1773. Hesketh, John. "History of the Turtle Mountain Chippewa." *CSHSND,* 5 (1923), 85–154.

Culture survey includes data on ceremonialism and legend and oration texts.

1774. Hickerson, Harold. "Notes on the Post-Contact Origin of the Midewiwin." *Eh,* 9 (1962), 404–23.

Argues that the Mide Society developed in response to social and political changes effected by EA contact.

1775. ———. "The Sociohistorical Significance of Two Chippewa Ceremonials." *AA*, 65 (1963), 67–85.

The abandonment of the Feast of the Dead and the substitution of the Mide Ceremony reflected changes in the group's community organization.

1776. Hilger, Sister M. Inez. "Chippewa Burial and Mourning Customs." *AA*, 46 (1944), 565–68.

Description of mortuary ceremonies performed for a World War II veteran.

1777. ———. *Chippewa Child Life and Its Cultural Background. BAEB* No. 146 (1951).

Survey of socialization practices includes descriptions of life cycle ceremonials. Includes two myth texts and some data on lullabies.

1778. ———. "Chippewa Customs." *PM*, 9 (1936), 17–24.

Life history of a woman written in 1930s. Contains data on ceremonialism.

1779. ———. "Chippewa Interpretations of Natural Phenomena." *ScM*, 45 (August 1937), 178–79.

Presents explanations of weather and biological events, some of which are based on myths.

1780. ———. "Naming a Chippewa Indian Child." *WA*, n. s. 39 (1958), 120–26.

Ceremonial description with prayer texts.

1781. Hoffman, Walter J. "The Midé'wiwin or 'Grand Medicine Society' of the Ojibwa." *ARBAE*, 7 (1885–1886), 143–300.

Description of the ceremonial society includes its origin myth and other narrative texts, description of ritual practices, and some song texts (words and music).

1782. ———. "Notes on Ojibwa Folk-Lore." *AA*, o.s. 2 (1889), 215–23.

Survey of materials collected in 1887, especially the ceremonies of the Mide Society and traditions about the culture hero.

1783. ———. "Pictography and Shamanistic Rites of the Ojibwa." *AA*, o.s. 1 (1888), 209–29.

Includes origin myth of the Mide Society with some description of the ceremonials.

1784. Howard, James H. "The Henry Davis Drum Rite: An Unusual Drum Religion Variant of the Minnesota Ojibwa." *PlA*, 11, No. 32 (1966), 117–26.

Description of a ritual observed in 1963.

1785. Hume, Christopher. "The New Age of Indian Art." *Mac*, 92 (22 January 1979), 24–28.

Discusses modern NA painters, especially Norval Morrisseau, whose work includes several mythic motifs. Contains account of Morrisseau's visionary experience with Thunderbird.

1786. Jenks, Albert Ernest. "The Bear Maiden. An Ojibwa Folk-Tale from Lac Courte Oreille Reservation, Wisconsin." *JAF*, 15 (1902), 33–35.

Unannotated myth text collected in 1899. Brief commentary on content.

1787. Jenness, Diamond. *The Ojibwa Indians of Parry Island, Their Social and Religious Life. NMCB*, Anthropological Series No. 17 (1935).

Ethnography based on fieldwork done in 1929. Contains data on ceremonialism and excerpts from myth and legend texts.

1788. Johnson, Frederick. "Notes on the Ojibwa and Potawatomi of the Parry Island Reservation, Ontario. *IN*, 6 (1929), 193–216.

Ethnographic sketch includes data on music and ceremonialism. With two unannotated myth texts.

1789. Johnston, Basil. *Ojibway Heritage*. New York: Columbia Univ. Press, 1976.

Focuses on ceremonialism, songs, dances, and prayers as keys to the tribe's cultural values.

1790. Jones, Peter [Kahkewaquonaby]. *History of the Ojebway* [sic] *Indians; with Especial Reference to Their Conversion to Christianity. With a Brief Memoir of the Writer; and Introductory Notice by the Rev. G. Osborn.* London: A. W. Bennett, [1861].

More ethnography than history. Includes texts of cosmogonic myths and descriptions of religious attitudes and ceremonials.

1791. Jones, William. "Ojibwa Tales from the North Shore of Lake Superior." *JAF*, 29 (1916), 368–91.

Sixty myth, legend, and folktale abstracts. No annotation or commentary.

1792. ———. *Ojibwa Texts.* Ed. Truman Michelson. *PAES* No. 7, Part 1 (1917); Part 2 (1919).

Sixty-three episodes in the Trickster cycle and seventy-eight miscellaneous myth and folktale texts collected in 1903–1905. Presented with free translations. Sketchy linguistic and comparative notes.

1793. Kinietz, W. Vernon. *Chippewa Village: The Story of Katikitegon.* Bloomfield Hills, Mich.: Cranbrook Institute of Science, 1947 (Bulletin No. 25).

Ethnography based on fieldwork done in 1939–1940. Includes fairly complete descriptions of games and ceremonials.

1794. Kinnaman, J. O. "Chippewa Legends." *AAOJ*, 32 (1910), 96–102, 137–44.

Six unannotated myth texts. No commentary.

1795. ———. "Chippewa History as Told by Themselves and French Documents." *AAOJ*, 33 (1911), 32–40.

Post-contact history, partially from oral traditions.

1796. ———. "History of the Chippewa Nation as Told by Themselves and Catholic Documents." *AAOJ*, 32 (1910), 183–90.

NA prehistory, based partially on oral traditions.

1797. Kinsey, Mabel C. "An Ojibwa Song." *JAF*, 46 (1933), 416–17.

Text collected in 1919. No commentary or annotation.

1798. Knight, Julia. "Ojibwa Tales from Sault Ste. Marie, Mich." *JAF*, 26 (1913), 91–96.

Four unannotated myth and folktale texts. No commentary.

1799. Kroeber, Karl. "Poem, Dream, and the Consuming Culture." *GR*, 32 (1978), 266–80.

Literary analysis of an Ojibwa Deer Dance Song.

1800. Kurath, Gertrude P. "Chippewa Sacred Songs in Religious Metamorphosis." *ScM*, 79 (November 1954), 311–17.

Shows how Christian hymns have arisen out of traditional sacred music of the group.

1801. Lafleur, Laurence J. "On the Midé of the Ojibway." *AA*, 42 (1940), 706–8.

Conflicting descriptions of the Mide Society, its myths, and its rituals result from the nature of informants' perspectives as priests or laity.

1802. Laidlaw, Col. G. E. "Ojibwa Myths and Tales." *WA*, n. s. 1 (1922), 28–38.

Fifteen myth and folktale texts collected in 1921. Some explanatory and comparative notes.

1803. Landes, Ruth. *Ojibwa Religion and the Midéwiwin.* Madison: Univ. of Wisconsin Press, 1968.

Thorough historical and descriptive work on the Society with attention to ceremonial procedures and oral narratives.

1804. ——. *The Ojibwa Woman. CUCA* No. 31 (1938).

Description of the course of life among Ojibwa women, including ceremonial participation. Includes three life histories collected in early 1930s.

1805. Lanman, Charles. "The Dancing Ghosts." *MH,* 2 (December 1905), 424–26.

Unannotated myth text. No commentary.

1806. ——. "The Maiden of the Moon." *MH,* 2 (October 1905), 273–75.

Unannotated myth text. No commentary.

1807. *Life, History, and Travels, of Kah-Ge-Ga-Gah-Bowh (George Copway), a Young Indian Chief of the Ojebwa [sic] Nation, a Convert to the Christian Faith, and a Missionary to His People for Twelve Years; with a Sketch of the Present State of the Ojebwa Nation, in Regard to Christianity and Their Future Prospects, The. Also an Appeal; with All the Names of the Chiefs Now Living, Who Have Been Christianized, and the Missionaries Now Laboring Among Them. Written by Himself.* Albany: Weed and Parsons, 1847.

Autobiography of a Christian Ojibwa. Early chapters describe native culture (ceremonialism, supernaturalism, some data on oral tradition), but with a strong overlay of Christian commentary and evaluation.

1808. Linderman, Frank B. *Indian Old-Man Stories. More Sparks from War Eagle's Lodge-Fire.* New York: Scribners, 1920.

Thirteen rewritten myth and folktale texts. No annotations. May be for children.

1809. McGee, W. J. "Ojibwa Feather Symbolism." *AA,* o. s. 11 (1898), 177–80.

Survey of feather usage, especially in ceremonial contexts.

1810. McKenney, Thomas L. *Sketches of a Tour to the Lakes, of the Character and Customs of the Chippeway Indians, and of Incidents Connected with the Treaty of Fond du Lac.* Baltimore: Fielding Lucas, Jun'r, 1827.

Travel diary from 1826. Includes description of Ojibwa ceremonials and text of hero myth. Some discussion of the character of Manabozho.

1811. "Medicine Men's Tales." *TT,* 4, No. 11 (November 1904), 337–39.

Rewritten flood myth.

1812. Michelson, Truman. "Ojibwa Tales." *JAF,* 24 (1911), 249–50.

Two myth texts collected in 1910. No commentary or annotation.

1813. Miller, Frank C. "Humor in a Chippewa Tribal Council." *Eth,* 6 (1967), 263–71.

Survey of types and functions of joking which occur at meetings of group's political body.

1814. Morgan, Fred. "Friday Night Drum." *DM,* 35, No. 1 (January 1961), 40–41.

Describes ceremonial singing and dancing.

1815. Morriseau, Norval. *Legends of My People, The Great Ojibway.* Ed. Selwyn Dewdney. Toronto: Ryerson, 1965.

Descriptions of beliefs, customs, and ceremonials with summarized myth and legend texts. No annotations.

1816. Moyne, Ernest J. "Manabozho, Tarenyawagon, and Hiawatha." *SFQ,* 29 (1965), 195–203.

Suggests that Longfellow's confusion of Ojibwa and Iroquois culture heroes is due to errors in Schoolcraft's work.

1817. Nichols, John, ed. "Gabekanaansing/At the End of the Trail. Memories of Chippewa Childhood in Minnesota with Texts in Ojibwe and English. Told by Maude Kegg." *JWIRI,* 5, No. 2 (June 1978), 1–85.

Life history selected from interview data collected between 1971 and 1977. Text with free and interlinear translations.

1818. Paredes, J. Anthony. "A Case Study of a 'Normal' Windigo." *An,* n. s. 14 (1972), 97–116.

Analysis of an informant's dream in terms of the tradition of a cannibalistic monster.

1819. Parker, Seymour. "Motives in Eskimo and Ojibwa Mythology." *Eth,* 1 (1962), 516–23.

Uses myth in a personality and culture study to show occurrence of achievement, power, and affiliation motives in the two cultures.

1820. ——. "The Wiitiko Psychosis in the Context of Ojibwa Personality and Culture." *AA,* 62 (1960), 603–23.

Shows how references to cannibalism and to frustrated children in Ojibwa folklore contribute to cultural basis of the Windigo psychosis.

1821. Parker, William Thornton. "Concerning Indian Burial Customs." *OC,* 26 (February 1902), 86–96.

Ceremonial description with song texts (words only).

1822. Radin, Paul. "Ethnological Notes on the Ojibwa of Southeastern Ontario." *AA,* 30 (1928), 659–68.

Surveys various aspects of the culture from the perspective of a Native informant. Some attention is paid to ceremonialism.

1823. ——. "Ojibwa Ethnological Chit-Chat." *AA,* 26 (1924), 491–530.

Reports items of personal reminiscence and gossip recorded in 1912–1916. Includes several personal narrative and legend texts.

1824. ——. *Some Myths and Tales of the Ojibwa of Southeastern Ontario. CGSMB,* Anthropological Series No. 2 (1914).

Forty-five myth texts collected in 1912. No commentary.

1825. ——, and Albert B. Reagan. "Ojibwa Myths and Tales." *JAF,* 41 (1928), 61–146.

Forty-two unannotated myth and folktale texts collected in 1911, 1913, and 1914. Some explanatory comments.

1826. Reagan, Albert B. "The Flood Myth of the Chippewas." *PIAS for 1919,* pp. 347–52.

Unannotated myth text. No commentary.

1827. ——. "Medicine Songs of George Farmer." *AA,* 24 (1922), 332–69.

Twenty-four song texts copied into a notebook by an Ojibwa informant. Work includes native texts, free translations, explanations, and comments on the Mide Society.

1828. ——. "Picture Writings of the Chippewa Indians." *WA,* n. s. 6 (1927), 80–83.

Song texts from Ojibwa birchbark picture-writing.

1829. ——. "Rainy Lakes Indians." *WA,* n. s. 2 (1923), 140–47.

Description of a visit to an Ojibwa community includes data on ceremonialism and some myth texts in storytelling context.

1830. ———. "Some Games of the Bois Fort Ojibwa." Ed. F. W. Waugh. *AA,* 21 (1919), 264–78.

Descriptions of games with some related song texts (words and music).

1831. ———. "A Trip Among the Rainy Lakes." *PIAS for 1919,* pp. 253–59.

Includes a myth text in storytelling context. No annotations or commentary.

1832. Reid, A. P. "Religious Belief of the Ojibois or Sauteux Indians, Resident in Manitoba and at Lake Winnipeg." *JAIGBI,* 3 (1874), 106–13.

Surveys mythically based religious ideas encountered during contact between 1860 and 1864.

1833. Ritzenthaler, Robert. "The Ceremonial Destruction of Sickness by the Wisconsin Chippewa." *AA,* 47 (1945), 320–22.

Description of a healing ceremony witnessed in 1915 and in 1943.

1834. ———. "Totemic Insult Among the Wisconsin Chippewa." *AA,* 47 (1945), 322–24.

Describes the Gorging Feast, during which an individual who had insulted a totemic figure was forced to gorge himself on food prepared by members of the totemic group.

1835. Rogers, John [Chief Snow Cloud]. *Red World and White. Memories of a Chippewa Boyhood.* Revised edition. Norman: Univ. of Oklahoma Press, 1974.

Memoirs cover from 1896 into early years of twentieth century. Some attention to ceremonialism. 1st edition = 1957.

1836. Róhrl, Vivian J. "The Drum Societies in a Southwestern Chippewa Community." *WA,* n. s. 49 (1968), 131–37.

Description of a Drum Dance held in 1963.

1837. ———. "Some Observations on the Drum Society of the Chippewa Indians." *Eh,* 19 (1972), 219–25.

History of the Drum Dance and speculation about its modern function.

1838. Roufs, Timothy G. *The Anishinabe of the Minnesota Chippewa Tribe.* Phoenix: Indian Tribal Series, 1975.

Tribal history includes several myth texts and descriptions of ceremonialism.

1839. Sagatoo, Mary A. *Wah Sash Kah Moqua; or, Thirty-Three Years Among the Indians.* Boston: Charles A. White, 1897.

Account of residence among the Ojibwa includes descriptions of creation and of eschatological myths. The former kind of myth is characterized as "ludicrous and absurd."

1840. Schoolcraft, Henry Rowe. *The Literary Voyager or Muzzeniegun.* Ed. Philip P. Mason. East Lansing: Michigan State Univ. Press, 1962.

Edited complete run of a ms. magazine edited by Schoolcraft in 1826–1827. Includes material on Ojibwa ceremonialism and myth texts. Much of the material written by NAs.

1841. ———. *The Myth of Hiawatha and Other Oral Legends, Mythologic and Allegoric, of the North American Indians.* Philadelphia: J. B. Lippincott, 1856.

Collection of myths and legends primarily from the Ojibwa and some Northeast groups. Some general

commentary.

1842. Seymour, E. S. *Sketches of Minnesota, the New England of the West. With Incidents of Travel in That Territory During the Summer of 1849.* New York: Harper & Brothers, 1850.

Description of Ojibwa and Sioux ceremonialism and oratory.

1843. Skinner, Alanson. "The Cultural Position of the Plains Ojibway." *AA,* 16 (1914), 314–18.

Finds that folklore of western Ojibwa resembles that of Plains groups.

1844. ———. "European Tales from the Plains Ojibwa." *JAF,* 29 (1916), 330–40.

Four folktale texts with very brief comparative notes. No commentary.

1845. ———. "Plains Ojibwa Tales." *JAF,* 32 (1919), 280–305.

Seven myth and folktale texts (including fifteen episodes from the culture hero cycle). Collected in 1913. Comparative notes, but no commentary.

1846. Smith, Harlan I. "Certain Shamanistic Ceremonies Among the Ojibwas." *AAOJ,* 18 (1896), 282–84.

Ceremonial descriptions.

1847. ———. "The Monster in the Tree: An Ojibwa Myth." *JAF,* 10 (1897), 324–25.

Unannotated myth text collected in 1894. With data on collecting situation and cultural background.

1848. ———. "Some Ojibwa Myths and Traditions." *JAF,* 19 (1906), 215–30.

Seven legend texts with very good data on collecting situation and informants. Collected in 1894. Some comparative notes.

1849. Tanner, Helen Hornbeck. *The Ojibwas. A Critical Bibliography.* Bloomington: Indiana Univ. Press, 1976.

Unannotated list of 275 books and articles. Introductory essay includes section on "Language and Traditions."

1850. Thomas, T. C. "Beliefs of the Aborigines of America." *AAOJ,* 35 (1913), 63–69.

Brief overview of Ojibwa mythic ideas.

1851. Thompson, Stith. "The Indian Legend of Hiawatha." *PMLA,* 37 (1922), 128–40.

Examines the mythic cycle of Manabozho and its relationship to Longfellow's epic hero.

1852. "Three Ojibway Folk Tales as Told by Paul Michel of the Lake Nipigon Ojibways to Arthur Lower." *QQ,* 75 (Winter 1968), 584–91.

Unannotated texts with brief comments on collecting situation.

1853. "Two Indian Stories." *B,* 299 (Summer 1968), 51.

Myth texts (Ojibwa and Chipewyan). Unannotated, but with some data on collecting situation.

1854. Vennum, Thomas, Jr. "Constructing the Ojibwa Dance Drum." *WA,* n. s. 54 (1973), 162–74.

Describes art of drum-making as it relates to the Drum Dance Ceremonial.

1855. ———. "Ojibwa Origin-Migration Songs of the *mitewiwin.*" *JAF,* 91 (1978), 753-91.

Shows how tribal origin and migration narratives have influenced the sacred songs of the Mide Society.

1856. Vizenor, Gerald. *Tribal Scenes and Ceremonies.* Minneapolis: Nodin, 1976.

Vignettes of contemporary Ojibwa life include data on

ceremonialism.

1857.   Walker, Louise J. "Jawinikom's Tale." *MWF*, 5 (1955), 35–36.

Unannotated folktale text. No commentary.

1858.   ———. "The Moccasin Flower. A Chippewa Legend Retold." *NM*, 48 (May 1955), 230.

Rewritten folktale text. No commentary or annotations.

1859.   ———. "Why the Pine Trees Weep. A Chippewa Legend Retold." *NM*, 48 (March 1955), 113.

Rewritten myth text. No commentary or annotations.

1860.   Warren, William W. "History of the Ojibways, Based Upon Traditions and Oral Statements." *CMHS*, 5 (1885), 21–394.

History and prehistory from oral accounts. Included are data on ceremonialism and religion.

1861.   ———. "Traditions of Descent." *DWM*, 3, No. 2 (December 1898), 40–47.

Attempts to prove that NAs are the lost tribes of Israel by citing Ojibwa tribal origin myth and religious practices.

1862.   Wheeler, Olin D., and A. G. Bernard. "The Lake of the Leech." *DWM*, 3, No. 1 (November 1898), 11–17.

Description of a Minnesota lake begins with an Ojibwa folktale about it.

1863.   Whittlesey, Charles. "Among the Otchipwees." *MWH*, 1 (1884–1885), 86–91, 177–92, 335–42.

Historical and cultural survey contains data on ceremonialism, storytelling, and the Windigo.

See also 509, 667, 813, 868, 908, 1606, 1609, 1620, 1628, 1629, 1678, 1892, 2077, 2078, 2169, 2263, 2358, 2535, 2536, 2537, 5106, 5156, 5169, 5171, 5176.

H. Osage

1864.   "Account of the War Customs of the Osages, Given by Red Corn (HapaɔüꞁsE), of the Tsiɔu Peace-Making Gens, to the Rev. J. Owen Dorsey, An." *AmN*, 18 (February 1884), 113–33.

Thorough description of ceremonialism with texts of ritual formulas.

1865.   Ashley Montagu, M. F. "An Indian Tradition Relating to the Mastodon." *AA*, 46 (1944), 568–71.

Reprints an account which appeared in an 1841 pamphlet accompanying the exhibit of a mastodon skeleton. The account describes an Osage ceremony designed to placate monsters.

1866.   Baird, W. David. *The Osage People*. Phoenix: Indian Tribal Series, 1972.

Tribal history begins with account of tribal origin myth and some legendary history.

1867.   Churchill, George W. "Dance of Triumph." *C*, 117 (29 June 1946), 22–23.

Describes a ceremony celebrating allied victory in World War II.

1868.   Dickerson, Philip J. *History of the Osage Nation*. Pawhuska, Okla.: *NP*, 1906.

Potpourri of data includes material on mythology, the Ghost Dance, and traditional ceremonialism.

1869.   Dorsey, George A. "The Osage Mourning-War Ceremony." *AA*, 4 (1902), 404–11.

Description of a ceremony designed to avenge a death.

1870.   ———. "Traditions of the Osage." *PFCM-AS*, 7, No. 1 (1904), 1–60.

Forty folktale texts with abstracts. Collected in 1901–1903. Some comparative notes.

1871.   Dorsey, J. Owen. "Osage Traditions." *ARBAE*, 6 (1884–1885), 373–97.

Myth texts collected in 1883. With interlinear and free translations. Some commentary on informants and cultural background.

1872.   Fitzgerald, Sister Mary Paul. *Beacon on the Plains*. Leavenworth, Kan.: Saint Mary College, 1939.

History of Catholic mission to the Kansas Osage includes some data on NA religion, prayer, and ceremonialism.

1873.   Geddes, Alice Spencer. "Recorder of the Red Man's Music." *Sun*, 32 (January 1914), 165–67.

Surveys the work of composer Charles Wakefield Cadman, who collected and transcribed Osage music.

1874.   Graves, Wm. W. *The First Osage Protestant Missions, 1820–1837*. Oswego, Kan.: Carpenter Press, 1949.

Account of mission work includes excerpts from missionaries' descriptions of Osage prayers and religion.

1875.   Ingenthron, Elmo. *Indians of the Ozark Plateau*. Point Lookout, Mo.: School of the Ozarks Press, 1970.

Chapter on Osage contains some data on ceremonialism. Rest of work is archeological and historical.

1876.   "Journal of Diron D'Artaguiette, 1722–1723," in 140, pp. 15–92.

Includes description of a healing ceremony.

1877.   La Flesche, Francis. *A Dictionary of the Osage Language*. BAEB No. 109 (1932).

Includes brief descriptions of rituals, song texts, proverbs, and myth texts.

1878.   ———. "The Osage Tribe: Rites of the Chiefs; Sayings of the Ancient Men." *ARBAE*, 36 (1914–1915), 37–597.

Text of verbal aspects of ritual in Osage with free and literal translations. Song texts include music. Introduced by cultural overview.

1879.   ———. "The Osage Tribe: The Rite of Vigil." *ARBAE*, 39 (1917–1918), 31–630.

Two texts of the ritual, presented in Osage with free and literal translations. Song texts include music.

1880.   ———. "The Osage Tribe: Rite of the Wa-xo'-be; Shrine Degree." *ARBAE*, 45 (1927–1928), 523–833.

Texts of songs (words and music) and other verbal formulas associated with war rituals. Presented in Osage with free and literal translations.

1881.   ———. "The Osage Tribe: Two Versions of the Child-Naming Rite." *ARBAE*, 43 (1925–1926), 23–164.

Describes ceremony in two Osage gentes. Presents texts of verbal elements in Osage and in free translations.

1882.   ———. "Right and Left in Osage Ceremonies," in *Holmes Anniversary Volume*. Washington: James William Bryan, 1916, pp. 278–87.

Treats positional arrangements in ceremonies with some attention to mythic bases. Reprinted in 144 (pp. 32-42).

1883.   ———. "The Symbolic Man of the Osage Tribe." *A&A*, 9 (February 1920), 68–72.

Brief survey of ceremonial complex. With one song text (words only).

1884. ———. *War Ceremony and Peace Ceremony of the Osage Indians.* BAEB No. 101 (1939).

Description of two ceremonials includes texts of prayers and songs (words and music). Osage language versions appear at the end of the English material.

1885. Marriott, Alice L. "Dancing Makes Fun," in 92, pp. 82–87.

Description of a dance in honor of Mother's Day.

1886. Mathews, John Joseph. *The Osages. Children of the Middle Waters.* Norman: Univ. of Oklahoma Press, 1961.

Historical work includes data on mythology and ceremonialism.

1887. ———. *Talking to the Moon.* Chicago: Univ. of Chicago Press, 1945.

Memoir of Osage life traces the group's annual cycle. Includes data on mythology and ceremonialism.

1888. ———. *Wah'kon-tah: The Osage and the White Man's Road.* Norman: Univ. of Oklahoma Press, 1932.

Describes process of acculturation, based on journal of Laban J. Miles, who served as agent to the Osage. One chapter describes a storytelling session; another presents a mourning ceremony.

1889. McDermott, John Francis, ed. *Tixier's Travels on the Osage Prairies.* Trans. Albert J. Salvan. Norman: Univ. of Oklahoma Press, 1940.

Originally published in French in 1844. Travel account based on journey in 1839–1840. Includes data on Osage ceremonialism and singing.

1890. Pinkley-Call, Cora. "Stories About the Origin of Eureka Springs." *AHQ,* 5 (1946), 297–307.

Accounts of origin of Arkansas spa include summary of an Osage myth.

1891. Williams, Alfred M. "The Giants of the Plain." *LM,* n. s. 6 (1883), 362–71.

Description of a visit to the Osage includes data on ceremonialism.

See also 357, 1292, 2065, 2345, 2458, 2502.

I. Ottawa

1892. Blackbird, Andrew J. *History of the Ottawa and Chippewa Indians of Michigan; a Grammar of Their Language, and Personal and Family History of the Author.* Ypsilanti, Mich.: Ypsilantian Job Printing, 1887.

Historical section includes descriptions of ceremonialism and myth and legend texts.

1893. Cash, Joseph H., and Gerald W. Wolff. *The Ottawa People.* Phoenix: Indian Tribal Series, 1976.

Historical survey includes summary of tribal origin myth.

1894. Ettawageshik, Fred. "Ghost Suppers." *AA,* 45 (1943), 491–93.

Describes ceremonials to honor the dead.

1895. Ettawageshik, Jane (Introduction by Gertrude P. Kurath). "Three True Tales from L'Arbre Croche." *MWF,* 7, No. 1 (Spring 1957), 38–40.

Unannotated legend texts. No commentary.

1896. Kurath, Gertrude P. "Modern Ottawa Dances." *MWF,* 5 (1955), 15–22.

Discusses status of dancing among the Ottawa and presents steps and song texts (words and music) of Bear Dance and Eagle Dance.

1897. Michelson, Truman. "Three Ottawa Tales." *JAF,* 44 (1931), 191–95.

Two folktales and one legend text. Brief comparative commentary.

J. Potawatomi

1898. Baerreis, David A. "Chieftainship Among the Potawatomi: An Exploration of Ethnohistoric Methodology." *WA,* n. s. 54 (1973), 114–34.

Attempts to reconstruct the group's pattern of chieftainship, in part by using folktale accounts.

1899. Bee, Robert L. "Potawatomi Peyotism: The Influence of Traditional Patterns." *SJA,* 22 (1966), 194–205.

Analysis of the effects of traditional ideas on organization and ritual behavior of peyotists.

1900. Clifton, James A. "Sociocultural Dynamics of the Prairie Potawatomi Drum Cult." *PlA,* 14, No. 44, Part 1 (May 1969), 85–93.

Treats contemporary cultural role of a revitalization movement which originated in 1872.

1901. Dundes, Alan. "The Study of Folklore in Literature and Culture: Identification and Interpretation." *JAF,* 78 (1965), 136–42.

Demonstrates that identification and interpretation are methodological steps shared by the study of folklore in literature and in culture. Uses a Potawatomi folktale as an example.

1902. Hockett, Charles F. "Potawatomi IV: Particles and Sample Texts." *IJAL,* 14 (1948), 213–25.

Last in a series of linguistic articles. Presents line-by-line analyses of two stories collected in 1937 and in 1940.

1903. Howard, James H. "When They Worship the Underwater Panther: A Prairie Potawatomi Bundle Ceremony." *SJA,* 16 (1960), 217–24.

Description of a ceremonial observed in 1956 with cross-cultural survey of the "underwater panther" in NA mythology.

1904. Landes, Ruth. *The Prairie Potawatomi. Tradition and Ritual in the Twentieth Century.* Madison: Univ. of Wisconsin Press, 1970.

Ethnography based on fieldwork done primarily in 1935. Includes extensive data on ceremonialism (traditional and peyotist).

1905. Lawson, Publius V. "The Potawatomi." *WA,* o. s. 19 (1920), 41–116.

Culture survey includes data on religion and ceremonialism.

1906. McDonald, Daniel. *Removal of the Pottawattomie Indians from Northern Indiana. Embracing Also a Brief Statement of the Indian Policy of the Government, and Other Historical Matter Relating to the Indian Question.* Plymouth, Ind.: by the Author, 1899.

Historical work contains Potawatomi and Menomini oration texts.

1907. Pokagan, Simon. "Indian Superstitions and Legends." *Fo,* 25 (1898), 618–29.

Miscellany of myths, legends, and descriptions of customs. Related from the perspective of a Christianized NA.

1908. ———. "The Massacre of Fort Dearborn at Chicago. Gathered from the Traditions of the Indian Tribes Engaged in the Massacre and from the Published Accounts." *H,* 98 (1898–1899), 649–56.

Account of 1812 massacre draws upon eyewitness description. Includes an oration text by Tecumseh.

1909. Salzer, Robert J. "Bear-Walking: A Shamanistic Phenomenon Among the Potawatomi Indians in Wisconsin." *WA,* n. s. 53 (1972), 110–46.

Survey of ritual behavior and paraphernalia. With legend texts.

1910. Skinner, Alanson. "The Mascoutens or Prairie Potawatomi Indians. Mythology and Folklore." *BPMCM,* 6, No. 3 (22 January 1927), 327–411.

Unannotated texts of myths, legends, and personal narratives. Brief introductory commentary.

1911. ———. "The Mascoutens or Prairie Potawatomi Indians. Social Life and Ceremonies." *BPMCM,* 2, No. 1 (10 November 1924), 1–262.

General ethnography based on fieldwork done in 1912. Contains extensive data on ceremonialism, including ritual origin myths, songs, and chants (from traditional and peyotist systems).

1912. Winslow, Charles S. *Indians of the Chicago Region.* Chicago: by the Author, 1946.

Includes Potawatomi creation myth, a folktale text, and survey of religious beliefs. Some data on the Miami and the Illinois as well.

See also 1584, 1603, 1609, 1629, 1671, 1788, 2458.

K. Quapaw

1913. Dorsey, J. Owen. "Kwapa Folk-Lore." *JAF,* 8 (1895), 130–31.

Miscellany of beliefs, allusions to myths, and ceremonial descriptions. Collected in 1883.

1914. Herndon, Dallas T. "When the Quapaws Went to Red River—A Translation." *PAHA,* 4 (1917), 326–31.

Free translation of a ms. dated 1826 dealing with removal of Quapaws. Contains one prayer text.

1915. Masterson, James R. *Tall Tales of Arkansaw.* Boston: Chapman and Grimes, 1942.

Incorrectly titled work on the image of Arkansas in folklore and popular tradition. Contains a chapter on NAs in Arkansas, which includes oration texts. Reprinted by Rose Publishing Company (Little Rock) in 1974 as *Arkansas Folklore.*

1916. Nieberding, Velma Seamster. *The Quapaws (Those Who Went Downstream).* Miami, Okla.: Dixon, 1976.

Cultural and historical survey includes some references to mythology, religion, and ceremonialism. With chapters on peyotism and the Ghost Dance.

L. Sauk

1917. Briggs, John Ely. "Wisaka." *Pal,* 7 (1926), 97–112.

Retelling of myth cycle of culture hero. No commentary or annotations.

1918. Jackson, Donald, ed. *Ma-ka-tai-me-she-kia-kiak. Black Hawk. An Autobiography.* Urbana: Univ. of Illinois Press, 1955.

Text of a work first published in 1822, supposedly dictated to John B. Patterson and Antoine Le Claire. Most of the work deals with relations with EAs, but there are some accounts of ceremonialism.

1919. Skinner, Alanson. "Sauk Tales." *JAF,* 41 (1928), 147–71.

Twenty myth texts, many dealing with the culture hero, collected in 1922–1923. No commentary or annotation. One text presented in Sauk with interlinear translation.

See also 1584, 1603, 1611, 1620, 1628, 1641, 1642, 1648, 1651.

M. Shawnee

1920. Alford, Thomas Wildcat. *Civilization.* Norman: Univ. of Oklahoma Press, 1936.

Autobiography of a Shawnee, narrated to Florence Drake. Focus is on acculturation, but one chapter deals with ceremonialism.

1921. Drake, Benjamin. *Life of Tecumseh and of His Brother The Prophet; with a Historical Sketch of the Shawanoe Indians.* Cincinnati: H. S. & J. Applegate, 1852.

"Historical Sketch" includes tribal origin myth and some data about theology.

1922. Galloway, William Albert. *Old Chillicothe: Shawnee and Pioneer History. Conflicts and Romances in the Northwest Territory.* Xenia, Ohio: Buckeye Press, 1934.

Includes descriptions of ceremonies, song texts, and a legend text.

1923. Harvey, Henry. *History of the Shawnee Indians, from the Year 1681 to 1854, Inclusive.* Cincinnati: Ephraim Morgan & Sons, 1855.

Contains two oration texts.

1924. Hayes, Mrs. Harriet H. "An Indian Death-Chant." *FL,* 1 (1892), 45–46.

Music of a death song in context.

1925. Kinietz, Vernon, and Erminie W. Voegelin, eds. *Shawnese Traditions: C. C. Trowbridge's Account. OCMAUM* No. 9 (1939).

Presents a ms. written in 1824, which includes myth and song texts and descriptions of customs and ceremonies. Material taken from two informants: The Prophet and Black Hoof.

1926. Nettl, Bruno. "The Shawnee Musical Style: Historical Perspective in Primitive Music." *SJA,* 9 (1953), 277–85.

Characterization of the style includes some music texts.

1927. Nieberding, Velma. "Shawnee Indian Festival: The Bread Dance." *CO,* 42 (1964), 253–61.

Ceremonial description and myth text excerpted from a pamphlet circulated among tribe members.

1928. Spencer, J. "Shawnee Folk-Lore." *JAF,* 22 (1909), 319–26.

Miscellany of material including myth texts, descriptions of ceremonialism, and accounts of singing.

1929. Voegelin, C. F. "From FL (Shawnee) to TL (English), Autobiography of a Woman." *IJAL,* 19 (1953), 1–25.

An exercise in translation and transcription practices. Uses the life history of a Shawnee, narrated in 1952. With free and literal translations.

1930. ——. *The Shawnee Female Deity.* YUPA No. 10 (1936).

Descriptions of a mythic figure. With myth texts collected in 1933–1934.

1931. ——, and Erminie W. Voegelin. "The Shawnee Female Deity in Historical Perspective." *AA,* 46 (1944), 370–75.

Suggests that change in sex from male to female of high god of the Shawnee resulted from contact with the Huron.

1932. ——, and Erminie W. Voegelin. "Shawnee Name Groups." *AA,* 37 (1935), 617–35.

Describes naming ceremonies and shows relationship of name groups to storytelling.

1933. ——, and John Yegerlehner. "Toward a Definition of Formal Style, with Examples from Shawnee," in 152, pp. 141–50.

Emphasizes the potential of style as a primary research matter. Cites Shawnee oral literature for illustrations.

1934. ——, Florence M. Robinett, and Nancy P. Hickerson. "From FL (Shawnee) to TL (English): Some Differences Between Two Versions of the Autobiography." *IJAL,* 19 (1953), 106–17.

Compares a life history which a Shawnee performed for a tape recorder with one performed for manual transcription.

1935. Voegelin, Erminie W. "Shawnee Musical Instruments." *AA,* 44 (1942), 463–75.

Describes physical features and functions of various accompaniments to Shawnee singing.

1936. Yegerlehner, John. "The First Five Minutes of Shawnee Laws in Multiple Stage Translation." *IJAL,* 20 (1954), 281–94.

Traces the process of translating a moralistic commentary from the tape-recorded Shawnee to printed English.

See also 912, 945, 1601, 1620, 1908, 2458.

N. Winnebago

1937. Atwater, Caleb. *The Indians of the Northwest, Their Manners, Customs, &c. &c. Or Remarks Made on a Tour to Prairie du Chien and Thence to Washington City in 1829.* Columbus, Ohio: NP, 1850.

Travel account includes descriptions of NA poetry and oratory. With one song text.

1938. Babcock-Abrahams, Barbara. " 'A Tolerated Margin of Mess': The Trickster and His Tales Reconsidered." *JFI,* 11 (1975), 147–86.

Argues that Trickster defines the boundaries of a culture by transgressing the normative limits of social behavior. Uses examples from Winnebago Trickster cycle.

1939. Bergen, Fanny D. "Some Customs and Beliefs of the Winnebago Indians." *JAF,* 9 (1896), 51–54.

Miscellany of beliefs, references to mythology, and brief descriptions of ceremonies. No comparative notes.

1940. Danker, Kathleen, and Felix White, Sr. *The Hollow of Echoes.* Lincoln: Nebraska Curriculum Development Center, 1978.

Myth texts related by White in 1973 and placed in fictionalized storytelling context by Danker.

1941. Densmore, Frances. "Winnebago Beliefs Concerning the Dead." *AA,* 33 (1931), 659–60.

Description of a funerary ritual.

1942. Dorsey, J. Owen. "Winnebago Folk-Lore Notes." *JAF,* 2 (1889), 140.

Two myth excerpts. No annotations or commentary.

1943. Enerson, Amy Rolfe. "The Origin of the Peace Pipe." *Me,* 10, No. 2 (November 1922), 44–46.

Retelling of a myth with some data on cultural background.

1944. Hexom, Charles Philip. *Indian History of Winneshiek County.* Decorah, Iowa: A. K. Bailey & Son, 1913.

Concerned with Winnebago settlements in Iowa. Some data on religion and traditional history.

1945. Lamere, Oliver. "Winnebago Legends." *WA,* n. s. 1 (1922), 66–68.

Three unannotated myth texts. No commentary.

1946. ——, and Paul Radin. "Description of a Winnebago Funeral." *AA,* 13 (1911), 437–44.

Description of a ceremony written by Lamere and edited by Radin.

1947. Lang, John D., and Samuel Taylor, Jr. *Report of a Visit to Some of the Tribes of Indians, Located West of the Mississippi River.* New York: M. Day, 1843.

Includes text of a Winnebago oration.

1948. Lawson, Publius V. "The Winnebago Tribe." *WA,* o. s. 6 (1907), 78–160.

Cultural survey includes data on religion and ceremonialism.

1949. Lévi-Strauss, Claude. "Four Winnebago Myths. A Structural Sketch," in 102, pp. 351–62.

Analyzes concept of fate in myths collected by Paul Radin.

1950. Lurie, Nancy Oestreich, ed. *Mountain Wolf Woman, Sister of Crashing Thunder: The Autobiography of a Winnebago Indian.* Foreword by Ruth Underhill. Ann Arbor: Univ. of Michigan Press, 1961.

Life history of a highly acculturated Winnebago, beginning with her birth in 1884. Includes descriptions of traditional and peyotist ceremonialism and some song texts.

1951. ——. "Winnebago Berdache." *AA,* 55 (1953), 708–12.

Surveys ritual transvestism. With legendary accounts of famous practitioners.

1952. Peet, Stephen D. *Prehistoric America.* 2 volumes. Chicago: American Antiquarian Office, 1890.

Discusses significance of prehistoric mounds by examining Winnebago mythology.

1953. Radin, Paul. "The Autobiography of a Winnebago Indian." *UCPAAE,* 16, No. 7 (1920), 381–473.

Life history of Sam Blowsnake written in syllabary and translated into English. Includes data on acculturation and ceremonialism (especially peyotist). Re-issued by Dover Publications in 1963.

1954. ——. "The Clan Organization of the Winnebago." *AA,* 12 (1910), 209–19.

Survey of Winnebago society includes references to myths and legends which validate the social system.

1955. ——. *Crashing Thunder. The Autobiography of an American Indian.* New York: D. Appleton, 1926.

Second published version of Sam Blowsnake's life history (see 1953), written in the syllabary. Included are a number of myth texts and descriptions of ceremonialism (traditional and peyotist). Extensive explanatory notes.

1956. ———. *The Culture of the Winnebago: As Described by Themselves.* MIJAL No. 2 (1949).

Four myth and legend texts with free translations and extensive linguistic and cultural notes.

1957. ———. "Literary Aspects of Winnebago Mythology." *JAF,* 39 (1926), 18–52.

Discussion of content and structure of Winnebago myths with four sample texts.

1958. ———. *The Origin Myth of the Medicine Rite: Three Versions. The Historical Origins of the Medicine Rite.* MIJAL No. 3 (1950).

Four myth texts with free translations. No annotations or commentary.

1959. ———. "Personal Reminiscences of a Winnebago Indian." *JAF,* 26 (1913), 293–318.

Text and free translation of personal narratives and mythological material collected from Sam Blowsnake. Some explanatory notes.

1960. ———. "The Ritual and Significance of the Winnebago Medicine Dance." *JAF,* 24 (1911), 149–208.

Thorough description of the ceremonial and of the Mide Society with analysis of functions. Attention paid to ritual origin myth, but no texts.

1961. ———. *The Road of Life and Death: A Ritual Drama of the American Indians.* Foreword by Mark Van Doren. New York: Pantheon, 1945 (Bollingen Series No. 5).

Text of the Medicine Rite collected from Sam Blowsnake in 1908–1909. Introduced by discussion of collection context, survey of Winnebago mythology, and account of traditional religion. Extensive explanatory notes.

1962. ———. *The Social Organization of the Winnebago Indians, An Interpretation.* CGSMB, Anthropological Series No. 5 (1915).

Describes Winnebago clan system. Considers mythical explanations of the system and the role of clans in ceremonialism.

1963. ———. "The Thunderbird Warclub. A Winnebago Tale." *JAF,* 44 (1931), 143–65.

Unannotated myth text. No commentary.

1964. ———. *The Trickster. A Study in American Indian Mythology.* New York: Philosophical Library, 1956.

Presents Sam Blowsnake's version of the Trickster and Hare cycles and compares Winnebago material with myths from the Assiniboin and Tlingit. Radin explains relationship of Trickster to Winnebago culture. Essays by Karl Kerenyi and C. G. Jung place Trickster in the traditions of international mythology and identify Trickster as an archetypal symbol.

1965. ———. *Winnebago Hero Cycles. A Study in Aboriginal Literature.* MIJAL No. 1 (1948).

Presents four myth cycles (Trickster, Hare, Red Horn, Twin) collected between 1909 and 1912. Extensive commentary on approaches to mythological interpretation. With explanatory notes.

1966. ———. "Winnebago Tales." *JAF,* 22 (1909), 288–313.

Four myth texts with explanatory notes. Collected in 1908. Some data on collecting situation.

1967. ———. "The Winnebago Tribe." *ARBAE,* 37 (1915–1916), 35–550.

Ethnography includes descriptions of ceremonials, texts of clan origin myths, religious narratives, oration texts, summaries of other myths, and song texts. Includes extensive data on peyotism.

1968. Sebeok, Thomas A. "Two Winnebago Texts." *IJAL,* 13 (1947), 167–70.

Religious legends recorded in 1945 with interlinear and free translations. Some linguistic commentary.

1969. Sieber, George W. "A 1964 Winnebago Funeral." *JWIRI,* 2, No. 1 (June 1966), 102–5.

Ritual description.

1970. Street, Brian V. "The Trickster Theme: Winnebago and Azande," in 156, pp. 82–104.

Comparison of Trickster in African and NA cultures.

1971. Susman, Amelia. "Word Play in Winnebago." *La,* 17 (1941), 342–44.

Cites five examples of word play: two occurring at speeches during peyote meetings; one is a traditional joke.

1972. Walle, Alf H. "The Morphology and Social Dynamics of an American Indian Folktale." *KFR,* 24, Nos. 3–4 (July–December 1978), 74–80.

Extension of Radin's analysis of Trickster (1964) to include a socio-economic dimension.

See also 368, 408, 1584, 1609, 1628, 2003, 3964.

V PLAINS

A. General Works

1973. Albers, Patricia, and Seymour Parker. "The Plains Vision Experience: A Study of Power and Privilege." *SJA,* 27 (1971), 203–33.

Suggests that visions function to justify personal attributes just as myths justify group attributes.

1974. Alexander, Hartley Burr. "Symbolism of the Pipe." *EP,* 31 (1931), 74–84.

Describes the ceremonial significance of the pipe in Plains groups. With prayer text.

1975. Aquila, Richard. "Plains Indian War Medicine." *JW,* 13, No. 2 (April 1974), 19–43.

Cross-cultural survey of war ceremonialism. With song texts (words only).

1976. Armstrong, Moses K. *The Early Empire Builders of the Great West.* St. Paul, Minn.: E. W. Porter, 1901.

EA settlement history includes four myth texts from Plains groups.

1977. Barbeau, Marius. *Indian Days on the Western Prairies.* NMCB No. 163 (1960).

Oral history material arranged by informant. Includes historical data and descriptions of ceremonies for Plains and Sub-Arctic groups.

1978. Benedict, Ruth Fulton. "The Vision in Plains Culture." *AA,* 24 (1922), 1–23.

Compares the vision quest in various Plains groups. Treats myths which validate the quest and narratives which the quest generates.

1979. Bennett, John. "The Development of Ethnological Theory as Illustrated by Studies of the Plains Sun Dance." *AA,* 46 (1944), 162–81.

Traces development of anthropological emphasis from historical reconstruction to concern with functional and cultural relationships. Focuses on studies of the Sun Dance.

1980. Blue Eagle, Acee. "Oklahoma Plains Indian Dances." *SAM,* 40 (June 1941), 327–29, 9a.

Cursory survey of Plains ceremonialism.

1981. Brady, Cyrus Townsend. *Indian Fights and Fighters.* Introduction by James T. King. Lincoln: Univ. of Nebraska Press, 1971.

Reprint of a book published in 1904. One chapter in this historical work includes an account of the Custer massacre supposedly narrated by Rain-in-the-Face and reprinted by Brady from *Outdoor Life* for March 1903.

1982. Branch, Douglas. "Buffalo Lore and Boudin Blanc," in 105, pp. 126–36.

Miscellaneous myths about the buffalo, primarily from Plains groups.

1983. Brown, Annora. "Prairie Totems." *CGJ,* 23, No. 3 (September 1941), 148–51.

Description of design patterns on tipis includes references to myth-based symbols.

1984. Brown, Dee, ed. *Pawnee, Blackfoot, and Cheyenne. History and Folklore of the Plains from the Writings of George Bird Grinnell.* New York: Scribners, 1961.

Selections from *Pawnee Hero Stories* (2474), *Blackfoot Lodge Tales* (2147), and *By Cheyenne Campfires* (2235).

1985. Brown, Joseph Epes. "Sun Dance: Sacrifice—Renewal—Identity." *P,* 3, No. 2 (May 1978), 12–15.

Interprets the ritual as a celebration of the cycle of life.

1986. Catlin, George. *North American Indians: Being Letters and Notes on Their Manners, Customs, and Conditions, Written During Eight Years' Travel Amongst the Wildest Tribes in North America, 1832–1839.* 2 volumes. Edinburgh: John Grant, 1926.

Letters by the pioneer artist contain descriptions of supernaturalism and ceremonialism among various Plains groups.

1987. Childears, Lucille. "Montana Place Names from Indian Myth and Legend." *WF,* 9 (1950), 263–64.

Brief references to myths from various Plains groups associated with Montana place names.

1988. Chittenden, Hiram Martin, and Alfred Talbot Richardson, eds. *Life, Letters and Travels of Father Pierre-Jean de Smet, S. J., 1801–1873, Missionary Labors and Adventures Among the Wild Tribes of the North American Indians, Embracing Minute Description of Their Manners, Customs, Games, Modes of Warfare and Torture, Legends, Tradition, etc., All from Personal Observations Made During Many Thousand Miles of Travel, with Sketches of the Country from St. Louis to Puget Sound and the Altrabasca.* 4 volumes. New York: Francis P. Harper, 1905.

Letters contain much relevant to folklore of NA groups in Plains, Midwest, Great Basin, and Northwest Coast: discussion of religious attitudes and ceremonialism, summaries of myths and legends (including that of the Piasa).

1989. Collier, Donald. "The Sun Dance of the Plains Indians." *IW,* 8, No. 8 (April 1940), 46–50.

Description and functional analysis of the ceremony.

1990. Cooper, John M. "The Shaking Tent Rite Among Plains and Forest Algonquians." *PM,* 17 (1944), 60–84.

Comparative treatment of the ritual among Plains and Midwest groups and the Gros Ventre. Contains some legend texts.

1991. Corrigan, Samuel W. "The Plains Indian Powwow: Cultural Integration in Manitoba and Saskatchewan." *An,* n. s. 12 (1970), 253–77.

Description of types, functions, and general nature of intertribal ceremonial.

1992. Culbertson, Thaddeus A. *Journal of an Expedition to the Mauvaises Terres and the Upper Missouri in 1850.* Ed. John Francis McDermott. *BAEB* No. 147 (1952).

Includes occasional comments on NA customs, particularly those of the Sioux, and several paraphrases of prayers. Culbertson's primary purpose for the journey was to study natural history.

1993. Davis, Theodore R. "A Summer on the Plains." *H*, 36 (1867–1868), 292–307.

Account of a summer tour of the Plains includes some highly ethnocentric accounts of NA life. Information on mythic ideas and supernaturalism.

1994. ———. "Winter on the Plains." *H*, 39 (1869), 22–34.

Discusses life during winter among various Plains groups, especially the Cheyenne. Some highly ethnocentric descriptions of ceremonials.

1995. De Smet, P. J. "The Indians of the Upper Missouri." *Mo*, 5 (September 1866), 322–30.

Survey of religious concepts.

1996. ———. *Western Missions and Missionaries: A Series of Letters.* New York: James B. Kirker, 1863.

Many of the letters deal with religion and ceremonialism among groups in the Plains, Midwest, and Plateau. See also 1988.

1997. Dodge, Richard Irving. *The Hunting Grounds of the Great West. A Description of the Plains, Game, and Indians of the Great North American Desert.* London: Chatto & Windus, 1877.

Geographical and cultural survey of the Plains includes descriptions of ceremonialism and singing. Ceremonials handled fairly thoroughly.

1998. Dorsey, J. Owen. "Camping Circles of the Siouan Tribes." *AA*, o.s. 2 (1889), 175–77.

Describes camp layouts and symbolic significance of those layouts among Siouan-speakers in the Plains.

1999. ———. "Nanibozhu in Siouan Mythology." *JAF*, 5 (1892), 293–304.

Describes Trickster and related figures in the mythologies of Siouan-speakers in the Plains.

2000. ———. "Siouan Folk-Lore and Mythologic Notes." *AAOJ*, 6 (1884), 174–76; 7 (1885), 105–8.

Summaries of myths from various Siouan-speaking groups in the Plains.

2001. ———. "Siouan Onomatopes." *AA*, o. s. 5 (1892), 1–8.

Surveys use of onomatopoeia among Siouan-speakers from Plains groups. Contains a folktale and song text (words and music) from the Omaha.

2002. ———. "Siouan Sociology, A Posthumous Paper." *ARBAE*, 15 (1893–1894), 205–44.

Primarily concerned with social organization of groups in Siouan language family (in Plains, Midwest, and Southeast). Some texts of verbal formulas used in selecting and arranging campsites.

2003. ———. "A Study of Siouan Cults. *ARBAE*, 11 (1889–1890), 351–544.

Survey of religious practices among several Siouan-speaking groups (Omaha, Ponca, Kansa, Winnebago, Iowa, Oto, Dakota) based, in part, on author's observations while a missionary to the Ponca in the early 1870s. Includes summaries of myths, prayers, and songs (texts in original and translations) and ceremonial descriptions.

2004. Draper, W. H. "Indian Dances of the Southwest." *Ou*, 37 (March 1901), 659–66.

Despite the title, the essay treats the Ghost Dance on the Plains. Song texts and myth excerpts included.

2005. Dyck, Paul. "The Plains Indian Shield." *AIAM*, 1 November 1975, pp. 33–41.

Ties shield into religious and mythic system.

2006. Eaton, Evelyn. *I Send a Voice.* Wheaton, Ill.: Theosophical Publishing House, 1978.

Account of author's experience in becoming a Pipe Woman. Contains ritual descriptions and texts of songs from various Plains groups.

2007. Erdoes, Richard, ed. *The Sound of Flutes and Other Indian Legends Told by Lame Deer, Jenny Leading Cloud, Leonard Crow Dog, and Others.* New York: Pantheon, 1976.

Twenty-nine myth and folktale texts. Unannotated, but introduced by a discussion of Plains storytelling traditions.

2008. ———. *The Sun Dance People: The Plains Indians, Their Past and Present.* New York: Alfred A. Knopf, 1972.

Contrasts traditional life of Plains groups with contemporary reservation life. Includes data on ceremonialism, with a photographic record of a contemporary Sun Dance. Uses chant and prayer texts as chapter epigraphs.

2009. Ewers, John C. "Plains Indian War Medicine." *To*, 4, No. 3 (Spring 1956), 85–90.

Survey of war ceremonials.

2010. Fletcher, Alice C. "The Indian Messiah." *JAF*, 4 (1891), 57–60.

Incorrect description of the origin of the Ghost Dance. Some descriptions of ceremonialism.

2011. Forbes, Allan, Jr. "The Plains *Agon*—A Gross Typology." *PlA*, 17 (1972), 143–55.

Categorizes kinds of military expeditions among Plains groups. Some data on ceremonialism and oratory.

2012. Gilmore, Melvin R. *Prairie Smoke.* New York: AMS Press, 1966.

Describes lifeways of Plains groups through depictions of theology, retellings of myths, and accounts of ceremonials.

2013. Grinnell, George Bird. "Coup and Scalp Among the Plains Indians." *AA*, 12 (1910), 296–310.

Describes ceremonials honoring warriors who had counted coup. Also treats the Scalp Dance.

2014. ———. *The Indians of To-Day.* Chicago: Herbert S. Stone, 1900.

Treats conditions of NAs at turn of the century. Includes myth texts and ceremonial descriptions from Plains groups.

2015. ———. "The Medicine Wheel." *AA*, 24 (1922), 299–310.

Describes and speculates about the origin of large stone design in Wyoming. Among relevant data is the career of the Cheyenne culture hero, Sweet Medicine.

2016. Herzog, George. "Plains Ghost Dance and Great Basin Music." *AA*, 37 (1935), 403–19.

Musicological analysis of eight tune texts from the Plains Ghost Dance. The tunes originated with the Paiute.

2017. Hewitt, J. N. B., ed. *Journal of Rudolph Friederich Kurz: An Account of His Experiences Among Fur Traders and American Indians on the Mississippi and Upper Missouri Rivers During the Years 1846 to 1852.* Trans. Myrtis Jarrell. *BAEB* No. 115 (1937).

Narrative by a Swiss artist recounts observations of NA life. Includes descriptions of ceremonialism and a text of an Assiniboin war song.

2018. Hoebel, E. Adamson. *The Plains Indians. A Critical Bibliography.* Bloomington: Indiana Univ. Press, 1977.

Unannotated list of 205 books and articles.
Bibliographical introduction includes sections on tribes.
2019. Howard, James H. "The Mescal Bean Cult of the Central and Southern Plains: An Ancestor of the Peyote Cult?" *AA,* 59 (1957), 75–87.
Describes features of mescal bean ceremonialism among Plains and Southwest groups and suggests that mescalism may have been the predecessor of peyotism. Relevant archeological data were added by T. N. Campbell in *AA,* 60 (1958), 156–60. Weston La Barre responded in *AA,* 59 (1957), 708–11.
2020. ———. "Peyote Jokes." *JAF,* 75 (1962), 10–14.
Presents texts of jokes told on mornings following all-night peyote rituals.
2021. ———. "The Plains Gourd Dance as a Revitalization Movement." *AE,* 3 (1976), 243–59.
Traces the Gourd Dance as a traditional practice of various Plains groups to its status as an intertribal event.
2022. Hunter, John D. *Manners and Customs of Several Indian Tribes Located West of the Mississippi; Including Some Account of the Soil, Climate, and Vegetable Productions, and the Indian Materia Medica: To Which Is Prefixed the History of the Author's Life During a Residence of Several Years Among Them.* Philadelphia: J. Maxwell, 1823.
Observations, beginning with captivity narrative, of Plains and Midwest cultures with data on religion, ceremonialism, singing, and oratory.
2023. Hurt, Wesley R. "Factors in the Persistence of Peyote in the Northern Plains." *PlA,* 5, No. 9 (May 1960), 16–27.
Suggests that the persistence of peyotism depends on its approval by tribal political leaders and on the size and homogeneity of the group.
2024. Jones, Hettie. *Coyote Tales.* New York: Holt, Rinehart and Winston, 1974.
Four myth texts rewritten from Plains sources. Some data on Coyote's role as Trickster.
2025. Judson, Katharine Berry, ed. *Myths and Legends of the Great Plains.* Chicago: A. C. McClurg, 1913.
Unannotated texts taken from BAE and other government publications. No commentary.
2026. Kehoe, Alice B. "The Ghost Dance Religion in Saskatchewan, Canada." *PlA,* 13, No. 42, Part 1 (November 1968), 296–304.
Historical work on spread of Ghost Dance into Saskatchewan in the 1880s.
2027. Kehoe, Thomas F., and Alice B. Kehoe. "Boulder Effigy Monuments in the Northern Plains." *JAF,* 72 (1959), 115–27.
Presents NA explanations for monumental rock constructions from Blackfoot, Sioux, Mandan, Hidatsa, and Crow.
2028. Laubin, Reginald, and Gladys Laubin. *The Indian Tipi. Its History, Construction, and Use.* Norman: Univ. of Oklahoma Press, 1957.
Primarily a material culture study, but some data on dedication rituals and associated mythology.
2029. Liberty, Margot P. "Priest and Shaman on the Plains: A False Dichotomy?" *PlA,* 15 (May 1970), 73–79.
Shows the inadequacy of conventional categories of religious practitioners.
2030. Little Duck (Interpreted by Roger St. Pierre). "How the First White Man Came to America." *CSHSND,* 3 (1910), 725–27.

Unannotated legend text. No commentary. Group not specified.
2031. Lowie, Robert H. "American Indian Dances." *AMJ,* 15 (1915), 95–102.
Survey of Plains ceremonialism.
2032. ———. "'Freemasons' Among North Dakota Indians." *AM,* 19 (February 1930), 192–96.
Overview of esoteric societies. With one song text (words only).
2033. ———. *Indians of the Plains.* New York: McGraw-Hill, 1954.
General introduction to Plains cultures with data on storytelling, mythology, and ceremonialism.
2034. ———. "Some Problems in Plains Indian Folklore." *JAF,* 60 (1947), 401–3.
Survey of folklore studies pertaining to Plains groups. Part of a report prepared by the AFS Committee on Research in Folklore.
2035. Mails, Thomas E. *Dog Soldiers, Bear Men and Buffalo Women: A Study of the Societies and Cults of the Plains Indians.* Englewood Cliffs, N. J.: Galahad, 1973.
Illustrated treatment of ceremonials among various Plains and Plateau groups includes descriptions of rituals and texts of songs, prayers, and ritual origin myths.
2036. Marriott, Alice. "The Opened Door." *NY,* 30 (25 September 1954), 80–91.
Description of the NA Church and its rituals.
2037. ———, and Carol K. Rachlin. *Peyote.* New York: Thomas Y. Crowell, 1971.
Historical account of the development of peyotism among Plains groups. Includes data on ritual procedure.
2038. ———, and Carol K. Rachlin. *Plains Indian Mythology.* New York: Thomas Y. Crowell, 1975.
Includes texts with explanatory notes and occasional comparative data and a general introduction.
2039. Maus, Marion P. "The New Indian Messiah." *HW,* 34 (6 December 1890), 947.
Account of the Ghost Dance.
2040. McCracken, Harold. "The Sacred White Buffalo." *NH,* 55 (1946), 304–9, 341.
Discusses place of white buffalo in Plains ceremonialism. Includes summary of legend text.
2041. McD., Max. "The Sun Dance." *OM,* n. s. 67 (1916), 138–40.
General description of the ritual.
2042. McGee, W. J. "The Siouan Indians. A Preliminary Sketch." *ARBAE,* 15 (1893–1894), 153–204.
Cultural survey of Siouan-speaking groups in Plains, Midwest, and Southeast. Some attention to mythology and music.
2043. McNickle, D'Arcy. "Peyote and the Indian." *ScM,* 57 (September 1943), 220–29.
Description of ritual procedure of NA Church with historical background on peyotism.
2044. McTaggart, Fred. "American Indian Literature: Contexts for Understanding," in 81, pp. 2–9.
Emphasizes sacred and didactic nature of Plains oral literature—qualities unrecognized by most EA readers.
2045. Mooney, James. "The Ghost-Dance Religion and the Sioux Outbreak of 1890," *ARBAE,* 14 (1892–1893), 641–1110.
Classic account of the revitalization movement which affected many NA groups in the Plains during the 1880s. Included is a history of the movement from its inception

through the Wounded Knee massacre. Presents descriptions of ceremonialism and song texts from following groups: Arapaho, Cheyenne, Comanche, Paiute, Sioux, Kiowa, and Caddo.

2046.   Morgan, Lewis Henry. *The Indian Journals, 1859–62.* Ed. Leslie A. White. Ann Arbor: Univ. of Michigan Press, 1959.

Narrative accounts of the pioneer ethnologist's field trips to the Plains and Midwest include descriptions of ceremonials—especially the Sun Dance. Introduction evaluates Morgan's career. With extensive annotations by White.

2047.   Muntsch, Albert. "The Relations Between Religion and Morality Among the Plains Indians." *PM,* 4 (1931), 22–29.

Examines mythology and ceremonialism of various Plains groups in order to construct moral codes.

2048.   *Nebraska Folklore Pamphlet Two. Indian Place Legends.* Lincoln: Federal Writers' Project, 1937.

Seven myth and folktale texts collected from Pawnee, Omaha, and Sioux sources. No commentary or annotations. Collected by the WPA.

2049.   Neihardt, John G. *Indian Tales and Others.* New York: Macmillan, 1926.

Sketches of Plains life include some narratives from NA sources and descriptions of storytelling situations.

2050.   Nelson, Bruce. *Land of the Dacotahs.* Minneapolis: Univ. Of Minnesota Press, 1946.

Popular history of the northern Plains includes data on NA ceremonials and storytelling.

2051.   Nettl, Bruno. "Observations on Meaningless Peyote Song Texts." *JAF,* 66 (1953), 161–64.

Examines text-tune relations of Plains songs consisting of meaningless syllables and associated with peyotism.

2052.   Newcomb, W. W., Jr. *The Indians of Texas from Prehistoric to Modern Times.* Austin: Univ. of Texas Press, 1961.

Survey work includes chapters on specific groups and a general introduction. Some discussion of supernaturalism and ceremonials for each group. Covers Plains and Southwest.

2052a.   O'Brien, Lynne Woods. *Plains Indian Autobiographies.* WWS No. 10 (1973).

Critical survey of written and oral life histories.

2053.   Overholt, Thomas W. "The Ghost Dance of 1890 and the Nature of the Prophetic Process." *Eh,* 21 (1974), 37–63.

Describes a model of the prophetic process which involves interaction among the supernatural, the prophet, his disciples, and the people as a way to view the Ghost Dance in the Plains and among the Paiute.

2054.   Pound, Louise. "The Nebraska Legend of Weeping Water." *WF,* 6 (1947), 305–16.

Rejects popular idea that a narrative about a stream called Weeping Water is of NA origin. Attributes source to French explorers and traders.

2055.   ———. "Nebraska Legends of Lovers' Leaps." *WF,* 8 (1949), 304–13.

Considers and rejects the popular notion that Lovers' Leap stories are of NA origin.

2056.   Ray, Verne F. "The Contrary Behavior Pattern in American Indian Ceremonialism." *SJA,* 1 (1945), 75–113.

Survey of the behavior of clowns and other ceremonial deviants in Plains and Southwest cultures.

2057.   Roe, Frank Gilbert. *The North American Buffalo: A Critical Study of the Species in Its Wild State.* Toronto: Univ. of Toronto Press, 1951.

Zoological study of the animal includes data on buffalo ceremonialism among Plains groups.

2058.   Schultes, Richard Evans. "The Appeal of Peyote (*Lophophora Williamsii*) as a Medicine." *AA,* 40 (1938), 698–715.

Argues that the principal appeal of peyote among NAs has been therapeutic and that its visionary aspect is relatively insignificant. Describes a curing ritual. Weston La Barre responded in *AA,* 41 (1939), 340–42.

2059.   ———. "Peyote and the American Indian." *NM,* 30 (September 1937), 155–57.

History of the spread of peyotism and description of ritual procedure of NA Church.

2060.   Shonle, Ruth. "Peyote, the Giver of Visions." *AA,* 27 (1925), 53–75.

Surveys peyote use among NAs and focuses on peyote ritualism among the Arapaho.

2061.   Sidoff, Phillip G. "An Ethnohistorical Investigation of the Medicine Bundle Complex Among Selected Tribes of the Great Plains." *WA,* n. s. 58 (1977), 173–204.

Cross-cultural survey of the ritual complex. It functions differently in hunting and agricultural societies.

2062.   Slotkin, J. S. *The Peyote Religion: A Study in Indian-White Relations.* Glencoe, Ill.: Free Press, 1956.

History of peyotism and NA Church primarily among Plains groups. Contains description of theology and ceremonialism with attention to praying and singing.

2063.   ———. "The Peyote Way." *To,* 4, No. 3 (Spring 1956), 64–70.

Description of peyotism as practiced by Plains and Midwest groups.

2064.   ———. "Peyotism, 1521–1891." *AA,* 57 (1955), 202–30.

Examination of the literature on pre-twentieth century peyotism among NAs. Includes appended descriptions of ceremonialism among Plains and Southwest groups.

2065.   Smith, Maurice Greer. "Political Organization of the Plains Indians, with Special Reference to the Council." *UNS,* 24, Nos. 1–2 (January-April 1924), 3–84.

Treats mythic and ritual aspects of political structure. Special attention to the Osage.

2066.   Stewart, Omer C. "The Peyote Religion and the Ghost Dance." *IH,* 5, No. 4 (Winter 1972), 27–30.

Argues that peyotism preceded the Ghost Dance among Plains groups. Contrary to conventional view.

2067.   "Sun Dance of the Plains Tribes, The." *IW,* 7, No. 2 (October 1939), 24–25.

General description of the ceremony.

2068.   Tilghman, Zoe A. "Source of the Buffalo Origin Legend." *AA,* 43 (1941), 487–88.

Suggests that myth that buffalo were created underground relates to animals' winter habitat in Palo Duro Canyon in Texas.

2069.   Troike, Rudolph C. "The Origins of Plains Mescalism." *AA,* 64 (1962), 946–63.

Surveys ethnographic materials relating to ceremonial uses of mescal bean among Plains groups. Some data on ritual procedures.

2070. Wake, C. Staniland. "Mythology of the Plains Indians." *AAOJ,* 27 (1905), 9–16.

Discusses concepts underlying mythology, especially animism.

2071. ———. "Mythology of the Plains Indians. Magical Animals." *AAOJ,* 28 (1906), 205–12.

Survey of animals portrayed in myths of various Plains groups.

2072. ———. "Mythology of the Plains' [sic] Indians. Nature Deities." *AAOJ,* 27 (1905), 73–80.

Treats personifications of natural phenomena in myths of various Plains groups.

2073. ———. "Mythology of the Plains Indians. Terrestial Objects." *AAOJ,* 27 (1905), 323–28.

Treats personified objects in myths of various Plains groups.

2074. Will, George F., and George E. Hyde. *Corn Among the Indians of the Upper Missouri.* St. Louis: Harvey Miner, 1917.

Discussion of use of corn by various Plains groups includes summaries of several corn origin myths and descriptions of corn ceremonialism.

2075. Wissler, Clark. "Ethnographical Problems of the Missouri Saskatchewan Area." *AA,* 10 (1908), 197–207.

Survey of research on Plains groups includes suggestion that study of oral literature should focus on comparisons with material from outside the Plains.

2076. ———. *Indian Cavalcade or Life on the Old-Time Indian Reservations.* New York: Sheridan House, 1938.

Recollections of reservation life include descriptions of ceremonials and an account of a storytelling session.

2077. ———, ed. "Societies of the Plains Indians." *APAMNH,* 11 (1916), 1–1031.

Collection of essays which treat ceremonialism—with occasional myth and song texts—of various Plains groups: by Robert H. Lowie (Eastern Dakota, Crow, Hidatsa, Arikara, Shoshoni, Kiowa), Wissler (Oglala, Blackfoot), Pliny Earle Goddard (Sarsi), Alanson Skinner (Ojibwa, Cree, Iowa, Kansa, Ponca), and James R. Murie (Pawnee).

2078. ———, ed. "Sun Dance of the Plains Indians." *APAMNH,* 16 (1921), 1–548.

Descriptions of the ceremonial in various groups prepared by different ethnographers: Robert H. Lowie (Crow, Ute, Shoshoni, Hidatsa), J. R. Walker (Oglala Sioux), Wissler (Blackfoot), Pliny Earle Goddard (Sarsi), Alanson Skinner (Ojibwa, Sisseton Sioux), Skinner and Goddard (Cree), W. D. Wallis (Canadian Sioux), and Leslie Spier (Kiowa). With myth and song texts.

2079. zu Wied, Prince Maximilian. *People of the First Man. Life Among the Plains Indians in Their Final Days of Glory. The Firsthand Account of Prince Maximilian's Expedition Up the Missouri River, 1833–34.* Ed. Davis Thomas and Karin Ronnefeldt. New York: E. P. Dutton, 1976.

Edition of a journal first published in English in 1843. Includes data on ceremonials of various groups in the Plains and an appended study of Mandan culture.

See also 30, 172, 313, 393, 425, 441, 479, 630, 1301, 1594, 1608, 1631, 1843, 2127, 2339, 2695, 2704, 3130, 4002, 4014, 4501, 4555, 4595, 4670, 4989, 5092, 5099, 5102, 5113.

B. Arapaho

2080. Bass, Althea. *The Arapaho Way: A Memoir of an Indian Boyhood.* Introduction by Frank Waters. New York: Clarkson N. Potter, 1966.

Reminiscences of Arapaho painter Carl Sweezy. Chapter on religion deals with traditional belief system, the Ghost Dance, and peyotism.

2081. Boyer, Warren E. "The Thunder Bird." *Sun,* 60 (June 1928), 19.

Describes Arapaho belief in the Thunderbird.

2082. Carter, John G. "The Northern Arapaho Flat Pipe and the Ceremony of Covering the Pipe." *BAEB* No. 119 (*AP* No. 2), 1938.

Description of a ceremony involving the use of the sacred medicine pipe.

2083. Dorsey, George A. "The Arapaho Sun Dance; The Ceremony of the Offerings Lodge." *PFCM-AS,* 4 (1903), 1–228.

Thorough ceremonial descriptions based on observations in 1901–1902. Treats symbolism and mythic associations. With prayer and origin myth texts.

2084. ———, and Alfred L. Kroeber. "Traditions of the Arapaho." *PFCM-AS,* 5 (1903), 1–475.

Translated myth texts (146) with abstracts and some comparative notes.

2085. Hilger, Sister M. Inez. *Arapaho Child Life and Its Cultural Background. BAEB* No. 148 (1952).

Treats socialization process with attention to lullabies and rites of passage. Based on fieldwork done in late 1930s and early 1940s.

2086. Hultkrantz, Åke. "Some Notes on the Arapaho Sun Dance." *En,* 17 (1952), 24–38.

Description of the ceremonial as observed in 1948. With extensive comparative notes.

2087. Kroeber, Alfred L. "The Arapaho: Ceremonial Organization." *BAMNH,* 18, Part 2 (1904), 151–230.

Includes descriptions of ceremonials with some song texts.

2088. ———. "Arapaho Dialects." *UCPAAE,* 12, No. 3 (1916), 71–138.

Linguistic survey based on fieldwork done in 1899-1901. Includes one prayer and two myth texts with interlinear translations and linguistic analyses. Short section on Gros Ventre contains one myth text.

2089. ———. "The Arapaho: General Description; Decorative Art and Symbolism." *BAMNH,* 18, Part 1 (1902), 1–150.

General ethnography section includes some material on ceremonialism. Discussion of symbolism suggests mythic associations.

2090. ———. "The Arapaho: Religion." *BAMNH,* 18, Part 4 (1907), 279–454.

Includes a thorough description of the Sun Dance and other ceremonials. With description of belief system and texts of prayers.

2091. ———. "Decorative Symbolism of the Arapaho." *AA,* 3 (1901), 308–36.

Survey of ornamentation of leather goods includes references to myths recounting design origins.

2092. ———. "Symbolism of the Arapaho Indians." *BAMNH,* 13 (1900), 69–86.
Treats designs in pictorial art. Some have mythic associations.

2093. Lemly, H. R. "Among the Arrapahoes." *H,* 60 (1879–1880), 494–501.
Random notes on Arapaho culture, including description of a dance preceding a buffalo hunt.

2094. Meriwether, Lee. "A Buckboard Trip Among the Indians." *Cos,* 4 (October 1887), 138–42.
Includes description of a ceremonial dance.

2095. Michelson, Truman. "Narrative of an Arapaho Woman." *AA,* 35 (1933), 595–610.
Life history collected from a seventy-seven-year-old informant in 1932. Outlines the cycle of woman's life.

2096. Nettl, Bruno, "Musical Culture of the Arapaho." *MQ,* 41 (1955), 325–31.
Survey of musical performance includes six texts (music only).

2097. ———. "Text-Music Relationships in Arapaho Songs." *SJA,* 10 (1954), 192–99.
Examination of correlations between words and music.

2098. Salzmann, Zdeněk. "Arapaho II: Texts." *IJAL,* 22 (1956), 151–58.
Five trickster tales collected from the same informant. With interlinear translations, but no commentary.

2099. ———. "Arapaho III: Additional Texts." *IJAL,* 22 (1956), 266–72.
Five narratives—one a tall tale—with interlinear translations. No commentary.

2100. ———. "Arapaho Tales III." *MWF,* 7, No. 1 (Spring 1957), 27–37.
Seven folktale texts with comparative commentary. Some data on informants.

2101. ———. "Contrastive Field Experience with Language and Values of the Arapaho." *IJAL,* 17 (1951), 98–101.
Explores relationship between language and the acculturation process. Shows English influence on storytelling and prayers.

2102. ———, and Joy Salzmann. "Arapaho Tales I." *HF,* 9 (1950), 80–96.
Two folktale texts with comparative notes and some commentary on storytelling contexts.

2103. ———, and Joy Salzmann. "Arapaho Tales II." *MWF,* 2 (1952), 21–42.
Two myth texts with comparative and explanatory notes.

2104. Underhill, Ruth, and Students. "Modern Arapaho." *SWL,* 17 (1951), 38–42.
Describes contemporary ceremonials.

2105. Voth, H. R. "Arapaho Tales." *JAF,* 25 (1912), 43–50.
Fifteen myth and folktale texts collected between 1882 and 1892. No commentary or annotations.

2106. Wake, C. Staniland. "Nihancan, the White Man." *AAOJ,* 26 (1904), 225–31.
Characterization of the Arapaho Trickster.

2107. ———. "Traits of an Ancient Egyptian Folk-Tale, Compared with Those of Aboriginal American Tales." *JAF,* 17 (1904), 255–64.
Shows parallels between an Arapaho folktale and the Egyptian story "The Two Brothers."

2108. Wildschut, William. "Arapaho Medicine Bundle."

IN, 4 (1927), 83–88.
Includes summary of ritual origin myth.

See also 187, 499, 761, 2045, 2060, 2225, 2226, 4061.

C. Arikara

2109. Alexander, Hartley Burr. "Lucky-in-the-House." *TAM,* 17 (August 1933), 616–26.
Description of an Arikara ceremonial observed in 1924.

2110. "Arikara Creation Myth." *JAF,* 22 (1909), 90–92.
Commentary on cosmogony from the unpublished notes of Rev. C. L. Hall. Written in 1881.

2111. *Arikara Indians of South Dakota.* Vermillion, S. D.: Univ. Museum, 1941.
Archeological and ethnographic survey. Includes chapter on mythology and accounts of ceremonials and games.

2112. Dorsey, George A. "An Arikara Story-Telling Contest." *AA,* 6 (1904), 240–43.
Presents a series of stories, mostly personal narratives, in the order in which they were related.

2113. ———. *Traditions of the Arikara.* Washington: Carnegie Institute, 1904.
Eighty-two myth texts with abstracts collected in 1903. Some general content commentary, but no annotations.

2114. Gilmore, Melvin R. "Arikara Account of the Origin of Tobacco and Catching of Eagles." *IN,* 6 (1929), 26–33.
Unannotated myth text. Some comments on cultural background.

2115. ———. "The Arikara Consolation Ceremony." *IN,* 3 (1926), 256–74.
Description of a ritual observed in 1922. Includes texts of orations.

2116. ———. "Arikara Genesis and Its Teachings. Told by Four-Rings, an Old Man of the Arikara Tribe, and Now Summarized in English." *IN,* 3 (1926), 188–93.
Cosmogonic myth and its allegorical implications.

2117. ———. "Arikara Household Shrine to Mother Corn." *IN,* 2 (1925), 31–34.
Description of ceremonial.

2118. ———. "Buffalo-Skull from the Arikara." *IN,* 3 (1926), 75–79.
Description of a ritual object includes account of Arikara cosmology.

2119. ———. "The Coyote's Boxelder Knife." *IN,* 4 (1927), 214–16.
Unannotated myth text with some context commentary.

2120. ———. "Origin of the Arikara Silverberry Drink." *IN,* 4 (1927), 125–27.
Unannotated text of an etiological myth. No commentary.

2121. Goddard, Pliny E. "Indian Ceremonies of Long Ago." *NH,* 22 (1922), 559–64.
Description of Arikara's revival of ceremonies which had ceased to be observed in the twentieth century.

2122. Howard, James H. "The Arikara Buffalo Society Medicine Bundle." *PlA,* 19 (1974), 241–71.

Description of ritual origin myth and ceremonial. With one song text.

2123. ———. "Arikara Native-Made Glass Pendants: Their Probable Function." *AAn,* 37 (1972), 93–97.

Beads found in sites in South Dakota seem related to ceremonials of the Arikara.

2124. Libby, O. G., ed. "The Arikara Narrative of the Campaign Against the Hostile Dakotas. June, 1876." *CSHSND,* 6 (1920), 5–209.

Accounts by nine surviving members of the Arikara scouts who served under Custer. Collected in 1912. No annotations, but some commentary on cultural background.

See also 2077, 2388.

D. Assiniboin

2125. Denig, Edwin Thompson. "Indian Tribes of the Upper Missouri." Ed. J. N. B. Hewitt. *ARBAE,* 46 (1928–1929), 375–628.

Ethnography based on observations in 1850s includes descriptions of ceremonials, religious conceptions, music, and oratory. Includes free translations of two prayers and one myth.

2126. Ewers, John C. "The Assiniboin Horse Medicine Cult." *AnQ,* 29 (1956), 57–68.

Ceremonial description includes text of ritual origin myth.

2127. ———. "The Bear Cult Among the Assiniboin and Their Neighbors of the Northern Plains." *SJA,* 11 (1955), 1–14.

Description of ceremonials with attention to comparisons with rituals of other Plains groups.

2128. Kennedy, Dan (Ochankugahe). *Recollections of an Assiniboine Chief.* Toronto: McClelland and Stewart, 1972.

Anecdotes, myths, and legends rewritten from oral accounts. No annotations, but extensive introduction to tribal culture (by James R. Stevens).

2129. Kennedy, Michael Stephen, ed. *The Assiniboines from the Accounts of the Old Ones Told to First Boy (James Larpenteur Long).* Norman: Univ. Of Oklahoma Press, 1961.

Oral history recounted in 1939. Includes myth texts, historical legends, and descriptions of customs. With brief descriptions of informants, but no annotations.

2130. Lowie, Robert H. "The Assiniboine." *APAMNH,* 4 (1910), 1–270.

Ethnography based on fieldwork done in 1907. Includes descriptions of ceremonials and eighty oral narrative texts (including the multi-episodic Trickster cycle). Includes comparative notes and four texts with interlinear translations.

2131. ———. "A Few Assiniboine Texts." *AnL,* 2, No. 8 (November 1960), 1–30.

Twelve myth and folktale texts and six song texts (words only) with interlinear translations. Collected between 1907 and 1913. No commentary, but some linguistic notes.

2132. Potts, William John. "Creation Myth of the Assinaboines." *JAF,* 5 (1892), 72–73.

Paraphrased myth text with some data on cultural background.

2133. Rodnick, David. "An Assiniboine Horse-Raiding Expedition." *AA,* 41 (1939), 611–16.

Excerpts an account of a horse-raiding expedition from a life history collected in 1935. Includes data on songs and prayers.

2134. ———. *The Fort Belknap Assiniboine of Montana. A Dissertation.* Philadelphia: NP, 1938.

Ethnography based on fieldwork done in 1935. Includes descriptions of ceremonials, dances, and games.

See also 1964, 2017.

E. Blackfoot

2135. Benedict, Ruth. "Primitive Freedom." *AtM,* 169 (1942), 756–63.

Cross-cultural survey of concepts of freedom includes synopsis of Blackfoot legends about Eagle in the Skies, a culture hero.

2136. Brasser, Ted J. "The Pedigree of the Hugging Bear Tipi in the Blackfoot Camp." *AIAM,* November 1979, pp. 32–39.

Describes traditional tipi decoration which depicts a mythic creature embracing the structure.

2137. Browne, John Mason. "Indian Medicine." *AtM,* 18 (1866), 113–19.

Examines "medicine" as a ceremonial system among NA groups. Includes descriptions of Blackfoot rituals and song texts.

2138. ———. "Traditions of the Blackfeet." *Gal,* 3 (15 January 1867), 157–64.

Survey of the group's mythic concepts.

2139. Comes at Night, George. *Roaming Days.* Browning, Mont.: Blackfeet Heritage Program, 1978.

Rewritten myth and legend texts placed in storytelling context. Also some brief ceremonial descriptions.

2140. Ewers, John C. "The Blackfoot War Lodge: Its Construction and Use." *AA,* 46 (1944), 182–92.

Includes personal narratives relating war adventures which help to clarify the varied uses of the lodge.

2141. ———. "The Case for Blackfoot Pottery." *AA,* 47 (1945), 289–99.

Tries to determine whether the Blackfoot made pottery by examining mythology and other oral traditions.

2142. ———. *The Horse in Blackfoot Indian Culture with Comparative Material from Other Western Tribes.* BAEB No. 159 (1955).

Primarily concerned with economics of horse use among the Blackfoot, but includes data on the Horse Medicine Cult, its origin myth, and ceremonial procedures. Also contains three myth texts on origin of the horse.

2143. ———. "A Unique Pictorial Interpretation of Blackfoot Indian Religion in 1846–1847." *Eh,* 18 (1971), 231–38.

Explains the iconography of a symbolic painting by a Blackfoot artist (1846 or 1847) depicting the group's religion.

2144. Gilles, George. "Three Indian Tales." *AHR*, 15, No. 1 (Winter 1967), 25–28.

Unannotated legend texts. Collected in 1890s.

2145. Goldfrank, Esther S. *Changing Configurations in the Social Organization of a Blackfoot Tribe During the Reserve Period (The Blood of Alberta, Canada)*. *MAES* No. 8 (1945).

Culture change study covering 1877 to 1940. Includes data on ceremonialism.

2146. Grinnell, George Bird. *Blackfeet Indian Stories.* New York: Scribner's, 1915.

Twenty-four unannotated myth and folktale texts. No commentary.

2147. ———. *Blackfoot Lodge Tales: The Story of a Prairie People.* New York: Scribner's, 1892.

Unannotated myth and legend texts introduced by general discussion of Blackfoot storytelling. Also includes a brief cultural survey, with data on ceremonialism.

2148. ———. "A Blackfoot Sun and Moon Myth." *JAF*, 6 (1893), 44–47.

Unannotated myth text with some explanatory commentary.

2149. ———. "Childbirth Among the Blackfeet." *AA*, o.s. 9 (1896), 286-87.

Discusses ceremonials and prayers associated with birth.

2150. ———. "Early Blackfoot History." *AA*, o. s. 5 (1892), 153–64.

Reconstruction of tribal history based in part on oral traditions.

2151. ———. "Little Friend Coyote." *H*, 102 (1900–1901), 288–93.

Rewritten folktale text.

2152. ———. "The Lodges of the Blackfeet." *AA*, 3 (1901), 650–68.

Architectural survey includes discussion of mythical symbols painted on lodges and of ceremonials which accompany the erection of lodges.

2153. Ground, Mary. *Grass Woman Stories.* Browning, Mont.: Blackfeet Heritage Program, 1978.

Pamphlet includes unannotated myth and legend texts. No commentary.

2154. Hale, Horatio. "Ethnology of the Blackfoot Tribes." *PSM*, 29 (June 1886), 204–12.

Cultural survey includes data on religion and mythology.

2155. ———. "Report on the Blackfoot Tribes." *Na*, 32 (1 October 1885), 531–33.

Brief cultural survey includes data on religion and mythology.

2156. Hanks, Lucien M., Jr. "A Psychological Exploration in the Blackfoot Language." *IJAL*, 20 (1954), 195–205.

Focuses on the word and concept *matsapsi*, "crazy." Includes several anecdotes to show how the concept is used and suggests how it fits into tribal value structure.

2157. ———, and Jane Richardson Hanks. *Tribe Under Trust. A Study of the Blackfoot Reserve of Alberta.* Toronto: Univ. of Toronto Press, 1950.

Ethnography based on fieldwork begun in 1938. Major interest is economic, but includes data on ceremonials such as the Sun Dance.

2158. Harrod, Howard L. *Mission Among the Blackfeet.* Norman: Univ. of Oklahoma Press, 1971.

History of missionary institutions among the tribe contains data on ceremonialism (including the Sun

Dance) and some myth texts.

2159. Hellson, John C. "The Pigeons, a Society of the Blackfoot Indians," in 166, pp. 181–220.

Thorough description of a ceremonial society and its rituals.

2160. Higgins, Kathleen. "The Blackfeet Medicine Lodge Ceremony." *IW*, 3, No. 23 (15 July 1936), 18–19.

Description of a ceremony.

2161. ———. "Origin of the Grass Dance." *IW*, 3, No. 23 (15 July 1936), 47.

Text of a ritual origin myth.

2162. Holterman, Jack. "Seven Blackfeet Stories." *IH*, 3, No. 4 (Fall 1970), 39–43.

Legend and folktale texts with explanatory notes. Introduction includes comparative data.

2163. Josselin de Jong, Jan P. *Blackfoot Texts from the Southern Piegans Blackfoot Reservation, Teton County Montana.* Amsterdam: J. Müller, 1914.

Not available for examination.

2164. Knox, Robert H. "A Blackfoot Version of the Magic Flight." *JAF*, 36 (1923), 401–3.

Unannotated folktale text collected in 1921. No commentary.

2165. Lancaster, Richard. "Why the White Man Will Never Reach the Sun," in 93, pp. 190–200.

Text of a myth collected in 1958 from the Chief of the Piegan Reservation. Preceded by data on informant and collection situation.

2166. Laut, Agnes C. "The Struggle for Life of the Blackfeet." *PM*, 46 (1926), 19–24.

Overview of the culture in the 1920s. With one myth summary.

2167. Lewis, Oscar. "Manly-Hearted Women Among the North Piegan." *AA*, 43 (1941), 173–87.

Description of women who adopt masculine roles, including solo singing and performance of other verbal art usually reserved for men.

2168. L'Heureux, Jean. "Ethnological Notes on the Astronomical Customs and Religious Ideas of the Chokitapia or Blackfeet Indians, Canada." *JAIGBI*, 15 (1886), 301–4.

Briefly describes ceremonialism associated with astronomy.

2169. Linderman, Frank B. [Co-Skee-See-Co-Cot]. *Indian Why Stories. Sparks from War Eagle's Lodge-Fire.* New York: Scribner's, 1915.

Etiological and bowdlerized Trickster myths and legends (200) from the Blackfoot, Ojibwa, and Cree. No annotations or commentary. Claims to be using NA storytelling style.

2170. Long Lance, Chief Buffalo Child. "The Ghost Horse," in 111, pp. 155–70.

Account of a wild horse hunt, which the author says was recounted many times. Reprinted from 2171.

2171. ———. *Long Lance: The Autobiography of a Blackfoot Indian Chief.* London: Faber & Faber, 1928.

Includes several descriptions of ceremonials.

2172. ———. "The Sun Dance." *GH*, 85 (August 1927), 64–65, 219.

Ceremonial description.

2173. Maclean, John. "Blackfoot Amusements." *AAOJ*, 23 (1901), 163–66.

Ceremonial descriptions with song texts (words only).

2174. ———. "Blackfoot Indian Legends." *JAF*, 3 (1890), 296–98.

Four unannotated myth texts with brief comments on cultural background.

2175. ——. "Blackfoot Mythology." *JAF,* 6 (1893), 165–72.

Eight unannotated myth and legend texts with some comments on cultural background.

2176. Many Guns, Tom. *Pinto Horse Rider.* Browning, Mont.: Blackfeet Heritage Program, 1979.

Ethnographic sketches and rewritten myth texts. No annotations.

2177. McClintock, Walter. *The Blackfoot Beaver Bundle. SWML* Nos. 2 & 3 (ND).

Description of object includes ritual procedures and origin myth.

2178. ——. "Blackfoot Legends (As Related by Bull Plume, of the Northern Piegan)." *M,* 7 (1933), 41–46, 70–73.

Two unannotated myth texts. No commentary.

2179. ——. "Blackfoot Medicine-Pipe Ceremony." *M,* 22 (1948), 12–16, 56–61.

Ceremonial description with song text. Reprinted as *SWML* No. 21 (ND).

2180. ——. "Blackfoot Warrior Societies." *M,* 11 (1937), 148–58, 198–204; 12 (1938), 11–23.

Based on fieldwork done in 1905. Survey of ceremonial organization includes song texts and ceremonial descriptions. Reprinted as *SWML* No. 8 (ND).

2181. ——. "Dances of the Blackfoot Indians." *M,* 11 (1937), 77–86, 111–21.

Description of the Grass Dance as observed in 1898. Reprinted as *SWML* No. 7 (ND).

2182. ——. "Four Days in a Medicine Lodge." *H,* 101 (1900), 519–32.

Account of Medicine-Lodge Ceremony includes summary of ritual origin legend and music from one of the songs.

2183. ——. *The Old North Trail or Life, Legends and Religion of the Blackfeet Indians.* London: Macmillan, 1910.

Account of Blackfoot culture written by employee of Forest Service. Includes a number of myth and legend texts in their storytelling contexts. With descriptions of ceremonials, especially a very thorough treatment of the Sun Dance.

2184. ——. *Painted Tipis and Picture-Writing of the Blackfoot Indians. SWML* No. 6 (ND).

Description of art work on tipis includes text of origin myth of the Snow Tipi.

2185. ——. "Saítsiko, the Blackfoot Doctor." *M,* 15 (1941), 80–86.

Description of a healing ritual includes prayer text.

2186. ——. *The Tragedy of the Blackfoot.* Los Angeles: Southwest Museum, 1930 (Museum Papers No. 3).

Includes anecdotes about life among the Blackfoot during initial acculturation period (1890s), ceremonial descriptions, and data on religion.

2187. Mezquida, Anna Blake. "The Door of Yesterday. An Intimate View of the Vanishing Race at the Panama-Pacific International Exposition." *OM,* n. s. 66 (July 1915), 3–11.

Describes storytelling and ceremonial performances of Blackfoot at the Exposition.

2188. Michelson, Truman, "A Piegan Tale." *JAF,* 29 (1916), 408–9.

Unannotated Trickster myth. No commentary.

2189. ——. "Piegan Tales." *JAF,* 24 (1911), 238–48.

Five myth and folktale texts collected in 1910. No commentary or annotations.

2190. ——. "Piegan Tales of European Origin." *JAF,* 29 (1916), 409.

Note on some narratives of EA origin among the Blackfoot.

2191. ——. "Trickster Marries His Daughter." *JAF,* 45 (1932), 265.

Blackfoot text of a Trickster tale.

2192. Nettl, Bruno. "Biography of a Blackfoot Indian Singer." *MQ,* 54 (1968), 199–207.

Based on data collected in 1966 and 1967. Presents the singer's development as a performer and describes the role of music in Blackfoot culture.

2193. Nevin, Arthur. "Impressions of Indian Music as Heard in the Woods, Prairies, Mountains and Wigwams. A Sketch of the Ceremonial Songs of the Blackfeet Indians." *Etu,* 38 (October 1920), 663–64.

Survey of musical performances among the group.

2194. Raczka, Paul. "Minípoka: Children of Plenty." *AIAM,* May 1979, pp. 62–67, 96.

Discusses concept of favorite child in Blackfoot culture, ceremonies performed for the child, and art objects manufactured for it.

2195. *Redman Echoes. Comprising the Writings of Chief Buffalo Child Long Lance and Biographical Sketches by His Friends.* Los Angeles: Frank Wiggins Trade School, 1933.

Collected writings include the description of the Sun Dance from *GH* (2172) and pieces on the acculturation process.

2196. Rides at the Door, Darnell Davis, comp. *Napi Stories.* Browning, Mont.: Blackfeet Heritage Program, 1979.

Pamphlet includes rewritten texts from the Trickster cycle. Some data on storytelling. No annotations.

2197. Schultz, James Willard. *Blackfeet and Buffalo. Memories of Life Among the Indians.* Norman: Univ. of Oklahoma Press, 1962.

Collection of periodical pieces, most published in the *Great Falls Tribune* and in magazines for boys. First section consists of autobiographical pieces; second section contains personal narratives from NA informants.

2198. ——. *Blackfeet Tales of Glacier National Park.* Boston: Houghton Mifflin, 1916.

Unannotated myth and legend texts with settings in the Park. Placed in fictionalized storytelling context.

2199. ——. *Friends of My Life as an Indian.* Boston: Houghton Mifflin, 1923.

Account of author's visits to old friends among Blackfoot includes many narrative texts—myths, legends, personal narratives—in storytelling contexts. Also some descriptions of ceremonials.

2200. ——. *In Enemy Country.* Boston: Houghton Mifflin, 1928.

Account of a Blackfoot's adventures in Crow and Cheyenne country, apparently written from his oral narration.

2201. ——. *My Life as an Indian. The Story of a Red Woman and a White Man in the Lodges of the Blackfeet.* New York: Doubleday, Page, 1907.

Account of author's marriage into Blackfoot tribe and participation in ceremonialism. Includes one legend text, attributed to a Kutenai.

2202. ———. *Signposts of Adventure: Glacier National Park as the Indians Know It.* Boston: Houghton Mifflin, 1926.

Contains two sections: one on Blackfoot names in the Park; the other on Kutenai names. Thorough discussions of sources for names include references to and summaries of myths.

2203. ———. *Why Gone Those Times? Blackfoot Tales.* Ed. Eugene Lee Silliman. Norman: Univ. of Oklahoma Press, 1974.

Anthology of NA oral narratives collected by Schultz.

2204. *Sta-Ai-Tsi-Nix-Sin Ghost Stories.* Browning, Mont.: Blackfeet Heritage Program, 1979.

Pamphlet includes unannotated legend texts. No commentary.

2205. "Torture Ordeal of the Blackfeet Sun Dance, The." *HW,* 34 (13 December 1890), 975-76.

Ceremonial description.

2206. Uhlenbeck, C. C. *A New Series of Blackfoot Texts from the Southern Piegans Blackfoot Reservation, Teton County, Montana.* Amsterdam: Johannes Müller, 1912.

Fifty-five myth, folktale, and legend texts collected in 1911 and presented with free translations. No commentary or annotations.

2207. ———. *Original Blackfoot Texts from the Southern Piegans Reservation, Teton County, Montana.* Amsterdam: J. Müller, 1911.

Myth and other narrative texts presented with free translations. Some commentary on informants and the mythological system.

2208. Walton, Eda Lou. *Dawn Boy. Blackfoot and Navajo Songs.* New York: E. P. Dutton, 1926.

Thirteen Blackfoot and thirty-six Navajo song texts (words only) and several verse renderings of myths from the groups. Some impressionistic commentary about poetic quality of the material. No annotations.

2209. Watt, Ellen. "Transferral of a Bundle." *B,* 298 (Summer 1967), 22-26.

Ceremonial description.

2210. Wildschut, William. "Blackfoot Pipe Bundles." *IN,* 5 (1928), 419-33.

Includes ritual origin myth and thorough description of ritual procedure.

2211. Wilson, R. N. "Blackfoot Star Myths—The Pleiades." *AAOJ,* 15 (1893), 149-50.

Unannotated myth text. No commentary.

2212. ———. "Blackfoot Star Myths—The Seven Stars." *AAOJ,* 15 (1893), 200-03.

Unannotated myth text. No commentary.

2213. ———. "The Sacrificial Rite of the Blackfoot." *PTRSC,* 3rd series, 3, section 2 (1909), 3-21.

Ceremonial description with text of ritual origin myth.

2214. Wissler, Clark, "Ceremonial Bundles of the Blackfoot Indians." *APAMNH,* 7 (1912), 65-289.

Description of bundles includes treatment of ceremonies associated with them. Also discusses ceremonial singing and presents one myth text ("Origin of the Horse").

2215. ———. "Societies and Dance Associations of the Blackfoot Indians." *APAMNH,* 11 (1913), 361-460.

Thorough coverage of Blackfoot ceremonialism based on fieldwork begun in 1903.

2216. ———, and D. C. Duvall. "Mythology of the Blackfoot Indians." *APAMNH,* 2 (1908), 1-163.

About 100 myth and legend texts collected in

1903-1907. Introductory commentary and notes provide some comparative data.

See also 436, 1984, 2027, 2077, 2078, 2514.

F. Cheyenne

2217. "Account of the Northern Cheyenne Concerning the Messiah Superstition." *JAF,* 4 (1891), 61-69.

Description of the Ghost Dance excerpted from George Bird Grinnell's interview for the *New York Tribune* for 23 November 1890, Grinnell's correspondence with *JAF* editor, and an account in the *Essex County Mercury* for 26 November 1890.

2218. Anderson, Robert. "The Buffalo Men, A Cheyenne Ceremony of Petition Deriving from the Sutaio." *SJA,* 12 (1956), 92-104.

History and description of a ceremony with one song text.

2219. ———. "The Northern Cheyenne War Mothers." *AnQ,* 29 (1956), 82-90.

Description of a ceremony which responded to United States military conscription.

2220. ———. "Notes on Northern Cheyenne Corn Ceremonialism." *M,* 32 (1958), 57-63.

Ritual description.

2221. Campbell, Stanley. "Two Cheyenne Stories." *JAF,* 29 (1916), 406-8.

Texts of etiological myths collected in 1913. No annotations, but with some data on informant.

2222. Chief Thunderbird. "Cheyenne Ceremony for Girls." *M,* 23 (1949), 178-79.

Description of an initiation ritual.

2223. "Cheyenne Marriage Customs." *JAF,* 11 (1898), 298-301.

Description of ceremonialism reprinted from the *Southern Workman* for July 1898.

2224. Cohoe. *A Cheyenne Sketchbook.* Commentary by E. Adamson Hoebel and Karen Daniels Petersen. Norman: Univ. of Oklahoma Press, 1964.

Collection of sketches of Cheyenne life done by an artist who died in 1924. Commentary deals with ceremonials, dances, and other subjects treated in the sketches.

2225. Densmore, Frances. *Cheyenne and Arapaho Music.* Los Angeles: Southwest Museum, 1936 (Museum Papers No. 10).

Seventy-two song texts (words and music) collected in 1935. General comments treat musical performance. Contextual and musicological notes accompany each text.

2226. ———. "A Study of Cheyenne and Arapaho Music." *M,* 9 (1935), 187-89.

Brief account of research sponsored by the Southwest Museum. With one song text.

2227. Dorsey, George A. "The Cheyenne: Ceremonial Organization." *PFCM-AS,* 9 (1905), 1-56.

Descriptions of ceremonial societies and texts of five myths (including tribal origin and origin of the Sun Dance) in English translations. No commentary or annotations.

2228. ——. "The Cheyenne: The Sun Dance." *PFCM-AS,* 9 (1905), 57–186.
Description of the ceremonial as observed in 1901, 1902, and 1903.

2229. Dundes, Alan. "A Cheyenne Version of Tale-Type 1176." *WF,* 23 (1964), 41–42.
Annotated folktale text collected in 1963. Fairly extensive comparative discussion.

2230. Ewers, John C. "Self-Torture in the Blood Indian Sun Dance." *JWAS,* 38 (1948), 166–73.
Ritual description with extensive use of personal narrative texts.

2231. Garrard, Lewis H. "In the Lodge of Vi-Po-Na." *AW,* 5, No. 4 (July 1968), 32–36.
Reprinted excerpt from a book published in 1850. Includes some data on oratorical performance.

2232. Goggin, John M. "A Note on Cheyenne Peyote." *NMA,* 3, No. 2 (November-December 1938), 26–30.
Description of ritual procedure.

2233. Goodbear, Paul Flying Eagle. "Southern Cheyenne Ghost Narratives." *PM,* 24 (1951), 10–20.
Six unannotated legend texts with comments on storytelling practices and ghost beliefs.

2234. Grinnell, George Bird. "A Buffalo Sweatlodge." *AA,* 21 (1919), 361–75.
Deals with ceremonial construction of the lodge and with songs performed in the lodge.

2235. ——. *By Cheyenne Campfires.* New Haven: Yale Univ. Press, 1926.
Myth and legend texts with some context data. No annotations. Texts seem to be rewritten.

2236. ——. *The Cheyenne Indians. Their History and Ways of Life.* 2 volumes. New Haven: Yale Univ. Press, 1924.
Thorough survey of Cheyenne culture based on contact begun in 1890. Contains data on storytelling, music, and ceremonialism.

2237. ——. "The Cheyenne Medicine Lodge." *AA,* 16 (1914), 245–56.
Describes Medicine Lodge ceremony from an informant's account.

2238. ——. "A Cheyenne Obstacle Myth." *JAF,* 16 (1903), 108–15.
Unannotated myth text with brief commentary on cultural background.

2239. ——. "Falling-Star." *JAF,* 34 (1921), 308–15.
Myth text collected in 1921. Some data on the informant. No comparative notes.

2240. ——. "The Great Mysteries of the Cheyenne." *AA,* 12 (1910), 542–75.
Discusses the medicine arrows and the sacred hat. Includes song and legend texts and ceremonial descriptions.

2241. ——. "Lone Wolf's Last War Trip." *M,* 17 (1943), 162–67, 219–24.
Account of a warrior's death.

2242. ——. "Notes on Some Cheyenne Songs." *AA,* 5 (1903), 312–22.
Texts and translations with some commentary about contexts. No music. Grinnell corrected some of his translations in *AA,* 5 (1903), 582–83.

2243. ——. "Some Early Cheyenne Tales." *JAF,* 20 (1907), 169–94.
Myth and folktale texts with commentary on content and cultural background. Some comparative discussion.

2244. ——. "Some Early Cheyenne Tales. II." *JAF,* 21 (1908), 269–320.
Continuation of 2243. This section focuses on myths about the culture hero.

2245. Habegger, Lois R. *Cheyenne Trails: A History of Mennonites and Cheyennes in Montana.* Newton, Kan.: Mennonite Publication Office, 1959.
Contains some data on Cheyenne ceremonials and summaries of myths.

2246. Hoebel, E. Adamson. *The Cheyennes, Indians of the Great Plains.* New York: Henry Holt, 1960.
Ethnography with sections on ceremonialism (Arrow Renewal, Sun Dance, Animal Dance) and world view.

2247. Kroeber, A. L. "Cheyenne Tales." *JAF,* 13 (1900), 161–90.
Thirty-three myth texts collected in 1899. Some comparative notes and data on collecting situation.

2248. Liberty, Margot. "The Northern Cheyenne Sun Dance and the Opening of the Sacred Medicine Hat, 1959." *PlA,* 12, No. 38 (November 1967), 367–80.
Description of a ceremonial with comparisons with previously published accounts.

2249. Llewellyn, K. N., and E. Adamson Hoebel. *The Cheyenne Way. Conflict and Case Law in Primitive Jurisprudence.* Norman: Univ. of Oklahoma Press, 1941.
Survey of Cheyenne legal system includes data on role of myth and ritual in the system.

2250. Marquis, Thomas B., comp. *Cheyenne and Sioux. The Reminiscences of Four Indians and a White Soldier.* Ed. Ronald H. Limbaugh. Stockton, Cal.: Pacific Center of Western Historical Studies, 1973 (Monograph No. 3).
Reminiscences of three Cheyenne and one Sioux: Iron Teeth, interviewed in 1929 and published in condensed form in *Cent* (1929); unnamed Cheyenne, interviewed in 1927; James Tangled Yellow Hair, interviewed in 1927; Oscar Good Shot, interviewed in 1926 and published in condensed form in *Cent* (1926). Contains some legend texts and descriptions of ceremonials.

2251. ——. *A Warrior Who Fought Custer.* Minneapolis: Midwest, 1931.
Biography based on interviews with subject and other Cheyenne. Contains material on religion, customary way of life, and personal narratives.

2252. Michelson, Truman. "The Narrative of a Southern Cheyenne Woman." *SMC,* 87, No 5 (1932), 1–13.
Life history collected in 1931. Some data on ceremonialism. Extensive explanatory notes.

2253. Ottaway, Harold N. "A Possible Origin for the Cheyenne Sacred Arrow Complex." *PlA,* 15 (May 1970), 94–98.
Examines ritual origin myth to trace origin of ceremonial.

2254. Petersen, Karen D. "Cheyenne Soldier Societies." *PlA,* 9, No 25 (August 1964), 146–72.
Synthesis of published information on the associations.

2255. ——. "On Hayden's List of Cheyenne Military Societies." *AA,* 67 (1965), 469–72.
In 1862, explorer F. V. Hayden published an ethnographic description of northern Plains groups. Petersen summarizes his list of Cheyenne dances.

2256. Petter, Rodolphe. "Sketch of the Cheyenne Grammar." *MAAA,* 1 (1905–1907), 443–78.
Includes examples with interlinear translations of speech usages for prayers, chants, and storytelling.

2257. Poteet, Chrystabel Berrong. "The Ending of a Cheyenne Legend." *CO,* 41, No. 1 (Spring 1963), 9–14.

Describes a tornado which hit Geary, Oklahoma, in 1961 despite Cheyenne oral traditions that the town was immune from such storms.

2258. Powell, Peter J. "The Enduring Beauty of Cheyenne Art." *AW,* 10, No. 4 (July 1973), 4–17.

Surveys various art forms. With some attention to their mythic associations.

2259. ———. *Sweet Medicine: The Continuing Role of the Sacred Arrows, the Sun Dance, and the Sacred Buffalo Hut in Northern Cheyenne History.* 2 volumes. Norman: Univ. of Oklahoma Press, 1969.

Volume I treats the history of Cheyenne ceremonialism as it was affected by contact with other NAs and with EAs. Volume II describes ritual procedures, presents song and prayer texts, and recounts myths.

2260. Stands In Timber, John, Margot Liberty, and Robert M. Utley. *Cheyenne Memories.* New Haven: Yale Univ. Press, 1967.

Attempt by self-appointed keeper of Cheyenne oral tradition to preserve tribal history and prehistory. Includes myth and legend texts and descriptions of ceremonialism and singing.

2261. Straus, Anne S. "The Meaning of Death in Northern Cheyenne Culture." *PlA,* 23 (February 1978), 1–6.

Examines mythic ideas underlying symbolism of death.

2262. ———. "Northern Cheyenne Ethnopsychology." *E,* 5 (1977), 326–57.

Treats concepts of the nature of the self and its maturation. Some data on ceremonialism and mythic concepts.

2263. Swanton, John R. "Some Neglected Data on Cheyenne, Chippewa, and Dakota History." *AA,* 32 (1930), 156–60.

Enters the debate over the historicity of NA traditions by citing material from David Thompson's *Narrative of His Explorations in Western America, 1784–1812,* which deals with Cheyenne southward migration.

2264. Weist, Katherine M. "Giving Away: The Ceremonial Distribution of Goods Among the Northern Cheyenne of Eastern Montana." *PlA,* 18 (May 1973), 97–103.

Description of a ceremonial. Viewed as a method for maintenance of inter- and intra-tribal ties.

2265. Wood, W. Raymond. *Biesterfeldt: A Post-Contact Coalescent Site on the Northeastern Plains. SmCA* No. 15 (1971).

Archeological investigation of a site, identified as Cheyenne, in North Dakota. Includes discussion of tribal origin myth.

See also 499, 1984, 1994, 2015, 2045, 2276, 2459.

G. Comanche

2266. Becker, Daniel A. "Comanche Civilization with History of Quanah Parker." *CO,* 1 (1923), 243–52.

Contains text of an oration delivered by Parker and some data on Comanche ceremonialism.

2267. Canonge, Elliott. *Comanche Texts.* Ed. Benjamin Elson. Norman: Summer Institute of Linguistics of the Univ. of Oklahoma, 1958.

Seven Coyote tales, fourteen anecdotes and descriptions of customs, and ten folktales. With literal translations. No commentary or annotations.

2268. [Eastman, Edwin]. *Seven and Nine Years Among the Camanches* [sic] *and Apaches. An Autobiography.* Jersey City, N. J.: Clark Johnson, 1879.

Captivity narrative includes fairly lengthy descriptions of ceremonialism.

2269. Ferguson, Charles A. "Baby Talk in Six Languages." *AA,* 66 (1964), 103–14.

Cross-cultural survey of language usage for infants includes Comanche. Part of a special issue of *AA* dealing with "The Ethnography of Communication."

2270. Gladwin, Thomas. "Comanche Kin Behavior." *AA,* 50 (1948), 73–94.

Surveys Comanche kinship patterns and contextual uses of kinship terminology. Some attention to use of the terminology in folktales.

2271. Harston, J. Emmor. *Comanche Land.* San Antonio: Naylor, 1963.

Historical and ethnological survey includes data on ceremonialism, singing, and dancing. Some song texts.

2272. Hunter, J. Marvin. "The Legend of the Valley of Paint," in 91, pp. 126–28.

Text of a narrative supposedly told to Hunter's informant by a NA storyteller (either Comanche or Kiowa).

2273. Jones, David E. *Sanapia. Comanche Medicine Woman.* New York: Holt, Rinehart and Winston, 1972.

Ethnographic portrait of a Comanche Eagle Doctor. Includes excerpts from interviews with the subject, texts of personal narratives and legends, and ceremonial descriptions.

2274. Kenner, Charles L. *A History of New Mexican-Plains Indian Relations.* Norman: Univ. of Oklahoma Press, 1969.

Primarily a political and social history, but argues that some New Mexican folk drama has a basis in Comanche songs.

2275. Linton, Ralph. "The Comanche Sun Dance." *AA,* 37 (1935), 420–28.

The last Comanche Sun Dance occurred in 1878. Linton reports an informant's recollections of the ceremony.

2276. McAllester, David P. *Peyote Music. VFPA* No. 13 (1949).

Song texts collected, for the most part, in 1940 and presented with thorough description of the ritual procedure. Included are informants' comments about the songs and a discussion of singing style. Groups represented are Comanche, Fox, Washo, Cheyenne.

2277. ———. "Riddles and Other Verbal Play Among the Comanches." *JAF,* 77 (1964), 250–57.

Discusses opinions about the state of NA riddling traditions, presents thirty-two riddle texts, and provides texts of other word play (puns, onomatopoeia, tongue-twisters, and metaphors).

2278. Reid, Mrs. Bruce. "An Indian Legend of the Blue Bonnet," in 104, pp. 197–200.

Rewritten legend text. Some commentary on variants.

2279. Tilghman, Zoe A. *Quanah, The Eagle of the Comanches.* Oklahoma City: Harlow, 1938.

Biography of Quanah Parker includes some song texts and ceremonial descriptions.

2280. Wallace, Ernest, and E. Adamson Hoebel. *The Comanches. Lords of the South Plains.* Norman: Univ. of Oklahoma Press, 1952.

Historical and ethnological work includes data on mythology and ceremonialism.

See also 2045, 2363, 2704, 4066.

H. Crow

2281. Denig, Edwin Thompson. "Of the Crow Nation." Ed. John C. Ewers. *BAEB* No. 151 (*AP* No. 33), 1953.

Essay on Crow culture written in 1856 contains information on tobacco-planting ceremony.

2282. Ehrlich, Clara. "Tribal Culture in Crow Mythology." *JAF,* 50 (1937), 307–408.

Thorough survey of Crow myths using "mirror of culture" approach. Compares ethnographic data from myths with that obtained through field research.

2283. Ewers, John C. "A Crow Chief's Tribute to the Unknown Soldier." *AW,* 8, No. 6 (November 1971), 30–35.

Describes the presence of Plenty Coups at the burial of the Unknown Soldier from World War I. Contains an English text of his speech.

2284. Kaschube, Dorothea V. *Crow Texts. IJAL-NATS* No. 2 (1978).

Texts gathered by the technique of domain-eliciting in 1953–1954. Presented with interlinear translations and extensive linguistic commentary. Most of the material is descriptions of culture.

2285. Linderman, Frank B. *American: The Life Story of a Great Indian.* New York: John Day, 1930.

Fictionalized biography of Plenty Coups. Has some information on storytelling and ceremonialism. Based on interviews with subject.

2286. ———. *Old Man Coyote (Crow).* New York: John Day, 1931.

Eleven rewritten myth texts with no annotations, but brief commentary on the role of Coyote as Trickster.

2287. ———. *Pretty-Shield. Medicine Woman of the Crows.* Lincoln: Univ. of Nebraska Press, 1960.

Life history includes myth and folktale texts. Reprinted from 1932 edition.

2288. Lowie, Robert H. "Crow Curses." *JAF,* 72 (1959), 105.

Examines three curse texts.

2289. ———. "The Crow Indian Sun Dance." *AMJ,* 15 (1915), 23–25.

Focuses on the sacred dolls used in the ceremonial.

2290. ———. *The Crow Indians.* New York: Holt, Rinehart and Winston, 1935.

Cultural survey based on fieldwork begun in 1907 includes data on ceremonials, storytelling, dances, songs, and world view.

2291. ———. "The Crow Indians of Montana." *AMJ,* 11 (1911), 179–81.

Notes on field trip to reservation include description of adoption ceremony.

2292. ———. "The Crow Language. Grammatical Sketch and Analyzed Text." *UCPAAE,* 39 (1942), 1–142.

Based on fieldwork done in 1931. Contains a myth text with free translation and linguistic analysis.

2293. ———. "Crow Prayers." *AA,* 35 (1933), 433–42.

Seven prayer texts and translations with data on the role of prayer in Crow religion.

2294. ———. "Crow Rapid-Speech Puzzles." *JAF,* 27 (1914), 330–31.

Two tongue-twister texts with grammatical analyses.

2295. ———. "The Crow Sun Dance." *JAF,* 27 (1914), 94–96.

Discusses psychological factors involved in the ceremonial.

2296. ———. "A Crow Tale." *AnQ,* 27 (1954), 1–22.

Myth text with explanatory notes. Collected in 1931. Some commentary on meaning.

2297. ———. "A Crow Text, with Grammatical Notes." *UCPAAE,* 29 (1930), 155–75.

Myth text with free translation and linguistic analysis.

2298. ———. *Crow Texts.* Berkeley: Univ. of California Press, 1960.

Thirty-two legend texts, thirty-two myth texts, songs, prayers, proverbs, tongue twisters, and curses presented with free and interlinear translations. No commentary or annotations.

2299. ———. "Indian Theologians." *AM,* 24 (December 1931), 472–79.

Crow religious ideas presented with summaries of myths.

2300. ———. "Minor Ceremonies of the Crow Indians." *APAMNH,* 21, Part 5 (1924), 323–65.

Description of the Horse Dance, Medicine Pipe Ritual, Bear Song Dance, and Cooked Meat Singing. Includes song texts (words only).

2301. ———. "Myths and Traditions of the Crow Indians." *APAMNH,* 25, Part 1 (1918), 3–308.

Sixty-nine myths and folktales and twelve legends with some comparative and explanatory notes. Introduction places Crow folklore into general Plains traditions.

2302. ———. "Observations on the Literary Style of the Crow Indians," in 112, pp. 271–83.

Examines stylistic features of two variants of a Crow myth.

2303. ———. "The Oral Literature of the Crow Indians." *JAF,* 72 (1959), 97–104.

Distinguishes among Native genres of oral literature, discusses literary style, and examines the contributions of individual storytellers.

2304. ———. "Proverbial Expressions Among the Crow Indians." *AA,* 34 (1932), 739–40.

Texts and meanings of six Crow proverbs. In Crow and free translations.

2305. ———. "The Religion of the Crow Indians." *APAMNH,* 25, Part 2 (1922), 309–444.

Includes extensive data on the Vision Quest, shamanism, and ceremonialism. Based on fieldwork done in 1907–1916.

2306. ———. "Social Life of the Crow Indians." *APAMNH,* 9, Part 2 (1912), 179–248.

Ethnography based on fieldwork done between 1907 and 1912. Contains song and oath texts and translations and descriptions of ceremonials.

2307. ———. "Some Problems in the Ethnology of the Crow and Village Indians." *AA,* 14 (1912), 60–71.

Discusses similarities between Crow and Hidatsa

mythology and ceremonialism.

2308. ———. "Studies in Plains Indian Folklore." *UC-PAAE,* 40, No. 1 (1942), 1–28.

Includes comparative analysis of a Hidatsa myth collected in 1910 and 1911 and "Some Cases of Repeated Reproduction," which presents cases of variation from storyteller to storyteller in Crow folklore. The latter is reprinted in 114 (pp. 259–64).

2309. ———. "The Tobacco Society of the Crow Indians." *APAMNH,* 21, Part 2 (1919), 101–200.

Includes data on ceremonialism as well as origin myths for various chapters of the Society and song texts (words only).

2310. McAllester, David. "Water as a Disciplinary Agent Among the Crow and Blackfoot." *AA,* 43 (1941), 593–604.

Shows parallels between use of water in discipline and beliefs in water monsters. Response by Jane Richardson and Lucien M. Hanks, Jr. in *AA,* 44 (1942), 331–33.

2311. McGinnis, Dale K., and Floyd W. Sharrock. *The Crow People.* Phoenix: Indian Tribal Series, 1972.

Tribal history begins with summary of migration legend.

2312. Nabokov, Peter. *Two Leggings: The Making of a Crow Warrior.* New York: Thomas Y. Crowell, 1967.

Life history based on interviews done by William Wildschut between 1919 and 1923. Includes data on storytelling and ceremonials such as the Sun Dance.

2313. Rollins, W. E. "Passing of the Dance." *OM,* n. s. 42 (August 1903), 111–15.

Description of a ceremonial.

2314. Simms, S. C. "Cultivation of 'Medicine Tobacco' by the Crows—A Preliminary Paper." *AA,* 6 (1904), 331–35.

Description of the ceremony associated with tobacco-planting. Includes English texts of several songs.

2315. ———. "Traditions of the Crows." *PFCM-AS,* 2, No. 6 (October 1903), 281–324.

Twenty-four myth texts and abstracts and two anecdotes collected in 1902. No commentary or annotations.

2316. Voget, Fred. "Individual Motivation in the Diffusion of the Wind River Shoshone Sundance to the Crow Indians." *AA,* 50 (1948), 634–46.

Shows how dissatisfaction with culture change caused the Crow to re-introduce the Sun Dance, which had disappeared from the culture in the 1800s, from Shoshoni sources. Includes description of the ceremonial.

2317. Wildschut, William. *Crow Indian Medicine Bundles.* Ed. John C. Ewers. New York: Museum of the American Indian, 1975.

Edition of a ms. written in 1927. Includes data on ceremonialism, vision quests, and dreams and visions.

2318. ———. "Crow Love Medicine." *IN,* 2 (1925), 211–14.

Includes myth treating origin of love magic.

2319. ———. "The Crow Skull Medicine Bundle." *IN,* 2 (1925), 119–22.

Includes description of ceremonial.

2320. ———. "Moccasin-Bundle of the Crows." *IN,* 3 (1926), 201–5.

Includes origin myth of a ritual object.

See also 2027, 2077, 2078, 2370, 3271, 3595, 4041, 4070.

I. Hidatsa

2321. Bowers, Alfred W. *Hidatsa Social and Ceremonial Organization.* BAEB No. 194 (1965).

Ethnography based on fieldwork done in early 1930s. Includes descriptions of ceremonialism and several myth texts.

2322. Lowie, Robert H. "Hidatsa Texts." Ed. Zellig Harris and C. F. Voegelin. *IHS-PRS,* 1 (1939), 173–239.

Four myth texts and translations collected by Lowie in 1911. With extensive linguistic notes.

2323. Matthews, Washington. *Ethnography and Philology of the Hidatsa Indians.* USGS, Miscellaneous Publication No. 7 (1877).

Based on fieldwork done in 1850s. Includes summary of mythology and folktale texts.

2324. ———. "A Folk-Tale of the Hidatsa Indians." *FLR,* 1 (1878), 136–43.

Unannotated text. No commentary. Reprinted from 2323.

2325. Pepper, George H., and Gilbert L. Wilson. "An Hidatsa Shrine and the Beliefs Respecting It." *MAAA,* 2 (1907–1915), 275–328.

Includes explanations of elements in the shrine from Hidatsa informants and myths about their origin.

2326. Scattered Corn. "The Story of the Grandson, A Hidatsa Legend." *CSHSND,* 4 (1913), 33–40.

Unannotated myth text. No commentary.

2327. Stewart, Frank Henderson. "Hidatsa Origin Traditions Reported by Lewis and Clark." *PlA,* 21 (May 1976), 89–92.

Critique of 2321. Its use of Hidatsa myths collected by Lewis and Clark fails to notice the explorers' vagueness on Plains tribal distinctions.

2328. Will, George F. "Some Hidatsa and Mandan Tales." *JAF,* 25 (1912), 93–94.

Unannotated folktale texts (three Hidatsa, two Mandan). No commentary.

2329. Wilson, Gilbert Livingstone. *Agriculture of the Hidatsa Indians. An Indian Interpretation.* UMSSS No. 9 (1917).

Data on agriculture as related by a woman informant between 1912 and 1915. Contains life history material, ceremonial descriptions, and song and story texts.

2330. ———. *Goodbird the Indian. His Story.* New York: Fleming H. Revell, 1914.

Oral life history rewritten by Wilson. Includes data on ceremonialism and acculturation and prayer and song texts.

2331. ———. "Hidatsa Eagle Trapping." *APAMNH,* 30, No. 4 (1928), 99–245.

Includes ceremonial data with song texts and legend texts.

2332. ———. *Waheenee. An Indian Girl's Story.* St. Paul: Webb, 1921.

Life history of Buffalo-Bird Woman, as related by the subject and her brother. Contains data on storytelling.

See also 813, 2027, 2077, 2078, 2307, 2308, 2382, 2383, 2384, 2385, 2388, 2391.

J. Iowa

2333. Blaine, Martha Royce. *The Ioway Indians.* Norman: Univ. of Oklahoma Press, 1979.
Historical work treats mythology and ceremonialism in early chapters.
2334. Dorsey, J. Owen. "The Dhegiha Language. II." *AAOJ,* 8 (1886), 366–68.
Summaries of eight myths with no commentary or annotations.
2335. ———. "The Sister and Brother. An Iowa Tradition." *AAOJ,* 4 (1882), 286–89.
Unannotated myth text without commentary. Song within myth presented in original with free translation and music.
2336. ———. "The Social Organization of the Siouan Tribes." *JAF,* 4 (1891), 331–42.
Description of Iowa social system includes myth of system's origin.
2337. Skinner, Alanson. "Traditions of the Iowa Indians." *JAF,* 38 (1925), 425–506.
Forty-eight myth texts collected in 1914 and 1922. No annotations. Brief comments on informants and storytelling customs.

See also 1603, 1629, 2003, 2077.

K. Kansa

2338. Unrau, William E. *The Kaw People.* Phoenix: Indian Tribal Series, 1975.
Tribal history includes origin myth, description of storytelling and singing, and presentation of traditional religious system.

See also 2003, 2077, 2458, 2502.

L. Kiowa

2339. Battey, Thomas C. *The Life and Adventures of a Quaker Among the Indians.* Boston: Lee and Shepard, 1876.
Account of contact as a teacher on reservations with various Plains groups, especially the Kiowa. Includes oration texts and descriptions of ceremonialism.
2340. Brant, Charles S. "Joe Blackbear's Story of the Origin of the Peyote Religion." *PlA,* 8, No. 21 (August 1963), 180–81.
Unannotated myth text. No commentary.
2341. Collier, Donald. "Conjuring Among the Kiowa." *PM,* 17 (1944), 45–49.
Brief description of ceremonialism.
2342. Corry, John. "A Man Called Perry Horse." *H,* October 1970, pp. 81–84.
Profile of a contemporary Kiowa includes some information of peyotism and traditional ceremonialism.
2343. Crawford, Isabel. *Kiowa: The History of a Blanket Indian Mission.* New York: Fleming H. Revell, 1915.

Reminiscences of ten years (1896–1906) at a Kiowa mission include accounts of storytelling, the Ghost Dance, and NA responses to Christianity.
2344. Garrett, Roland. "The Notion of Language in Some Kiowa Folktales." *IH,* 5, No. 2 (Summer 1972), 32–37, 42.
Shows sensitivity to language revealed in narratives in *The Way to Rainy Mountain* (2360).
2345. Griffis, Joseph K. *Tahan: Out of Savagery into Civilization. An Autobiography.* New York: George H. Doran, 1915.
Although born of an Osage mother, Griffis was captured as a child by the Kiowa. Deals with prayer, mythology, and ceremonialism in the group.
2346. Harrington, John P. "Three Kiowa Texts." *IJAL,* 12 (1946), 237–42.
Myth texts with interlinear translations.
2347. ———. *Vocabulary of the Kiowa Language. BAEB* No. 84 (1928).
Linguistic survey concludes with narrative text in Kiowa with free and interlinear translations.
2348. Haskins, Frederick J. "Sign Talk of Red Men." *TT,* 4 (July 1902), 242–44.
Includes synopses of two Kiowa folktales.
2349. La Barre, Weston. "Kiowa Folk Sciences." *JAF,* 60 (1947), 105–14.
Outlines tribal ethnobotany, ethnozoology, folk physiology, and folk anthropology.
2350. Marriott, Alice. *Saynday's People. The Kiowa Indians and the Stories They Told.* Lincoln: Univ. of Nebraska Press, 1963.
Combines two volumes which grew out of fieldwork in 1934–1936: *Winter-Telling Stories* contains thirteen episodes from the Saynday cycle (no annotations or commentary); *Indians on Horseback* is an ethnography.
2351. ———. *The Ten Grandmothers.* Norman: Univ. of Oklahoma Press, 1945.
Vignettes of Kiowa life include data on ceremonialism and mythology.
2352. Mayhall, Mildred P. *The Kiowas.* Norman: Univ. of Oklahoma Press, 1962.
Historical work begins with an account of pre-contact culture, including data on storytelling and ceremonialism.
2353. McKenzie, Parker, and John P. Harrington. *Popular Account of the Kiowa Indian Language.* Santa Fe: School of American Research and Museum of New Mexico, 1948 (Monograph No. 12).
Contains legend text with interlinear translation and explanatory comments.
2354. McRae, William E. "Peyote Rituals of the Kiowas." *SWR,* 60 (1975), 217–33.
Unannotated transcripts of two interviews about peyotism conducted in 1975.
2355. Momaday, N. Scott. "Kiowa Legends from *The Journey of Tai-Me.*" *ST,* 3, No. 1 (Fall 1976), 6–8.
Six legend texts from a privately printed book.
2356. ———. "The Morality of Indian Hating." *Ram,* 3 (Summer 1964), 29–40.
Includes data on Kiowa legendary history and ceremonialism and on Pueblo ceremonialism.
2357. ———. "To the Singing, to the Drums." *NH,* February 1975, pp. 38–45.
Treats dances and ceremonialism in contemporary Kiowa culture. With myth and song texts.

2358. ———. "A Vision Beyond Time and Place." *L,* 71 (2 July 1971), 67.
Describes a Kiowa elder and his world view. Contains text of an Ojibwa song (words only).

2359. ———. "The Way to Rainy Mountain." *Rep,* 26 January 1967, pp. 41–43.
Contrasts grandmother's house during family and tribal gathering with silence after her death. Some data on traditional history.

2360. ———. *The Way to Rainy Mountain.* Albuquerque: Univ. of New Mexico Press, 1969.
Intertwines Kiowa mythology and historical legends with an account of own pilgrimage to birthplace in Oklahoma.

2361. Mooney, James. "Calendar History of the Kiowa Indians." *ARBAE,* 17 (1895–1896), 129–445.
Year-by-year analysis of pictographic calendars. Includes history of the group, ethnographic data, references to mythology, and analysis of symbols.

2362. ———. "A Kiowa Mescal Rattle." *AA,* o. s. 5 (1892), 64–65.
Description of an artifact, the designs of which represent elements in peyote ritual.

2363. Nichols, George Ward. "The Indian: What We Should Do with Him." *H,* 40 (1869–1870), 732–39.
Discussion of federal policy toward NAs includes texts of Kiowa and Comanche orations.

2364. Nye, Wilbur Sturtevant. *Bad Medicine & Good. Tales of the Kiowas.* Norman: Univ. of Oklahoma Press, 1962.
Forty-four rewritten historical legends with no annotations. Collected in 1933–1937. General introduction treats Kiowa history and collecting situations. Good material, but poorly presented.

2365. Parsons, Elsie Clews. *Kiowa Tales. MAFS* No. 22 (1929).
Ninety-seven myth, legend, and folktale texts collected in 1927. Extensive explanatory and comparative notes. Introduction treats storytelling situations.

2366. Richardson, Jane. *Law and Status Among the Kiowa Indians. MAES* No. 1 (1940).
Includes data on the Sun Dance and other ceremonials. Based on fieldwork done in 1935.

2367. Rister, C. C. "Santanta, Orator of the Plains." *SWR,* 17, No. 1 (October 1931), 77–99.
Biographical essay contains texts of Santanta's speeches.

2368. Roemer, Kenneth M. "Survey Courses, Indian Literature, and *The Way to Rainy Mountain.*" *CE,* 37, No. 6 (February 1976), 619–24.
Argues that Momaday's book (2360) is the best single work for introducing NA literature. It provides a range of oral literary genres and ironically treats stereotypes of NAs.

2369. Scott, Hugh Lenox. "Notes on the Kado, or Sun Dance of the Kiowa." *AA,* 13 (1911), 345–79.
Description of the ceremonial. Includes text of ritual origin myth.

2370. Voegelin, Erminie W. "Kiowa-Crow Mythological Affiliations." *AA,* 35 (1933), 470–74.
Tabulates correspondences between forty-four Kiowa myths and analogues in other Plains cultures. Concludes that Kiowa mythology is most closely related to that of the Crow.

2371. Wharton, Clarence. *Santanta: The Great Chief of the Kiowas and His People.* Dallas: Banks Upshaw, 1935.
Biographical work includes summary of tribal origin myth.

See also 2045, 2077, 2078, 2272, 3064.

M. Kiowa-Apache

2372. Beatty, John. "Kiowa-Apache Music and Dance." *UNCMA-OP-ES,* 31 (1974), 1–80.
Ethnomusicological analysis of tradition considers style, context of performance, and song types. Includes thirteen music texts and twelve word texts collected in 1965.

2373. Bittle, William E. "The Manatidie. A Focus for Kiowa Apache Tribal Identity." *PlA,* 7, No. 17 (August 1962), 152–63.
Views a modern dancing society as focus of tribal identity.

2374. Brant, Charles S. "The Cultural Position of the Kiowa-Apache." *SJA,* 5 (1949), 56–61.
Discusses group's relationship with other NA groups. Includes comparative treatment of folklore.

2375. ———, ed. *Jim Whitewolf. The Life of a Kiowa Apache Indian.* New York: Dover, 1969.
Life history based on material collected in 1948–1949. Includes descriptions of ceremonials including the Ghost Dance and some legend texts.

2376. ———. "Kiowa Apache Culture History: Some Further Observations." *SJA,* 9 (1953), 195–202.
Attempts to place the group in cultural context by discussing folklore and ceremonialism.

2377. ———. "Peyotism Among the Kiowa-Apache and Neighboring Tribes." *SJA,* 6 (1950), 212–22.
History and description of ritualism. Contains text of ritual origin myth.

2378. McAllister, J. Gilbert. "The Four Quartz Rocks Medicine Bundle of the Kiowa-Apache." *Eth,* 4 (1965), 210–24.
Description of ritual object includes its origin myth.

2379. ———. "Kiowa-Apache Tales," in 90, pp. 1–141.
Forty-six narrative texts collected in 1930s. Includes some cultural background, thorough descriptions of informants and translators, and general comparative data.

2380. ———. "Kiowa-Apache Tales," in 94, pp. 1–11.
Six myth texts with no annotation or commentary.

2381. Opler, Morris E., and William E. Bittle. "The Death Practices and Eschatology of the Kiowa Apache." *SJA,* 17 (1961), 383–94.
Survey of funeral ceremonials and attitudes toward death.

N. Mandan

2382. Beckwith, Martha Warren. "Mandan and Hidatsa Tales. Third Series." *PFF,* 14 (1934), 269–320.
Fifteen myth and legend texts collected in 1929–1932. Good comparative notes.

2383. ———. *Mandan-Hidatsa Myths and Ceremonies.* *MAFS* No. 32 (1938).

Forty-eight myths and ceremonial texts collected in 1929–1932. With comparative notes and brief introduction on storytelling customs.

2384. ———. "Myths and Ceremonies of the Mandan and Hidatsa. Second Series." *PFF,* 12 (1932), 117–267.

Ritual descriptions and origin myths collected in 1931–1932. Good comparative notes, but no commentary.

2385. ———. "Myths and Hunting Stories of the Mandan and Hidatsa Sioux." *PFF,* 10 (1930), 1–116.

Twelve myth and folktale texts collected in 1929. Good comparative notes, but no commentary.

2386. Boller, Henry A. *Among the Indians. Eight Years in the Far West 1858–1866.* Ed. Milo Milton Quaife. Chicago: R. R. Donnelley, 1959.

Edition of book originally published in 1868. Includes detailed descriptions of Mandan ceremonials.

2387. Bowers, Alfred W. *Mandan Social and Ceremonial Organization.* Chicago: Univ. of Chicago Press, 1950.

Thorough survey of ceremonialism contains texts of a number of ritual origin myths.

2388. Cash, Joseph H., and Gerald W. Wolff. *The Three Affiliated Tribes (Mandan, Arikara, and Hidatsa).* Phoenix: Indian Tribal Series, 1974.

Tribal history includes data on ceremonialism and oratory.

2389. Catlin, George. *O-Kee-Pa: A Religious Ceremony; and Other Customs of the Mandans.* London: Trübner, 1867.

Thorough description of the ceremony with texts of and references to myths.

2390. DeLand, Charles E. "The Aborigines of South Dakota. Part II. The Mandan Indians." *CSHSSD,* 4 (1908), 275–730.

Culture survey includes data on ceremonialism and mythology.

2391. Densmore, Frances. *Mandan and Hidatsa Music.* *BAEB* No. 80 (1923).

Song texts (110 – words and music) collected in 1912, 1915, and 1918. Each text accompanied by musicological analysis. General comments on performance contexts, informants, and cultural background.

2392. Kennard, Edward. "Mandan Grammar." *IJAL,* 9 (1936–1939), 1–43.

General linguistic survey contains myth texts with interlinear and free translations and grammatical commentary.

2393. Kessel, Ralph. "A Structural Analysis of a Mandan Myth." *PlA,* 17 (February 1972), 11–19.

Analysis of three myths associated with the Shell Robe Bundle based on the opposing categories of Summer and Winter.

2394. Kipp, James. "On the Accuracy of Catlin's Account of Mandan Ceremonies." *ARSI for 1872,* pp. 436–38.

Defends validity of Catlin's description in response to criticism by Schoolcraft.

2395. Libby, O. G. "The Story of Corn Silk, An Ancient Mandan Legend." *CSHSND,* 3 (1910), 688–707.

Unannotated myth text. No commentary.

2396. Packeneau, Joseph. "The Story of Corn Silk—A Mandan Legend." *CSHSND,* 2 (1908), 494–97.

Unannotated myth text. No commentary.

2397. "Story of a Medal, Related by Its Owner, Gun-That-Guards-the-House." *CSHSND,* 2 (1908), 470–73.

Legend text with some historical notes. No commentary.

2398. Will, George F. "No-Tongue, A Mandan Tale." *JAF,* 26 (1913), 331–37.

First part of a myth text. No annotation. Brief comment on collecting situation.

2399. ———. "The Story of No-Tongue." *JAF,* 29 (1916), 402–6.

Continuation of 2398. No annotation or commentary.

2400. ———, and H. J. Spinden. "The Mandans. A Study of Their Culture, Archaeology and Language." *PPM,* 3 (1906), 81–219.

Ethnography based on fieldwork done in 1905. Contains survey of mythology and religious attitudes.

See also 2027, 2079, 2328.

O. Omaha

2401. Abbott, Keene. "From Moccasin to Motor-Car." *H,* 133 (1916), 113–20.

Survey of post-contact Omaha life with description of singing and praying at a Christian worship service.

2402. Arth, Malcolm J. "A Functional View of Peyotism in Omaha Culture." *PlA,* No. 7 (October 1956), 25–29.

Suggests that a function of male participation in peyotism is prestige acquisition.

2403. Densmore, Frances. "The Survival of Omaha Songs." *AA,* 46 (1944), 418–20.

Reports similarities between three songs recorded in 1941 and the same songs as recorded by Alice C. Fletcher fifty years earlier.

2404. Dorsey, J. Owen. "Abstracts of Omaha and Ponka Myths." *JAF,* 1 (1888), 74–78, 204–8.

Eight unannotated summaries. No commentary.

2405. ———. "How the Rabbit Killed the (Male) Winter. An Omaha Fable." *AAOJ,* 2 (1880), 128–32.

Myth text with free and interlinear translations and linguistic notes.

2406. ———. "Omaha Folk-Lore Notes." *JAF,* 1 (1888), 213–14.

Summary of creation myth. No commentary.

2407. ———. "Omaha Folk-Lore Notes." *JAF,* 2 (1889), 190.

Unannotated legend text and miscellaneous beliefs. Collected in 1878.

2408. ———. "Omaha Sociology." *ARBAE,* 3 (1881–1882), 205–370.

Ethnography includes descriptions of ceremonialism and story and song texts.

2409. ———. "Omaha Songs." *JAF,* 1 (1888), 209–13.

Nine song texts (words only) with interlinear translations. Comments on cultural background and collecting situation.

2410. ———. "On the Gentile System of the Omahas." *AAOJ,* 5 (1883), 312–18.

Includes descriptions of rituals and origin stories of sub-groups in system.

2411. ———. "The Orphan Myth. The Dhegiha Language III." *AAOJ,* 9 (1887), 95–97.

Summaries of seven myths concerning the culture hero.

2412. ——. "Ponka and Omaha Songs." *JAF,* 2 (1889), 271–76.

Nine Omaha and four Ponca song texts (words and music) with free translations. Some commentary on performance contexts.

2413. ——. "The Religion of the Omahas and the Ponkas." *AAOJ,* 5 (1883), 271–75.

Survey of beliefs and ceremonials.

2414. ——. "Songs of the He¢ucka Society." *JAF,* 1 (1888), 65–68.

Seven song texts (words and music) with interlinear translations. Some commentary on informants and contexts.

2415. ——. "The Young Chief and the Thunders; An Omaha Myth." *AAOJ,* 3 (1881), 303–7.

Unannotated text. No commentary.

2416. Evers, Lawrence J. "Native American Oral Literatures in the College English Classroom: An Omaha Example." *CE,* 36, No. 6 (February 1975), 649–62.

Provides an illustration of how a myth can be interpreted from a literary perspective.

2417. Fillmore, John Comfort. "An Omaha Tribal Festival." *LS,* 10 (1899), 326–33.

Impressionistic description of a ceremonial.

2418. Fletcher, Alice C. "An Evening in Camp Among the Omahas." *S,* 6 (31 July 1885), 88–90.

Description of storytelling session.

2419. ——. "Glimpses of Child-Life Among the Omaha Tribe of Indians." *JAF,* 1 (1888), 115–23.

Descriptions of games and pastimes. With folktale and song texts (words and music).

2420. ——. "Hae-Thu-Ska Society of the Omaha Tribe." *JAF,* 5 (1892), 135–44.

Descriptions of the ceremonials of the society. With song texts (words only).

2421. ——. "Home Life Among the Indians. Records of Personal Experience." *Cent,* n. s. 32 (1897), 252–63.

Contains descriptions of ceremonials and a prayer text.

2422. ——. "Hunting Customs of the Omahas. Personal Studies of Indian Life." *Cent,* n. s. 28 (1895), 691–702.

Includes descriptions of ceremonials.

2423. ——. "Indian Songs. Personal Studies of Indian Life." *Cent,* n. s. 25 (1893–1894), 421–31.

Contextual discussion presents ritual background for two texts (words and music).

2424. ——. "The 'Lazy Man' in Indian Lore." *JAF,* 14 (1901), 100–104.

Survey of references and responses to laziness in Omaha folklore, especially proverbs.

2425. ——. "Leaves from My Omaha Note-Book." *JAF,* 2 (1889), 219–26.

Includes data on marriage and courtship. With one song text (words only).

2426. ——. "Nature and the Indian Tribe." *A&A,* 4 (December 1916), 291–96.

Relates ceremonialism associated with nature among the Omaha.

2427. ——. "Personal Studies of Indian Life. Politics and 'Pipe-Dancing.' " *Cent,* n. s. 23 (1892–1893), 441–55.

Thorough description of the Pipe Dance.

2428. ——. "The Sacred Pole of the Omaha Tribe."

AAOJ, 17 (1895), 257–68.

Ceremonial description and text of ritual origin myth.

2429. ——. "The Significance of the Scalp-Lock. A Study of an Omaha Ritual." *JAIGBI,* 27 (1898), 436–50.

Ceremonial description with song texts (words and music).

2430. ——. "A Study from the Omaha Tribe: The Import of the Totem." *ARSI for 1897,* pp. 577–86.

Study of personal and group totems with their associated rites and myths.

2431. ——. "Wakondagi." *AA,* 14 (1912), 106–8.

Survey of usages of the Omaha term *wakondagi,* including its application to mythical monsters as a synonym for "mystery."

2432. ——. "The Wa-Wa*n,* or Pipe Dance of the Omahas." *Mu,* 4 (1893), 468–77.

Ceremonial description with song texts (words and music). Excerpted from 2434.

2433. ——, and Francis La Flesche. "The Omaha Tribe." *ARBAE,* 27 (1905–1906), 17–642.

General ethnography includes texts of tribal and ritual origin myths and song texts (words and music), descriptions of ceremonialism, and accounts of musical performances.

2434. ——, and Francis La Flesche. "A Study of Omaha Indian Music." *PPM,* 1, No. 5 (1893), 1–152.

Ninety-two song texts (words and music). Some discussion of collecting and performance contexts. Includes "Structural Peculiarities of the Music" by John Comfort Fillmore.

2435. Fortune, R. F. *Omaha Secret Societies. CUCA* No. 14 (1932).

Descriptions of traditional and peyotist ceremonials. With song and personal narrative texts.

2436. Giffen, Fannie Reed. *Oo-Mah-Ha Ta-Wa-Tha (Omaha City).* Illustrations by Susette La Flesche Tibbles. Lincoln, Neb.: by the Authors, 1898.

Miscellany of data relating to Omaha culture contains two story texts and two song texts.

2437. Gilmore, Melvin R. "Meaning of the Word Dakota." *AA,* 24 (1922), 242–45.

Speculates that "Dakota" comes from the Omaha language. Basis of argument is occurrence of a similar word in an Omaha song.

2438. ——. "Teoka*n*ha's Sacred Bundle." *IN,* 1 (1924), 52–62.

Description of bundle includes data on its ceremonial usage and a song text.

2439. Hocart, A. M. "Childhood Ceremonies." *F,* 46 (1935), 281–83.

International survey cites an Omaha example.

2440. Howard, James H. "An Oto-Omaha Peyote Ritual." *SJA,* 12 (1956), 432–36.

Description of the ritual as performed in 1949.

2441. Huntington, Mary. "Man and Music." *NH,* 44 (1939), 107–15.

Considers the role of music in human cultures with some treatment of NA materials and the text of an Omaha song (music only).

2442. La Flesche, Francis. "Death and Funeral Customs Among the Omahas." *JAF,* 2 (1889), 3–11.

Covers eschatology and ceremonialism. With one song text (words and music).

2443. ———. "The Omaha Buffalo Medicine-Men. An Account of Their Method of Practice." *JAF,* 3 (1891), 215–21.

Ritual descriptions with song texts (words and music).

2444. Lurie, Nancy Oestreich. "The Lady from Boston and the Omaha Indians." *AW,* 3, No. 4 (Fall 1966), 31–33, 80–85.

Contrasts the career of Alice C. Fletcher as an ethnologist with her role in the federal dispersal of tribal lands.

2445. Mullin, Cora Phebe. "Council of the Omahas." *PS,* 3 (1929), 201–6.

Description of Tribal Council Meetings includes free translations of six songs and chants.

2446. Olson, Paul A., ed. *The Book of the Omaha: Literature of the Omaha People.* Lincoln: Nebraska Curriculum Development Center, 1979.

Rewritten texts of myths, folktales, legends, and songs. Designed as a secondary school textbook.

2447. Ta-De-Win. "Indian Sing: Indian Pray." *IW,* 3, No. 23 (15 July 1936), 39–42.

Describes Omaha ceremonial singing.

2448. Tibbles, Thomas Henry. *Buckskin and Blanket Days. Memoirs of a Friend of the Indians.* Garden City, N. Y.: Doubleday, 1957.

Autobiography written in 1905 by early supporter of NA rights. Description of life among Omaha includes data on storytelling, singing, and ceremonialism.

2449. Welsch, Roger L. *A Treasury of Nebraska Pioneer Folklore.* Lincoln: Univ. of Nebraska Press, 1966.

Contains twenty-one myths and legends collected from Omaha, Sioux, and Pawnee storytellers during the 1930s. All material previously published in *Nebraska Folklore Pamphlets.* Welsch has supplied a headnote for each text.

2450. ———. " 'We Are What We Eat': Omaha Food as Symbol." *KF,* 16 (1971), 165–70.

Discusses ceremonial and symbolic uses of food in the culture.

See also 200, 296, 440, 502, 743, 748, 2001, 2003, 2048, 2452.

P. Oto

2451. Dorsey, J. Owen. "The Rabbit and the Grasshopper: An Otoe Myth." *AAOJ,* 3 (1880), 24–27.

Text with free translation and linguistic and explanatory notes.

2452. Kercheval, George Truman. "An Otoe and an Omaha Tale." *JAF,* 6 (1893), 199–204.

Two folktale texts with some explanatory notes. No comparative annotations.

2453. Whitman, William. "Origin Legends of the Oto." *JAF,* 51 (1938), 173–205.

Texts collected in 1935 which relate to Oto social structure and ceremonial life.

2454. ———. *The Oto. CUCA* No. 28 (1937).

Ethnography based on fieldwork done in 1935. Contains data on religion and ceremonialism (traditional and peyotist).

See also 2003.

Q. Pawnee

2455. Critcher, Marge, Carolyn Boyum, Patti Huff, and Paul Olson, eds. *The Book of the Pawnee: Pawnee Stories for Study and Enjoyment.* Lincoln: Nebraska Curriculum Development Center, 1979.

Rewritten myth and folktale texts from previously published sources. No annotations, but some commentary on content and cultural background. Designed as a textbook.

2456. DeLand, Charles E. "The Aborigines of South Dakota. Part I." *CSHSSD,* 3 (1906), 271–586.

Culture survey includes data on religion and ceremonialism.

2457. Densmore, Frances. *Pawnee Music.* BAEB No. 93 (1929).

Eighty-six song texts (words and music), each accompanied by musicological and contextual analysis. Recorded in 1919–1920. Introduction compares Pawnee songs to those of other NA groups.

2458. De Voe, Carrie. *Legends of the Kaw. The Folk-Lore of the Indians of the Kansas River Valley.* Kansas City: Franklin Hudson, 1904.

Ethnographic notes and summaries of myths from the Pawnee, Sioux, Kansa, Osage, Delaware, Wyandot, Potawatomi, and Shawnee.

2459. Dorsey, George A. "How the Pawnee Captured the Cheyenne Medicine Arrows." *AA,* 5 (1903), 644–58.

Two versions of a Pawnee historical legend about the theft of sacred objects from the Cheyenne.

2460. ———. *The Pawnee. Mythology (Part I).* Washington: Carnegie Institution, 1906.

Myth texts with abstracts (148) based on fieldwork begun in 1903. Includes brief cultural commentary, but no comparative notes.

2461. ———. "A Pawnee Personal Medicine Shrine." *AA,* 7 (1905), 496–98.

Text of a legend which elucidates the role of personal medicine shrines in Pawnee culture.

2462. ———. "Pawnee War Tales." *AA,* 8 (1906), 337–45.

Texts of two historical legends. No annotations or commentary.

2463. ———. *Traditions of the Skidi Pawnee. MAFS* No. 8 (1904).

Ninety myth and folktale texts with extensive explanatory and comparative notes. Introduction describes cultural background.

2464. Fletcher, Alice C. "Giving Thanks: A Pawnee Ceremony." *JAF,* 13 (1900), 261–66.

Description of a ceremonial. With prayer texts.

2465. ———. "The Hako: A Pawnee Ceremony." *ARBAE,* 22, Part 2 (1900–1901), 5–368.

Thorough ceremonial description includes step-by-step explanation of each ritual and presentation of relevant song texts (words and music). Based primarily on the description of a Pawnee informant.

2466. ———. "A Pawnee Ritual Used When Changing a Man's Name." *AA,* 1 (1899), 82–97.

Ceremonial description.

2467. ———. "Pawnee Star Lore." *JAF,* 16 (1903), 10–15.

Survey of starlore includes miscellaneous beliefs, mythology, and ceremonialism.

2468. ———. "Star Cult Among the Pawnee—A Preliminary Report." *AA,* 4 (1902), 730–36.

Includes texts of origin myth and discussion of its relevance to cultic practices.

2469. Gerrard, Ernest A. "A Gruesome War Dance. A Deer-Hunting Experience Among the Pawnee Indians." *Ou,* 39 (January 1902), 404–7.

Ceremonial description.

2470. Grinnell, George Bird. "Development of a Pawnee Myth." *JAF,* 5 (1892), 127–34.

Unannotated myth text with speculation about how it developed.

2471. ———. "The Girl Who Was the Ring." *H,* 102 (1900–1901), 425–30.

Rewritten folktale text.

2472. ———. "Marriage Among the Pawnees." *AA,* o. s. 4 (1891), 275–81.

Description of the ceremonial complex surrounding courtship and marriage.

2473. ———. "The Medicine Grizzly Bear." *H,* 102 (1900–1901), 736–44.

Rewritten folktale text.

2474. ———. *Pawnee Hero Stories and Folk-Tales with Notes on the Origin, Customs and Character of the Pawnee People.* New York: Forest and Stream, 1889.

Twenty-one unannotated narrative texts. An appended section on Pawnee culture covers ceremonialism and religion.

2475. ———. "Pawnee Mythology." *JAF,* 6 (1893), 113–30.

Survey and discussion of tribal religious ideas, cosmogonic myths, and hero myths.

2476. ———. "A Pawnee Star Myth." *JAF,* 7 (1894), 197–200.

Unannotated myth text. No commentary.

2477. ———. "The Young Dog's Dance." *JAF,* 4 (1891), 307–13.

Text of a ritual origin myth and a description of the ritual.

2478. Hazen, R. W. *History of the Pawnee Indians.* NP: Fremont Tribune, 1893.

Focuses on Pawnee-EA relations as presented through explorers' journals. Some data on religion and a marriage ceremony.

2479. Hyde, George E. *The Pawnee Indians.* Foreword by Savoie Lottinville. Revised edition. Norman: Univ of Oklahoma Press, 1974.

History of the tribe includes data on ceremonialism and mythology.

2480. Irving, John T., Jr. *Indian Sketches, Taken During an Expedition to the Pawnee Tribes.* 2 volumes. Philadelphia: Carey, Lea, and Blanchard, 1835.

Account of a visit to the Plains undertaken in 1833. Contains data on ceremonialism, oratory, and singing and one legend text.

2481. Lesser, Alexander. *The Pawnee Ghost Dance Hand Game. A Study of Cultural Change.* CUCA No. 16 (1933).

Historical treatment of the development of Ghost Dance among the Pawnee, and its effects on the traditional Hand Game. Contains several song texts (words only) and translations.

2482. Lillie, Gordon Wm. (Pawnee Bill). "Sacred Dances of the Pawnees." *AAOJ,* 7 (1885), 208–12.

Brief descriptions of several ceremonials.

2483. Linton, Ralph. *Annual Ceremony of the Pawnee Medicine Men.* FMNH-DAL No. 8 (1923).

Pamphlet describes ceremonial procedure.

2484. ———. "The Origin of the Skidi Pawnee Sacrifice to the Morning Star." *AA,* 28 (1926), 457–66.

Discusses the sacrifice of a captive girl to the Morning Star. Includes several myth texts. Supplementary material came from Barbara Aitken in *AA,* 29 (1927), 731–32; and John Owen Clark in *AA,* 29 (1927), 732–33.

2485. ———. *Purification of the Sacred Bundles, A Ceremony of the Pawnee.* FMNH-DAL No. 7 (1923).

Pamphlet describes ceremonial procedure.

2486. ———. *The Sacrifice to the Morning Star by the Skidi Pawnee.* FMNH-DAL No. 6 (1922).

Pamphlet describes ceremonial procedure and presents texts of ritual origin myth.

2487. ———. *The Thunder Ceremony of the Pawnee.* FMNH-DAL No. 5 (1922).

Pamphlet presents ritual procedure and song texts.

2488. Murray, Charles Augustus. *Travels in North America During the Years 1834, 1835, & 1836. Including a Summer Residence with the Pawnee Tribe of Indians, in the Remote Prairies of the Missouri, and a Visit to Cuba and the Azore Islands.* 2 volumes. London: Richard Bentley, 1839.

During stay with Pawnee, Murray witnessed several ceremonials and oration performances.

2489. *Nebraska Folklore Pamphlet Six. Animal Legends.* Lincoln: Federal Writers' Project, 1937.

Four unannotated myth and folktale texts. No commentary. Collected by the WPA.

2490. *Nebraska Folklore Pamphlet Twelve. Indian Ghost Legends.* Lincoln: Federal Writers' Project, 1937.

Eight unannotated legend texts. No commentary. Collected by the WPA.

2491. Spencer, Lilian White. "Fairy Tales of Archaeology—III." *SWL,* 3 (1937), 10–12.

Account of the Morning Star Sacrifice.

2492. Thurman, Melburn D. "A Case of Historical Mythology: The Skidi Pawnee Morning Star Sacrifice of 1833." *PlA,* 15 (November 1970), 309–11.

Suggests that the belief that the Pawnee engaged in human sacrifice is untrue.

2493. Weltfish, Gene. *Caddoan Texts. Pawnee, South Band Dialect.* PAES No. 17 (1937).

Forty-four texts of myths, legends, folktales, and reminiscences with free and interlinear translations. Collected in 1928–1929. No commentary or annotation.

2494. ———. "The Linguistic Study of Material Culture." *IJAL,* 24 (1958), 301–11.

Examination of the relationship of language to a group's perception of the material world. Uses a Pawnee vision story for illustration.

2495. ———. *The Lost Universe with a Closing Chapter on "The Universe Regained."* New York: Basic Books, 1965.

Account of Pawnee history and culture until 1876 based on interview data. Includes information on ceremonialism and myth and legend texts.

2496. ———. "The Vision Story of Fox-Boy, A South Band Pawnee Text." *IJAL,* 9 (1936–1939), 44–75.

Text of the story used in 2494. Includes interlinear and free translations and extensive linguistic commentary.

2497. Wissler, Clark. "The Sacred Bundles of the Pawnee." *NH,* 20 (1920), 569–71.

Describes medicine bundles, their ceremonial role, and related mythology.

2498. ———, and Herbert J. Spinden. "The Pawnee Human Sacrifice to the Morningstar." *AMJ,* 16 (1916), 48–55.

Compares Pawnee ceremony with Aztec sacrifice.

See also 426, 699, 791, 858, 1984, 2048, 2077, 2449, 2706, 3395.

R. Ponca

2499. Cash, Joseph H., and Gerald W. Wolff. *The Ponca People.* Phoenix: Indian Tribal Series, 1975.

Tribal history includes references to legendary accounts of prehistoric animals, excerpts from oratory, and descriptions of traditional and peyotist religious beliefs and practices.

2500. Dorsey, George A. "The Ponca Sun Dance." *PFCM-AS,* 7, No. 2 (1905), 61–88.

Thorough description of the ritual based on observation and interviews.

2501. Dorsey, James Owen. *The Çegiha Language. CNAE* No. 6 (1890).

Includes myth and legend texts from the Ponca (collected 1871–1873) and the Omaha (collected 1878–1880). Presented with free and interlinear translations and linguistic commentary.

2502. ———. "The Myths of the Raccoon and the Crawfish Among the Dakotah Tribes." *AAOJ,* 6 (1884), 237.

Unannotated myth texts from the Ponca, Osage, and Kansa. No commentary.

2503. ———. "Ponka Stories, Told by Tim Potter, or Big Grizzly Bear, in 1872, at Ponka Agency, Dakota Territory." *JAF,* 1 (1888), 73.

Unannotated summaries of legend texts. No commentary.

2504. Fletcher, Alice C. "The Indian and Nature." *AA,* 9 (1907), 440–43.

Uses a legend text about a Vision Quest to generalize about NA concepts of nature.

2505. Howard, James H. *The Ponca Tribe. BAEB* No. 195 (1965).

Ethnography based on fieldwork done in 1949 and 1954. Includes references to mythic figures and descriptions of ceremonialism (traditional and peyotist). Contains an essay on Ponca history, written in 1947 by tribal historian Peter Le Claire.

2506. McGee, W. J. "Ponka Feather Symbolism." *AA,* o. s. 11 (1898), 156–59.

Survey of feather usage, particularly in ceremonialism.

2507. "Sun Dance of the Ponca Indians." *AAOJ,* 25 (1903), 372–74.

Ceremonial description.

2508. Whitman, William. "Xube, A Ponca Autobiography." *JAF,* 52 (1939), 180–93.

Life history of a subject born in 1899, who was one of the last of his group to have the supernatural power called *xube.* Based on Black Eagle's reminiscences collected in 1935.

2509. Zimmerman, Charles Leroy. *White Eagle, Chief of the Poncas.* Harrisburg, Penn.: Telegraph Press, 1941.

Historical and biographical work with data on religious beliefs and ceremonials including the Sun Dance. Much of the data is highly generalized, not specific to the Ponca.

2510. Zylyff [Thomas Henry Tibbles] and Inshtatheamba. *The Ponca Chiefs: An Indian's Attempt to Appeal from the Tomahawk to the Courts.* Boston: Lockwood, Brooks, 1880.

NA case against federal seizure of tribal lands includes texts of orations, particularly those delivered by the Ponca leader Standing Bear.

See also 1629, 2003, 2077, 2404, 2412, 2413.

S. Sioux

2511. Amiotte, Arthur. "Eagles Fly Over." *P,* 1, No. 3 (Spring 1976), 28–41.

Describes Pipe Fast. With prayer text.

2512. Bartlett, S. C. *Historic Sketch of the Missions of the American Board Among the North American Indians.* Boston: American Board of Missions, 1880.

Section dealing with the Sioux has highly ethnocentric description of ceremonialism.

2513. Beach, Rex E. "The Great Sioux Festival." *ApJ,* 6 (September 1905), 305–16.

Unsympathetic description of ceremonies associated with a Fourth of July festival.

2514. Beaudoin, Kenneth Lawrence. *4 Sioux Myths and 2 Blackfoot Legends.* Mexico City: Amerind Press, 1950.

Pamphlet includes unannotated texts with no commentary. Collected from "reservation students."

2515. Beckwith, Martha Warren. "Mythology of the Oglala Dakota." *JAF,* 43 (1930), 338–442.

Thirty-seven myth and legend texts with personal narratives, descriptions of customs, and a winter count. All collected in 1926. With data on role of myths in the culture and comparative notes.

2516. Beckwith, Paul. "Notes on Customs of the Dakotahs." *ARSI for 1886,* pp. 245–57.

Survey includes sections on ceremonial dances and religion.

2517. Biallas, Leonard J. "Let Black Elk Speak." *ChrC,* 91 (9 October 1974), 932–34.

Suggests positive contributions that Black Elk's teachings can make to modern society.

2518. Blish, Helen H. "The Ceremony of the Sacred Bow of the Oglala Dakota." *AA,* 36 (1934), 180–87.

Description of a ceremonial involving war preparations. With summary of ritual origin myth.

2519. ———. "The Drama of the Sioux Sun Dance." *TAM,* 17, No. 8 (August 1933), 629–34.

Views the ritual as a manifestation of the will to live.

2520. ———. *A Pictographic History of the Oglala Sioux.* Drawings by Amos Bad Heart Bull. Introduction by Mari Sandoz. Lincoln: Univ. of Nebraska Press, 1967.

Pictographic record of history and culture of the group kept by a Sioux artist between 1890 and 1913.

Commentary treats such matters as ceremonialism
(including the Sun Dance and the Ghost Dance).

2521. Boas, Franz. "Teton Sioux Music." *JAF,* 38
(1925), 319–24.

Discusses problems in transcribing NA music.
Compares own attempts with Sioux music with attempts
by Frances Densmore.

2522. Brown, Joseph Epes, ed. *The Sacred Pipe. Black
Elk's Account of the Seven Rites of the Oglala Sioux.* Norman:
Univ. of Oklahoma Press, 1953.

Texts of Black Elk's descriptions of Oglala rituals
recorded in 1947–1948. Includes texts of ritual origin
myths, songs, and prayers. Longest section deals with the
Sun Dance.

2523. Brown, Vinson. *Great Upon the Mountain. Crazy
Horse of America.* Healdsburg, Cal.: Naturegraph, 1971.

Account of "spiritual crises" in life of Crazy Horse
and emphasis on their didactic potential. Includes data
on Sioux ceremonialism and supernaturalism.

2524. Burton, Henrietta K. "Their Fun and Humor."
IW, 3, No. 9 (15 December 1935), 24.

Note on joking behavior among Sioux women.

2525. Bushotter, George. "A Teton Dakota Ghost
Story." Ed. J. Owen Dorsey. *JAF,* 1 (1888), 68–72.

Unannotated legend text with free and interlinear
translations. No commentary.

2526. Collins, Mary C. "The Religion of the Sioux
Indians." *MRW,* 25, No. 11 (November 1902), 827–31.

Survey of belief system.

2527. *Contemporary Sioux Painting.* Rapid City, S. D.:
Tipi Shop, 1970.

Catalogue of an exhibition released through the Sioux
Indian Museum and Crafts Center. Introduction (by
Myles Libhart) surveys traditional culture, including
religion and ceremonialism.

2528. Deloria, Ella Cara. *Dakota Texts.* New York: G. E.
Stechert, 1932.

Sixty-four myth and folktale texts with free and literal
translations. Collected in 1931. Includes linguistic and
explanatory notes.

2529. ———. "Dakota Treatment of Murderers."
PAPS, 88 (1944), 368–71.

Description of judicial system includes data on oratory.

2530. ———. "Short Dakota Texts, Including Conversations." *IJAL,* 20 (1954), 17–22.

Included are a greeting formula and a proverb with
translations and extensive ethnographic commentary.

2531. ———. "The Sun Dance of the Oglala Sioux."
JAF, 42 (1929), 354–413.

Text of a ceremonial description written in the Native
language and presented with free and interlinear
translations. Includes explanatory notes and prayer and
song texts.

2532. DeMallie, Raymond J. "Teton Dakota Time Concepts: Methodological Foundations for the Writing of Ethnohistory," in 136, pp. 7–17.

Cites necessity of employing NA time concepts for
understanding group's history and oral literature.

2533. Densmore, Frances. "A Collection of Specimens
from the Teton Sioux." *IN&M,* 11, No. 3 (1948), 163–204.

Describes artifacts collected in 1911–1914. With data
on ceremonialism and singing.

2534. ———. "For the Sake of Indian Songs." *M,* 29
(1955), 27–29.

Account of a fieldwork experience which illustrates NA
attitude toward music.

2535. ———. *Poems from Sioux and Chippewa Songs.*
Washington: NP, 1917.

Collection of poems based on NA songs. For each
poem, a translation of the song on which it is based is
provided.

2536. ———. "The Rhythm of Sioux and Chippewa
Music." *A&A,* 9 (February 1920), 59–67.

Focuses on various cadences in the music. With
several song texts (words and music).

2537. ———. *Teton Sioux Music. BAEB* No. 61 (1918).

Song texts (240—words and music), each accompanied
with musicological and contextual analysis. Introduction
treats cultural background and compares material with
Ojibwa music.

2538. Dorsey, George A. "Legend of the Teton Sioux
Medicine Pipe." *JAF,* 19 (1906), 326–29.

Unannotated myth text with brief description of
Medicine Pipe Ceremony.

2539. Dorsey, J. Owen. "Games of Teton Dakota Children." *AA,* o. s. 4 (1891), 329–45.

Classified listing and brief descriptions of games.

2540. ———. "Teton Folk-Lore." *AA,* o. s. 2 (1889),
143–58.

Includes ghostlore recorded by George Bushotter in
1887. With legend texts.

2541. ———. "Teton Folk-Lore Notes." *JAF,* 2 (1889),
133–39.

Miscellany includes myth and legend summaries and
song texts (words and music).

2542. Duratschek, Sister Mary Claudia. *Crusading Along
Sioux Trails: A History of the Catholic Indian Missions of South
Dakota.* Yankton, S. D.: Benedictine Convent of the Sacred
Heart, 1947.

Contains some descriptions of "superstitions"—i.e.,
ceremonials.

2543. Eastman, Charles A. *From the Deep Woods to Civilization. Chapters in the Autobiography of an Indian.* Boston: Little,
Brown, 1916.

Sequel to 2544. Contains a chapter on the Ghost
Dance.

2544. ———. *Indian Boyhood.* Garden City, N. Y.: Doubleday, Page, 1915.

Autobiography includes several myth, legend, and
song texts and descriptions of ceremonialism.

2545. ———. *Red Hunters and the Animal People.* New
York: Harper, 1904.

Retellings of twelve folktales.

2546. ———. "The Sioux Mythology." *PSM,* 46 (November 1894), 88–91.

Overview of the group's mythic world view.

2547. ———. "Sioux Mythology," in 79, pp. 221–26.

Emphasizes ideas underlying myths.

2548. ———. *The Soul of the Indian. An Interpretation.*
Boston: Houghton Mifflin, 1911.

Generalized account of NA spiritual life. Chapter on
"The Unwritten Scriptures" includes rewritten Sioux
myths. Also some vague descriptions of ceremonials.

2549. ———, and Elaine Goodale Eastman. *Wigwam
Evenings: Sioux Folk Tales Retold.* Boston: Little, Brown,
[1909].

Twenty-seven rewritten myth and folktale texts. No
annotations or substantive commentary.

2550. Eastman, Mary. *Dahcotah; or Life and Legends of the Sioux Around Fort Snelling.* New York: John Wiley, 1849.

Sketches of NA life focus on oral literature (including rewritten myth and legend texts), oratory, ceremonialism, and supernaturalism.

2551. Ebell, Adrian J. "The Indian Massacres and War of 1862." *H,* 27 (June 1863), 1–24.

Description of NA-EA conflict includes some data on Sioux culture. With a song text (words and music).

2552. Ewers, John C. *Teton Dakota Ethnology and History.* Revised edition. Berkeley, Cal.: National Park Service (Western Museum Laboratories), 1938.

Ethnography designed for museum use. Contains data on religion and ceremonialism including the Sun Dance and the Ghost Dance, but major focus is on material culture.

2553. Feraca, Stephen. "The Yuwipi Cult of the Oglala and Sicangu Teton Sioux." *PlA,* 6, No. 13 (August 1961), 155–63.

Description of a healing ceremony as observed in 1956.

2554. Fire, John (Lame Deer), and Richard Erdoes. *Lame Deer: Seeker of Visions.* New York: Simon and Schuster, 1972.

Autobiography (oral?) includes extensive data on ceremonialism and song texts. Emphasizes NA-EA relations.

2555. Fiske, Frank. *The Taming of the Sioux.* Bismarck, N. D.: Bismarck Tribune, 1917.

Historical account of the waning of Sioux culture includes chapters on religion and the Ghost Dance.

2556. Fletcher, Alice C. "The Emblematic Use of the Tree in the Dakotan Group." *S,* n. s. 4 (2 October 1896), 475–87.

Surveys mythic and ritual significance of trees and poles.

2557. Frerichs, Robert, and Paul A. Olson, eds. *A Few Great Stories of the Santee People Told by Many Nineteenth Century Santee and by Edna Peniska and Paul Robertson of the Modern Santee.* Lincoln: Nebraska Curriculum Development Center, 1979.

Eleven unannotated myth and folktale texts. Includes a content commentary for each text and a general introduction on storytelling customs. Designed as a textbook.

2558. Gardner, W. H. "Ethnology of the Indians of the Valley of the Red River of the North." *ARSI for 1870,* pp. 369–73.

Culture survey includes references to theology and mythology.

2559. Gilmore, Melvin R. "The Dakota Ceremony of Hunká." *IN,* 6 (1929), 75–79.

Ritual descriptions

2560. ———. "The Pasque Flower. Bloom of Dakota Folklore." *NM,* 21 (January 1933), 17.

Rewritten folktale.

2561. ———. "Some Cosmogonic Ideas of the Dakota." *AA,* 28 (1926), 570–72.

Survey of mythic ideas about the origin and nature of the universe.

2562. Grobsmith, Elizabeth S. "The Lakhota Giveaway: A System of Social Reciprocity." *PlA,* 24 (May 1979), 123–31.

Ceremony promotes social alliance, interdependence, and redistribution of wealth.

2563. ———. "Wakunza: Uses of *Yuwipi* Medicine Power in Contemporary Teton Dakota Culture." *PlA,* 19 (May 1974), 129–33.

Surveys the belief in supernatural retribution and its functions.

2564. Hallam, John. "A Sioux Vision—Thick-Headed-Horse's Dream," in 83, pp. 126–44.

Narrative of a dream experience. Originally published in *Inland Magazine* for June 1876.

2565. Hans, Fred M. *The Great Sioux Nation. A Complete History of Indian Life and Warfare in America.* Chicago: M. A. Donahue, 1907.

Ethnocentric history of the Sioux with data on religion, ceremonialism, and oratory.

2566. Hassrick, Royal B. (in collaboration with Dorothy Maxwell and Cile M. Bach). *The Sioux. Life and Customs of a Warrior Society.* Norman: Univ. of Oklahoma Press, 1964.

Survey of history and culture includes data on ceremonialism and mythology.

2567. Herman, Jake. "The Sacred Pole." *M,* 37 (1963), 35–38.

Rewritten text of ritual origin myth. No commentary or annotations.

2568. Holly, Carol T. "*Black Elk Speaks* and the Making of Indian Autobiography." *G,* 12 (1979), 117–36.

Examines effects of Neihardt's editing on Black Elk's orally performed life history.

2569. Holy Dance, Robert. "The Seven Pipes of the Dakota Sioux." *PlA,* 15 (May 1970), 81–82.

Describes ceremonial usages of the pipes.

2570. Hoover, Herbert T. *The Sioux. A Critical Bibliography.* Bloomington: Indiana Univ. Press, 1979.

Unannotated list of 213 books and articles. Introductory essay includes sections on "Autobiographies and Biographies," "Religion," and "Legends."

2571. Howard, James H. "The Dakota Heyóka Cult." *ScM,* 78 (April 1954), 254–58.

Description of ceremonial clowning with one song text (words and music).

2572. ———. "Notes on the Dakota Grass Dance." *SJA,* 7 (1951), 82–85.

Surveys the historical development of the ceremonial.

2573. ——— "Notes on the Ethnogeography of the Yankton Dakota." *PlA,* 17 (November 1972), 281–307.

Surveys geographical knowledge with attention to folklore references. With one personal narrative text.

2574. ———. "The Tree Dweller Cults of the Dakota." *JAF,* 68 (1955), 169–74.

Describes belief in a malevolent wood spirit and includes personal narratives about encounters with it.

2575. ———. "Yanktonai Dakota Eagle Trapping." *SJA,* 10 (1954), 69–74.

Description of ceremonial activity. With one song text.

2576. Howe, M. A. DeWolfe. "An Apostle to the Sioux: Bishop Hare of South Dakota." *AtM,* 108 (1911), 359–70.

Account of the career of Episcopal clergyman William Hobart Hare, who went to South Dakota in 1873. Contains text of origin myth of the Sacred Pipe.

2577. ———. *The Life and Labors of Bishop Hare, Apostle to the Sioux.* New York: Sturgis & Walton, 1912.

Biography of the clergyman includes some data on Sioux ceremonialism and an account of the Ghost Dance.

2578. Huggins, Captain E. L. "The Story of Hépi and Winona. A Dakota Legend." *FL,* 1 (1893), 89–95.

Text with some commentary.

2579. Humfreville, J. Lee. *Twenty Years Among Our Hostile Indians. Describing the Characteristics, Customs, Habits, Religion, Marriages, Dances and Battles of the Wild Indians in Their Natural State, Together with the Entrance of Civilization Through Their Hunting Grounds, Also the Fur Companies, Overland Stage, Pony Express, Electric Telegraph, and Other Phases of Life in the Pathless Regions of the Wild West.* New York: Hunter, 1899.

Includes descriptions of Sioux religion, ceremonialism (including the Sun Dance), and games.

2580. Hurt, Wesley R. "A Yuwipi Ceremony at Pine Ridge." *PlA,* 5, No. 10 (November 1960), 48–52.

Description of the final phase of a healing ceremony observed in 1958.

2581. ———, and James H. Howard. "A Dakota Conjuring Ceremony." *SJA,* 8 (1952), 286–96.

Description of the *Yuwipi* ceremony and its parallels with ceremonials of other NA groups.

2582. Hyde, George E. *A Sioux Chronicle.* Norman: Univ. of Oklahoma Press, 1956.

Historical work covering period 1877–1891 contains material on the Ghost Dance.

2583. "Indian Stories as Related by Andrew Knife at Pine Ridge Reservation, to the Boys and Girls of the Fifth Grade at Oglala Community School, South Dakota." *IW,* 3, No. 17 (15 April 1936), 43–45.

Seven personal narrative texts.

2584. Jahner, Elaine. "The Spiritual Landscape." *P,* 2, No. 3 (1977), 32–38.

Interprets a creation myth as providing validation for the Vision Quest's function as physical and spiritual experience.

2585. Johnson, W. Fletcher. *Life of Sitting Bull and History of the Indian War of 1890–91.* NP: Edgewood, 1891.

Includes chapters on "Legends and Creeds," "Feasting and Dancing," and "The Ghost Dances."

2586. Kemnitzer, Luis S. "Structure, Content, and Cultural Meaning of *yuwipi:* A Modern Lakota Healing Ritual." *AE,* 3 (1976), 261–80.

Analysis of ritual reveals tribal beliefs about human nature, man's relationship to the cosmos, and acculturation.

2587. ———. "Yuwipi." *IH,* 11 No. 2 (Spring 1978), 2–5.

Description of a healing ceremony.

2588. Koch, William E. "The Sioux Trickster." *Kan,* 1960, pp. 18–26.

Seven myth texts collected in 1950s with general discussion of the role of Trickster.

2589. La Framboise, Julia. "Canktewin, The Ill-Fated Woman: A Dakota (Sioux) Legend." *FL,* 1 (1892), 37–43.

Unannotated text. No commentary.

2590. Lanman, Charles. "The Lone Buffalo." *MH,* 2 (November 1905), 356–58.

Unannotated myth text. No commentary.

2591. La Pointe, Frank. *The Sioux Today.* New York: Crowell-Collier, 1972.

Collection of case studies about contemporary Sioux life. Some data on ceremonialism.

2592. La Pointe, James. *Legends of the Lakota.* San Francisco: Indian Historian Press, 1976.

Myths, legends, songs, and ceremonial descriptions

written by an Oglala Sioux elder.

2593. Lewis, Thomas H. "The *heyoka* Cult in Historical and Contemporary Oglala Sioux Society." *A,* 69 (1974), 17–32.

Description of the ceremonial role of the "contrary" with case studies of particular personalities.

2594. ———. "The Oglala (Teton Dakota) Sun Dance: Vicissitudes of Its Structures and Functions." *PlA,* 17 (February 1972), 44–49.

Compares traditional and modern versions of the ceremonial.

2595. Lowie, Robert H. "Dance Associations of the Eastern Dakota." *APAMNH,* 11, Part 2 (1913), 101–42.

Descriptions of dances and dance societies based on fieldwork done in 1911–1912. Includes some ritual origin myths.

2596. Mails, Thomas E. *Fools Crow.* Garden City, N.Y.: Doubleday, 1979.

Life history of subject born in 1890. Includes extensive data on ceremonialism. Good explanatory notes.

2597. ———. *Sundancing at Rosebud and Pine Ridge.* Sioux Falls, S. D.: Center for Western Studies, 1978.

Thorough description of the Sun Dance based on fieldwork in the 1970s and accounts of earlier observers. Profusely illustrated.

2598. Malan, Vernon D., and Clinton J. Jesser. *The Dakota Indian Religion: A Study of Conflict in Values.* SDSCB No. 473 (1959).

Includes descriptions of ceremonials and a few myth and song texts.

2599. McCluskey, Sally. *"Black Elk Speaks:* and So Does John Neihardt." *WAL,* 6, No. 4 (Winter 1972), 231–42.

Literary analysis of the life history explores Neihardt's editorial role and the persona projected by Black Elk.

2600. McCreight, M. I. *Firewater and Forked Tongues: A Sioux Chief Interprets U. S. History.* Pasadena, Cal.: Trail's End, 1947.

Includes some personal narratives recorded from Flying Hawk, but major focus is on the Sioux informant's ideas about NA-EA relations.

2601. McLaughlin, Mrs. Marie L. *Myths and Legends of the Sioux.* Bismarck, N. D.: Bismarck Tribune, 1916.

Rewritten texts of thirty-eight narratives. No annotations.

2602. Medicine, Beatrice. "Oral History as Truth: Validity in Recent Court Cases Involving Native Americans," in 136, pp. 1–5.

Focuses on cases involving the Wounded Knee incident to treat the admissability of NA oral history in the American judicial system.

2603. Meeker, Louis L. "Siouan Mythological Tales." *JAF,* 14 (1901), 161–64.

Summaries of narratives used for instruction of initiates into Medicine Lodge. No annotation, but some commentary on cultural background.

2604. ———. "White Man. A Siouan Myth." *JAF,* 15 (1902), 84–87.

Unannotated myth text. No commentary.

2605. Mekeel, Scudder. "An Indian Christmas." *IW,* 3, No. 9 (15 December 1935), 7–8.

Description of festivities at the Pine Ridge Reservation in 1932. Some attention to hymn-singing.

2606. ———. "Sioux New Year's Celebration." *IW*, 3, No. 10 (1 January 1936), 7–9.

Description of ceremonials observed in 1932.

2607. Melody, Michael Edward. "Maka's Story: A Study of a Lakota Cosmogony." *JAF*, 90 (1977), 149–67.

Discusses a creation story apparently from a ms. by J. R. Walker. Treats textual history and the tribal cosmology.

2608. Miller, David Humphreys. *Ghost Dance*. New York: Duell, Sloan and Pearce, 1959.

Popular history of the revitalization movement among the Sioux. With descriptions of ceremonials and song texts.

2609. Moorehead, Warren K. "The Indian Messiah and the Ghost Dance." *AAOJ*, 13 (1891), 161–67.

Description of the Ghost Dance on the Pine Ridge Reservation. With song text (words only).

2610. *Nebraska Folklore Pamphlet Twenty-One. Santee-Sioux Indian Legends*. Lincoln: Federal Writers' Project, 1939.

Eight unannotated myth and folktale texts. No commentary. Collected by the WPA.

2611. *Nebraska Folklore Pamphlet Twenty-Three. More Santee-Sioux Indian Legends*. Lincoln: Federal Writers' Project, 1939.

Eight unannotated myth and folktale texts. No commentary. Collected by the WPA.

2612. Neihardt, John G. *Black Elk Speaks, Being the Life Story of a Holy Man of the Ogalala Sioux*. New York: William Morrow, 1932.

Most famous life history of a NA ever published. Black Elk, who witnessed the Custer massacre, recounts his visionary experiences, describes ceremonies, sings songs, and recounts personal narratives. Frequently reprinted.

2613. ———. "The Book That Would Not Die." *WAL*, 6, No. 4 (Winter 1972), 227–30.

Reprint of the Pocket Books introduction to 2612.

2614. "Oath-Taking Among the Dakota." *IN*, 4 (1927), 81–83.

Comments on public oaths from the notes of George Bushotter.

2615. Olden, Sarah Emilia. *The People of Tipi Sapa (The Dakotas). Tipi Sapa Mitaoyate Kin*. Milwaukee: Morehouse, 1918.

History and ceremonialism as presented by an Episcopal priest of Sioux ancestry (P. J. Deloria). Includes myth and legend texts, song texts with translations, and thorough descriptions of ceremonials.

2616. Paige, Darcy. "George W. Hill's Account of the Sioux Sun Dance of 1866." *PlA*, 24 (May 1979), 99–112.

Publication of a ms. account of the Sun Dance with comparison to other accounts.

2617. Paige, Harry W. "A Death on the Prairie." *Ame*, 138 (24 June 1978), 507–09.

Description of fieldwork in collecting Sioux songs with data on death of principal informant. Includes text of his death song.

2618. ———. *Songs of the Teton Sioux*. Los Angeles: Westernlore, 1970.

Thorough description of function, style, and context of musical performances as observed in the 1960s. Includes texts (words only) and literary analysis.

2619. Parker, Donald Dean, ed. *The Recollections of Philander Prescott, Frontiersman of the Old Northwest, 1819–1862*. Lincoln: Univ. of Nebraska Press, 1966.

Reminiscences of a fur trader and agricultural adviser to the Sioux. Section on "Sioux Lore" contains data on ceremonialism and some oration texts.

2620. Pidgeon, William, *Traditions of De-coo-dah and Antiquarian Researches: Comprising Extensive Explorations, Surveys, and Excavations of the Wonderful and Mysterious Earthen Remains of the Mound-Builders in America; the Traditions of the Last Prophet of the Elk Nation Relative to Their Origin and Use; and the Evidences of an Ancient Population More Numerous Than the Present Aborigines*. New York: Horace Thayer, 1858.

Describes mounds and similar antiquities in the Upper Mississippi Valley with elucidation of traditions about the prehistoric Elk tribe from a Sioux informant.

2621. Powers, William K. *Oglala Religion*. Lincoln: Univ. of Nebraska Press, 1977.

Historical and ethnographic presentation with attention to cosmology and ceremonialism. Some data on the effects of culture change.

2622. Reese, Montana Lisle, ed. *Legends of the Mighty Sioux*. Chicago: Albert Whitman, 1941.

Some forty-five unannotated myth, folktale, and legend texts collected by the South Dakota Writers' Project, WPA. No commentary. May be for children.

2623. Riggs, Stephen Return. *Dakota Grammar, Texts, and Ethnography*. Ed. James Owen Dorsey. *CNAE* No. 9 (1893).

Based on Riggs' long association with the Sioux (1837–1883). Contains eight myth and folktale texts with free and interlinear translations and explanatory notes. Ethnographic data include treatments of religion and supernaturalism.

2624. ———. "Mythology of the Dakotas." *AAOJ*, 5 (1883), 147–49.

Argues that mythology helps to establish a group's origin and relations with other groups.

2625. ———, trans. "Narrative of Paul Mazakootemane." *CMHS*, 3 (1880), 81–90.

Written autobiography by a Sioux. Includes data on ceremonialism and a song text.

2626. ———. *Tah-Koo Wah-Kán; or, The Gospel Among the Dakotas*. Boston: Congregational Sabbath-School and Publishing Society, [c. 1869].

Historical work on missions contains chapters on Dakota religion which outline the group's supernaturalism and describe the ceremonialism.

2627. ———. "The Theogony of the Sioux." *AAOJ*, 2 (1880), 265–70.

Survey of Sioux religious ideas with summaries of myths, song texts, and ceremonial descriptions.

2628. Robinson, Doane. *A History of the Dakota or Sioux Indians from Their Earliest Traditions and First Contact with White Men to the Final Settlement of the Last of Them Upon Reservations and the Consequent Abandonment of the Old Tribal Life*. Pierre: State of South Dakota, 1904.

Historical work includes some good descriptions of ceremonials and an oration text. With a section on the Ghost Dance. Re-issued by Ross & Haines in 1956.

2629. ———. "The Legend of Medicine Knoll." *CSHSSD*, 12 (1924), 179.

Unannotated legend text collected from an EA in 1923, but probably of NA origin. No commentary.

2630. ———. "Tales of the Dakota. One Hundred Anecdotes Illustrative of Sioux Life and Thinking." *CSHSSD*, 14 (1928), 485–537.

Brief vignettes of Sioux life. Included are a few historical legends and ceremonial descriptions. Mostly *about,* not of, the group.

2631. Sandoz, Mari. *These Were the Sioux.* New York: Hastings House, 1961.

Recollections of contact with the Sioux as a child leads into general treatment of the culture, including religion, world view, and ceremonialism.

2632. Sayre, Robert F. "Vision and Experience in *Black Elk Speaks.*" *CE,* 32, No. 5 (February 1971), 509–35.

Treats the role of Black Elk as a perpetrator of a visionary world view. Includes some treatment of the relationship between Black Elk and Neihardt.

2633. Schwatka, Frederick. "The Sun Dance of the Sioux." *Cent,* n. s. 17 (March 1890), 753–59.

Description of the ceremonial.

2634. Shelton, Rosa T. "In the Country of Sitting Bull." *O,* 60 (5 November 1898), 617–21.

Some data on ceremonialism and an oration text.

2635. Skinner, Alanson. "A Sketch of Eastern Dakota Ethnology." *AA,* 21 (1919), 164–74.

Data gathered during fieldwork in 1914 include a brief section on folklore, which explores analogues with traditions of neighboring NA groups.

2636. Smith, G. Hubert. "The Winona Legend." *MnH,* 13 (1932), 367–76.

Traces history of a Lovers' Leap story back to a Sioux informant.

2637. Smith, J. L. "A Ceremony for the Preparation of the Offering Cloths for Presentation to the Sacred Calf Pipe of the Teton Sioux." *PlA,* 9, No. 25 (August 1964), 190–96.

Description of a ceremonial observed in 1964.

2638. ———. "The Sacred Calf Bundle: It's [sic] Effect on the Present Teton Dakota." *PlA,* 15 (May 1970), 87–93.

Considers role of the Bundle in contemporary culture. With ritual origin myth.

2639. Smith, Rex Alan. *Moon of Popping Trees.* New York: Readers' Digest Press, 1975.

Historical account of events leading up to Wounded Knee Massacre includes several chapters on the Ghost Dance. With song texts.

2640. [Snelling, William Joseph]. *Tales of the Northwest; or, Sketches of Indian Life and Character.* Boston: Hilliard, Gray, Little, and Wilkins, 1830.

Anecdotes about Sioux life include data on ceremonialism and religion. Re-issued by the Univ. of Minnesota Press in 1936.

2641. Sobosan, Jeffrey C. "The Philosopher and the Indian: Correlations Between Plotinus and Black Elk." *IH,* 7, No. 2 (Spring 1974), 47–48.

Points out similarities between the two mystics.

2642. Standing Bear, Luther. *Land of the Spotted Eagle.* Boston: Houghton Mifflin, 1933.

Description of lifeways with extensive data on religion and ceremonialism.

2643. ———. *My People the Sioux.* Ed. E. A. Brininstool. Introduction by William S. Hart. Boston: Houghton Mifflin, 1928.

Autobiography of Standing Bear (born 1868). Describes games and ceremonials including the Sun Dance.

2644. "Sun Dance of the Sioux Nation, The." *LH,* 1882, pp. 174–77.

Description of a ceremonial observed in 1878.

2645. Sword, Major George. "The Story of the Ghost Dance." *FL,* 1 (1892), 28–36.

Description of the Ghost Dance with nineteen song texts (with free translations). Written by an Oglala Sioux policeman.

2646. Terrell, John Upton. *Sioux Trail.* New York: McGraw-Hill, 1974.

General treatment of Sioux history and culture includes data on mythology and ceremonialism.

2647. Theisz, R. D. *Buckskin Totems: Contemporary Oral Narratives of the Lakota.* Aberdeen, S. D.: North Plains Press, 1975.

Not available for examination.

2648. Thomas, Sidney J. "A Sioux Medicine Bundle." *AA,* 43 (1941), 605–9.

Includes references to origin myth of Bundle and description of ceremonialism.

2649. Trimble, Bessie. "Sioux Give-Away Ceremony." *IW,* 2, No. 24 (1 August 1935), 38–39.

Description of a ceremony.

2650. Vestal, Stanley. *New Sources of Indian History, 1850–1891: The Ghost Dance—The Prairie Sioux.* Norman: Univ. of Oklahoma Press, 1934.

Anthology of documents, one section pertaining to the Ghost Dance and the other focusing on general aspects of Sioux culture. Included are government reports, statements by eyewitnesses (NA and EA) to events, and excerpts from ethnographic materials.

2651. ———. *Sitting Bull, Champion of the Sioux. A Biography.* Boston: Houghton Mifflin, 1932.

Based to a large degree on accounts of NA and EA storytellers. Includes some song texts and descriptions of ceremonialism. Treats the Ghost Dance.

2652. ———. "The Works of Sitting Bull, Real and Imaginary." *SWR,* 19, No. 3 (April 1934), 265–78.

Contrasts authentic poems attributed to Sitting Bull with those composed by EAs and passed off as his work.

2653. Walker, F. R. "Sioux Games. I." *JAF,* 18 (1905), 277–90.

Descriptions of games with song texts (words only).

2654. Wallis, Wilson D. "Beliefs and Tales of the Canadian Dakota." *JAF,* 36 (1923), 36–101.

Includes twenty-six episodes from the Iktomi cycle, four animal tales, and descriptions of cosmology and cosmogony. Collected in 1914. No comparative notes.

2655. ———. "The Canadian Dakota." *APAMNH,* 41, Part 1 (1947), 1–225.

Ethnography based on fieldwork done in 1914 includes data on ceremonialism and myth and legend texts.

2656. Wassell, William H. "The Religion of the Sioux." *H,* 89 (1894), 943–52.

Emphasizes involvement with Christianity, but includes some data on traditional ceremonialism. With one music text.

2657. Wilson, Thomas. "Dakota Legend of the Head of Gold." *JAF,* 13 (1900), 294–96.

Comparative comments on a narrative published in 2623.

2658. Wissler, Clark. "Some Dakota Myths. I." *JAF,* 20 (1907), 121–31.

Five unannotated myth texts. No commentary.

2659. ———. "Some Dakota Myths. II." *JAF,* 20 (1907), 195–206.

Five unannotated myth texts. No commentary. Continuation of 2658.

2660. ———. "The Whirlwind and the Elk in the Mythology of the Dakota." *JAF,* 18 (1905), 257–68.

Survey of Sioux ideas about the supernatural power embodied in the whirlwind and elk. With myth texts.

2661. Yarrow, H. C. "Some Superstitions of the Live Indians." *AAOJ,* 4 (1882), 136–44.

Description of burial customs with long, unannotated myth text.

2662. Zitkala-Ša. "Impressions of an Indian Childhood." *AtM,* 85 (1900), 37–47.

Random reminiscences include description of a storytelling session.

2663. ———. *Old Indian Legends.* Boston: Ginn, 1901.

Fourteen rewritten narrative texts, some of which deal with Iktomi. No annotations or substantive commentary.

See also 502, 509, 573, 667, 1603, 1629, 1755, 1842, 1992, 2003, 2027, 2045, 2048, 2077, 2078, 2250, 2263, 2437, 2449, 2458, 4470.

T. Wichita

2664. Dorsey, George A. "Hand or Guessing Game Among the Wichitas." *AAOJ,* 23 (1901), 363–70.

Description of play activity and related songs.

2665. ———. *The Mythology of the Wichita.* Washington: Carnegie Institution, 1904.

Sixty myth texts with abstracts. Collected in 1903. Some commentary on cultural background, but no comparative notes.

2666. ——— "Wichita Tales." *JAF,* 15 (1902), 215–39.

Text of creation myth collected in 1902. No annotations, but brief data on informant.

2667. ———. "Wichita Tales." *JAF,* 16 (1903), 160–79.

Unannotated myth text. No commentary.

2668. "Wichita Tales." *JAF,* 17 (1904), 153–60.

Unannotated myth text. No commentary.

2669. Mooney, James. "Quivira and the Wichitas." *H,* 99 (1899), 126–35.

Suggests that the Wichita were contacted by Coronado in 1541. Ethnographic data include treatment of singing style.

2670. Scarborough, Dorothy. "Traditions of the Waco Indians," in 164, pp. 50–54.

Survey of culture of a sub-group of the Wichita includes summaries of several legends.

See also 813.

VI SOUTHWEST

A. General Works

2671. Alexander, Hartley Burr. "The Serpent Symbol and Maize Culture." *NMQ*, 22 (1952), 315–21.

Mostly concerned with Mexican groups, but includes some data on relationship among serpent symbolism, Messiah beliefs, and corn cultivation in the Southwest.

2672. Alliot, Hector. *Bibliography of Arizona. Being the Record of Literature Collected by Joseph Amasa Munk, M. D., and Donated by Him to the Southwest Museum of Los Angeles, California.* Los Angeles: Southwest Museum, 1914.

Unannotated list includes the following relevant sections: "Folklore," "Indians," and "Ethnology."

2673. Applegate, Frank G. *Native Tales of New Mexico.* Introduction by Mary Austin. Philadelphia: Lippincott, 1932.

Sketches of New Mexico history and culture. Some chapters contain narratives rewritten from NA storytellers and placed in performance contexts.

2674. Austin, Mary. "Primitive Stage Setting." *TAM*, 12 (January 1928), 49-59.

Argues that primitive magical drama still occurs among Southwest groups.

2675. ———. "Sekala Ka'ajma. An Interpretive Dance–Drama of the Southwest." *TAM*, 13 (April 1929), 267–78.

Dramatic rendition of a myth about the triumph of life over the transitory vicissitudes of existence.

2676. Bahti, Tom. *Southwestern Indian Ceremonials.* Las Vegas: KC Publications, 1970.

Profusely illustrated booklet contains summaries of myths, descriptions of belief systems and of ceremonialism, and a bibliography.

2677. Bailey, Virginia. "Indian Music of the Southwest." *EP*, 44 (1938), 1–4.

Survey of the styles and contexts of musical performances.

2678. Bailey, Wilfrid C. "Birds in Southwestern Indian Life." *Ki*, 5, No. 5 (February 1940), 17–20.

Includes data on birds associated with myths and ceremonies.

2679. Bandelier, Adolf F., ed. *The Journey of Alvar Nuñez Cabeza de Vaca and His Companions from Florida to the Pacific, 1528–1536. Translated from His Own Narrative by Fanny Bandelier. Together with the Report of Father Marcos of Nizza and a Letter from the Viceroy Mendoza.* New York: A. S. Barnes, 1905.

Travel narrative includes general descriptions of religious attitudes and ceremonialism.

2680. Bascom, William. "The Myth-Ritual Theory." *JAF*, 70 (1957), 103–14.

Critique of the theories of Lord Raglan pays special attention to the applications of his theories in the Southwest.

2681. Biggs, Bruce. "Testing Intelligibility Among Yuman Languages." *IJAL*, 23 (1957), 57–62.

An experiment in mutual intelligibility among speakers of various Yuman languages (Walapai, Yavapai, Havasupai, Yuma, Mohave, Maricopa) involved recording a folklore text and evaluating listeners' comprehension of it.

2682. Boyer, Mary G. *Arizona in Literature: A Collection of the Best Writings of Arizona Authors from Early Spanish Days to the Present Time.* Glendale, Cal.: Arthur H. Clark, 1934.

Includes narrative texts from the Pima (rewritten by J. William Lloyd) and Navajo (by Mary E. Thompson, Lulu Wade Wetherill, and Byron Cummings) and a description of the Hopi Snake Dance (by Kate T. Corey).

2683. Brown, Donald N. "Ethnomusicology and the Prehistoric Southwest." *Em*, 15 (1971), 363–78.

Uses historical accounts of musical performances among NAs in the Southwest to complement archeological findings of musical instruments and ceremonial objects.

2684. Bryan, Bruce. "A Possible Clue to Mimbres Mythology." *M*, 52 (1978), 63–66.

Suggests that the design on a pottery bowl may depict a scene relevant to the prehistoric group's mythology.

2685. Carlisle, Veronica M. "Notes on the Coyote in Southwestern Folktales." *Aff*, 3, No. 4 (Winter 1973), 38–47.

Survey of Coyote's character in narratives from various Southwest groups.

2686. Chesky, Jane. "Indian Music of the Southwest." *Ki*, 7, No. 3 (December 1941), 9–12.

Survey of types and functions of songs. With some musicological commentary.

2687. Collier, John. *American Indian Ceremonial Dances.* Introduction by John Sloan. Preface by Harry L. Shapiro. New York: Bounty Books, 1972.

Survey of ceremonials of the Navajo, Apache, and Zuni and other Pueblo groups. With some chant texts. Profusely illustrated by Ira Moskowitz.

2688. ———. *On the Gleaming Way: Navajos, Eastern Pueblos, Zunis, Hopis, Apaches, and Their Land; and Their Meaning to the World.* Denver: Swallow, 1969.

Explores reasons behind survival of Southwest cultures and describes various group's ceremonials. With chant and song texts. Written by Commissioner of Indian Affairs, 1933–1945.

2689. Conklin, E. *Picturesque Arizona. Being the Result of Travels and Observations in Arizona During the Fall and Winter of 1877.* New York: Mining Record, 1878.

Includes descriptions of Hopi and Zuni games and ceremonies.

2690. Cowan, John L. "Indian Ceremonial Dances." *OM*, n. s. 59 (1912), 505–12.

Survey of ceremonialism in the Southwest.

2691. Cozzens, Samuel Woodworth. *The Marvelous Country; or Three Years in Arizona and New Mexico, the Apaches'*

Home. Comprising a Description of This Wonderful Country, Its Immense Mineral Wealth, Its Magnificent Mountain Scenery, the Ruins of Ancient Towns and Cities Found Therein, with a Complete History of the Apache Tribe, and a Description of the Author's Guide, Cochise, the Great Apache War Chief. The Whole Interspersed with Strange Events and Adventures. London: Sampson Low, Marston, Low & Searle, 1874.

Historical and travel work presents accounts of ceremonialism and some myth texts, including the Zuni cosmogony.

2692.   Crawford, Roselle Williams. *Survival of Legends. Legends and Their Relation to History, Literature and Life of the Southwest.* San Antonio: Naylor, 1952.

Survey of Southwest legendry and its relationship to history, ethnicity, and ceremonial observances.

2693.   Curtis, Edward S. "Vanishing Indian Types." *Scr,* 39 (May 1906), 513–29.

Historical and cultural survey of Southwest groups includes data on ceremonialism.

2694.   ———. "Village Tribes of the Desert Land." *Scr,* 45 (March 1909), 275–87.

Cultural survey of groups in southwestern Arizona. With data on mythology and ceremonialism.

2695.   Dobie, J. Frank. *Guide to Life and Literature of the Southwest. Revised and Enlarged with Knowledge and Wisdom.* Dallas: Southern Methodist Univ. Press, 1952.

Bibliographic guide includes chapters on Pueblo and non-Pueblo NA groups in the Southwest and Plains.

2696.   Dorsey, George A. *Indians of the Southwest.* NP: NP, 1903.

Tourist guide published for the Sante Fe Railroad includes surveys of various NA cultures with attention to their ceremonials. Special focus on Hopi rituals with thorough descriptions of the Snake Dance and Antelope Dance.

2697.   Downing, Orlando Cuadra. *The Adventures of Don Coyote. American Indian Folk Tales.* New York: Exposition, 1955.

Twenty-five coyote tales taken from published sources on Navajo and Pueblo folklore. Brief introduction summarizes Coyote's role as a folk character. May be for children.

2698.   Duff, U. Francis. "Some Exploded Theories Concerning Southwestern Archeology." *AA,* 6 (1904), 303–6.

One fallacy is the idea of massive migrations in prehistory in the Southwest. Thus, migration legends of NAs are false.

2699.   Dunn, Dorothy. *American Indian Painting of the Southwest and Plains Areas.* Albuquerque: Univ. of Mexico Press, 1968.

Survey of painting from pre-contact period into twentieth century includes data on the relationship between symbolism in paintings and in ceremonialism and singing.

2700.   Dustin, C. Burton. *Peyotism and New Mexico.* Santa Fe: Vergara, 1960.

Pamphlet treats peyotism among various groups in the Southwest. With ritual descriptions.

2701.   Estabrook, Emma Franklin. "The Living Past." *EP,* 20 (1926), 40–48.

Effusive celebration of contributions of NAs in the Southwest to civilization. Includes one rewritten song text.

2702.   Evans, Bessie, and May G. Evans. *American Indian Dance Steps.* New York: A. S. Barnes, 1931.

Primarily a how-to book, but contains descriptions of dances and related song texts from Southwest groups.

2703.   Fergusson, Erna. *Dancing Gods. Indian Ceremonials of New Mexico and Arizona.* New York: Alfred A. Knopf, 1931.

Survey of ceremonials of various Southwest groups. Describes ritual procedures and cultural background.

2704.   Gilles, Albert S., Sr. "The Southwestern Indian and His Drugs." *SWR,* 55 (1970), 196–203.

Survey of stimulants and sedatives used by Southwest and Plains groups. With a description of a Comanche peyote ritual.

2705.   Hall, D. J. *Enchanted Sand. A New Mexican Pilgrimage.* New York: William Morrow, 1933.

Englishman's account of visit to Southwest includes excerpts from songs, chants, and myths.

2706.   Hodge, George Meany. *Four Winds. Poems from Indian Rituals.* Santa Fe: Sunstone Press, 1972.

Pamphlet includes unannotated song texts from Southwest groups and the Pawnee.

2707.   Holtz, R. D. "La Fiesta de los Vaqueros." *IW,* 3, No. 23 (15 July 1936), 28–29.

Description of an intertribal festival.

2708.   Ickes, Anna Wilmarth. "Indian Ceremonial Dances of the Southwest." *IW,* 2, No. 24 (1 August 1935), 5–6.

Overview of ceremonials of various Southwest groups.

2709.   Ives, Ronald L. "Anent Unipeds." *AA,* 41 (1939), 336–37.

Treats references to one-footed creatures in Southwest mythologies.

2710.   James, George Wharton. *The Indians of the Painted Desert Region: Hopis, Navahoes, Wallapais, Havasupais.* Boston: Little, Brown, 1903.

Popular survey includes descriptions of ceremonials and rewritten myths and legends.

2711.   Jares, Edward E. "Tepee Tales." *Aff,* 4, No. 3 (Fall 1974), 7–10.

Texts of five stories collected from various Southwest groups. No commentary.

2712.   Jett, Stephen C. "Testimony of the Sacredness of Rainbow Natural Bridge to Puebloans, Navajos, and Paiutes." *Plat,* 45, No. 4 (September 1973), 133–42.

Examines traditions about Rainbow Bridge which suggest its sacredness to various Southwest and Great Basin groups.

2713.   La Farge, Oliver. "Plastic Prayers. Dances of the Southwestern Indians." *TAM,* 14 (March 1930), 218–24.

Describes ceremonials, emphasizing that they are primarily religious events.

2714.   ———. "Unscientific Expedition." *WW,* January 1931, pp. 50–55; February 1931, pp. 76–80; March 1931, pp. 72–76; May 1931, pp. 69–73; July 1931, pp. 54–59.

Account of visit to several Southwest groups includes data on ceremonials.

2715.   Lane, Edith C. "The Legend of Cheetwah," in 104, pp. 130–32.

Rewritten text of a historical legend. Brief commentary on possible function, but no annotation or tribal identification.

2716.   Lange, Charles H., and Carroll L. Riley (with the assistance of Elizabeth M. Lange), eds. *The Southwestern Journals of Adolph F. Bandelier, 1883–1884.* Albuquerque: Univ. of New Mexico Press, 1970.

Description of field experiences includes data on ceremonialism of various groups.

2717. Matthews, Washington. "Ichthyophobia." *JAF*, 11 (1898), 105–12.

Surveys taboos among various Southwest groups on killing and eating fish. With data on relationship between taboos and mythology.

2718. McAllester, David P. *Indian Music in the Southwest.* Colorado Springs: Taylor Museum, 1961.

Pamphlet describes musical traditions of various Southwest groups. Song texts (words only).

2719. McGill, Anna Blanche. "Old Mission Music." *MQ*, 24 (1938), 186–93.

Treats continuing tradition of hymn-singing among NAs, inherited from the mission experience in the Southwest. With five texts (words and music).

2720. McKee, Louise, and Richard Summers. *Dusty Desert Tales.* Caldwell, Ida.: Caxton, 1941.

Unannotated myth texts from the Pima (nine), Apache (seven), Hopi (eight), and Yuma (four). Brief commentaries on cultural backgrounds.

2721. Meaders, Margaret Inman. "Indian Christmas." *T*, 116 (December 1961), 36–38.

Describes Christmas ceremonials among various Southwest groups.

2722. Moon, Carl. "An Aboriginal Thanksgiving. The Harvest Festival of America's First Farmers, Before the Pilgrims Came." *Sun*, 43 (November 1919), 35–37, 52.

Brief overview of harvest ceremonialism in the Southwest.

2723. Parsons, Elsie Clews. "Masks in the Southwest of the United States." *MF*, 5, No. 3 (July–September 1929), 152–56.

Survey of mask designs and functions in various Southwest groups. Written in Spanish and English.

2724. Pearce, T. M. "The Rainbow in Southwestern Folklore." *NMFR*, 12 (1969–1970), 29–34.

Survey of the occurrence of the rainbow in myths and ceremonials of various groups.

2725. Peet, Stephen D. "The Worship of the Rain-God." *AAOJ*, 16 (1894), 341–56.

Treats myths and ceremonials associated with rain in the Southwest.

2726. Reagan, Albert B. "Some Notes on the Occult and Hypnotic Ceremonies of Indians." *UASAL*, 11 (1934), 65–71.

Description of rituals among Southwest and Northwest Coast groups.

2727. Roberts, Helen. "Indian Music from the Southwest." *NH*, 27 (1927), 257–65.

History of collecting NA music in the Southwest. With seven song texts (words and music).

2728. Rush, Olive. "The Young Indian's Work in Old Forms." *TAM*, 17, No. 8 (August 1933), 635-38.

Examination of NAs' retention of traditional culture—especially dance, prayer, and story—in contemporary art forms. Focuses on Southwest groups.

2729. Siettle, Nicholas. "Indian Legend." *IW*, 3, No. 4 (1 October 1935), 40–41.

Myth text with some data on the storyteller. From an unspecified Southwest group.

2730. Simmons, Marc. *Witchcraft in the Southwest. Spanish and Indian Supernaturalism on the Rio Grande.* Flagstaff, Ari.: Northland Press, 1974.

Survey of witch beliefs and practices among various Southwest groups. Includes several case histories, some apparently based on oral accounts.

2731. Simpson, Ruth De Ette. "The Coyote in Southwestern Indian Tradition." *M*, 32 (1958), 43–55.

Survey of oral literature about Coyote among various Southwest groups.

2731a. Smith, Victor J. "Indian Pictographs of the Big Bend in Texas," in 103, pp. 18–30.

Illustrated survey deals with associated myths of various Southwest groups.

2732. Spicer, Edward H. *Circles of Conquest. The Impact of Spain, Mexico, and the United States on the Indians of the Southwest, 1533–1960.* Tucson: Univ of Arizona Press, 1962.

Massive historical work contains material on religious acculturation which describes traditional and modern ceremonialism.

2733. Spinden, Herbert J. *Fine Art and the First Americans.* New York: Exposition of Indian Tribal Arts, 1931.

Pamphlet treats NA painting and textile art. Relates artistic attitudes to NA poetry, especially among Southwest groups.

2734. Taub, Amos. "On the Trail of Song." *SWR*, 34, No. 1 (Winter 1949), 83–88.

Surveys singing among Southwest groups. With several texts.

2735. ———. "Southwestern Indian Poetry." *ArQ*, 6 (1950), 236–43.

Consideration of the study of the poetry. Concludes that while collecting has been extensive, little literary analysis has occurred.

2736. Thompson, S. W. R. "La Fiesta de los Vaqueros." *IW*, 2, No. 24 (1 August 1935), 26–27.

Description of games and dances at an intertribal festival.

2737. Underhill, Ruth M. *Ceremonial Patterns in the Greater Southwest. MAES* No. 13 (1948).

Treats four ritual complexes—the Vision, Corn Ceremonialism, Hunting Ceremonialism, shamanism—with thorough descriptions of ritual procedures. With prayer and song texts.

2738. Wallrich, William Jones. "Tecohote—The Owl in Southwestern Folklore." *SWL*, 15 (June 1949), 15–21.

Surveys the role of the owl in Southwest mythology.

2739. Warner, Louis H. "The Dance of the Redskin." *NR*, 17 (November 1929), 16–17, 42.

Very general survey of ceremonialism among various Southwest groups.

2740. Watson, Edith L. "The Cult of the Mountain Lion." *EP*, 34 (1933), 95–109.

Survey of religious significance of the animal among various Southwest groups. Includes songs, myths, and ceremonial descriptions.

2741. Williams, Jack R. "From My Notebook." *SWL*, 17 (1951), 59–61.

Myth and legend texts from various Southwest groups.

2742. Wilson, Eddie W. "The Gourd in the Southwest." *M*, 24 (1950), 84–88.

Some data on ceremonial usages. With excerpt from a Zuni song text.

See also 172, 192, 250, 283, 384, 427, 479, 546, 627, 630, 721, 1247, 1304, 2019, 2056, 2064, 2919, 4118, 4143, 4184, 5117, 5213.

B. Apache

2743.   Ball, Eve. *In the Days of Victorio. Recollections of a Warm Springs Apache.* Tucson: Univ. of Arizona Press, 1970.
Orally recounted life history of James Kaywaykla (b. 1870s). One chapter focuses on ceremonialism.

2744.   Basso, Keith H. "The Gift of Changing Woman." *BAEB* No. 196 (*AP* No. 76), 1967.
Description and analysis of symbolic content of girl's puberty ritual in early 1960s. Includes summary of ritual origin myth.

2745.   ———. " 'To Give Up on Words': Silence in Western Apache Culture." *SJA*, 26 (1970), 213–30.
One context in which the Western Apache refrain from speech is the curing ceremonial, where chanting is the only permitted verbalization. Also published in 80 (pp. 151–61).

2746.   ———, ed. (with the assistance of E. W. Jernigan and W. B. Kessell). *Western Apache Raiding and Warfare from the Notes of Grenville Goodwin.* Tucson: Univ. of Arizona Press, 1971.
Texts of personal narratives and historical legends collected by Goodwin in 1930s. With introductory account of Goodwin's career and extensive explanatory notes.

2747.   ———. *Western Apache Witchcraft. APUAZ* No. 15 (1969).
Treats witchcraft beliefs, practices, and ceremonials.

2748.   Betzinez, Jason (with Wilbur Sturtevant Nye). *I Fought with Geronimo.* Harrisburg, Penn.: Stackpole, 1959.
Memoirs include description of girl's puberty ritual and a Medicine Dance.

2749.   Bourke, John G. "The Medicine-Men of the Apache." *ARBAE,* 9 (1887–1888), 443–603.
Description of shamanistic practices.

2750.   ———. "Notes on Apache Mythology." *JAF,* 3 (1890), 209–12.
Survey of cosmology and cosmogony collected in 1884.

2751.   ———. "Notes Upon the Religion of the Apache Indians." *F,* 2 (1891), 419–54.
Treats belief system and ceremonialism. With prayer and song texts (words only).

2752.   Boyer, L. Bryce. *Childhood and Folklore. A Psychoanalytic Study of Apache Personality.* New York: Library of Psychological Anthropology, 1979.
Basic Personality Structure study based on an examination of tribal mythology and ceremonialism. Includes a number of field-collected texts.

2753.   ———. "An Example of Legend Distortion from the Apaches of the Mescalero Indian Reservation." *JAF,* 77 (1964), 118–42.
Compares texts of the same story collected from a woman and her teenage grandson. The boy's transformations in the story reflect his personal problems and changes in tribal social structure resulting from acculturation.

2754.   ———. "Stone as a Symbol in Apache Mythology." *AI,* 22 (1965), 14–39.
Analysis of two myths reveals pre-oedipal and oedipal conflicts created by socialization. Stones in the myths vary from vaginal to phallic symbolism.

2755.   Boyer, Ruth M. "A Mescalero Apache Tale: The Bat and the Flood." *WF,* 31 (1972), 189–97.
Story collected in 1958. Embodies religious concepts, interpersonal relationships, and attitudes toward success and leadership.

2756.   Clark, Laverne Harrell. "The Girl's Puberty Ceremony of the San Carlos Apaches." *JPC,* 10, No. 2 (Fall 1976), 431–48.
Illustrated description of ceremonial, focusing on that observed in 1971.

2757.   Cochise, Ciyé "Niño" (as told to A. Kinney Griffith). *The First Hundred Years of Niño Cochise. The Untold Story of an Apache Indian Chief.* New York: Abelard-Schuman, 1971.
Life history beginning in 1874. Includes data on ceremonialism.

2758.   Corbusier, Wm. M. "The Apache-Yumas and Apache-Mojaves." *AAOJ,* 8 (1886), 325–39.
Culture survey includes data on shamanism and ceremonialism.

2759.   Cornwall, Claude C. "Apache 'Devil' Dance." *IW,* 4, No. 4 (1 October 1936), 11–12.
Description of a ceremonial.

2760.   Cremony, John C. *Life Among the Apaches.* San Francisco: A. Roman, 1868.
Account of soldier's tenure in Southwest between 1849 and 1850. Contains some very ethnocentric descriptions of Apache ceremonials. Reprinted by Rio Grande Press in 1969.

2761.   Cummings, Byron. "An Apache Girl Comes of Age." *IW,* 7, No. 1 (September 1939), 37–39.
Description of the puberty ritual.

2762.   ———. "Apache Puberty Ceremony for Girls." *Ki,* 5, No. 1 (October 1939), 1–4.
Description of a ceremonial.

2763.   Daklugie, Asa (as told to Eve Ball). "Coyote and the Flies." *NMFR,* 10 (1955–1956), 12–13.
Myth text with sketchy comparative notes.

2764.   Dobie, J. Frank. "The Apache and His Secret," in 90, pp. 142–54.
Second-hand account of the experience of a member of Victorio's band. Also includes some vague material on Apache buried treasure tradition.

2765.   Evers, Lawrence. "*Báts'oosee,* An Apache Trickster Cycle." *SWF,* 3, No. 4 (Fall 1979), 1–15.
Annotated transcript of a storytelling performance recorded in 1977.

2766.   Fergusson, Erna. "Modern Apaches of New Mexico." *AIn,* 6, No. 1 (Summer 1951), 3–14.
Surveys cultures of Mescalero and Jicarilla with some attention to ceremonials.

2767.   "Ghost Dance in Arizona." *JAF,* 5 (1892), 65–68.
Description of Ghost Dance among Apache and Walapai reprinted from the *Chicago Inter-Ocean* for 25 June 1891.

2768.   Goddard, Pliny Earle. "Jicarilla Apache Texts." *APAMNH,* 8 (1911), 1–276.
Twenty-five myths, twenty-eight folktales, sixteen personal narratives, and seventeen descriptions of customs presented with free and interlinear translations. Collected in 1909. Very brief introduction presents cultural background. Some comparative notes.

2769.   ———. "Myths and Tales from the San Carlos Apache." *APAMNH,* 24, Part 1 (1918), 1–86.

Twenty-three myths and folktales collected in 1905 and 1910. With some explanatory notes.

2770. ———. "Myths and Tales from the White Mountain Apache." *APAMNH,* 24, Part 2 (1919), 87–139.

Thirteen myth texts collected in 1910. With some explanatory notes.

2771. ———. "San Carlos Apache Texts." *APAMNH,* 24, Part 3 (1919), 141–367.

Twenty-four myth and folktale texts with literal translations (free translation for some in 2769). With occasional explanatory notes.

2772. ———. "White Mountain Apache Texts." *APAMNH,* 24, Part 4 (1920), 369–527.

Eighteen myth texts and descriptions of customs with literal translations (free translation for some in 2770). With occasional explanatory notes.

2773. Goodwin, Grenville. "The Characteristics and Function of Clan in a Southern Athapascan Culture." *AA,* 39 (1937), 394–407.

Mentions clan legends which describe early settlement patterns and acquisition of clan names.

2774. ———. *Myths and Tales of the White Mountain Apache. MAFS* No. 33 (1939).

Fifty-seven myth and folktale texts collected in 1931, 1932, and 1936. With extensive explanatory notes and an overview of tribal oral traditions.

2775. ———. "White Mountain Apache Religion." *AA,* 40 (1938), 24–37.

Based on fieldwork done in mid-1930s. Includes data on cosmogony, cosmology, supernaturalism, and ceremonialism.

2776. ———, and Charles Kaut. "A Native Religious Movement Among the White Mountain and Cibecue Apache." *SJA,* 10 (1954), 385–404.

Text of a historical legend about a nativistic movement. Recorded in 1936.

2777. Gordon, B. L. "Heroes and Ethos of the Jicarilla Apache." *M,* 44 (1970), 54–62.

Myth text about culture heroes and legend text illustrate environmental influences on Apache ethos.

2778. Gould, M. K. "Two Legends of the Mojave-Apache, Told by Captain Jim (Hoo-Kut-A-Go-Che, 'Nose-Tied-Up') of That Tribe." *JAF,* 34 (1921), 319–20.

Unannotated myth texts. No commentary.

2779. Hoijer, Harry. *Chiricahua and Mescalero Apache Texts.* Ethnological Notes by Morris Edward Opler. Chicago: Univ. of Chicago Press, 1938.

Forty-six Chiricahua myths, legends, songs, prayers, and descriptions of customs; and nine Mescalero myths. Collected in 1930s and presented with free translations and linguistic analysis. Brief ethnographic commentary, but no annotations.

2780. ———. "The History and Customs of the Lipan, as Told by Augustina Zuazua." *Lin,* 161 (1975), 5–37.

Ethnographic account recorded in 1930s. Presented with literal translation and some data on the cultural background.

2781. Hrdlička, Aleš. "Notes on the San Carlos Apache." *AA,* 7 (1905), 480–95.

Ethnography includes data on folklore and ceremonialism. Based on observations in 1900 and 1905.

2782. Kane, Henry. "The Apache Secret Devil Dance." *EP,* 42 (1937), 93–94.

Brief description of a ritual.

2783. Kaut, Charles. "The Clan System as an Epiphenomenal Element of Western Apache Social Organization." *Eth,* 13 (1974), 45–70.

Includes references to traditional history and a legend text collected in 1954.

2784. ———. "Notes on Western Apache Religious and Social Organizations." *AA,* 61 (1959), 99–102.

Relates social organization of the Cibecue Apache to funeral ceremonials observed in 1953 and 1954.

2785. Kessell, William B. "The Battle of Cibecue and Its Aftermath: A White Mountain Apache's Account." *Eh,* 21 (1974), 123–34.

Oral narrative by son of one of the Apache participants in the 1881 battle. Compares NA and EA perceptions of the event.

2786. Lewis, Enola C. "The Mescalero Feast of 1936." *IW,* 4, No. 5 (15 October 1936), 29–31.

Description of a ceremony.

2787. Lupan, Nantan. "An Apache Dance." *Ou,* 22 (June 1893), 189–91.

Ceremonial description.

2788. Mails, Thomas E. *The People Called Apache.* Englewood Cliffs, N. J.: Prentice-Hall, 1974.

Profusely illustrated volume describes cultures of several Apache groups (Western, Chiricahua, Mescalero, Jicarilla). Includes lengthy descriptions of ceremonials and games and song texts.

2789. McAllester, David P. "The Role of Music in Western Apache Culture," in 165, pp. 468–72.

Compares and contrasts Apache and NA attitudes toward music.

2790. Meader, Forrest W., Jr. "'Na'ilde': The Ghost Dance of the White Mountain Apache." *Ki,* 33 (October 1967), 15–24.

Describes the 1881 revitalization movement and relates it to the 1870 Paiute Ghost Dance.

2791. Melody, Michael Edward. *The Apaches. A Critical Bibliography.* Bloomington: Indiana Univ. Press, 1977.

Unannotated list of 223 books and articles. Introductory essay includes sections on mythology and religion.

2792. Mooney, James. "The Jicarilla Genesis." *AA,* o. s. 11 (1898), 197–209.

Origin myth collected in 1897. With some explanatory notes.

2793. Nicholas, Dan. "Mescalero Apache Girls' Puberty Ceremony." *EP,* 46 (1939), 193–204.

Description of the ceremony in 1939.

2794. Opler, Morris Edward. "Adolescence Rite of the Jicarilla." *EP,* 49 (1942), 25–38.

Thorough description of the ritual, obtained during fieldwork in 1934–1935.

2795. ———. *Apache Odyssey. A Journey Between Two Worlds.* New York: Holt, Rinehart and Winston, 1969.

Life history of Chris collected in 1934–1936. Includes data on ceremonialism, shamanism, and acculturation. With extensive explanatory notes.

2796. ———. "Cause and Effect in Apachean Agriculture, Division of Labor, Residence Patterns, and Girls' Puberty Rites." *AA,* 74 (1972), 1133–46.

Cites Jicarilla myth of the origin of agriculture to argue for important role of males in Apache culture. Part of an interchange with Harold E. Driver, who responded in *AA,,* 74 (1972), 1147–51.

2797. ———. "The Character and Derivation of the Jicarilla Holiness Rite." *UNMB-AS,* 4, No. 3 (June 1943), 1–98.
Description of a ritual with comparisons with Ute and Navajo ceremonialism.
2798. ———. *Childhood and Youth in Jicarilla Apache Society.* Los Angeles: Southwest Museum, 1946 (Hodge Anniversary Publication No. 5).
Thorough description of socialization processes includes accounts of ceremonials and some folktale texts.
2799. ———. "Chiricahua Apache Material Relating to Sorcery." *PM,* 19 (1946), 81–92.
Five legend texts with explanatory notes.
2800. ———. "Component, Assemblage, and Theme in Cultural Integration and Differentiation." *AA,* 61 (1955), 955–64.
Compares reactions to death among the Lipan and Jicarilla. Shows how cultural components cluster into assemblages, which relate to value affirmations in the culture called themes. Mythical ideas about death comprise a component of the death reaction assemblage in the Apache cultures.
2801. ———. "The Concept of Supernatural Power Among the Chiricahua and Mescalero Apaches." *AA,* 37 (1935), 65–70.
Survey of the uses in the cultures of supernatural aids. Some attention to ceremonialism.
2802. ———. "The Creative Role of Shamanism in Mescalero Apache Mythology." *JAF,* 59 (1946), 268–81.
Presents a myth text, collected in 1933, which shows how a storyteller's shamanistic powers may contribute a religious aura to a story.
2803. ———. *Dirty Boy: A Jicarilla Tale of Raid and War. MAAA* No. 52 (1938).
Long folktale text collected in 1934–1935. Presented with extensive comparative and explanatory notes.
2804. ———. "Examples of Ceremonial Interchanges Among Southwestern Tribes." *M,* 16 (1942), 77–80.
Two accounts of Apaches' hiring shamans from other groups for ceremonials.
2805. ———. "The Influence of Aboriginal Pattern and White Contact on a Recently Introduced Ceremony, the Mescalero Peyote Rite." *JAF,* 49 (1936), 143–66.
Study of religious acculturation: the effects of traditional and EA religious ideas on peyotism. Includes personal narrative and anecdote texts.
2806. ———. "The Jicarilla Apache Ceremonial Relay Race." *AA,* 46 (1944), 75–97.
Describes the ceremonial race as it occurred in the 1930s. With text of ritual origin myth.
2807. ———. "A Jicarilla Apache Expedition and Scalp Dance." *JAF,* 54 (1941), 10–23.
Text of a historical narrative collected in 1935. With description of a Victory Dance.
2808. ———. "Jicarilla Apache Fertility Aids, and Practices for Preventing Conception." *AA,* 50 (1948), 359–61.
Includes mythic validations for some of the techniques.
2809. ———. "Jicarilla Apache Territory, Economy, and Society in 1850." *SJA,* 27 (1971), 309–29.
Establishes extent of tribal territory in 1850 by using legendary narratives.
2810. ———. "The Lipan Apache Death Complex and Its Extensions." *SJA,* 1 (1945), 122–41.

Describes eschatology and death ceremonialism.
2811. ———. "A Mescalero Apache Account of the Origin of the Peyote Ceremony." *EP,* 52 (1945), 210–12.
Unannotated legend text. No commentary.
2812. ———. "Mountain Spirits of the Chiricahua Apache." *M,* 24 (1946), 125–31.
Three legend texts with explanatory notes and background data on belief system.
2813. ———. "Myth and Practice in Jicarilla Apache Eschatology." *JAF,* 73 (1960), 133–53.
Describes tribal deathlore.
2814. ———. "Mythology and Folk Belief in the Maintenance of Jicarilla Apache Tribal Endogamy." *JAF,* 60 (1947), 126–29.
Shows how mythology supports endogamy by characterizing alien peoples as descendants of animals or birds.
2815. ———. *Myths and Legends of the Lipan Apache Indians. MAFS* No. 36 (1940).
Myth, folktale, and legend texts (170)—including seventy-five episodes from the Coyote cycle—collected in 1935. Introduction surveys tribal oral traditions. With some explanatory notes.
2816. ———. *Myths and Tales of the Chiricahua Apache Indians. MAFS* No. 37 (1942).
Myth and folktale texts (102)—including fifty-eight episodes from the Coyote cycle—collected in 1931–1935. With extensive explanatory notes. Comparative annotations provided by David French.
2817. ———. *Myths and Tales of the Jicarilla Apache Indians. MAFS* No. 31 (1938).
Myth and folktale texts (140)—including sixty-six episodes from the Coyote cycle—collected in 1934–1935. Introduction surveys the scope of tribal mythology. With some explanatory and comparative notes.
2818. ———. "Navaho Shamanistic Practice Among the Jicarilla Apache." *NMA,* 6–7, No. 1 (January-March 1943), 13–18.
Describes Navajo ceremonials among the Jicarilla. With personal narrative texts.
2819. ———. "Notes on Chiricahua Apache Culture. I. Supernatural Power and the Shaman." *PM,* 20 (1947), 1–14.
Miscellany of shamanistic beliefs and practices.
2820. ———. "Reaction to Death Among the Mescalero Apache." *SJA,* 2 (1946), 254–67.
Treats eschatology and death ceremonialism.
2821. ———. "Remuneration to Supernaturals and Man in Apachean Ceremonialism." *Eth,* 7 (1968), 356–93.
Survey of payments made to ceremonial performers and supernatural beings in various Apache groups. Opler added further data in *Eth,* 8 (1969), 122–24.
2822. ———. "The Sacred Clowns of the Chiricahua and Mescalero Indians." *EP,* 44 (1938), 75–79.
Description of the role of ritual clowns.
2823. ———. "The Slaying of the Monsters, A Mescalero Apache Myth." *EP,* 53 (1946), 215–25, 242–58.
Myth text collected in 1933. With some explanatory notes.
2824. ———. "A Summary of Jicarilla Apache Culture." *AA,* 38 (1936), 202–23.
Ethnographical survey based on fieldwork done in 1934–1935. Treats cosmogony, cosmology, and other myth cycles and ceremonialism.

2825. ———. "Themes as Dynamic Forces in Culture." *AJS*, 51 (1945), 198–206.

Uses Apache ceremonial life to illustrate the concept of *theme*, one of the basic assertions of a culture. Albert K. Cohen evaluated the *theme* concept in *AJS*, 52 (1946), 41–42; and Opler responded in *AJS*, 52 (1946), 43–44.

2826. ———. "The Use of Peyote by the Carrizo and Lipan Apache Tribes." *AA*, 40 (1938), 271–85.

Presents an informant's recollections of peyote use and a thorough description of ceremonialism. Recorded in 1935.

2827. Reagan, Albert B. "Twinkling Star." *PIAS for 1922*, pp. 75–81.

Description of a healing ritual. In the form of a scenario.

2828. Russell, Frank. "An Apache Medicine Dance." *AA*, o. s. 11 (1898), 367–72.

Description of a ritual.

2829. ———. "Myths of the Jicarilla Apaches." *JAF*, 11 (1898), 253–71.

Sixteen unannotated myth texts. Brief commentary on cultural background.

2830. Scully, Vincent. "In Praise of Women: The Mescalero Puberty Ceremony." *AiA*, 60 (July-August 1972), 70–77.

Fairly good description of the ritual.

2831. Sirdofsky, Arthur. "An Apache Girl Comes of Age." *T*, 138 (July 1972), 40–43.

Sketchy description of a puberty ceremony at San Carlos.

2832. Sjoberg, Andrée F. "Lipan Apache Culture in Historical Perspective." *SJA*, 9 (1953), 76–98.

Survey of historical material on the culture yields some data on ceremonialism.

2833. Stewart, Omer C. "Origin of the Peyote Religion in the United States." *PlA*, 19 (August 1974), 211–23.

Suggests that Lipan Apache learned of peyotism from Mexican NAs and spread knowledge northward.

2834. Tweedie, M. Jean. "Notes on the History and Adaptation of the Apache Tribes." *AA*, 70 (1968), 1132–42.

Folklore of various Apache groups provides data into prehistoric tribal movements.

2835. Whitaker, Kathleen. "Na Ih Es. An Apache Puberty Ceremony." *M*, 45 (1971), 4–12.

Description of the girls' puberty ceremony as observed in 1969.

2836. ———. "Na Ih Es at San Carlos." *M*, 43 (1969), 151.

Description of the puberty ceremony.

2837. Whiteman, A. L. "Indian Reminiscence on Lost Mines." *NMFR*, 1 (1946–1947), 5–6.

Unannotated buried treasure legend. Some data on historical background.

See also 22, 499, 813, 1080, 1562, 1760, 2268, 2687, 2688, 2691, 2720, 2929, 2978, 2979, 3017, 3047, 3219, 3412, 3899, 3982.

C. Cocopa

2838. Alvarez de Williams, Anita. *The Cocopah People.* Phoenix: Indian Tribal Series, 1974.

Tribal history includes text of creation myth, descriptions of games, and data on singing.

2839. Crawford, James M. "More on Cocopa Baby Talk." *IJAL*, 44 (1978), 17–23.

List of words and phrases collected in 1973. With linguistic analysis.

2840. Gifford, E. W. "The Cocopa." *UCPAAE*, 31, No. 5 (1933), 257–334.

Ethnography includes data on ceremonialism, theology, song cycles, and shamanism.

2841. Kelly, William H. "Cocopa Attitudes and Practices with Respect to Death and Mourning." *SJA*, 5 (1949), 151–64.

Includes data on eschatology and ceremonialism.

2842. ———. *Cocopa Ethnography.* APUAZ No. 29 (1977).

Based on fieldwork done between 1940 and 1952. Includes data on ceremonialism and several unannotated myth texts.

2843. Langdon, Margaret. "Animal Talk in Cocopa." *IJAL*, 44 (1978), 10–16.

Study of speech attributed to animals and addressed to animals. Animals which appear in Cocopa folklore also have distinctive speech patterns.

See also 3990.

D. Havasupai

2844. Cushing, Frank Hamilton. *The Nation of the Willows.* Flagstaff, Ari.: Northland, 1965.

Account of a visit to the Havasupai in 1881 includes data on mythology and ceremonialism. Reprinted from *AtM* for 1882.

2845. Dobyns, Henry F., and Robert C. Euler. *The Ghost Dance of 1889 Among the Pai Indians of Northwestern Arizona.* Prescott, Ari.: Prescott College Press, 1967.

Study of the effects of the Ghost Dance on the Havasupai and Walapai. Contains several contemporary accounts of ritual behavior.

2846. Janson, Donald. "People of the Blue-Green Waters." *Au*, 68, No. 6 (November-December 1966), 464–68.

View of Havasupai life includes a summary of the creation myth.

2847. Madden, Ross. "An Indian Arcadia in the Southwest." *T*, 84 (March 1945), 22–24, 32.

Culture survey includes data on ceremonialism.

2848. Reilly, P. T. "The Disappearing Havasupai Corn-Planting Ceremony." *M*, 44 (1970), 30–34.

Brief survey of published accounts of the ritual.

2849. Sinyella, Juan. "Havasupai Traditions." Ed. J. Donald Hughes. *SWF*, 1, No. 2 (Spring 1977), 35–52.

Stories and descriptions of customs recorded in 1964 by a member of the Havasupai Tribal Council. Includes myths and legends.

2850. Smithson, Carma Lee. *The Havasupai Woman.* APUU No. 38 (1959).

Traces life cycle of typical woman with data on ceremonialism and shamanism.

2851. ———, and Robert C. Euler. *Havasupai Religion and Mythology.* APUU No. 68 (1964).

Material collected by Smithson in the 1950s includes data on shamanism and ceremonialism and twenty-six unannotated myth texts.

2852. Spier, Leslie. *Comparative Vocabularies and Parallel Texts in Two Yuman Languages of Arizona. APUNM* No. 2 (1946).

Contains parallel myth texts in Havasupai and Maricopa with free and interlinear translations.

2853. ———. "Havasupai Ethnography." *APAMNH,* 29, Part 3 (1928), 81–392.

Based on fieldwork in 1918, 1919, and 1921. Includes data on shamanism and ceremonialism and texts of songs (words only) and legends (with explanatory notes).

2854. ———. "Havasupai (Yuman) Texts." *IJAL,* 3, No. 1 (1924–1925), 109–16.

Text with interlinear and free translations of two stories collected in 1921.

2855. ———. "Problems Arising from the Cultural Position of the Havasupai." *AA,* 31 (1929), 213–22.

Studies relationship between Havasupai and neighboring groups from the perspective of folklore, among other factors.

2856. Walkup, Lucy. "A Collection of Folklore from the Flagstaff, Arizona, Area." *Aff,* 2, No. 4 (Winter 1973), 29–40.

Contains Havasupai creation myth and some legend texts.

See also 2681, 2710, 3954, 3955.

E. Jumano

2857. Kelley, J. Charles. "Juan Sabeata and Diffusion in Aboriginal Texas." *AA,* 57 (1955), 981–95.

Sabeata, chief of the Jumano and Cibola in the late 1600s, made several journeys across Texas, during which he avidly collected and recounted rumor and gossip. He is perceived as a factor in the diffusion of culture traits, especially oral tradition.

F. Mohave

2858. Allen, George A. "Manners and Customs of the Mohaves." *ARSI for 1890,* pp. 615–16.

Brief note includes some data on theology and supernaturalism.

2859. Bourke, John G. "Notes on the Cosmogony and Theogony of the Mojave Indians of the Rio Colorado, Arizona." *JAF,* 2 (1889), 169–89.

Myth texts collected in 1896. Presented with commentary on their religious significance.

2860. Devereux, George. "Amusements and Sports of Mohave Children." *M,* 24 (1950), 143–52.

Includes a description of musical performances.

2861. ———. "Dream Learning and Individual Ritual Differences in Mohave Shamanism." *AA,* 59 (1957), 1036–45.

Assesses the role of dreams in the acquisition of magical power.

2862. ———. "Mohave Beliefs Concerning Twins." *AA,* 43 (1941), 573–92.

Cites mythic bases for two patterns of belief about twins.

2863. ———. "Mohave Chieftainship in Action: A Narrative of the First Contacts of the Mohave Indians with the United States." *Plat,* 23 (1951), 33–43.

Historical narrative based on oral accounts.

2864. ———. "Mohave Coyote Tales." *JAF,* 61 (1948), 233–55.

Texts of four narratives with descriptions of storytelling situations and psychoanalytic interpretations.

2865. ———. "Mohave Dreams of Omen and Power." *To,* 4, No.3 (Spring 1956), 17–24.

Discusses content and function of dream life.

2866. ———. *Mohave Ethnopsychiatry and Suicide: The Psychiatric Knowledge and the Psychic Disturbances of an Indian Tribe. BAEB* No. 175 (1961).

Systematic study of Mohave psychiatric theories and practices considers role of songs in therapy and mythic models for deviant behavior. With ceremonial descriptions.

2867. ———. "The Mohave Neonate and Its Cradle." *PM,* 21 (1948), 1–18.

Study of infant care includes lullaby and other song texts (words only) with interlinear translations.

2868. ———. "Mohave Obstetrics: A Psychoanalytic Study." *AI,* 5 (1948), 95–139.

Examines from a psychoanalytic perspective myths, songs, and ceremonials associated with childbirth.

2869. ———. "Mohave Soul Concepts." *AA,* 39 (1937), 417–22.

Treats ideas about the soul and its fate.

2870. ———. "Psychodynamics of Mohave Gambling." *AI,* 7 (1950), 55–65.

Sees gambling as a temporary return to omnipotence fantasies. Tribal interest in gambling is apparent in the mythology.

2871. ———. "Some Mohave Gestures." *AA,* 51 (1949), 325–26.

List and description of eight gestures which accompany Mohave verbal performances.

2872. Fathauer, George H. "The Mohave 'Ghost Doctor.'" *AA,* 53 (1951), 605–07.

Discussion of the ceremonial role of the Mohave specialist in supernaturalism.

2873. Grey, Herman. *Tales from the Mohave.* Foreword by Alice Marriott. Norman: Univ. of Oklahoma Press, 1970.

Eight unannotated texts. General commentary surveys role of oral literature in Mohave life and its relationship to dreams.

2874. Kroeber, A. L. "Ethnographic Interpretations 1–6." *UCPAAE,* 47, No. 2 (1957), 191–234.

Two of the brief essays are relevant: "Ad Hoc Reassurance Dreams" (pp. 205–08) covers dream life of Mohave and Yurok informants; "Mohave Clairvoyance" (pp. 226–31) describes ritual procedure and includes song texts (words only).

2875. ———. "Ethnographic Interpretations 7–11." *UCPAAE,* 47, No. 3 (1959), 235–310.

Two of the brief essays are relevant: "Desert Mohave: Fact or Fancy" (pp. 294–307) reproduces ethnographic notes, collected in 1934 by Richard F. Van Valkenburgh and Malcolm Farmer, which include legends and personal narratives; "Yurok National Character" (pp. 235–40) describes the value system of the group.

2876. ———. "A Mohave Historical Epic." *UCPAR*, 11, No. 2 (1951), 71–176.

Translated myth text with extensive explanatory notes and commentary on literary qualities.

2877. ———. *More Mohave Myths*. *UCPAR* No. 27 (1972).

Myth texts with extensive explanatory and comparative notes, descriptions of informants, and data on contexts.

2878. ———. "Preliminary Sketch of the Mohave Indians." *AA*, 4 (1902), 276–85.

Ethnography includes data on ceremonialism, singing, and mythology.

2879. ———. "Seven Mohave Myths." *UCPAR*, 11, No. 1 (1948), 1–70.

Translated texts with extensive data on informants, cultural background, and performance style. Collected between 1900 and 1910.

2880. Stewart, Kenneth M. "An Account of the Mohave Mourning Ceremony." *AA*, 49 (1947), 146–48.

Description of a ceremony from an informant's recollections.

2881. ———. "The Amatpathenya—Mohave Leprechauns?" *Aff*, 3, No. 1 (Spring 1973), 40–41.

Note on Mohave anecdotes about "little people." Includes summaries of five accounts.

2882. ———. "Mojave Indian Ghosts and the Land of the Dead." *M*, 51 (1977), 14–21.

Survey of ghostlore with extensive quotations from informants.

2883. ———. "Mojave Indian Shamanism." *M*, 44 (1970), 15–24.

Describes types of shamans with attention to mythic concepts and ceremonials.

2884. ———. "Mojave Shamanistic Specialists." *M*, 48 (1974), 4–13.

Lists and describes twenty-three shaman types with some attention to their rituals.

2885. ———. "Mohave Warfare." *SJA*, 3 (1947), 257–78.

Includes texts of historical legends and descriptions of ceremonialism.

2886. ———. "Mortuary Practices of the Mohave Indians." *EP*, 79 (1974), 2–12.

Thorough description of ceremonial.

2887. ———. "The Owl in Mohave Indian Culture." *Aff*, 2, No. 3 (October 1972), 17–23.

Treats supernatural attributes assigned to the bird. With five legend texts.

2888. ———. "Witchcraft Among the Mohave Indians." *Eth*, 12 (1973), 315–24.

Includes ceremonial descriptions and references to narratives by and about witches.

2889. Underhill, Ruth, trans. "The Battle at Spirit Mountain." *M*, 10 (1936), 10–14.

Unannotated excerpts from a song narrative. No commentary.

2890. Wallace, W. J. "The Dream in Mohave Life." *JAF*, 60 (1947), 252–58.

Compares two types of dreams and their relationship to folklore.

See also 2681, 2758, 2778, 3982, 3990, 3995, 4182, 4229, 4232.

G. Navajo

2891. Aberle, David F. "Mythology of the Navaho Game Stick-Dice." *JAF*, 55 (1942), 144–54.

Mythology associated with gambling game reveals tribal attitudes toward gambling and the place of women.

2892. ———. "The Navaho Singer's 'Fee': Payment or Prestation?" in 128, pp. 15–32.

Consideration of transactions between ceremonial performers and audiences.

2893. ———. *The Peyote Religion Among the Navaho*. *VFPA* No. 42 (1966).

Historical and ethnographic study of Navajo peyotism based on fieldwork done between 1949 and 1953. Contains thorough description of ritual procedures.

2894. Adair, John, and Evon Vogt. "Navaho and Zuni Veterans: A Study of Contrasting Modes of Culture Change." *AA*, 51 (1949), 547–61.

Compares modes of reintegrating soldiers after World War II. While the Zuni regarded the veterans as threats, the Navajo saw them as potential leaders. Describes reintegrating ceremonies.

2895. Adair, John, and Sol Worth. "The Navajo as Filmmaker: A Brief Report of Research in the Cross-Cultural Aspects of Film Communication." *AA*, 69 (1967), 76–78.

Survey of field methodology in ethnographic filmmaking. Some attention to folklore implications.

2896. Adair, Mildred Lee. "Folktales of the Navajo Indian." *SFQ*, 11 (1947), 211–14.

Two unannotated texts with some commentary on cultural background.

2897. Adams, William Y. *Shonto. A Study of the Role of the Trader in a Modern Navaho Community*. *BAEB* No. 188 (1963).

Investigation of the influence of Shonto Trading Post on 100 families in its vicinity, based on fieldwork done in 1954–1956. Some attention to ritual life of the community and the role of the singer.

2898. Allen, T. D. *Navahos Have Five Fingers*. Norman: Univ. of Oklahoma Press, 1963.

Study of NA-EA contact emphasizes medical practices. Includes descriptions of Navajo healing rituals.

2899. Altman, George J. "A Navaho Wedding." *M*, 20 (1946), 159–64.

Description of a ceremony.

2900. Armer, Laura Adams. "The Crawler, Navaho Healer." *M*, 27 (1953), 5–10.

Character sketch with ceremonial description and song text.

2901. ———. "Navaho Sand-Paintings." *AA*, 33 (1931), 657.

Describes paintings used in stellar prognostication. With ritual description.

2902. ———. "The Navajo Sand-Painters at Work." *T*, 53 (August 1929), 25–27, 49.

Treats ceremonial functions and mythic bases of the paintings.

2903. ———. "Two Navaho Sand-Paintings, with Certain Comparisons." *M*, 24 (1950), 79–83.

Descriptions with attention to mythological and ritual backgrounds.

2904. Astrov, Margot. "The Concept of Motion as the Psychological Leitmotif of Navaho Life and Literature." *JAF*, 63 (1950), 45–56.

Sees the theme of motion in creation and other myths.

2905.   Austin, Mary. "One-Smoke Stories." *GBM,* 12 (October 1930), 37–38.

Two unannotated narrative texts with brief context data.

2906.   ———. "One Smoke Stories." *YR,* 22 (1933), 525–32.

Rewritten texts of five narratives with some general context data.

2907.   ———. *One-Smoke Stories.* Boston: Houghton Mifflin, 1934.

Thirty-eight rewritten narrative texts. Brief description of storytelling situations.

2908.   Bailey, Flora L. "Navaho Motor Habits." *AA,* 44 (1942), 210–34.

Catalogue of gestures used in various contexts including storytelling and ritual singing.

2909.   Ballinger, Franchot. "The Responsible Center: Man and Nature in Pueblo and Navaho Songs and Prayers." *AQ,* 30 (1978), 90–107.

Examines ritual songs and prayers to reveal tribal conceptions of nature and of man's central position in the cosmos.

2910.   Begay, Beyal, Yohe Hatrale, and Mary C. Wheelwright. *Atsah or Eagle Catching Myth and Yohe or Bead Myth.* BMNCA No. 3 (1945).

Unannotated myth texts in English.

2911.   Bennett, Kay. *Kaibah: Recollection of a Navajo Girlhood.* Los Angeles: Westernlore, 1964.

Memoir of a childhood between 1928 and 1935. Contains rewritten myth texts and descriptions of ceremonials.

2912.   ———, and Russ Bennett. *A Navajo Saga.* San Antonio: Naylor, 1969.

Family history (may be fictionalized) covering period 1846–1870. Contains some ceremonial descriptions and song texts (words only).

2913.   Berlant, Anthony, and Mary Hunt Kahlenberg. *Walk in Beauty: The Navajo and Their Blankets.* Boston: New York Graphic Society, 1977.

Illustrated survey of blanket-making contains discussion of ceremonial life, summaries of myths, song texts, and excerpts from myth texts.

2914.   Berry, Rose V. S. "The Navajo Shaman and His Sacred Sand-Paintings." *EP,* 26 (1929), 23–38.

Description of healing rituals and related paintings. Also published in *A&A,* 27 (January 1929), 2–16.

2915.   Boas, Franz. "Northern Elements in the Mythology of the Navaho." *AA,* o. s. 10 (1897), 371–76.

Enumeration of motifs in Navajo myths which show affinity with folklore from northern NA groups.

2916.   Breed, Jack. "Better Days for the Navajos." *NG,* 114 (December 1958), 800–47.

Survey of contemporary lifeways includes data on healing ceremonies.

2917.   Brink, L. P. "The Religion of the Navahoes." *NR,* 22 (November 1934), 16–18, 33.

Survey of theology, mythology, and ceremonialism.

2918.   Brown, Mrs. Lottie. "Navajo Legend." *IW,* 7, No. 2 (October 1939), 27.

Story of Shiprock.

2919.   Brugge, David M. "A Comparative Study of Navajo Mortuary Practices." *AIQ,* 4 (1978), 309–28.

Compares Navajo death ceremonials with practices of

Southwest, California, and Northwest Coast groups.

2920.   Buckland, A. W. "Points of Contact Between Old World Myths and Customs and the Navajo Myth, Entitled 'The Mountain Chant.' " *JAIGBI,* 22 (1893), 346–55.

Point-by-point comparison of myth and ceremony to EA analogues.

2921.   Buxton, L. H. Dudley. "Some Navajo Folktales and Customs." *F,* 34 (1923), 293–313.

Includes some rewritten myths and descriptions of ceremonials.

2922.   Campbell, Isabel. "Navajo Sandpaintings." *SWR,* 25, No. 2 (January 1940), 143–50.

Description of the ceremonial function and mythological basis of sandpaintings.

2923.   Case, Charles C. "Blessing Way, the Core Ritual of Navajo Ceremony." *Plat,* 41, No. 2 (Fall 1968), 35–42.

Description of the ritual as a central force in Navajo life.

2924.   Cassidy, Ina Sizer. "Translations from the Navajo." *Po,* 43, No. 3 (December 1933), 119–23.

Five very free translations of Navajo songs, chants, and prayers.

2925.   Chapin, Gretchen. "A Navajo Myth from the Chaco Canyon." *NMA,* 4, No. 4 (October–December 1940), 63–67.

Text of the Gambler Myth. Annotated and with commentary on cultural context.

2926.   Chapman, Arthur. "The Sand Painters of the American Desert." *T,* 36 (January 1921), 15–17, 39.

Superficial ceremonial descriptions.

2927.   Chelf, Carl R. "Good Luck for Gray Head." *M,* 32 (1958), 21–28.

Description of a healing ceremony.

2928.   Chisholm, James Stewart. "The Social Organization of Ceremonial Practitioners at Navajo Mountain, Utah." *Plat,* 47, No. 3 (Winter 1975), 82–104.

Suggests that recent changes in ceremonial organization have resulted in concentration of practitioners, who inherit ceremonial items patrilineally, in a few kinship groups.

2929.   Clark, Laverne Harrell. *They Sang for Horses: The Impact of the Horse on Navajo and Apache Folklore.* Tucson: Univ. of Arizona Press, 1966.

Examines horselore among the two groups. With excerpts from myths and song texts. One chapter deals with the role of the horse in ceremonialism.

2930.   Coolidge, Dane, and Mary Roberts Coolidge. *The Navajo Indians.* Boston: Houghton Mifflin, 1930.

Culture survey includes retelling of creation myth and descriptions of ceremonials. Song texts are used as epigraphs for each section.

2931.   Crapanzano, Vincent. *The Fifth World of Forster Bennett. Portrait of a Navajo.* New York: Viking, 1972.

Journal of experiences as a graduate student doing fieldwork with emphasis on contact with a middle-aged Navajo. Contains retellings of myths and first- and second-hand descriptions of ceremonies.

2932.   Cummin, Hazel E. "The Bayeta of the Navaho." *HB,* 65 (May 1929), 644–45, 662, 664–65, 669.

Description of weaving practices especially for blankets. Included are accounts of ceremonialism and song texts.

2933.   Cummings, Byron. "The Bride of the Sun." *Ki,* 1, No. 5 (January 1936), 1–4.

Unannotated myth text in storytelling context.

2934. ———. "Kivas of the San Juan Drainage." *AA,* 17 (1915), 272–82.

Description of kiva construction involves emergence myths of the Navajo, Hopi, and Zuni.

2935. ———. "Navajo Sand Paintings." *Ki,* 1, No. 7 (March 1936), 1–2.

Brief description of the Yebatchai Ceremony.

2936. Cummings, Emma. "Sand Paintings in the Arizona State Museum at Tucson." *Ki,* 1, No. 7 (March 1936), 2–4.

Interprets mythic and ceremonial significance of sandpaintings.

2937. "Death of a Medicine Man as Told to Grace French Evans by Mrs. Richard Wetherill." *Scr,* 91 (May 1932), 304–8.

Account of a death ritual with some song texts.

2938. DeHuff, Elizabeth Willis. "Navajo Creation Myths," in 109, pp. 127–34.

Two myth texts with some data on storytelling contexts.

2939. de Johly, Hastéen, Estsán Hatráli B'yásh, and Mary C. Wheelwright. *Myth of Willa-Chee-Ji Deginnh-Keygo Hatrál and Myth of Natóhe Bakáji Hatrál (Male Shooting Chant).* BMNCA No. 7 (1958).

Myth texts recounted in 1932 and 1933 and rewritten by Wheelwright. No annotations or commentary.

2940. Dimock, A. W. "Among the Navaho." *O,* 76 (6 February 1904), 349–59.

Culture survey contains some data on ceremonialism and religion.

2941. Dory, William. "Navajo Land." *NH,* 23 (1923), 486–505.

Description of environment and culture of Navajo includes descriptions of healing ritual and singing style. With one prayer text.

2942. Dutton, Bertha P. "The Navaho Wind Way Ceremonial." *EP,* 48 (1941), 73–82.

Description of a ritual and interpretation of sandpaintings.

2943. Duxbury, William Crocker. "A Legend of the Navajoes." *Cos,* 22 (November 1896), 73–79.

Treats a narrative which deals with NA-EA warfare.

2944. Dyk, Walter. *A Navaho Autobiography.* VFPA No. 8 (1947).

Life history collected in 1933 of a subject born c. 1865. Contains data on ceremonialism and a few prayer texts.

2945. ———. *Son of Old Man Hat. A Navaho Autobiography.* Foreword by Edward Sapir. New York: Harcourt, Brace, 1938.

Oral life history of Left Handed, born in 1868 and interviewed in 1934. Contains descriptions of singing and ceremonialism.

2946. Eickemeyer, Carl. *Over the Great Navajo Trail.* NP: NP, 1900.

Account of travels among the Navajo includes a rewritten myth text and a description of a healing ceremonial.

2947. Elmore, Francis H. "The Deer, and His Importance to the Navaho." *EP,* 60 (1953), 371–84.

Surveys economic, ceremonial, and mythological roles of the deer.

2948. *An Ethnologic Dictionary of the Navaho Language.* St.

Michaels, Ari.: Franciscan Fathers, 1910.

Thorough catalogue of Navajo culture with tribal terms for various elements. Includes summary of mythology and exhaustive description of ceremonialism.

2949. Evans, Will. "Eclipse of Moon Mars Navajo Fire Dance." *SWL,* 5 (1940), 78–79.

Description of a ceremonial observed in 1939.

2950. ———. "Hosteen Bear Loses the Second Fall (Sequel to The White-Haired One Wrestles the Bear). A Navajo Folk Story." *SWL,* 14 (1948), 3–4.

Unannotated folktale text in storytelling context. No commentary.

2951. ———. "How Jackrabbit Got His Long Ears. A Navaho Folk Story." *SWL,* 13 (1947), 41–42.

Unannotated folktale text in storytelling context. No commentary.

2952. ———. "Navajo Folk Lore." *SWL,* 14 (1948), 45–68.

Ten unannotated folktale texts in storytelling context. No commentary.

2953. ———. "The Origin of Navajo Sandpainting." *NMFR,* 9 (1954–1955), 4–7.

Retelling of ritual origin myth. With some context data.

2954. ———. "The White Haired One Wrestles with Hosteen Bear. A Navajo Folk Story." *SWL,* 13 (1948), 53–55.

Unannotated folktale text in storytelling context. No commentary.

2955. Evers, Lawrence J. "On Structuring a Lesson: Comments on Two Navajo Songs." *SWF,* 1, No. 1 (Winter 1977), 30–47.

Texts and discussion of two songs which framed a Navajo lecturer's treatment of ceremonialism. Recorded in 1975.

2956. Fillmore, John Comfort. "Songs of the Navajos. From the Musician's Point of View." *LS,* 5, No. 6 (November 1896), 238–41.

Musicological analysis of four songs collected by Washington Matthews. See 3091.

2957. Fishler, Stanley A. *In the Beginning. A Navaho Creation Myth.* APUU No. 13 (1953).

Translated text collected in 1950. Introduction treats cultural background.

2958. ———. "Navaho Buffalo Hunting." *EP,* 62 (1955), 43–57.

Includes an informant's reminiscences about hunting and data on the buffalo's role in ceremonialism.

2959. ———. "A Navaho Version of the 'Bear's Son' Folktale." *JAF,* 66 (1953), 70–74.

Presentation of a folktale text collected in 1950.

2960. ———. "Symbolism of a Navaho 'Wedding' Basket." *M,* 28 (1954), 205–15.

Shows relationship of basketry symbols to mythology and ceremonialism.

2961. Forrest, Earle R. *With a Camera in Old Navaholand.* Foreword by Katharine Barlett. Norman: Univ. of Oklahoma Press, 1970.

Account of a photographic expedition to Navajo and Ute reservations in 1902. Contains descriptions of ceremonials and summaries of myths.

2962. Frisbie, Charlotte Johnson. *Kinaaldá: A Study of the Navaho Girl's Puberty Ceremony.* Middletown, Conn.: Wesleyan Univ. Press, 1967.

Thorough description of ritual based on fieldwork done in 1963–1964. Contains myth and song texts (words and music), comparative analysis, informant data, and complete coverage of the ritual procedure.

2963. ——. "The Navajo House Blessing Ceremonial." *EP,* 75 (1968), 27–35.

Description of the ceremonial. With one prayer text.

2964. ——, and David P. McAllester, eds. *Navajo Blessingway Singer. The Autobiography of Frank Mitchell, 1881–1967.* Tucson: Univ. of Arizona Press, 1978.

Life history with extensive data on collecting situation and explanatory notes and documents. Treats Mitchell's ceremonial participation.

2965. Gardner, William A. "Place of the Gods." *NH,* 45 (1940), 40–43, 54–55.

Account of visit to northeastern Arizona contains descriptions of sites important in Navajo ceremonialism and references to myths.

2966. Gayton, A. H. "Giant and Turkey: A Navajo Myth." *NMFR,* 2 (1947–1948), 24–25.

Text collected in 1941. With some data on storytelling style.

2967. Gill, Sam D. "The Color of Navajo Ritual Symbolism: An Evaluation of Methods." *JAR,* 31 (1975), 350–63.

Criticizes previous discussions of tribal symbolism and discusses importance of color symbolism in the Emergence Myth.

2968. ——. " 'It's Where You Put Your Eyes.' " *P,* 4, No. 4 (November 1979), 91–97.

Focuses on sandpainting to discuss ways in which NA art is perceived.

2969. ——. "Prayer as Person: The Performative Force in Navajo Prayer Acts." *HR,* 17, No. 2 (November 1977), 143–57.

Analyzes Navajo praying as an act whose very performance has pragmatic effects. Praying is viewed in personified terms by the Navajo.

2970. ——. "The Prayer of the Navajo Carved Figurine. An Interpretation of the Navajo Remaking Rite." *Plat,* 47, No. 2 (Fall 1974), 59–69.

Views a figurine carved for ceremonial usage as a representative of the life principle.

2971. ——. "The Shadow of a Vision Yonder," in 96, pp. 44–57.

Sees the power of Navajo ceremonialism in the participants' recognition of the values of performance.

2972. ——. "The Trees Stood Deep Rooted." *P,* 2, No. 2 (Spring 1977), 6–12.

Shows how Navajo creation myth provides a paradigm for creative activity. Sees ritual songs as providing a link between myth and human behavior.

2973. ——. "Whirling Logs and Coloured Sands," in 166, pp. 151–63.

Describes a sandpainting in ritual, mythological, and cultural contexts. With a response by Karl Luckert (pp. 163–64).

2974. Gillmor, Frances, and Louisa Wade Wetherill. *Traders to the Navajos. The Story of the Wetherills of Kayenta.* Boston: Houghton Mifflin, 1934.

History of a family of traders includes ceremonial descriptions and song texts.

2975. Goddard, Pliny Earle. "Navajo Texts." *APAMNH,* 34, Part 1 (1933), 3–179.

Seven myth texts collected in 1923–1924. With free and interlinear translations, occasional explanatory notes, and some data on collecting situation.

2976. ——. "The Night Chant as Represented in the New Navajo Group at the American Museum." *NH,* 25 (1925), 49–53.

Brief description of the ceremonial. With one song text.

2977. Goldfrank, Esther S. "Irrigation Agriculture and Navaho Community Leadership: Case Material on Environment and Culture." *AA,* 47 (1945), 262–77.

Discussion of Navajo agriculture includes references to origin myth as a guide to prehistory.

2978. Goodwin, Grenville. "A Comparison of Navaho and White Mountain Apache Ceremonial Forms and Categories." *SJA,* 1 (1945), 498–506.

List of ceremonials common to both groups. Considers differences in their performance.

2979. ——. "The Southern Athapascans." *Ki,* 4, No. 2 (November 1938), 5–10.

Cultural survey of Navajo and Apache includes data on religion and ceremonialism.

2980. Gorman, Carl N. "Navajo Vision of Earth and Man." *IH,* 6, No. 1 (Winter 1973), 19–22.

Defines tribal philosophy as manifested in chant and ceremonialism.

2981. Grant, Campbell. *Canyon de Chelly: Its People and Rock Art.* Tucson: Univ. of Arizona Press, 1978.

Treats geography, history, and ethnography of the site. With attention to Navajo myths represented in the rock art and to ceremonialism.

2982. Griffen, Joyce. "Variations on a Rite of Passage: Some Recent Navajo Funerals." *AIQ,* 4 (1978), 367–81.

Surveys differences occurring among Navajo funerals.

2983. Guernsey, S. J. "Notes on a Navajo War Dance." *AA,* 22 (1920), 304–7.

Description of a ceremonial observed in 1914.

2984. Haile, Father Berard. *Head and Face Masks in Navaho Ceremonialism.* St. Michaels, Ari.: St. Michaels Press, 1947.

Describes masks, their ceremonial uses, and mythological background.

2985. ——. *Learning Navaho.* 4 volumes. St. Michaels, Ari.: St. Michaels Press, 1941–1948.

Series of textbooks for learning the language. Some of the lessons involve materials regarding ceremonialism and storytelling.

2986. ——. *Legend of the Ghostway Ritual in the Male Branch of the Shootingway.* St. Michaels, Ari.: St. Michaels Press, 1950.

Navajo text of the ritual with free and interlinear translations and linguistic commentary. Collected in 1933.

2987. ——. "Navaho Chantways and Ceremonials." *AA,* 40 (1938), 639–52.

Primarily concerned with terminology associated with Navajo ritual.

2988. ——. *The Navaho Fire Dance or Corral Dance. A Brief Account of Its Practice and Meaning.* St. Michaels, Ari.: St. Michaels Press, 1946.

Pamphlet describes procedures of the ceremony.

2989. ——. "Navaho Games of Chance and Taboo." *PM,* 6 (1933), 35–40.

Describes games. With some attention to mythological references.

2990. ———. *Navaho Sacrificial Figurines.* Chicago: Univ. of Chicago Press, 1947.

Describes private ceremonials, which are interpreted as excerpts of public ceremonials. With song texts and interlinear translations.

2991. ———. "Navaho Upward-Reaching Way and Emergence Place." *AA,* 44 (1942), 407–20.

Close linguistic analysis of the ceremony. Views it as the paradigm for funeral ceremonialism. Treats myth about the first death.

2992. ———. *The Navaho War Dance. A Brief Narrative of Its Meaning and Practice.* St. Michaels, Ari.: St. Michaels Press, 1946.

Pamphlet describes function and procedures of the dance.

2993. ———. "A Note on the Navaho Visionary." *AA,* 42 (1940), 359.

Contrasts legendary figures, who receive power through dreams and visions, with real-life Navaho.

2994. ———. *Origin Legend of the Navaho Flintway.* Chicago: Univ. of Chicago Press, 1943.

Text and free translation of the ceremonial with extensive notes and commentary.

2995. ———. *Prayer Stick Cutting in a Five Night Navaho Ceremonial of the Male Branch of Shootingway.* Chicago: Univ. of Chicago Press, 1947.

Text with free and interlinear translations of ceremonial. Collected in 1929–1930. With extensive commentary and ethnographic and linguistic notes.

2996. ———. "Property Concepts of the Navaho Indians." *CUAAS,* 17 (1954), 1–56.

Includes data on ownership of songs and ceremonials.

2997. ———. *Soul Concepts of the Navaho.* Vatican: Typografia Poliglotta Vaticana, 1943.

Pamphlet relates belief system about the soul to creation mythology.

2998. ———. *Starlore Among the Navaho.* Santa Fe: Museum of Navaho Ceremonial Art, 1947.

Treats mythic significance of stars and constellations.

2999. ———. *Suckingway. Its Legend and Practice.* St. Michaels, Ari.: St. Michaels Press, 1950.

Ritual text with free and interlinear translations. Collected in early 1930s. With some linguistic commentary.

3000. ———. "Why the Navaho Hogan?" *PM,* 15 (1942), 39–56.

Considers mythic and ceremonial sanctions for hogan design and construction. With excerpt from a chant.

3001. ———, and Irvy W. Goossen. *Love-Magic and Butterfly People. The Slim Curly Version of Ajitee and Mothway Myths.* Ed. Karl W. Luckert. Flagstaff: Museum of Northern Arizona Press, 1978 (American Tribal Religions No. 2).

Navajo and English texts of myths collected by Haile in 1930–1931.

3002. ———, and Irvy W. Goossen. *Waterway. A Navajo Ceremonial Myth Told by Black Mustache Circle.* Appendix by Karl W. Luckert. Flagstaff: Museum of Northern Arizona Press, 1979 (American Tribal Religions, No. 5).

Account of Waterway Ceremonial collected in 1929. Presented with free translation. Appendix presents sandpaintings associated with the ceremonial.

3003. ———, and Mary C. Wheelwright. *Emergence Myth*

According to Hanelthnayhe or Upward-Reaching Rite. Santa Fe: Museum of Navajo Ceremonial Art, 1949 (Navajo Religion Series No. 3).

Includes myth text recorded by Haile in 1908 and two texts recorded by Wheelwright in 1931 and 1940. With descriptions of associated ceremonials, reproductions of sandpaintings, and explanatory commentary.

3004. Hall, Manly P. "The Sand Magic of the Navaho." *OM,* n. s. 87 (1929), 137, 154, 160.

Survey of healing rituals.

3005. Harman, Robert. "Change in a Navajo Ceremonial." *EP,* 7 (1964), 20–26.

Examines changes in the Enemy Way since 1938, especially in the behavior of young Navajo.

3006. Hausman, Gerald. *Sitting on the Blue-Eyed Bear: Navajo Myths and Legends.* Westport, Conn.: Lawrence Hill, 1975.

Poetic renderings of myths with some general data about the cultural background.

3007. Hill, Gertrude. "The Use of Turquoise Among the Navajo." *Ki,* 4, No. 3 (December 1938), 11–14.

Includes retelling of the creation myth, emphasizing references to turquoise.

3008. Hill, W. W. *The Agricultural and Hunting Methods of the Navaho Indians. YUPA* No. 18 (1938).

Includes data on rituals and mythological background. With texts of agricultural songs (words only).

3009. ———. "The Hand Trembling Ceremony of the Navaho." *EP,* 38 (1935), 65–68.

Ritual description includes ritual origin myth and song text.

3010. ———. "The Navaho Indians and the Ghost Dance of 1890." *AA,* 46 (1944), 523–27.

Speculates about Navajo failure to respond to Ghost Dance and presents eight oral history texts.

3011. ———. "Navaho Rites for Dispelling Insanity and Delirium." *EP,* 41 (1936), 71–74.

Description of a ritual.

3012. ———. "Navaho Trading and Trading Ritual: A Study of Cultural Dynamics." *SJA,* 4 (1948), 371–96.

Includes descriptions of ceremonials with song texts (words only).

3013. ———. *Navaho Warfare. YUPA* No. 5 (1936).

Includes several legend texts and descriptions of ceremonials.

3014. ———. "Stability in Culture and Pattern." *AA,* 41 (1939), 258–60.

Illustrates resistance to culture change by describing the Navajo Night Chant. Changes in that ceremonial are not merely responses to external influence.

3015. ———. "The Status of the Hermaphrodite and Transvestite in Navaho Culture." *AA,* 37 (1935), 273–79.

Cultural role of the two figures—regarded with favor by the Navajo—is confirmed by mythology.

3016. ———, and Dorothy W. Hill. "The Legend of the Navajo Eagle-Catching-Way." *NMA,* 6–7, No. 2 (April-June 1943), 31–36.

Myth text with some introductory data on cultural background. No annotation.

3017. ———, and Dorothy W. Hill. "Navaho Coyote Tales and Their Position in the Southern Athabaskan Group." *JAF,* 58 (1945), 317–43.

Nineteen texts and fourteen abstracts of Coyote tales.

With comparisons to similar material among Apache groups.

3018. ———, and Dorothy W. Hill. "Two Navajo Myths." *NMA,* 6–7, No. 3 (July-September 1943), 111–14.

Texts with brief annotations and data on collecting situation. Collected in 1934–1935.

3019. Hodge, Carle. "Don't Laugh at the Navajo Medicine Man." *C,* 130 (25 October 1952), 66–71.

Description of Navajo therapeutic techniques.

3020. Hodge, William H. "Navaho Pentecostalism." *AnQ,* 37 (1964), 73–93.

Examines introduction of a Christian religious movement. With several personal narrative texts.

3021. Hogner, Dorothy Childs. "Hogan Tales." *NMQ,* 4 (1934), 77–86.

Three rewritten myth texts. No commentary or annotations.

3022. Hogner, Nils. "Navajo Art." *SAM,* 30 (March 1931), 465–66, ix.

Covers several art forms and includes an etiological myth about weaving.

3023. Honigmann, John J. "Northern and Southern Athapaskan Eschatology." *AA,* 47 (1945), 467–69.

Compares Navajo and Sarsi beliefs and ceremonials regarding death.

3024. Iverson, Peter. *The Navajos. A Critical Bibliography.* Bloomington: Indiana Univ. Press, 1976.

Unannotated list of 189 books and articles. Introductory essay contains section on "Health and Religion."

3025. Jacobson, Doranne. "Navajo Enemy Way Exchanges." *EP,* 7 (1964), 7–19.

Description of the ritual, emphasizing exchanges of goods and services.

3026. James, George Wharton. *House Blessing Ceremony and Guest Book.* Pasadena, Cal.: Radiant Life Press, 1917.

First half of the volume is a text of the ceremony. Second half is a guestbook.

3027. ———. *Indian Blankets and Their Makers.* Chicago: A. C. McClurg, 1914.

Popular survey of blanket art among the Navajo and Pueblo groups. With data on ceremonialism and religion.

3028. Joe, Eugene Baatsoslanii, and Marle Bahti. *Navajo Sandpainting Art.* Tucson: Treasure Chest, 1978.

Pamphlet describes various sandpainting designs in terms of their mythical associations.

3029. Karam, A. H. "Medicine Man from the East." *SWR,* 52 (1967), 393–403.

Doctor who worked on Navajo Reservation learned need to consider traditional healing rituals when dealing with patients.

3030. Keegan, Marcia. *Mother Earth, Father Sky: Navajo and Pueblo Indians of the Southwest.* New York: Grossman, 1974.

Photographic album. Each picture is captioned with an excerpt from a NA song or chant.

3031. Keith, Anne B. "The Navajo Girls' Puberty Ceremony: Function and Meaning for the Adolescent." *EP,* 7 (1964), 27–36.

The ceremony brings changes in the subject's attitudes, status, potential, and actual behavior. A straight functional analysis.

3032. Kelly, Roger E., R. W. Lang, and Harry Walters. *Navaho Figurines Called Dolls.* Santa Fe: Museum of Navaho Ceremonial Art, 1972.

Two essays: "Navaho Ritual Human Figurines: Form and Function" by Kelly treats form and ritual uses of the figures (with prayer texts); Lang and Walters' "The Remaking Rites of the Navaho: Causal Factors of Illness and Its Nature" offers a survey of theories of disease.

3033. King, Jeff. *Where the Two Came to Their Father. A Navaho War Ceremonial.* Recorded by Maud Oakes. Commentary by Joseph Campbell. New York: Pantheon, 1943.

Text of the ritual with reproductions of sandpaintings. Campbell's commentary points out international parallels. Re-issued by Princeton Univ. Press in 1969.

3034. Klah, Hosteen, and Mary C. Wheelwright. *Navajo Creation Myth.* BMNCA No. 6 (1953).

Unannotated myth text. No commentary.

3035. ———, and Mary C. Wheelwright. *Tleji or Yehbechai Myth.* BMNCA No. 1 (1938).

Unannotated myth text. No commentary.

3036. ———, and Mary C. Wheelwright. *Wind Chant and Feather Chant.* BMNCA No. 4 (1946).

Unannotated myth texts. No commentary.

3037. ———, Hosteen Gahni, and Mary C. Wheelwright. *Myth of Mountain Chant and Beauty Chant.* BMNCA No. 5 (1951).

Unannotated myth texts. No commentary.

3038. Kluckhohn, Clyde E. "The Dance of Hasjelti, Being an Account of the Yeibitchai Held at Thoreau, N. M., Nov. 9th to 18th." *EP,* 15 (1923), 187–92.

Description of a healing ritual.

3039. ———. "The Great Chants of the Navajo." *TAM,* 17, No. 8 (August 1933), 639–45.

Describes Night Chant and Mountain Chant.

3040. ———. "Navaho Categories," in 102, pp. 65–98.

Treats correspondences between categories of supernaturals and categories of rituals.

3041. ———. "A Navaho Personal Document with a Brief Paretian Analysis." *SJA,* 1 (1945), 260–83.

Presents personal narrative text collected in 1938. With analysis from Pareto's concept of social equilibrium.

3042. ———. "Navaho Witchcraft." *PPM,* 22, No. 2 (1944), 1–149.

Survey of the witch belief system with data on ceremonials. Includes functional analysis of witchcraft.

3043. ———. "Navaho Women's Knowledge of Their Song Ceremonials." *EP,* 45 (1938), 87–92.

Finds women have a good deal of knowledge about rituals in which they do not participate.

3044. ———. "Notes on the Navajo Eagle Way." *NMA,* 5, No. 1 (January-March 1941), 6–14.

Description of the ceremonial with excerpts from ritual origin myth and reproduction of sandpaintings.

3045. ———. "Participation in Ceremonials in a Navaho Community." *AA,* 40 (1938), 359–69.

Examines knowledge of song ceremonials among the Navajo, finding that a good deal of familiarity with ritual system exists.

3046. ———, and Dorothea Leighton. *The Navaho.* Cambridge: Harvard Univ. Press, 1946.

Ethnography includes data on mythology and folktales, descriptions of ceremonials, and an outline of the world view. A revised edition was published by Doubleday in 1962.

3047. ———, and Leland C. Wyman. *An Introduction to Navaho Chant Practice with an Account of the Behaviors Observed in Four Chants. MAAA* No. 53 (1940).

Survey of personnel, equipment, medicines, and procedures characteristic of chant performances with special attention to the Navajo Windway, the Chiricahua Windway, the Female Shooting Holyway, and the Hand Trembling Evilway.

3048. ———, W. W. Hill, and Lucy Wales Kluckhohn. *Navaho Material Culture.* Cambridge: Harvard Univ. Press, 1971.

Survey of architecture, clothing, and artifacts, including those associated with ceremonialism. Descriptions of the last include ritual procedure and song texts.

3049. Kroeber, Henriette Rothschild. "A Navajo's Fairy Tale." *OM,* n. s. 54 (November 1909), 456–58.

Unannotated Coyote myth with brief introduction about NA oral traditions.

3050. Lamphere, Louise. "Loose-Structuring as Exhibited in a Case Study of Navajo Religious Learning." *EP,* 7 (1964), 37–44.

Argues that the loosely structured society of the Navajo facilitates ritual and religious instruction.

3051. ———. "Symbolic Elements in Navajo Ritual." *SJA,* 25 (1969), 279–305.

Suggests that Navajo rituals are a symbolic system which communicates a model of the natural and supernatural realms. Myths help to elucidate the symbolism of aspects of the rituals.

3052. Landar, Herbert J. "Four Navaho Summer Tales." *JAF,* 72 (1959), 161–64, 248–51, 298–309.

Four stories collected in 1956 are explored for recurrent themes related to the central values of the culture.

3053. ———. "A Note on the Navaho Word for Coyote." *IJAL,* 27 (1961), 86–88.

Etymological analysis involves references to mythology.

3054. ———. "Theme of Incest in Navaho Folklore," in 118, pp. 118–33.

Text of a myth collected in 1956 and presented with free translation. Analyzed in terms of cultural values and deep structure.

3055. "Legend of Canyon de Chelly, The." *Aff,* 1, No. 4 (January 1972), 10.

Navajo story about cliff dwellings. Reprinted from the May 1939 issue of *Scenic Southwest Magazine.*

3056. Leighton, Alexander H., and Dorothea C. Leighton. "Gregorio, the Hand-Trembler. A Psychobiological Personality Study of a Navaho Indian." *PPM,* 40, No. 1 (1949), 1–177.

Life history of a ceremonial practitioner with extensive commentary on cultural and psychological factors shaping his personality. Collected in 1940.

3057. Leighton, Dorothea, and Clyde Kluckhohn. *Children of the People: The Navaho Individual and His Development.* Cambridge: Harvard Univ. Press, 1947.

Personality and culture study focusing on socialization processes. Includes some descriptions of ceremonials and song texts.

3058. Levy, Jerrold E. "The Fate of Navajo Twins." *AA,* 66 (1964), 883–87.

Describes ambivalence about birth of twins as related

to mythology.

3059. Link, Margaret Schevill. *The Pollen Path. A Collection of Navajo Myths.* With a Psychological Commentary by Joseph L. Henderson. Stanford: Stanford Univ. Press, 1956.

Twelve myth texts, rewritten and unannotated. Henderson's stance is Jungian. An appendix describes Link's fieldwork experiences, presents song texts, and summarizes the religious system.

3060. Lipps, Oscar H. *The Navajos.* Cedar Rapids, Iowa: Torch Press, 1909.

Contains myth texts and descriptions of ceremonials.

3061. Locke, Raymond Friday. *The Book of the Navajo.* Los Angeles: Mankind, 1976.

General survey of Navajo culture with emphasis on mythic concepts of prehistory and contact history. Contains retellings of five myths.

3062. Lockett, Clay. "Midwives and Childbirth Among the Navajo." *Plat,* 12, No. 1 (1939), 15–17.

Some data on ceremonials associated with childbirth.

3063. Loganbill, Dean. "Collecting Folklore on the Alamo Reservation: Some Preliminary Observations." *Aff,* 3, No. 4 (Winter 1973), 34–36.

Discusses problems in doing fieldwork on the reservation.

3064. ———. "Some Navajo and Kiowa Folktales." *NMFR,* 13 (1973–1974), 7–10.

Unannotated legend texts with some data about collecting situation.

3065. Looney, Ralph. "The Navajos." *NG,* 142 (December 1972), 740–81.

Historical and cultural survey includes data on ceremonialism and mythology.

3066. Lovering, J. "The Two Vases. The Navajo Legend of the Creation." *OM,* n. s. 55 (1910), 528–29.

Unannotated, rewritten myth.

3067. Luckert, Karl W. "An Approach to Navajo Mythology," in 166, pp. 117–31.

Treats the time-space structure of the Hunter myth as key to Navajo world view. Response by Sam Gill (pp. 131–32).

3068. ———. *Coyoteway. A Navajo Holyway Healing Ceremonial.* Tucson: Univ. of Arizona Press; Flagstaff: Museum of Northern Arizona Press, 1979.

Text of the ceremony with song and prayer texts and ritual description. Includes some previously recorded texts and data on cultural and mythological background.

3069. ———. *The Navajo Hunter Tradition.* Tucson: Univ. of Arizona Press, 1975.

Texts of hunter mythology and ritual procedure with a presentation of underlying belief system. Thorough cross-cultural survey of related mythology.

3070. ———. *Navajo Mountain and Rainbow Bridge Religion.* Flagstaff: Museum of Northern Arizona Press, 1977.

Discusses sacred significance of the Rainbow Bridge region. Interviews with eight informants include prayers, myths, and songs.

3071. ———, Johnny C. Cooke, and Irvy W. Goossen. *A Navajo Bringing-Home Ceremony. The Claus Chee Sonny Version of Deerway Ajitee.* Flagstaff: Museum of Northern Arizona Press, 1978 (American Tribal Religions No. 3).

Thorough ritual description with song texts and mythology. Collected in 1976–1977.

3072. Luomala, Katherine. "The Ear-Sleeper Motif in Navaho Mythology?" *JAF,* 90 (1977), 467–71.

Questions whether a folk-narrative motif popular in Eurasia and used in a novel about Navajo life actually occurs in tribal folklore.

3073. Marshall, Louise R. "A Drum for the Navajo Chorus." *Etu,* 59 (February 1941), 126.

Treats the significance of the drum in Navajo ceremonialism.

3074. Matthews, Washington. "The Gentile System of the Navajo Indians." *JAF,* 3 (1890), 89–110.

Survey of social organization includes treatment of its mythological basis.

3075. ———. "The Mountain Chant. A Navajo Ceremony." *ARBAE,* 5 (1883–1884), 379–467.

Description of the ceremony includes texts of its origin myth, prayers, and songs.

3076. ———. "Mythic Dry Paintings of the Navajos." *AmN,* 19 (October 1885), 931–939.

Description of healing ceremonialism.

3077. ———. *Navaho Legends. MAFS* No. 5 (1897).

Lengthy texts of creation myth and two other myths. Very good introduction on cultural background and explanatory notes to the texts. Contains music for songs in myths.

3078. ———. "Navaho Myths, Prayers, and Songs with Texts and Translations." Ed. Pliny Earle Goddard. *UC-PAAE,* 5 (1907–1910), 21–63.

Includes various oral literary forms associated with the Night Chant. Texts of myths, prayers, and songs with interlinear and free translations. No commentary or annotations.

3079. ———. "Navaho Night Chant." *JAF,* 14 (1901), 12–19.

Description of the ceremonial with song and chant texts.

3080. ———. "Navajo Gambling Songs." *AA,* o. s. 2 (1889), 1–19.

Texts and free translations of twenty-one songs with descriptions of the games associated with them.

3081. ———. "A Navajo Initiation." *LS,* 15 (November 1901), 353–56.

Description of a ritual associated with the Night Chant.

3082. ———. "The Night Chant, A Navaho Ceremony." *MAMNH,* 6 (1902), 3–332.

Thorough description of the ritual with prayer and chant texts. Extensive data on ceremonial context. Fieldwork done on Hyde Expedition.

3083. ———. "Noqoìlpi, the Gambler: A Navajo Myth." *JAF,* 2 (1889), 89–94.

Unannotated myth text with brief comments on cultural background.

3084. ———. "The Origin of the Utes. A Navajo Myth." *AAOJ,* 7 (1885), 271.

Unannotated text. No commentary.

3085. ———. "A Part of the Navajo's Mythology." *AAOJ,* 5 (1883), 207–24.

Portions of the creation myth retold and explicated.

3086. ———, trans. "Prayer from the Night Chant." *SWR,* 34, No. 1 (Winter 1949), 89–91.

Unannotated text. No commentary.

3087. ———. "The Prayer of a Navajo Shaman." *AA,* o. s. 1 (1888), 149–71.

Text with free translation. Includes context description.

3088. ———. "Serpent Worship Among the Navajos." *LS,* 9 (September 1898), 228–35.

Survey of serpent symbolism in Navajo ritual and mythology.

3089. ———. "Some Deities and Demons of the Navajos." *AmN,* 20 (October 1886), 841–50.

Summary of supernaturalism includes song text and rewritten myth.

3090. ———. "Some Sacred Objects of the Navajo Rites," in 79, pp. 227–47.

Description of ceremonial objects includes one song text (words only).

3091. ———. "Songs of the Navajos." *LS,* 5 (October 1896), 197–201.

Includes several song texts (words only), but the emphasis is on collecting experiences. An analysis of the music of the songs appears in 2956.

3092. ———. "Songs of Sequence of the Navajos." *JAF,* 7 (1894), 185–94.

Texts and analysis of ritual songs which follow a standardized sequence in ceremonial performances.

3093. ———. "The Treatment of Ailing Gods." *JAF,* 14 (1901), 20–23.

Text of a ritual origin myth with some comment on cultural background.

3094. ———. "A Vigil of the Gods—A Navaho Ceremony." *AA,* o. s. 9 (1896), 50–57.

Thorough description of a ceremonial with attention to its myth associations. Includes one song text (words only) with free translation.

3095. McAllester, David P. "Enemy Way Music. A Study of Social and Esthetic Values as Seen in Navaho Music." *PPM,* 41, No. 3 (1954), 1–96.

Seventy-five song texts (words and music) with extensive data on ceremonial context, musicological features, and relationship to cultural values.

3096. ———. "A Paradigm of Navajo Dance." *P,* 4, No. 2 (May 1979), 28–35.

Discusses sacredness of three kinds of dancing among the Navajo: traditional, pan-Indian, and disco. Description of first includes mythic background and song texts.

3097. McGibbeny, J. H. "Navajos Are My Subjects." *AzH,* 29, No. 7 (July 1953), 16–29.

Photographer's notes include data on ceremonialism.

3098. Mills, George. *Navaho Art and Culture.* Colorado Springs: Taylor Museum, 1959.

Examines how Navajo art reflects the values of the culture. Attempts to relate art—especially sandpainting—to mythology.

3099. Mindeleff, Cosmos. "Houses and House Dedication of the Navahos." *ScA,* 82 (14 April 1900), 233–34.

Ceremonial description with song and chant texts (words only).

3100. ———. "Navaho Houses." *ARBAE,* 17 (1895–1896), 469–517.

Architectural survey which analyzes descriptions of houses which appear in myths.

3101. Mitchell, Emerson Blackhorse, and T. D. Allen. *Miracle Hill. The Story of a Navaho Boy.* Norman: Univ. of Oklahoma Press, 1967.

Autobiography rewritten from Mitchell's ms. by Allen. Focuses on acculturation and ceremonialism.

3102. Moon, Sheila. *A Magic Dwells: A Poetic and Psychological Study of the Navaho Emergence Myth.* Middletown, Conn.: Wesleyan Univ. Press, 1970.
Jungian analysis of the myth with a synopsis of the text.

3103. Morgan, William. *Human-Wolves Among the Navaho.* YUPA No. 11 (1936).
Description of shapeshifters includes myth and legend texts.

3104. ———. "Navaho Dreams." *AA,* 34 (1932), 390–405.
Discusses methods of dream interpretation and influence of myths on Navajo dreaming.

3105. ———. "Navaho Treatment of Sickness: Diagnosticians." *AA,* 33 (1931), 390–402.
Distinguishes the diagnostician from the shaman. The former creates his own songs, while the shaman performs traditional pieces.

3106. ———. "The Organization of a Story and a Tale." Preface by Alfred North Whitehead. *JAF,* 58 (1945), 169–94.
Discusses the processes involved in folktale formation. Explores the folktale as an event interrelated with the cultural and psychological pasts of the storyteller and his audience. Uses Navajo materials in this anticipation of the performance approach to folklore story.

3107. Nabokov, Peter. "The Peyote Road." *NYTM,* 9 March 1969, pp. 30–31, 129–34.
Description of the belief system and rituals of the NA Church among the Navajo.

3108. "Navajo and Pueblo Indian Dancing." *IW,* 5, No. 1 (1 October 1937), 27–34.
Survey of ceremonial behavior. With one song text.

3109. "Navajo Witchcraft." *EP,* 80 (1974), 38–42.
Includes several witchcraft legends collected by Clyde Kluckhohn. With some data on cultural background.

3110. Newcomb, Franc Johnson. "'Fire Lore' in Navajo Legend and Ceremony." *NMFR,* 3 (1948–1949), 3–9.
Survey of symbolic significance of fire in Navajo mythology and ceremonialism.

3111. ———. *Hosteen Klah: Navaho Medicine Man and Sand Painter.* Norman: Univ. of Oklahoma Press, 1964.
Biography of Navajo spiritual leader and artist (1867–1937), based on interviews conducted with him and others. Includes some oral history material and data on ceremonialism.

3112. ———. "How the Navajo Adopt Rites." *EP,* 46 (1939), 25–27.
Brief note on religious acculturation.

3113. ———. *Navaho Folk Tales.* Santa Fe: Museum of Navaho Ceremonial Art, 1967.
Seventeen rewritten myths. No commentary or annotations. May be for children.

3114. ———. "The Navajo Listening Rite." *EP,* 45 (1938), 46–49.
Ceremonial description.

3115. ———. *Navajo Omens and Taboos.* Santa Fe: Rydal Press, 1940.
Classifies taboos and relates them to supernaturalism, mythology, and ceremonialism.

3116. ———. "Navajo Symbols of the Sun." *NMQ,* 6 (1936), 305–07.
Treats the role of the sun in Navajo mythology and ritual.

3117. ———. "Origin Legend of the Navaho Eagle Chant." *JAF,* 53 (1940), 50–77.
Text of a ritual origin myth.

3118. ———, and Gladys A. Reichard. *Sandpaintings of the Navajo Shooting Chant.* New York: J. J. Augustin, ND.
Reproductions of paintings are introduced with thorough description of the ceremonial and a retelling of its myth.

3119. Northshield, Robert. "The Healing of Robert Lee." *Sm,* 5, No. 9 (December 1974), 74–77.
Ceremonial description.

3120. O'Bryan, Aileen. *The Diné: Origin Myths of the Navaho Indians.* BAEB No. 163 (1956).
Myth and chant texts recorded in 1928 and presented in free translations. Some commentary on informant and explanatory notes.

3121. Oglesby, Catharine. *Modern Primitive Arts of Mexico, Guatemala, and the Southwest.* New York: Whittlesey House, 1939.
Includes some treatment of mythic origins of art forms among Navajo, Hopi, and other Pueblo groups. With some chant texts.

3122. Overholt, Mary Elisabeth. "Pictures in Sand." *A&A,* 34 (September-October 1933), 262–66.
Description of healing ceremony with summary of ritual origin myth.

3123. Parsons, Elsie Clews. "Navaho Folk Tales." *JAF,* 36 (1923), 368–75.
Thirteen myth and folktale texts with some comparative notes. Includes brief description of collecting situation.

3124. ———. "Note on Navajo War Dance." *AA,* 21 (1919), 465–67.
Description of a part of the ritual as observed in 1918.

3125. ———. "Note on the Night Chant at Tuwelchedu Which Came to an End on December 6, 1920." *AA,* 23 (1921), 240–43.
Description of a Navajo ceremonial and a summary of a myth relating to Hopi clan affiliations.

3126. Pepper, George H. "Ah-Jih-Lee-Hah-Neh, a Navajo Legend." *JAF,* 21 (1908), 178–83.
Unannotated myth text collected in 1904. No commentary.

3127. Reagan, Albert B. "The Influenza and the Navajo." *PIAS for 1919,* pp. 243–47.
Account of NA response to disease includes some references to mythology and ceremonials.

3128. ———. "A Navaho Fire Dance." *AA,* 36 (1934), 434–37.
Describes the ritual as observed in 1923.

3129. Reichard, Gladys A. *Dezba, Woman of the Desert.* New York: J. J. Augustin, 1939.
Description of lifeways of Navajo women. One chapter focuses on religious beliefs and ceremonialism.

3130. ———. "Distinctive Features of Navaho Religion." *SJA,* 1 (1945), 199–220.
Compares features characteristic of Navajo religion to Pueblo and Plains religions.

3131. ———. "Good Characters in Myth: The Navaho Sun God." *JAF,* 56 (1943), 141–43.
Description of the deity based on myths.

3132. ———. "Individualism and Mythological Style." *JAF,* 57 (1944), 16–25.

Uses Navajo myths to show how the nature of the narratives provides information about the characters of the storytellers. Myths reflect the individual as well as his culture.

3133. ———. "Language and Cultural Pattern." *AA,* 52 (1950), 194–204.

Uses linguistic and ethnological approaches to investigate patterns in Navajo prayers and greeting formulas. Sees them as reflecting values of the culture.

3134. ———. "Linguistic Diversity Among the Navaho Indians." *IJAL,* 11 (1940), 156–68.

Study of language variation among the Navajo includes text of a myth which accounts for such variations.

3135. ———. "The Navaho and Christianity." *AA,* 51 (1949), 66–71.

Points out incompatibilities between Christianity and the Navajo world view. Cites ceremonials and prayers to show why missionary work has been generally unsuccessful.

3136. ———. *Navaho Grammar. PAES* No. 21 (1951).

Linguistic survey includes one life history text with free and literal translations and linguistic analysis.

3137. ———. *Navaho Religion. A Study of Symbolism.* 2 volumes. New York: Pantheon, 1950.

Very thorough treatment of the Navajo religious system with section on dogma (with myths), symbolism, and ritual (with songs). Includes descriptive lists of supernatural beings and ritual ideas.

3138. ———. *Navajo Shepherd and Weaver.* New York: J. J. Augustin, 1936.

Survey of the woolen industry. Includes a description of the role of the ritual performer as a purveyor of power. Reprinted by the Rio Grande Press in 1968.

3139. ———. *Prayer: The Compulsive Word. MonAES* No. 7 (1944).

Thorough discussion of the function, structure, and content of Navajo prayers includes several texts. With exhaustive analysis of a prayer for the Male Shooting Chant.

3140. ———. *Social Life of the Navajo Indians with Some Attention to Minor Ceremonies. CUCA* No. 7 (1928).

Describes ceremonials, witchcraft, and religious attitudes. Based on fieldwork done in 1923–1925.

3141. ———. *Spider Woman. A Story of Navajo Weavers and Chanters.* New York: Macmillan, 1934.

Anecdotal description of Navajo culture focusing on various ceremonials such as sandpainting and chanting. Includes some freely translated song texts. Reprinted by the Rio Grande Press in 1968.

3142. ———. *The Story of the Navajo Hail Chant.* New York: NP, 1944.

Text and translation recorded in 1938. Some general introductory commentary and explanatory notes.

3143. ———. "The Translation of Two Navaho Chant Words." *AA,* 44 (1942), 421–24.

Argues that the "Moving Up Way" should be translated as "Chant of Waning Endurance." Berard Haile responded in *AA,* 45 (1943), 306–11.

3144. Roberts, Kenneth L. "Navaho Land." *SEP,* 197 (15 September 1924), 28, 175–78.

Popularized culture survey includes data on ceremonialism and mythology.

3145. Roessel, Ruth, ed. *Navajo Stories of the Long Walk*

Period. Tsaile, Ari.: Navajo Community College Press, 1973.

Accounts from forty narrators of events associated with the Long Walk of the 1860s. Some general contextual data, but no information about specific texts.

3146. Rogers, George. "Klah, the Pagan." *Me,* 12, No. 3 (March 1924), 46–48.

Characterization of ceremonial practitioner contains summaries of myths and data on rituals.

3147. Rollins, Warren E. "Passing of the Spirit Dance." *EP,* 7 (1919), 187–91.

Description of a ritual.

3148. ———. "The Spirit of the Dead (A Navajo Ceremony)." *EP,* 12 (1922), 71–73.

Description of a ritual. With song texts.

3149. Roosevelt, Theodore. "Across the Navajo Desert." *O,* 105 (11 October 1913), 309–17.

Description of a visit to northeastern Arizona includes texts of several Navajo prayers.

3150. Rudhyar, Dane. "The Navajo 'Male Mountain Chant' Once More Resounds Before the Assembled Tribes." *NMQ,* 9 (1939), 29–38.

Description of a ceremonial.

3151. Runke, Walter. "How Arizona Became the Navajo's Home." *TT,* 4 (July 1902), 197–98.

Comic myth text.

3152. Rush, Emmy Matt. "Indian Legends." *EP,* 32 (1932), 137–54.

Unannotated myth texts and ritual descriptions from Navajo, Hopi, and a southern California group.

3153. "Sand Paintings of the Navajo, The." *IW,* 3, No. 11 (15 January 1936), 25–26.

Description of sandpainting designs in a New Mexico hotel, their mythic significance, and their ritual context.

3154. Sapir, Edward. "A Navaho Sand Painting Blanket." *AA,* 37 (1935), 609–16.

Describes how a weaver transforms the pattern of a sandpainting enough to avoid accusations of tampering with the sacred.

3155. ———. *Navaho Texts.* Ed. and with supplementary texts by Harry Hoijer. Iowa City, Iowa: Linguistic Society of America, 1942.

Fifteen myths, two prayers, two personal narratives, and thirty descriptions of customs collected in 1929. Presented with free translations and linguistic and explanatory notes.

3156. Sawyer, Marileta. "The Navajo Hand Trembling Ceremony." *Aff,* 3, No. 2 (Summer 1973), 33–42.

Thorough description of the ceremonial as observed in 1970. Includes prayer and song texts.

3157. Schevill, Margaret Erwin. "Navajo Sandpainting." *ArQ,* 1, No. 2 (1945), 7–16.

Brief descriptions of sandpainting designs with Jungian interpretations. Includes excerpts from myths associated with the paintings.

3158. Shepardson, Mary. "Changes in Navajo Mortuary Practices and Beliefs." *AIQ,* 4 (1978), 383–95.

Focuses on transformations brought about by Christianity.

3159. Sleight, Frederick W. "The Navajo Sacred Mountain of the East—A Controversy." *EP,* 58 (1951), 379–97.

Outlines disagreements over location of sacred mountain mentioned in Navajo oral literature.

3160. Spencer, Katherine. *Mythology and Values. An Analysis of Navaho Chantway Myths. MAFS* No. 48 (1957).

Using published materials and the unpublished mss. of
Fr. Berard Haile, Spencer shows how Navajo myths
reflect cultural values.

3161. ———. *Reflection of Social Life in the Navaho Origin
Myth.* APUNM No. 3 (1947).
Considers the manner and extent of cultural reflection
in mythology.

3162. Stephen, A. M. "The Navajo." *AA,* o. s. 6 (1893),
345–62.
Ethnographic notes include data on mythology and
ceremonialism. With song texts.

3163. ———. "Navajo Origin Legend." *JAF,* 43 (1930),
88–104.
Unannotated myth text collected in 1885. Some
commentary with diagrams on Navajo cosmology.

3164. Stevenson, James. "Ceremonial of Hasjelti Dail-
jis and Mythical Sand Painting of the Navajo Indians." *AR-
BAE,* 8 (1886–1887), 229–85.
Thorough description of a healing ritual includes
prayer and song texts. With six myth texts.

3165. Stuckey, William. "Navajo Medicine Men." *SD,*
December 1975, pp. 34–40.
Describes traditional healing practices still in use.
Includes summary of myths and accounts of rituals.

3166. Swinnerton, Louise Scher. "Making War on Evil
Thoughts." *Sun,* 58 (January 1927), 36–37.
Description of a ceremonial.

3167. Toelken, J. Barre. "A Circular World: The Vision
of Navajo Crafts." *P,* 1, No. 1 (Winter 1976), 30–37.
Examination of material culture as a reflection of the
Navajo world view—especially the tendency to see things
as cyclic.

3168. ———. "The Demands of Harmony: An Appreci-
ation of Navajo Relations." *P,* 2, No. 4 (1977), 74–81.
Treats view of relationships between people and
people, people and nature, and people and the sacred.
Some data on healing rituals.

3169. ———. *"Ma'i Joldloshi:* Legendary Styles and
Navaho Myth," in 122, pp. 203–11.
The study of Navajo legends blurs many of the
distinctions used when dealing with EA oral materials.
Toelken illustrates by using Coyote tales.

3170. ———. "The 'Pretty Languages' of Yellowman:
Genre, Mode, and Texture in Navaho Coyote Narratives."
G, 2 (1969), 211–36.
Treats the performance of a Coyote tale by a Navajo
storyteller. Discusses text of the story and comments
extensively on the performer. Reprinted in 84 (pp.
145–70).

3171. Tozzer, Alfred M. "A Note on Star-Lore Among
the Navajos." *JAF,* 21 (1908), 28–32.
Describes sandpainting and rattles used in the Night
Chant with attention to depictions of star formations.
Some data on star mythology.

3172. Tschopik, Harry, Jr. "Taboo as a Possible Factor
involved in the Obsolescence of Navaho Pottery and Basketry." *AA,* 40 (1938), 257–62.
Elaborate taboos associated with ceremonial objects
discouraged potters and basketmakers from practicing
their crafts. Omer C. Stewart responded in *AA,* 40
(1938), 758–59.

3173. Udall, Stewart L. "Navajos: They Walk with
Beauty in the Land of Dineh." *NW,* 10, No. 4 (June-July
1972), 4–9.

Brief account of Navajo relationship to nature includes
song texts (words only).

3174. Van Valkenburgh, Richard. "The Government of
the Navajos." *ArQ,* 1, No. 4 (1945), 63–73.
Description of political system includes mythic basis
for the system.

3175. ———. "Sacred Places and Shrines of the Navajos. Part II. Navajo Rock and Twig Piles, Called Tsenad-
jihih." *Plat,* 13, No. 1 (July 1940), 6–9.
Describes sacred sites in terms of their mythic or
legendary sanctions.

3176. ———, and Scotty Begay. "Sacred Places and
Shrines of the Navajo. Part I. The Sacred Mountains."
MNMNA, 11, No. 3 (September 1938), 29–34.
List of sacred places with some of their mythic and
legendary significance.

3177. Van Vleet, T. Stanton. "Legendary Evolution of
the Navajo Indians." *AmN,* 27 (January 1893), 69–79.
Four myth texts with some explanatory notes. Brief
data on the informant.

3178. Villasenor, David D. *Tapestries in Sand: The Spirit of
Indian Sandpainting.* Ed. Vinson Brown. Healdsburg, Cal.:
Naturegraph, 1963.
Paintings and commentary. Latter includes myths,
symbolism and ceremonial descriptions.

3179. Wagner, Roland M. "Pattern and Process in
Ritual Syncretism: The Case of Peyotism Among the
Navajo." *JAR,* 31 (1975), 162–81.
Focuses on religious acculturation by describing a
ceremony which blends peyotism with traditional
religious practices.

3180. Wake, C. Staniland. "The Navaho Origin Legend." *AAOJ,* 26 (1904), 265–71.
Retelling of the myth with some attention to its
cultural significance.

3181. Walsh, Patrick. "The Skinwalker." *Aff,* 4, No. 1
(Spring 1974), 20–22.
Three legend texts about shapeshifters. Collected from
Navajo students at Northern Arizona University.

3182. Walton, Eda Lou. "Navaho Poetry: An Interpretation." *TR,* 7 (1922), 198–210.
Relates song texts (words only) to cultural values.

3183. ———, trans. "Navaho Songs." *N,* 110 (17 April
1920), 517.
Twelve unannotated texts (words only). No
commentary.

3184. ———. "Navajo Song Patterning." *JAF,* 43
(1930), 105–18.
Discussion of the use of parallelism in Navajo songs
and chants.

3185. ———. "Navajo Verse Rhythms." *Po,* 24, No. 1
(April 1924), 40–44.
Brief survey of metrical patterns in Navajo oral poetry.

3186. Waters, Frank. *Masked Gods. Navaho and Pueblo
Ceremonialism.* Chicago: Swallow, 1950.
Draws parallels between ceremonialism in the
Southwest, Western rationalism, and Eastern mysticism.
Includes rewritten myths and song texts.

3187. ———. "Navajo Yei-Bet-Chai." *YR,* 28 (1938–
1939), 558–71.
Description of ceremonialism with excerpts from song
texts.

3188. Watkins, Frances E. *The Navaho.* SWML No. 16
(ND).

Culture survey includes data on cosmology, singing, and ceremonialism.

3189. Wattles, Ruth Jocelyn. "Sketches of Indian Life. The Navajo Wedding." *OM,* n. s. 68 (August 1916), 170–73.

Description of a ceremonial.

3190. Wetherill, Hilda Faunce. *Navajo Indian Poems.* New York: Vantage, 1952.

Forty-one unannotated song texts (words only). No commentary.

3191. ———. "The Trading Post: Letters from a Primitive Land." *AtM* 142 (1928), 289–300, 510–21.

Letters from the wife of a trader on the Navajo Reservation. Contains data on ceremonialism, especially healing rituals.

3192. Wetherill, Louisa Wade. "The Story of the First Lie." *Ki,* 12, No. 3 (March 1947), 36–38.

Unannotated myth text. No commentary.

3193. ———. "The Woman Whose Nose Was Cut Off Twelve Times or The Woman Who Controls the Weather." *Ki,* 12, No. 2 (January 1947), 25–26.

Unannotated myth text. No commentary.

3194. Wetherill, Lulu Wade, and Byron Cummings. "A Navaho Folk Tale of Pueblo Bonito." *A&A,* 14 (September 1922), 132–36.

Unannotated folktale text with introductory data on cultural background.

3195. Wheelwright, Mary C. *Hail Chant and Water Chant.* Santa Fe: Museum of Navajo Ceremonial Art, 1946 (Navajo Religion Series No. 2).

Texts with descriptions of ritual procedures and reproductions of sandpaintings. Some explanatory comments.

3196. ———. *Myth of Sontso (Big Star).* BMNCA No. 2 (1940).

Unannotated myth text. No commentary.

3197. ———. *The Myths and Prayers of the Great Star Chant and The Myth of the Coyote Chant.* Ed. David P. McAllester. Santa Fe: Museum of Navajo Ceremonial Art, 1956 (Navajo Religion Series No. 4).

Myth and prayer texts with commentary by McAllester and descriptions of ceremonial procedures by Sontso-Hatrali and Yoh Hatrali. Texts recorded in 1930s by Wheelwright and Fr. Berard Haile.

3198. ———. "Notes on Some Navajo Coyote Myths." *NMFR,* 4 (1949–1950), 17–19.

Summaries of three myths with discussion of their relationship to Navajo religion.

3199. Wilson, Alan, and Gene Dennison. *Laughter: The Navajo Way.* Gallup: Univ. of New Mexico, Gallup Branch, 1970.

Twenty-one jokes and anecdotes in Navajo with translation and linguistic commentary. Designed as an aid in learning the language.

3200. Witherspoon, Gary. "The Central Concepts of Navajo World View." *Lin,* 119 (1 January 1974), 41–59; 161 (1 October 1975), 69–87.

Draws extensively on myth and chant to characterize the group's ethos.

3201. ———. "A New Look at Navajo Social Organization." *AA,* 72 (1970), 55–65.

Basic symbol underlying social system is motherhood, which is rooted in mythology.

3202. Worth, Sol, and John Adair. "Navajo Filmmakers." *AA,* 72 (1970), 9–34.

Films made by Navajo informants reflected cultural storytelling style.

3203. Wright, Mrs. James. "Navajo and Hopi Tales." *Aff,* 3, No. 3 (Fall 1973), 23–38.

Stories collected from high school students in Tuba City, Arizona.

3204. Wyman, Leland C., ed. *Beautyway: A Navaho Ceremonial.* Myth recorded by Fr. Berard Haile. Variant recorded by Maud Oakes. Sandpaintings recorded by Laura A. Armer, Franc J. Newcomb, and Maud Oakes. New York: Pantheon, 1957.

Ceremonial description with myth texts recorded in 1932 and 1942. With extensive commentary and reproductions of sandpaintings.

3205. ———. *Blessingway. With Three Versions of the Myth Recorded and Translated from the Navajo by Father Berard Haile, OFM.* Tucson: Univ of Arizona Press, 1970.

Versions of the Blessingway with introductory comments on cultural and mythological backgrounds.

3206. ———. "The Female Shooting Life Chant; A Minor Navaho Ceremony." *AA,* 38 (1936), 634–53.

Description of a healing ceremonial observed in 1935.

3207. ———. *The Mountainway of the Navajo. With a Myth of the Female Branch Recorded and Translated by Father Berard Haile, OFM.* Tucson: Univ. of Arizona Press, 1975.

Description of the ceremonial procedure, mythology, and sandpaintings of the Mountainway.

3208. ———. "Navaho Diagnosticians." *AA,* 38 (1936), 236–46.

Describes various means of divination such as hand-trembling, their ceremonies, and origin myths.

3209. ———. *Navaho Indian Painting: Symbolism, Artistry, and Psychology.* Boston: Boston Univ. Press, 1959.

Pamphlet surveys the functions and techniques of sandpainting and relates paintings to mythological sources.

3210. ———. *Navaho Sandpainting: The Huckel Collection.* Colorado Springs: Taylor Museum, 1960.

Describes ceremonialism, role of paintings in ritual, and myths associated with the paintings.

3211. ———. "Note on Obsolete Navaho Ceremonies." *Plat,* 23, No. 3 (January 1951), 44–48.

Descriptions of four rituals from the notes of Louisa Wade Wetherill: Raven Chant, Spider Chant, Lizard Chant, and Star-Gazing.

3212. ———. "Origin Legends of Navaho Divinatory Rites." *JAF,* 49 (1936), 134–42.

Two ritual origin myths with brief introductory commentary on ceremonial contexts.

3213. ———. "Psychotherapy of the Navaho." *To,* 4, No. 3 (Spring 1956), 77–84.

Overview of healing rituals.

3214. ———. *The Red Antway of the Navaho.* Santa Fe: Museum of Navajo Ceremonial Art, 1965 (Navajo Religion Series No. 5).

Thorough analysis of myths and procedures associated with a healing ritual. Includes prayer and song texts, myth texts, index of motifs, and description of function and context of the ritual.

3215. ———. *The Sandpaintings of the Kayenta Navaho. An Analysis of the Louisa Wade Wetherill Collection.* APUNM, No. 7 (1952).

Describes designs in terms of mythic backgrounds and ceremonial associations.

3216. ———. *Sandpaintings of the Navaho Shootingway and the Walcott Collection. SmCA,* 13 (1970).

Brief account of ritualism and mythology introduces treatment of sandpaintings. Includes thorough discussion of the mythology of Shootingway.

3217. ———. "Snakeskins and Hoops." *Plat,* 39, No. 1 (Summer 1966), 4–25.

Interprets Navajo Big Hoop Ceremony as a rite of transformation. View is reinforced by the myth of the ceremony.

3218. ———. "The Sandpaintings from Male Shootingway." *Plat,* 45, No. 2 (Fall 1972), 55–67.

Describes symbolism of ten designs.

3219. ———. *The Windways of the Navaho.* Colorado Springs: Taylor Museum, 1962.

Includes texts of Navajo and Apache Windway myths (collected by Fr. Berard Haile) and extensive comparative commentary.

3220. ———, and Flora L. Bailey. "Idea and Action Patterns in Navaho Flintway." *SJA,* 1 (1945), 356–77.

Catalogue of the elements comprising Flintway.

3221. ———, and Flora L. Bailey. "Navaho Girl's Puberty Rite." *NMA,* 6–7, No. 1 (January-March 1943), 3–12.

Ceremonial description.

3222. ———, and Flora L. Bailey. *Navaho Indian Ethnoentomology. APUNM,* No. 12 (1964).

Survey of insect lore includes data on insects in myths and representations of insects in sandpaintings.

3223. ———, and Flora L. Bailey. "Navaho Striped Windway, An Injury-Way Chant." *SJA,* 2 (1946), 213–38.

Description of the ceremonial, its mythology, and sandpaintings.

3224. ———, and Flora L. Bailey. "Navaho Upward-Reaching-Way: Objective Behavior, Rationale and Sanction." *UNMB-AS,* 4, No. 2 (May 1943), 3–47.

Thorough description of the ceremony including its mythological basis.

3225. ———, and Flora L. Bailey. "Two Examples of Navaho Physiotherapy." *AA,* 46 (1944), 329–37.

Ceremonial descriptions with attention to mythic bases.

3226. ———, and Stuart K. Harris. *Navajo Indian Medical Ethnobotany. UNMB-AS,* 3, No. 5 (1941).

Contains data on ceremonial usages of plants.

3227. ———, and Clyde Kluckhohn. *Navaho Classification of Their Song Ceremonials. MAAA,* No. 50 (1938).

Presents system of cataloging ceremonials.

3228. ———, and Franc J. Newcomb. "Drypaintings Used in Divination by the Navajo." *Plat,* 36, No. 1 (Summer 1963), 18–24.

Survey of symbolism of paintings.

3229. ———, and Franc J. Newcomb. "Sandpaintings of Beautyway." *Plat,* 35 (1962), 37–52.

Interprets symbolism used in the ritual paintings.

3230. ———, W. W. Hill, and Iva Ósanai. *Navaho Eschatology. UNMB-AS,* 4, No. 1 (1942).

Survey of beliefs about ghosts and the afterworld.

3231. Yanh-na-bah. "Navajo Sketches," in 110, pp. 142–54.

Two rewritten legend texts. No commentary or annotation.

3232. Yazzie, Ethelou, ed. *Navajo History. Vol. I.* Many Farms, Ari.: Navajo Community College Press, 1971.

Eight unannotated myth texts dealing with tribal

prehistory. No commentary.

3233. Yuinth-Nezi, Yoh Hatráli, and Mary C. Wheelwright. *Myth of Sóntso Hatrál (Big Star Chant) and The Myth of Má-ih Hatrál (Coyote Chant).* Revised edition. *BMNCA,* No. 2 (1957).

Myth texts rewritten by Wheelwright. No commentary or annotations.

See also 453, 519, 520, 667, 797, 988, 2208, 2682, 2687, 2688, 2697, 2710, 2712, 2797, 2818, 3445, 3577, 3587, 3899.

H. Papago

3234. Beaudoin, Kenneth Lawrence. *The Papago Genesis and Two Other Legends of Origin.* Mexico City: Amerind Press, 1950.

Pamphlet contains translations of Papago, Hopi, and Nez Perce myths with some comments on cultural backgrounds. Collected from "reservation students."

3235. Castetter, Edward F., and Ruth M. Underhill. "Ethnobiological Studies in the American Southwest. II. The Ethnobiology of the Papago Indians." *UNMB-BS,* 4, No. 3 (October 1935), 1–84.

Consideration of animal and plant lore includes data on ceremonialism.

3236. Chesky, Jane. "The Wiikita." *Ki,* 8, No. 1 (November 1942), 3–5.

Description of a ceremonial.

3237. Childs, Thomas (as written to Henry F. Dobyns). "Sketch of the 'Sand Indians.'" *Ki,* 19, Nos. 2–4 (Spring 1954), 27–39.

Culture survey includes data on ceremonialism and religion.

3238. Davis, Edward H. "The Papago Ceremony of Víkita." *IN&M,* 3, No. 4 (1920), 157–77.

Description of ceremony with text of ritual origin myth.

3239. Densmore, Frances. *Papago Music. BAEB* No. 90 (1929).

Song texts (167 — words and music), each accompanied by musicological and contextual analysis. Introduction compares Papago songs wth those of other NA groups. Collected in 1920.

3240. ———. "Poems from Desert Indians." *N,* 122 (14 April 1926), 407.

Six song texts (words only). No commentary or annotation.

3241. Enos, Susie Ignacio. "Papago Legend of the Sahuaro." *ArQ,* 1, No. 1 (1945), 64–69.

Retelling of a myth text. No commentary.

3242. Gaillard, D. D. "Papago of Arizona and Sonora." *AA,* o. s. 7 (1894), 293–96.

Ethnographic survey includes data on ceremonialism and theology.

3243. Hanlon, Capistran J., OFM. "Papago Funeral Customs." *Ki,* 37, No. 2 (Winter 1972), 104–13.

Description of traditional and Christian ceremonials.

3244. Hayden, Julian D. "Wihom-Ki." *Ki,* 43, No. 1 (Fall 1977), 31–35.

Place legend with data on collecting situation.

3245. Henderson, Esther. "Well of Sacrifice." *AzH,* 29, No. 2 (February 1953), 3–4.

Description of ceremonial and summary of creation myth.

3246. Hill, Gertrude. "Papago Legends from Santa Rosa, Arizona." *SWL,* 6 (June 1940), 18–20; 6 (September 1940), 34–37.

Unannotated myth texts collected in 1935. No commentary.

3247. Ives, Ronald L. "Geologic Verification of a Papago Legend." *M,* 9 (1935), 160–61.

Cites proof for legends about a volcanic eruption.

3248. ———. "The Monster of Quitovac." *M,* 15 (1941), 195–99.

Text and comparative analysis of a Papago myth.

3249. Johnson, Barbara. "The Wind Ceremony: A Papago Sand-Painting." *EP,* 67 (1960), 28–31.

Description of painting with summary of related myth.

3250. Joseph, Alice, Rosamond B. Spicer, and Jane Chesky. *The Desert People: A Study of the Papago Indians.* Chicago: Univ. of Chicago Press, 1949.

Primarily a personality and culture study emphasizing socialization. Includes data on religion (traditional and Christian) and a summary of tribal origin myth.

3251. Kroeber, Henriette Rothschild. "Papago Coyote Tales." *JAF,* 22 (1909), 339–42.

Two unannotated myth texts. No commentary.

3252. ———. "Traditions of the Papago Indians." *JAF,* 25 (1912), 95–105.

Three unannotated myth texts. With brief commentary on cultural background.

3253. Kurath, William. "A Brief Introduction to Papago, A Native Language of Arizona." *UAB,* 16, No. 2 (1945), 1–43.

Contains four myths and two songs with free translations. Some general discussion of performance contexts.

3254. Mason, J. Alden. "The Papago Harvest Festival." *AA,* 22 (1920), 13–25.

Describes the ceremony as observed in 1919. With eight song texts.

3255. ———. "The Papago Migration Legend." *JAF,* 34 (1921), 254–68.

Myth text collected in 1919. Includes some comparative annotation and explanatory comments.

3256. Norman, Rosamond. "A Look at the Papago 'Vikita.'" *M,* 34 (1960), 98–101.

Description of the ritual as observed in 1921.

3257. O'Neale, Lila M., and Juan Dolores. "Notes on Papago Color Designations." *AA,* 45 (1943), 387–97.

Analysis of color terminology includes text of a ritual origin myth.

3258. "Papago, The." *ASTCB,* 20, No. 3 (October 1939), 5–16.

Ethnographic notes compiled by Federal Writers' Project include some myth summaries and descriptions of ceremonialism and singing.

3259. Pinkley, Edna Townsley. "The Shrine of the Children (A Papago Folk Tale)." *EP,* 20 (1926), 119–22.

Unannotated myth text. With some commentary on cultural background.

3260. Rumbley, Darrell. "Papago Stories." *ST,* 2, No. 1 (Fall 1975), 11–17.

Three legend texts and one life history. No commentary or annotations.

3261. Saxton, Dean, and Lucille Saxton. *O'othham Hoho-'ok A'agitha. Legends and Lore of the Papago and Pima Indians.* Tucson: Univ. of Arizona Press, 1973.

Thirty-eight myth texts with free translations. Includes explanatory notes and linguistic analysis.

3262. Spicer, Edward. "The Papago Indians." *Ki,* 6, No. 6 (March 1941), 21–24.

Culture survey includes data on religion and ceremonialism.

3263. Stricklen, E. G. "Notes on Eight Papago Songs." *UCPAAE,* 20 (1923), 361–66.

Musical texts with sketchy musicological analysis.

3264. Underhill, Ruth M. *The Autobiography of a Papago Woman. MAAA,* No. 46 (1936).

Life history of Chona. Includes descriptions of ceremonials and numerous song texts. Re-issued by Holt, Rinehart and Winston in 1979.

3265. ———. "Note on Easter Devils at Kawori'k on the Papago Reservation." *AA,* 36 (1934), 515–16.

Describes figures who appear in devil masks during Passion week. Includes text of traditional recitation performed by these figures, who function as scapegoats.

3266. ———. *Papago Indian Religion. CUCA,* No. 33 (1946).

Survey based on fieldwork done between 1931 and 1935. Includes extensive data on ceremonialism and texts of songs, prayers, and oratory.

3267. ———. *Singing for Power. The Song Magic of the Papago Indians of Southern Arizona.* Berkeley: Univ. of California Press, 1938.

Includes texts of songs placed into ritual contexts. With a summary of the mythological system. Based on fieldwork done in 1931–1933.

3268. ———. *Social Organization of the Papago Indians. CUCA,* No. 30 (1939).

Ethnography based on fieldwork done between 1931 and 1935. Includes data on ceremonialism and the role of storytelling in maintaining social stability.

3269. ———. "Vocabulary and Style in an Indian Language." *AS,* 9 (1934), 279–82.

Examination of stylistic and grammatical features of Papago, especially as manifested in song and oratory.

3270. ———. "War Poems of the Papago Indians." *NMQ,* 7, No. 1 (February 1937), 16–22.

Texts with some data on performance context.

3271. Woodruff, Janette, and Cecil Dryden. *Indian Oasis.* Caldwell, Ida.: Caxton, 1939.

Memoirs of a federal employee on Crow, Paiute, and Papago reservations. Includes five Papago myth texts and fairly good descriptions of Papago ceremonials. Sketchy accounts of Crow and Paiute ceremonialism.

3272. Wright, Harold Bell. *Long Ago Told (Huh-Kew Ah-Kah). Legends of the Papago Indians.* New York: D. Appleton, 1929.

Twenty-three rewritten myths. With no commentary or annotations.

See also 667, 3267, 3277, 3279, 3282, 3288, 3291.

I. Pima

3273. *Aw-Aw-Tam Indian Nights. Being the Myths and Legends of the Pimas of Arizona as Received by J. William Lloyd from Comalk-Hawk-Kih (Thin Buckskin) Thru the Interpretation of Edward Hubert Wood.* Westfield, N. J.: The Lloyd Group, 1911.

Narrative texts collected in 1903. Introduction describes collecting situation. Includes some explanatory comments with individual narratives.

3274. Bahr, Donald. "Breath in Shamanic Curing," in 86, pp. 29–40.

Considers the role of sucking in Pima shamanistic ritual.

3275. ———. "On the Complexity of Southwest Indian Emergence Myths." *JAR*, 33 (1977), 317–49.

Compares three emergence myth texts and one war oration from the Pima and Zuni. Concerned with differences arising from generic factors and with cross-cultural variation.

3276. ———. *Pima and Papago Ritual Oratory. A Study of Three Texts.* San Francisco: Indian Historian Press, 1975.

Three oration texts recorded in 1960s are presented with literal translations. With very extensive commentary on linguistics, the oratory tradition, and the mythological context.

3277. ———. "Who Were the Hohokam? The Evidence from Pima-Papago Myths." *Eh*, 18 (1971), 245–66.

Thirteen myth texts are examined for references to the prehistoric group. Most of the texts express a death and rebirth ideology.

3278. ———, and J. Richard Haefer. "Song in Piman Curing." *Em*, 22 (1978), 89–122.

Treats Pima classification for songs, the role of songs in curing, and restrictions on their use. Includes five texts with context data.

3279. ———, Joseph Giff, and Manuel Hairer. "Piman Songs on Hunting." *Em*, 23 (1979), 245–96.

Examination of three cycles of curing songs whose subject matter is hunting. Primarily concerned with literary qualities. From the Pima and Papago.

3280. ———, Juan Gregoria, David I. Lopez, and Albert Alvarez. *Piman Shamanism and Staying Sickness: Ka':cim Múmkidag.* Tucson: Univ. of Arizona Press, 1974.

Treats medical concepts and associated ceremonialism. Extensive interview data from Juan Gregorio, a shaman, presented in original with free translations.

3281. Brown, Herbert. "A Pima-Maricopa Ceremony." *AA*, 8 (1906), 688–90.

Description of the Harvest or Corn Festival.

3282. Castetter, Edward F., and Willis H. Bell. *Pima and Papago Indian Agriculture.* Albuquerque: Univ. of New Mexico Press, 1942.

Section on tobacco includes text of etiological myth and descriptions of ritualism. Also contains a chapter on agricultural ceremonialism in general.

3283. Ezell, Paul H. *The Hispanic Acculturation of the Gila River Pimas.* MAAA No. 90 (1961).

Historical work shows the Hispanic influence on Pima myths and legends, particularly the incorporation of Christian supernaturalism into NA traditions.

3284. Fewkes, Jesse Walter. "Casa Grande, Arizona." *ARBAE*, 28 (1906–1907), 25–179.

Description of archeological researches at a site in central Arizona. Includes texts of seven Pima myths and legends which relate to the site.

3285. Grossmann, Capt. F. E. "The Pima Indians of Arizona." *ARSI for 1871,* pp. 407–19.

Ethnological notes include some data on ceremonialism and summaries of myths.

3286. ———. "Three Pima Fables." *Ki*, 24 (October 1958), 24.

Unannotated texts. No commentary.

3287. Herzog, George. "Note of Pima Moieties." *AA*, 38 (1936), 520–21.

Reports myths which suggest that clans once existed among the Pima.

3288. Hill, W. W. "Note on the Pima Berdache." *AA*, 40 (1938), 338–40.

Since the Pima have no cultural role for the sexual deviant, their myths suggest that such behavior arose among the Papago.

3289. Hrdlička, Aleš. "Notes on the Pima of Arizona." *AA*, 8 (1906), 39–46.

Ethnographic data collected in 1902 and 1905 include brief survey of ceremonialism.

3290. Kroeber, Henriette Rothschild. "Pima Tales." *AA*, 10 (1908), 231–35.

Two narrative texts. No commentary.

3291. Neff, Mary L. "Pima and Papago Legends." *JAF*, 25 (1912), 51–65.

Twelve myth and folktale texts written by a student at an industrial school in 1907. No commentary or annotations.

3292. Parsons, Elsie Clews. "Notes on the Pima, 1926." *AA*, 30 (1928), 445–64.

Ethnographic survey includes references to myths which validate the social structure and a description of ceremonialism, especially as it compares to that of the Pueblos.

3293. Robinson, Will H., ed. *When the Red Gods Made Men. Legends of Superstition Mountain as Told by a Pima Indian Boy, Joe Buckskin.* 2nd edition. Phoenix: Hubbard, 1935.

Pamphlet includes text of creation myth and song texts. With data on collecting situation.

3294. Russell, Frank. "Pima Annals." *AA*, 5 (1903), 76–80.

Extracts from historical legends recalled by an informant who used notched sticks as mnemonic devices to keep track of chronology.

3295. ———. "The Pima Indians." *ARBAE*, 26 (1904–1905), 3–389.

Ethnography contains much folklore material: texts and abstracts of myths and "nursery tales," song texts (with free and interlinear translations), and descriptions of ceremonials.

3296. Shaw, Anna Moore. *Pima Indian Legends.* Tucson: Univ. of Arizona Press, 1968.

Twenty-four rewritten myth texts. No commentary or annotations.

3297. ———. *A Pima Past.* Tucson: Univ. of Arizona Press, 1974.

Account of growing up as a Pima in the twentieth century. Includes description of puberty ritual and some narrative texts.

3298. Webb, George. *A Pima Remembers.* Tucson: Univ. of Arizona Press, 1959.

Account of Pima traditions includes oration, myth, and song texts. Written "with the young Pima Indians in mind."

3299. Woodward, Arthur. "Historical Notes on the Pima." *M*, 23 (1949), 144–47.

Data collected by Joseph P. Allyn in 1864 and by Woodward in 1930 include some descriptions of ceremonials.

See also 797, 2682, 2720, 3359.

J.1. Pueblo: General

3300. Anderson, Bruce A. "Kokopelli: The Humpbacked Flute-Player." *AIAM*, 1 February 1976, pp. 36–40.

Considers artistic depictions of Kokopelli and summarizes mythic material about him.

3301. Anderson, Frank G. "Early Documentary Material on the Pueblo Kachina Cult." *AnQ*, 29 (1956), 31–44.

Presents data on Pueblo ceremonialism from sixteenth and seventeenth century sources.

3302. ———. "Intertribal Relations in the Pueblo Kachina Cult," in 165, pp. 377–83.

Examines contributions of various Pueblo groups to Kachina ceremonialism and belief.

3303. ———. "The Pueblo Kachina Cult: A Historical Reconstruction." *SJA*, 11 (1955), 404–19.

Survey of the history of the cult since EA contact.

3304. Applegate, Frank G. *Indian Stories from the Pueblos.* Glorieta, N. M.: Rio Grande Press, 1971.

Rewritten narrative texts. Prepared by an artist of the Taos-Santa Fe group. Originally published in 1929.

3305. Austin, Mary. "American Indian Dance Drama." *YR*, 19 (1929–1930), 732–45.

Discusses NA ceremonialism as drama. With examples from various Pueblo groups.

3306. ———. "The Days of Our Ancients." *Su*, 53 (1 October 1924), 33–38.

Survey of Pueblo lifeways includes references to myths and ceremonials.

3307. ———. "Folk Plays of the Southwest." *TAM*, 17 (August 1933), 599–606.

Treats dramas with Christian themes performed seasonally at several Pueblos.

3308. ———. "Songs of the American Indian." *H*, 143 (1921), 77–80.

Free translations of six songs from the Paiute and various Pueblo groups. Includes some data on the nature of NA oral poetry and on collecting situations.

3309. Bandelier, Adolf F. *The Gilded Man* (*El Dorado*) *and Other Pictures of the Spanish Occupancy of North America.* New York: D. Appleton, 1893.

Historical work with some data on ceremonialism among the Pueblo groups.

3310. ———. "The 'Montezuma' of the Pueblo Indians." *AA*, o. s. 5 (1892), 319–26.

Discusses the spread of the reputation of Montezuma northward until legends about him became prominent among Pueblo groups.

3311. Blaumenschein, Ernest L. "San Geronimo Day: The Pueblo Indian's Holiday." *HW*, 42 (10 December

1898), 1207.

Ceremonial description.

3312. Bloom, Lansing B. "The Indian Ceremonies." *EP*, 15 (1923), 96–97.

List and brief descriptions of dances performed by Pueblo groups at the Santa Fe Fiesta.

3313. Boas, Franz. *Keresan Texts.* 2 volumes. *PAES* No. 8 (1928; 1925).

Collected in 1919–1921. Part I includes translations of myths, songs, folktales, legends, personal narrative, prayers, orations, and descriptions of customs. Comparative and contextual commentary accompanies the abstracts. Part II contains Keresan texts of the material.

3314. Cassidy, Ina Sizer. "Some Pueblo Ideas." *WF*, 10 (1951), 78.

Brief account of a creation myth.

3315. Chavez, Fray Angelico. "Pohé-Yemo's Representative and the Pueblo Revolt of 1680." *NMHR*, 42 (1967), 85–126.

Treats the role of a mythical figure in the 1680 uprising.

3316. Colton, Harold S. "What Is a Kachina?" *Plat*, 19, No. 3 (January 1947), 40–47.

Attempts to define the kachina and to delineate types.

3317. Coolidge, Mary Roberts. *The Rain-Makers. Indians of Arizona and New Mexico.* Boston: Houghton Mifflin, 1929.

Survey of NA cultures in the Southwest, focusing primarily on Pueblo groups. Includes descriptions of ceremonials such as the Hopi Snake Dance and texts of songs, chants, and myths.

3318. Cowan, John L. "Legend of Pose-weve." *OM*, n. s. 53 (May 1909), 433–36.

Rewritten myth text with some data on historical and cultural background.

3319. Coze, Paul. "Kachinas: Masked Dancers of the Southwest." *NG*, 112, No. 2 (August 1957), 219–36.

Survey of ceremonialism.

3320. Crane, Leo. *Desert Drums. The Pueblo Indians of New Mexico, 1540–1928.* Boston: Little, Brown, 1928.

Surveys historical roots of problems confronting federal Indian policy in the Southwest. Includes descriptions of ceremonials.

3321. Curtin, L. S. M. *Preparation of Sacred Corn Meal in the Rio Grande Pueblos. SWML* No. 32 (1968).

Pueblo-by-Pueblo survey of ceremonial preparation of corn.

3322. ———. "Spanish and Indian Witchcraft in New Mexico." *M*, 45 (1971), 89–101.

Texts of four witchcraft legends with some historical commentary.

3323. Curtis, Edward S. "Indians of the Stone Houses." *Scr*, 45 (February 1909), 161–75.

Culture survey includes data on mythology and ceremonialism.

3324. Curtis, Natalie. "The Pueblo Singer: A Bit of Native American History." *Cr*, 24, No. 4 (July 1913), 400–01.

In-context description of song performance with translated text (words only).

3325. DeHuff, Elizabeth Willis. "Four Pueblo Folk-Tales." *YR*, 15 (1925–1926), 768–85.

Unannotated texts with sparse introductory commentary. Three from Taos and one from San Ildefonso.

3326. ———. "Fox-Woman and Bear-Woman." *NMFR,* 1 (1946–1947), 15–17.
Rewritten myth text. No annotation or commentary.
3327. ———. "More Pueblo Tales." *EP,* 11 (1921), 140–44.
Five unannotated legend texts from various Pueblos. No commentary.
3328. ———. "Myths Told by the Pueblos." *EP,* 11 (1921), 86–92.
Nine unannotated myth texts from various Pueblos. No commentary.
3329. ———. "A Pueblo Child's Party." *EP,* 14 (1923), 184.
Description of children's games from an unspecified Pueblo group.
3330. ———. "Pueblo Versions of Old World Tales," in 109, pp. 104–26.
Texts of seven narratives which have affinities with European folktales. Some data on storytelling context.
3331. ———. "Telling Stories to Primitives." *Bo,* 62 (February 1926), 689–91.
Description of Pueblo response to storytelling. With some attention to themes of Pueblo oral narratives.
3332. Densmore, Frances. *Music of Acoma, Isleta, Cochiti and Zuñi Pueblos. BAEB* No. 165 (1957).
Eighty-two song texts (words and music), each accompanied by musicological and contextual analysis. Includes comparative notes with music from other NA groups. Collected throughout 1930s.
3333. ———. "A Resemblance Between Yuman and Pueblo Songs." *AA,* 34 (1932), 694–700.
Emphasizes importance of rhythm in NA music. Shows rhythmic correspondences between material from the Yuma and Pueblo groups (Acoma, Isleta, Cochiti).
3334. Dozier, Edward P. "Rio Grande Pueblo Ceremonial Patterns." *NMQ,* 27 (1957), 27–34.
Describes the dual system of Pueblo ceremonials: the Spanish-Catholic and the NA.
3335. ———. "Spanish-Catholic Influences on Rio Grande Pueblo Religion." *AA,* 60 (1958), 441–48.
Treats religious acculturation. Suggests that NA and Spanish-Catholic ceremonials share common goals.
3336. Dutton, Bertha P. "The New Year of the Pueblo Indians of New Mexico." *EP,* 78 (1972), 3–13.
Description of the ceremony at various Pueblos.
3337. Edelman, Prewitt. "Working Back: The New Physics and Pueblo Mythology." *SWR,* 58 (1973), 302–6.
Comparison of Pueblo cosmology with relativistic physics.
3338. Eickemeyer, Carl, and Lilian Westcott Eickemeyer. *Among the Pueblo Indians.* New York: Merriam, 1895.
Travel narrative includes descriptions of ceremonials and games, including the chicken pull at Cochiti.
3339. Ellis, Florence Hawley. "Patterns of Aggression and the War Cult in Southwestern Pueblos." *SJA,* 7 (1951), 177–201.
Description of religious basis of defense among Pueblo groups and of the duties of the War Priest.
3340. Espinosa, Aurelio M. "All-Souls Day at Zuñi, Acoma, and Laguna." *JAF,* 31 (1918), 550–52.
Descriptions of ceremonials. With texts of formulaic recitations.
3341. ———. "Miscellaneous Materials from the Pueblo Indians of New Mexico." *PQ,* 21 (1942), 121–27.

Includes songs (words only), prayers, and legends. Some in original with free translations. With linguistic and comparative notes.
3342. ———. "Pueblo Indian Folk Tales." *JAF,* 49 (1936), 69–133.
Sixty-seven myth and folktale texts collected from various Pueblos in 1931. No commentary. Occasional explanatory notes by Elsie Clews Parsons.
3343. Estabrook, Emma Franklin. *Givers of Life. The American Indians as Contributors to Civilization.* Boston: Marshall Jones, 1931.
Concentrates on Pueblo groups to show the contributions of NAs to general culture. One chapter deals with Pueblo ceremonials as poetry and drama and includes song texts (words only).
3345. Fergusson, Erna. "Ceremonial Dances of the Pueblos." *T,* 58 (December 1931), 15–19, 58.
Survey of Pueblo ceremonialism.
3346. ———. "Laughing Priests." *TAM,* 17, No. 8 (August 1933), 657–62.
Discusses the function of sacred clown, particularly the koshare of the Rio Grande Pueblos.
3347. ———. "Perpetual Pagans." *Scr,* 92 (November 1932), 293–95.
Treats the effects of Christianity on Pueblo cultures.
3348. Fisher, Reginald G. "Kivas of the Living Pueblos." *EP,* 43 (1937), 91–97.
Survey of the ritual function of kivas among various Pueblo groups.
3349. ———. "An Outline of Pueblo Indian Religion." *EP,* 44 (1938), 169–78.
Survey emphasizes mythic concepts and functions of religion.
3350. Fynn, A. J. *The American Indian as a Product of Environment with Special Reference to the Pueblos.* Boston: Little, Brown, 1907.
Discusses religious, ceremonial, and mythic responses to the desert environment on the part of Pueblo groups. With a description of the Hopi Snake Dance.
3351. Gallenkamp, Charles. "The Pueblo Indian Today." *DM,* 28, No. 3 (March 1954), 23–29.
Describes various Pueblo ceremonials.
3352. Goldfrank, Esther S. "Socialization, Personality, and the Structure of Pueblo Society (with Particular Reference to Hopi and Zuni)." *AA,* 47 (1945), 516–39.
Socialization study with attention paid to bogey tales and initiation ceremonies.
3353. Gwyther, George. "Pueblo Indians." *OM,* o. s. 6 (March 1871), 260–67.
Culture survey includes data on ceremonialism.
3354. H., F. W. "Masked Kachinas in Spanish Times." *M,* 26 (1952), 17–20.
Extracts from seventeenth-century accounts of Pueblo ceremonialism.
3355. Hartley, Marsden. "The Scientific Esthetic of the Redman." *A&A,* 13 (March 1922), 113–19; 14 (September 1922), 137–39.
Describes esthetic qualities of the Green Corn Ceremony at Taos and of the Fiesta of San Geronimo at Santo Domingo.
3356. ———. "Tribal Esthetics." *Di,* 65 (16 November 1918), 399–401.
Treats artistic qualities of NA dances with special reference to Pueblo groups.

3357. Harvey, Byron, III. "An Overview of Pueblo Religion," in 147, pp. 197–217.

Survey considers various aspects of religion at the Pueblos: world view, mythology, and ceremonialism.

3358. Henderson, Alice Corbin. "The Dance-Rituals of the Pueblo Indians." *TAM,* 7 (April 1923), 109–15.

Ceremonial description.

3359. Herzog, George. "A Comparison of Pueblo and Pima Musical Styles." *JAF,* 49 (1936), 283–417.

Comparison of fifty-seven song texts collected in 1927. Considers singing style, structure, melody, and rhythm.

3360. Hewett, Edgar L. "The Indian Ceremonies." *A&A,* 18 (November-December 1924), 207–14.

Descriptions of dances performed at the Santa Fe Fiesta in 1924.

3361. ———. "My Neighbors, the Pueblo Indians." *A&A,* 16 (July 1923), 3–24.

General culture survey includes data on religion and ceremonialism.

3362. ———, and Bertha P. Dutton. *The Pueblo Indian World. Studies on the Natural History of the Rio Grande Valley in Relation to Pueblo Indian Culture.* Albuquerque: Univ. of New Mexico and School of American Research, 1945.

Handbook designed to present to the general reader the findings of research undertaken by the School of American Research. Focus is on world view with references to a number of relevant myths.

3363. Hodge, F. W. "Pueblo Snake Ceremonials." *AA,* o. s. 9 (1896), 133–36.

Overview of snake clans and their rituals among various Pueblo groups.

3364. Hodge, Gene Meany. *The Kachinas Are Coming. Pueblo Indian Kachina Dolls with Related Folktales.* Flagstaff, Ari.: Northland, 1967.

Rewritten myth texts accompanied by paintings of kachina dolls and commentary on cultural significance.

3365. Holien, Elaine Baran. "Kachinas." *EP,* 76, No. 4 (September 1970), 1–15.

Survey of the role of the kachina in Pueblo ritual and mythology.

3366. Hunt, Irvin, Julia Seelatsee, and Caleb Carter. "The Meeting of Two Cultures at Christmas." *IH,* 1, No. 1 (December 1967), 6–9.

Accounts of Christmas festivities among Pueblo groups, the Yakima, and the Nez Perce.

3367. "Indian Ceremonies, The." *EP,* 17 (1924), 109–23.

List and brief descriptions of dances performed by Pueblo groups at the Santa Fe Fiesta.

3368. Jacobi, Frederick. "On Indian Music." *AIn,* 1, No. 4 (Summer 1944), 23–25.

General comments on performance style of Pueblo music.

3369. Kurath, Gertrude P. "Calling the Rain Gods." *JAF,* 73 (1960), 312–16.

Describes ceremonials to summon rain gods at Keresan Pueblos. With two song texts.

3370. ———. "Game Animal Dances of the Rio Grande Pueblos." *SJA,* 14 (1958), 438–48.

Survey of the ceremonial complex.

3371. ———. "The Origin of the Pueblo Indian Matachines." *EP,* 64 (1957), 259–64.

Traces origin of the dance-drama to the European Middle Ages.

3372. La Farge, Oliver. "The Ancient Strength." *NY,* 39 (31 August 1963), 26–34.

Treats Pueblo land dispute and suggests that claimants' strength lies in their ceremonial heritage.

3373. Lange, Charles H. "The Keresan Component of Southwestern Pueblo Culture." *SJA,* 14 (1958), 34–50.

Survey of Keresan influence on other Pueblo groups in such areas as ceremonialism.

3374. Laughlin, Ruth. "Christmas Ceremonies in New Mexico." *EP,* 40 (1936), 1–5.

Describes ceremonial observances at various Pueblos.

3375. Law, George Warrington. "Preface to Kiva Religion." *NMQ,* 6 (1936), 203–6.

Describes the kiva as the spiritual center of Pueblo religion.

3376. Lawrence, D. H. "The Dance of the Sprouting Corn." *TAM,* 8 (July 1924), 447–57.

Ceremonial description.

3377. LeViness, W. Thetford. "The Pueblo Indians Have Made Music the Heart and Soul of Their Well-Balanced Lives." *MuA,* 76 (May 1956), 18–20.

Treats the role of singing and dancing in various Pueblo cultures. With one song text (words only).

3378. ———. "The Three Cultures of New Mexico." *Ams,* 18, No. 6 (June 1966), 8–15.

Considers Pueblo, Spanish, and Anglo influences on the culture of the state. With data on Pueblo ceremonialism (traditional and Christian).

3379. Lummis, Charles F. "The Indian Who Is Not Poor." *Scr,* 12 (September 1892), 361–72.

Survey of Pueblo history and culture includes data on ceremonialism, singing, and storytelling.

3380. ———. *The Man Who Married the Moon and Other Pueblo Indian Folk-Stories.* New York: Century, 1894.

Thirty-two unannotated myth and folktale texts. No commentary.

3381. ———. *Pueblo Indian Folk-Stories.* New York: Century, 1920.

Thirty-three unannotated myth and folktale texts, one presented in "Indian" with interlinear translation. With general introduction on Pueblo storytelling. Parts of this volume were previously published in 3380.

3382. Milford, Stanley J. "The Twin War God Myth Cycle." *EP,* 43 (1937), 1–13, 19–28.

Analysis and texts of myth cycle common to various Pueblo groups. Emphasizes fertility aspect.

3383. Ortiz, Alfonso, ed. *Handbook of North American Indians. Volume 9. Southwest.* Washington: Smithsonian Institution, 1979.

Thorough survey of Pueblo cultures with chapters on individual groups, most of which include data on mythology and ceremonialism. Three chapters with special focus are "Zuni Religion and World View" (by Dennis Tedlock), "Hopi Ceremonial Organization" (by Arlette Frigout), and "The Pueblo Mythological Triangle: Poseyemu, Montezuma, and Jesus in the Pueblos" (by Richard J. Parmentier).

3384. ———. "Ritual Drama and the Pueblo World View," in 147, pp. 135–61.

Shows how world view is manifest in calendrical dramas. Includes description of various aspects of the dramatic performances.

3385. Ortiz y Silva, Marga. "Easter in the Desert." *HW,* 60 (3 April 1915), 316–17.

Ceremonial description.

3386. Pach, Walter. "Notes on Indian Water-Colours." *Di,* 68 (March 1920), 343–45.

Describes three paintings of ceremonials done by NA artists. Includes summary of a ritual origin myth from a Pueblo source.

3387. Paloheimo, Leonora Curtin. "The Antelope Are Fat in Summer." *M,* 24 (1950), 73–78.

Description of a hunting ceremony.

3388. Parsons, Elsie Clews. "All-Souls Day at Zuñi, Acoma, and Laguna." *JAF,* 30 (1917), 495–96.

Description of ceremonial observances.

3389. ———. "The Antelope Clan in Keresan Custom and Myth." *Man,* 17 (1917), 190–93.

Includes text of ritual origin myth and description of ceremonials.

3390. ———. "Notes on Isleta, Santa Ana, and Acoma." *AA,* 22 (1920), 56–69.

Random ethnographic data collected from an informant's description include data on ceremonialism.

3391. ———. "The Pueblo Indian Clan in Folk-Lore." *JAF,* 34 (1921), 209–16.

Treats clan migration legends among various Pueblo groups, especially the Hopi.

3392. ———. "Pueblo-Indian Folk-Tales, Probably of Spanish Provenience." *JAF,* 31 (1918), 216–55.

Seventeen folktale texts from various Pueblos. With extensive explanatory and comparative notes.

3393. ———. *Pueblo Indian Religion.* 2 volumes. Chicago: Univ. of Chicago Press, 1939.

Massive treatment of religious systems of Pueblo groups. With extensive data on ceremonialism.

3394. ———. "Riddles and Metaphors Among Indian Peoples." *JAF,* 49 (1936), 171–74.

Treats riddling traditions and metaphorical language among Pueblo groups.

3395. ———. "Ritual Parallels in Pueblo and Plains Cultures, with a Special Reference to the Pawnee." *AA,* 31 (1929), 642–54.

Comparison of Pueblo and Pawnee deities, spirits, and creation myths.

3396. ———. "Witchcraft Among the Pueblos: Indian or Spanish?" *Man,* 27 (1927), 106–12, 125–28.

Discusses mythic basis for witchcraft beliefs and practices and presents two folktales with witchcraft themes.

3397. ———, and Ralph L. Beals. "The Sacred Clowns of the Pueblo and Mayo-Yaqui Indians." *AA,* 36 (1934), 491–514.

Compares the functions of clowns which figure in Christian ceremonialism. A chart compares creation myths from various Pueblo groups and the Yaqui.

3398. Pedro, Joe A., Teofila Lucero, and Juan Aragon. "Pueblo Folk Tales." *NMQ,* 2 (1932), 251–54.

Three unannotated texts from Laguna and Taos. No commentary.

3399. Peet, Stephen D. "Agriculture Among the Pueblos and Cliff-Dwellers." *AAOJ,* 21 (1899), 209–32.

Includes some data on ceremonialism.

3400. ———. "The Religious Life and Works of the Cliff Dwellers." *AAOJ,* 20 (1898), 275–98.

Reconstructs prehistoric religious practices by comparing with Pueblo system.

3401. Pradt, George H. "Shakok and Miochin: Origin

of Summer and Winter." *JAF,* 15 (1902), 88–90.

Unannotated myth text. No commentary.

3402. "Pueblo Rabbit Hunt, A." *JAF,* 8 (1895), 324–27.

Ceremony description reprinted from the *New York Evening Post* for 20 July 1895.

3403. "Puppets in Paradise." *De,* 127 (September 1935), 7, 48–49.

Survey of ceremonialism.

3404. Purley, Anthony F. "Keres Pueblo Concepts of Deity." *AICRJ,* 1, No. 1 (1974), 29–32.

Not available for examination.

3405. Reagan, Albert B. *Don Diego or The Pueblo Indian Uprising of 1680.* New York: Alice Harriman, 1914.

Historical work includes song texts (words and music) and ceremonial descriptions.

3406. Reed, Verner Z. "Ancient Po-Who-Geh. The Montezuma and Other Legends of the Pueblos." *OM,* n. s. 28 (December 1896), 644–56.

Rewritten myths and legends from various Pueblo groups.

3407. Renaud, Etienne B. "Kokopelli. A Study in Pueblo Mythology." *SWL,* 14 (1948), 25–40.

Treats rock art portrayals of the hump-backed flute player.

3408. Roberts, Don L. "The Ethnomusicology of the Eastern Pueblos," in 147, pp. 243–55.

Survey treats previous research on Pueblo music, current status of musical tradition, and suggestions for future study.

3409. Roberts, Kenneth L. "The First Families of America." *SEP,* 197 (18 October 1924), 23, 166–74.

Culture survey has extensive data on various Pueblo ceremonials.

3410. Roediger, Virginia More. *Ceremonial Costumes of the Pueblo Indians: Their Evolution, Fabrication, and Significance in the Prayer Drama.* Berkeley: Univ. of California Press, 1941.

Focus is on material culture, but includes data on the role of costumes in ceremonials. Also treats mythological sources for costumes.

3411. Sabin, Edwin L. " 'Mucha Fiesta' in the Southwest." *OM,* n. s. 64 (November 1914), 427–36.

Overview of Pueblo ceremonialism.

3412. Scully, Vincent. *Pueblo: Mountain, Village, Dance.* New York: Viking, 1975.

Focuses on Pueblo architecture, but includes ceremonial descriptions. One chapter deals with Mescalero Apache puberty ritual.

3413. Sergeant, Elizabeth Shepley. "Christmas in the Pueblos." *Su,* 51 (1 December 1923), 252–56.

Description of ceremonials. With one song text (words only).

3414. ———. "Death to the Golden Age." *NRep,* 35 (22 August 1923), 354–57.

Laments EA attempts to curtail Pueblo ceremonialism. With ritual descriptions and song texts.

3415. ———. "Earth Horizon." *N,* 124 (29 June 1927), 714–16.

Treats spiritual life (with songs and myths) of Pueblo cultures.

3416. ———. "The Principales Speak." *NRep,* 33 (7 February 1923), 273–75.

Description of Pueblo council to discuss loss of land and water rights. Includes oration texts.

3417. Sharp, J. H. "The Pueblo Indian Dance." *HW,* 37 (14 October 1893), 982–83.

Ceremonial description.

3418. Silverberg, Robert. *The Old Ones. Indians of the American Southwest.* New York: New York Graphic Society, 1965.

Describes Pueblo cultures before and after Spanish contact. With song texts and descriptions of ceremonials.

3419. Smith, Helena Huntington. "The Red Man Dances." *NAR,* 228 (July 1929), 78–84.

Treats controversy aroused by federal opposition to Pueblo dances. With some descriptions of the dance.

3420. Spinden, Herbert J. "Indian Dances of the Southwest." *AMJ,* 15 (1915), 103–15.

Survey of Pueblo ceremonialism. With one song text (words only).

3421. Stewart, Dorothy N. *Handbook of Indian Dances: New Mexico Pueblos.* [Santa Fe]: Museum of New Mexico, 1952.

Pamphlet describes Pueblo ceremonials.

3422. Strong, William Duncan. "An Analysis of Southwestern Society." *AA,* 29 (1927), 1–61.

Primarily concerned with parallels in social organization between Pueblo and southern California groups, but shows how mythology reflects the social structure. Supplementary data provided by Philip Drucker in *AA,* 39 (1941), 644–47.

3423. Terrell, John Upton. *Pueblos, Gods and Spaniards.* New York: Dial, 1973.

Year-by-year history of Spanish-NA relationships in the Southwest through the end of the seventeenth century. With references to origin myths of various Pueblos.

3424. Tyler, Hamilton A. *Pueblo Animals and Myths.* Norman: Univ. of Oklahoma Press, 1975.

Study of major animals which figure in Pueblo ceremonialism and mythology. Chapter is devoted to each animal.

3425. ———. *Pueblo Birds and Myths.* Norman: Univ. of Oklahoma Press, 1979.

Survey of the roles of birds in myths and rituals of various Pueblo groups.

3426. ———. *Pueblo Gods and Myths.* Norman: Univ. of Oklahoma Press, 1964.

Includes survey of Pueblo theology with attention to relevant myths and rituals. Includes excerpts from myth and song texts and a general discussion of animism.

3427. Van Stone, Mary R. "The Matachina Dance." *EP,* 38 (1935), 10–12.

Brief description of a ritual performed as a Christmas observance at various Pueblos.

3428. Waldron, Marion, and Webb Waldron. "Christmas in New Mexico." *H&G,* 76 (December 1939), 53, 64.

Superficial description of a ceremony.

3429. Walter, Paul A. "The Fiesta of Santa Fe." *A&A,* 9 (January 1920), 15–23.

Overview of the activities at the annual event.

3430. White, Leslie A. "A Ceremonial Vocabulary Among the Pueblos." *IJAL,* 10 (1939), 161–67.

List of terms used at various Pueblos for such sacred functions as the narration of myths.

3431. ———. "The World of the Keresan Pueblo Indians," in 102, pp. 53–64.

Consideration of the contemporary and mythological physical environments.

3432. Wittfogel, Karl A., and Esther S. Goldfrank. "Some Aspects of Pueblo Mythology and Society." *JAF,* 56 (1943), 17–30.

Shows how mythology serves as a mirror of culture.

3433. Wright, Barton. "Tabletas, A Pueblo Art." *AIAM,* 1 May 1976, pp. 56–65.

Describes headgear worn on ceremonial and social occasions.

See also 240, 368, 425, 797, 1760, 2356, 2687, 2688, 2695, 2697, 2712, 2909, 3027, 3030, 3121, 3130, 3186, 3292, 3628, 3675, 3960.

J.2. Pueblo: Acoma

3434. Benedict, Ruth. "Eight Stories from Acoma." *JAF,* 43 (1930), 59–87.

Myth texts with some explanatory notes.

3435. Bunzel, Ruth L. *The Pueblo Potter: A Study of Creative Imagination in Primitive Art.* New York: Columbia Univ. Press, 1929.

Primarily a study of material culture, but chapter on symbolism suggests mythic bases for some pottery designs. Treats pottery traditions of Acoma, San Ildefonso, Hopi, and Zuni.

3436. Kennedy, Keith. "The Dance in the Mist." *M,* 4 (1930), 123–26.

Ceremonial description.

3437. Miller, Wick R. *Acoma Grammar and Texts. UCPL* No. 40 (1965).

Texts include descriptions of ceremonials and other customs collected between 1956 and 1959. With free translations. Only one text is analyzed.

3438. Sedgwick, Mrs. William T. *Acoma, the Sky City: A Study in Pueblo-Indian History and Civilization.* Cambridge: Harvard Univ. Press, 1926.

Includes chapters on oral narratives (with texts), mythological system, ceremonial life, and religious beliefs. Primarily a compilation of previously published data.

3439. Shelp, C. Lillian A. "The Eyes of the Gambling God." *OM,* n. s. 54 (October 1909), 420–22.

Rewritten myth with comments on cultural background.

3440. Stirling, Matthew W. *Origin Myth of Acoma and Other Records. BAEB* No. 135 (1942).

Texts of creation and hero myths and miscellaneous notes on customs. Collected from residents of Acoma and Santa Ana visiting Washington in 1928 and presented in English only. With explanatory notes.

3441. White, Leslie A. "The Acoma Indians." *ARBAE,* 47 (1929–1930), 17–192.

Ethnography with strong emphasis on ceremonialism. Includes texts of fifteen narratives in free translations.

3442. ———. "New Material from Acoma." *BAEB* No. 136 (*AP* No. 32), 1943.

Ethnographic notes include myth texts and the life history of a seventy-three-year-old informant.

3443. ———. "Summary Report of Field Work at Acoma." *AA,* 30 (1928), 559–68.

Reports findings from research done in 1926–1927. Includes data on cults and their ceremonials.

See also 3332, 3333, 3340, 3388, 3390, 3735.

J.3. Pueblo: Cochiti

3444. Benedict, Ruth. *Tales of the Cochiti Indians. BAEB* No. 98 (1931).
Includes myths, legends, folktales from European sources, and other narratives collected in 1924. Includes some commentary on cultural background.

3445. Curtin, L. S. M. "The Navaho Slave and the Talking Scalp." *NMFR,* 3 (1948–1949), 18–20.
Legend texts with some informant data and explanatory notes.

3446. Dumarest, Fr. Noël. "Notes on Cochiti, New Mexico." Ed. Elsie Clews Parsons. *MAAA,* 6 (1919), 137–236.
Ethnography based on observations in 1890s. Includes extensive data on ceremonialism and seven myth texts with explanatory notes by Parsons.

3447. Goldfrank, Esther Schiff. *The Social and Ceremonial Organization of Cochiti. MAAA* No. 33 (1927).
Thorough presentation of ceremonial patterns. With prayer texts.

3448. Lange, Charles H. *Cochiti: A New Mexico Pueblo, Past and Present.* Austin: Univ. of Texas Press, 1959.
Ethnography based on fieldwork done in 1947–1948. Includes data on ceremonialism and mythology.

3449. ———. "The Role of Economics in Cochiti Pueblo Culture Change." *AA,* 55 (1953), 674–94.
Shows how economic changes were causing disappearance of secret societies, which survived only in pageantry and oral tradition.

3450. Lummis, Charles F. "The Wanderings of Cochiti." *Scr,* 13 (January 1893), 92–102.
Historical and culture survey includes data on mythology and ceremonialism.

3451. Mason, Edith Hart. "Enemy Bear." *M,* 22 (1948), 80–85.
Anecdote associated with the Bear Ceremony.

See also 3332, 3333, 3338.

J.4. Pueblo: Hopi

3452. A., C. " 'Those Beautiful Straight Rows.' A Hopi Indian Legend of Corn." *M,* 2 (1929), 17–19.
Unannotated myth text in storytelling context.

3453. Aitken, Barbara. "A Trance Experience." *Plat,* 28, No. 3 (January 1956), 67–70.
Reminiscence of experience in curing ritual. Collected in 1913.

3454. Akin, Louis. "Hopi Indians—Gentle Folk: A People Without Need of Courts, Jails or Asylums." *Cr,* 10, No. 3 (June 1906), 314–29.
Culture survey includes data on religion, ceremonialism, and singing.

3455. Baxter, Rupert H. "The Moqui Snake Dance." *AAOJ,* 17 (1895), 205–7.
Ceremonial description.

3456. Beaglehole, Ernest. *Hopi Hunting and Hunting Ritual. YUPA* No. 4 (1936).
Includes ceremonial descriptions, myth excerpts, and

song texts (words only).

3457. ———. *Notes on Hopi Economic Life. YUPA* No. 15 (1937).
Ethnographic notes based on fieldwork done in 1932 and 1934. Includes data on ceremonialism.

3458. ———, and Pearl Beaglehole. *Hopi of the Second Mesa. MAAA* No. 44 (1935).
Includes two relevant essays: "A Note on Hopi Sorcery" (pp. 5–10), which has data on ceremonial behavior; and "Hopi Death Customs" (pp. 11–14), which treats eschatology and funeral ritual.

3459. Black, Robert A. "Hopi Grievance Chants: A Mechanism of Social Control," in 128, pp. 54–67.
Includes texts, translations, and analyses of a kind of secular chant.

3460. ———. "Hopi Rabbit-Hunt Chants: A Ritualized Language," in 125, pp. 7–11.
Describes form and content of ritual chanting.

3461. Boelter, Homer H. *Portfolio of Hopi Kachinas.* Hollywood, Cal.: Homer H. Boelter Lithography, 1969.
Collection of paintings with an introduction dealing with ceremonials.

3462. Bogert, C. M. "The Hopi Snake Dance." *NH,* 47 (1941), 276–83.
Description of the ceremonial.

3463. Bourke, John G. "The Snake Ceremonials at Walpi." *AA,* o. s. 8 (1895), 192–96.
Discussion of ceremonial based on observations in 1880.

3464. ———. *The Snake-Dance of the Moquis of Arizona, Being a Narrative of a Journey from Santa Fe, New Mexico, to the Villages of the Moqui Indians of Arizona, with a Description of the Manners and Customs of This Peculiar People, and Especially of the Revolting Religious Rite, the Snake-Dance; to Which Is Added a Brief Dissertation Upon Serpent-Worship in General with an Account of the Tablet Dance of the Pueblo of Santo Domingo, New Mexico, Etc.* New York: Scribner's, 1884.
Highly ethnocentric account of visit to Hopis in 1881. Includes ceremonial descriptions and texts of myths and legends. With comparison of Snake Dance to international ceremonial traditions and an account of a ceremony at Santo Domingo.

3465. Broder, Patricia Janis. *Hopi Painting. The World of the Hopis.* New York: E. P. Dutton, 1978.
Relates paintings to Hopi ethnohistory, mythology, and ceremonialism. With story and song texts.

3466. Burbank, E. A. (as told to Ernest Roya). *Burbank Among the Indians.* Ed. Frank J. Taylor. Caldwell, Ida.: Caxton, 1944.
Reminiscences of an artist include text of origin myth of Hopi Snake Dance and ceremonial descriptions of the Hopi and other groups.

3467. Bushby, D. Maitland (Chief Whispering Pine). "The Dance of the Snake." *OM,* n. s. 87 (1929), 167–68.
Ceremonial description. With song text.

3468. Cody, Bertha Parker. "Kachina Dolls." *M,* 13 (1939), 25–30.
Describes kachina ceremonials and physical appearance of dolls.

3469. Colton, Harold S. "Hopi Dieties [sic]." *Plat,* 20, No. 1 (July 1947), 10–16.
List and brief description of figures in the Hopi pantheon.

3470. ———. *Hopi Kachina Dolls with a Key to Their Identification.* Revised edition. Albuquerque: Univ. of New Mexico Press, 1959.

Contains some treatment of Hopi deities.

3471. ———, and Edmund Nequatewa. "The Ladder Dance." *MNMNA,* 5, No. 2 (August 1932), 5–12.

Two legend texts about an extinct ceremonial.

3472. Colton, Mary Russell F., and Harold S. Colton. "Petroglyphs, the Record of a Great Adventure." *AA,* 33 (1931), 32–37.

Carvings on a boulder near Willow Springs, Arizona, are interpreted by a Hopi informant, who associated the designs with mythology.

3473. ———, Edmund Nequatewa, and Harold S. Colton. "Hopi Legends of the Sunset Crater Region." *MNMNA,* 5, No. 4 (October 1932), 17–23.

Two myths and one legend with extensive commentary on cultural background. No annotations.

3474. Coston, Ruth C. "The Hopis Pray for Rain." *ScT,* 62, No. 13 (6 May 1953), 28, 39.

Description of the Snake Dance.

3475. Courlander, Harold. *The Fourth World of the Hopis.* New York: Crown, 1971.

Rewritten myths and legends with data on informants and comparative notes.

3476. ———. *People of the Short Blue Corn. Tales and Legends of the Hopi Indians.* New York: Harcourt Brace Jovanovich, 1970.

Seventeen myth and legend texts with general treatment of storytelling traditions and fairly good explanatory and comparative notes.

3477. Craig, Edna L. "The Basket Dance." *SAM,* 40 (November 1940), 99–100, 9a–10a.

Description of a ceremonial. With one music text.

3478 Crane, Leo. *Indians of the Enchanted Desert.* Boston: Little, Brown, 1925.

Memoirs of an Indian agent. One chapter treats the Hopi Snake Dance; another deals with the ritual calendar and life cycle.

3479. ———. "Let Joy Be Unrefined!" *AtM,* 136 (August 1925), 188–99.

Description of the Snake Dance.

3480. Curtis, Natalie. "An American-Indian Composer." *H,* 107 (1903), 626–32.

Survey of Hopi singing styles and contexts. With focus on a performer and his songs (words and music).

3481. Cushing, Frank Hamilton. "Origin Myth from Oraibi." *JAF,* 36 (1923), 163–70.

Text collected by Cushing in 1883 and extensively annotated by Elsie Clews Parsons.

3482. ———, J. Walter Fewkes, and Elsie Clews Parsons. "Contributions to Hopi History." *AA,* 24 (1922), 253–98.

Reports on Oraibi in 1883 (by Cushing), in 1890 (by Fewkes), and in 1920 (by Parsons) include descriptions of ceremonialism. Also included is a description of Shöhmo'pavi Pueblo by Parsons.

3483. "Dancing with Rattlesnakes to Incline the Gods to Send Rain." *LD,* 67 (16 October 1920), 58–61.

Ceremonial description reprinted from the Dearborn *Independent.*

3484. Davis, Lawrence M. "Three Hopi Tales." *Aff,* 2, No. 2 (September 1972), 23–31.

Unannotated myth and folktale texts. No commentary.

Collected in 1964.

3485. DeHuff, Elizabeth Willis. "The Witch." *EP,* 31 (1931), 37–39.

Unannotated myth text. No commentary.

3486. Dellenbaugh, F. S. "The Somaikoli Dance at Sichumovi." *AMJ,* 15 (1915), 256–58.

Description of a ceremonial observed in 1884.

3487. Dennis, Wayne. *The Hopi Child.* New York: John Wiley, 1965.

Socialization study includes data on ceremonialism. Originally published in 1940.

3488. ———. "The Socialization of the Hopi Child," in 161, pp. 259–71.

Considers the role of the kachinas in enculturation. With ceremonial descriptions.

3489. Dockstader, Frederick. "The Hopi Kachina Cult." *To,* 4, No. 3 (Spring 1956), 57–63.

Survey of the tribal religious system.

3490. ———. *The Kachina and the White Man: A Study of the Influences of White Culture on the Hopi Kachina Cult.* Bloomfield Hills, Mich.: Cranbrook Institute of Science, 1954 (Bulletin No. 35).

Acculturation study includes extensive descriptions of Hopi beliefs and ceremonials. Traces the history of Hopi-EA relations.

3491. Donaldson, Thomas. *Moqui Pueblo Indians of Arizona and Pueblo Indians of New Mexico.* Washington: United States Census Printing Office, 1893 (Extra Census Bulletin).

Includes descriptions of ceremonials. A long section treats the Hopi Snake Dance.

3492. Dorsey, George A. "The Hopi Indians of Arizona." *PSM,* 55 (October 1899), 732–50.

Culture survey includes data on ceremonialism.

3493. ———, and H. R. Voth. "The Mishongnovi Ceremonies or the Snake and Antelope Fraternities." *PFCM-AS,* 3, No. 3 (June 1902), 159–261.

Thorough descriptions of the Antelope Race and Snake Dance with English text of ritual origin myth.

3494. ———, and H. R. Voth. "The Oraibi Soyal Ceremony." *PFCM-AS,* 3, No. 1 (March 1901), 1–59.

Description of the nine-day ceremony based chiefly on observations in 1897. Some attention to singing.

3495. Dozier, Edward P. "The Hopi and the Tewa." *ScA,* 196, No. 6 (June 1957), 127–36.

Treats assimilation of Hopi and Tewa cultures. Emphasizes contrasting elements present in aspects of the cultures, such as songs and ceremonials.

3496. ———. "Resistance to Acculturation and Assimilation in an Indian Pueblo." *AA,* 53 (1951), 56–66.

Describes ways a Hopi village has persisted in traditional lifestyle. With references to village origin and migration myths.

3497. ———. "The Role of the Hopi-Tewa Migration Legend in Reinforcing Cultural Patterns and Prescribing Social Behavior." *JAF,* 69 (1956), 176–80.

Shows how folk narrative functions to maintain self-esteem and perpetuate distinctive cultural characteristics.

3498. Earle, Edwin. *Hopi Kachinas.* Text by Edward A. Kennard. New York: J. J. Augustin, 1938.

Paintings of kachinas are introduction on ceremonial context. With prayer texts from the Niman Kachina Ceremony.

3499. Eggan, Dorothy. "Instruction and Affect in Hopi Cultural Continuity." *SJA,* 12 (1956), 347–70.

Socialization study deals with role of kachinas in transmission of culture.

3500. ———. "The Personal Use of Myth in Dreams." *JAF,* 68 (1955), 445–53.

Shows how a Hopi, troubled by acculturation, invests his dreams with symbols from tribal myths and thus identifies with culture heroes. Reprinted in 155 (pp. 67–75).

3501. ———. "The Significance of Dreams for Anthropological Research." *AA,* 51 (1949), 177–98.

Dreams recorded from Don C. Talayevsa in the 1940s reveal recurrent patterns, clarify psychological processes in the dreamer's life, and make good stories.

3502. Eggan, Fred. "From History to Myth: A Hopi Example," in 128, pp. 33–53.

Study of the way a historical narrative takes on mythic features.

3503. Eiseman, Fred B., Jr. "Notes on the Hopi Ceremonial Cycles." *Plat,* 34, No. 1 (July 1961), 18–22.

Summaries of the cycles at the four Hopi religious centers.

3504. Fewkes, J. Walter. "The Alósaka Cult of the Hopi Indians." *AA,* 1 (1899), 522–44.

Description of ceremonial with related mythology.

3505. ———. "Ancestor Worship of the Hopi Indians." *ARSI for 1921,* pp. 485–506.

Description of ceremonies with some attention to their validating myths.

3506. ———. "A-Wá-To Bi: An Archeological Verification of a Tusayan Legend." *AA,* o. s. 6 (1893), 363–76.

Excavation of a destroyed pueblo confirms Hopi legend of its destruction.

3507. ———. "The Butterfly in Hopi Myth and Ritual." *AA,* 12 (1910), 576–94.

Treats occurrences of the butterfly in Hopi art. Describes the Butterfly Dance and interprets butterfly's symbolic significance on the basis of myth.

3508. ———. "A Central American Ceremony Which Suggests the Snake Dance of the Tusayan Villagers." *AA,* o. s. 6 (1893), 285–306.

Comparison of Hopi and Nahuatl ceremonialism.

3509. ———. "The Ceremonial Circuit Among the Village Indians of Northeastern Arizona." *JAF,* 5 (1892), 33–42.

Discusses the importance of circular movement and the cardinal directions in Hopi ceremonialism.

3510. ———. "A Comparison of Sia and Tusayan Snake Ceremonials." *AA,* o. s. 8 (1895), 118–41.

Comparison takes into account the ceremonials themselves as well as theological background and ritual paraphernalia.

3511. ———. "Designs on Prehistoric Hopi Pottery." *ARBAE,* 33 (1911–1912), 207–84.

Interprets some designs as representing gods and other mythic beings.

3512. ———. "The Destruction of the Tusayan Monsters." *JAF,* 8 (1895), 132–37.

Four myth texts with some explanatory notes. Includes general comments on the mythological system.

3513. ———. "Dolls of the Tusayan Indians." *IAE,* 7 (1894), 45–74.

Reproduction and description of figures with

commentary on their ritual and mythological significance.

3514. ———. "The Feather Symbol in Ancient Hopi Designs." *AA,* o. s. 11 (1898), 1–14.

Treats use of feathers in Hopi graphic art and the ceremonial and mythic associations of feathers.

3515. ———. "A Few Summer Ceremonials at the Tusayan Pueblos." *JAEA,* 2 (1892), 1–159.

Thorough description of Hopi ceremonials as observed in 1890s as a member of the Hemenway Southwestern Expedition.

3516. ———. "A Few Tusayan Pictographs." *AA,* o. s. 5 (1892), 9–26.

Describes several examples of rock art and oral traditions about their significance.

3517. ———. "Fire Worship of the Hopi Indians." *ARSI for 1920,* pp. 589–610.

Describes ceremonialism, singing, and mythic basis for the worship.

3518. ———. "The Growth of the Hopi Ritual." *JAF,* 11 (1898), 173–94.

Study of the additions through history of rituals to the Hopi calendar. Based on archeological data, but refers to mythic traditions about clan migrations.

3519. ———. "Hopi Basket Dances." *JAF,* 12 (1899), 81–96.

Description of ceremonials observed in 1898. Some attention to myths associated with the rituals.

3520. ———. "Hopi Ceremonial Frames from Cañon de Chelly, Arizona." *AA,* 8 (1906), 664–70.

Material culture study used to confirm a Hopi migration legend.

3521. ———. "Hopi Katcinas Drawn by Native Artists." *ARBAE,* 21 (1899–1900), 3–126.

Thorough treatment of the Hopi kachina system with data on ceremonial calendar. Data on specific ceremonials appear as commentary for paintings of kachinas done by Kutcahonauû (White Bear).

3522. ———. "Hopi Shrines Near the East Mesa, Arizona." *AA,* 8 (1906), 346–75.

Descriptions of shrine sites with data on associated ceremonials and myths.

3523. ———. "Hopi Snake Washing." *AA,* o. s. 11 (1898), 313–18.

Treats variations in the snake-washing segment of the Snake Dances at two communities.

3524. ———. "An Interpretation of Katcina Worship." *JAF,* 14 (1901), 81–94.

Argues that kachinas originally represented founders of clans and that the symbolism of kachina masks is totemic.

3525. ———. "The Katcina Altars in Hopi Worship." *ARSI for 1926,* pp. 469–86.

Descriptions of four Hopi altars, their ritual usage, and myth associations.

3526. ———. "The Lesser New-Fire Ceremony at Walpi." *AA,* 3 (1901), 438–53.

Account of the ceremony based on observation in 1900. Treats praying and singing.

3527. ———. "The Micoñinovi Flute Altars." *JAF,* 9 (1896), 241–55.

Describes ceremonial observances at Micoñinovi as compared with those at other Hopi communities. Particular focus on material apparatus.

3528. ———. "Minor Hopi Festivals." *AA*, 4 (1902), 482–511.

Describes several ceremonials. With special attention to songs and prayers.

3529. ———. "Morphology of Tusayan Altars." *AA*, o. s. 10 (1897), 129–45.

Descriptions of altars with associated rituals and symbolic significance.

3530. ———. "The New-Fire Ceremony at Walpi." *AA*, 2 (1900), 80–138.

Description of the ceremonial as observed in 1898. Includes data on singing.

3531. ———. "On Certain Personages Who Appear in a Tusayan Ceremony." *AA*, o. s. 7 (1894), 32–52.

Describes figures disguised as monsters who appear during the Powamu Ceremony.

3532. ———. "The Oraibi Flute Altar." *JAF*, 8 (1895), 265–84.

Data on two ceremonials including the 1895 Snake Dance.

3533. ———. "The Owakülti Altar at Sichomovi Pueblo." *AA*, 3 (1901), 211–26.

Describes sacred objects—including effigies which represent mythic beings—used in ceremonialism.

3534. ———. "The Prehistoric Culture of Tusayan." *AA*, o. s. 9 (1896), 151–74.

Attempt to reconstruct Hopi prehistory relies, in part, on mythology and legends.

3535. ———. "Provisional List of Annual Ceremonies at Walpi." *IAE*, 8 (1895), 215–36.

Summary of the Hopi ceremonial calendar.

3536. ———. "The Sacrificial Element in Hopi Worship." *JAF*, 10 (1897), 187–201.

Surveys sacrifice and prayer in Hopi ceremonials. With attention to mythic background.

3537. ———. "Sky-God Personations in Hopi Worship." *JAF*, 15 (1902), 14–32.

Describes kachina ceremonies and costumes, especially those associated with sky-god figures. Some attention to mythic bases for impersonations.

3538. ———. "A Suggestion as to the Meaning of the Moki Snake Dance." *JAF*, 4 (1891), 129–38.

Sees the ritual as designed to promote fertility.

3539. ———. "Sun Worship of the Hopi Indians." *ARSI for 1918*, pp. 493–526.

Presents ceremonials and mythic concepts associated with sun worship.

3540. ———. "A Theatrical Performance at Walpi." *PWAS*, 2 (1900), 605–29.

Thorough description of the Ritual of the Great Serpent as drama.

3541. ———. "Tusayan Flute and Snake Ceremonies." *ARBAE*, 19 (1897–1898), 957–1011.

Describes ceremonies observed in 1896 and 1897 at Mishongnovi and Walpi.

3542. ———. "Tusayan Katcinas." *ARBAE*, 15 (1893–1894), 245–313.

Describes seasonal round of ceremonials with comparisons to rituals at Zuni and Cibola. Includes summaries of myth texts.

3543. ———. "Tusayan Migration Traditions." *ARBAE*, 19 (1897–1898), 573–633.

Synthesis of fragments of Hopi legendary history which traces clan movements. With some data on clan ceremonial activities.

3544. ———. "Tusayan Snake Ceremonies." *ARBAE*, 16 (1894–1895), 267–312.

Describes snake ceremonials at Cipaulovi, Cuñopavi, and Oraibi. With data on singing and summaries of myths.

3545. ———. "The Use of Idols in Hopi Worship." *ARSI for 1922*, pp. 377–97.

Survey of idols in Hopi ceremonialism. With references to mythic concepts.

3546. ———. "The Walpi Flute Observance: A Study of Primitive Dramatization." *JAF*, 7 (1894), 265–88.

Thorough description of the ritual with some attention to mythological background.

3547. ———. "The Winter Solstice Ceremony at Walpi." *AA*, o. s. 11 (1898), 65–87, 101–15.

Thorough description of the ritual as observed in 1891.

3548. ———, and J. G. Owens. "The Lā'-Lā-Kōn-Ta: A Tusayan Dance." *AA*, o. s. 5 (1892), 105–29.

Thorough description of a ritual observed in 1891.

3549. ———, and A. M. Stephen. "The Mam-Zrau'-Ti: A Tusayan Ceremony." *AA*, o. s. 5 (1892), 217–45.

Describes a ritual observed in 1891.

3550. ———, and A. M. Stephen. "The Nā-Ác-Nai-Ya: A Tusayan Initiation Ceremony." *JAF*, 5 (1892), 189–221.

Thorough description of a ceremonial observed in 1891.

3551. ———, and A. M. Stephen. "The Pá-Lü-Lü-Koñ-Ti: A Tusayan Ceremony." *JAF*, 6 (1893), 269–84.

Describes a ceremonial observed in 1893.

3552. ———, A. M. Stephen, and J. G. Owens. "The Snake Ceremonials at Walpi." *JAEA*, 4 (1894), 3–126.

Very thorough description of the nine-day ceremonial. Based on observations as members of the Hemenway Southwestern Expedition.

3553. Finnigan, Mrs. Charles. "A Visit to the Moquis." *GS*, 2, No. 6 (September 1907), 153, 160–61.

Includes description of the Snake Dance.

3554. Forde, C. Daryll. "Hopi Agriculture and Land Ownership." *JAIGBI*, 61 (1931), 357–99.

Contains data on ceremonialism.

3555. Forrest, Earle R. *The Snake Dance of the Hopi Indians*. Los Angeles: Westernlore Press, 1961.

Description of the ritual as it occurred early in this century with attention to its myth of origin.

3556. ———. "The Snake Dance in the Painted Desert." *T*, 40 (January 1923), 16–20, 36.

Fairly thorough ceremonial description.

3557. Garland, Hamlin. "Among the Moki Indians." *HW*, 40 (15 August 1896), 801–7.

Description of a visit to the Hopi includes account of Snake Dance.

3558. Gianini, Charles A. "The Hopi Snake Dance." *EP*, 25 (1928), 439–49.

Ritual description.

3559. Gill, Sam D. "Disenchantment." *P*, 1, No. 3 (Spring 1976), 6–13.

Cross-cultural survey of initiation rituals which seem to defame the sacred includes a description of unmasking of kachinas among Hopi.

3560. Gilman, Benjamin Ives. "Hopi Songs." *JAEA*, 5 (1908), 3–226.

Thorough study of Hopi singing from a musicological perspective. Includes a number of music texts with extensive analysis. Based on work done by the Hemenway Southwestern Expedition in the 1890s.

3561. Glenn, Nan Ashton. "Points of View: Snake Dance at Moenkopi." *SWR*, 19, No. 1 (October 1933), 11–12.

Description of the ceremonial.

3562. Goldfrank, Esther S. "The Impact of Situation and Personality on Four Hopi Emergence Myths." *SJA*, 4 (1948), 241–62.

Examines environmental factors which affect the performance of myths.

3563. Hall, Thelma Bonney. "Dancing the Snakes." *AzH*, 29, No. 7 (July 1953), 4–11.

Description of the Snake Dance.

3564. Harrington, Isis L. "'The Good-Bringing': A Tale from the Hopi Pueblo of Oraibi." *NMHR*, 6 (1931), 227–30.

Unannotated legend text. Some data on informant.

3565. Harrison, Michael. "First Mention in Print of the Hopi Snake Dance." *M*, 38 (1964), 150–55.

Text of an article by W. R. Mateer, published originally in *The Long-Islander* for 10 October 1879.

3566. Harvey, Byron, III. *Ritual in Pueblo Art. Hopi Life and Hopi Painting. CMAI* No. 24 (1970).

Collection of paintings by five contemporary Hopi artists arranged according to depictions of Hopi life cycle and annual cycle. Many of the paintings are captioned with descriptions of ceremonials.

3567. ———. "Song of the Dog Kachina." *M*, 40 (1966), 106-8.

Description of a mythic figure with analysis of a song and text of a myth.

3568. Hawley, Florence. "Kokopelli, of the Prehistoic Southwestern Pueblo Pantheon." *AA*, 39 (1937), 644–46.

Reports of the kachina's appearance as dolls, in pictographs, and on pottery sherds. Emphasis on Kokopelli's insect-like qualities added by Elsie Clews Parsons in *AA*, 40 (1938), 337–38.

3569. Hieb, Louis B. "Masks and Meaning: A Contextual Approach to the Hopi *Tüvi'kü*," in 98, pp. 123–34.

Studies two Hopi kachina masks in terms of bipartition as a cultural theme.

3570. Holder, Charles Frederick. "The Snake Dancers of Tusayan." *NEM*, n.s. 25 (December 1901), 512–19.

Ritual description.

3571. "Hopi Snake Dance as a Magnet for 2,500 Motorists." *LD*, 88 (6 March 1926), 50–52.

Description of the ceremonial.

3572. Hough, Walter. *The Moki Snake Dance.* Sante Fe Route: Passenger Department, 1898.

Description of the ceremony at Walpi in 1897.

3573. ———. "Music of the Hopi Flute Ceremony." *AA*, o. s. 10 (1897), 162–63.

Non-technical, impressionistic description of musical performance.

3574. ———. "The Sio Shalako at the First Mesa, July 9, 1916." Commentary by J. Walter Fewkes. *AA*, 19 (1917), 410–15.

Description of a Hopi ceremonial, adopted from the Zuni. Fewkes describes his observations in 1894.

3575. Hungry Wolf, Adolph. *A Hopi Dream by the Old*

People. Invermere, B. C., Canada: Good Medicine Books, 1974.

Selected stories from *The Traditions of the Hopi* (3695).

3576. James, George Wharton. "The Hopi Snake Dance." *Ou*, 36 (June 1900), 302–10.

Fairly thorough ceremonial description.

3577. ———. "Moki and Navaho Indian Sports." *Ou*, 39 (October 1901), 10–15.

Treats ceremonial games and dances.

3578. ———. "The Snake Dance of the Mokis." *ScA*, 80 (24 June 1899), 408–9; 81 (9 September 1899), 167.

Ritual description includes texts of ritual formulas.

3579. James, Harry C. *The Hopi Indians. Their History and Their Culture.* Caldwell, Ida.: Caxton, 1956.

Popular history and culture survey includes references to myths, description of the religious system, and accounts of ceremonials.

3580. ———. *Pages from Hopi History.* Tucson: Univ. of Arizona Press, 1974.

Unannotated accounts of Hopi prehistory and history. Material has been extensively reorganized and rewritten from oral originals.

3581. Jones, Hester. "Niman Katcina Dance at Walpi." *EP*, 33 (1932), 68–71.

Description of a ritual.

3582. Josephy, Alvin M., Jr. "The Hopi Way." *AH*, 24, No. 2 (February 1973), 49–55.

Account of Hopi response to acculturation, especially coal mining on Black Mesa. Treats ceremonialism and summarizes emergence myth.

3583. Kennard, Edward A. "Hopi Reactions to Death." *AA*, 39 (1937), 491–96.

Includes texts of kachinas' speeches and narratives.

3584. ———. "Linguistic Acculturation in Hopi." *IJAL*, 29 (1963), 36–41.

Personal narrative text, presented in interlinear and free translations, illustrates the occurrences of English loan-words in Hopi. Recorded in 1961.

3585. ———. "Metaphor and Magic: Key Concepts in Hopi Culture and Their Linguistic Forms," in 158, pp. 468–73.

Identifies key concepts underlying Hopi religion and their manifestations in songs and myths.

3586. Klauber, L. M. "A Herpetological Review of the Hopi Snake Dance." *BZSSD* No. 9 (1932).

Describes the Snake Dance in 1931 with speculations about methods of handling poisonous snakes during the ritual.

3587. Kluckhohn, Clyde. "Hopi and Navajo." *NMQ*, 3 (1933), 56–64.

Contrasts the cultures. In ceremonialism Hopi emphasis is on the community, and Navajo is on the individual.

3588. L'Allemand, Gordon. "Pageantry on the Mesa." *T*, 61 (June 1933), 15–17, 46.

Description of the Butterfly Dance.

3589. Lawrence, D. H. "The Hopi Snake Dance." *TAM*, 8 (December 1924), 836–60.

Ceremonial description.

3590. List, George. "Musical Concepts in Traditional Cultures," in 101, pp. 335–46.

Discusses values of eliciting performers' concepts regarding the songs they sing. Draws upon Hopi materials for illustrations.

3591. Lockett, Hattie Greene. *The Unwritten Literature of the Hopi. UAB*-Social Sciences No. 2 (1933).

Survey of Hopi culture with special attention to myth and religion. Includes general discussion of storytelling and the function of myth. With seven unannotated myth texts.

3592. Longembaugh, May M. "The Snake Dance at Chimopovy." *OM,* n. s. 68 (1916), 280–88.

Description of the ritual.

3593. Lowie, Robert H. "The Emergence Hole and the Foot Drum." *AA,* 40 (1938), 174.

Describes Hopi and Zuni practice of dancing on planks placed across a hole, and the Maidu foot drum, which involves a sheet of bark stretched across a hole. Sees possible connection with emergence myths.

3594. ——. "Noted in Hopiland." *AMJ,* 17 (1917), 569–73.

Description of a kachina dance observed in 1916. Performed by someone who had recovered from a serious illness.

3595. ——. "Religion in Human Life." *AA,* 65 (1963), 532–42.

Emphasizes integrative functions of religion by citing mythology and ceremonialism from the Hopi and Crow.

3596. ——. "A Women's Ceremony Among the Hopi." *NH,* 25 (1925), 178–83.

Description of the Majau ritual as observed in 1916.

3597. Lundahl, William D. "About Hopi Kachinas." *M,* 32 (1958), 122–26.

Survey of the nature and role of kachinas.

3598. MacLeish, Kenneth. "A Few Hopi Songs from Moenkopi." *M,* 15 (1941), 178–84.

Six song texts (words and music) collected in 1938. With some musicological commentary.

3599. ——. "Notes on Folk Medicine in the Hopi Village of Moenkopi." *JAF,* 56 (1943), 62–68.

Texts of anecdotes and personal narratives concerning Hopi curing practices.

3600. Malotki, Ekkehart. *Hopitutuwutsi. Hopi Tales. A Bilingual Collection of Hopi Indian Stories.* Flagstaff: Museum of Northern Arizona Press, 1978.

Ten myth and folktale texts with free translations and some linguistic analysis. Includes commentary on Hopi storytelling traditions, but no annotations.

3601. McCormick, Howard. "The Artist's Southwest." *AMJ,* 13 (1913), 119–25.

Photographs of Hopi kachinas and Snake Dances with accompanying commentary.

3602. McDonald, Thomas F. "Does Liturgy Need Something We Don't Have? 'Hopi Indians Still Have It.' " *NCW,* 215 (July–August 1975), 159–61, 188–89.

Argues that the Hopi assign to their religion a vitality absent from Catholicism. Some data on ceremonialism.

3603. McIntire, Elliot G., and Sandra R. Gordon. "Ten Kate's Account of the Walpi Snake Dance: 1883." *Plat,* 41, No. 1 (Summer 1968), 27–33.

Translation of H. F. C. Ten Kate's description of the ceremonial, which was originally published in Dutch in 1885.

3604. McLaughlin, Ruth. "The Hopi Snake Dance." *OM,* n. s. 63 (May 1914), 419–26.

Description of the ceremonial.

3605. *Me and Mine. The Life Story of Helen Sekaquaptewa as Told to Louise Udall.* Tucson: Univ. of Arizona Press, 1969.

Oral life history with extensive data on ceremonialism and storytelling.

3606. Mearns, Edgar A. "Ornithological Vocabulary of the Moki Indians." *AA,* o. s. 9 (1896), 391–403.

Word list preceded by data on the role of birds in Hopi ceremonialism.

3607. Milford, Stanley J. "Why the Coyote Has a Black Spot on His Tail." *EP,* 48 (1941), 83–84.

Myth text recorded in 1940. No annotation or commentary.

3608. Mindeleff, Cosmos. "Localization of Tusayan Clans." *ARBAE,* 19 (1897–1898), 635–53.

Treats reasons for clan migrations, some of which are preserved in myths.

3609. Mindeleff, Victor. "A Study of Pueblo Architecture: Tusayan and Cibola." *ARBAE,* 8 (1886–1887), 3–228.

Primarily an archeological study, but presents the traditional history of Tusayan. Includes myth texts and summaries.

3610. Monroe, Harriet. "To the Snake-Dance." *FR,* n. s. 78 (1905), 665–77.

Describes visit to Arizona and the Hopi ceremonial.

3611. Monsen, Frederick. "Festivals of the Hopi: Religion the Inspiration, and Dancing an Expression in All Their National Ceremonies." *Cr,* 12, No. 3 (June 1907), 269–85.

Descriptions of ceremonials, including the Snake Dance.

3612. Mullett, G. M. *Spider Woman Stories.* Foreword by Fred Eggan. Tucson: Univ. of Arizona Press, 1979.

Eleven rewritten myths and folktales. No annotations. Foreword treats Mullett's career as a journalist and illustrator for the BAE.

3613. Munk, Joseph A. *Arizona Sketches.* New York: Grafton, ND [c. 1905].

Collection of vignettes about Arizona life includes a lengthy description of the Hopi Snake Dance.

3614. Nequatewa, Edmund. "The Destruction of Elden Pueblo, A Hopi Story." *Plat,* 28, No. 2 (October 1955), 37–44.

Unannotated legend text. No commentary.

3615. ——. "Dr. Fewkes and Masauwu. The Birth of a Legend." *MNMNA,* 11, No. 2 (August 1938), 25–27.

Legend text about Fewkes's reasons for abandoning his work at Walpi in 1898.

3616. ——. "A Flute Ceremony at Hotevilla." *Plat,* 19, No. 2 (October 1946), 35–36.

Description of a ritual observed in 1939.

3617. ——. "A Mexican Raid on the Hopi Pueblo of Oraibi." *Plat,* 16, No. 3 (January 1944), 45–52.

Unannotated legend text. With some data about storytelling style.

3618. ——. "The Place of Corn and Feathers in Hopi Ceremonies." *Plat,* 19, No. 1 (July 1946), 15–16.

Brief description of ceremonial usages.

3619. ——. *Truth of a Hopi and Other Clan Stories of Shung-opovi.* Ed. Mary-Russell F. Colton. *BMNA* No. 8 (1936).

Sixteen myth texts with some explanatory notes. No commentary or comparative annotation.

3620. ——, and K. Bartlett. "Hopi Hopiwime: The Hopi Ceremonial Calendar." *MNMNA,* 3, No. 9 (March 1931), 1–4.

Treats calendrical customs of the Hopi.

3621. ——, and Mary-Russell F. Colton. "Hopi Courtship and Marriage, Second Mesa." *MNMNA*, 5, No. 9 (March 1933), 41–54.

Description of ceremonialism.

3622. Nusbaum, Mary Aileen. "Another Tower of Babel." *EP*, 18, No. 1 (January 1925), 9–12.

Unannotated myth text. With comparison to classical traditions.

3623. O'Kane, Walter Collins. *The Hopis: Portrait of a Desert People.* Norman: Univ. of Oklahoma Press, 1953.

Culture survey centered on photographs of Hopi individuals. With data on religion and ceremonialism.

3624. ——. *Sun in the Sky.* Norman: Univ. of Oklahoma Press, 1950.

Culture survey with chapters on ceremonialism and supernaturalism. Includes one song text.

3625. Oliver, Marion L. "The Snake Dance." *NG*, 22, No. 2 (February 1911), 107–37.

Ceremonial description. With text of ritual origin myth.

3626. Owens, J. G. "Natal Ceremonies of the Hopi Indians." *JAEA*, 2 (1892), 163–75.

Description of rituals based on observations while a member of the Hemenway Southwestern Expedition.

3627. Page, James K., Jr. "A Rare Glimpse into the Evolving Way of the Hopi." *Sm*, 6, No. 8 (November 1975), 90–100.

Examination of culture change with attention to ceremonialism. Includes summary of clan origin myth.

3628. Parsons, Elsie Clews. "Early Relations Between Hopi and Keres." *AA*, 38 (1936), 554–60.

Traditions about early associations between groups are reinforced by Hopi songs which include Keresan words.

3629. ——. "Getting Married on First Mesa, Arizona." *ScM*, 13 (September 1921), 259–65.

Description of a ceremonial from an informant's account.

3630. ——. *Hopi and Zuni Ceremonialism.* *MAAA* No. 39 (1933).

Comparative treatment includes material on functions, procedures, and theology.

3631. ——. "The Hopi Buffalo Dance." *Man*, 23 (1923), 21–26.

Description of the ceremonial.

3632. ——. "A Hopi Ceremonial." *Cent*, n. s. 49 (1920–1921), 177–80.

Description of the author's adoption into the Hopi community.

3633. ——, ed. *Hopi Journal of Alexander M. Stephen.* 2 volumes. *CUCA* No. 23 (1936).

Edition of Stephen's notebooks from 1891 to 1894, while he was a member of the Hemenway Southwestern Expedition. Very extensive data on ceremonialism. With song texts.

3634. ——. "Hopi Mothers and Children." *Man*, 21 (1921), 98–103.

Socialization study includes data on ceremonialism.

3635. ——. "The Hopi *Wöwöchim* Ceremony in 1920." *AA*, 25 (1923), 156–87.

Ceremonial description compares its 1920 performance with observances in 1892, 1893, and 1898.

3636. ——. *A Pueblo Indian Journal, 1920–1921.* *MAAA* No. 32 (1925).

Daily record written by Crow-Wing contains much data on ceremonialism. Extensive explanatory notes and introduction on the writer's purpose provided by Parsons.

3637. ——. "Some Aztec and Pueblo Parallels." *AA*, 35 (1933), 611–31.

Treats parallels such as masked depictions of gods, curing societies, eschatological beliefs, traditions about water spirits, and general ceremonialism. Focuses on Hopi and Zuni cultures.

3638. Pearson, Charles S. "Idols in Hopi Worship." *Me*, 16, No. 8 (September 1928), 53–54.

Description of ceremonials.

3639. Peet, Stephen D. "History and Architecture of the Tusayans." *AAOJ*, 18 (1896), 1–21.

Includes summaries and texts of creation myths and migration legends.

3640. Qoyawayma, Polingaysi [Elizabeth Q. White] (as told to Vada F. Carlson). *No Turning Back. A True Account of a Hopi Indian Girl's struggle to Bridge the Gap Between the World of Her People and the World of the White Man.* Albuquerque: Univ. of New Mexico Press, 1964.

Rewritten life history which focuses on acculturation. Includes song texts.

3641. Reagan, Albert B. "Who Made the Kayenta-National Monument Ruins." *AA*, 22 (1920), 387–88.

Hypothesizes that some of the ruins are of Hopi manufacture. Based on NA interpretation of pictographs and on Hopi mythology.

3642. Rollins, W. E. "Story of the Sacred Stone." *EP*, 6 (1919), 36–39.

Unannotated myth text. With some data on storytelling context.

3643. Roosevelt, Theodore. "The Hopi Snake Dance." *O*, 105 (18 October 1913), 365–73.

Account of a trip to Arizona includes description of the ceremonial.

3644. Sands, Kathleen M., and Emory Sekaquaptewa. "Four Hopi Lullabies." *AIQ*, 4 (1978), 195–210.

Four song texts (words only) represent two types of Hopi children's songs: reproving and admonishing.

3645. Schlegel, Alice. "The Adolescent Socialization of the Hopi Girl." *Eth*, 12 (1973), 449–62.

Treats role of kachinas in socialization and women's ceremonial activities.

3646. ——. "Sexual Antagonism Among the Sexually Egalitarian Hopi." *E*, 7 (1979), 124–41.

Includes data on ceremonial recognition of sexual relationships.

3647. Sekaquaptewa, Emory. "A Clown Story." *ST*, 5 (1979), 1–2.

Unannotated legend text with some commentary on cultural significance.

3648. ——. "Hopi Indian Ceremonies," in 96, pp. 35–43.

Uses the kachina ceremony to show how the NA can adjust and adapt to contemporary life.

3649. ——. "One More Smile for a Hopi Clown." *P*, 4, No. 1 (February 1979), 6–9.

Treats role of the ritual clown in Hopi life. Refers to myth of clown's origin.

3650. Sheldon, Charles M. "The Hopi Snake Dance." *Ind*, 57 (3 November 1904), 1026–31.

Description of the ceremonial as observed in 1904.

3651. Simmons, Leo W., ed. *Sun Chief: The Autobiography of a Hopi Indian.* New Haven: Yale Univ. Press, 1942.

Life history of Don C. Talayesva based on diaries and interviews. Includes data on religious beliefs and ceremonials. Appendix contains texts of thirteen myths and legends.

3652. Simpson, Ruth DeEtte. *The Hopi Indians. SWML* No. 25 (1953).

Extensive cultural and historical survey includes data on religion and ceremonialism.

3653. Smith, Dama Margaret. "Thou Shalt Have No Other Gods." *GH,* 77 (December 1923), 33–37, 189–92.

Description of the Snake Dance.

3654. Stephen, Alexander M. "Description of a Hopi Ti-Hü." *FL,* 1 (1893), 83–88.

Description of a ceremonial.

3655. ———. "Hopi Indians of Arizona." *M,* 13 (1939), 197–204; 14 (1940), 20–27, 102–9, 143–49, 170–79, 207–15.

Culture survey based on fieldwork done in 1881. Contains ceremonial descriptions and song texts.

3656. ———. "Hopi Tales." *JAF,* 42 (1929), 1–72.

Twenty-eight myth texts recorded in 1883 and 1893. Includes some comparative and explanatory notes by Elsie Clews Parsons.

3657. ———. "Legend of the Snake Order of the Moquis, as Told by Outsiders." *JAF,* 1 (1888), 109–14.

Unannotated ritual origin myth. With comments on cultural background by Washington Matthews.

3658. ———. "Pigments in Ceremonials of the Hopi," in 79, pp. 260–65.

Surveys color symbolism in Hopi ceremonialism.

3659. ———. "The Po-Boc-Tu Among the Hopi." *AAOJ,* 16 (1894), 212–14.

Description of a sorcerer and his ceremonies.

3660. Steward, Julian H. "Notes on Hopi Ceremonies in Their Initiatory Form in 1927–1928." *AA,* 33 (1931), 56–79.

Describes three winter ceremonies of the Hopi: Wuwuchim, Powamu, and Soyala.

3661. Stirling, Matthew W. "Snake Bites and the Hopi Snake Dance." *ARSI for 1941,* pp. 551–55.

Examines techniques of rattlesnake-handling during the ritual.

3662. Sutton, Anne. "Indian Legends. Mesa Verde, Colorado." *CW,* 126 (February 1928), 639–42.

Rewritten myth texts. No commentary or annotations.

3663. Sykes, Godfrey. "Hopi Snake-Washing: 1893." *ArQ,* 1, No. 4 (1945), 34–36.

Description of ceremonial behavior written by a trading post manager.

3664. Talayesva, Don. "Twins Twisted Into One." *P,* 4, No. 3 (August 1979), 7–12.

Excerpt from *Sun Chief* (3651).

3665. Thayer, Lee I. "The Hopi Indians and Their Religion." *MRW,* 40, No. 7 (July 1917), 507–13.

Survey of belief and ceremonial system.

3666. Thompson, Laura. *Culture in Crisis. A Study of the Hopi Indians.* New York: Harper and Brothers, 1950.

Acculturation study includes summaries of myths and descriptions of ceremonials. Appendix by Benjamin Lee Whorf treats linguistic basis for Hopi concepts of space and time.

3667. ———. "Logico-Aesthetic Integration in Hopi Culture." *AA,* 47 (1945), 540–53.

Overview of Hopi philosophy as embodied in myth and expressed in ceremonialism and daily behavior.

3668. ———, and Alice Joseph. *The Hopi Way.* Chicago: Univ. of Chicago Press, 1945.

Psychological study of socialization practices includes data on ceremonialism.

3669. ———, and Alice Joseph. "White Pressures on Indian Personality and Culture." *AJS,* 53, No. 1 (July 1947), 17–22.

Acculturation study shows how ceremonialism maintains balance between the Hopi social system and the individual personality.

3670. Titiev, Mischa. "A Hopi Salt Expedition." *AA,* 39 (1937), 244–58.

Account of a journey made for salt in 1912. Recalls ritual behavior and ritual origin myth. Material collected in 1933–1934.

3671. ———. "Hopi Snake Handling." *ScM,* 57 (July 1943), 44–51.

Description of the Snake Dance with emphasis on ways in which snakebite is avoided.

3672. ———. *Old Oraibi. A Study of the Hopi Indians of Third Mesa. PPM* No. 22 (1944).

Ethnography based on fieldwork done in 1932, 1933, and 1934. Contains extensive data on ceremonialism with some myth texts and references.

3673. ———. "The Problem of Cross-Cousin Marriage Among the Hopi." *AA,* 40 (1938), 105–11.

Supports past occurrences of cross-cousin marriages among the Hopi by referring to ceremonialism and legends.

3674. ———. "Shamans, Witches and Chiefs Among the Hopi." *To,* 4, No. 3 (Spring 1956), 51–56.

Describes varieties of religious practitioners.

3675. ———. "The Story of Kokopele." *AA,* 41 (1939), 91–98.

Presents myth text and draws comparisons with Keresan material collected by Leslie A. White. Relates mythology to kachina ceremonials.

3676. ———. "Two Hopi Myths and Rites." *JAF,* 61 (1948), 31–43.

Attempts to relate myth texts collected in 1933–1934 to the Water Serpent Dance and the Powamu.

3677. ———. "Two Hopi Tales from Oraibi." *PMASAL,* 29 (1943), 425–37.

Folktale texts with extensive explanatory notes.

3678. ———. "The Use of Kinship Terms in Hopi Ritual." *MNMNA,* 10, No. 3 (September 1937), 9–11.

Examines significance of ritual terms denoting relationships.

3679. Townshend, R. B. "The Snake-Dancers of Mishongnovi." *NC,* 55 (March 1904), 429–43.

Description of the ceremonial.

3680. True, Webster P. "Sun Worship Among the American Aborigines. The Ceremonies Attached to the Deification of the Orb of the Day." *ScAM,* October 1921, pp. 329–31.

Description of Hopi ceremonialism.

3681. Voegelin, C. F. "Pregnancy Couvade Attested by Term and Text in Hopi." *AA,* 62 (1960), 491–94.

Presents three Hopi descriptions of couvade which involve jokes and puns. Shows correlation between the texts and their intended audience.

3682. ——, and Robert C. Euler. "Introduction to Hopi Chants." *JAF,* 70 (1957), 115–36.

Application of componential analysis to Hopi chanting. With discussion of the relationship of chanting to cultural background.

3683. von Berckefeldt, Susan. "The Humpback Flute Player." *M,* 51 (1977), 113–15.

Description of Kokopelli in graphic art and in Hopi and Zuni mythology.

3684. Voth, H. R. "Four Hopi Tales." *PFCM-AS,* 11, No. 2 (February 1912), 139–43.

Unannotated myth texts.

3685. ——. "Hopi Marriage Rites on the Wedding Morning." *PFCM-AS,* 11, No. 2 (February 1912), 147–49.

Ceremonial description based on observation in 1904.

3686. ——. "Notes on the Eagle Cult of the Hopi." *PFCM-AS,* 11, No. 2 (February 1912), 106–9.

Surveys ritual procedure.

3687. ——. "The Oraibi Marau Ceremony." *PFCM-AS,* 11, No. 1 (February 1912), 1–88.

Thorough description of the nine-day ceremony. With song texts and translations.

3688. ——. "Oraibi Marriage Customs." *AA,* 2 (1900), 238–46.

Ceremonial description.

3689. ——. "Oraibi Natal Customs and Ceremonies." *PFCM-AS,* 6, No. 2 (February 1905), 47–61.

Survey of ceremonialism beginning with birth and ending with naming. Includes texts of ritual formulas.

3690. ——. "The Oraibi New Year Ceremony." *PFCM-AS,* 11, No. 2 (February 1912), 113–19.

Description of the ceremony as observed in 1897 and 1901.

3691. ——. "The Oraibi Oáqöl Ceremony." *PFCM-AS,* 6, No. 1 (December 1903), 1–46.

Thorough description of the nine-day event with song and chant texts and translations.

3692. ——. "The Oraibi Powamu Ceremony." *PFCM-AS,* 3, No. 2 (December 1901), 60–158.

Thorough description of the ten-day event. Includes song and oration texts and translations.

3693. ——. "The Oraibi Summer Snake Ceremony." *PFCM-AS,* 3, No. 4 (November 1903), 262–358.

Description of the ceremonial as observed in 1896 and 1898. With prayer text and text of ritual origin myth.

3694. ——. "Tawa Baholawu of the Oraibi Flute Societies." *PFCM-AS,* 11, No. 2 (February 1912), 123–36.

Descriptions of rituals as observed in January 1898 (winter ceremony) and June 1901 (summer ceremony).

3695. ——. *The Traditions of the Hopi. PFCM-AS* No. 8 (1905).

Myth, folktale, and legend texts (110) in English translations with abstracts. Selections appear in 3575.

3696. Wade, Edwin, and David Evans. "The Kachina Sash: A Native Model of the Hopi World." *WF,* 32 (1973), 1–18.

Presents Native interpretations of the symbolism of a ceremonial sash worn by most Hopi kachina dancers. Some treatment of cosmology.

3697. Wallis, Wilson D. "Folk Tales from Shumopovi, Second Mesa." *JAF,* 49 (1936), 1–68.

Twenty-one myth texts collected in 1912. Occasional comparative notes by Elsie Clews Parsons, but no commentary.

3698. Waters, Frank. *Book of the Hopi.* New York: Viking, 1963.

Presents mythology, ritual procedures, and historical legends of the Hopi as recorded by Oswald White Bear Fredericks. Material seems to be rewritten. No annotations.

3699. ——. *Pumpkin Seed Point.* Chicago: Swallow, 1969.

Anecdotal account of three years of field research to gather material for 3698. Although focus is on Waters' relationships with the Hopi, some myths and ceremonials are described. Informed by a Jungian perspective.

3700. Wheeler-Jones, C. G. *The Returned Katchinas.* Tucson: Desert Press, 1940.

Pamphlet describes several kachinas with attention to mythological and ritual background.

3701. Whiting, Alfred F. "The Bride Wore White." *Plat,* 37, No. 4 (Spring 1965), 128–40.

Description of a wedding ceremony.

3702. ——. *Ethnobotany of the Hopi. BMNA* No. 15 (1939).

List of plants used by the Hopi includes some accounts of ceremonial usages.

3703. ——. "Hopi Kachinas." *Plat,* 37, No. 1 (Summer 1964), 1–7.

Attempts to define kachinas and their ritual context.

3704. Wright, Barton. "Anasazi Murals." *AIAM,* 1 February 1976, pp. 62–67.

Description of prehistoric group's art includes summaries of Hopi migration legends, which seem to relate to the art.

3705. ——. *Hopi Kachinas: The Complete Guide to Collecting Kachina Dolls.* Flagstaff, Ari.: Northland, 1977.

Guide to kachinas provides description and mythic background for each. Some data on ceremonialism.

3706. ——, and Evelyn Roat. *This Is a Hopi Kachina.* Flagstaff: Northern Arizona Society of Science and Art, 1962.

Illustrated pamphlet describes kachina dances and symbolism.

See also 24, 519, 667, 705, 2682, 2688, 2689, 2696, 2710, 2720, 2934, 3121, 3125, 3203, 3234, 3317, 3350, 3352, 3383, 3391, 3435, 3808, 3846, 4774, 4837.

J.5. Pueblo: Isleta

3707. Gatschet, Albert S. "A Mythic Tale of the Isleta Indians." *PAPS,* 29 (1891), 208–18.

Two myth texts with free and interlinear translations. Some commentary on religious significance.

3708. Goldfrank, Esther S. *The Artist of "Isleta Paintings" in Pueblo Society. SmCA* No. 5 (1967).

Biographical data, including ceremonial role, of Joe B. Lente, the artist who painted the materials included in Parsons' *Isleta Paintings* (3715). Contains some of Lente's letters, which describe ceremonialism.

3709. ——. "Isleta Variants: A Study in Flexibility." *JAF,* 39 (1926), 70–78.

Comparative treatment of texts collected by Goldfrank in 1924 and Parsons in 1925. Sees a personal element explaining textual variation.

3710. Gordon, Dudley. "An Example of Indian Oratory." *M*, 39 (1965), 154–56.

Text of a speech delivered by the governor of Isleta in 1940.

3711. Harvey, Byron, III. "Masks at a Maskless Pueblo: The Laguna Colony Kachina Organization at Isleta." *Eth*, 2 (1963), 478–89.

Study of the adoption of the Kachina Cult into the ceremonial calendar at Isleta, where Christianity had driven out the Native religion. Contains one song text.

3712. Lange, Charles H. "Notes on a Winter Ceremony at Isleta Pueblo, January 7, 1940." *EP*, 60 (1953), 116–23.

Ceremonial description.

3713. Parsons, Elsie Clews. "Further Notes on Isleta." *AA*, 23 (1921), 149–69.

Random ethnographic notes include data on dances and the ceremonial calendar.

3714. ———. "Isleta, New Mexico." *ARBAE*, 47 (1929–1930), 193–466.

Ethnography based on fieldwork done in 1925. Covers ceremonial calendar with excerpts from song texts. With narrative texts in free translations.

3715. ———. *Isleta Paintings.* 2 volumes. *BAEB* No. 181 (1962).

Paintings (140), many of which depict ceremonial occasions and apparatus. Parsons' commentary, written in the 1930s, serves to relate content of paintings to ethnographic background. For data on the painter, see 3708.

See also 3332, 3333, 3390, 3738.

J.6. Pueblo: Jemez

3716. Alexander, Hartley B. "The Pecos Bull." *EP*, 39 (1935), 121–24.

Description of a ritual.

3717. Ellis, Florence Hawley. "Jemez Kiva Magic and Its Relation to Features of Prehistoric Kivas." *SJA*, 8 (1952), 147–63.

Explains features of prehistoric kivas by decribing contemporary kiva ceremonialism, especially the ritual of kiva dedication.

3718. ———. *A Reconstruction of the Basic Jemez Pattern of Social Organization, with Comparisons to Other Tanoan Social Structures.* *APUNM* No. 11 (1964).

Includes data on religious cults and their ceremonials.

3719. Ewart, Wilfrid. "The Dance of the Jemez Indians." *CM*, n. s. 55 (December 1923), 547–55.

Ceremonial description.

3720. Jones, J. Robert. "A Jemez Corn Grinding." *EP*, 54 (1947), 43–44.

Description of a communal work activity accompanied by singing. Observed in 1939.

3721. Keech, Roy A. "The Pecos Ceremony at Jemez, August 2, 1932." *EP*, 36 (1934), 129–34.

Description of a ritual.

3722. ———. "Two Days and Nights in a Pueblo." *EP*, 35 (1933), 185–95.

Includes descriptions of ceremonials.

3723. Kluckhohn, Jane. "Traditional Forms of Greet-ing in Jemez Pueblo." *NMFR*, 3 (1948–1949), 31.

Brief description of greeting formulas.

3724. Parsons, Elsie Clews. *The Pueblo of Jemez. PSWE* No. 3 (1925).

Ethnography based on fieldwork done in 1921–1922. Includes data on ceremonialism and five myth texts.

3725. Reagan, Albert B. "The Jemez Indians." *EP*, 4 (1917), 25–72.

Ethnographic survey includes myth and song texts and descriptions of ceremonials.

3726. ———. "Notes on Jemez Ethnography." *AA*, 29 (1927), 719–28.

Describes election ceremony at the Pueblo. Includes two prayers and two myth texts. Based on observations in 1900.

3727. Reagan, James B. "The Jemez Indians." *EP*, 16 (1924), 168–73.

Historical notes with a text of the creation myth.

3728. Roberts, Helen H. "The Reason for the Departure of the Pecos Indians for Jemez Pueblo." *AA*, 34 (1932), 359–60.

Summary of tribal migration legend.

3729. Thompson, Gilbert. "An Indian Dance at Jemez, New Mexico." *AA*, o. s. 2 (1889), 351–55.

Description of a ceremony observed in 1874.

See also 3889.

J.7. Pueblo: Laguna

3730. Boas, Franz. "A Keresan Text." *IJAL*, 2, Nos. 3–4 (1921–1923), 171–80.

Portion of a Laguna Coyote story with extensive linguistic notes. No translation.

3731. Curtis, Natalie. "A Bit of American Folk-Music: Two Pueblo Indian Grinding Songs." *Cr*, 7, No. 1 (October 1904), 35–41.

Texts (words and music) with description of performance context.

3732. Dutton, Bertha P., and Miriam A. Marmon. *The Laguna Calendar. UNMB-AS*, 1, No. 2 (1936).

Description of the ceremonial cycle.

3733. Gordon, Dudley. "An Early Fiesta at Laguna." *M*, 46 (1972), 34–37.

Description of a Christmas dance in 1894 from a letter written by Charles F. Lummis.

3734. Grinnell, George Bird. "The Salt Story of Laguna Pueblo, New Mexico." *M*, 14 (1940), 80–82.

Unannotated myth text collected in 1919. No commentary.

3735. Gunn, John Malcolm. *Schat-chen: History, Traditions and Naratives* [sic] *of the Queres Indians of Laguna and Acoma.* Albuquerque: Albright & Anderson, 1916.

Twenty-two unannotated myth texts with no commentary. Preceded by historical survey of the two Keresan cultures.

3736. Hrdlička, Aleš. "A Laguna Ceremonial Language." *AA*, 5 (1903), 730–32.

Word list of an archaic language used exclusively in rituals.

3737. Marmon, Miriam A. "The Laguna Wedding Gift Ceremony." *EP,* 42 (1937), 55–57.
Ritual description.
3738. Parsons, Elsie Clews. "The Laguna Migration to Isleta." *AA,* 30 (1928), 602–13.
Primarily concerned with acculturation resulting from tribal contact, especially in regard to ceremonialism. Some data on oral traditions about the Laguna migration to Isleta in 1880.
3739. ———. "Laguna Tales." *JAF,* 44 (1931), 137–42.
Seven myth and folktale texts collected between 1917 and 1920. No commentary or comparative annotation.
3740. ———. "Mothers and Children at Laguna." *Man,* 19 (1919), 34–38.
Socialization study includes description of ceremonialism and song and prayer texts.
3741. Schiff, Esther. "A Note on Twins." *AA,* 23 (1921), 387–88.
Describes ceremonial to counteract evil influences of birth of twins at Laguna.
3742. Vogt, Evon Z. "A Study of the Southwestern Fiesta System as Exemplified by the Laguna Fiesta." *AA,* 57 (1955), 820–39.
Uses festival in honor of St. Joseph to represent the tradition of village festivals in the Southwest. Shows how Catholic ceremonies and traditional ritualism attract visitors from other groups.

See also 3340, 3388, 3398, 3711, 3782, 3908, 3922, 3925.

J.8. Pueblo: Picuris

3743. Harrington, J. P., and Helen H. Roberts. "Picurís Children's Stories with Texts and Songs." *ARBAE,* 43 (1925–1926), 289–447.
Twenty-one narrative and eleven song texts collected from Rosendo Vargas. Presented with free translations. Includes some background commentary and musicological analysis of the songs.
3744. Pancoast, Chalmers Lowell. "Last Dance of the Picuris." *AMJ,* 18 (1918), 309–11.
Description of a festival in honor of San Lorenzo in 1917.
3745. Parsons, Elsie Clews. "Picurís, New Mexico." *AA,* 41 (1939), 206–22.
Describes layout and culture of the pueblo with attention to ceremonialism and narrative traditions.

J.9. Pueblo: San Felipe

3746. Bunzel, Ruth. "The Emergence." *JAF,* 41 (1928), 288–90.
Unannotated text of creation myth. No commentary.
3747. ———. "Notes on the Katcina Cult in San Felipe." *JAF,* 41 (1928), 290–92.
Description of ceremonialism. With some ritual language texts.

3748. Parsons, Elsie Clews. "Notes on San Felipe and Santo Domingo." *AA,* 25 (1923), 485–94.
Ethnographic notes include data on ceremonial terminology and behavior.
3749. White, Leslie A. *The Pueblo of San Felipe. MAAA* No. 38 (1932).
Ethnography focuses on ceremonialism.

J.10. Pueblo: Santa Ana

3750. Davis, Irvine. "The Language of Santa Ana Pueblo." *BAEB* No. 191 (*AP* No. 69), 1964.
Linguistic survey includes text of a myth (with Christian overtones) with interlinear and free translations. Collected in 1950s.
3751. Parsons, Elsie Clews. "Fiesta at Sant'ana, New Mexico." *ScM,* 16 (February 1923), 178–183.
Ceremonial description with song text (words only).
3752. White, Leslie A. *The Pueblo of Santa Ana, New Mexico. MAAA* No. 60 (1942).
Ethnography based on fieldwork done between 1928 and 1941 includes data on ceremonialism, song texts (words only), and legend texts.
See also 3390, 3440.

J.11. Pueblo: Santo Domingo

3753. Anderson, Arnold M. "The Corn Dance of Santo Domingo." *GS,* 4, No. 4 (September 1908), 100–102, 110–11.
Description of the annual August ceremony.
3754. Densmore, Frances. *Music of Santo Domingo Pueblo, New Mexico.* Los Angeles: Southwest Museum, 1938 (Museum Paper No. 12).
Song texts (103 with words and music), each with musicological and context notes. With general description of cultural background. Collected in mid-1930s.
3755. Dougherty, John. "New Mexico Indians Greet the Christ Child in Ancient Ceremonial Dance." *DM,* 35, No. 12 (December 1961), 24–25.
Ceremonial description.
3756. Gaastra, Mrs. T. Charles. "Santo Domingo 'Bull and Horse' Ceremony." *EP,* 18 (1925), 67–69.
Ritual description.
3757. "Green Corn Ceremony, The." *EP,* 27 (1929), 48–50.
Description of a ceremonial.
3758. Hewett, Edgar L. "The Corn Ceremony at Santo Domingo." *EP,* 5 (1918), 69–74.
Ritual description.
3759. Huebener, G. "The Green Corn Dance at Santo Domingo." *EP,* 45 (1938), 1–17.
Examines aspects of the ritual from a comparative perspective.
3760. Lange, Charles H. "An Animal Dance at Santo Domingo Pueblo, January 26, 1940." *EP,* 61 (1954), 151–55.
Description of a ceremonial.

3761. ———. "King's Day Ceremonies at a Rio Grande Pueblo, January 6, 1940." *EP,* 58 (1951), 398–406.
Good description of the ceremony.

3762. Moore, Allen. "Impressions of Corn Dance." *EP,* 15 (1923), 77–78.
Generalized ritual description.

3763. Rosenfeld, Paul. "Musical Chronicle." *Di,* 81 (December 1926), 529–34.
Impressionistic description of a ceremonial dance.

3764. "Tablet Dance at Santo Domingo, The." *HW,* 34 (7 June 1890), 447.
Ceremonial description.

3765. Terry, Walter. "Adventure into a Celestial Sphere." *SR,* 2 September 1967, pp. 40–41.
Description of the Corn Dance.

3766. White, Leslie A. *The Pueblo of Santo Domingo, New Mexico.* MAAA No. 43 (1935).
Ethnography includes data on ceremonialism and twelve myth texts with explanatory notes.

See also 3355, 3464, 3748.

J.12. Pueblo: Sia

3767. DeHuff, Elizabeth Willis. "Pueblo Myths and Legends." *EP,* 11 (1921), 98–99.
Unannotated myth text reported from Sia and San Juan Pueblos. No commentary.

3768. Halseth, Odd S. "Report of Economic and Social Survey of the Keres Pueblo of Zia, New Mexico." *EP,* 16 (1924), 67–75.
Ethnographic notes collected in 1923 contain data on religion and singing.

3769. Keech, Roy A. "Green Corn Ceremony at the Pueblo of Zia, 1932." *EP,* 36 (1934), 145–49.
Description of a ritual.

3770. Stevenson, Matilda Coxe. "The Sia." *ARBAE,* 11 (1889–1890), 3–157.
Ethnographic notes emphasize religious and ceremonial concerns. Includes a summary of the group's mythology, thorough descriptions of various rituals, song and prayer texts with interlinear and free translations, and four myths (three about Coyote) in free translations.

3771. White, Leslie A. *The Pueblo of Sia, New Mexico.* BAEB No. 184 (1962).
Ethnography based on fieldwork done in 1928 contains descriptions of ceremonials and summaries of myths.

See also 3510.

J.13. Pueblo: Taos

3772. Bailey, Florence Merriam. "Poetic Children of the Pueblos." *T,* 43 (August 1924), 23–26.
Culture survey with attention to group's esthetics, particularly as manifested in myths and ceremonials.

3773. ———. "Some Plays and Dances of the Taos In-

dians." *NH,* 24 (1924), 85–95.
Describes several ceremonials.

3774. Brown, Donald Nelson. "Taos Dance Classification." *EP,* 67 (1960), 203–9.
Describes ceremonialism from a NA perspective.

3775. Collins, John James. "A Descriptive Introduction to the Taos Peyote Ceremony." *Eth,* 7 (1968), 427–49.
Survey of the ceremony includes song texts, references to myths, and descriptions of other verbal performances.

3776. DeHuff, Elizabeth Willis. "The Bear and the Deer." *EP,* 31 (1931), 2–4.
Unannotated myth text. No commentary.

3777. ———. "The Fate of Yellow Corn and Blue Corn. A Story of Taos Pueblo." *EP,* 16 (1924), 53–55.
Unannotated myth text. No commentary.

3778. ———. "The Greedy Fox." *EP,* 31 (1931), 20–22.
Unannotated myth text. No commentary.

3779. ———. "Infidelity." *EP,* 31 (1931), 200–01.
Unannotated myth text. No commentary.

3780. ———. "The Red Winged Hawk. A Story of Taos Pueblo." *EP,* 16 (1924), 51–53.
Unannotated myth text. No commentary.

3781. ———. "The Witches' Feast Is Interrupted." *EP,* 45 (1938), 69–73.
Unannotated myth text. No commentary.

3782. Goldfrank Esther S. "Notes on Two Pueblo Feasts." *AA,* 25 (1923), 188–96.
Descriptions of ceremonials at Taos and Laguna include oration and song texts and a catalogue of gestures. Pays attention to Christian-NA assimilation.

3783. Grant, Blanche C. *Taos Indians.* Taos, N.M.: Santa Fe New Mexican, 1925.
Survey of history and culture has references to mythology and ceremonialism. With legend texts. Most of the material is from oral sources.

3784. Jeancon, Jean Allard. "Taos Notes." *EP,* 28 (1930), 3–11.
Ethnographic notes compare Taos mythology to traditions of other groups.

3785. Lawrence, D. H. "New Mexico." *Su,* 66 (1 May 1931), 153–55.
Impressions of northern New Mexico include description of Taos ceremonialism.

3786. LeRoy, James A. "The Indian Festival at Taos." *Ou,* 43 (December 1903), 282–88.
Ceremonial description.

3787. Miller, Merton Leland. *A Preliminary Study of the Pueblo of Taos, New Mexico.* Chicago: Univ. of Chicago Press, 1898.
Ethnography based on fieldwork done in 1896 includes data on ceremonialism and summaries of myths.

3788. Parsons, Elsie Clews. *Taos Pueblo.* Menasha, Wis.: George Banta, 1936.
Ethnography with extensive data on ceremonialism.

3789. ———. *Taos Tales.* MAFS 34 (1940).
Ninety-eight myth, folktale, and legend texts with some linguistic and explanatory notes. No comparative annotation. Appended are two texts with free and interlinear translations collected by George L. Trager.

3790. Reno, Philip. *Taos Pueblo.* Denver: Swallow, 1963.
Historical pamphlet includes a chapter on "Dances and Ceremonies."

3791.   Vorse, Mary Heaton. "Deer Dance in Taos." *N*, 131 (13 August 1930), 178–79.
Ceremonial description.
3792.   Wood, Nancy. *Hollering Sun*. New York: Simon and Schuster, 1972.
Legend texts and philosophy rendered as poetry and illustrated with photographs.
3793.   ———. *Many Winters. Prose and Poetry of the Pueblos*. Garden City, N.Y.: Doubleday, 1974.
Reminiscences and descriptions of customs collected from Taos and rendered as poetry.

See also 3325, 3355, 3398, 4084.

J.14. Pueblo: Tewa

3794.   "Animal Dance at San Ildefonso, The." *EP*, 24 (1928), 119–22.
Ritual description.
3795.   Arnold, Charlotte. "The Dance at Nambe." *EP*, 24 (1928), 26–28.
Description of a ceremonial.
3796.   Bayliss, Clara Kern. "A Tewa Sun Myth." *JAF*, 22 (1909), 333–35.
Unannotated myth text. No commentary.
3797.   Burlin, Natalie Curtis. "The Indians' Part in the Dedication of the New Museum." *A&A*, 7 (January-February 1918), 31–32.
Describes NA contributions to opening of New Mexico Art Museum. With song texts (words only).
3798.   Cata, Regina Alvarado. "Two Stories from San Juan Pueblo." *WF*, 15 (1956), 106–9.
Unannotated myth texts with some comparative and cultural commentary.
3799.   Chapman, Kate Muller. "Sun Basket Dance at Santa Clara." *EP*, 18 (1925), 45–46.
Ritual description.
3800.   Cody, Bertha Parker. "A Tale of Witchcraft as Told by a Tewa Indian of New Mexico." *M*, 13 (1939), 188–89.
Unannotated legend text. No commentary.
3801.   "Comanche Dances at San Ildefonso, Jan. 23, 1921." *EP*, 10, No. 4 (January 1921), 5–7.
Ritual description.
3802.   Curtis, Natalie. "A Plea for Our Native Art." *MQ*, 6 (1920), 175–78.
Illustrates NA artistic accomplishments with a chant from the San Ildefonso Eagle Dance.
3803.   DeHuff, Elizabeth Willis. "The Princess of Monarca." *NMFR*, 2 (1947–1948), 14–19.
Annotated folktale texts with data on collecting situation.
3804.   ———. "The Venomous Snake-Girl." *EP*, 31 (1931), 73–74.
Unannotated myth text. No commentary.
3805.   Dougan, Rose. "The Capture of Santiago and Crooked Neck." *EP*, 6 (1919), 34–35.
Two unannotated legend texts. No commentary.
3806.   Dozier, Edward P. "Cultural Matrix of Singing and Chanting in Tewa Pueblos." *IJAL*, 24 (1958), 268–72.

General survey of ceremonial contexts for verbal performance.
3807.   ———. *Hano: A Tewa Indian Community in Arizona*. New York: Holt, Rinehart and Winston, 1966.
Ethnography includes data on ceremonialism.
3808.   ———. "The Hopi-Tewa of Arizona." *UCPAAE*, 44, No. 3 (October 1954), 259–376.
Ethnography based on fieldwork done in 1949. Contains data on ceremonialism.
3809.   Dutton, Bertha P. "San Ildefonso's Snowbird Dance, 1949." *EP*, 56 (1949), 123–24.
Description of a ceremonial.
3810.   Edelman, Sandra Prewitt. "Ascension Motifs and Reversals in Tewa Narratives." *JAR*, 30 (1974), 35–40.
Pattern of ascent and return which marks the progress of the hero in Tewa narratives reverses the pattern in EA folklore.
3811.   Fay, George E. "Some Notes on the Cow Dance, Santa Clara Pueblo." *EP*, 59 (1952), 186–88.
Ceremonial description.
3812.   Fewkes, J. Walter. "The Pueblo Settlements Near El Paso, Texas." *AA*, 4 (1902), 57–75.
Ethnography of the Tewa at Ysleta Pueblo includes description of ceremonialism and singing.
3813.   ———. "The Winter Solstice Altars at Hano Pueblo." *AA*, 1 (1899), 251–76.
Ceremonial description with some attention to oral narratives.
3814.   Ford, Richard I. "Communication Networks and Information Hierarchies in Native American Folk Medicine: Tewa Pueblos, New Mexico," in 123, pp. 143–57.
Examines degree to which medical knowledge is a specialization among the Tewa. Includes data on ceremonialism.
3815.   Green, Thomas A. "Folk History and Cultural Reorganization: A Tigua Example." *JAF*, 89 (1976), 310–18.
Oral history of the Tewa at Ysleta Pueblo portrays them as adversaries of the Spanish during the seventeenth century.
3816.   ———. "The Legends of the Tigua," in 78, pp. 16–19.
Paraphrased texts of oral history.
3817.   ———. "Stereotype Manipulation in Contemporary Native American Humor." *MJLF*, 4 (1978), 18–26.
Analysis of three joke texts as manifestation of NA response to EA dominance.
3818.   H., H. "A Midsummer Fête in the Pueblo of San Juan." *AtM*, 49 (1882), 101–8.
Description of observance of St. John's Day. With data on singing.
3819.   Harrington, John Peabody. "The Ethnogeography of the Tewa Indians." *ARBAE*, 29 (1907–1908), 29–618.
Presentation of geographical knowledge focuses primarily on place names, but includes data on cosmography and places in mythology.
3820.   ———. "The Tewa Indian Game of 'Cañute.'" *AA*, 14 (1912), 243–86.
Thorough description of a game of divination. Includes description of singing and one song text (words and music).
3821.   ———. "Three Tewa Texts." *IJAL*, 13 (1947), 112–16.
Narratives with interlinear translations. No commentary.

3822. Henderson, Junius, and John Peabody Harrington. *Ethnozoology of the Tewa Indians. BAEB* No. 56 (1914).
List of animals includes data on their occurrence in mythology and ceremonialism.
3823. Hewett, Edgar L. "Archeology of Pajarito Park, New Mexico." *AA,* 6 (1904), 629–59.
Among the discoveries reported is a pictograph associated with a Tewa legend.
3824. ———. "The Excavations at El Rito de los Frijoles in 1909." *AA,* 11 (1909), 651–73.
Description of a site in New Mexico. Tewa excavators provided linguistic and mythological data.
3825. James, Ahlee. "Crow Dance at San Ildefonso." *EP,* 18 (1925), 229–30.
Ritual description.
3826. ———. *Tewa Firelight Tales.* New York: Longmans, Green, 1927.
Twenty-seven myths and folktales. No commentary or annotations.
3827. Kellogg, Harold. "It's an Old Indian Custom." *EP,* 33 (1932), 1–4.
Description of the Woman's Dance at San Ildefonso.
3828. Kurath, Gertrude P. "Two Line Dances of San Juan Pueblo, New Mexico." *MWF,* 8 (1958), 155–58.
Description of the Yellow Corn Dance and the Deer Dance. With music texts.
3829. ———, and Antonio Garcia. *Music and Dance of the Tewa Pueblos. MNMRR* No. 8 (1970).
About 100 song texts (words and music) with related dance steps. Placed in ceremonial context with choreographic and musicological commentary.
3830. Laski, Vera P. "The Raingod Ceremony of the Tewa, A Religious Drama." *M,* 31 (1957), 76–84.
Description of a ceremonial in dramatic terms. With song texts.
3831. ———. *Seeking Life.* Philadelphia: American Folklore Society, 1958.
Considers two aspects of religious life at San Juan Pueblo. The Raingod Drama is presented with interpretation of its elements. Shamanistic healing ceremonies are described. Includes myth text which validates sacred healing.
3832. Lewis, Orian Louise. "Fiesta at Nambé Pueblo, October 4, 1953." *EP,* 60 (1953), 409–13.
Description of the Arrow Dance.
3833. Ortiz, Alfonso. "Dual Organization as an Operational Concept in the Pueblo Southwest." *Eth,* 4 (1965), 389–96.
Discussion of social structure involves the Tewa creation myth.
3834. ———. *The Tewa World. Space, Time, Being, and Becoming in a Pueblo Society.* Chicago: Univ. of Chicago Press, 1969.
Relates cosmology and ritual life to social institutions. Includes summaries of myths and texts of prayers and songs.
3835. ———. "The Tewa World View," in 163, pp. 179–89.
Outline of the group's ethos.
3836. Parsons, Elsie Clews. "The Ceremonial Calendar of the Tewa of Arizona." *AA,* 28 (1926), 209–29.
Surveys the seasonal cycle of ceremonies.
3837. ———. *The Social Organization of the Tewa of New Mexico. MAAA* No. 36 (1929).

Study of social system deals with ceremonialism and place of supernaturals in the system. Appended are ten myths and legends with some explanatory notes.
3838. ———. "Tewa Mothers and Children." *Man,* 24 (1924), 148–51.
Socialization study includes data on ceremonialism and bogey figures.
3839. ———. *Tewa Tales. MAFS,* No. 19 (1926).
Myth and folktale texts (106) collected in 1920s. Extensive explanatory notes. Introduction places material in cross-cultural perspective.
3840. Reichard, Gladys A. "Good Stories: Water Jar Boy." *JAF,* 56 (1943), 69–71.
Retelling of a folktale taken from 3839.
3841. Robbins, Wilfred William, John Peabody Harrington, and Barbara Freire-Marreco. *Ethnobotany of the Tewa Indians. BAEB* No. 55 (1916).
List of plants includes references to their appearances in myth and song and to their ceremonial uses.
3842. Spinden, Herbert J. "Home Songs of the Tewa Indians." *AMJ,* 15 (1915), 73–78.
Survey of singing tradition with texts (words only).
3843. ———, trans. "The Lover's Lament. A Tewa Indian Song." *GBM,* 12, No. 70 (October 1930), 38.
Unannotated song text. No commentary.
3844. ———. *Songs of the Tewa.* New York: Exposition of Indian Tribal Arts, 1933.
Fifty translated texts collected between 1909 and 1912. Notes deal with contexts and provide samples of original language. Includes a general essay on NA poetry.
3845. Whitman, William, 3rd. *The Pueblo Indians of San Ildefonso. A Changing Culture. CUCA* No. 34 (1947).
Ethnography based on fieldwork done in 1936, 1937, and 1939. Contains data on religion and ceremonialism.
3846. Yava, Albert. *Big Falling Snow: A Tewa-Hopi Indian's Life and Times and the History and Traditions of His People.* Ed. Harold Courlander. New York: Crown, 1978.
Life history contains much contextual data. With thorough annotation by Courlander. Appended are three song texts (words and music) and two myth texts.
3847. Yegerlehner, John. "Structure of Arizona Tewa Words, Spoken and Sung." *IJAL,* 24 (1958), 264–67.
Compares sung and spoken language using a dozen songs collected in 1957.

See also 3495, 3497.

J.15. Pueblo: Zuni

3848. Bartlett, Florence. "The Creation of the Zunis." *OSF,* 2, No. 1 (July 1914), 79–87.
Rewritten creation myth with no commentary or annotation.
3849. Bartlett, Mrs. W. H. "The Shalako Dance." *OW,* 22, No. 6 (June 1905), 389–402.
Description of a ceremonial with summary of related myth.
3850. Baxter, Sylvester. "The Father of the Pueblos." *H,* 65 (1882), 72–91.
Culture survey includes data on oral traditions and ceremonialism. Based on discussions with Frank Hamilton Cushing.

3851. ———. "Zuni Revisited." *AABN,* 13 (17 March 1883), 124–26.

Account of a visit to Cushing at Zuni includes description of ceremonials.

3852. "Belief of Indians in Evolution." *S,* n. s. 74 (24 July 1931), supplement p. 12.

Points out parallels between Zuni creation myth and Darwinian evolution.

3853. Benedict, Ruth. *Zuni Mythology.* 2 volumes. New York: Columbia Univ. Press, 1935.

Narrative texts collected in 1922 and 1923 introduced by extensive discussion of themes in Zuni oral literature and their relationship to the rest of the culture.

3854. Boas, Franz. "Tales of Spanish Provenience from Zuñi." *JAF,* 35 (1922), 62–98.

Eight folktale and legend texts collected in 1900. With occasional comparative and explanatory notes. No commentary.

3855. Bohrer, Vorsila L. "Zuni Agriculture." *EP,* 67 (1960), 181–202.

Survey of Zuni crops includes data on planting ceremonials. With a song text.

3856. Bunzel, Ruth L. "Introduction to Zuñi Ceremonialism." *ARBAE,* 47 (1929–1930), 467–544.

Survey of cosmology and ritual calendar includes excerpts from prayer texts. Based on fieldwork done in 1928.

3857. ———. "Zuñi Katcinas: An Analytical Study." *ARBAE,* 47 (1929–1930), 837–1086.

Focuses on ceremonialism of the most important Zuni cult. Includes song texts and myth texts.

3858. ———. "Zuñi Origin Myths." *ARBAE,* 47 (1929–1930), 545–609.

Texts with interlinear and free translations. Some commentary of comparisons with previously published Zuni creation myths.

3859. ———. "Zuñi Ritual Poetry." *ARBAE,* 47 (1929–1930), 611–835.

Texts and free translations of poetic prayers. Some commentary on Zuni poetic style.

3860. ———. *Zuni Texts. PAES* No. 15 (1933).

Fifteen myth and folktale texts, one life history, and several legends and descriptions of customs collected in 1926. Presented with free translations. No commentary or annotations.

3861. Cazeneuve, Jean. "Some Observations on the Zuñi Shalako." *EP,* 62 (1955), 347–56.

Comparison of ceremonial in 1954 with those described in ethnographic literature.

3862. Chapman, K. M. "The Shalako Ceremony at Zuni." *EP,* 23 (1927), 622–27.

Ritual description.

3863. Chauvenet, Beatrice. "A Zuni Shalako." *EP,* 27 (1929), 299–306.

Ritual description.

3864. Curtis, William E. *Children of the Sun.* Chicago: Inter-Ocean, 1883.

Account of a visit to Zuni while Cushing was in residence. Includes many references to myths and legends and general discussion of the religious system.

3865. Cushing, Frank Hamilton. "Manual Concepts: A Study of the Influence of Hand-Usage on Culture-Growth." *AA,* o. s. 5 (1892), 289–317.

International survey of the effects of right- and left-handedness includes discussion of its role in Zuni ceremonialism.

3866. ———. "My Adventures in Zuñi." *Cent,* 25 (1882), 191–207, 500–11; 26 (1883), 28–47.

Account of field trip to Zuni includes much on ceremonial and religious life.

3867. ———. "Outlines of Zuni Creation Myths." *ARBAE,* 13 (1891–1892), 321–447.

Seventy-seven texts of creation and etiological myths introduced by data on Zuni history, ceremonial organization, and religion.

3868. ———. *Zuñi Breadstuff. IN&M* No. 8 (1920).

A NA "cookbook" includes data on ceremonialism and mythological system.

3869. ———. *Zuñi Fetiches. ARBAE,* 2 (1880–1881), 3–45.

Survey of the group's religion with special reference to animal worship. Includes texts of myths which validate particular worship patterns.

3870. ———. "A Zuñi Folk-Tale of the Underworld." *JAF,* 5 (1892), 49–56.

Myth text with extensive explanatory notes. Data on cultural background.

3871. ———. *Zuni Folk Tales.* Introduction by John Wesley Powell. New York: Putnam, 1901.

Thirty-three myth and folktale texts with occasional explanatory notes. No comparative annotation. Powell's introduction generalizes about mythology with special reference to Zuni.

3872. ———. "The Zuñi Social, Mythic, and Religious Systems." *PSM,* 21 (June 1882), 186–92.

Survey of the group's mythology and its expression in social and religious life.

3873. Custer, Augusta H. "Zuni Katcinas." *SAM,* 33 (September 1933), 36–38.

Describes three kachina figures and their mythic and ritual significance.

3874. de Lemos, Pedro. "Zuni Hunt Fetishes." *SAM,* 43 (November 1943), 86–87.

Description of fetish stones, their functions, and mythic sanction.

3875. Fewkes, J. Walter. "A Few Summer Ceremonials at Zuñi Pueblo." *JAEA,* 1 (1891), 1–61.

Thorough description of ceremonialism based on observations while a member of the Hemenway Southwestern Expedition.

3876. Fillmore, John Comfort. "The Zuni Music as Translated by Mr. Benjamin Ives Gilman." *Mu,* 5 (1893), 39–46.

Analysis of Gilman's findings reported in *JAEA* (3878).

3877. Fine, Elizabeth C. "Six Versions of the Zuni Deer Boy Tale: An Analysis." *FA,* 7–8 (1977), 12–27.

Structuralist approach reveals raw/cooked dualism as theme of narrative.

3878. Gilman, Benjamin Ives. "Zuñi Melodies." *JAEA,* 1 (1891), 65–91.

Musicological analysis of nine tunes collected by J. Walter Fewkes while a member of the Hemenway Southwestern Expedition. See 3876.

3879. Gonzales, Clara. "The Shalakos Are Coming." *EP,* 73, No. 3 (Autumn 1966), 5–17.

Description of the ceremonial. With one song text.

3880. Green, Jesse, ed. *Zuñi: Selected Writings of Frank Hamilton Cushing.* Lincoln: Univ. of Nebraska Press, 1979.

Includes full texts and excerpts from 3866, 3867, 3868, 3869, and 3871; texts of several lectures; and texts of unpublished letters. Introduction surveys Cushing's career.

3881. Handy, Edward L. "Zuñi Tales." *JAF,* 31 (1918), 451–71.

Nineteen myth and folktale texts with occasional comparative and explanatory notes. No commentary.

3882. Harrington, M. R. "Ruins and Legends of Zuni Land." *M,* 3 (1929), 5–16.

Myth texts collected on a tour of the Southwest are placed in storytelling context.

3883. Hieb, Louis A. "Meaning and Mismeaning: Toward an Understanding of the Ritual Clown," in 147, pp. 163–95.

Views the clown figure in Zuni ritual both as a mediator between man and nature and as a creator of "communitas."

3884. Hill, Gertrude. "Turquoise and the Zuni Indian." *Ki,* 12, No. 4 (May 1947), 42–52.

Treats mythic and ceremonial significance of the stone.

3885. Hodge, F. Webb. "A Zuni Foot-Race." *AA,* o. s. 3 (1890), 227–31.

Description of a ceremonial race.

3886. James, George Wharton. "With the Zunis in New Mexico." *OM,* n. s. 72 (1918), 105–12, 254–60, 285–99.

Historical and culture survey includes data on ceremonialism and prayer texts.

3887. Jones, Hester. "Mythology Comes to Life at Zuñi." *EP,* 32 (1932), 57–66.

Treats mythic backgrounds of ceremonialism.

3888. ———. "Zuni Shalako Ceremony." *EP,* 30 (1931), 1–10.

Ritual description.

3889. Judd, Neil M. "When the Jemez Medicine Men Came to Zuni." *JAF,* 60 (1947), 182–84.

Describes a curing ceremony conducted by Jemez curers for the Zuni in 1926.

3890. Kaplan, Bert. "Psychological Themes in Zuni Mythology and Zuni TAT's," in 143, Vol. 2, pp. 255–62.

Finds similarities in content, but differences in function.

3891. Kennedy, Katharine. "Poems from the Zuñi." *SWR,* 25, No. 2 (January 1940), 151–55.

Free translations of four texts. No commentary or annotations.

3892. ———, trans. "Zuni Rituals." *Po,* 50, No. 5 (August 1937), 254–57.

Five very free translations of Zuni myths, songs, and prayers.

3893. Kirk, Ruth F. "Introduction to Zuni Fetishism." *EP,* 50 (1943), 117–29, 146–59, 183–98, 206–19, 235–45.

Thorough description of the Zuni religious system pays special attention to venerated objects.

3894. ———. "Zuñi Fetish Worship." *M,* 17 (1943), 129–35.

Survey of sacred objects among the Zuni.

3895. Klett, Francis. "The Zuni Indians of New Mexico." *PSM,* 5 (September 1874), 580–91.

Culture survey with data on ceremonialism and mythology.

3896. Kroeber, A. L. "The Oldest Town in America and Its People." *AMJ,* 16 (1916), 80–85.

Description of Zuni emphasizes the importance of mythology and ceremonialism.

3897. Lévi-Strauss, Claude. "The Structural Study of Myth." *JAF,* 68 (1955), 428–44.

Demonstrates structuralist approach to myth interpretation by analyzing the Zuni emergence myth. Reprinted in 155 (pp. 50–66) and 455 (pp. 206–31). For critiques, see 683 and 684.

3898. Li An-che. "Zuñi: Some Observations and Queries." *AA,* 39 (1937), 62–76.

Reassesses ideas of previous ethnographers about Zuni prayers and ceremonials.

3899. Loeb, Edwin M. "A Note on Two Far-Travelled Kachinas." *JAF,* 56 (1943), 192–99.

Theorizes that Kachina Cult of the Zuni and Hopi diffused to the Navajo and Apache in the Southwest and to the Pomo and other groups in California.

3900. Mariager, Dagmar. "A Zuñi Genesis." *OM,* n. s. 13 (1889), 383–85.

Rewritten creation myth. No commentary or annotation.

3901. Mason, O. T. "The Planting and Exhuming of a Prayer." *S,* 8 (9 July 1886), 24–25.

Description of a ceremonial.

3902. Owens, John G. "Some Games of the Zuñi." *PSM,* 39 (May 1891), 39–50.

Describes games, ceremonial races, and hunting.

3903. Pandey, Triloki Nath. "Anthropologists at Zuni." *PAPS,* 116 (1972), 321–27.

Examines NA reactions to anthropological visitors. With legend and anecdote texts.

3904. Parsons, Elsie Clews. "The Favorite Number of the Zuñi." *ScM,* 3 (December 1916), 596–600.

Treats significance of the number four in Zuni ceremonialism.

3905. ———. "A Few Zuni Death Beliefs and Practices." *AA,* 18 (1916), 245–56.

Discussion of ceremonials associated with death and witchcraft.

3906. ———. "Increase by Magic: A Zuñi Pattern." *AA,* 21 (1919), 279–86.

Describes ritual designed to increase various resources. With texts of chants and prayers.

3907. ———. "Mothers and Children at Zuni, New Mexico." *Man,* 19 (1919), 168–73.

Socialization study includes data on ceremonialism and a prayer text.

3908. ———. "Nativity Myth at Laguna and Zuñi." *JAF,* 31 (1918), 256–63.

Retelling of the Christian Nativity collected at Laguna and several Christian miracle legends collected at Zuni. Extensive explanatory notes.

3909. ———. "Notes on Zuni." *MAAA,* 4 (1917), 151–327.

Focuses on ceremonialism. With thorough descriptions of Shalako (in 1915), Hilili (1917), and Mahedinasha (1917).

3910. ———. "The Origin Myth of Zuñi." *JAF,* 36 (1923), 135–62.

Extensively annotated myth text.

3911. ———. "Reasoning from Analogy at Zuñi." *ScM,* 4 (April 1917), 365–68.

Describes thought patterns and their ceremonial manifestations.

3912. ———. *The Scalp Ceremonial of Zuñi. MAAA* No. 31 (1924).

Compares ceremonial observances in 1891 and 1921.

3913. ———. "Spring Days in Zuni, New Mexico." *ScM,* 36 (January 1933), 49–54.

Description of ceremonialism. With song text.

3914. ———. Waiyautitsa of Zuñi, New Mexico." *ScM,* 9 (November 1919), 443–57.

Treats ceremonial life of a Zuni girl.

3915. ———. "Winter and Summer Dance Series in Zuñi in 1918." *UCPAAE,* 17, No. 3 (1922), 171–216.

Thorough description of ceremonials. With song texts and translations.

3916. ———. "The Zuñi A'Doshlĕ and Suukĕ." *AA,* 18 (1916), 338–47.

Treats use of bogey figures in disciplining children. With data on ceremonies and anecdotes involving bogeys.

3917. ———. "Zuñi Inoculative Magic." *S,* n. s. 44 (29 September 1916), 469–70.

Description of sympathetic magic practices.

3918. ———. "The Zuñi La' Mana." *AA,* 18 (1916), 521–28.

Describes hermaphroditic figures in Zuni culture, their ceremonials, and myths which explain their existence.

3919. ———. "The Zuñi Mo'lawia." *JAF,* 29 (1916), 392–99.

Description of a ceremonial observed in 1915. With myth text.

3920. ———. "Zuñi Names and Naming Practices." *JAF,* 36 (1923), 171–76.

Describes naming patterns. With appended list of names.

3921. ———. "Zuñi Tales." *JAF,* 43 (1930), 1–58.

Nineteen myths collected in 1918 and 1920. Two presented in Zuni with interlinear translations. Commentary on informant and explanatory notes included.

3922. ———, and Franz Boas. "Spanish Tales from Laguna and Zuñi, N. Mex." *JAF,* 33 (1920), 47–72.

Nine folktale texts with comparative notes. No commentary.

3923. Proctor, Edna Dean. *The Song of the Ancient People.* Preface and Notes by John Fiske. Commentary by Frank Hamilton Cushing. Boston: Houghton Mifflin, 1893.

Original poem dealing with Zuni culture. Commentary and notes discuss the mythic and ceremonial allusions made by the poet.

3924. Risser, Anna. "Seven Zuñi Folk Tales." *EP,* 48 (1941), 215–26.

Unannotated myth and folktale texts collected in 1929. No commentary.

3925. Roberts, Helen H. "Chakewa Songs of Zuñi and Laguna." *JAF,* 36 (1923), 177–84.

Comparison of three texts of a ceremonial song. Considers words, rhythm, and metric structure.

3926. Roberts, John M., and Malcolm J. Arth. "Dyadic Elicitation in Zuni." *EP,* 73, No. 2 (Summer 1966), 27–41.

Demonstrates an interviewing technique by citing Zuni illustrations. Includes reminiscences and descriptions of ceremonials.

3927. Rollins, Warren E. "Zuni Indian Fire Dance." *EP,* 5 (1918), 307.

Ritual description. With song excerpt.

3928. Schaafsma, Polly F., and Curtis F. Schaafsma.

"Evidence for the Origins of the Pueblo Katchina Cult as Suggested by Southwestern Rock Art." *AAn,* 39 (1974), 535–45.

Myths about origins of kachina cult among Zuni, Hopi, and Keresan groups are supported by rock art, which depicts mythological figures associated with the cult.

3929. Schlater, Katharine. "An Easterner Visits the Shalako." *EP,* 54 (1947), 35–42.

Ceremonial description.

3930. Simpson, Ruth De Ette. "An Ancient Custom in Modern Zuni—A Sword-Swallowing Ceremony." *M,* 22 (1948), 102–4.

Description of a ritual.

3931. Stevenson, Matilda Coxe. "Ethnobotany of the Zuñi Indians." *ARBAE,* 30 (1908–1909), 31–102.

Catalogue of plants used for various functions includes data on ceremonial usage. Includes some data on plants in mythology.

3932. ———. "Zuñi Ancestral Gods and Masks." *AA,* o. s. 11 (1898), 33–40.

Concerned with tribal theology and theogony. Includes summaries of creation myths.

3933. ———. "Zuñi Games." *AA,* 5 (1903), 468–97.

Thorough description of seventeen games. Includes data on singing.

3934. ———. "The Zuñi Indians: Their Mythology, Esoteric Fraternities, and Ceremonies." *ARBAE,* 23 (1901–1902), 3–608.

Includes myth texts and paraphrases, song texts, prayer texts, and descriptions of ceremonials. Some of the material is presented in Zuni with free and interlinear translations.

3935. Stevenson, Tilly E. "The Religious Life of the Zuñi Child." *ARBAE,* 5 (1883–1884), 533–55.

Describes initiation for male children. With summaries of myths.

3936. Tedlock, Barbara. "Boundaries of Belief." *P,* 4, No. 1 (February 1979), 70–77.

Examines Zuni clowning as a response to challenges to traditional beliefs from Christianity, pan-Indianism, and modern technology.

3937. Tedlock, Dennis. "An American Indian View of Death," in 163, pp. 248–71.

Ceremonial description with song texts and myth excerpt.

3938. ———. "The Analogical Tradition and the Emergence of a Dialogical Anthropology." *JAR,* 35 (1979), 387–400.

Suggests possibility of using oral literature to reveal elements of culture in which it occurs and to reflect general human nature. Cites Zuni examples.

3939. ———. "The Boy and the Deer: A Zuni Tale." *Ki,* 33, No. 2 (December 1967), 67–79.

Prose translation of a folktale with summary of Zuni interpretations of the story.

3940. ———. *Finding the Center. Narrative Poetry of the Zuni Indians.* Introduction by Jerome Rothenberg. New York: Dial, 1972.

Innovative translations of nine Zuni myths and folktales. Uses a system of typographic variation to indicate features of oral performance. With explanatory notes.

3941. ———. "On the Translation of Style in Oral Narrative." *JAF,* 84 (1971), 114–33.

Describes translation practices used in 3940. Reprinted in 149 (pp. 114–33).

3942. ———. "Pueblo Literature: Style and Verisimilitude," in 147, pp. 219–42.

Focuses on aspects of Zuni narrative style which are associated with distortions of reality. Includes one text.

3943. Ten Kate, H. F. C. "A Zuñi Folk-Tale." *JAF,* 30 (1917), 496–99.

Myth text with explanatory notes and description of collecting situation.

3944. Troyer, Carlos. *Indian Music Lecture: The Zuñi Indians and Their Music: An Address Designed for Reading at Musical Gatherings, Describing the Lives, Customs, Religions, Occult Practices, and the Surprising Musical Development of the Cliff Dwellers of the South West.* Philadelphia: Theo. Presser, 1913.

Pamphlet surveys Zuni Culture and discusses function of ritual singing. Some attention to singing style.

3945. Wengerd, Stephanie K. "The Role and Use of Color in the Zuni Culture." *Plat,* 44, No. 3 (Winter 1972), 113–24.

Color symbolism in Zuni life relates to six cardinal directions.

3946. Wetherill, Betty. "A Zuñi Legend." *M,* 12 (1938), 196–98.

Unannotated myth text. No commentary.

3947. Whitaker, Kathleen. "The Zuni Shalako Festival." *M,* 48 (1974), 84–97, 136–47.

Thorough description of the ritual with attention to mythic background.

3948. Wilson, Edmund. "A Reporter in New Mexico: Shalako." *NY,* 25 (9 August 1949), 62–73; (16 August 1949), 70–82.

Describes Zuni ceremonialism and the response of Zunis to EA attitudes toward their religion.

3949. "Witches in Zuni." *M,* 38 (1964), 35–38.

Anecdotes and descriptions of witch behavior. For the mss. of F. W. Hodge.

3950. Woodward, Arthur. "Concerning Witches." *M,* 24 (1950), 183–88.

Witch legend with explanatory notes.

3951. Wyman, Anne. "Zuñi Dance." *M,* 10 (1936), 22–26.

Description of a ritual.

3952. The Zuni People. *The Zunis: Self-Portrayals.* Trans. Alvina Quam. Albuquerque: Univ. of New Mexico Press, 1972.

Results of an oral history project include unannotated myth and legend texts. No commentary.

See also 61, 202, 327, 340, 406, 2688, 2689, 2691, 2742, 2894, 2934, 3275, 3332, 3352, 3383, 3388, 3435, 3542, 3574, 3593, 3630, 3637, 3683.

K. Walapai

3953. Dobyns, Henry F., and Robert C. Euler. *The Walapai People.* Phoenix: Indian Tribal Series, 1976.

Tribal history includes summary of creation myth and data on the Ghost Dance.

3954. Ewing, Henry P. "The Pai Tribes." Ed. Robert. C Euler and Henry F. Dobyns. *Eh,* 7 (1960), 61–80.

Culture survey written in 1903 contains data on storytelling and ceremonialism among the Walapai, Yavapai, and Havasupai.

3955. Iliff, Flora Gregg. *People of the Blue Water. My Adventures Among the Walapai and Havasupai Indians.* New York: Harper and Brothers, 1954.

Reminiscences of time spent as a schoolteacher in reservation schools focus on acculturation. Includes retellings of myths and legends.

3956. Kroeber, A. L., ed. *Walapai Ethnography. MAAA* No. 42 (1935).

Results of team fieldwork (Fred Kniffen, Gordon MacGregor, Robert McKennan, Scudder Mekeel, and Maurice Mook) in 1929. Contains data on music, shamanism, and ceremonialism. With four life histories and twenty-two myths and folktales. With explanatory notes.

3957. Winter, Werner. "Stories and Songs of the Walapai." *Plat,* 35 (1962), 114–22.

Legend and song texts recorded in 1956. Includes data on informant and explanatory notes, but no comparative annotation.

3958. ———. "Yuman Languages II: Wolf's Son—A Walapai Text." *IJAL,* 32 (1966), 17–40.

Text of a Coyote story collected in 1956. With literal translation and linguistic analysis.

See also 2681, 2710, 2767, 2845.

L. Yaqui

3959. Altman, George J. "The Yaqui Easter Play at Guadalupe, Arizona." *M,* 20 (1946), 181–89; 21 (1947), 19–23, 67–71.

Thorough description of a ceremonial.

3960. Barker, George C. "Some Functions of Catholic Processions in Pueblo and Yaqui Culture Change." *AA,* 60 (1958), 449–55.

Contrasts the place of Christian ceremonialism in Yaqui and Keresan-speaking Pueblo cultures: Fusion occurs in the former; compartmentalization occurs in the latter.

3961. Beals, Ralph L. *The Contemporary Culture of the Cáhita Indians. BAEB* No. 142 (1945).

Attempts to reconstruct pre-contact culture on the basis of fieldwork among Yaqui and Mexican NAs. Includes data on ceremonialism and thirteen myth texts (including a narrative about Jesus and St. Peter).

3962. Bogan, Phebe M. *Yaqui Indian Dances of Tucson, Arizona.* Tucson: Archeological Society, 1925.

Describes ceremonial behavior, especially during the Christian Holy Week.

3963. Crumrine, Lynne S. *The Phonology of Arizona Yaqui with Texts. APUAZ* No. 5 (1961).

Contains one personal narrative and one legend text with free and interlinear translations and linguistic analysis.

3964. Densmore, Frances. "Native Songs of Two Hybrid Ceremonies Among the American Indians." *AA,* 43 (1941), 77–82.

Treats musical performances during Yaqui Holy Week ceremonies (1922) and among the Winnebago during NA Church rituals (1927).

3965. Getty, Harry T. "Some Characteristics of the Folklore of the Indians of Arizona," in 145, pp. 29–42.

Generalizations about narrative traditions of various Southwest groups followed by annotated texts of six Yaqui stories collected in 1942 and 1943.

3966. Giddings, Ruth Warner. *Yaqui Myths and Legends. APUAZ* No. 2 (1959).

Sixty-one myth and legend texts collected in 1942. With general discussion of storytelling and data on informants. Some explanatory and comparative notes.

3967. Jensen, Marguerite. "The Yaqui." *IH,* 4, No. 3 (Fall 1971), 41–42, 43.

Focuses on religion and ceremonialism.

3968. Johnson, Barbara. "Holy Saturday: A Yaqui Ceremony in Pascua Village." *EP,* 67 (1960), 102–4.

Description of a Christian ceremony.

3969. Kaczkurkin, Mini Valenzuela. *Yoeme: Lore of the Arizona Yaqui People.* Tucson: Sun Tracks, 1977.

Collection of myths, folktales, legends, beliefs, and historical anecdotes. No annotation, but good commentary on informants.

3970. Kelley, Jane Holden. *Yaqui Women. Contemporary Life Histories.* Lincoln: Univ. of Nebraska Press, 1978.

Four life histories collected between 1968 and 1972. Emphasis is on NA-EA relations, but with some data on ceremonialism. Thorough data on collecting situation.

3971. Lindenfeld, Jacqueline. *Yaqui Syntax. UCPL* No. 76 (1973).

Includes a personal narrative text with free and interlinear translations and linguistic analysis. Collected between 1965 and 1971.

3972. Mason, J. Alden. "A Preliminary Sketch of the Yaqui Language." *UCPAAE,* 20 (1923), 195–212.

Legend texts with interlinear and free translations and linguistic analysis.

3973. Moisés, Rosalio, Jane Holden Kelley, and William Curry Holden. *The Tall Candle. The Personal Chronicle of a Yaqui Indian.* Lincoln: Univ. of Nebraska Press, 1971.

Life history of Moisés (1896–1969) includes data on ceremonialism. With introductory comments on cultural background and collecting situation.

3974. Montell, G. "Yaqui Dances." *En,* 3 (1938), 145–66.

Survey of the group's ceremonialism.

3975. Painter, Muriel Thayer, Refugio Savala, and Ignacio Alvarez, eds. "A Yaqui Easter Sermon." *UAB—Social Sciences,* 26, No. 6 (October 1955), 5–89.

Text with free and interlinear translations recorded in 1941. Includes linguistic analysis and thorough description of performance context.

3976. Savala, Refugio. "Two Yaqui Legends." *ArQ,* 1, No. 1 (1945), 21–27.

Rewritten myth texts. A note on the author, a Yaqui, is provided by Harry T. Getty.

3977. Shutler, Mary Elizabeth. "Disease and Curing in a Yaqui Community," in 160, pp. 169–237.

Survey of the Yaqui medical system treats role of prayer in curing procedure.

3978. Spicer, Edward H. *Pascua. A Yaqui Village in Arizona.* Chicago: Univ. of Chicago Press, 1940.

Ethnography includes data on ceremonialism.

3979. ———. "Social Structure and Cultural Process in Yaqui Religious Acculturation." *AA,* 60 (1958), 433–41.

Shows how Christianity has fused with traditional Yaqui religious system to produce distinctive myths and symbols.

3980. ———. "The Yaqui Indians of Arizona." *Ki,* 5, No. 6 (March 1940), 21–24.

Culture survey includes data on religion and ceremonialism.

3981. Wilder, Carleton Stafford. "The Yaqui Deer Dance: A Study in Cultural Change." *BAEB* No. 186 (*AP* No. 66), 1963.

Describes the ceremony as observed in 1940. Includes twenty song texts with interlinear and free translations.

See also 3397, 3990.

M. Yavapai

3982. Freire-Marreco, Barbara. "The 'Dreamers' of the Mohave-Apache Tribe." *F,* 23 (1912), 172–74.

Abstract of a presentation dealing with shamans and their ceremonialism.

3983. Gifford, E. W. "Northeastern and Western Yavapai." *UCPAAE,* 34, No. 4 (1936), 247–354.

Ethnography based on fieldwork done in 1932 contains data on ceremonialism and shamanism. With thirteen unannotated legend texts. Appendix treats the Ghost Dance.

3984. ———. "Northeastern and Western Yavapai Myths." *JAF,* 46 (1933), 347–415.

Twenty-nine texts collected in 1932. Introduction comments on mythological system. With some comparative annotation.

3985. ———. "The Southeastern Yavapai." *UCPAAE,* 29, No. 3 (1932), 177–252.

Ethnography based on fieldwork done in 1929–1930. Includes data on shamanism and ceremonialism. With four unannotated myth texts.

3986. Morris, C. Patrick. "Bears, Juniper Trees, and Deer, the Metaphors of a Domestic Life. An Analysis of a Yavapai Variant of the Bear Maiden Story." *JAR,* 32 (1976), 246–54.

Study of three episodes in a monster-slayer myth reveals that elements are organized into metaphoric reflections of aspects of Yavapai domesticity.

See also 2681, 3954, 3995.

N. Yuma

3987. Castetter, Edward F., and Willis H. Bell. *Yuman Indian Agriculture. Primitive Subsistence on the Lower Colorado and Gila Rivers.* Albuquerque: Univ. of New Mexico Press, 1951.

Contains data on agricultural rituals and singing.

3988. Curtis, Natalie. "Creation Myth of the Cochans (Yuma Indians)." *Cr,* 16, No. 5 (August 1909), 559–67.

Unannotated text with brief comment on cultural background.

3989. Deane, Reubena. "The Legend of Singing Water." *OM*, n. s. 77 (1921), 24–28.

Rewritten legend text. No commentary or annotation.

3990. Densmore, Frances. *Yuman and Yaqui Music.* *BAEB* No. 110 (1932).

Song texts (130—translated words and music), each with musicological analysis. Introduction provides cultural background and makes musicological comparisons with material from other NA cultures. Data collected in 1922 from Yuma, Yaqui, Cocopa, Mohave, and Mayo singers.

3991. Forbes, Jack D. *Warriors of the Colorado. The Yumas of the Quechan Nation and Their Neighbors.* Norman: Univ. of Oklahoma Press, 1965.

Historical and cultural survey includes data on ceremonialism and mythology.

3992. Forde, C. Daryll. "Ethnography of the Yuma Indians." *UCPAAE*, 28, No. 4 (1931), 83–278.

Based on fieldwork done in 1928–1929. Includes data on prayer, ceremonialism, and singing. With some texts of ritual origin myths.

3993. Gifford, Edward Winslow. "Yuma Dreams and Omens." *JAF*, 39 (1926), 58–69.

Texts of several dreams with a discussion of effects of traditional culture, including folklore, on their content and their role in the culture.

3994. Harrington, John Peabody. "A Yuma Account of Origins." *JAF*, 21 (1908), 324–48.

Text of creation myth with some explanatory notes. Introduction treats historical and cultural backgrounds and the informant.

3995. Herzog, George. "The Yuman Musical Style." *JAF*, 41 (1928), 183–231.

Thirty-nine song texts (words and music) collected in 1927 from Yuma, Mohave, Diegueño, Maricopa, and Yavapai singers. Extensive discussion of song structure, melodic contour, and singing style.

3996. Putnam, G. R. "A Yuma Cremation." *AA*, o. s. 8 (1895), 264–67.

Description of mortuary rites observed in 1892.

3997. "Yuma Puberty Ceremony." *M*, 26 (1952), 69–70.

Ritual as reported by Juan Bautista de Anza.

See also 2681, 2720, 2758, 3333.

VII GREAT BASIN

Community-by-community survey of Paiute and Shoshoni political entities in the Great Basin. Includes data on ceremonial occasions in each community.

See also 172, 721, 1988, 4040a, 4126, 4138, 4184, 4986.

A. General Works

3998. Du Bois, Cora. "The 1870 Ghost Dance." *UC-PAR*, 3, No. 1 (1939), 1–151.
Historical treatment of the messianic movement among Great Basin and California groups. Includes legend texts and data on ceremonialism.

3999. Fife, Austin E. "A Utah Parallel of Logan's Speech." *JAF*, 66 (1953), 134.
Reports a speech delivered by a NA leader which ended the Black Hawk War of 1873.

4000. Forbes, Jack D., ed. *Nevada Indians Speak*. Reno: Univ. of Nevada Press, 1967.
Collection of documents relating the NA viewpoint on NA-EA relations in the Great Basin. Some material comes from life histories, but most is from newspapers and government documents.

4001. Fowler, Don D., and Catherine S. Fowler, eds. *Anthropology of the Numa: John Wesley Powell's Manuscripts on the Numic Peoples of Western North America, 1868–1880. SmCA* No. 14 (1971).
Edited text of Powell's mss. from fieldwork among various Great Basin groups. Includes summaries and texts of myths, song texts, and descriptions of ceremonials. Introduction treats Powell's research methods and interests.

4002. Greenway, John. "The Ghost Dance." *AW*, 6, No. 4 (July 1969), 42–47.
Describes the Ghost Dance movement in the Great Basin and Plains. With text of a letter recounting a visit to Wovoka in 1891 and excerpts from an interview with George Bird Grinnell which appeared in the *New York Tribune* in 1890.

4003. Lowie, Robert H. "Notes on Shoshonean Ethnography." *APAMNH*, 20, Part 3 (1924), 187–314.
Data on Shoshonean-speaking groups in the Great Basin include information on religion and ceremonialism.

4004. ———. "Shoshonean Tales." *JAF*, 37 (1924), 1–242.
Fifty-seven Ute myth, legend, and folktale texts; fifty-four Paiute myths; and twenty-three Paviotso myths and legends. Collected in 1912, 1914, and 1915. No commentary or annotation.

4005. Park, Willard Z. "Culture Succession in the Great Basin," in 161, pp. 180–88.
Considers the distribution through time and space of ceremonial dances among various Great Basin groups.

4006. Steward, Julian H. *Basin-Plateau Aboriginal Sociopolitical Groups. BAEB* No. 120 (1938).

B. Gosiute

4007. Hayes, Alden. "Peyote Cult on the Goshiute Reservation at Deep Creek, Utah." *NMA*, 4, No. 2 (April–June 1940), 34–36.
Note on status of the NA Church.

4008. Malouf, Carling. "Gosiute Peyotism." *AA*, 44 (1942), 93–103.
Describes two peyote cults extant among the Gosiute in the 1930s: The Tipi Way and The Sioux Way. The former evinces Christian influences.

4009. ———, and Elmer R. Smith. "Some Gosiute Mythological Characters and Concepts." *UHR*, 1 (1942), 369–77.
Surveys tribal geographical and historical conceptions as manifested in myths and legends.

C. Mono

4010. Chalfant, William A. "Medicine Men of the Eastern Mono." *M*, 5 (1931), 50–54.
Survey of shamanism and its ceremonials.

4011. Gifford, E. W. "The Northfork Mono." *UCPAAE*, 31, No. 2 (1932), 15–65.
Ethnography includes data on ceremonialism and shamanism.

4012. ———. "Western Mono Myths." *JAF*, 36 (1923), 302–67.
Thirty-four myth and folktale texts collected in 1918. Includes some general comparative commentary.

4013. Townsend, George Elliot. "Indian Mythology of Yosemite Valley." *OM*, n. s. 41 (June 1903), 454–59.
Survey of Mono myths and legends localized in Yosemite.

See also 4447–4451.

D. Paiute

4014. Bailey, Paul. *Wovoka the Indian Messiah*. Los Angeles: Westernlore, 1957.
Biography of the prophet of the Ghost Dance includes second-hand descriptions of Ghost Dance rituals and account of spread of the movement to the Plains.

4015. Brooks, Cecil R., William M. Clements, Jo Ann Kantner, and Genevieve Y. Poirier. *A Land Use History of Coso Hot Springs, Inyo County, California.* China Lake, Cal.: Naval Weapons Center, 1979 (Administrative Publication No. 200).

Assessment of NA claims that a mineral springs on a weapons proving grounds has sacred significance involves analysis of the myths and legends of the Owens Valley Paiute.

4016. Bruce, Irma Irene. "A Legend of Pyramid Lake." *CW,* 154 (February 1942), 597–98.

Rewritten text. No commentary or annotation.

4017. Kelly, Isabel T. "The Ethnography of the Surprise Valley Paiute." *UCPAAE,* 31, No. 3 (1932), 67–210.

Based on fieldwork done in 1930. Contains data on shamanism, concepts of the soul, and ceremonialism.

4018. ———. "Northern Paiute Tales." *JAF,* 51 (1938), 363–438.

Thirty-eight narrative texts collected in 1930. Includes information on informants.

4019. ———. "Southern Paiute Ethnography." *APUU,* 69 (1964), 1–194.

Based on fieldwork done in 1932. Includes data on ceremonialism, supernaturalism, and storytelling.

4020. ———. "Southern Paiute Shamanism." *UCPAR,* 2, No. 4 (1939), 151–67.

Description of ceremonials with legend and personal narrative texts.

4021. Marsden, W. L. "The Northern Paiute Language of Oregon." *UCPAAE,* 20 (1923), 175–91.

Linguistic survey includes five myth texts with literal translations. No commentary or annotation.

4022. Martin, Al H. "The Will of the Lake Spirit. An Indian Legend of the High Sierras." *OM,* n. s. 57 (February 1911), 167–68.

Unannotated myth text. No commentary.

4023. Meighan, Clement W. "More on Folk Traditions." *JAF,* 73 (1960), 59–60.

Adds evidence to the case developed by him and Pendergast (4028) that Paiute oral traditions concerning prehistory may have some historical validity.

4024. Natches, Gilbert. "Northern Paiute Verbs." *UCPAAE,* 20 (1923), 245–59.

Linguistic analysis includes three myths, three songs, and one personal experience narrative. With literal translations. Collected in 1914.

4025. Olofson, Harold. "Northern Paiute Shamanism Revisited." *A,* 74 (1979), 11–24.

Survey of shamanistic practices includes acquisition of power, ritual structure, and impact of Christianity and peyotism.

4026. Palmer, William R. *Pahute Indian Legends.* Salt Lake City: Deseret, 1946.

Rewritten texts of twenty-five myths. No annotations.

4027. ———. *Why the North Star Stands Still and Other Indian Legends.* Englewood Cliffs, N.J.: Prentice-Hall, 1957.

Rewritten myth texts. No commentary or annotation.

4028. Pendergast, David M., and Clement W. Meighan. "Folk Traditions as Historical Fact: A Paiute Example." *JAF,* 72 (1959), 128–33.

Analyzes verbal traditions about prehistoric inhabitants of Paiute territory in southern Utah.

4029. Phister, Nat. P. "The Indian Messiah." *AA,* o. s. 4 (1891), 105–8.

Description of Wovoka and his successor.

4030. Raglan, Lord. "Folk Traditions as Historical Fact." *JAF,* 73 (1960), 58–59.

Critical comment on 4028.

4031. Roberts, Bertram L. "Descendants of the Numu." *M,* 39 (1965), 13–22, 66–76.

Ethnographic sketch of Owens Valley Paiute based on fieldwork done in 1963. With data on storytelling.

4032. Rush, Emmy Matt. "Legenda [sic] of the Paiutes of the Owens River Valley in California." *EP,* 28 (1930), 72–87.

Six rewritten myth and legend texts with some context description. No annotation.

4033. Sapir, Edward. "Song Recitative in Paiute Mythology." *JAF,* 23 (1910), 455–72.

Ten song texts (words and music) which occur in Paiute myths. Treats place of songs in narrative development. With some musicological analysis.

4034. Scott, Lalla. *Karnee. A. Paiute Narrative.* Reno: Univ. of Nevada Press, 1966.

Biography based on oral accounts of subject's daughter, related in 1936. With some data on storytelling. Extensive notes and commentary by Charles R. Craig.

4035. Steward, Julian H. "Ethnography of the Owens Valley Paiute." *UCPAAE,* 33, No. 3 (1933), 233–350.

Based on fieldwork done in 1927, 1928, and 1931. Includes data on ceremonialism and shamanism. With eighteen song texts (words and music) and excerpts from myths.

4036. ———. "Myths of the Owens Valley Paiute." *UCPAAE,* 34, No. 5 (1936), 355–440.

Forty-seven myth texts and eleven song texts (words and music) collected in 1927 and 1928. General introduction on literary aspects of mythology and some explanatory notes.

4037. ———. "Two Paiute Autobiographies." *UCPAAE,* 33, No. 5 (1934), 423–38.

Life histories collected in Owens Valley in 1927 and 1928. With extensive explanatory notes.

4038. Stewart, Omer C. "Contemporary Document on Wovoka (Jack Wilson) Prophet of the Ghost Dance in 1890." *Eh,* 24 (1977), 219–22.

Reproduces report of Inspector L. A. Dovington from the Nevada Indian Agency which briefly characterizes Wovoka.

4039. Trejo, Judy. "Coyote Tales: A Paiute Commentary." *JAF,* 87 (1974), 66–71.

Four Coyote stories with description of storytelling situation and an interpretation of their meaning. Also published in *IH,* 10, No. 1 (Winter 1977), 27–30 (shorter version) and Jan Harold Brunvand, ed., *Readings in American Folklore* (New York: Norton, 1979), pp. 192–98.

See also 813, 2016, 2045, 2053, 2712, 2790, 3308, 4004, 4006, 4042, 4067, 4085, 4097, 4114, 4179.

E. Paviotso

4040. Park, Willard Z. "Paviotso Shamanism." *AA,* 36 (1934), 98–113.

Survey of shamanistic beliefs and practices with personal narrative and anecdote texts. Based on fieldwork done in 1933.

4040a. ———. *Shamanism in Western North America. A Study in Cultural Relationships.* Evanston: Northwestern Univ. Press, 1938.

Describes myths and rituals associated with Paviotso shamanism and relates the material to that of other Great Basin and Plateau groups.

See also 4004.

F. Shoshoni

4041. Allen, W. A. *The Sheep Eaters.* New York: Shakespeare Press, 1913.

Investigation of an extinct NA group, thought to be related to Shoshoni and Crow. Includes several legends narrated by a 115-year-old woman, the group's last member.

4042. Austin, Mary. "Medicine Songs Transcribed from the Indian Originals." *Ev,* 31 (September 1914), 413–15.

Words of two songs (Shoshoni and Paiute). No commentary or annotation.

4043. Boyd, Doug. *Rolling Thunder. A Personal Exploration into the Secret Healing Powers of an American Indian Medicine Man.* New York: Random House, 1974.

Record of an attempt to understand NA shamanism. Contains song texts, ceremonial descriptions, comparisons with oriental traditions, and data on peyotism. Rolling Thunder characterized as Shoshoni and Cherokee.

4044. Brackett, Albert G. "The Shoshonis, or Snake Indians, Their Religion, Superstitions, and Manners." *ARSI for 1879,* pp. 328–33.

Survey of culture includes descriptions of storytelling and religious attitudes.

4045. Dorn, Edward, and Leroy Lucas. *The Shoshoneans. The People of the Basin-Plateau.* New York: William Morrow, 1966.

Photograph album. Accompanying text includes information on ceremonials such as the Sun Dance and a prayer text.

4046. Findley, Palmer. "The Sun Dance as Celebrated by the Shoshone Indians." *Hy,* 5 (May 1927), 236–37.

Ceremonial description.

4047. Heady, Eleanor B. *Sage Smoke. Tales of the Shoshoni-Bannock Indians.* Chicago: Follett, 1973.

Twenty myth and folktale texts. No annotation. General comments on cultural background. May be for children.

4048. Hebard, Grace Raymond. *Sacajawea. A Guide and Interpreter of the Lewis and Clark Expedition, with an Account of the Travels of Toussaint Charbonneau, and of Jean Baptiste, the Expedition Papoose.* Glendale, Cal.: Arthur H. Clark, 1957.

Biographical and historical work. Appendix includes texts of oral history accounts by several Shoshoni informants, mostly related in the 1920s.

4049. ———. *Washakie. An Account of Indian Resistance of the Covered Wagon and Union Pacific Railroad Invasions of Their Territory.* Cleveland: Arthur H. Clark, 1930.

Biography includes an appendix on Shoshoni culture which describes ceremonials such as the Sun Dance and summarizes myths and legends.

4050. Hoebel, E. Adamson. "The Sun Dance of the Hekandika Shoshone." *AA,* 37 (1935), 570–81.

Describes the ritual as it occurred in 1934. Includes data on prayers and songs.

4051. Holthoff, Cyd McMullen. "A Preliminary Survey: Northeastern Nevada Folklore." *SWF,* 3, No. 2 (Spring 1979), 1–17.

Includes texts of five Shoshoni stories: a family legend and four Coyote tales.

4052. Hultkrantz, Åke. "The Concept of the Soul Held by the Wind River Shoshone." *En,* 16 (1951), 18–44.

Analyzes concepts of the soul with attention to cross-cultural comparisons.

4053. ———. "An Ideological Dichotomy: Myths and Folk Beliefs Among the Shoshoni Indians of Wyoming." *HR,* 11, No. 4 (May 1972), 339–53.

Argues that Shoshoni myths have little relationship to other aspects of religious system.

4054. ———. "The Masters of the Animals Among the Wind River Shoshoni." *En,* 26 (1961), 198–218.

Treats individuals with supernatural control of animals. Some attention to myths and ceremonials.

4055. ———. "The Origin of Death Myth as Found Among the Wind River Shoshoni Indians." *En,* 20 (1955), 127–36.

Shows how two versions of the origin of death relate to group's religious system.

4056. ———. "Religious Aspects of the Wind River Shoshoni Folk Literature," in 102, pp. 552–69.

Survey of the religious significance of various types of oral narratives.

4057. Jorgensen, Joseph G. *The Sun Dance Religion.* Chicago: Univ. of Chicago Press, 1972.

Historical and descriptive treatment of the ceremonial among the Shoshoni. With some comparison to Ute practices.

4058. Lowie, Robert H. "The Northern Shoshone." *APAMNH,* 2 (1909), 165–306.

Ethnography based on fieldwork done in 1906 contains data on religious attitudes and cosmology. Contains thirty-nine translated myth and legend texts with comparative notes.

4059. Miller, Wick R. "Newe Natekwinappeh: Shoshoni Stories and Dictionary." *APUU,* 94 (June 1972), 1–172.

Fourteen legend and folktale texts with free translations, explanatory notes, and linguistic analysis. Collected in 1960s.

4060. Randle, Martha Champion. "A Shoshone Hand Game Gambling Song." *JAF,* 66 (1953), 155–59.

Description of a game with tune of a song performed in association with it.

4061. Ross, Adeline R. "Indian Life in Wyoming." *SeR,* 19 (1911), 61–70.

Describes life among Shoshoni and Arapaho on the Wind River Reservation. With attention to ceremonialism, dancing, and singing.

4062. Shimkin, D. B. "Childhood and Development Among the Wind River Shoshone." *UCPAR,* 5, No. 5 (1947), 289–326.

Includes some data on ceremonialism and some life history texts.

4063. ———. "Shoshone, I: Linguistic Sketch and Text." *IJAL*, 15 (1949), 175–88.

Mythological narrative with free and analytical translations. Preceded by linguistic survey.

4064. ———. "Wind River Shoshone Literary Forms: An Introduction." *JWAS*, 37 (1947), 329–52.

Characterizes three finest forms of verbal expression: myth, song, prayer. Describes performance style for each.

4065. ———. "The Wind River Shoshone Sun Dance." *BAEB* No. 151 (*AP* No. 41), 1953.

Compares observation of the ritual in 1937 with accounts from 1800s. Includes song texts (with interlinear translations) and a reminiscence of the 1908 ritual. Thorough description of ceremonial procedure.

4066. St. Clair, H. H. "Shoshone and Comanche Tales." Ed. Robert H. Lowie. *JAF*, 22 (1909), 265–82.

Ten Shoshoni and eight Comanche myths and folktales. With some comparative notes and commentary on content.

4067. Steward, Julian H. "Some Western Shoshoni Myths." *BAEB* No. 136 (*AP* No. 31), 1943.

Thirty-five texts collected from Shoshoni and Paiute storytellers in 1935. Presented only in English.

4068. Trenholm, Virginia Cole, and Maurine Carley. *The Shoshonis, Sentinels of the Rockies.* Norman: Univ. of Oklahoma Press, 1964.

Historical account begins with some data on mythology and ceremonialism.

4069. Voget, Fred W. "Current Trends in the Wind River Shoshone Sun Dance." *BAEB* No. 151 (*AP* No. 42), 1953.

Treats modern developments in the ritual, including role of songs and prayers.

4070. ———. "A Shoshone Innovator." *AA*, 52 (1950), 53–63.

Treats role of John Truhujo in the spread of the Sun Dance to the Crow in the 1940s. Used to develop general concepts of acculturation.

See also 2077, 2078, 2316, 4006.

G. Ute

4071. Barber, Edwin A. "Gaming Among the Utah Indians." *AmN*, 11 (June 1877), 351–53.

Description of games. With a song text (words and music).

4072. Casey, Pearle R. "Two Tales of the Utes." *SWL*, 3 (1937), 7–10.

Unannotated myth texts. No commentary.

4073. Densmore, Frances. *Northern Ute Music. BAEB* No. 75 (1922).

Song texts (110—music and occasional words) and four texts of story songs, each with contextual and musicological commentary. General ethnographic survey introduces the songs. Collected in 1914 and 1916.

4074. Goss, James A. "Ute Language, Kin, Myth, and Nature: A Demonstration of a Multi-Dimensional Folk Taxonomy." *AnL*, 9, No. 9 (December 1967), 1–11.

Examines the correlation between kinship terms and names of spiritual animals in myths.

4075. Hartzell, Grace L. "Sidelights on the Ute." *M*, 37 (1963), 15–17.

Descriptions of ceremonials observed in 1910–1914. Including the Sun Dance.

4076. Ives, Ronald L. "Folklore of Eastern Middle Park, Colorado." *JAF*, 54 (1941), 24–43.

Presents miscellany of folklore collected in an isolated section of the state. Some of the material seems to be of Ute origin.

4077. Jones, J. A. "The Sun Dance of the Northern Ute." *BAEB* No. 157 (*AP* No. 47), 1955.

Interprets the ceremonial as a nativistic movement. With attention to songs and prayers.

4078. Kroeber, A. L. "Notes on the Ute Language." *AA*, 10 (1908), 74–87.

Linguistic survey includes the text of a narrative with interlinear translations. Collected in 1901.

4079. ———. "Ute Tales." *JAF*, 14 (1901), 252–85.

Twelve unannotated myth and folktale texts collected in 1900. With comments on affinities of material with other NA narrative traditions.

4080. Mason, J. Alden. "Myths of the Uintah Utes." *JAF*, 23 (1910), 299–363.

Thirty myth texts collected in 1909. With some comparative notes and content commentary.

4081. Opler, Marvin K. "The Character and History of the Southern Ute Peyote Rite." *AA*, 42 (1940), 463–78.

Treats how and why peyotism was adopted by the Colorado Utes. With thorough ritual description. Omer C. Stewart responded in *AA*, 43 (1941), 303–8; Opler added data in *AA*, 44 (1942), 151–59.

4082. ———. "A Colorado Ute Indian Bear Dance." *SWL*, 7 (September 1941), 21–30.

Ceremonial description. With text of ritual origin myth.

4083. ———. "The Integration of the Sun Dance in Ute Religion." *AA*, 43 (1941), 550–72.

Ritual description with text of ritual origin myth and anecdotes about its efficacy. With attention to singing and chanting.

4084. ———. "The Southern Ute Dog-Dance and Its Reported Transmission to Taos." *NMA*, 3, No. 5 (September–December 1937), 66–72.

Ritual description with history of its development.

4085. ———. "The Ute and Paiute Indians of the Great Basin Southern Rim," in 134, pp. 257–88.

Ethnological and historical survey includes data on narrative traditions, supernaturalism, cosmology, and ceremonialism.

4086. Parkhill, Forbes. *The Last of the Indian Wars.* NP: Crowell-Collier, 1961.

Account of Ute War of 1915 includes description of the Bear Dance and two myth texts.

4087. Powell, John Wesley. "Sketch of the Mythology of the North American Indians." *ARBAE*, 1 (1879–1880), 17–56.

Conceives of mythology as a stage in philosophy. Treats this primitive thought pattern in reference to Ute culture. With four Ute texts.

4088. Reagan, Albert B. "Some Games by the Northern Utes." *NWS*, 8 (March 1934), 12–16.

Describes three games. With some attention to singing.

4089. Reed, Verner Z. "The Southern Ute Indians." *Cal*, 4, No. 4 (September 1893), 488–505.

Culture survey includes data on religion, shamanism, and ceremonialism.

4090. ——. "The Ute Bear Dances." *AA,* o. s. 9 (1896), 237–44.

Description of the ritual as observed in 1893.

4091. Smith, Anne M. *Ethnography of the Northern Utes.* Santa Fe: Museum of New Mexico Press, 1974 (Anthropological Paper No. 17).

Based on fieldwork done in 1936–1937. Contains data on ceremonialism (including peyotism and the Sun Dance), shamanism, and mythology.

4092. Steward, Julian H. "A Uintah Ute Bear Dance, March, 1931." *AA,* 34 (1932), 263–73.

Ritual description with text of ritual origin myth.

4093. Tufford, Wil V. "The Saguache Legend." *TT,* 4 (July 1902), 201–2.

Retelling of a historical legend.

4094. ——. "The Utes' Legend of the Flood." *TT,* 4 (May 1902), 127–29.

Myth text.

4095. "Ute Legend of Creation, The." *EP,* 14 (1923), 104–5.

Unannotated myth text. No commentary.

See also 2078, 2797, 2961, 4004, 4057.

H. Washo

4096. Barrett, Samuel Alfred. *The Washo Indians. MPMB,* 2, No. 1 (1917).

Ethnography includes data on ceremonialism.

4097. Brandeis, Erich. "Indian Legends for Profit." *OM,* n. s. 71 (February 1918), 115–19.

Describes Washo and Paiute storytellers who entertain tourists at Lake Tahoe. With two myth texts.

4098. Dangberg, Grace. *Washo Tales.* Carson City: Nevada State Museum, 1968.

Pamphlet includes three myth texts with extensive commentary on cultural background.

4099. ——. "Washo Texts." *UCPAAE,* 22, No. 3 (1927), 391–443.

Six myth texts collected in 1919–1920. With literal translations. No commentary or annotation.

4100. Downs, James F. *The Two Worlds of the Washo. An Indian Tribe of California and Nevada.* New York: Holt, Rinehart and Winston, 1966.

Ethnography includes data on ceremonialism and mythology.

4101. Freed, Stanley A., and Ruth S. Freed. "A Configuration of Aboriginal Washo Culture," in 100, pp. 41–56.

Sees the prevalence of fear among the group as related to ghost beliefs.

4102. ——. "The Persistence of Aboriginal Ceremonies Among the Washo Indians," in 100, pp. 25–40.

Describes several ceremonials. Theorizes that those requiring no specialists are most likely to survive.

4103. Handelman, Don. "Aspects of the Moral Compact of a Washo Shaman." *AnQ,* 45 (1972), 84–101.

Examines the moral ambiguity attributed to shamans in folktales and effects of shamans' relations with others.

4104. ——. "The Development of a Washo Shaman." *Eth,* 6 (1967), 444–64.

Life history of Henry Rupert, last shaman among the Washo in eastern California and western Nevada. Text includes some verbatim material, but is heavily edited. Includes descriptions of ceremonials.

4105. ——. "Transcultural Shamanic Healing: A Washo Example." *En,* 32 (1967), 149–67.

Examines healing procedures used by a Washo shaman when treating EAs and non-Washo NAs.

4106. Hickson, Jane Green. *Dat So La Lee. Queen of the Washo Basket Makers.* Carson City: Nevada State Museum, 1967.

Biography of a basketmaker. Primary concern is with craft, but includes summary of a myth.

4107. James, George Wharton. *The Lake of the Sky, Lake Tahoe, in the High Sierras of California and Nevada. Its History, Indians, Discovery by Fremont, Legendary Lore, Various Namings, Physical Characteristics, Glacial Phenomena, Geology, Single Outlet, Automobile Routes, Historic Towns, Early Mining Excitements, Steamer Ride, Mineral Springs, Mountain and Lake Resorts, Trail and Camping Out Trips, Summer Residences, Fishing, Hunting, Flowers, Birds, Animals, Trees and Chapparal, with a Full Account of the Tahoe National Forest, the Public Use of the Water of Lake Tahoe and Much Other Interesting Matter.* Pasadena, Cal.: by the Author, 1915.

Includes six myth and legend texts.

4108. Kroeber, A. L. "The Washo Language of East Central California and Nevada." *UCPAAE,* 4 (1906–1907), 252–317.

Linguistic survey includes texts of personal narratives with interlinear translations and linguistic notes.

4109. Lowie, Robert H. "Ethnographic Notes on the Washo." *UCPAAE,* 36, No. 5 (1939), 301–52.

Based on fieldwork done in 1926. Includes data on ceremonialism and shamanism and nineteen myth texts and fragments. With explanatory notes.

4110. ——. "Washo Texts." *AnL,* 5, No. 7 (October 1963), 1–30.

Myths, orations, and descriptions of customs presented with interlinear translations. Collected in 1926. No commentary or annotation.

4111. Merriam, Alan P., and Warren L. d'Azevedo. "Washo Peyote Songs." *AA,* 59 (1957), 615–41.

Analysis of songs used in peyote rituals in terms of types, origin, content, structure, and style. Includes five music texts and comparison with peyote music from other NA groups.

4112. Price, John A. "Some Aspects of Washo Life Cycle," in 100, pp. 96–114.

Describes several life crises and accompanying ceremonials. Includes a prayer text.

4113. Rich, George W. "New Tales from Old: Two Washoe Examples." *WF,* 32 (1973), 274–76.

Illustrates the fragmentation of long oral narratives by citing Washo texts which are episodes from longer creation myths.

4114. Stewart, Omer C. "Washo-Northern Paiute Peyotism. A Study in Acculturation." *UCPAAE,* 40, No. 3 (1944), 63–142.

Based on fieldwork done in 1937–1938. Historical and ethnographic treatment of peyotism in the two groups. With thorough descriptions of ritual procedures.

See also 2276.

VIII CALIFORNIA

A. General Works

4115. Applegate, Richard B. *?Atishwin: The Dream Helper in South-Central California.* Socorro, N. M.: Ballena Press, 1978 (Anthropology Paper No. 13).
Cross-cultural survey of power concept derived from dreams. With references to and texts of myths and songs from various California groups.

4116. ———. "Native California Concepts of the Afterlife," in 86, pp. 105–19.
Treats mythological and religious ideas concerning the fate of the soul.

4117. Bancroft, Hubert Howe. *The Works of Hubert Howe Bancroft. Vol. I. The Native Races: Wild Tribes.* San Francisco: History, 1886.
Ethnographic survey of California, Northwest Coast, and some Arctic groups includes data on ceremonialism and religious concepts.

4118. ———. *The Works of Hubert Howe Bancroft. Vol. III. The Native Races: Myths and Languages.* San Francisco: History, 1886.
Includes rewritten myths, descriptions of ceremonials, and data on belief systems of groups in California, the Northwest Coast, and the Southwest.

4119. Bean, Lowell John. "California Indian Shamanism and Folk Curing," in 123, pp. 109–23.
Description of aspects of shamanism among various California groups.

4120. Bowles, E. E. "The Legend of La Piedra Pintada. California's Mysterious Painted Rock." *T,* 34 (February 1920), 42.
Account of sources of pictographs near San Luis Obispo. From a NA of unspecified group.

4121. Brooks, Joseph C. "The Caverns of Castle Rock. An Indian Legend of Santa Clara Valley." *OM,* n. s. 54 (September 1909), 289–95.
Retelling of a myth. No commentary.

4122. Caballeria, Rev. Father Juan. *History of San Bernardino Valley from the Padres to the Pioneers, 1810–1851.* San Bernardino, Cal.: Times-Index, 1902.
Includes several chapters on the "Diggers." With data on religion and ceremonialism.

4123. Chandler, Katherine. *In the Reign of Coyote. Folklore from the Pacific Coast.* Boston: Ginn, 1905.
Twenty-seven rewritten myths and folktales from various California and Northwest Coast groups. No commentary or annotation. May be for children.

4124. Chever, Edward F. "The Indians of California." *AmN,* 4 (May 1870), 129–48.

Cultural survey of "Diggers" includes data on religion and theology.

4125. Dangel, R. "Bears and Fawns." *JAF,* 42 (1929), 307–8.
Historic-geographic note on a narrative collected from various California groups.

4126. Demetracopoulou, D. "The Loon Woman Myth: A Study in Synthesis." *JAF,* 46, (1933), 101–28.
Examines how episodes cluster to form a coherent myth text, which is found among California and Great Basin groups. With one Wintun Text.

4127. Dixon, Roland B. "Some Shamans of Northern California." *JAF,* 17 (1904), 23–27.
Survey of ceremonial practices of shamans from various northern California groups.

4128. Fleming, Lizzie Park. "Legends of Mount Shasta." *OM,* n. s. 62 (August 1913), 132–36.
Two rewritten myth texts. No commentary.

4129. Forbes, Jack D. "Indian Horticulture West and Northwest of the Colorado River." *JW,* 2 (1963), 1–14.
Overview of agriculture of various groups with attention to the place of horticulture in their cosmogonies.

4130. Gayton, A. H. "Areal Affiliations of California Folktales." *AA,* 37 (1935), 582–99.
Shows how narrative traditions of California groups fall into three categories: North, Central, and South. Generalizes about narrative repertoires of each category.

4131. ———. "The Ghost Dance of 1870 in South-Central California." *UCPAAE,* 28, No. 3 (1930), 57–82.
Historical work on predecessor of more famous revitalization movement. Includes data on ceremonialism with song and myth texts.

4132. Gifford, Edward W., and Gwendolyn Harris Block. *Californian Indian Nights Entertainments. Stories of the Creation of the World, of Man, of Fire, of the Sun, of Thunder, etc., of Coyote, the Land of the Dead, the Sky Land, Monsters, Animal People, etc.* Glendale, Cal.: Arthur H. Clark, 1930.
Extensive collection of myths from various California groups. Adapted from scholarly collections. Introduction treats the supernatural bases for the material and the cultural backgrounds.

4133. Gill, Don. "The Coyote and the Sequential Occupants of the Los Angeles Basin." *AA,* 72 (1970), 821–26.
Focus is primarily on zoogeography, but includes some data on the role of Coyote in verbal art in southern California.

4134. Groff, William S., Jr. "California Indian Cannibal Tales." *M,* 34 (1960), 152–65.
Survey of cannibalism and cannibal types in the oral narratives of various California groups.

4135. Harrington, M. R. *Ancient Life Among the Southern California Indians. SWML* No. 26 (1955).
Reconstruction of lifeways includes descriptions of ceremonials and summary of creation myth.

4136. ———. "California Eagle Dance." *M,* 19 (1945), 5–6.
Survey of the ceremonial as performed by various southern California groups.

4137. Heizer, Robert F., ed. *California. Volume 8. Handbook of North American Indians.* Washington: Smithsonian Institution, 1978.

Contains chapters on tribal groups, many of which deal with folklore and its contexts. Also included are the following chapters of folklore interest: "Music and Musical Instruments" (William J. Wallace); "Natural Forces and Native World View" (Robert F. Heizer); "Mythology: Regional Patterns and History of Research" (Heizer); "Comparative Literature" (Wallace); and "Cults and Their Transformations" (Lowell John Bean and Sylvia Brakke Vane).

4138. ———. "Fishermen and Foragers of the West," in 167, pp. 203–52.

General survey of NA cultures in California, the Northwest Coast, the Great Basin, and Plateau includes song texts, references to mythology, and descriptions of ceremonials.

4139. ———. *The Indians of California. A Critical Bibliography.* Bloomington: Indiana Univ. Press, 1976.

Unannotated list of 193 books and articles. Introductory essay contains section on "World View."

4140. ———, Albert B. Elsasser, James C. Bard, Edward D. Castillo, and Karen M. Nissen. *A Bibliography of California Indians: Archaeology, Ethnography, Indian History.* New York: Garland, 1977.

Classified list of 3303 unannotated items. One section treats folklore and music.

4141. Holder, Charles Frederick. "The Early Californians." *Ch,* 9 (May 1889), 478–81.

Culture survey of "Mission Indians" includes data on ceremonialism.

4142. Johnson, Mary Elizabeth. *Indian Legends of the Cuyamaca Mountains.* NP: NP, 1914.

Pamphlet includes eleven myth texts from unspecified southern California groups. No commentary or annotation.

4143. Judson, Katharine Berry, ed. *Myths and Legends of California and the Old Southwest.* Chicago: A. C. McClurg, 1912.

Rewritten myth and legend texts identified by group.

4144. Kroeber, A. L. "The Anthropology of California." *S,* n. s. 27 (1908), 281–90.

Survey of cultures in area includes some data on mythology.

4145. ———. "Elements of Culture in Native California." *UCPAAE,* 13, No. 8 (1922), 259–328.

Ethnographic survey includes data on religion, ceremonialism, and the Ghost Dance.

4146. ———. "Games of the California Indians." *AA,* 22 (1920), 272–77.

Survey of games of dexterity and of chance among various California groups. With data on singing.

4147. ———. *Handbook of the Indians of California.* BAEB No. 78 (1925).

Arranged by tribal group. Each section contains data on religion and ceremonials. With occasional song and myth texts.

4148. ———. "Indian Myths of South Central California." *UCPAAE,* 4 (1906–1907), 169–250.

Forty-one myth texts with abstracts. With comparative notes. Material comes from Costanoan, Miwok, Yokuts, and Shoshonean-speaking groups.

4149. ———. "The Languages of the Coast of Califor-

nia North of San Francisco." *UCPAAE,* 9, No. 3 (1911), 273–435.

Contains myth and personal narrative texts from Miwok, Pomo, Yuki, Wiyot, Yurok, and Karok.

4150. ———. "A Mission Record of the California Indians from a Manuscript in the Bancroft Library." *UCPAAE,* 8, No. 1 (1908), 1–27.

Culture survey based on data collected through a questionnaire submitted to the missions in 1811. With data on singing, ceremonialism, and supernaturalism.

4151. ———. "The Religion of the Indians of California." *UCPAAE,* 4 (1906–1907), 321–56.

Survey treats such topics as shamanism, ceremonialism, and mythology. Emphasizes three culture area concept of California groups (North, Central, and South).

4152. ———. "A Southern California Ceremony." *JAF,* 21 (1908), 40.

Description of a ritual performed to cause earthquakes.

4153. ———. "Two Myths of the Mission Indians of California." *JAF,* 19 (1906), 309–21.

Texts and comparative discussion of mythology of several southern California groups.

4154. ———. "Types of Indian Culture in California." *UCPAAE,* 2 (1904–1907), 81–103.

Cross-cultural survey includes data on shamanism, ceremonialism, and mythology.

4155. ———, and E. W. Gifford. "World Renewal: A Cult System of Native Northwest California." *UCPAR,* 13, No. 1 (1949), 1–156.

Intertribal survey of cult system includes data on ceremonialism and prayers. With seventeen myth texts and fragments.

4156. Kroeber, Henriette Rothschild. "Told by the California Indians." *OM,* n. s. 51 (1908), 553–54.

Rewritten legend text with some general culture background.

4157. Kroeber, Theodora. *The Inland Whale.* Foreword by Oliver La Farge. Bloomington: Indiana Univ. Press, 1959.

Nine rewritten myth and folktale texts from various California groups. Includes explanatory notes and general comments on NA storytelling.

4158. ———. "A Note on a California Theme." *JAF,* 70 (1957), 72–74.

Shows how colors of the sunset figure in the verbal art and ceremonialism of several California groups: Yurok, Wintun, Modoc, Hupa.

4159. Loeb, E. M. "The Religious Organizations of North Central California and Tierra del Fuego." *AA,* 33 (1931), 517-56.

Compares religious systems of Fuegians with the Kuksu Cult among various California groups (Pomo, Kato, Yuki, Wailaki, Wappo, Miwok). Includes data on mythology.

4160. ———. "The Western Kuksu Cult." *UCPAAE,* 33, No. 1 (1932), 1–137.

Survey of the cult in various California groups (Pomo, Kato, Yuki, Wappo, Miwok, Wailaki) includes descriptions of ceremonials and creation myths. Based on fieldwork done in 1930.

4161. Lowie, Robert H. "The Cultural Connections of California and Plateau Shoshonean Tribes." *UCPAAE,* 20

(1923), 145–56.

Parallels include aspects of ceremonialism and mythology.

4162. Marrant, Doris E. "Variations on a Theme: Some Northern California Indian Horror Stories." *WF,* 29 (1970), 257–67.

Presentation of six categories of horror stories collected from various northern California groups.

4163. Merriam, C. Hart. "Totemism in California." *AA,* 10 (1908), 558–62.

Survey of individual, patriarchal, and matriarchal totems among various California groups. Includes a legend text.

4164. ———. "Transmigration in California." *JAF,* 22 (1909), 433–34.

Treats beliefs about transmigration of souls and their mythological basis among various California groups.

4165. Morris, C. Patrick. "Heart and Feces: Symbols of Mortality in the Dying God Myth," in 86, pp. 41–57.

Analysis of recurrent elements in a myth from several southern California groups.

4166. Pierce, Harry Willard. "The Legend of Lake Jonive." *OM,* n. s. 46 (August 1905), 145–49.

Rewritten myth text. No commentary.

4167. Potts, William John. "Creation Myth of the California Indians." *JAF,* 5 (1892), 73–74.

Myth text reprinted from *The Evening Wisconsin* for 27 August 1890.

4168. Powers, Stephen. "California Indian Characteristics." *OM,* o. s. 14 (1875), 297–309.

One trait is lack of belief in a high god. Illustrated by myths.

4169. ———. "The Northern California Indians." *OM,* o. s. 8 (1872), 325–33, 425–35, 530–39; 9 (1872), 155–64, 305–13, 498–507; 10 (1873), 322–33, 535–45; 11 (1873), 105–16; 12 (1874), 21–31, 412–24, 530–40; 13 (1874), 542–50.

Survey of tribal cultures includes a number of myth texts from various groups: Karok, Hupa, Yuki, Pomo, Yurok, Miwok, Modoc, Patwin, Wishram, Wintun, Yokuts.

4170. ———. *Tribes of California.* CNAE No. 3 (1877).

Survey of northern and central California groups with myth texts and descriptions of ceremonials.

4171. Ray, Verne F. "Far Western Indian Folklore." *JAF,* 60 (1947), 406–16.

Treats folklore study among California, Plateau, and Northwest Coast groups. Part of a report prepared by the AFS Committee on Research in Folklore.

4172. Roberts, Elizabeth Judson. *Indian Stories of the Southwest.* San Francisco: Harr Wagner, 1917.

Miscellany of myths, legends, and descriptions of customs collected from a woman from an unspecified southern California group.

4173. Roberts, Helen H. *Form in Primitive Music. An Analytical and Comparative Study of the Melodic Form of Some Ancient Southern California Indian Songs.* New York: Norton, 1933.

Texts (words and music) from Luiseño, Gabrielino, and Catalineno singers. Collected in 1926. With musicological analysis and explanatory notes.

4174. Romero, John Bruno. *The Botanical Lore of the California Indians with Side Lights on Historical Incidents in California.* New York: Vantage, 1954.

Primarily a herbal, but contains a legend text about a medicinal spring.

4175. Rust, Horatio N. "A Puberty Ceremony of the Mission Indians." *AA,* 8 (1906), 28–32.

Ceremonial description based on observation in 1889. Notes added by A. L. Kroeber.

4176. Shinn, G. Hazen. *Shoshonean Days. Recollections of a Residence of Five Years Among the Indians of Southern California 1885–1889.* Glendale, Cal.: Arthur H. Clark, 1941.

Contains some rewritten myth texts with fairly extensive comparative commentary. With some data on ceremonialism. Treats Cahuilla, Gabrielino, and Serrano.

4177. Strong, William Duncan. "Aboriginal Society in Southern California." *UCPAAE,* 26 (1929), 1–358.

Survey of social structure of Serrano, Cahuilla, Cupeno, and Luiseño. With some data on ceremonialism.

4178. "Superstitions of the Indians." *AAOJ,* 27 (1905), 132–36.

Describes sorcery and witchcraft among southern California groups. Reprinted from the *Chicago Inter-Ocean.*

4179. Voegelin, Erminie W. "Suicide in Northeastern California." *AA,* 39 (1937), 445–56.

Presents accounts of suicides from Wintun, Atsugewi, Achomawi, Paiute, Modoc, Klamath, Nisenan, Shasta, and Maidu.

4180. Walker, Edwin F. *Indians of Southern California.* SWML No. 10 (ND).

Culture survey includes some data on music and ceremonialism.

4181. Wallace, William J. "Listen to the Chief! Harangues of the California Indians." *M,* 52 (1978), 54–58.

Texts and analysis of daily exhortations delivered by leaders of various California groups.

4182. Waterman, Thomas T. "Analysis of the Mission Indian Creation Story." *AA,* 11 (1909), 41–55.

Compares creation myths collected from Luiseño, Cahuilla, Diegueño, and Mohave storytellers. Devises five categories for the myths.

4183. Weltfish, Gene. *The Origins of Art.* Indianapolis: Bobbs-Merrill, 1953.

Anthropological treatment of artistic activity includes material on how art, religion, and mythology interrelate among California and Southwest groups.

4184. Wherry, Joseph H. *Indian Masks and Myths of the West.* New York: Funk & Wagnalls, 1969.

Rewritten myths, depictions of masks, and descriptions of ceremonials from various groups in California, Southwest, Great Basin, Plateau, Northwest Coast, Sub-Arctic, and Arctic.

See also 172, 192, 609, 721, 2919, 3152, 3422, 3899, 3998, 4600, 4986, 5117.

B. Achomawi

4185. Curtin, Jeremiah. "Achomawi Myths." Ed. Roland B. Dixon. *JAF,* 22 (1909), 283–287.

Five unannotated myth texts. No commentary.

4186. Dixon, Roland B. "Achomawi and Atsugewi Tales." *JAF,* 21 (1908), 159–77.

Unannotated myth texts (ten Achomawi, two Atsugewi) collected in 1900 and 1903. No commentary.

4187. ———. "Notes on the Achomawi and Atsugewi Indians of Northern California." *AA,* 10 (1908), 208–20.

Ethnographic survey contains data on ceremonials at puberty, childbirth, and death and on shamanistic rituals.

4188. de Angulo, Jaime, and L. S. Freeland. "Two Achumawi Tales." *JAF,* 44 (1931), 125–36.

Two unannotated myth texts. No substantive commentary.

4189. Merriam, C. Hart, ed. *An-nik-a-del: The History of the Universe as Told by the Mo-des'-se Indians of California.* Boston: Stratford, 1928.

Twenty myth texts without comparative annotation. Extensive explanatory notes. With brief data on informant.

See also 4179, 4393.

C. Atsugewi

4190. de Angulo, Jaime. "The Background of the Religious Feeling in a Primitive Tribe." *AA,* 28 (1926), 352–60.

Places Atsugewi religion in cultural context. Includes data on mythology and the text of a shamanistic personal narrative.

4191. ———. "Indians in Overalls." *HuR,* 3 (1950), 327–77.

Account of fieldwork, especially linguistic, among the Atsugewi. Includes texts of narratives, songs, and orations.

4192. ———. *Indian Tales.* Foreword by Carl Carmer. New York: A. A. Wyn, 1953.

Anthology includes some original materials and some translated field texts. No annotation, but an appendix includes data from 4191.

4193. ———. "Seven Indian Tales." *HuR,* 5 (1952), 165–98.

Texts selected from 4192.

4194. Garth, Thomas R. "Atsugewi Ethnography." *UCPAR,* 14, No 2 (1953), 129–212.

Based on fieldwork done in 1938–1939. Includes data on religion, ceremonialism, and shamanism. With personal narrative texts and summary of creation myth.

4195. ———. "Emphasis on Industriousness Among the Atsugewi." *AA,* 47 (1945), 554–66.

Sees industriousness as dominant feature in group's ethos. Finds it expressed in supernaturalism and ceremonialism.

See also 4179, 4186, 4187.

D. Cahuilla

4196. Barrows, David Prescott. *The Ethno-Botany of the Coahuilla Indians of Southern California.* Chicago: Univ. of Chicago Press, 1900.

Survey of plant usage includes data on shamanism.

4197. ———. "Some Coahuia Songs and Dances." *LS,* 4, No. 1 (December 1895), 38–41.

Five song texts (words and music) with good descriptions of context.

4198. Heizer, Robert F. "An Early Cahuilla Ethnographic Sketch." *M,* 48 (1974), 14–21.

Account dated 31 January 1854 by C. C. Lovell includes data on religion, mythology, and ceremonialism.

4199. Hooper, Lucile. "The Cahuilla Indians." *UCPAAE,* 16, No. 6 (1920), 315–80.

Ethnographic survey based on fieldwork done in 1918. Includes summaries of myths and descriptions of supernaturalism and ceremonialism.

4200. James, George Wharton. *Through Ramona's Country.* Boston: Little, Brown, 1909.

Examination of sources of Helen Hunt Jackson's *Ramona* includes rewritten legends, ceremonial descriptions, and survey of folklore studies in California.

4201. Kroeber, A. L. "Ethnography of the Cahuilla Indians." *UCPAAE,* 8, No. 2 (1908), 29–68.

Ethnographic notes include sketchy data on mythology and supernaturalism.

4202. *Legends and History of the San Jacinto Mountains.* Long Beach, Cal.: K. P. Frederick, 1926.

Pamphlet includes rewritten myths and legends with some explanatory comments.

4203. Miles, Josephine. "A Double for King Midas." *CJ,* 23 (1927), 209–10.

Note on a Cahuilla folktale which resembles the King Midas story.

4204. Patencio, Chief Francisco (as told to Kate Collins). *Desert Hours with Chief Patencio.* Ed. Roy F. Hudson. [Palm Springs, Cal.]: Palm Springs Desert Museum, 1971.

Pamphlet includes miscellany of reminiscences and ceremonial data. Sequel to 4205.

4205. ———, and Margaret Boynton. *Stories and Legends of the Palm Springs Indians.* Los Angeles: Times-Mirror, 1943.

Fifteen unannotated myth and legend texts followed by Patencio's autobiography. Latter includes more legend texts and descriptions of ceremonials.

4206. Rush, Emmy Matt. "The Indians of the Coachella Valley Celebrate. Fiesta of the Choom-Ni." *EP,* 32 (1932), 1–19.

Thorough ritual description.

4207. Ryterband, Roman. "Agua Caliente and Their Music." *IH,* 12, No. 4 (1979), 2–9.

Musicological analysis of Cahuilla music with one text (words and music).

4208. Saubel, Catherine Siva. "Adventures of Konvaxmal." *IH,* 1, No. 4 (Fall 1968), 28.

Unannotated myth text. No commentary.

4209. Seiler, Hansjakob. *Cahuilla Texts with an Introduction.* Bloomington: Indiana Univ. Research Center for the Language Sciences, 1970 (Language Science Monograph No. 6).

Texts of myths and legends with literal translations. With linguistic commentary.

4210. Woosley, David J. "Cahuilla Tales." *JAF,* 21 (1908), 239–40.

Outlines of two myths. No commentary or annotation.

See also 4176, 4177, 4182.

E. Chemehuevi

4211.   Kroeber, A. L. "Origin Tradition of the Chemehuevi Indians." *JAF,* 21 (1908), 240–42.
Two unannotated myth texts with no commentary. Some sketchy data on ceremonials.
4212.   Laird, Carobeth. "Behavioral Patterns in Chemehuevi Myths," in 86, pp. 97–103.
Comparison of behavior in myth and in actual life.

F. Chimariko

4213.   Dixon, Roland B. "The Chimariko Indians and Language." *UCPAAE,* 5, No. 5 (1910), 293–380.
Culture survey includes brief data on ceremonialism. With six myth texts with free and interlinear translations and linguistic notes.

See also 4423.

G. Chumash

4214.   Blackburn, Thomas C., ed. *December's Child: A Book of Chumash Oral Narratives.* Berkeley: Univ. of California Press, 1975.
Narrative texts (111) collected by John P. Harrington. Includes data on cultural background and informants. Shows how the material reflects Chumash culture.
4215.   Dougan, Marcia. "Why Humming-Bird Became Eagle." *M,* 39 (1965), 77–78.
Unannotated myth text. No commentary.
4216.   Geiger, Maynard. *The Indians of Mission Santa Barbara in Paganism and Christianity.* Santa Barbara, Cal.: Franciscan Fathers, 1960.
Pamphlet deals with Christianizing of Chumash and describes ceremonials.
4217.   Grant, Campbell. *The Rock Paintings of the Chumash: A Study of a California Indian Culture.* Foreword by Robert F. Heizer. Berkeley: Univ. of California Press, 1965.
Commentary preceding paintings includes description of Chumash ceremonialism.
4218.   Heizer, Robert F. "Two Chumash Legends." *JAF,* 68 (1955), 34, 56, 72.
Texts collected in 1887 and included in BAE ms. collection.
4219.   Hudson, Travis. "Chumash Indian Astronomy in South Coastal California." *M,* 53 (1979), 84–88.
Focuses on rock art, but includes data on beliefs and ceremonials.
4220.   ———, and Ernest Underhay. *Crystals in the Sky: An Intellectual Odyssey Involving Chumash Astronomy, Cosmology and Rock Art.* Socorro, N. M.: Ballena Press, 1978 (Anthropological Paper No. 10).
Survey of Chumash astronomical and cosmological knowledge. Seen as key to understanding entire culture.
4221.   ———, Thomas Blackburn, Rosario Curletti, and Janice Timbrook, eds. *The Eye of the Flute: Chumash Traditional History and Ritual as Told by Fernando Librado Kitsepawit to John P. Harrington.* Santa Barbara, Cal.: Museum of Natural History, 1977.
Myth, legend, and song texts and ritual descriptions collected in 1912 and presented with extensive explanatory notes and commentary.
4222.   Kroeber, A. L. "The Chumash and Costanoan Languages." *UCPAAE,* 9, No. 2 (1910), 237–71.
Includes song and myth texts with interlinear translations. Based on work of Fr. Felipe Arroyo de la Cuesta.
4223.   Matthiessen, Peter. "Last Stand at the Western Gate." *N,* 229 (25 August–1 September 1979), 135-38.
Treats resistance to construction of a natural gas facility by NAs who recall that the designated area was a traditional sacred site.
4224.   Mohr, Albert, and L. L. Sample. "The Religious Importance of the Swordfish in the Santa Barbara Area and Its Possible Implications." *M,* 29 (1955), 62–68.
Includes data on ceremonialism.

H. Cupeno

4225.   Faye, Paul-Louis. "Christmas Fiestas of the Cupeño." *AA,* 30 (1928), 651–58.
Describes ceremonials observed in 1919. Most of the songs performed have associations with tribal mythology.
4226.   Hill, Jane H., and Rosinda Nolasquez. *Mulu'wetam: The First People. Cupeño Oral History and Language.* Banning, Cal.: Malki Museum Press, 1973.
Texts of legends, descriptions of customs, songs, personal narratives, and animal tales collected in 1920s by Paul-Louis Faye and in the 1960s by Hill. Presented with literal translations and extensive ethnographic and linguistic notes.

See also 4177.

I. Diegueno

4227.   Davis, Edward H. "The Diegueño Ceremony of the Death Images." *CMAI,* 5, No. 2 (1919), 7–33.
Thorough description of the ritual as observed in 1908.
4228.   Du Bois, Constance Goddard. "Ceremonies and Traditions of the Diegueño Indians." *JAF,* 21 (1908), 228–36.
Includes one myth text, ceremonial descriptions, and translations and summaries of song texts (words only).
4229.   ———. "Diegueño Myths and Their Connections with the Mohave." *ICA,* 15, No. 2 (1906), 129–33.
Briefly summarizes Diegueno mythological system and provides analogues from the Mohave.
4230.   ———. "The Mythology of the Diegueños." *JAF,* 14 (1901), 181–85.
Four myth texts with some commentary on cultural background. Sketchy comparative notes.

4231. ———. "The Mythology of the Dieguenos, Mission Indians of San Diego County, California, as Proving Their Status to be Higher Than Is Generally Believed." *ICA,* 11 (1902), 101–6.

Text of Chaup story is used to illustrate the quality of Dieguено oral literature.

4232. ———. "Mythology of the Mission Indians." *JAF,* 19 (1906), 145–64.

Texts and commentary on a myth previously collected from the Mohave. Includes data on collecting situation.

4233. ———. "Religious Ceremonies and Myths of the Mission Indians." *AA,* 7 (1905), 620–29.

Reconstructs Dieguено religious life from reminiscences of informants. Includes one myth text.

4234. ———. "The Story of Chaup. A Myth of the Diegueños." *JAF,* 17 (1904). 217–42.

Unannotated myth text. No commentary.

4235. Gifford, E. W. *The Kamia of the Imperial Valley.* BAEB No. 97 (1931).

Ethnography contains data on religious and ceremonial life, song cycles, and belief system. With three myth texts and one joke. Based on material collected from six informants in 1928 and 1929.

4236. Jensen, Joan M. "The Indian Legends of Maria Alto." *WE,* 3, No. 3 (April 1965), 25–28.

Describes a pamphlet published in 1914 which contained twelve oral narratives. Includes one myth text and comments on cultural background.

4237. Langdon, Margaret. *A Grammar of Diegueño. The Mesa Grande Dialect.* UCPL No. 66 (1970).

Sample text describes acorn gathering. With free translation and syntactic analysis.

4238. Robertson, Rosalie Pinto. *The Autobiography of Delfina Cuero, A Diegueño Indian as Told to Florence C. Shipek.* Los Angeles: Dawson's Book Shop, 1968.

Life history of a woman born about 1900. Includes data on ceremonialism.

4239. Spier, Leslie. "Southern Diegueño Customs." *UCPAAE,* 20 (1923), 297–358.

Notes based on fieldwork done in 1920 include data on ceremonialism, shamanism, and song cycles. With three unannotated myth texts. No commentary.

4240. Waterman, Thomas T. "Diegueño Identification of Color with the Cardinal Points." *JAF,* 21 (1908), 40–42.

Presents songs and recitations which include parallels between colors and directions.

4241. ———. "The Religious Practices of the Diegueño Indians." *UCPAAE,* 8, No. 6 (1910), 271–358.

Descriptions of ceremonials include song and chant texts. With annotated text of creation myth.

4242. Woodward, John A. "The Anniversary: A Contemporary Diegueño Complex." *Eth,* 7 (1968), 86–94.

Description of a ceremony honoring a person one year after his death. With data on singing.

See also 3995, 4182, 4293.

J. Gabrielino

4243. Harrington, John P. "A New Original Version of Boscana's Historical Account of the San Juan Capistrano

Indians of Southern California." *SMC,* 92, No. 4 (1934), 1–62.

Presents a ms. written in 1820s which contains data on religious beliefs and ceremonials and a summary of the creation myth.

4244. Johnston, Bernice Eastman. *California's Gabrielino Indians.* Los Angeles: Southwest Museum, 1962.

Historical and cultural survey includes summaries of myths and descriptions of ceremonials and singing.

4245. Wey, Auguste. "The Captain's Song." *LS,* 6, No. 1 (December 1896), 3–8.

Describes a song associated with the Dance of the Capitan.

See also 4173, 4176.

K. Hupa

4246. Bushnell, John H. "From American Indian to Indian American: The Changing Identity of the Hupa." *AA,* 70 (1968), 1108–16.

Traces a century of Hupa culture history to show that despite rapid modernization, many Hupa evince an interest in traditional culture, including folklore.

4247. ———. "Hupa Reaction to the Trinity River Floods: Post-Hoc Recourse to Aboriginal Belief." *AnQ,* 42 (1969), 316–24.

Reactions to severe flooding placed responsibility on those who had violated ceremonial proscriptions.

4248. ———, and Donna Bushnell. "Wealth, Work and World View in Native Northwest California: Sacred Significance and Psychoanalytic Symbolism," in 86, pp. 120–82.

Psychoanalytic study of myth, ritual, and customary behavior shows recurrent theme of the quest for spiritual power.

4249. Fry, Winifred. "Humboldt Indians. A Sketch." *OW,* 21 (1904), 503–14.

Survey of Hupa culture with data on ceremonialism and mythology.

4250. Goddard, Pliny Earle. "Chilula Texts." *UCPAAE,* 10, No. 7 (1914), 289–379.

Twenty-nine myth texts with free and interlinear translations. Some explanatory and comparative notes.

4251. ———. "Hupa Texts." *UCPAAE,* 1, No. 2 (1903–1904), 89–368.

Fourteen myth and folktale texts and thirty-six prayers, formulas, and other ceremonial texts. Collected in 1901 and 1902. With free and interlinear translations and explanatory notes.

4252. ———. "Life and Culture of the Hupa." *UCPAAE,* 1, No. 1 (1903–1904), 1–88.

Ethnography based on fieldwork done between 1897 and 1900 contains data on shamanism, religion, and ceremonialism.

4253. Goldschmidt, Walter R., and Harold E. Driver. "The Hupa White Deerskin Dance." *UCPAAE,* 35 (1943), 103–41.

Describes ceremonial observed in 1930s. With musicological analysis of song text.

4254. Lindgren, Louise. "Brush Dance at Hoopa Reservation." *IW,* 3, No. 5 (15 October 1935), 43–45.

Description of a ceremonial.

4255.   Wallace, William J. "Hupa Narrative Tales." *JAF*, 61 (1948), 345–55.

Twelve narrative texts with some commentary. All the texts are anecdotes about persons or events.

4256.   ———. "The Role of Humor in the Hupa Indian Tribe." *JAF*, 66 (1953), 135–41.

Discusses occasions for humor and its categories and functions.

4257.   ———, and Edith S. Taylor. "Hupa Sorcery." *SJA*, 6 (1950), 188–96.

Survey of sorcery types with data on ritual responses to sorcery.

4258.   Woodruff, Charles E. "Dances of the Hupa Indians." *AA*, o. s. 5 (1892), 53–61.

Describes four ceremonial dances with a song text (words and music).

See also 4158, 4169.

L. Karok

4259.   Bright, William. *The Karok Language. UCPL* No. 13 (1957).

Includes ninety-two texts (myths, folktales, personal narratives, descriptions of customs) with free translations and explanatory notes. Collected between 1949 and 1954.

4260.   de Angulo, Jaime, and L. S. Freeland. "Karok Texts." *IJAL*, 6 (1931), 194–226.

Seven narratives with interlinear and free translations. Three myths, one legend, and three personal narratives collected in 1927.

4261.   Drucker, Philip. "A Karuk World-Renewal Ceremony at Panaminik." *UCPAAE*, 35 (1943), 23–28.

Description of a ceremonial based on accounts of participants.

4262.   Harrington, John P. *Karuk Indian Myths. BAEB* No. 107 (1932).

Twelve texts with free translations. Some explanatory notes.

4263.   ———. "Karuk Texts." *IJAL*, 6 (1931), 121–61.

Fourteen narratives with interlinear and free translations. With some ethnographic notes.

4264.   ———. *Tobacco Among the Karũk Indians of California. BAEB* No. 94 (1932).

Introductory notes on Karok culture prepared for testimony about tobacco use, presented in Karok and in free translation. Some material on myths and songs.

4265.   Kroeber, A. L. "A Ghost-Dance in California." *JAF*, 17 (1904), 32–35.

Description of a Ghost Dance which occurred shortly before the Modoc War. Based on informant's description.

4266.   ———. "A Karok Orpheus Myth." *JAF*, 59 (1946), 13–19.

Two texts of story with Orpheus theme are presented with comparison with analogous materials.

4267.   Olden, Sarah Emilia. *Karoc Indian Stories.* San Francisco: Harr Wagner, 1923.

Rewritten myths and legends with no annotations. Introduced by general survey of cultural background.

4268.   Roberts, Helen H. "The First Salmon Ceremony of the Karuk Indians." *AA*, 34 (1932), 426–40.

Based on recollections secured in 1926. Ceremonial description with song texts (words and music).

4269.   Saindon, Carolyn. "The Taming of Fire: A Karok Fable." *IH*, 1, No. 2 (Spring 1968), 19.

Unannotated retelling of a folktale. No commentary.

See also 4149, 4169.

M. Kato

4270.   Goddard, Pliny Earle. "Kato Texts." *UCPAAE*, 5 (1907–1910), 67–238.

Thirty-seven myth and folktale texts with free and interlinear translations and linguistic notes. Collected in 1906.

See also 4159, 4160.

N. Kawaiisu

4271.   Zigmond, Maurice. "The Supernatural World of the Kawaiisu," in 86, pp. 59–95.

Survey of religious and mythological conceptions.

O. Klamath

4272.   Barker, M. A. R. *Klamath Texts. UCPL* No. 30 (1963).

Twenty-one myths and eighteen descriptions of customs with free translations and linguistic commentary. Collected in 1955–1957.

4273.   Carlson, Roy L. "Klamath *Henwas* and Other Stone Sculpture." *AA*, 61 (1959), 88–96.

Description of three types of Klamath sculpture. One type, a category of anthropomorphic figures called *henwas*, is associated with shamanistic incantations and myths.

4274.   Chambers, G. A. "A Ghost Dance on the Klamath River." *JAF*, 19 (1906), 141–42.

Legend about incident during Modoc War. No commentary or annotation.

4275.   ———. "Tradition Formerly Obtained at Chico." *JAF*, 19 (1906), 141.

Unannotated legend text. No commentary.

4276.   Gatschet, Albert Samuel. *The Klamath Indians of Southwestern Oregon. CNAE*, 2, Part 1 (1890).

Texts of historical legends, songs, incantations, and myths with free and interlinear translations and linguistic notes.

4277.   Opsahl, Josephine. "Crater Lake." *NM*, 26 (July 1935), 24, 63.

Description of scenic site includes retelling of a Klamath myth.

4278. Phillips, Alice. "Legend of the Cricket." *TT*, 4, No. 12 (December 1904), 368–69.

Myth text.

4279. ———. "Profamepa." *TT*, 5, No. 4 (April 1903), 150–51.

Myth text.

4280. Schmitt, Frank. "The Legend of the Half Moon. A Tale of the Klamath River Indians." *OM*, n. s. 46 (October 1905), 311–14.

Rewritten myth text.

4281. Spencer, Robert F. "Exhortation and the Klamath Ethos." *PAPS*, 100 (1956), 77–86.

Treats role of exhortations and harangues in inculcating ethical concepts.

4282. ———. "Native Myth and Modern Religion Among the Klamath Indians." *JAF*, 65 (1952), 217–26.

Describes religious acculturation which involves identification of culture heroes with Christian supernatural figures.

4283. Spier, Leslie. "The Ghost Dance of 1870 Among the Klamath of Oregon." *UWPA*, 2, No. 2 (November 1927), 39–56.

Historical work on revitalization movement. Contains song texts and translations and descriptions of ceremonials.

4284. ———. "Klamath Ethnography." *UCPAAE*, 30 (1930), 1–338.

Based on fieldwork done in 1925–1926. Includes data on ceremonialism and shamanism. With song texts (words only).

4285. Stern, Theodore. "Ideal and Expected Behavior as Seen in Klamath Mythology." *JAF*, 76 (1963), 21–30.

Analysis of fifty-five narratives which present an emic view of the group's expectations of ideal social behavior.

4286. ———. "Klamath Myth Abstracts." *JAF*, 76 (1963), 31–41.

Summaries of forty-two myths with several variant texts.

4287. ———. *The Klamath Tribe. A People and Their Reservation. MonAES* No. 41 (1965).

Ethnography based on fieldwork done between 1949 and 1956 includes brief survey of religious response to acculturation.

4288. ———, ed. "Nolis Gaeni." *NWR*, 5 (Summer 1962), 106–12.

Myth text collected in 1951. With explanatory notes and general introduction to Klamath mythology.

4289. ———. "Some Sources of Variability in Klamath Mythology." *JAF*, 69 (1956), 1–12, 135–46, 377–86.

Concludes that patterns of variation in storytelling respond to audiences.

4290. ———. "The Trickster in Klamath Mythology." *WF*, 12 (1953), 158–74.

Describes several figures who appear as Trickster in the tradition.

4291. Thompson, Lucy. *To the American Indian.* Eureka, Cal.: Cummins Print Shop, ND.

Culture survey includes some rewritten myths and descriptions of ceremonials.

See also 200, 4179.

P. Luiseno

4292. Cody, Iron Eyes. "Traditions of the American Indians: Coming of Age in Southern California." *M*, 52 (1978), 113–14.

Description of an initiation ceremony.

4293. Davis, Edward H. "Early Cremation Ceremonies of the Luiseño and Diegueño Indians of Southern California." *IN&M*, 7, No. 3 (1921), 91–110.

Description of a ritual. With myth summary.

4294. Dougan, Marcia. "The Memorial Ceremony of the Luiseno Indians." *M*, 38 (1964), 140–49.

Description of the ceremonial as observed in 1938.

4295. Du Bois, Constance Goddard. "Mythology of the Mission Indians." *JAF*, 17 (1904), 185–88.

Two myth texts. With comparative commentary.

4296. ———. "Mythology of the Mission Indians." *JAF*, 19 (1906), 52–60.

Four myth texts with explanatory notes.

4297. ———. "The Religion of the Luiseño Indians of Southern California." *UCPAAE*, 8, No. 3 (1908), 69–186.

Descriptions of ceremonials, myth texts, and song texts (with some music) from fieldwork done in 1906.

4298. Henshaw, H. W. "The Luiseno Creation Myth." *M*, 46 (1972), 93–100.

Unannotated myth text collected in 1884. Commentary on previously published texts by Robert F. Heizer.

4299. James, George Wharton. "The Legend of Tauquitch and Algoot." *JAF*, 16 (1903), 153–59.

Unannotated myth text with brief comment on cultural background.

4300. ———. "A Saboba Origin-Myth." *JAF*, 15 (1902), 36–39.

Unannotated myth text with some data on the informant.

4301. Kroeber, A. L. "Inheritance by Magic." *AA*, 18 (1916), 19–40.

Cross-cultural survey of the idea of "cosmic evolution" includes summary of Luiseno creation myth.

4302. ———, and George William Grace. *The Sparkman Grammar of Luiseño. UCPL* No. 16 (1960).

Texts recorded in 1909 and 1951 include legends, reminiscences, descriptions of customs, and ritual formulas. With literal translations.

4303. Malécot, André. "Luiseño, A Structural Analysis. III: Texts and Lexicon." *IJAL*, 30 (1964), 14–31.

Contains personal narrative text with free translation and linguistic analysis.

4304. Sparkman, Philip Stedman. "The Culture of the Luiseño Indians." *UCPAAE*, 8, No. 4 (1908), 187–234.

Ethnographic survey includes data on shamanism and ceremonialism.

4305. ———. "A Luiseño Tale." *JAF*, 21 (1908), 35–36.

Unannotated myth text. No commentary.

4306. White, Raymond C. "Luiseño Social Organization." *UCPAAE*, 48, No. 2 (1963), 91–194.

Treats role of religion and ceremonialism in the social system.

4307. ———. "The Luiseño Theory of 'Knowledge.' " *AA*, 59 (1957), 1–19.

Shows how *ayelkwi,* similar to "mana," relates to tribal mores. Relates the creation myth which charters the concept.

4308. ———. "Two Surviving Luiseño Indian Ceremonies." *AA,* 55 (1953), 569–78.

Describes the rituals as they occurred in 1952.

See also 340, 4173, 4177, 4182.

Q. Maidu

4309. Azbill, Henry. "How Death Came to the People." *IH,* 2, No. 2 (Summer 1969), 13–14, 29.

Unannotated myth text.

4310. ———. "World Maker." *IH,* 2, No. 1 (Spring 1969), 20.

Unannotated myth text.

4311. Beals, Ralph L. "Ethnology of the Nisenan." *UCPAAE,* 31, No. 6 (1933), 335–414.

Based on fieldwork done in 1929. Includes data on ceremonialism and shamanism.

4311a. Cody, Bertha Parker. "A Maidu Myth of the Creation of Indian Women." *M,* 13 (1939), 83.

Unannotated myth text. No commentary.

4312. ———. "A Maidu Myth of the First Death." *M,* 13 (1939), 144.

Unannotated myth text. No commentary.

4313. Densmore, Frances. *Music of the Maidu Indians of California.* Los Angeles: Southwest Museum, 1958 (Hodge Publication No. 8).

Fifty-three song texts (words and music) collected in 1937. Each text is accompanied by context and musicological comments. With data on cultural background.

4314. ———. "Musical Instruments of the Maidu Indians." *AA,* 41 (1939), 113–18.

Describes instruments in use in 1937: drums, rattles, flutes, whistles, musical bows.

4315. Dixon, Roland B. "Maidu Myths." *BAMNH,* 17, Part 2 (1902), 33–118.

Twenty-two myth texts with abstracts and comments on cultural background. No comparative notes.

4316. ———. *Maidu Texts. PAES* No. 4 (1912).

Eighteen myth texts collected in 1902–1903. Presented with free translations (interlinear translation for one text). No commentary or annotation.

4317. ———. "The Northern Maidu." *BAMNH,* 17 (1902), 119–346.

Ethnography includes data on music, religion, ceremonialism, shamanism, and mythology.

4318. ———. "Some Coyote Stories from the Maidu Indians of California." *JAF,* 13 (1900), 267–70.

Four unannotated myth texts collected in 1899. With brief comments on cultural background. Reprinted in Jan Harold Brunvand, ed., *Readings in American Folklore* (New York: Norton, 1979), pp. 16–21.

4319. ———. "System and Sequence in Maidu Mythology." *JAF,* 16 (1903), 32–36.

Describes systematic features of two myth cycles.

4320. Faye, Paul-Louis. "Notes on the Southern Maidu." *UCPAAE,* 20 (1923), 35–53.

Data collected from one informant in 1919 include material on shamanism and ceremonialism.

4321. Gifford, Edward Winslow. "Southern Maidu Religious Ceremonies." *AA,* 29 (1927), 214–57.

Ceremonial descriptions with attention to shamanism and supernaturalism.

4322. Kroeber, A. L. "The Valley Nisenan." *UCPAAE,* 24, No. 4 (1929), 253–90.

Ethnographic survey based on fieldwork done in 1920s. With data on ceremonialism and shamanism and eight unannotated myth texts.

4323. Loeb, E. M. "The Eastern Kuksu Cult." *UCPAAE,* 33, No. 2 (1933), 139–232.

Describes the cult among the Maidu and Patwin. Includes data on ceremonialism and creation mythology. Based on fieldwork done in 1931.

4324. Miller, Mabel L. "The So-Called California 'Diggers.'" *PSM,* 50 (December 1896), 201–14.

Culture survey includes data on religion. With a legend text.

4325. Read, William E. "Indian Traditions of Their Origin." *OM,* n. s. 20 (December 1892), 577–84.

Summary of myth cycle placed in storytelling context.

4326. Shipley, William F. *Maidu Grammar. UCPL* No. 41 (1964).

Includes text of a personal narrative with free translation and linguistic analysis. Collected in 1950s.

4327. ———. *Maidu Texts and Dictionary. UCPL* No. 33 (1963).

Fifteen myths and folktales, five personal narratives, a prayer, and three descriptions of customs. With free translations and some explanatory notes. Part of the material reconstituted from Roland B. Dixon's collectanea published in 1912 (4316).

4328. Simpson, Richard. *Ooti, A Maidu Legacy.* Mimbre, Cal.: Celestial Arts, 1977.

Biography of Lizzie Enos is introduced by retelling of cosmogony. Includes material from subject's reminiscences.

4329. Spencer, D. L. "Notes on the Maidu Indians of Butte County, California." *JAF,* 21 (1908), 242–45.

Miscellany of beliefs and customs includes a myth text.

4330. Splitter, H. W. "Ceremonial and Legend of Central California Indians." *WF,* 7 (1948), 266–71.

Newspaper accounts include descriptions of three Nisenan ceremonials and a myth text.

4331. Thurston, Bertha Parker. "How a Haidu [sic]-Medicine Man Lost His Power." *M,* 9 (1935), 28–29.

Unannotated legend text. No commentary.

4332. ———. "How He Became a Medicine-Man." *M,* 8 (1934), 79–81.

Unannotated personal narrative text. No commentary.

4333. ———. "A Night in a Maidu Shaman's House." *M,* 7 (1933), 111–16.

Description of a healing ceremony.

4334. ———. "A Rare Treat at a Maidu Medicine-Man's Feast." *M,* 10 (1936), 16–21.

Description of festivities with some data on storytelling.

4335. Uldall, Hans Jorgen, and William Shipley. *Nisenan Texts and Dictionary. UCPL* No. 46 (1966).

Myth and legend texts and descriptions of customs with free translations and some explanatory notes.

See also 3, 3593, 4179.

R. Miwok

4336.   Barrett, S. A. "Myths of the Southern Sierra Miwok." *UCPAAE,* 16, No. 1 (1919), 1–28.

Fifteen myth texts collected in 1906. With explanatory and comparative notes.

4337.   ———. "Totemism Among the Miwok Indians." *JAF,* 21 (1908), 237.

Brief description of clan system.

4338.   Broadbent, Sylvia M. *The Southern Sierra Miwok Language. UCPL* No. 38 (1964).

Texts include myths, legends, and descriptions of customs, with free translations. No commentary. Collected between 1955 and 1961.

4339.   Clark, Galen. *Indians of the Yosemite Valley and Vicinity. Their History, Customs and Traditions.* Yosemite Valley, Cal.: By the Author, 1904.

Describes various aspects of culture including ceremonialism. With several rewritten myth and legend texts.

4340.   de Angulo, Jaime. "Five Thousand Years." *Ind,* 115 (4 July 1925), 11–12.

Retelling of a myth.

4341.   ———, and L. S. Freeland. "Miwok and Pomo Myths." *JAF,* 41 (1928), 232–52.

Myth texts with explanatory notes and discussion of themes.

4342.   Freeland, L. S. *Language of the Sierra Miwok. IUPAL* No. 6 (1951).

Includes autobiographical narratives, folktales, and descriptions of customs with free and interlinear translations. Linguistic notes.

4343.   ———. "Western Miwok Texts with Linguistic Sketch." *IJAL,* 13 (1947), 31–46.

General linguistic survey introduces two narratives with interlinear and free translations. Collected in 1922.

4344.   ———, and Sylvia M. Broadbent. *Central Sierra Miwok Dictionary with Texts. UCPL* No. 23 (1960).

Includes texts of a myth, several shaman legends, and descriptions of dances. With free translations. No commentary.

4345.   Gifford, E. W. "Central Miwok Ceremonies." *UCPAR,* 14, No. 4 (1955), 261–318.

Thorough survey of ceremonialism based on interview data.

4346.   ———. "Miwok Cults." *UCPAAE,* 18, No. 3 (1926), 391–408.

Based on fieldwork begun in 1913. Surveys ceremonial and cultic organization.

4347.   ———. "Miwok Moieties." *UCPAAE,* 12, No. 4 (1916), 139–94.

Study of social organization includes some data on ceremonialism.

4348.   ———. "Miwok Myths." *UCPAAE,* 12, No. 8 (1917), 283–338.

Fourteen myth texts with abstracts collected in 1913–1914. No commentary or annotations.

4349.   Hudson, J. W. "An Indian Myth of the San Joaquin Basin." *JAF,* 15 (1902), 104–6.

Two texts of the same folktale collected from different informants. Some discussion of variation.

4350.   Lehmer, Derrick Norman. "The First People. Miwok Indian Myths." *OM,* n. s. 87 (1929), 378–79.

Survey of tribal mythology.

4351.   Merriam, C. Hart. *The Dawn of the World. Myths and Weird Tales Told by the Mewan Indians of California.* Cleveland: Arthur H. Clark, 1910.

Thirty-three unannotated myth texts and descriptions of customs. Some data on cultural milieu.

4352.   Peterson, Bonnie J., ed. *Dawn of the World. Coast Miwok Myths.* NP: Marin Museum Society, 1976.

Excerpts from 4351. With a brief note on Miwok culture.

4353.   Smith, Bertha H. *Yosemite Legends.* San Francisco: Paul Elder, 1904.

Six rewritten myth and legend texts. No commentary or annotations.

4354.   Townsend, George Elliot. "Indian Mythology of Yosemite Valley." *OM,* n. s. 41 (June 1903), 454–59.

Summaries of myths and legends associated with specific sites in Yosemite.

See also 4148, 4149, 4159, 4160, 4169.

S. Modoc

4355.   Curtin, Jeremiah. *Myths of the Modocs. Indian Legends of the Northwest.* Boston: Little, Brown, 1912.

Narrative texts collected in 1884. With explanatory notes.

4356.   Gatschet, A. S. "Animism Among the Modocs." *JAF,* 2 (1889), 236–37.

Legend text collected in 1885 with commentary on its religious significance.

4357.   ———. "Oregonian Folk-Lore." *JAF,* 4 (1891), 139–43.

Three Modoc myths and one Kalapuya myth. No annotations. Some data on content and collecting situation.

4358.   ———. "Songs of the Modoc Indians." *AA,* o. s. 7 (1894), 26–31.

Three song texts (words only) with interlinear translations. Includes fairly thorough analysis of their content.

4359.   Hall, Jody C., and Bruno Nettl. "Musical Style of the Modoc." *SJA,* 11 (1955), 58–66.

Characterization of the style includes some musical texts.

4360.   Lockley, Fred. "How the Modoc Indian War Started." *OM,* n. s. 81 (1923), 12–14, 43.

Historical reminiscence collected from a descendant of participants in the Modoc War.

4361.   Meacham, A. B. *Wi-ne-ma (The Woman-Chief) and Her People.* Hartford, Conn.: American, 1876.

Biographical and historical work includes descriptions of Modoc ceremonialism and data on mythology, prayer, and oratory.

4362.   Miller, Joaquin. *Unwritten History. Life Amongst the Modocs.* Hartford, Conn.: American, 1874.

Focuses on NA perspective on Modoc War. Includes text of creation myth and descriptions of ceremonials.

4363.   Ray, Verne F. *Primitive Pragmatists. The Modoc Indians of Northern California. MonAES* No. 38 (1963).

Ethnography based on fieldwork done during 1930s contains data on religion, shamanism, ceremonialism, and world view.

See also 4158, 4169, 4179.

T. Pomo

4364.   Aginsky, Burt W. "The Socio-Psychological Significance of Death Among the Pomo Indians." *AI,* 1, No. 3 (June 1940), 1–11.

Describes ceremonials used to counteract supernatural threat, which was seen as the cause of most deaths. Response by George B. Wilbur (pp. 12–18).

4365.   ———, and Ethel G. Aginsky. "The Pomo: A Profile of Gambling Among Indians." *AAAPSS,* 269 (May 1950), 108–13.

Includes data in myths on gambling and information on ways in which gamblers enlist supernatural aid.

4366.   Barrett, S. A. "Ceremonies of the Pomo Indians." *UCPAAE,* 12, No. 10 (1917), 397–441.

Survey of the group's ceremonialism.

4367.   ———. "A Composite Myth of the Pomo Indians." *JAF,* 19 (1906), 37–51.

Myth text collected in 1904. With explanatory notes and data on collecting situation.

4368.   ———. "Pomo Bear Doctors." *UCPAAE,* 12, No. 11 (1917), 443–65.

Survey of shamanism includes text of shamanistic origin myth and descriptions of ceremonials.

4369.   ———. *Pomo Myths. MPMB* No. 15 (1933).

Texts and abstracts (108) collected between 1903 and 1906 and 1914–1915. With explanatory notes, index, and thorough treatment of religious background.

4370.   Clark, Cora, and Texa Bowen Williams. *Pomo Indian Myths and Some of Their Sacred Meanings.* New York: Vantage, 1954.

Forty-three myth texts with a commentary by a Pomo "priest." With general data on nature of myth. No comparative notes.

4370a.   Cody, Bertha Parker. "Pomo Bear Impersonators." *M,* 14 (1940), 132–37.

Description of shamanism.

4371.   Colson, Elizabeth. *Autobiographies of Three Pomo Women.* Berkeley: Univ. of California Anthropological Research Facility, 1974.

Life histories collected in 1941. With data on ceremonialism, extensive explanatory notes, and brief survey of cultural background.

4372.   de Angulo, Jaime. "Pomo Creation Myth." *JAF,* 48 (1935), 203–62.

Myth text with literal translation of first seventeen paragraphs and free translation of entire narrative.

4373.   ———, and William Ralganal Benson. "The Creation Myth of the Pomo Indians." *A,* 27 (1932), 261–74, 779–95.

Translated text of myth dictated by Benson. Some explanatory notes and data on cultural background.

4374.   ———, and L. S. Freeland. "A New Religious Movement in North-Central California." *AA,* 31 (1929), 265–70.

Describes developing revitalization movement in the Clear Lake region of California. With some data on singing.

4375.   Freeland, L. S. "Pomo Doctors and Poisoners." *UCPAAE,* 20 (1923), 57–73.

Survey of shamanistic beliefs and rituals.

4376.   Gifford, Edward Winslow. "Clear Lake Pomo Society." *UCPAAE,* 18, No. 2 (1926), 287–390.

Ethnographic survey based on interviews obtained in 1919. With data on shamanism and ceremonialism.

4377.   ———. "Notes on Central Pomo and Northern Yana Society." *AA,* 30 (1928), 675–84.

Ethnographic survey includes some data on myth narration.

4378.   Gorringe, Katherine. "The Ukiah Big-Time." *Di,* 86 (July 1929), 580–85.

Describes festive singing and dancing.

4379.   Hastings, Cristel. "Lu-Po-Yoma—A Legend." *OM,* n. s. 86 (April 1928), 116, 119.

Rewritten myth text. No commentary.

4380.   Hudson, John W. "Pomo Wampum Makers. An Aboriginal Double Standard." *OM,* n. s. 30 (1897), 101–8.

Description of wampum-making process includes excerpts from a song text with free translation.

4381.   Loeb, Edwin M. "The Creator Concept Among the Indians of North Central California." *AA,* 28 (1926), 467–93.

Three Pomo myth texts collected in 1924–1925 with data on creator figure among neighboring groups.

4382.   ———. "Pomo Folkways." *UCPAAE,* 19, No. 2 (1926), 149–404.

Ethnographic survey includes extensive data on religion and ceremonialism.

4383.   McLendon, Sally. *A Grammar of Eastern Pomo. UCPL* No. 74 (1975).

Includes a folktale text with free and interlinear translations and linguistic analysis. Collected between 1959 and 1964.

4384.   Meighan, Clement W., and Francis A. Riddell. *The Maru Cult of the Pomo Indians. A California Ghost Dance Survival.* Los Angeles: Southwest Museum, 1972 (Museum Paper No. 23).

Thorough description of the ritual as observed between 1949 and 1959. Includes some musical texts. With emphasis on traits retained from Ghost Dance.

4385.   Merriam, C. Hart. "How Mah'-tah, the Turkey Buzzard, Lost His Speech." *AMJ,* 17 (1917), 557.

Myth collected near Clear Lake, California.

4386.   Moshinsky, Julius. *A Grammar of Southeastern Pomo. UCPL* No. 72 (1974).

Includes text of personal narrative with free translation and linguistic analysis. Collected in 1965.

4387.   Oswalt, Robert L. *Kashaya Texts. UCPL* No. 36 (1964).

Texts of myths, legends, oratory, prayers, and descriptions of customs with free translations. No annotations, but extensive commentary on cultural background. Collected between 1957 and 1961.

4388.   Treganza, Adan E., Edith S. Taylor, and William J. Wallace. "The Hindil, a Pomo Indian Dance in 1946." *M,* 21 (1947), 119–25.

Ritual description.

See also 3899, 4149, 4159, 4160, 4169, 4331.

U. Salina

4389.   Mason, J. Alden. "The Ethnology of the Salinan Indians." *UCPAAE*, 10, No. 4 (1912), 97–240.
Based on fieldwork done in 1910. Includes data on ceremonialism and supernaturalism and three myths and six legends.
4390.   ———. "The Language of the Salinan Indians." *UCPAAE*, 14, No. 1 (1918), 1–154.
Linguistic survey based on fieldwork begun in 1910. Includes thirty-eight myth and legend texts with free and interlinear translations.

V. Serrano

4391.   Benedict, Ruth Fulton. "A Brief Sketch of Serrano Culture." *AA*, 26 (1924), 366–92.
Ethnography includes descriptions of ceremonials, excerpts from song texts, and data on shamanism.
4392.   ———. "Serrano Tales." *JAF*, 39 (1926), 1–17.
Seventeen myth texts. No commentary or annotations.

See also 4176, 4177.

W. Shasta

4393.   Dixon, Roland B. "The Mythology of the Shasta-Achomawi." *AA*, 7 (1905), 607–12.
Summaries of myths. With comparisons to traditions of other California groups.
4394.   ———. "The Shasta." *BAMNH*, 17 (1902), 381–498.
Ethnography based on fieldwork done between 1900 and 1904 includes data on music, religion, ceremonialism, shamanism, and mythology.
4395.   ———. "Shasta Myths." *JAF*, 23 (1910), 8–37, 364–70.
Thirty-four myth and folktale texts. No commentary or annotations.
4396.   Farrand, Livingston. "Shasta and Athapascan Myths from Oregon." Ed. Leo J. Frachtenberg. *JAF*, 28 (1915), 207–42.
Twenty-two myth texts collected in 1900 (fifteen Shasta, five Joshua, two Tututuni). With very extensive comparative notes.
4397.   Holt, Catharine. "Shasta Ethnography." *UCPAR*, 3, No. 4 (1946), 299–350.
Based on fieldwork done in 1937. Includes data on religion, ceremonialism, shamanism, and storytelling.
4398.   Murdock, George Peter. "Tenino Shamanism." *Eth*, 4 (1965), 165–71.
Survey includes descriptions of ceremonials.
4399.   Voegelin, Erminie W. "Three Shasta Myths, Including 'Orpheus.' " *JAF*, 60 (1947), 52–58.
Narratives collected in 1936. Compares the Orpheus myth to similar narratives in various NA cultures.

See also 4179, 4423.

X. Southern Athapaskans

4400.   Goddard, Pliny Earle. "Lassik Tales." *JAF*, 19 (1906), 133–40.
Nine unannotated myth texts collected in 1903. With data on cultural background.
4401.   ———. "Wailaki Texts." *IJAL*, 2, Nos. 3 and 4 (1921–1923), 77–135.
Texts and translations of thirty-six narratives collected in 1901 and 1906.
4402.   Jacobs, Elizabeth D. "A Chetco Athabaskan Myth Text from Southwestern Oregon." *IJAL*, 34 (1968), 192–93.
Text with literal translation. Collected in 1935.
4403.   ———. "A Chetco Athabaskan Text and Translation." *IJAL*, 43 (1977), 269–73.
Narrative collected in 1935. With literal and free translations.
4404.   Kroeber, A. L. "Sinkyone Tales." *JAF*, 32 (1919), 346–51.
Eleven myth and folktale texts collected in 1902. Some commentary on cultural background.
4405.   Li, Fang-Kuei. *Mattole. An Athabaskan Language.* Chicago: Univ. of Chicago Press, 1930.
Contains text of a Coyote myth with free and interlinear translations. No commentary.
4406.   Nomland, Gladys Ayer. "Bear River Ethnography." *UCPAR*, 2, No. 2 (1938), 91–124.
Based on fieldwork among Mattole done in 1928–1931. Includes data on religion, shamanism, and ceremonialism. With sixteen unannotated myth texts.
4407.   ———. "A Bear River Shaman's Curative Dance." *AA*, 33 (1931), 38–41.
Description of a ceremonial observed in 1930.
4408.   ———. "Sinkyone Notes." *UCPAAE*, 36, No. 2 (1935), 149–78.
Ethnographic sketch based on fieldwork done in 1928–1929 includes descriptions of ceremonials and eleven myth texts.
4409.   Seaburg, William R. "A Wailaki (Athapaskan) Text with Comparative Notes." *IJAL*, 43 (1977), 327–32.
Narrative collected in 1927. With literal translation and linguistic analysis.

Y. Tubatulabal

4410.   Voegelin, Charles F. "Tübatulabal Grammar." *UCPAAE*, 34, No. 2 (1935), 55–190.
Contains a personal narrative text with free and interlinear translations and linguistic analysis. Based on fieldwork done in 1931–1933.
4411.   ———. "Tübatulabal Texts." *UCPAAE*, 34, No. 3 (1935), 191–246.
Includes fourteen myths, ten personal narratives, an oration, and two descriptions of customs, With translations and linguistic notes. Collected in 1931.
4412.   Voegelin, Erminie W. "Initial and Final Elements in Tübatulabal Myths." *SJA*, 4 (1948), 71–75.
List of opening and closing formulas for narratives.

4413. ———. "Tübatulabal Ethnography." *UCPAR*, 2, No. 1 (1938), 1–84.

Includes data on religion, shamanism, and ceremonialism. With one myth and one life history.

Z. Wappo

4414. Driver, Harold E. "Wappo Ethnography." *UCPAAE*, 36, No. 3 (1936), 179–220.

Based on fieldwork done in 1932. Contains brief survey of mythological system.

4415. Kroeber, Henriette Rothschild. "Wappo Myths." *JAF*, 21 (1908), 321–23.

Two unannotated texts. No commentary.

4416. Radin, Paul. "A Grammar of the Wappo Language." *UCPAAE*, 27 (1929), 1–194.

Linguistic survey with analysis of a myth text. Presented with free and interlinear translations.

4417. ———. "Wappo Texts. First Series." *UCPAAE*, 19, No. 1 (1924), 1–147.

Eleven myth texts collected in 1918 with free and interlinear translations. With explanatory notes and data on informant.

See also 4159, 4160.

AA. Wintun

4418. Barrett, S. A. "Indian Opinions of the Earthquake of April, 1906." *JAF*, 19 (1906), 324–25.

Responses to the earthquake based on cosmological mythology.

4419. ———. "The Wintun Hesi Ceremony." *UCPAAE*, 14, No. 4 (1919), 437–88.

Thorough description of the ceremonial as observed in 1906. With song, prayer, and oration texts.

4420. Curtin, Jeremiah. *Creation Myths of Primitive America in Relation to the Religious History and Mental Development of Mankind.* Boston: Little, Brown, 1898.

Myth texts collected from Wintun and Yana in 1890s. Introductory commentary treats types of creation myths among NAs and compares them to world mythology. Includes explanatory and comparative notes for each text.

4421. Demetracopoulou, D. "Wintu Songs." *A*, 30 (1935), 483–94.

Forty-nine song texts (words only) collected in 1929–1931. With data on context.

4422. ———, and Cora Du Bois. "A Study of Wintu Mythology." *JAF*, 45 (1932), 373–500.

Sixty-nine myth texts collected in 1929–1930. With data on context, performance style, and informants.

4423. Dixon, Roland B. "Water Monsters in Northern California." *JAF*, 19 (1906), 323.

Brief survey of accounts of water monsters among Wintun, Chimariko, and Shasta.

4424. Du Bois, Cora. "Wintu Ethnography." *UCPAAE*, 36, No. 1 (1935), 1–148.

Includes data on various aspects of religion: prayer,

cosmology, shamanism, theology.

4425. ———, and Dorothy Demetracopoulou. "Wintu Myths." *UCPAAE*, 28, No. 5 (1931), 279–403.

Seventy-five texts collected in 1929. With occasional comparative notes.

4426. Goldschmidt, Walter. "Nomlaki Ethnography." *UCPAAE*, 42, No. 4 (1951), 303–443.

Includes data on cosmology, cosmography, and shamanism. With song, myth, and life history texts.

4427. Knudtson, Peter H. "Flora, Shaman of the Wintu." *NH*, May 1975, pp. 6–17.

Description of ceremonialism as recalled and practiced by a female shaman. With excerpt from a song text.

4428. Kroeber, A. L. "The Patwin and Their Neighbors." *UCPAAE*, 29, No. 4 (1932), 253–423.

Ethnography based on fieldwork done in 1923–1924 includes data on ceremonialism and shamanism. With eleven legend and twelve myth texts (all unannotated).

4429. Lee, D. Demetracopoulou. "Categories of the Generic and the Particular in Wintu'." *AA*, 46 (1944), 362–69.

Shows how linguistic preference for the generic over the particular is manifested in mythology.

4430. ———. "The Place of Kinship Terms in Wintu' Speech." *AA*, 42 (1940), 604–16.

Uses myths to show practical uses of kinship terminology.

4431. ———. "Reflections on Wintu' Thought." *IJAL*, 10 (1939), 181–87.

Analysis of the tribal world view based on language. Includes a prayer text.

4432. ———. "Stylistic Use of the Negative in Wintu'." *IJAL*, 12 (1946), 79–81.

Illustrates use of negative indirection in storytelling.

4433. ———. "A Wintu· Girls' Puberty Ceremony." *NMA*, 4, No. 4 (October-December 1940), 57–60.

Description of a ritual observed in 1938.

4434. Masson, Marcelle. *A Bag of Bones. The Wintu Myths of a Trinity River Indian.* [Healdsburg, Cal.]: Naturegraph, 1966.

Fifteen myth texts written by a Wintun informant. No annotations, but with extensive data on informant and cultural background.

4435. Sargent, Lucy. "Indian Dances in Northern California." *Cal*, 1 (1880), 464–69.

Describes ceremonialism.

See also 4126, 4158, 4169, 4179.

BB. Wiyot

4436. Herrick, Mrs. R. F. "Origin of the White Deer Dance." *AAOJ*, 30 (1908), 210–14.

Text of ritual origin myth. Collected in 1859.

4437. Kroeber, A. L. "Wishosk Myths." *JAF*, 18 (1905), 85–107.

Twenty-four unannotated myth texts with abstracts. Preceded by data on cultural background, comparison with mythology of other California groups, and data on general mythological system.

4438. ———. "Wiyot Folk-Lore." *JAF*, 21 (1908), 37–39.

Miscellany of beliefs and brief descriptions of ceremonials.

4439. Reichard, Gladys A. "Wiyot Grammar and Texts." *UCPAAE*, 22, No. 1 (1925), 1–215.

Linguistic survey includes forty-four myth texts with literal translations. Collected in 1922 and 1923.

4440. Teeter, Karl V. *The Wiyot Language.* UCPL No. 37 (1964).

Texts include twenty-four myths and folktales, eighteen personal narratives, and thirty-eight descriptions of customs. With free translations and explanatory notes. Collected between 1956 and 1959.

See also 4149.

CC. Yana

4441. Sapir, Edward. "Text Analyses of Three Yana Dialects." *UCPAAE*, 20 (1923), 263–94.

Thorough linguistic analyses of two myths and one personal narrative. With free and interlinear translations.

4442. ———. "Yana Texts. Together with Yana Myths Collected by Roland B. Dixon." *UCPAAE*, 9, No. 1 (1910), 1–235.

Fifteen myth texts and nine descriptions of customs, collected in 1907. Presented with free and interlinear translations and explanatory and comparative notes.

4443. ———, and Leslie Spier. "Notes on the Culture of the Yana." *UCPAR*, 3, No. 3 (1943), 239–98.

Sapir's ms. written c. 1910 includes data on religion, ceremonialism, and shamanism. Annotated by Spier.

See also 4377, 4420.

DD. Yokuts

4444. Beeler, Madison S. "Nuptinte Yokuts," in 153, pp. 11–76.

Linguistic analyses of Christian religious texts and descriptions of traditional customs.

4445. Gamble, Geoffrey. *Wikchamni Grammar.* UCPL No. 89 (1978).

Myth text with free and interlinear translations and linguistic commentary. Collected in 1974.

4446. Gayton, A. H. "Culture-Environment Integration: External References in Yokuts Life." *SJA*, 2 (1946), 252–68.

Shows how ceremonialism and mythology help to integrate the lifestyle with the natural environment.

4447. ———. "Yokuts and Western Mono Ethnography. I: Tulare Lake, Southern Valley, and Central Foothill Yokuts." *UCPAR*, 10, No. 1 (1948), 1–142.

Based on fieldwork done in 1925 and 1930. Includes data on religion, shamanism, and ceremonials such as the Ghost Dance of 1870.

4448. ———. "Yokuts and Western Mono Ethnography. II: Northern Foothill Yokuts and Western Mono." *UCPAR*, 10, No. 2 (1948), 148–302.

Based on fieldwork done in 1925 and 1930. Includes data on religion, shamanism, and ceremonials such as the Ghost Dance of 1870.

4449. ———. "Yokuts and Western Mono Social Organization." *AA*, 47 (1945), 409–26.

Includes some data on totemic animals and ceremonials associated with units in the social structure.

4450. ———. "Yokuts-Mono Chiefs and Shamans." *UCPAAE*, 24, No. 8 (1930), 361–420.

Treats political and ceremonial leaders by citing mythic bases for offices and related ceremonialism.

4451. ———, and Stanley S. Newman. "Yokuts and Western Mono Myths." *UCPAR*, 5, No. 1 (1940), 1–110.

Fifty-five texts with abstracts, comparative notes, and commentary on cultural background and performance style.

4452. Kroeber, A. L. "The Yokuts Language of South Central California." *UCPAAE*, 2 (1904–1907), 165–377.

Includes several myth texts with interlinear translations and linguistic analyses. Collected between 1900 and 1904.

4453. ———. "Yokuts Names." *JAF*, 19 (1906), 142–43.

Describes naming patterns. With appended list of names.

4454. Latta, F. F. *California Indian Folklore.* Shafter, Cal.: by the Author, 1936.

Thirty-two unannotated myth texts with explanatory notes and data on storytelling customs.

4455. Pietroforte, Alfred. *Songs of the Yokuts and Paiutes.* Ed. Vinson Brown. Healdsburg, Cal.: Naturegraph, 1965.

Twenty-five song texts (words and music) with context data and descriptions of singers. Collected in 1959.

4456. Riddell, Francis A. "Notes on Yokuts Weather Shamanism and the Rattlesnake Ceremony." *M*, 29 (1955), 94–98.

Data on ceremonialism collected in 1949.

4457. Rogers, Barbara Thrall, and A. H. Gayton. "Twenty-Seven Chukchansi Yokuts Myths." *JAF*, 57 (1944), 190–207.

Texts collected in 1938. With some comparative notes.

4458. Stewart, Geo. W. "Two Yokuts Traditions." *JAF*, 21 (1908), 237–39.

Myth texts collected in 1907. With sketchy comparative notes.

4459. ———. "A Yokuts Creation Myth." *JAF*, 19 (1906), 322.

Unannotated text collected in 1903. No commentary.

See also 4148, 4169.

EE. Yuki

4460. Foster, George M. "A Summary of Yuki Culture." *UCPAR*, 5, No. 3 (1944), 155–244.

Based on fieldwork done in 1937. Includes data on religion (including Pentecostalism), ceremonialism, shamanism, and humor.

4461. Gifford, E. W. "The Coast Yuki." *A,* 34 (1939), 292–375.

Ethnography based on fieldwork done in 1926 and 1929 includes data on religion, ceremonialism, and shamanism.

4462. ———. "Coast Yuki Myths." *JAF,* 50 (1937), 115–72.

Thirty-nine unannotated myth texts collected in 1926 and 1929. With some data on context.

4463. Goldschmidt, Walter, George Foster, and Frank Essene. "War Stories from Two Enemy Tribes." *JAF,* 50 (1939), 141–54.

Nine historical legends, collected from the Yuki and Nomlaki, about warfare between the two groups. The legends reflect the groups' attitudes toward each other and present ethnographic data about traditional warfare.

4464. Kroeber, A. L. "Yuki Myths." *A,* 27 (1932), 905–39.

Nine translated myth texts collected in 1902. Presented with linguistic notes and some data on collecting situation.

See also 4149, 4159, 4160, 4169.

FF. Yurok

4465. Buckley, Thomas. "Doing Your Thinking." *P,* 4, No. 4 (November 1979), 29–37.

Socialization study includes data on role of mythology, historical legends, and prayers in the past and of metaphorical songs today.

4466. Cody, Bertha Parker. "Some Yurok Customs and Beliefs." *M,* 16 (1942), 157–62; 17 (1943), 81–87.

Material collected in 1940 and 1941 consists primarily of orally recounted reminiscences.

4467. ———. "Yurok Fish-Dam Dance. As Told by Jane Van Stralen." *M,* 16 (1942), 81–86.

Description of a ritual narrated in 1941.

4468. ———. "Yurok Tales. As Told by Jane Van Stralen." *M,* 15 (1941), 228–31.

Four myth and legend texts with explanatory notes. Collected in 1940.

4469. Denny, Melcena Burns. "Orleans Indian Legends." *OW,* 25 (1906), 37–40, 161–66, 268–71, 373–75, 451–54; 26 (1907), 73–80, 168–70, 267–68.

Eleven unannotated myth texts dealing with Coyote. No commentary.

4470. Erikson, Erik H. "Erikson Among the Indians." *Ho,* 14, No. 4 (Autumn 1972), 80–85.

Comparison of Yurok and Sioux childrearing practices and resulting Basic Personality Structure. Some references to mythic reflections of the personalities.

4471. ———. "Observations on the Yurok: Childhood and World Image." *UCPAAE,* 35 (1943), 257–301.

Personality and culture study takes creation myth and ceremonialism into account.

4472. Kroeber, A. L. "The Yurok Culture." *RS,* 28, No. 3 (September 1960), 567–69 (Monograph Supplement No. 2).

Compares Yurok and Twana cosmologies and ceremonial complexes.

4473. ———. *Yurok Myths.* Berkeley: Univ. of California Press, 1976.

Presentation of texts accompanied by "Folkloristic Commentary" by Alan Dundes and an assessment of Kroeber's fieldwork among the Yurok by Timothy N. Thorsen. With data on cultural background for myths.

4474. ———. "A Yurok War Reminiscence: The Use of Autobiographical Evidence." *SJA,* 1 (1945), 318–32.

Excerpts from two life histories are used to show the place of autobiography in ethnography.

4475. O'Neil, Michael R. "Doomed Sons of the Redwoods." *T,* 52 (February 1929), 33–37, 46–48.

Survey of declining Yurok culture includes data on ceremonialism.

4476. Posinsky, S. H. "The Problem of Yurok Anality." *AI,* 14 (1957), 3–31.

Passion for wealth, revealed in myths and rituals, results from infantile deprivation.

4477. Robins, R. H. *The Yurok Language: Grammar, Texts, Lexicon. UCPL* No. 15 (1958).

Eight myth and folktale texts. Presented with free translations and linguistic notes.

4478. Sapir, Jean. "Yurok Tales." *JAF,* 41 (1928), 253–61.

Eleven folktale texts collected in 1927. No commentary or annotation.

4479. Spott, Robert, and A. L. Kroeber. "Yurok Narratives." *UCPAAE,* 35 (1943), 143–256.

Thirty-seven legend texts with commentary on cultural background. No annotation.

4480. Waterman, T. T., and A. L. Kroeber. "The Kepel Fish Dam." *UCPAAE,* 35 (1943), 49–80.

Description of a ceremonial based on material collected in 1901.

See also 2874, 2875, 4149, 4158, 4169.

IX NORTHWEST COAST

A. General Works

4481. Allen, Rosemary A. "The Potlatch and Social Equilibrium." *DJA,* 2, No. 1 (Winter 1955), 43–54.
Describes ways in which the ceremonial contributes to social equilibrium.
4482. Ames, Michael. "Indians of the Northwest Coast." *AW,* 10, No. 4 (July 1973), 12–17.
Survey includes data on several tribal groups and an extensive description of the potlatch.
4483. "Appeal by the Indians of Vancouver Island, An." *JAF,* 36 (1923), 295–97.
Text of letter written to "Indian Department of Canada" asking for permission to engage in traditional ceremonialism.
4484. Badlam, Alexander. *The Wonders of Alaska.* San Francisco: Bancroft, 1890.
Historical, geographical, and ethnological survey includes a legend text and description of ceremonialism and supernaturalism among Northwest Coast and Arctic groups.
4485. Ballard, Arthur C. "Mythology of Southern Puget Sound." *UWPA,* 3, No. 2 (December 1929), 31–150.
Translated myth texts from various groups (Puyallup, Snuqualmi, Duwamish, Skagit, and Yakima). No annotations. With some data on informants.
4486. Barbeau, Marius. *Alaska Beckons.* Caldwell, Ida.: Caxton, 1947.
Rewritten myth and legend texts from various Northwest Coast and Arctic groups are used to introduce NA cultures, Alaskan history, and current problems in the state.
4487. ———. "Asiatic Survivals in Indian Songs." *MQ,* 20 (1934), 107–16.
Examines five song texts (words and music) for parallels with oriental traditions. Reprinted in *QQ,* 47 (Spring 1940), 67–76; and *ScM,* 54 (April 1942), 303–7.
4488. ———. "Buddhist Dirges on the North Pacific Coast." *JIFMC,* 14 (1962), 16–21.
Compares song texts from various Northwest Coast groups to materials from China and Siberia.
4489. ———. "How Totem Poles Originated." *QQ,* 46 (Autumn 1939), 304–11.
Argues that totem pole art is a recent development (beginning in 1800s). Retells an anecdote about a totem pole carver from Nass River.
4490. ———. *Medicine-Men on the North Pacific Coast.* NMCB No. 152 (1958).
Surveys shamanistic practices among various

Northwest Coast groups. With three legend texts.
4491. ———. "The Modern Growth of the Totem Pole on the Northwest Coast." *JWAS,* 28 (1938), 385–93.
Includes data on ceremonialism and mythic interpretations of totem pole art.
4492. ———. *Totem Poles.* 2 volumes. *NMCB* No. 119 (1950).
Catalogue of pole designs and locations with extensive use of myth texts and excerpts to account for designs.
4493. ———. "Totem Poles: A By-Product of the Fur Trade." *ScM,* 55 (December 1942), 507–14.
Argues for recent origin (c. 1830) for totem pole art on Northwest Coast.
4494. ———. "Totem Poles: A Recent Native Art of the Northwest Coast of America." *ARSI for 1931,* pp. 559–70.
General survey of art form with attention to origin of symbols in folklore. Reprinted from the *Geographical Review* for April 1930.
4495. ———. "Songs of the Northwest." *MQ,* 19 (1933), 101–11.
Seven song texts (words and music) from various groups. With descriptions of contexts and explanatory notes.
4496. ———. " 'Totemic Atmosphere' on the North Pacific Coast." *JAF,* 67 (1954), 103–22.
Argues that totemism does not exist among Northwest Coast groups.
4497. ———. "Totemism, A Modern Growth on the North Pacific Coast." *JAF,* 57 (1944), 51–58.
Argues that Northwest Coast totemism results from acculturation with EA and Oceanic groups.
4498. Barnett, H. G. *Indian Shakers. A Messianic Cult of the Pacific Northwest.* Carbondale: Southern Illinois Univ. Press, 1957.
Historical account of a revitalization movement includes data on ceremonialism.
4499. ———. "The Nature of the Potlatch." *AA,* 40 (1938), 349–58.
Attempts to correct misconceptions about the ritual.
4500. Beck, Mary. "The Oral Literature of Native Alaska." *IH,* 4, No. 2 (Summer 1971), 17–19.
Survey of Northwest Coast mythology as artistic expression.
4501. Bemister, Margaret. *Thirty Indian Legends of Canada.* Vancouver: J. J. Douglas, 1973.
Rewritten myth texts from groups in Northwest Coast, Sub-Artic, Plains, and Plateau. No commentary or annotations. First published in 1917.
4502. Blackman, Margaret B. "Creativity in Acculturation: Art, Architecture and Ceremony from the Northwest Coast." *Eh,* 23 (1976), 387–413.
Surveys positive effects of acculturation on various Northwest Coast groups, including developments in rituals such as the potlatch.
4503. Boas, Franz. "The Development of the Culture of North-West America." *S,* 12 (26 October 1888), 194–96.
Cross-cultural ethnographic survey includes data on mythology, legendry, and ceremonialism.

4504. ———. "The Growth of Indian Mythologies." *JAF*, 9 (1896), 1–11.

Evaluates cases for independent invention and for diffusion as ways of accounting for the development of the mythologies of various Northwest Coast groups.

4505. ———. "The Indians of British Columbia." *PSM*, 32 (March 1888), 628–36.

Cultural survey includes data on ceremonialism with song texts (words only).

4506. ———. "The Indians of British Columbia." *PTRSC*, 1st series, 6, section 2 (1888), 47–57.

Culture survey focuses on language and oral literature. With myth and legend texts.

4507. Bogoras, Waldemar. "The Folklore of Northeastern Asia, as Compared with That of Northwestern America." *AA*, 4 (1902), 577–683.

Demonstrates parallels between traditions of Siberian groups and of Northwest Coast and Arctic groups.

4508. Bruce, Miner W. *Alaska. Its History and Resources, Gold Fields, Routes and Scenery.* Seattle: Lowman & Hanford, 1895.

Historical, geographical, and ethnological survey includes summary of a Tlingit legend and data on ceremonials of various Northwest Coast and Arctic groups.

4509. Chowning, Ann. "Raven Myths in Northwestern North America and Northeastern Asia." *ArA*, 1, No. 1 (1962), 1–5.

Suggests that Raven myths offer evidence of diffusion between NAs and Asia.

4510. Clark, Ella E. "The Bridge of the Gods in Fact and Fancy." *OHQ*, 53 (March 1952), 29–38.

Comparative treatment of a myth known among several Northwest Coast groups.

4511. ———. "George Gibbs' Account of Indian Mythology in Oregon and Washington Territories." *OHQ*, 56 (December 1955), 293–325; 57 (June 1956), 125–67.

Excerpts from Gibbs' ms. dated 1865. May be earliest collection of oral literature from the Northwest Coast.

4512. ———. *Indian Legends of the Pacific Northwest.* Berkeley: Univ. of California Press, 1953.

Myth, folktale, and legend texts (109) from various Northwest Coast groups. Most of the material is rewritten from previously published or ms. sources. With explanatory comments.

4513. ———. "Indian Story-Telling of Old in the Pacific Northwest." *OHQ*, 54 (June 1953), 91–101.

Survey of storytelling customs among various Northwest Coast and Plateau groups.

4514. ———. "The Mythology of the Indians in the Pacific Northwest." *OHQ*, 54 (September 1953), 163–89.

Survey of themes in the mythologies of various Northwest Coast and Plateau groups.

4515. ———, ed. "Origin of Hot Springs." *NWR*, 5 (Summer 1962), 100–05.

Unannotated Coyote myth with general data on Coyote as a folklore figure. Collected from an informant on the Warm Springs Reservation.

4516. Collins, June McCormick. "The Indian Shaker Church: A Study of Continuity and Change in Religion." *SJA*, 6 (1950), 399–411.

Historical treatment of the revitalization movement includes ritual descriptions.

4517. Corser, H. P. *Totem Lore and the Land of the Totem.*

Including Totem Lore, Sixth Edition, and Through the Ten Thousand Islands of Alaska, Second Edition. Juneau: Nugget Shop, ND.

Hodgepodge of essays on Northwest Coast cultures includes data on totem pole art, mythology, and "Tlingit Intellectual Life."

4518. Curtis, Natalie. "The People of the Totem-Poles: Their Art and Legends." *Cr*, 16, No. 6 (September 1909), 612–21.

Culture survey contains summaries of myths.

4519. Davis, Robert Tyler. *Native Arts of the Pacific Northwest from the Rasmussen Collection of the Portland Art Museum.* Stanford, Cal.: Stanford Univ. Press, 1949.

Pictorial survey has commentary which treats beliefs in spirit world and their relationship to art.

4520. Deans, James. "Legendary Lore of the Coast Tribes of Northwestern America," in 79, pp. 266–77.

Describes myth types of various Northwest Coast groups.

4521. ———. "The Moon Symbol on the Totem Posts on the Northwest Coast." *AAOJ*, 13 (1891), 341–46.

Considers myths and legends about the moon illustrated on totem poles.

4522. ———. "The Raven in the Mythology of Northwest America." *AAOJ*, 10 (1888), 109–14.

Survey of Raven's role in the myths of various Northwest Coast groups.

4523. ———. "The Raven Myth of the Northwest Coast. Resemblance to Certain Bible Stories and Greek Constellations." *AAOJ*, 11 (1889), 297–301.

Points out several correspondences with Old World traditions.

4524. ———. "The Raven's Place in the Mythology of Northwestern America." *AAOJ*, 10 (1888), 273–78.

Continuation of 4522.

4525. ———. "Totem-Post Stories." *FL*, 1 (1893), 185–88.

Texts of two stories represented on a totem pole exhibition at the Chicago World's Fair.

4526. ———. "What Patlatches [sic] Are." *AAOJ*, 18 (1896), 274–76.

Ceremonial description.

4527. ———. "When Patlatches [sic] Are Observed." *AAOJ*, 18 (1896), 329–31.

Treats functions of the ceremony.

4528. Densmore, Frances. "Music of the Indians of British Columbia." *BAEB* No. 136 (*AP* No. 27), 1943.

Ninety-eight song texts (words and music) with musicological and contextual notes. Collected in 1926.

4529. ———. *Nootka and Quileute Music. BAEB* No. 124 (1939).

Song texts (210—words and music) with musicological and contextual notes. Introduction presents cultural background and compares material with songs of other NA groups. Collected in 1923 and 1926 from the Makah, Clayoquot, Quileute, Nootka, Quinault, and Yakima.

4530. Dickason, Olive Patricia. *Indian Arts in Canada.* Ottawa: Department of Indian Affairs and Northern Development, 1972.

Pictorial survey includes treatment of relationship between art and ceremonialism among various Northwest Coast and Sub-Arctic groups.

4531. Dorsey, J. Owen. "Indians of Siletz Reservation, Oregon." *AA*, o. s. 2 (1889), 55–62.

Ethnographic notes collected in 1884 include a creation myth narrated in Chinook.

4532. "Double Headed Serpent and the Migration of Symbols." *AAOJ,* 24 (1902), 482–83.

Comparative discussion of a symbol in Northwest Coast cultures with attention to its mythic background.

4533. Drucker, Philip. "The Antiquity of the Northwest Coast Totem Pole." *JWAS,* 38 (1948), 389–97.

Argues that totem pole art predated EA contact.

4534. ———. *Indians of the Northwest Coast.* Garden City, N.Y.: Doubleday, 1955.

Culture survey includes data on ceremonialism and mythology. Ceremonials are viewed as dramatic cycles.

4535. Eells, Myron. "Do-Ki-Batt; Or; The God of the Puget Sound Indians." *AAOJ,* 6 (1884), 389–93.

Description of high god shared by several Northwest Coast groups.

4536. ———. "Myths of the Puget Sound Indians." *AAOJ,* 12 (1890), 160–65.

Assorted texts of oral literature collected from various Northwest Coast groups: myths, folktales, children's stories, proverbs.

4537. ———. "The Potlatches of Puget Sound." *AAOJ,* 5 (1883), 135–37.

Fairly thorough description of the ceremonial.

4538. ———. "The Religion of the Indians of Puget Sound." *AAOJ,* 12 (1890), 69–84.

Survey of religious system treats theology and supernaturalism. With myth texts.

4539. ———. "The Thunder Bird." *AA,* o. s. 2 (1889), 329–36.

Focuses on Northwest Coast groups to describe the mythic creature.

4540. ———. "Traditions and History of the Puget Sound Indians." *AAOJ,* 9 (1887), 97–104.

Includes myths, legends, and folktales from various Northwest Coast groups.

4541. ———. "Traditions of the 'Deluge' Among the Tribes of the North-West." *AAOJ,* 1 (1878), 70–72.

Excerpts from flood myths of various Northwest Coast groups.

4542. Emmons, George T. "The Art of the Northwest Coast Indians." *NH,* 30 (1930), 282–92.

Survey of painting and carving. Some designs respresent mythical beings.

4543. ———. "Copper Neck-Rings of Southern Alaska." *AA,* 10 (1908), 644–49.

Survey of traditional ornamentation includes paraphrase of "The Salmon Doctor," a story known in several Northwest Coast groups.

4544. ———. "Portraiture Among the North Pacific Coast Tribes." *AA,* 16 (1914), 59–67.

Treats portraits of mythical beings and references to protraiture in the narrative traditions of the Tlingit and Tsimshian.

4545. Ernst, Alice Henson. "Masks of the Northwest Coast." *TAM,* 17, No. 8 (August 1933), 646-56.

Describes masks, their functions, and their mythic associations.

4546. ———. "Northwest Coast Animal Dances." *TAM,* 23 (September 1939), 661–72.

Description of ceremonials.

4547. ———. "Thunderbird Dance. Native North American Theatre." *TAM,* 29 (February 1945), 118–25.

Interprets ceremonial performed by various Northwest Coast groups as drama.

4548. Florida, R. E. "Claude Lévi-Strauss Meets *The Girl Who Married the Bear:* A Structural Analysis of a Canadian Indian Myth," in 157, pp. 81–94.

Analysis of a narrative popular among Northwest Coast and Sub-Arctic groups reveals concern with social relationships, clothing, and economics.

4549. Fullerton, Aubrey. "The Passing of the Totem-Pole." *Be,* 7 September 1918, pp. 263–65.

Survey of the role of the totem pole in Northwest Coast cultures.

4550. Garfield, Viola E., and Linn A. Forrest. *The Wolf and the Raven. Totem Poles of Southeastern Alaska.* Seattle: Univ. of Washington Press, 1961.

Descriptions of totem poles at four sites include mythological bases of designs.

4551. Gibbs, George. *Tribes of Western Washington and Northwestern Oregon.* CNAE No. 1 (1877).

Ethnographic survey includes data on ceremonialism.

4552. Grant, Rena V. "The Chinook Jargon, Past and Present." *CFQ,* 3 (1944), 259–76.

Historical treatment of the lingua franca of the Northwest Coast includes glossary and some hymn texts.

4553. Grinnell, George Bird. "Bluejay Visits the Ghost." *H,* 101 (1900), 840–45.

Rewritten folktale.

4554. ———. "The Punishment of the Stingy—A Bluejay Story." *H,* 101 (1900), 323–28.

Rewritten folktale.

4555. ———. *The Punishment of the Stingy and Other Indian Stories.* New York: Harper and Brothers, 1901.

Rewritten myth and folktale texts from various Northwest Coast and Plains groups. No commentary or annotations.

4556. Grumet, Robert Steven. *Native Americans of the Northwest Coast. A Critical Bibliography.* Bloomington: Indiana Univ. Press, 1979.

Unannotated list of 222 books and articles. Introductory essay focuses on specific groups and on general topics such as the potlatch.

4557. Grunfeld, Frederic V. "Indian Giving." *Ho,* 11 (Winter 1969), 46–47.

Description of the potlatch.

4558. ———. "Render unto Cedar." *Ho,* 10, No. 4 (Autumn 1968), 64–68.

Treats decay of totem poles among Northwest Coast groups. With excerpt from myth text.

4559. Guie, Heister Dean. "Nature and the Northwestern Red Man." *NM,* 32 (February 1939), 71–73.

Survey of ceremonial and medicinal uses of plants.

4560. Gunther, Erna. "Accretion in the Folktales of the American Indians." *F,* 38 (1927), 40–54.

Examines narratives from various Northwest Coast groups to determine whether or not they are developed from foreign accretions.

4561. ———. "An Analysis of the First Salmon Ceremony." *AA,* 28 (1926), 605–17.

Ceremonial description with prayer texts.

4562. ———. "A Further Analysis of the First Salmon Ceremony." *UWPA,* 2, No. 5 (June 1928), 129–73.

Amplification of 4561 includes description of the ceremonial and treatment of its relationship to mythology.

4563. ———. *Indian Life on the Northwest Coast of North America as Seen by the Early Explorers and Fur Traders During the Last Decades of the Eighteenth Century.* Chicago: Univ. of Chicago Press, 1972.

Ethnohistory based on accounts of early observers includes data on ceremonial singing and a myth text (Nootka) and historical legendry and singing (Tlingit).

4564. ———. "The Shaker Religion of the Northwest," in 159, pp. 37–76.

Historical account of revitalization movement. With ceremonial description.

4565. Haeberlin, Hermann. "Mythology of Puget Sound." *JAF,* 37 (1924), 371–438.

Forty-one myth and legend texts from various groups. No annotations. With brief introductory comments by Franz Boas.

4566. ———, and Erna Gunther. "The Indians of Puget Sound." *UWPA,* 4, No. 1 (September 1930), 1–84.

Ethnographic notes on Snohomish, Snuqualmi, Nisqually, Skykomish, and Skagit include data on religion, ceremonialism, and shamanism. Originally published in *Zeitschrift für Ethnologie* for 1924.

4567. Hall, Manly P. "The Mystery of the Thunderbird." *OM,* n. s. 87 (1929), 109–10, 128.

Description of the Northwest Coast Thunderbird figure. With comparison to traditions of other groups.

4568. Halpern, Ida. "On the Interpretation of 'Meaningless-Nonsensical Syllables' in the Music of the Pacific Northwest Indians." *Em,* 20 (1976), 253–71.

Shows deep significance of apparently meaningless syllables sung among Kwakiutl, Nootka, Salish, and Hinikeet.

4569. Harrington, Lyn. "Art of the Totem Pole." *SAM,* 50 (May 1951), 293–95.

Views the poles as representing myth and legend narratives.

4570. Hawthorn, H. B., C. S. Belshaw, and S. M. Jamieson. *The Indians of British Columbia. A Study of Contemporary Social Adjustment.* Berkeley: Univ. of California Press, 1958.

Acculturation study with some attention to ceremonials such as the potlatch.

4571. Hays, H. R. *Children of the Raven. The Seven Indian Nations of the Northwest Coast.* New York: McGraw-Hill, 1975.

Ethnography and history of Tlingit, Tsimshian, Haida, Kwakiutl, Bella Coola, Nootka, and Coast Salish include data on ceremonialism, the Raven Trickster cycle, other mythology, and songs.

4572. Henderson, Alice Palmer. *The Rainbow's End: Alaska.* Chicago: Herbert S. Stone, 1898.

Historical, geographical, and ethnological survey includes data on potlatch and funerary customs among Northwest Coast and Arctic groups.

4573. Hill-Tout, Charles. "The Origin of the Totemism of the Aborigines of British Columbia." *PTRSC,* 2nd series, 7, section 2 (1901), 3–15.

Cites clan origin myths and describes clan and personal totems in various Northwest Coast groups.

4574. Holm, Bill. *Crooked Beak of Heaven. Masks and Other Ceremonial Art of the Northwest Coast.* Seattle: Univ. of Washington Press, 1972.

Description of artifacts of several Northwest Coast groups includes some data on ceremonial background.

4575. Hughes, J. C. "A Bit of Indian Folk-Lore." *OM,* n. s. 1 (1883), 351–54.

Rewritten myth text from an unspecified Northwest Coast group.

4576. Ingersoll, Ernest. "From the Fraser to the Columbia." *H,* 68 (1883–1884), 706–21, 869–82.

Account of trip in Washington includes summary of a NA geographical legend.

4577. Inverarity, Robert Bruce. *Art of the Northwest Coast Indians.* Berkeley: Univ. of California Press, 1950.

Pictorial survey includes general description of ceremonialism and the text of a Raven myth.

4578. Irvin, Terry T. "The Northwest Coast Potlatch Since Boas, 1897–1972." *Ant,* 1, No. 1 (May 1977), 65–77.

Survey of interpretations of the ritual.

4579. Jackson, Sheldon. *Alaska, and Missions on the North Pacific Coast.* New York: Dodd, Mead, 1880.

Includes some descriptions of ceremonials from various groups in the Northwest Coast and Arctic. With one oration text.

4580. Jacobs, Melville. "Areal Spread of Indian Oral Genre Features in the Northwest States." *JFI,* 9 (1972), 10–17.

Lists twenty-one stylistic features characteristic of Northwest Coast oral literature.

4581. ———. "The Fate of Indian Oral Literatures in Oregon." *NWR,* 5 (Summer 1962), 90–99.

History of fieldwork among Northwest Coast groups.

4582. ———. "An Historical Event Text from a Galice Athabaskan in Southwestern Oregon." *IJAL,* 34 (1968), 183–91.

Legend text with free translation and linguistic analysis. Collected in 1930s.

4583. ———. "Texts in Chinook Jargon." *UWPA,* 7, No. 1 (November 1936), 1–27.

Fifteen myths and descriptions of culture recorded in Chinook from members of various Northwest Coast groups. Presented with free translations and explanatory notes.

4584. Jenness, Diamond. "Canadian Indian Religion." *An,* 1 (1955), 1–17.

Survey of religious systems of Northwest Coast, Sub-Arctic, and Arctic groups. Treats lack of distinction between myth and folktale among NAs.

4585. Johnston, Thomas F. "Alaskan Eskimo and Indian Musical Performance: Its Many Psychological and Social Ramifications," in 136, pp. 117–31.

Argues that form is more stable than function in music of Alaskan NA groups.

4586. Judson, Katharine Berry, ed. *Myths and Legends of Alaska.* Chicago: A. C. McClurg, 1911.

Rewritten texts from various Northwest Coast and Arctic groups.

4587. ———. *Myths and Legends of the Pacific Northwest Especially of Washington and Oregon.* Chicago: A. C. McClurg, 1910.

Rewritten texts from various Northwest Coast groups.

4588. Keithahn, Edward L. *Monuments in Cedar.* Seattle: Superior, 1963.

Treats the totem pole and its mythological associations. With a chapter on oral literature of various Northwest Coast groups.

4589. Kiefer, Thomas M. "Continuous Geographical Distribution of Musical Patterns: A Test Case from the Northwest Coast." *AA,* 71 (1969), 701–6.

Shows how variations between musical styles of Northwest Coast and Arctic groups relate to distance between groups.

4590. King, J. C. H. *Portrait Masks from the Northwest Coast of America.* [London]: Thames and Hudson, 1979.

Masks of five groups (Tlingit, Tsimshian, Haida, Nootka, Kwakiutl) are described in terms of ritual functions. With data on shamanism and the potlatch.

4591. Krieger, Herbert W. "Indian Villages of Southeast Alaska." *ARSI for 1927,* pp. 345–49.

Includes brief discussion of mythological designs in totem pole art.

4592. Lerman, Norman H. *Once Upon an Indian Tale. Authentic Folk Tales.* New York: Carlton Press, 1968.

Nine myth and folktale texts collected from female informants in British Columbia. No annotation, but some commentary on plot development. "Phrased in grammatical English" by Helen S. Carkin.

4593. Lévi-Strauss, Claude. "How Myths Die." *NLH,* 5, No. 2 (Winter 1974), 269–81.

Uses a myth extant among Northwest Coast and Plateau groups to show how dissemination of a text through space may disintegrate the narrative formula.

4594. Lewis, Albert Buell. "Tribes of the Columbia Valley and the Coast of Washington and Oregon." *MAAA,* 1 (1905–1907), 147–209.

Ethnographic survey of Northwest Coast and Plateau groups includes data on mythology.

4595. Long Lance, Chief Buffalo Child. "Indians of the Northwest and West Coast." *Me,* 12, No. 2 (March 1924), 3–40.

Historical and cultural survey of Northwest Coast, Plateau, and Plains groups includes data on ceremonialism and a joke text.

4596. Lyman, William D. "Indian Myths of the Northwest." *PAAS,* n. s. 25 (1915), 375–95.

Bibliographical essay surveys the sources of Northwest Coast mythologies.

4597. Malin, Edward. *A World of Faces: Masks of the Northwest Coast Indians.* Portland: Timber, 1978.

Includes data on ceremonial uses and mythological sources of masks.

4598. Marriott, Crittenden. "The Measles Cannibal." *ScA,* 99 (26 December 1908), 475.

Response by Northwest Coast shamans to measles epidemic. Personified as ogre.

4599. McClellan, Catharine. "Indian Stories About the First Whites in Northwestern America," in 132, pp. 103–33.

Surveys function, content, and style of NA accounts of first EA contact. From Northwest Coast and Sub-Artic groups.

4600. Meacham, A. B. *Wigwam and War-Path; or The Royal Chief in Chains.* 2nd edition. Boston: John P. Dale, 1875.

Sympathetic account of federal mistreatment of NAs by Superintendent of Indian Affairs in Oregon contains legend summaries and ceremonial descriptions for Northwest Coast and California groups.

4601. Morgan, Lael, ed. *Alaska's Native People.* AG, 6, No. 3 (1979).

Guide to various NA groups in Alaska includes some data on Tlingit supernaturalism (by William Paul), text of an Eskimo chant (by Howard Rock), and retellings of myths and legends from various groups.

4602. Morice, A. G. "The Fur Trader in Anthropology: And a Few Related Questions." *AA,* 30 (1928), 60–84.

Examines the ethnographic values of diaries and other mss. kept by fur traders, primarily in Northwest Coast area. Some of the excerpts from the mss. include data on NA ceremonials such as the potlatch.

4603. Ober, Sarah Endicott. "A New Religion Among the West Coast Indians." *OM,* n. s. 56 (1910), 583–94.

Description and history of Shakerism.

4604. Olson, Ronald L. "The Indians of the Northwest Coast." *NH,* 35 (1935), 182–97.

Culture survey includes a brief description of the potlatch.

4605. Phillips, W. S. *Totem Tales. Indian Stories Indian Told. Gathered in the Pacific Northwest.* Chicago: Star, 1896.

Thirty-one unannotated myth and folktale texts. No commentary. May be for children.

4606. Ramsey, Jarold. "The Indian Literature of Oregon," in 85, pp. 3–19.

Survey of forms and subjects of the oral literatures of various Northwest Coast groups.

4607. Randall, Betty Uchitelle. "The Cinderella Theme in Northwest Coast Folklore," in 159, pp. 243–85.

Cross-cultural survey of Northwest Coast variants of EA "Cinderella" folktales.

4608. Ravenhill, Alice. *The Native Tribes of British Columbia.* Victoria, B. C.: Charles F. Banfield, 1938.

Survey of cultures of various groups includes data on songs, myths, and oratory. With descriptions of ceremonialism such as the potlatch.

4609. Reagan, Albert B. "Some Traditions of the West Coast Indians." *UASAL,* 11 (1934), 73–93.

Unannotated myth and legend texts from various Northwest Coast groups. No commentary.

4610. Rich, John M. *Chief Seattle's Unanswered Challenge.* Seattle: Lowman & Hanford, 1932.

Impressionistic treatment of results of Seattle's oration of 1854.

4611. Rosman, Abraham, and Paula G. Rubel. *Feasting with Mine Enemy: Rank and Exchange Among Northwest Coast Societies.* New York: Columbia Univ. Press, 1971.

Relates the potlatch to social structures of various Northwest Coast groups. Views the ritual as an affirmation of individual and group status.

4612. Rousseau, B. G. "Legends of the Far West." *Be,* 23 (1 September 1917), 234–38.

Five rewritten myth texts. With some data on cultural background.

4613. Seaman, N. G. *Indian Relics of the Pacific Northwest.* Portland, Ore.: Binfords & Mort, 1967.

Archeological survey includes data on mythology and religion of various Northwest Coast groups.

4614. Smith, Harlan I. "Totem Poles of the North Pacific Coast." *AMJ,* 11 (1911), 77–82.

Description of artwork, some of which depicts mythical monsters.

4615. ———. "A Visit to the Indian Tribes of the Northwest Coast." *AMJ,* 10 (1910), 31–42.

Account of visit to various Northwest Coast groups includes description of potlatch.

4616. Smith, Marian W. "Shamanism in the Shaker Religion of Northwest America." *Man,* 54 (1954), 119–22.

Shows the role of traditional shamanism in the revitalization movement.

4617. Smith, Silas B. "Primitive Customs and Religious Beliefs of the Indians of the Pacific Northwest Coast." *OHQ,* 2 (1901), 255–65.

Cross-cultural survey of religious beliefs includes a myth text.

4618. Strong, William Duncan. "The Occurrence and Wider Implications of a 'Ghost Cult' on the Columbia River Suggested by Carvings in Wood, Bone and Stone." *AA,* 47 (1945), 244–61.

Examines effigies among various Northwest Coast groups as evidence of a ghost cult. Suggests ties of cult to the Ghost Dance.

4619. Swan, James G. *The Northwest Coast; or, Three Years' Residence in Washington Territory.* New York: Harper and Brothers, 1857.

Travel narrative includes summaries of myths and legends and descriptions of ceremonials and games from various Northwest Coast groups.

4620. Swanton, John R. "The Development of the Clan System and of Secret Societies Among the Northwestern Tribes." *AA,* 6 (1904), 477–85.

Survey of social systems of Northwest Coast, Arctic, and Sub-Arctic groups includes clan and tribal origin myths. Swanton added further material in *AA,* 6 (1904), 743–44.

4621. Teall, Gardner C. "The House of the Kumuque." *AAOJ,* 18 (1896), 47–54.

Unannotated myth text from an unspecified group. No commentary.

4622. ———. "The Soil Which Made the Earth. A Legend from the Northwest Coast." *AAOJ,* 17 (1895), 203–4.

Unannotated creation myth text from an unspecified group.

4623. Thornton, Mildred Valley. *Indian Lives and Legends.* Vancouver, B. C.: Mitchell Press, 1966.

Painter's reminiscences include some retellings of myths and descriptions of ceremonials.

4624. Vanderwall, Judith. "Indian Woodcarvers of the Northwest Coast." *AAr,* 36 (April 1972), 50–56, 80–83.

Treats totem pole art and the use of carved objects in rituals.

4625. Von Wrangell, Ferdinand Petrovich. "The Inhabitants of the Northwest Coast of America." Ed. James W. Vanstone. *ArA,* 6, No. 2 (1970), 5–20.

Descriptions of various groups in the Northwest Coast and Arctic, written by a Russian in 1839, include data on ceremonialism and a song text.

4626. Wade, Edwin L., and Lorraine Laurel Wade. "Voices of the Supernaturals: Rattles of the Northwest Coast." *AIAM,* 1 November 1976, pp. 32–39, 58–59.

Considers artistic and ceremonial significance of rattles used to accompany singing among various Northwest Coast groups. With a song text.

4627. Walker, Deward E., Jr. "New Light on the Prophet Dance Controversy." *Eh,* 16 (1969), 245–55.

Argues that the Prophet Dance was inspired by EA influence.

4628. Waterman, T. T. *Notes on the Ethnology of the Indians of Puget Sound. IN&M,* Miscellaneous Series No. 59 (1973).

Emphasizes material culture, but includes data on potlatch. Collected in 1918–1919.

4629. ———. "The Shaker Religion of Puget Sound." *ARSI for 1922,* pp. 499–507.

Description of revitalization movement includes data on preaching and prayer.

4630. ———. "Some Conundrums in Northwest Coast Art." *AA,* 25 (1923), 435–51.

Argues that totem poles do not represent family history. Their topic is mythology.

4631. Webber, W. L. *The Thunderbird "Tootooch" Legends: Folk Tales of the Indian Tribes of the Pacific Northwest Coast Indians.* Seattle: Ace, 1936.

Catalogue of animals appearing in totem pole carvings with attention to mythic and ritual significance.

4632. Yampolsky, Helene Boas. "Excerpts from the Letter Diary of Franz Boas on His First Field Trip to the Northwest Coast." *IJAL,* 24 (1958), 312–20.

Selections from Boas' diary from 1886 expedition include data on folklore performance and collection.

See also 19, 29, 30, 172, 192, 283, 384, 385, 433, 466, 512, 721, 851, 857, 865, 1596, 1988, 2726, 2919, 4117, 4118, 4123, 4138, 4171, 4184, 4701, 4732, 4986, 4988, 4993, 5092, 5099, 5113, 5362, 5369.

B. Alsea

4633. Drucker, Philip. "Contributions to Alsea Ethnography." *UCPAAE,* 35 (1943), 81–101

Includes data on shamanism and ceremonialism. Collected in 1933.

4634. Farrand, Livingston. "Notes on the Alsea Indians of Oregon." *AA,* 3 (1901), 239–47.

Ethnographic survey includes data on narrative traditions and descriptions of ceremonialism.

4635. Frachtenberg, Leo J. *Alsea Texts and Myths. BAEB* No. 67 (1920).

Twenty-two myths, two legends, three sets of exorcism formulas, and a description of a game with interlinear and free translations. Collected by Frachtenberg in 1910 and 1913 and by Livingston Farrand in 1900.

4636. ———. *Lower Umpqua Texts and Notes on the Kusan Dialects. CUCA* No. 4 (1914).

Twenty-three myths, folktales, and descriptions of customs collected in 1911. With free translations, data on collecting situations, and occasional explanatory notes.

4637. ———. "Myths of the Alsea Indians of Northwestern Oregon." *IJAL,* 1, No. 1 (1917), 64–75.

Four narrative texts with free translations and comparative and linguistic notes. Collected in 1900, 1910, and 1913.

C. Bella Bella

4638. Boas, Franz. *Bella Bella Tales. MAFS* No. 25 (1932).

Myths (including episodes from the Raven cycle), folktales, and legends with comparative notes. One text is presented in the Kwakiutl language.

4639. ———. *Bella Bella Texts. CUCA* No. 5 (1928).

Thirty-one myth, folktale, legend, and oration texts with free translations. Collected in 1897 and 1923. No commentary or annotations.

4640. Olson, Ronald L. "Notes on the Bella Bella Kwakiutl." *UCPAR,* 14, No. 5 (1955), 319–48.

Based on fieldwork done in 1935 and 1949. Includes data on religion, shamanism, and ceremonialism. With myth, folktale, and life history texts.

See also 4952.

D. Bella Coola

4641. Boas, Franz. "The Mythology of the Bella Coola Indians." *MAMNH,* 2, Part 2 (1898), 25–127.

Twenty-six myth texts with extensive commentary on conceptual and theological background. Collected by Jesup North Pacific Expedition.

4642. Haekel, Josef. "The Concept of a Supreme Being Among the Northwest Coast Tribes of North America." *WVM,* 2, No. 2 (1954), 171–82.

Survey of Bella Coola theology, especially the major deity conceived of as a chieftain figure.

4643. McIlwraith, T. F. *The Bella Coola Indians.* 2 volumes. Toronto: Univ. of Toronto Press, 1948.

Ethnography based on fieldwork done in 1922–1924 includes data on religion, the potlatch, and other ceremonials. With myth, legend, and song texts.

E. Chicoltin

4644. Farrand, Livingston. "Traditions of the Chicoltin." *MAMNH,* 4, Part 1 (1900), 1–54.

Thirty-two myth texts with abstracts and comparative notes. Collected in 1897 on the Jesup North Pacific Expedition.

F. Chinook

4645. Boas, Franz. "Chinook Songs." *JAF,* 1 (1888), 220–26.

Thirty-eight song texts with free translations and data on cultural background. Includes music for three of the songs.

4646. ———. *Chinook Texts.* BAEB No. 20 (1894).

Eighteen myth texts and assorted descriptions of customs collected in 1890–1891. With free and interlinear translations.

4647. ———. "The Doctrine of Souls and of Disease Among the Chinook Indians." *JAF,* 6 (1893), 39–43.

Texts of myth and personal narrative and description of a healing ritual. Collected in 1891. See comparative data in 417.

4648. ———. *Kathlamet Texts.* BAEB No. 26 (1901).

Thirty-three myth and folktale texts narrated by Charles Cultee in 1890, 1891, and 1894. With free and interlinear translations and data on informant.

4649. Franchère, Gabriel. *A Voyage to the Northwest Coast of America.* Ed. Milo Milton Quaife. Chicago: R. R. Donnelly, 1954.

Travel narrative (1810–1814) includes data on Chinook supernaturalism. Published in French in 1819 and in English in 1854.

4650. French, David. "Cultural Matrices of Chinookan Non-Casual Language." *IJAL,* 24 (1958), 258–63.

Surveys use of specialized language in myths, orations, public announcements, and ceremonial discourse.

4651. Hymes, Dell. "Discovering Oral Performance and Measured Verse in American Indian Narrative." *NLH,* 8 (1977), 431–57.

Uses Chinook oral narratives to show how performances are organized in terms of lines, verses, stanzas, scenes, and acts.

4652. ———. "Folklore's Nature and the Sun's Myth." *JAF,* 88 (1975), 345–69.

Analysis of a myth collected by Boas in 1901 considers genre, tradition, situation, creativity, and performance. Preceded by a survey of American folklore scholarship.

4653. ———. "Linguistic Features Peculiar to Chinookan Myths." *IJAL,* 24 (1958), 253–57.

Treats special features of language used in myth narration.

4654. ———. "Myth and Tale Titles of the Lower Chinook." *JAF,* 72 (1959), 139–45.

Analyzes titles of a body of Chinookan oral literature collected by Boas (4646, 4648). Deals with genre, syntactic style, and function.

4655. ———. "Two Wasco Motifs." *JAF,* 66 (1953), 69–70.

Explanation of characters appearing in myths. From an informant.

4656. ———. "The 'Wife' Who 'Goes Out' Like a Man: Reinterpretation of a Clackamas Chinook Myth," in 137, pp. 49–80.

Structural analysis of a myth previously interpreted by Jacobs in *The People Are Coming Soon* (4662). This was previously published in Julia Kristeva, ed., *Essays in Semiotics* (The Hague: Mouton, 1971).

4657. Jacobs, Melville. *Clackamas Chinook Texts. Part I.* IUPAL No. 8 (1958).

Thirty myth texts with free translations and explanatory notes. Collected in 1929–1930. With commentary on informant.

4658. ———. *The Content and Style of an Oral Literature: Clackamas Chinook Myths and Tales.* Chicago: Univ. of Chicago Press, 1959.

Literary analysis of eight narratives includes emphasis on role and intent of performer. Includes texts with literal and free translations.

4659. ———. "A Few Observations on the World View of the Clackamas Chinook Indians." *JAF,* 68 (1955), 283–89.

Presents a translation of a Coyote myth and shows how the text treats interrelationships among food, kindred, spirit powers, and people.

4660. ———. "Humor and Social Structure in an Oral Literature." in 102, pp. 181–89.

Examines comic situations in Chinook myths.

4661. ———. "Notes on the Structure of Chinook Jargon." *La,* 8, No. 1 (March 1932), 27–50.

Linguistic analysis includes excerpt from a myth text collected in 1930. With free and interlinear translations.

4662. ———. *The People Are Coming Soon: Analyses of Clackamas Chinook Myths and Tales.* Seattle: Univ. of Washington Press, 1960.

Interpretations of narratives collected in 1929–1930 involve sociocultural, psychological, and literary levels. With emphasis on dramatic aspects of myths.

4663. ———. "Psychological Inferences from a Chinook Myth." *JAF*, 65 (1952), 121–37.

Finds evidences for oral and genital stages of psychic development in a long myth text.

4664. ———. "Thoughts on Methodology for Comprehension of an Oral Literature," in 165, pp. 123–29.

Suggests analyses of storytellers, content, and style of Chinook narratives as method for comprehensive understanding.

4665. ———. "Titles in Oral Literature." *JAF*, 70 (1957), 157–72.

Emphasizes esthetic qualities of titles of Chinook oral narratives.

4666. Johnson, E. Pauline (Tekahionwake). *Legends of Vancouver.* New Edition. Toronto: McClelland, Goodchild & Stewart, 1911.

Fifteen unannotated myth and legend texts. No commentary. Originally published in the *Vancouver Daily Province.*

4667. Leechman, Douglas. "The Chinook Jargon." *AS*, 1 (1925–1926), 531–34.

Linguistic survey includes two song texts with free translations.

4667a. Ramsey, Jarold. "Three Warm Springs-Wasco Stories." *WF*, 31 (1972), 116–19.

Texts collected in 1969.

4668. ———. "The Wife Who Goes Out Like a Man, Comes Back as a Hero: The Art of Two Oregon Indian Narratives." *PMLA*, 92 (1977), 9–18.

Structural analysis of similar narratives from Clackamas Chinook and Coos groups reveals complementary factors which represent NA narrative art at its best.

4669. Ray, Verne F. "Lower Chinook Ethnographic Notes." *UWPA*, 7, No. 2 (May 1938), 29–165.

Contains data on ceremonials and four myth texts. Collected between 1931 and 1936.

4670. Sapir, Edward. "Preliminary Report on the Language and Mythology of the Upper Chinook." *AA*, 9 (1907), 533–44.

Survey of the mythological material of the Wishram concludes that it has affinities with both Northwest Coast and Plains groups.

4671. ———, and Jeremiah Curtin. *Wishram Texts, Together with Wasco Tales and Myths.* PAES No. 2 (1909).

Wishram material collected by Sapir in 1905 includes eighteen myths, four legends, four letters, descriptions of customs with free translations. Wasco material collected by Curtin in 1885 (English only) and edited by Sapir includes twenty-five myths and folktales. Also contains a Wasco myth and a Clackamas myth collected by Franz Boas. With linguistic and comparative notes.

4672. Scharbach, Alexander. "Aspects of Existentialism in Clackamas Chinook Myths." *JAF*, 75 (1962), 15–22.

Compares Clackamas Chinook myths to existential drama of Jean-Paul Sartre. Finds that both use myth and ritual as devices to communicate social and philosophical attitudes concerning human existence.

4673. Spier, Leslie, and Edward Sapir. "Wishram Ethnography." *UWPA*, 3, No. 3 (May 1930), 151–300.

Based on fieldwork done in 1905 by Sapir and in 1924–1925 by Spier. Includes data on religion, shamanism, and ceremonialism. With nine myth and folktale texts.

4674. Wade, M. S. "The Modernized Chinook." *T*, 36 (April 1921), 25–27, 32.

Examination of culture change with some data on mythology and ceremonialism.

See also 3, 417.

G. Coos

4675. Clark, Ella E. "The Mortal Who Married a Merman." *JAF*, 62 (1949), 64–65.

Parallels a Coos folktale to a Danish narrative used by Matthew Arnold in his poem "A Forsaken Merman."

4676. Frachtenberg, Leo J. *Coos Texts.* CUCA No. 1 (1913).

Thirty-two myth texts collected in 1903 and 1909 with free and a few interlinear translations. No annotations or commentary. Material for 1903 collected by Harry Hull St. Clair, 2nd.

4677. Jacobs, Melville. "Coos Myth Texts." *UWPA*, 8, No. 2 (1940), 127–260.

Forty-five texts and abstracts collected in 1933–1934. With free translations, data on informant, and comparative notes.

4678. ———. "Coos Narrative and Ethnologic Texts." *UWPA*, 8, No. 1 (April 1939), 1–126.

Twenty myth and legend texts and seventy-one descriptions of customs collected in 1933–1934. Presented with free translations, occasional explanatory notes, and phonetic commentary.

4679. St. Clair, Harry Hull, 2nd. "Traditions of the Coos Indians of Oregon." Ed. Leo J. Frachtenberg. *JAF*, 22 (1909), 25–39.

Thirteen unannotated myth and folktale texts collected in 1903. With some ethnographic notes on religious and ceremonial behavior.

4680. Wasson, Will, and Jim Metzner. "How Salmon Got Greasy Eyes." *P*, 4, No. 1 (February 1979), 66–69.

Coyote tale told by Wasson, of Coos-Coquille descent, to Metzner.

See also 3, 519, 4668.

H. Gitksan

4681. Barbeau, Marius. *Totem Poles of the Gitksan, Upper Skeena River, British Columbia.* NMCB No. 61 (1929).

Description of fifty-two poles with accounts of myths and legends associated with them.

4682. Emmons, George T. "The Kitikshan and Their Totem Poles." *NH*, 25 (1925), 33–48.

Argues that each totem pole represents an account of a mythical event.

4683. ———. "Some Kitksan Totem Poles." *AMJ*, 13 (1913), 362–69.

Contains tribal historical legends in summary. Suggests that poles serve as mnemonic devices for clan origin myths and hero tales.

4684. Kihn, W. Langdon. "The Gitksan on the Skeena." *Scr*, 79 (February 1926), 170–76.

Culture survey includes data on ceremonialism and the mythic bases of art.

4685. "Wee-Gat the Spirit." *B*, 303 (Summer 1972), 15–17.

Unannotated myth text. No commentary.

4686. *We-Gyet Wanders On: Legends of the Northwest.* Saanichton, B. C.: Hancock House, 1977.

Presents myth cycle in Gitksan and free translation. With brief comments on cultural background. No annotations.

I. Haida

4687. Barbeau, Marius. *Haida Myths Illustrated in Argillite Carvings.* NMCB No. 127 (1953).

Extensive collection of myths and legends illustrated by carvings in ivory. Each text is accompanied by data on collecting situation. No comparative notes.

4688. ———. "How the Raven Stole the Sun." *PTRSC*, 3rd series, 38, section 2 (1944), 59–69.

Describes representations in totem pole art of episodes from the Raven cycle.

4689. Blackman, Margaret B. "Ethnohistoric Changes in the Haida Potlatch Complex." *ArA*, 14, No. 1 (1977), 39–53.

Shows effects of acculturation on Haida potlatch: Feasts have come to replace the potlatch.

4690. ———. "Totems to Tombstones: Culture Change as Viewed Through the Haida Mortuary Complex, 1877–1971." *Eth*, 12 (1973), 47–56.

Historical survey of changes in funeral ceremonialism.

4691. Bursill-Hall, G. L. "The Linguistic Analysis of North American Indian Songs." *CJL*, 10, No. 1 (Fall 1964), 15–36.

Parallel analysis of words and music of two Haida love songs.

4692. Dawson, George M. "The Haidas." *H*, 65 (1882), 401–8.

Culture survey includes description of dancing and myth summaries.

4693. Deans, James. "Carved Columns or Totem Posts of the Haidas." *AAOJ*, 13 (1891), 282–87.

Account of origin myths for designs and carving techniques.

4694. ———. "The Feast of Ne-Kilst-Luss, the Raven God. A Tradition of the Queen Charlette [sic] Haidas." *AAOJ*, 10 (1888), 383.

Unannotated myth text. Possibly associated with potlatch.

4695. ———. "Hidery Prayers." *AAOJ*, 22 (1900), 31–32.

Texts with data on context.

4696. ———. "The Hidery Story of Creation." *AAOJ*, 17 (1895), 61–67.

Texts with discussion of cultural background.

4697. ———. "Legend of the Fin-Back Whale Crest of the Haidas, Queen Charlotte's Island, B. C." *JAF*, 5 (1892), 43–47.

Unannotated myth text with some data on the cultural background.

4698. ———. "A Little Known Civilization." *AAOJ*, 17 (1895), 208–13.

Ethnographic sketch contains a myth text.

4699. ———. "The Story of Skaga Belus." *AAOJ*, 13 (1891), 81–84.

Shaman legend with some comparative discussion.

4700. ———. "The Story of the Bear and His Indian Wife. A Legend of the Haidas of Queen Charlotte's Island, B. C." *JAF*, 2 (1889), 255–60.

Unannotated myth text collected in 1873. With explanatory comments.

4701. ———. *Tales from the Totems of the Hidery.* Ed. Oscar Lovell Triggs. *AIFA* No. 2 (1889).

Twenty-five myth and legend texts from the Haida and other Northwest Coast groups. Includes data on contexts. No comparative notes.

4702. ———. "Totem Posts at the World's Fair." *AAOJ*, 15 (1893), 281–86.

Relates traditional narratives associated with exhibited poles.

4703. ———. "A Weird Mourning Song of the Haidas." *AAOJ*, 13 (1891), 52–54.

Description of a ceremonial associated with a smallpox plague.

4704. ———. "What Befell the Slave-Seekers. A Story of the Haidahs on Queen Charlotte's Island, B. C." *JAF*, 1 (1888), 123–24.

Unannotated legend text. No commentary.

4705. Duff, Wilson. "Mute Relics of Haida Tribe's Ghost Villages." *Sm*, 7, No. 6 (September 1976), 84–91.

Examination of totem poles, which may be only structures at abandoned Haida communities, and their mythological significance.

4706. Guernsey, Egbert. "The Alaskan Natives of Ft. Wrangel." *AAOJ*, 13 (1891), 79–81.

Culture survey includes summary of creation myth.

4707. Harrison, Charles. "Religion and Family Among the Haidas (Queen Charlotte Islands)." *JAIGBI*, 21 (1892), 14–29.

Describes pantheon and cosmogony.

4708. Kaufmann, Carole N. "Functional Aspects of Haida Argillite Carvings," in 120, pp. 56–69.

Sees sculptured and painted art forms as the visual correlates of oral tradition.

4709. Leighton, Margaret Wentworth. "The Haidah Indians." *OM*, n. s. 37 (June 1901), 1083–86.

Culture survey includes data on totem pole art and belief in the Thunderbird.

4710. Murdock, George Peter. "Kinship and Social Behavior Among the Haida." *AA*, 36 (1934), 355–85.

Identifies kin relationships in terms of who performs verbal art for whom.

4711. ———. *Rank and Potlatch Among the Haida. YUPA* No. 13 (1936).

Describes five types of the ceremonial.

4712. Smyly, John, and Carolyn Smyly. "Koona: Life and Death of a Haida Village." *AW,* 13, No. 1 (January–February 1976), 14–19.

Describes cultural dissolution with some attention to mythic bases for social structure and art.

4713. Snyder, Gary. *He Who Hunted Birds in His Father's Village. The Dimensions of a Haida Myth.* Bolinas, Cal.: Grey Fox Press, 1979.

Analysis of a myth text from Freudian, Jungian, and historic-geographic perspectives.

4714. Stearns, Mary Lee. "The Reorganization of Ceremonial Relations in Haida Society." *ArA,* 14, No. 1 (1977), 54–63.

Focuses on a mortuary ritual to show how changes in kinship system affect ceremonialism.

4715. Swan, James G. *The Haidah Indians of Queen Charlotte's Islands, British Columbia. With a Brief Description of Their Carvings, Tattoo Designs, etc. SCK* No. 267 (1874).

Focuses on traditional carving and points out mythological associations of some designs.

4716. Swanton, John R. "Haida Songs." *PAES,* 3 (1912), 1–63.

Song texts (106—words only) collected in 1900–1901 and presented with free and interlinear translations. With sketchy context data.

4717. ———. *Haida Texts and Myths. Skidegate Dialect. BAEB* No. 29 (1905).

Seventy-two narrative texts collected in 1900–1901. Two texts (one in Skidegate, one in Masset) are presented with interlinear and free translations. Twelve texts are in Haida with free translations. No substantive commentary.

4718. ———. "Haida Texts—Masset Dialect." *MAMNH,* 14, No. 2 (1908), 271–802.

Ninety-one myth texts with free translations and occasional explanatory notes. From the Jesup North Pacific Expedition.

4719. ———. "Notes on the Haida Language." *AA,* 4 (1902), 392–403.

Linguistic survey includes text and interlinear translation of a narrative excerpt.

4720. ———. "Types of Haida and Tlingit Myths." *AA,* 7 (1905), 94–103.

Abstracts of thirty-six narratives. With little commentary.

4721. Tylor, Edward B. "On the Totem-Post from the Haida Village of Masset, Queen Charlotte Islands, Now Erected in the Grounds of Fox Warren, near Weybridge." *JAIGBI,* 28 (1899), 133–35.

Summarizes myths and describes ceremonials associated with Haida totemism.

4722. ———. "On Two British Columbian House-Posts with Totemic Carvings, in the Pitt-Rivers Museum, Oxford." *JAIGBI,* 28 (1899), 136–37.

Summarizes myths associated with carved designs. Either Haida or Tsimshian.

4723. Watkins, Frances E. "Potlatches and a Haida Potlatch Hat." *M,* 13 (1939), 11–17.

Description of the ritual.

See also 3, 4571, 4590, 4765, 4898, 4905, 4950.

J. Kalapuya

4724. de Angulo, Jaime. "A Tfalati Dance-Song in Parts." *AA,* 31 (1929), 496–98.

Text of a polyphonic song.

4724a. Gatschet, Albert S., Leo J. Frachtenberg, and Melville Jacobs. "Kalapuya Texts. Part III. Kalapuya Texts." *UWPA,* 11 (June 1945), 143–386.

Thirty-five myth and folktale texts with some descriptions of customs. Collected in 1877 (by Gatschet) and 1914 (by Frachtenberg). With free translations, comparative notes, and abstracts.

4725. Jacobs, Melville. "Kalapuya Texts. Part I. Santiam Kalapuya Ethnologic Texts." *UWPA,* 11 (June 1945), 3–81.

Descriptions of customs collected between 1928 and 1936. Presented with free translations. No commentary or annotations.

4726. ———. "Kalapuya Texts. Part II. Santiam Kalapuya Myth Texts." *UWPA,* 11 (June 1945), 83–142.

Nineteen myth texts collected in 1928. With free translations and brief data on collecting situation.

4727. Preston, W. D. "Problems of Text Attestation in Ethnography and Linguistics." *IJAL,* 12 (1946), 173–77.

Suggests proper presentation methods for texts collected for ethnographic and linguistic purposes. Uses material collected by Melville Jacobs (4725, 4726) to illustrate.

4728. Rumberger, J. P., Jr. "Ethnolinguistic Observations Based on Kalapuya Texts." *IJAL,* 15 (1949), 158–62.

Uses myths published by Melville Jacobs (4726) to develop linguistic theories about the nature of the language used in the stories.

See also 4357.

K. Klikitat

4729. Bunnell, Clarence Orvel. *Legends of the Klickitats: A Klickitat Version of the Story of the Bridge of the Gods.* Portland, Ore.: Metropolitan Press, 1935.

Eight episodes of the myth. Rewritten, unannotated, and with no substantive commentary.

4730. Jacobs, Melville. "Northwest Sahaptin Texts. I." *UWPA,* 2, No. 6 (June 1929), 175–244.

Thirteen myth texts collected in 1926 and 1928 and presented with free and interlinear translations. With commentary on cultural backgound.

4731. ———. "A Sketch of Northern Sahaptin Grammar." *UWPA,* 4, No. 2 (March 1931), 85–292.

Contains texts of two Coyote myths (Klikitat and Cowlitz) with interlinear translations and linguistic notes.

4732. Lyman, William D. "Myths and Superstitions of the Oregon Indians." *PAAS,* n. s. 16 (1903–1904), 221–51.

Survey of Klikitat mythology and religious beliefs with comparisons to traditions of other Northwest Coast groups.

4733. Shackleford, Mrs. R. S. "Legend of the Klickitat Basket." *AA,* 2 (1900), 779–80.

Paraphrases narrative about origin of basketweaving technique.

L. Kwakiutl

4734. Attenborough, David. *The Tribal Eye.* New York: Norton, 1976.

Cross-cultural survey of primitive art includes material on Kwakiutl totem poles and Eskimo carving.

4735. Bayliss, Clara Kern. "A Kwakiutl Fragment." *JAF,* 22 (1909), 335.

Unannotated myth text. No commentary.

4736. Beasley, Walter L. "The Secret Cannibal Society of the Kwakiutl." *ScA,* 89 (15 August 1903), 120–22.

Describes ritual procedures of the Hamatsa Society.

4737. Boas, Franz. *Contributions to the Ethnology of the Kwakiutl. CUCA* No. 3 (1925).

Texts of sixty-eight dreams and various customs in Kwakiutl with free translations. No annotation or commentary.

4738. ———. "Current Beliefs of the Kwakiutl Indians." *JAF,* 45 (1932), 177–260.

List of 759 beliefs based on over forty years of fieldwork (1886–1931) includes some ceremonial data.

4739. ———. "Ethnology of the Kwakiutl, Based on Data Collected by George Hunt." *ARBAE,* 35 (1913–1914), 43–1473.

Ethnographic notes in Kwakiutl and English include data on contexts for verbal performances. With texts of prayers, orations, and songs.

4740. ———. *Kwakiutl Culture as Reflected in Mythology. MAFS* No. 28 (1935).

Ethnographic description of the culture based on reflections in the folklore of the culture.

4741. ———. *Kwakiutl Ethnography.* Ed. Helen Codere. Chicago: Univ. of Chicago Press, 1966.

Ms. incomplete at Boas' death in 1943. Includes lengthy description of the potlatch and the Winter Ceremonial. Chapter on mythology comes from 4740.

4742. ———. *Kwakiutl Tales. CUCA* No. 2 (1910).

Fifty-two myth and folktale texts and fragments with free translations. No commentary or annotations.

4743. ———. *Kwakiutl Tales. New Series. Part I—Translations. CUCA* No. 26, Part 1 (1935).

Free translations of sixty-five myths and folktales, most of which were collected in 1930–1931. With extensive comparative notes.

4744. ———. *Kwakiutl Tales. New Series. Part II. CUCA* No. 26, Part 2 (1943).

Sixty-two untranslated and unannotated myth texts. See 4743 for translations.

4745. ———. "On Certain Songs and Dances of the Kwakiutl of British Columbia." *JAF,* 1 (1888), 49–64.

Miscellany of songs (words and music), myths, and ceremonial descriptions. Collected in 1886–1887.

4746. ———. "The Origin of Totemism." *AA,* 18 (1916), 319–26.

Suggests that totemic systems develop in a variety of ways.

4747. ———. *The Religion of the Kwakiutl Indians. Part I. Texts. CUCA* No. 10, Part 1 (1930).

Untranslated and unannotated texts of myths, prayers, personal narratives, and descriptions of ceremonials and other customs. See 4748 for translations.

4748. ———. *The Religion of the Kwakiutl Indians. Part II. Translations. CUCA* No. 10, Part 2 (1930).

Free translations of material presented in 4747. No commentary or annotations.

4749. ———. "Sketch of the Kwakiutl Language." *AA,* 2 (1900), 708–21.

Linguistic survey includes a narrative text with interlinear and free translations.

4750. ———. "The Social Organization and the Secret Societies of the Kwakiutl Indians." *RUSNM for 1895,* pp. 311–737.

Discusses ceremonials such as the potlatch and rituals of secret societies. With ritual and clan origin myths and song texts.

4751. Codere, Helen. "The Amiable Side of Kwakiutl Life: The Potlatch and the Play Potlatch." *AA,* 58 (1956), 334–51.

Characterizes the funmaking and horseplay at potlatches and the institution of the play potlatch. Response from Victor Barnouw in *AA,* 59 (1957), 532–35.

4752. ———. *Fighting with Property. A Study of Kwakiutl Potlatching and Warfare 1792–1930. MonAES* No. 18 (1950).

Sees the potlatch as a substitution for physical violence. Includes several song texts (words only).

4753. ———. "The Swai'xwe Myth of the Middle Fraser River: The Integration of Two Northwest Coast Cultural Ideas." *JAF,* 61 (1948), 1–18.

Compares three texts of a myth explaining the origin of a mask. The myth combines world views of the Kwakiutl and the Puyallup-Nisqually.

4754. Crumrine, N. Ross. "Mediating Roles in Ritual and Symbolism: Northwest Mexico and the Pacific Northwest." *An,* n. s. 18 (1976), 131–52.

Discusses the Wild Man of the Woods as a mediating figure for the Kwakiutl.

4755. Dawson, George M. "Notes and Observations on the Kwakiool People of the Northern Part of Vancouver Island and Adjacent Coasts, Made During the Summer of 1885; with a Vocabulary of About Seven Hundred Words." *PTRSC,* 1st series, 5, section 2 (1887), 63–98.

Ethnography contains data on religion and ceremonialism (such as the potlatch). With several myth texts.

4756. Drucker, Philip. "Kwakiutl Dancing Societies." *UCPAR,* 2, No. 6 (1940), 201–30.

Extensive data on ceremonialism.

4757. Fillmore, John Comfort. "A Woman's Song of the Kwakiutl Indians." *JAF,* 6 (1893), 285–90.

Text (words and music) of a potlatch song collected in 1893. With description of collecting situation and musicological analysis.

4758. Ford, Clellan S. *Smoke from Their Fires: The Life of a Kwakiutl Chief.* New Haven: Yale Univ. Press, 1941.

Life history of a subject born in 1870 includes data on ceremonialism and myth and song texts. Edited from oral narration.

4759. Grant, Rena V. "The Konikillah—A Kwakiutl Tale." *JAF,* 59 (1946), 194–96.

Text of a story narrated in 1898.

4760. Halliday, W. M. *Potlatch and Totem and the Recollections of an Indian Agent.* London: J. M. Dent, 1935.

Thorough description of a hypothetical potlatch.

4761. Hawthorn, Audrey. *Art of the Kwakiutl Indians and Other Northwest Coast Tribes.* Seattle: Univ. of Washington Press, 1967.

Thorough pictorial survey includes commentary on Kwakiutl mythology, the potlatch, and other ceremonials.

4762. Holm, Bill. "Traditional and Contemporary Kwakiutl Winter Dance." *ArA,* 14, No. 1 (1977), 5–24.

Compares past and present performances of a ceremonial which has served as a method for displaying hereditary prestige.

4763. Hunt, George. "Kwakiutl Texts." Ed. Franz Boas. *MAMNH,* 5, Part 1 (1902), 1–270.

Unannotated myth texts with free translations. From the Jesup North Pacific Expedition.

4764. ———. "Kwakiutl Texts—Second Series." Ed. Franz Boas. *MAMNH,* 14, Part 1 (1906), 1–269.

Fifty-six myth texts with free translations and occasional explanatory notes. Comparative notes accompany the abstracts. From the Jesup North Pacific Expedition.

4765. Hymes, Dell. "Some North Pacific Coast Poems: A Problem in Anthropological Philology." *AA,* 67 (1965), 316–41.

Argues that NA poetry should be evaluated from a linguistic perspective before anthropological and literary concerns are considered. Illustrates with Kwakiutl and Haida material.

4766. Large, R. Geddes. *Soogwillis. A Collection of Kwakiutl Indian Designs & Legends.* Toronto: Ryerson Press, 1951.

Rewritten hero cycle.

4767. Lindblom, Gerhard. "A Kwakiutl Totem Pole in Stockholm." *En,* 1 (1936), 137–41.

Description of the carving includes narrative of events that led to its erection.

4768. Lopatin, Ivan A. *Social Life and Religion of the Indians of Kitimat, British Columbia.* Foreword by Frederick W. Hodge. Los Angeles: Univ. of Southern California Press, 1945 (Social Science Series No. 26).

Ethnographic notes collected in 1930 include data on religious system, shamanism, the potlatch, ceremonialism, and cosmogony.

4769. McLaren, Carol Sheehan. "Moment of Death: Gift of Life. A Reinterpretation of the Northwest Coast Image 'Hawk.'" *An,* n. s. 20 (1978), 65–90.

Argues that images in Kwakiutl art identified by Boas as hawks are, in fact, salmon. This parallels the latter's mythological significance.

4770. Olson, Ronald L. "Social Life of the Owikeno Kwakiutl." *UCPAR,* 14, No. 3 (1954), 213–60.

Includes data on ceremonialism such as the potlatch, religion, and shamanism. With three myth texts.

4771. ———. "The Social Organization of the Haisla of British Columbia." *UCPAR,* 2, No. 5 (1940), 169–200.

Includes texts of several clan origin myths and some data on ceremonials such as the potlatch. Fieldwork done in 1935.

4772. Parker, Seymour. "The Kwakiutl Indians: 'Amiable' and 'Atrocious.'" *An,* n. s. 6 (1964), 131–58.

Personality and culture study with particular attention to potlatch and winter ceremonials.

4773. Piddocke, Stuart. "The Potlatch System of the Southern Kwakiutl: A New Perspective." *SJA,* 21 (1965), 244–64.

Sees the ritual as responsive to population decline and introduction of new wealth.

4774. Postal, Susan Koessler. "Body-Image and Identity: A Comparison of Kwakiutl and Hopi." *AA,* 67 (1965), 455–62.

Analyzes groups' folklore to reveal attitudes toward the body. Body-image reflects world view.

4775. Reid, Susan. "The Kwakiutl Man Eater." *An,* n. s. 21 (1979), 247–75.

Surveys cannibalism in myth and ritual. Relates theme to group's concepts of social space.

4776. Rohner, Ronald P. *The People of Gilford: A Contemporary Kwakiutl Village.* NMCB No. 225 (1967).

Ethnography based on fieldwork done between 1962 and 1964 includes several creation myth texts.

4777. Spradley, James P. *Guests Never Leave Hungry. The Autobiography of James Sewid, a Kwakiutl Indian.* New Haven: Yale Univ. Press, 1969.

Life history with data on the potlatch (including a song text) and other ceremonials. Appended is an analysis of the informant's adaptation to culture change.

4778. Stover, Dale. "Santa and the Man-Eater Spirit: Immigrants and Indians." *ChrC,* 95 (20 December 1978), 1238–39.

Compares EA Christmas ceremonials with winter rituals of the Kwakiutl.

4779. Teall, Gardner C. "The Salmon Wife—A Kwakiutl Legend." *AAOJ,* 16 (1894), 140–42.

Unannotated myth text. With data on storytelling context.

See also 3, 568, 4571, 4590, 4638, 4640.

M. Nootka

4780. Carmichael, Alfred. *Indian Legends of Vancouver Island.* Toronto: Musson, 1922.

Rewritten myth and folktale texts. No annotations or substantive commentary.

4781. Colson, Elizabeth. *The Makah Indians: A Study of an Indian Tribe in Modern American Society.* Minneapolis: Univ. of Minnesota Press, 1953.

Study of culture change based on fieldwork done in 1941–1942. Includes description of NA attitude toward traditional culture forms such as the potlatch.

4782. Densmore, Frances. "Conscious Effort Toward Physical Perfection Among the Makah Indians." *AA,* 25 (1923), 564–67.

Study of song texts reveals the ideals of physical beauty for women and strength for men.

4783. ———. "Musical Composition Among the American Indians." *AS,* 2 (1926–1927), 393–94.

Note of the compositional techniques used by Makah and Squamish performers.

4784. ———. "The True Story of a Little Stone Image." *AA,* 30 (1928), 311–13.

Includes summaries of personal narratives which deal with encounters with a sea creature.

4785. Drucker, Philip. *The Northern and Central Nootkan Tribes.* BAEB No. 144 (1951).

Ethnography based on fieldwork done in 1935–1936 includes data on religion and ceremonialism. With summaries of legend texts.

4786. Ernst, Alice Henson. *The Wolf Ritual of the Northwest Coast.* Eugene: Univ. of Oregon Press, 1952.

Describes occurrences of the ceremonial among the Makah and Quileute. With summary of ritual origin myth and functional analysis.

4787. Irvine, Albert. *How the Makah Obtained Possession of Cape Flattery.* Trans. Luke Markistun. *IN&M,* Miscellaneous Series No. 6 (1921).

Unannotated legend text. No commentary.

4788. Kenyon, Susan M. "Traditional Trends in Modern Nootka Ceremonies." *ArA,* 14, No. 1 (1977), 25–38.

Treats traditional aspects of contemporary ceremonialism—especially types of occasions celebrated, theatrical nature of ceremonials, and attitudes of participants.

4789. Koppert, Vincent A. *Contributions to Clayoquot Ethnology. CUAAS* No. 1 (1930).

Based on fieldwork done in 1923 and 1929. Includes data on shamanism and the potlatch.

4790. ———. "The Nootka Family." *PM,* 3 (1930), 49–55.

Fairly good description of marriage ceremonials. With data on singing.

4791. McCurdy, James G. *Indian Days at Neah Bay.* Ed. Gordon Newell. Seattle: Superior, 1961.

Account of a childhood among the Makah in 1870s includes data on ceremonials such as the potlatch and summary of a myth.

4792. Miller, Robert J. "Situation and Sequence in the Study of Folklore." *JAF,* 65 (1952), 29–48.

Uses twenty-one Makah folktales to show importance of collecting situations and of the order in which stories are narrated to collector.

4793. *Narrative of the Adventures and Sufferings of John R. Jewitt; Only Survivor of the Crew of the Ship Boston, During a Captivity of Nearly Three Years Among the Savages of Nootka Sound: with an Account of the Manners, Mode of Living and Religious Opinions of the Natives.* New York: NP, [c. 1815].

Captivity narrative beginning in 1803 includes data on Nootka singing and ceremonies.

4794. Roberts, Helen H., and Morris Swadesh. "Songs of the Nootka Indians of Western Vancouver Island." *TAPS,* n. s. 45, Part 3 (1955), 199–327.

Musicological, linguistic, and ethnological analysis of songs collected by Edward Sapir in 1910 and 1913–1914. With ninety-nine texts.

4795. Sapir, Edward. "A Flood Legend of the Nootka Indians of Vancouver Island." *JAF,* 32 (1919), 351–55.

Myth text with explanatory notes and commentary on status of oral literature among the group.

4796. ———. "A Girl's Puberty Ceremony Among the Nootka Indians." *PTRSC,* 3rd series, 7, section 2 (1913), 67–80.

Description of a ceremony observed in 1910.

4797. ———. "Indian Legends from Vancouver Island." *JAF,* 72 (1959), 106–14.

Two narrative texts collected from Nootka informants.

4798. ———. "The Rival Whalers, A Nitinat Story." *IJAL,* 3, No. 1 (1924–1925), 76–102.

Text, interlinear and free translations, and grammatical analysis of a story collected from a Nootka storyteller in 1913.

4799. ———. "Some Aspects of Nootka Language and Culture." *AA,* 13 (1911), 15–28.

Includes a description of the Wolf Ritual witnessed in 1910.

4800. ———. "Songs for a Comox Dancing Mask." Ed. Leslie Spier. *En,* 4, No. 2 (April-June 1939), 49–55.

Song texts (words and music) and origin myth texts associated with Grizzly Bear Dance.

4801. ———, and Morris Swadesh. *Nootka Texts. Tales and Ethnological Narratives with Grammatical Notes and Lexical Materials.* Philadelphia: Linguistic Society of America, 1939.

Twenty-two myth and folktale texts and twenty-two personal narratives and descriptions of customs with free translations. Five texts have interlinear translations also. With explanatory notes and linguistic commentary.

4802. Swadesh, Mary Haas, and Morris Swadesh. "A Visit to the Other World, A Nitinat Text." *IJAL,* 7 (1932), 195–208.

Narrative collected in 1931. With free and interlinear translations and grammatical analysis.

4803. Swadesh, Morris. "Motivations in Nootka Warfare." *SJA,* 4 (1948), 76–93.

Includes summaries of historical legends dealing with warfare.

4804. Swan, James G. *The Indians of Cape Flattery, at the Entrance to the Strait of Fuca, Washington Territory. SCK* No. 220 (1870).

Ethnographic notes based on contact in 1850s include data on ceremonialism, mythology, and songs. With myth and legend texts.

4805. Waterman, T. T. "The Whaling Equipment of the Makah Indians." *UWPA,* 1, No. 1 (June 1920), 1–67.

Contains data on ceremonialism.

See also 4529, 4563, 4568, 4571, 4590, 4952.

N. Quileute

4806. Andrade, Manuel J. "Quileute," in 87, pp. 151–292.

Contains a myth text with interlinear translation and linguistic analysis.

4807. ———. *Quileute Texts. CUCA* No. 12 (1931).

Seventy myth texts and descriptions of customs with free translations and occasional explanatory notes. Some material collected by Leo J. Frachtenberg.

4808. Farrand, Livingston. "Quileute Tales." Ed. Theresa Mayer. *JAF,* 32 (1919), 251–79.

Eighteen myth, folktale, and legend texts with comparative notes. No commentary.

4809. Frachtenberg, Leo J. "The Ceremonial Societies of the Quileute Indians." *AA,* 23 (1921), 320–52.

Survey of ceremonialism.

4810. ———. "Eschatology of the Quileute Indians." *AA,* 22 (1920), 330–40.

Survey tribal beliefs about the fate of the soul.

4811. Pettitt, George A. "The Quileute of La Push, 1775–1945." *UCPAR,* 14, No. 1 (1950), 1–128.

Ethnography and history include data on religious beliefs, shamanism, and ceremonialism. With four myth texts.

4812. Reagan, Albert B. "A Double-Headed Monster." *EP,* 40 (1936), 113–15.

Description of a healing ceremony brought about by a dream.

4813. ———. "Some Additional Myths of the Hoh and Quileute Indians." *UASAL,* 11 (1934), 17–37.
Fourteen myth texts collected between 1905 and 1909. No commentary or annotation.
4814. ———. "Some Myths of the Hoh and Quillayute Indians." *TKAS,* 38 (1935), 43–85.
Forty-one unannotated texts collected between 1905 and 1909. No commentary.
4815. ———. "Traditions of the Hoh and Quillayute Indians." *WHQ,* 20 (1929), 178–89.
Six unannotated folktale and legend texts. No commentary.
4816. ———. "Whaling of the Olympic Peninsula Indians of Washington." *NH,* 25 (1925), 24–32.
Description of hunting methods includes summaries of myths which are part of the education of a whaler.
4817. ———, and L. V. W. Walters. "Tales from the Hoh and Quileute." *JAF,* 46 (1933), 297–346.
Fifty-two myth texts (including several from the Raven cycle) collected between 1905 and 1909. Brief introductory comments by Walters. No annotations.

See also 4529, 4786.

O. Quinault

4818. Farrand, Livingston, and W. S. Kahnweiler. "Traditions of the Quinault Indians." *MAMNH,* 4, Part 3 (1902), 77–132.
Seventeen myth texts with abstracts and comparative notes. From the Jesup North Pacific Expedition.
4819. Olson, Ronald L. "The Quinault Indians." *UWPA,* 6, No. 1 (November 1936), 1–190.
Ethnography based on fieldwork done between 1925 and 1927 includes data on ceremonials such as the potlatch, religion, music, and shamanism. With a life history text.
4820. Willoughby, C. "Indians of the Quinaielt Agency, Washington Territory." *ARSI for 1886,* pp. 267–82.
Ethnographic notes include two myth texts and some data on religious system.

See also 4529.

P. Salish

4821. Adamson, Thelma. *Folk-Tales of the Coast Salish. MAFS* No. 27 (1934).
Myth and folktale texts (190) from various Salish-speaking groups (Chehalis, Cowlitz, Puyallup, Humptulip, Wynoochee, Satsop, Skokomish) collected in 1926–1927. With abstracts, comparative notes, and explanatory notes.
4822. "Address by Chief Seattle." *HuR,* 23 (1970), 492–94.
Text of a speech delivered to Commissioner of Indian Affairs for Washington Territory in 1854.
4823. Altman, George J. "Guardian Spirit Dances of the Salish." *M,* 21 (1947), 155–60.
Ceremonial description.
4824. Amoss, Pamela. *Coast Salish Spirit Dancing. The Survival of an Ancestral Religion.* Seattle: Univ. of Washington Press, 1978.
Describes resurgence of ceremonialism in terms of traditional belief system and Christianity.
4825. ———. "Strategies of Reorientation: The Contribution of Contemporary Winter Dancing to Coast Salish Identity and Solidarity." *ArA,* 17, No. 1 (1977), 77–83.
As a link with the cultural heritage, Winter Dancing helps participants cope with social and psychological pressures of modern life.
4826. Ballard, Arthur C. "Some Tales of the Southern Puget Sound Salish." *UWPA,* 2, No. 3 (December 1927), 57–81.
Twenty-one myth and folktale texts with explanatory notes.
4827. Barnett, H. G. "The Coast Salish of Canada." *AA,* 40 (1938), 118–41.
Ethnography based on fieldwork done in 1935–1936 includes data on ceremonialism.
4828. Beaty, S. A. "A Big Indian Wedding." *Cal,* 6 (1882), 433–36.
Description of a ceremonial.
4829. Boas, Franz. "A Chehalis Text." *IJAL,* 8 (1935), 103–10.
Myth text with interlinear translation and extensive linguistic commentary.
4830. ———. "Myths and Legends of the Catloltq of Vancouver Island." *AAOJ,* 10 (1888), 201–11, 366–73.
Six unannotated myth and folktale texts with some data on cultural background. Also includes a cycle of narratives with Mink as Trickster.
4831. ———. "Notes on the Snanaimuq." *AA,* o. s. 2 (1889), 321–28.
Ethnographic survey includes data on mortuary customs and two myth texts.
4832. Calhoun, Francy. "Four Puget Sound Folktales." *JAF,* 59 (1946), 40–44.
Texts collected in 1945 from Snuqualmi, Yakima, and Puyallup informants.
4833. Collins, June M. "John Fornsby: The Personal Document of a Coast Salish Indian," in 159, pp. 287–341.
Life history collected in 1942 and 1947. With extensive explanatory notes and commentary.
4834. ———. "The Mythological Basis for Attitudes Toward Animals Among Salish-Speaking Indians." *JAF,* 65 (1952), 353–59.
Shows how myths validate ways in which men and animals interrelate.
4835. ———. *Valley of the Spirits: The Upper Skagit Indians of Western Washington. MonAES* No. 56 (1974).
Ethnography based on fieldwork done in 1942 and 1947 includes data on the potlatch and other ceremonials, shamanism, supernaturalism, and mythology.
4836. Crosby, Thomas. *Among the An-ko-me-nums or Flathead Tribes of Indians of the Pacific Coast.* Toronto: William Briggs, 1907.
Missionary's memoirs include highly ethnocentric descriptions of ceremonials such as the potlatch and religious attitudes.
4837. Curtis, Edward S. *Indian Days of the Long Ago.* Yonkers-on-Hudson, N. Y.: World Book, 1915.

Melange of material primarily from the Salish and Hopi includes song and myth texts and a description of the Hopi Snake Dance.

4838. Dewhirst, John. "Coast Salish Summer Festivals: Rituals for Upgrading Social Identity." *An,* n. s. 18 (1976), 231–73.

Functional analysis of contemporary ceremonials.

4839. Eells, Myron. "Indian Music." *AAOJ,* 1 (1879), 249–53.

Discusses performance styles and types of songs among the Klallam and Twana.

4840. ———. "The Religion of the Clallam and Twana Indians." *AAOJ,* 2 (1879), 8–14.

Describes religious systems and their mythological bases.

4841. Elmendorf, William W. "Coastal and Interior Salish Power Concepts: A Structural Comparison." *ArA,* 14, No. 1 (1977), 64–76.

Finds correlations between attitudes toward power among Northwest Coast and Plateau Salish. Attributes variations to differences in kinship systems.

4842. ———. "The Cultural Setting of the Twana Secret Society." *AA,* 50 (1948), 625–33.

Describes initiation ritual for secret society and makes comparisons with the potlatch.

4843. ———. "The Structure of Twana Culture." *RS,* 28, No. 3 (September 1960), 1–566 (Monograph Supplement No. 2).

Ethnography based on fieldwork done in 1930s and 1940s includes data on ceremonial cycle, religion, shamanism, and cosmology.

4844. ———. "Word Taboo and Lexical Change in Coast Salish." *IJAL,* 17 (1951), 205–08.

Describes a ceremony among the Twana which involves the imposition of a taboo on using a deceased person's name.

4845. Gunther, Erna. "Klallam Ethnography." *UWPA,* 1, No. 5 (January 1927), 171–314.

Based on fieldwork in 1924–1925. Contains data on religion, shamanism, the potlatch, and other ceremonials. With song and myth texts.

4846. ———. "Klallam Folk Tales." *UWPA,* 1, No. 4 (August 1925), 113–70.

Translated texts of myths and folktales with explanatory and comparative notes.

4847. Herzog, George. "Salish Music," in 159, pp. 93–109.

Musicological survey focuses on rhythm and melodic range.

4848. Hill-Tout, Charles. "Curious and Interesting Marriage Customs of Some of the Aboriginal Tribes of British Columbia." *AAOJ,* 24 (1902), 85–87.

Ceremonial description.

4849. ———. "Ethnological Report on the Stseélis and Skaúlits Tribes of the Halōkmélem Division of the Salish of British Columbia." *JAIGBI,* 34 (1904), 311–76.

Ethnography includes data on ceremonialism, shamanism, and religion. With fourteen myth texts and linguistic notes.

4850. ———. "Notes on the Cosmogony and History of the Squamish Indians of British Columbia." *PTRSC,* 2nd series, 3, section 2 (1897), 85–90.

Text of creation myth with some discussion of Asian affinities.

4851. ———. "Report on the Ethnology of the Síciatl of British Columbia, A Coast Division of the Salish Stock." *JAIGBI,* 34 (1904), 20–91.

Includes data on ceremonialism and shamanism. With nine myth texts with free and interlinear translations and linguistic notes.

4852. ———. *Report on the Ethnology of the South-Eastern Tribes of Vancouver Island, British Columbia.* London: Royal Anthropological Institute of Great Britain and Ireland, ND.

Ethnography of various Salish-speaking groups includes data on ceremonialism and myth and legend texts. With flood and earthquake myths from the Cowichan.

4853. ———. "Report on the Ethnology of the Stlatlumh of British Columbia." *JAIGBI,* 35 (1905), 126–218.

Ethnography includes data on ceremonialism. With myth texts with free and interlinear translations and linguistic notes.

4854. ———. "Some Features of the Language and Culture of the Salish." *AA,* 7 (1905), 674–87.

Linguistic survey includes data on ceremonialism and shamanism.

4855. Holden, Madronna. " 'Making All the Crooked Ways Straight': The Satirical Portrait of Whites in Coast Salish Folklore." *JAF,* 89 (1976), 271–93.

Shows how the Salish use jokes, songs, and folktales to poke fun at EAs.

4856. Jacobs, Melville. *Northwest Sahaptin Texts. Part I. CUCA,* 19, Part 1 (1934).

Eighty-three myth texts and descriptions of customs collected in 1926–1930 from the Cowlitz, Klikitat, and Kittitas. With explanatory and comparative notes.

4857. ———. *Northwest Sahaptin Texts. Part II. CUCA,* 19, Part 2 (1937).

Original language texts of material in 4856.

4858. Kuipers, Aert H. *The Squamish Language: Grammar, Texts, Dictionary.* The Hague: Mouton, 1967.

Four myth and legend texts collected in 1950s. With free translations and linguistic notes.

4859. ———. *The Squamish Language. Grammar, Texts, Dictionary. Part II.* The Hague: Mouton, 1969.

Contains five myth texts, an oration, and a song. With free translations and linguistic analysis. Collected in 1967.

4860. Lewis, William S. "The Case of Spokane Garry." *BSHS,* 1, No. 1 (January 1917), 1–68.

Biography of a Spokane leader (1811–1892) includes some data on his oratorical ability.

4861. Mannenbach, Stephen. "Tradition Maintenance Facilitation, Experiential Continuation, and the Native American Point of View," in 136, pp. 27–57.

Presents NA views about their traditions and treats folklorist's role in maintaining those traditions. With interview excerpts from Colville, Makah, and Flathead informants.

4862. Matina, Tony. "Blue Jay." *P,* 2, No. 4 (1977), 63–73.

Unannotated myth text. No commentary.

4863. Maud, Ralph, ed. *The Salish People. The Local Contributions of Charles Hill-Tout.* 4 volumes. Vancouver, B. C.: Talonbooks, 1978.

Anthology of fifteen of Hill-Tout's studies of Northwest Coast cultures. Includes previously unpublished letters and biographical and bibliographical introductions.

4864. Ray, Verne F. "The Kalaskin Cult: A Prophet Movement of 1870 in Northeastern Washington." *AA*, 38 (1936), 67–75.

Survey of a revitalization movement among the Spokane, Sanpoil, and Okanagan.

4865. ———. "Sanpoil Folk Tales." *JAF*, 46 (1933), 129–87.

Twenty-five myth texts (including some Coyote tales), eleven historical legends, and four anecdotes collected between 1928 and 1931. Includes some data on cultural background.

4866. Reagan, Albert B. "Certain 'Writings' of Northwestern Indians." *AA*, 30 (1928), 345–47.

Describes Lummi drawings and recounts a myth associated with them.

4867. Riley, Carroll L. "The Story of Skalaxt, A Lummi Training Myth." *DJA*, 1, No. 2 (Winter 1955), 133–40.

Hero myth with brief introduction.

4868. Roberts, Helen H., and Hermann K. Haeberlin. "Some Songs of the Puget Sound Salish." *JAF*, 31 (1918), 496–520.

Ten song texts (words and music) collected in 1916. With extensive contextual and musicological commentary.

4869. Smith, Marian W. *The Puyallup-Nisqually. CUCA* No. 32 (1940).

Ethnography based on fieldwork done in 1935–1936 includes data on shamanism, ceremonials, and mythological beings.

4870. Snyder, Sally. "Quest for the Sacred in Northern Puget Sound: An Interpretation of Potlatch." *Eth*, 14 (1975), 149–61.

Views the ritual performed by the Skagit as an attempt to transcend human carnality.

4871. ———. "Stylistic Satisfaction in an Oral Tradition." *An*, n. s. 10 (1968), 234–59.

Examination of content and style of Skagit folktales and myths. Arranges narration processes on a continuum from "yarn spinning" to "myth making."

4872. Snyder, Warren A. *Southern Puget Sound Salish: Texts, Place Names, and Dictionary.* Sacramento: Sacramento Anthropological Society, 1968 (Paper No. 9).

Seventeen myth texts, one personal narrative, and several notes on customs collected in the 1950s. With free translations. No commentary or annotations.

4873. Stern, Bernard J. *The Lummi Indians of Northwest Washington. CUCA* No. 17 (1934).

Ethnography includes data on shamanism and ceremonialism and eight unannotated myth texts.

4874. Street, Eloise. *Sepass Poems. The Songs of Y-ail-mihth.* New York: Vantage, 1963.

Song texts (words only) collected between 1911 and 1915 from a Colville informant. With thorough data on the singer.

4875. Suttles, Wayne. "The Persistence of Intervillage Ties Among the Coast Salish." *Eth*, 2 (1963), 512–25.

One indication of Salish sense of community is the occurrence of intertribal dances where traditional singing takes place.

4876. ———. "The Plateau Prophet Dance Among the Coast Salish." *SJA*, 13 (1957), 352–96.

Historical treatment of the spread of a ceremonial from the Plateau among Salish-speaking groups in the Northwest Coast.

4877. ———. "Private Knowledge, Morality, and Social Classes Among the Coast Salish." *AA*, 60 (1958), 497–507.

Study of social stratification includes texts of folktales used to validate the lower status of others.

4878. Teit, James H. "The Middle Columbia Salish." Ed. Franz Boas. *UWPA*, 2, No. 4 (June 1928), 83–128.

Ethnography based on fieldwork done in 1908 contains data about ceremonialism and myths.

4879. Wade, Edwin L. "The Art of the Salish Power Dances." *AIAM*, 1 August 1976, pp. 64–67.

Description of costumes and masks with attention to their mythic significance.

4880. Waterman, T. T. "The Paraphernalia of the Duwamish 'Spirit-Canoe' Ceremony." *IN*, 7 (1930), 129–48, 295–312, 535–61.

Thorough description of a ceremony includes its mythic background and song texts.

4881. Wickersham, James. "Nusqually Mythology. Studies of the Washington Indians." *OM*, n. s. 32 (1898), 345–51.

Survey of tribal mythology.

4882. Wingert, Paul S. "Coast Salish Painting," in 159, pp. 77–91.

Considers the meanings of paintings used in shamanistic ritual.

See also 4568, 4571, 5106.

Q. Takelma

4883. Hymes, Dell. "How to Talk Like a Bear in Takelma." *IJAL*, 45 (1979), 101–6.

Study of prefixes added to discourse of animal characters (especially Bear and Coyote) in Takelma myths.

4884. Sapir, Edward. "Notes on the Takelma Indians of Southwestern Oregon." *AA*, 9 (1907). 251–75.

Ethnographic survey includes data on dances.

4885. ———. "Religous Ideas of the Takelma Indians of Southwestern Oregon." *JAF*, 20 (1907), 33–49.

Describes ceremonials. With prayer and song texts.

See also 3.

R. Tanana

4886. McKennan, Robert A. *The Upper Tanana Indians. YUPA* No. 55 (1959).

Ethnography based on fieldwork done in 1929–1930 includes data on ceremonials such as the potlatch and religion. With unannotated myth and legend texts.

S. Tillamook

4887. Boas, Franz. "Notes on the Tillamook." *UC-PAAE,* 20 (1923), 3–16.
Ethnographic notes collected in 1890 include data on shamanism and ceremonialism and four summarized myths.

4888. ———. "Traditions of the Tillamook Indians." *JAF,* 11 (1898), 23–38.
Four unannotated myth texts collected in 1890. With data on cultural background.

4889. ———. "Traditions of the Tillamook Indians. II." *JAF,* 11 (1898), 133–50.
Eight unannotated myth and folktale texts. With a few explanatory notes.

4890. Edel, May M. "Stability in Tillamook Folklore." *JAF,* 57 (1944), 116–27.
Demonstrates the emphasis on plot fixity in the culture.

4891. ———. "The Tillamook Language." *IJAL,* 10 (1939), 1–57.
Linguistic survey includes a myth text with interlinear translation and grammatical commentary.

4892. Jacobs, Elizabeth Derr. *Nehalem Tillamook Tales.* Ed. Melville Jacobs. *UOMA,* No. 3 (1959).
Sixty myth and legend texts with abstracts collected in 1934. With some data on informant and comparative notes.

T. Tlingit

4893. Averkieva, Julia. "The Tlingit Indians," in 134, pp. 317–42.
Ethnographic and historical survey contains data on the potlatch.

4894. Beasley, Walter L. "Chilkat Ceremonial Canoe. A Realistic Exhibit at the Museum of Natural History." *ScA* Supplement No. 1894 (20 April 1912), 249–50.
Includes a description of the Potlatch.

4895. Beck, Mary L. "Raven: Benefactor, Transformer, Trickster, Thief." *IH,* 12, No. 2 (Summer 1979), 50–53, 62.
Characterization of the Tlingit culture hero.

4896. Billman, Esther. "A Potlatch Feast at Sitka, Alaska." *APUAK,* 14, No. 2 (1969), 55–64.
Description of the potlatch written by William Wells, a Tlingit, in 1885.

4897. Boas, Franz. "Gleanings from the Emmons Collection of Ethnological Specimens from Alaska." *JAF,* 1 (1888), 215–19.
Notes from a catalogue of artifacts donated to the American Museum of Natural History include myth and legend texts.

4898. ———. "Vocabularies of the Tlingit, Haida, and Tsimshian Languages." *PAPS,* 29 (1891), 173–208.
Includes Tlingit texts of a legend, song (words only), and prayers. With interlinear translations. No commentary or annotations.

4899. Bugbee, Anna M. "The Dance of Peace." *OM,* n. s. 21 (May 1893), 488–91.
Description of a ritual among the "Sitka" NAs.

4900. Dauenhauer, Richard. "The Narrative Frame: Style and Personality in Tlingit Prose Narratives," in 136, pp. 65–81.
Treats frame as a unit of Tlingit narrative tradition reflecting storyteller's cultural and psychological backgrounds.

4901. Deans, James. "The Doom of the Katt-a-Quins. From the Aboriginal Folk-Lore of Southern Alaska." *JAF,* 5 (1892), 232–35.
Unannotated myth text collected in 1862. With some data on cultural background.

4902. de Laguna, Frederica. *The Story of a Tlingit Community: A Problem in the Relationship Between Archeological, Ethnological, and Historical Methods.* *BAEB* No. 172 (1960).
Based on fieldwork done in 1949–1950. Tries to integrate archeological data with ethnographic material such as myths and legends to construct a history of Tlingit culture.

4903. ———. "Tlingit Ideas About the Individual." *SJA,* 10 (1954), 172–91.
Traces the concept of the individual from birth through the afterlife. Emphasizes spiritual identity.

4904. ———. *Under Mount Saint Elias: The History and Culture of the Yakitat Tlingit.* *SmCA* No. 7 (1972).
Ethnography based on fieldwork done between 1949 and 1954 contains myth, legend, and song texts (including extensive material from the Raven cycle). With thorough treatment of ceremonialism.

4905. Dixon, Roland B. "Tobacco Chewing on the Northwest Coast." *AA,* 35 (1933), 146–50.
Description of the practice among the Tlingit and Haida includes summary of etiological myth.

4906. Dockstader, Frederick J. "Totem Poles: Family Trees." *NH,* October 1964, pp. 62–63.
Describes the symbolism of four Tlingit totem poles.

4907. Eifert, Virginia S. "Lincoln on a Totem Pole." *NH,* 56 (1947), 64–66.
Account of how figure of Abraham Lincoln was assimilated into mythological motifs by Tlingit woodcarvers.

4908. Emmons, George T. "Native Account of the Meeting Between La Perouse and the Tlingit." *AA,* 13 (1911), 294–98.
Legend text collected in 1886 dealing with Tlingit contact with a French explorer in 1786. With data on sea monster narratives.

4909. ———. "Petroglyphs in Southeastern Alaska." *AA,* 10 (1908), 221–30.
Describes Tlingit rock art designs, one of which depicts the groups's creation myth.

4910. ———. "The Potlatch of the North Pacific Coast." *AMJ,* 10 (1910), 229–34.
Ceremonial description.

4911. ———. "The Whale House of the Chilkat." *AMJ,* 16 (1916), 451–64.
Ethnographic survey focuses on most important of the group's ceremonial houses. With myth texts and summaries.

4912. Fox, Hugh. "Mythology of the Ancient Tlingit." *IH,* 4, No. 4 (Winter 1971), 12–15.
Sees the mythology of the group as reflecting a "comfortable" world view.

4913. Garfield, Viola E. "Historical Aspects of Tlingit Clans in Angoon, Alaska." *AA,* 49 (1947), 438–52.

Includes clan origin myths and legends about important clan members. Collected in 1945.

4914. Gerrish, Theodore. *Life in the World's Wonderland. A Graphic Description of the Great Northwest, from St. Paul, Minnesota, to the Land of the Midnight Sun.* Biddeford, Maine: Press of the Biddeford Journal, 1887.

Travelogue includes description of Tlingit ceremonialism and a rewritten myth.

4915. Golder, F. A. "Tlingit Myths." *JAF,* 20 (1907), 290–95.

Two unannotated texts. With brief comment on mythological system.

4916. Higginson, Ella. *Alaska, the Great Country.* New York: Macmillan, 1909.

Historical, geographical, and cultural survey includes summaries of Tlingit myths and descriptions of ceremonials.

4917. Johnston, Thomas F. "Alaskan Native Social Adjustment and the Role of Eskimo and Indian Music." *JES,* 3, No. 4 (Winter 1976), 21–36.

Music plays a role in establishing identity and in adapting to EA culture among the Tlingit and Eskimo.

4918. ———. "A Historical Perspective on Tlingit Music." *IH,* 8, No. 1 (Spring 1975), 3–10.

Collection of photographs depicting musical performances. With musicological and cultural commentary.

4919. Jonaitis, Aldona. "Land Otters and Shamans: Some Interpretations of Tlingit Charms." *AIAM,* November 1978, pp. 62–66.

Describes carved-bone charms which represent animal familiars of Tlingit shamans.

4920. Jones, Livingston F. *A Study of the Thlingets of Alaska.* New York: Fleming H. Revell, 1914.

Culture survey includes descriptions of ceremonials such as the potlatch, shamanism, and music. With summaries of myths and legends. Based on twenty years' residence with the group.

4921. Kaiper, Dan, and Nan Kaiper. *Tlingit: Their Art, Culture & Legends.* Seattle: Hancock House, 1978.

Culture survey includes data on shamanism and the potlatch. With ten unannotated myth texts. Some commentary on their cultural significance.

4922. Knapp, Frances, and Rheta Louise Childe. *The Thlinkets of Southeastern Alaska.* Chicago: Stone & Kimball, 1896.

Culture survey includes descriptions of ceremonials such as the potlatch, summaries of myths and legends, and song texts.

4923. Krause, Aurel. *The Tlingit Indians. Results of a Trip to the Northwest Coast of America and the Bering Straits.* Trans. Erna Gunther. *MonAES* No. 26 (1956).

Translation of an ethnography based on fieldwork done in 1880s. Contains data on ceremonialism and shamanism. With survey of the Raven cycle of myths.

4924. McClellan, Catharine. *The Girl Who Married a Bear: A Masterpiece of Indian Oral Tradition.* NMMCPE No. 2 (1970).

Plot and style analysis of eleven texts of a folktale collected between 1948 and 1968. Each text is thoroughly annotated.

4925. ———. "The Interrelations of Social Structure with Northern Tlingit Ceremonialism." *SJA,* 10 (1954), 75–96.

Relates the potlatch to tribal social organization.

4926. Miller, Ray E. "A Strobophotographic Analysis of a Tlingit Indian's Speech." *IJAL,* 6 (1931), 47–68.

An experiment in graphic representation of speech uses a legendary narrative recorded by a Tlingit storyteller.

4927. Oberg, Kalervo. "Crime and Punishment in Tlingit Society." *AA,* 36 (1934), 145–56.

Describes the Peace Dance as one of several responses to crime among the Tlingit.

4928. ———. *The Social Economy of the Tlingit Indians.* MonAES No. 55 (1973).

Ethnography completed in 1933 includes extensive data on the potlatch.

4929. Olson, Ronald L. *Social Structure and Social Life of the Tlingit in Alaska.* UCPAR No. 26 (1967).

Ethnographic data collected in 1933, 1934, 1949, and 1954 include texts of clan origin myths and historical legends and material on the potlatch.

4930. Rosman, Abraham, and Paula G. Rubel. "The Potlatch: A Structural Analysis." *AA,* 74 (1972), 658–71.

Shows different functions of the ceremonial among different groups: for the Tlingit it relates to marriage rules; for the Kwakiutl it reflects rules for succession.

4931. Salisbury, O. M. *Quoth and Raven: A Little Journey into the Primitive.* Seattle: Superior, 1962.

Memoirs of a government official who lived among the Tlingit in the 1920s contain data on ceremonialism and summaries of myths.

4932. Schwatka, Frederick. *Along Alaska's Great River. A Popular Account of the Travels of the Alaska Exploring Expedition of 1883, Along the Great Yukon River, from Its Source to Its Mouth, in the British North-West Territory, and in the Territory of Alaska.* New York: Cassell, 1885.

Contains data on Chilkat supernaturalism and ceremonialism.

4933. Scidmore, E. Ruhamah. *Alaska. Its Southern Coast and the Sitkan Archipelago.* Boston: D. Lothrop, 1885.

Describes Tlingit mythology, totem pole art, and ceremonialism.

4934. Swanton, John R. "Explanation of the Seattle Totem Pole." *JAF,* 18 (1905), 108–10.

Interprets the mythic significance of a Tlingit totem pole.

4935. ———. "Social Condition, Beliefs, and Linguistic Relationship of the Tlingit Indians." *ARBAE,* 26 (1904–1905), 391–485.

Emphasizes social events such as the potlatch. With some data on mythology.

4936. ———. *Tlingit Myths and Texts.* BAEB No. 39 (1909).

Eighty-eight myth texts collected in English and eighteen recorded in Tlingit, song texts, and oration texts collected in 1904. With free and interlinear translations of Tlingit material and abstracts of myths.

4937. Velten, H. V. "Three Tlingit Stories." *IJAL,* 10 (1939), 168–80.

Texts with interlinear and free translations. With some prefatory linguistic analysis.

4938. ———. "Two Southern Tlingit Tales." *IJAL,* 10 (1939), 65–74.

Texts, interlinear and free translations, and grammatical analysis.

4939. Wallis, W. D. "Ethical Aspects of Chilkat Culture." *AJP,* 29 (1918), 67–80.

Ethnographic notes collected in 1912–1913 include data on storytelling and a myth text.

4940. Williams, Frank, and Emma Williams. *Tongass Texts.* Ed. Jeff Leer. Fairbanks: Alaska Native Language Center, Univ. of Alaska, 1978.

Texts and free translations of descriptions of Tlingit culture. With extensive linguistic analysis and occasional explanatory notes.

See also 3, 202, 1964, 4508, 4517, 4544, 4563, 4571, 4590, 4601, 4720.

U. Tolowa

4941. Drucker, Philip. "The Tolowa and Their Southwest Oregon Kin." *UCPAAE,* 36, No. 4 (1937), 221–300.

Ethnography based on fieldwork done in 1933–1934. Includes data on shamanism, ceremonialism, and mythology.

4942. Du Bois, Cora A. "Tolowa Notes." *AA,* 34 (1932), 248–62.

Miscellany includes ceremonial descriptions and folklore texts: prayer used during girls' puberty ceremony, legends, and folktales.

4943. Gould, Richard A. "Indian and White Versions of 'The Burnt Ranch Massacre': A Study in Comparative Ethnohistory." *JFI,* 3 (1966), 30–42.

Compares three Tolowa legend texts about an incident occurring in 1853 with written accounts by EAs.

V. Tsetsaut

4944. Boas, Franz. "Traditions of the Ts'ets'a'ut." *JAF,* 9 (1896), 257–68.

Eight unannotated myth texts collected in 1894–1895. Includes an analogue from the Hare for one of the texts. With data on cultural background.

4945. ——— "Traditions of the Ts'ets'a'ut. II." *JAF,* 10 (1897), 35–48.

Continuation of 4944. Ten myth texts with occasional comparative notes. No commentary.

4946. ———, and Pliny Earle Goddard. "Ts'ets'aut, An Athapascan Language from Portland Canal, British Columbia." *IJAL,* 3, No. 1 (1924–1925), 1–35.

Linguistic material collected by Boas in 1894 includes a narrative text. Goddard provides an interlinear translation.

4947. Clutesi, George. *Potlatch.* Sidney, B. C.: Gray's, 1969.

Semi-fictional reconstruction of the ceremony. Extensive use of poems, songs, and orations.

4948. ———. *Son of Raven, Son of Deer. Fables of the Tse-shaht People.* Sidney, B. C.: Gray's, 1967.

Twelve unannotated myth texts. With some commentary on their pedagogical value.

W. Tsimshian

4949. Arctander, John W. *The Apostle of Alaska. The Story of William Duncan of Metlakahtla.* New York: Fleming H. Revell, 1909.

Biography of a missionary contains data on Tsimshian ceremonialism and supernaturalism. With a myth text.

4950. Barbeau, Marius. "Bear Mother." *JAF,* 59 (1946), 1–12.

Examines carved representations of the Bear Mother in Northwest Coast art. Their significance is partially explained by Tsimshian and Haida myths.

4951. ———. *Tsimsyan Myths. NMCB* No. 174 (1961).

Fifteen texts with some data on collection situations. With occasional explanatory notes.

4952. Boas, Franz. "Tsimshian Mythology." *ARBAE,* 31 (1909–1910), 29–1037.

Sixty-seven narrative texts (including thirty-eight episodes from the Raven cycle) collected by Henry W. Tate and freely translated by Boas. Uses the material to construct a description of Tsimshian culture. Appendix includes Bella Bella and Nootka texts.

4953. ———. *Tsimshian Texts. BAEB* No. 27 (1902).

Twenty-two narrative texts collected in 1894. With free and interlinear translations. No substantive commentary.

4954. ———. "Tsimshian Texts (New Series)." *PAES,* 3 (1912), 65–285.

Six myth texts with free translations. As written by a Tsimshian informant. No annotations.

4955. Davis, George T. B. *Metlakahtla: A True Narrative of the Red Man.* Chicago: Ram's Horn, 1904.

Account of the establishment of a Christian mission among the Tsimshian includes ethnocentric descriptions of dancing and other ceremonialism.

4956. Deans, James. "A Creation Myth of the Tsimshians of Northwest British Columbia." *JAF,* 4 (1891), 34.

Unannotated myth text. No commentary. Comparative note added by *JAF* editor.

4957. ———. "The Daughter of the Sun. A Legend of the Tsimshians of British Columbia." *JAF,* 4 (1891), 32–33.

Unannotated myth text collected in 1889. No commentary.

4958. Dorsey, G. A. "The Geography of the Tsimshian Indians." *AAOJ,* 19 (1897), 276–82.

Describes distribution of Tsimshian communities. With summary of creation myth.

4959. Emmons, George T. "Tsimshian Stories in Carved Wood." *AMJ,* 15 (1915), 363–66.

Four myth texts collected in 1913. With description of related totem pole art.

4960. Garfield, Viola E. "Tsimshian Clan and Society." *UWPA,* 7, No. 3 (February 1939), 167–340.

Based on fieldwork done in 1932, 1935, 1937. Includes data on ceremonials such as the potlatch.

4961. ———, and Paul S. Wingert. *The Tsimshian Indians and Their Arts.* Seattle: Univ. of Washington Press, ND.

Includes data on ceremonialism, mythology, and sculpture.

4962. Gunther, Erna. "A Tsimshian Version of the Test Theme." *JAF,* 38 (1925), 619.

Unannotated folktale text. No commentary.

4963. Halpin, Marjorie. "Confronting Looking-Glass Men: A Preliminary Examination of the Mask," in 98, pp. 41–61.

Suggests that ritual masking allows anti-social license during ceremonialism.

4964. Hoebel, E. Adamson. "The Asiatic Origin of a Myth of the Northwest Coast." *JAF,* 54 (1941), 1–9.

Shows Asiatic parallels for a narrative from 4952.

4965. "Indian Witchcraft." *JAF,* 34 (1921), 390–93.

Testimony from a witchcraft trial in British Columbia includes some personal narratives.

4966. Krappe, Alexander H. "A Solomon Legend Among the Indians of the North Pacific." *JAF,* 59 (1946), 309–14.

Comparison of a folktale collected by Franz Boas to Old World analogues.

4967. Lévi-Strauss, Claude. "The Story of Asdiwal," in 133, pp. 1–47.

Structural analysis of a Tsimshian myth. See the critique by Mary Douglas (574).

4968. Moore, John H. "Asdiwal, Boas, and Henry Tate. A Note on Structuralist Methodology." *A,* 70 (1975), 926–30.

Critique of 4967 emphasizes selectivity and ignorance of ethnographic background.

4969. Morison, Mrs. O. "Tsimshian Proverbs." *JAF,* 2 (1889), 285–86.

Sixteen proverb texts with free translations and interpretations.

4970. Robinson, Will, and Walter Wright. *Men of Medeek.* 2nd edition. NP: Northern Sentinel Press, [1962].

Narrated by Wright in 1935–1936 and rewritten by Robinson. History begins with mythic times and continues to EA contact. Contains heavily edited myths.

4971. Sapir, Edward. *A Sketch of the Social Organization of the Nass River Indians. NMCB,* Anthropological Series No. 7 (1915).

Includes some data on ceremonialism.

4972. Spier, Leslie. "Historical Interrelation of Cultural Traits: Franz Boas' Study of Tsimshian Mythology," in 151, pp. 449–57.

Evaluation of "mirror of culture" approach as illustrated by 4952.

4973. Thomas, L. L., J. Z. Kronenfeld, and D. B. Kronenfeld. "Asdiwal Crumbles: A Critique of Lévi-Straussian Myth Analysis." *AE,* 3 (1976), 147–73.

Suggests that 4967 is arbitrary, inconsistent, and circular.

4974. Wilson, E. F. "The Zimshian Indians." *CI,* 1 (1890–1891), 77–86.

Culture survey includes myth summary and data on ceremonialism.

See also, 3, 574, 4544, 4571, 4590, 4722, 4898.

X. Yakima

4975. Daughtery, Richard D. *The Yakima People.* Phoenix: Indian Tribal Series, 1973.

Tribal history includes description of revitalization movements such as the Smohalla Cult.

4977. McWhorter, Lucullus Virgil. *Tragedy of the Wahkshum. Prelude to the Yakima Indian War, 1855–56. The Killing of Major Andrew J. Bolon. Eyewitness Account by Su-el-lil Locating the Place of Bolon's Death and Indian Legends. Addendum: Definitions of "Yakima."* Yakima, Wash.: by the Author, 1937.

Pamphlet includes oral history, myth, and legend texts collected from Yakima and Klikitat storytellers.

4978. Weeks, Thelma E. "Child-Naming Customs Among the Yakima Indians." *Nam,* 19, No. 4 (December 1971), 252–56.

Includes description of naming ceremonials.

See also 3366, 4485, 4529, 4832.

X PLATEAU

A. General Works

4979. Aberle, David F. "The Prophet Dance and Reactions to White Contact." *SJA*, 15 (1959), 74–83.

Treats the effects of EA contact on the development and spread of a ceremonial complex. Sees the dance as a response to deprivation. Responses by Leslie Spier, Wayne Suttles, and Melville J. Herskovits in *SJA*, 15 (1959), 84–88.

4980. Boas, Franz, ed. *Folk-Tales of Salishan and Sahaptin Tribes. MAFS* No. 11 (1917).

Texts collected by James A. Teit (Thompson, Okanagan, Pend d'Oreille, Coeur d'Alene), Marian K. Gould (Sanpoil), Livingston Farrand (Sahaptin), and Herbert J. Spinden (Nez Perce). No commentary. With occasional comparative notes.

4981. Clark, Ella E. *Indian Legends from the Northern Rockies.* Norman: Univ. of Oklahoma Press, 1966.

Unannotated texts from NAs living in Idaho, Montana, and Wyoming. From own collecting, mss., and previously published collections. Most of the material is rewritten.

4982. Fisher, Vardis. *Idaho Lore.* Caldwell, Ida.: Caxton, 1939.

Includes sections on oral narratives and ceremonials of various Plateau groups. Prepared by Federal Writers' Project.

4983. Hines, Donald M. "The History and Traditional Lore of the Inland Pacific Northwest: Archival Materials." *JFI*, 13 (1976), 91–103.

Survey of archival holdings relating to folk cultures in northwestern states includes materials on various NA groups in the Plateau.

4984. Hultkrantz, Åke. "The Indians and the Wonders of Yellowstone: A Study of the Interrelations of Religion, Nature and Culture." *En*, 19 (1954), 34–68.

Suggests how the phenomena in Yellowstone National Park fit into religious concepts of various Plateau groups.

4985. Miller, Harriet, and Elizabeth Harrison. *Coyote Tales of the Montana Salish.* NP: Museum of the Plains Indian and Craft Center, 1974.

Pamphlet includes retellings of thirteen myths collected from Pierre Pichette. Designed to accompany museum exhibition.

4986. Ramsey, Jarold, ed. *Coyote Was Going There. Indian Literature of the Oregon Country.* Seattle: Univ. of Washington Press, 1977.

Myth, folktale, and song texts from unpublished mss. and previously published collections. With comparative and explanatory notes and data on collecting situations.

From Plateau, Northwest Coast, Great Basin, and California groups.

4987. Ray, Verne F. "The Bluejay Character in the Plateau Spirit Dance." *AA*, 39 (1937), 593–601.

Survey of the guardian spirit complex among Plateau groups includes focus on the character of Bluejay.

4988. ———. *Cultural Relations in the Plateau of Northwestern America.* Los Angeles: Southwest Museum, 1939 (Hodge Publication No. 3).

Description of cultural elements held in common by Plateau and some Northwest Coast groups includes data on ceremonialism.

4989. ———. "Historic Backgrounds of the Conjuring Complex in the Plateau and the Plains," in 161, pp. 204–16.

Survey of ritual behavior among various Plateau and Plains groups.

4990. ———. "The Sanpoil and Nespelem: Salishan Peoples of Northeastern Washington." *UWPA*, 5 (December 1932), 1–237.

Ethnography based on fieldwork done in 1928–1930 includes data on ceremonialism, religion, theology, and shamanism.

4991. Sanders, Helen Fitzgerald. *Trails Through Western Woods.* New York: Alice Harriman, 1910.

Description of life among Plateau Salish includes some myth and folktale texts in storytelling contexts.

4992. "Serpent-Woman of Hatton Lake, The." *JAF*, 5 (1892), 329.

Account of belief in water monster among NAs in Wyoming. Reprinted from the *St. Louis Republic* for 25 June 1892.

4993. Spier, Leslie. *The Prophet Dance of the Northwest and Its Derivatives: The Source of the Ghost Dance.* Menasha, Wis.: George Banta, 1935.

Describes the Prophet Dance among various Plateau and Northwest Coast groups. With emphasis on its influence on the Ghost Dance and Smohalla Cult.

4994. Teit, James A. "The Salishan Tribes of the Western Plateaus." Ed. Franz Boas. *ARBAE*, 45 (1927–1928), 23–396.

Ethnographies of three groups (Coeur d'Alene, Okanagan, Flathead) with descriptions of ceremonials and summaries of myths.

4995. Turney-High, Harry. "The Bluejay Dance." *AA*, 35 (1933), 103–7.

Description of a ceremonial among the Montana Salish.

4996. Young, Egerton Ryerson. *Indian Wigwams and Northern Camp-Fires.* London: Charles H. Kelly, 1893.

Missionary's account of experiences among various Plateau and Sub-Arctic groups includes data on storytelling and oratory. With some rewritten texts.

See also 30, 172, 192, 1996, 2026, 2035, 4040a, 4138, 4161, 4174, 4184, 4501, 4513, 4514, 4593–4595, 4841, 4876, 5113.

B. Bannock

4997. Fitzgerald, LaVerne Harriet. *Black Feather: Trapper Jim's Fables of Sheepeater Indians in the Yellowstone.* Caldwell, Ida.: Caxton, 1938.
Twenty-three rewritten myth and folktale texts. No annotations. Some data on the informant, a EA.
4998. Madsen, Brigham D. *The Bannock of Idaho.* Caldwell, Ida.: Caxton, 1958.
Historical work focuses on NA-EA contact. Includes some data on ceremonialism, prayer, and singing.

See also 4047.

C. Coeur d'Alene

4999. Reichard, Gladys A. *An Analysis of Coeur d'Alene Indian Myths.* MAFS 41 (1947).
Forty-eight myth and legend texts collected in 1927 and 1929. With discussion of literary style and application of "mirror of culture" theory. Comparative notes provided by Adele Froelich.
5000. ———. "Coeur d'Alene," in 87, pp. 521–707.
Contains a myth text with interlinear translation and linguistic analysis.
5001. ———. "Imagery in an Indian Vocabulary." *AS,* 18 (1943), 96–102.
The Coeur d'Alene vocabulary is concrete even when dealing with abstractions. With data on storytelling.

See also 4980, 4994, 5049.

D. Flathead

5002. Bigart, Robert James. "The Ideal Personality Form Seen in Ten Animal Tales of the Salish Flathead Indians of Montana." *PlA,* 17 (February 1972), 36–43.
Psychological analysis of folktales allows reconstruction of pre-contact world view.
5003. Clark, Ella E., ed. "Northwest Indian Coyote Tales." *NWR,* 6 (Summer 1963), 21–36.
Five myth texts from Flathead and Colville informants. Unannotated, but with data on informants and on the role of Coyote in NA folklore.
5004. Dusenberry, Verne. "Gabriel Nattau's Soul Speaks." *JAF,* 72 (1959), 155–60.
A ghost story heard by a priest while living among the Flathead in Montana reveals the influence of Christianity on NA culture.
5005. Fahey, John. *The Flathead Indians.* Norman: Univ. of Oklahoma Press, 1974.
Historical work contains data on ceremonials and mythology.
5006. McDermott, Louisa. "Folk-Lore of the Flathead Indians of Idaho: Adventures of Coyote." *JAF,* 14 (1901), 240–51.
Eleven unannotated Coyote tales. No commentary.
5007. Merriam, Alan P. *Ethnomusicology of the Flathead Indians.* VFPA No. 44 (1967).
Song texts (138) with musicological, contextual, functional, and esthetic analysis. Collected in 1950s.
5008. ———. "Flathead Indian Instruments and Their Music." *MQ,* 37 (1951), 368–75.

Describes flute and drum. With some music texts.
5009. ———. "The Hand Game of the Flathead Indians." *JAF,* 68 (1955), 313–24.
Describes the gambling activity. With attention to associated singing.
5010. ———. "Music of the Flathead Indians." *To,* 4, No. 3 (Spring 1956), 103–7.
Overview of the group's musical traditions.
5011. ———. "The Use of Music in the Study of a Problem of Acculturation." *AA,* 57 (1955), 28–34.
Shows how Flathead contact with EA culture has affected construction of musical instruments and song texts more than vocal quality and scale structure.
5012. Nixon, O. W. *Whitman's Ride Through Savage Lands with Sketches of Indian Life.* Introduction by James G. K. McClure. NP: Winona, 1905.
Biography of Marcus Whitman includes text of an oration delivered by a Flathead in 1831.
5013. Turney-High, Harry Holbert. *The Flathead Indians of Montana.* MAAA No. 48 (1937).
Ethnography includes data on religion, shamanism, and ceremonialism.
5014. Weisel, George P. "A Flathead Indian Tale." *JAF,* 65 (1952), 359–60.
Narrative text collected in Montana.

See also 4836, 4861, 4994.

E. Gros Ventre

5015. Cooper, John M. *The Gros Ventres of Montana: Part II. Religion and Ritual.* Ed. Regina Flannery. CUAAS No. 16 (1956).
Thorough survey of ceremonialism includes data on theology and supernaturalism. With eleven myth texts and comparative notes.
5016. Dusenberry, Verne. "Ceremonial Sweat Lodges of the Gros Ventres Indians." *En,* 28 (1963), 46–62.
Description of sweat lodge ceremonialism as recounted by an informant in 1941. With extensive explanatory notes.
5017. ———. "The Significance of the Sacred Pipes to the Gros Ventre of Montana." *En,* 26 (1961), 12–29.
Text of a historical legend collected in 1958. With data on cultural background.
5018. Flannery, Regina. "The Changing Form and Functions of the Gros Ventre Grass Dance." *PM,* 20 (1947), 39–70.
Historical treatment of the development of a ceremonial.
5019. ———. "The Gros Ventre Shaking Tent." *PM,* 17 (1944), 54–59.
Ceremonial description.
5020. ———. "Two Concepts of Power," in 162, pp. 185–89.
Discusses ideas about supernatural power as an outright gift or as involving continued relations with the supernatural. Data from Gros Ventre, Paviotso, and Klamath.
5021. ———, and John M. Cooper. "Social Mechanisms in Gros Ventre Gambling." *SJA,* 2 (1946), 391–419.

Includes legend texts about memorable games and players.

5022. Foolish Bear. "Origin of the Sacred Buffalo Horn." Trans. Arthur Mandan. *IW,* 5, No. 7 (March 1938), 35–36.

Legend text.

5023. Kroeber, A. L. "Ethnology of the Gros Ventre." *APAMNH,* 1, Part 4 (1908), 141–281.

Based on fieldwork done in 1901. Includes data on ceremonialism and mythology. With three personal narrative texts.

5024. ———. "Gros Ventre Myths and Tales." *APAMNH,* 1, Part 3 (1907), 55–139.

Fifty myth and folktale texts collected in 1901. With abstracts and comparative notes.

5025. Stallcop, Emmett A. "The So-Called Sun Dance of the Gros Ventre." *PlA,* 13, No. 40 (May 1968), 148–51.

Description of a ritual last conducted in 1884. Based on legendary accounts collected in 1967.

See also 1990, 2088.

F. Kalispel

5026. Carriker, Robert C. *The Kalispel People.* Phoenix: Indian Tribal Series, 1973.

Tribal history includes data on the role of the storyteller.

5027. Dusenberry, Verne. "Visions Among the Pend d'Oreille Indians." *En,* 24 (1959), 52–57.

Treats role of the visionary experience with attention to narratives about visions.

G. Kutenai

5028. Boas, Franz. "Additional Notes on the Kutenai Language." *IJAL,* 4 (1927), 85–104.

Linguistic survey includes a text of "The Star Husband" with interlinear translation and grammatical analysis.

5029. ———. *Kutenai Tales.* BAEB No. 59 (1918).

Seventy-seven narrative texts with interlinear and free translations. Collected by Alexander F. Chamberlain in 1891 and by Boas in 1914. With comparative notes.

5030. Chamberlain, Alexander F. "The Human Side of the Indian." *PSM,* 68 (June 1906), 503–14.

Survey of character traits of the Kutenai includes oral literature material: song and proverb texts, references to myths.

5031. ———. "A Kootenay Legend: The Coyote and the Mountain-Spirit." *JAF,* 7 (1894), 195–96.

Unannotated myth text collected in 1891. No commentary.

5032. ———. "Kootenay 'Medicine-Men.'" *JAF,* 14 (1901), 95–99.

Data on shamanism include translated song text and descriptions of ceremonials.

5033. ———. "Notes on the Kootenay Indians. Mythol-

ogy and Folklore." *AAOJ,* 17 (1895), 68–72.

Four unannotated myth texts with survey of tribal cosmology.

5034. ———. "Some Kutenai Linguistic Material." *AA,* 11 (1909), 13–26.

Includes five narrative texts and translations. Collected in 1891.

5035. Garvin, Paul L. "Colloquial Kutenai Text: Conversation II." *IJAL,* 20 (1954), 316–34.

Transcription of a tape-recorded conversation among three Kutenai speakers. With interlinear and free translations.

5036. ———. "Short Kutenai Texts." *IJAL,* 19 (1953), 305–11.

Seven anecdotes with interlinear translations. No commentary.

5037. Linderman, Frank B. *Kootenai Why Stories.* New York: Scribners, 1926.

Fifteen rewritten myth and folktale texts. No commentary or annotations. May be for children.

5038. Schaeffer, Claude. "The Bear Foster Parent Tale: A Kutenai Version." *JAF,* 60 (1947), 286–88.

Text of a folktale known most widely among Northeast groups. Collected in 1937.

5039. ———. "The Kutenai Female Berdache: Courier, Guide, Prophetess, and Warrior." *Eh,* 12 (1965), 193–236.

Describes role and ceremonial functions of women who assume masculine status among the Kutenai.

5040. ———. "Wolf and Two-Pointed Buck: A Lower Kutenai Tale of the Supernatural Period." *PM,* 22 (1949), 1–22.

Myth text collected in 1947. With extensive explanatory notes and data on supernaturalism.

5041. "Some Characteristics of Northwestern Indians." *PSM,* 43 (October 1893), 823–31.

Cultural notes taken from works by Alexander F. Chamberlain and George W. Dawson include data on ceremonialism and supernaturalism and myth summaries.

5042. Teit, James A. "Traditions and Information Regarding the Tona'xa." *AA,* 32 (1930), 625–32.

Data on an extinct tribal group include tribal origin myth. Collected from Kutenai and Salish.

5043. Turney-High, Harry Holbert. *Ethnography of the Kutenai.* MAAA No. 56 (1941).

Based on fieldwork done in 1939–1940. Includes data on religion, music, and ceremonialism.

5044. ———. "Two Kutenai Stories." *JAF,* 54 (1941), 191–96.

Two narratives dealing with the Sun Dance collected in 1939.

See also 2201, 2202.

H. Lillooet

5045. Elliott, W. C. "Lake Lillooet Tales." *JAF,* 44 (1931), 166–81.

Twelve myth and folktale texts. No commentary. With occasional comparative notes.

5046. Teit, James. "The Lillooet Indians." Ed. Franz Boas. *MAMNH,* 4, Part 6 (1906), 193–300.

Ethnography includes data on mythology and ceremonialism. From the Jesup North Pacific Expedition.

5047. ———. "Traditions of the Lillooet Indians of British Columbia." *JAF,* 25 (1912), 287–371.

Fifty myth and folktale texts with comparative and explanatory notes. Includes some data on cultural background.

See also 5090.

I. Nez Perce

5048. Ackerman, Lillian A. "Marital Instability and Juvenile Delinquency Among the Nez Perces." *AA,* 73 (1971), 595–603.

Blames Nez Perce social problems partially on lack of discipline. Formerly, cultural values were transmitted to children through storytelling.

5049. Aoki, Haruo. "The East Plateau Linguistic Diffusion Area." *IJAL,* 41 (1975), 183–99.

Linguistic survey of the Nez Perce and Coeur d'Alene. Correlations in myth repertoires elucidate intertribal relations.

5050. ———. *Nez Perce Grammar.* UCPL No. 62 (1970).

Includes legend excerpt with free translation and linguistic analysis. Collected in 1960.

5051. ———. *Nez Perce Texts.* UCPL No. 90 (1979).

Nine myths, eight legends, three songs, and four descriptions of customs collected between 1960 and 1972. With free and interlinear translations. Good annotations.

5052. Butterfield, Grace. "Romantic Historical Tale of the Nez Perces." *OHQ,* 43 (1942), 150–59.

Retelling of a folktale. No commentary or annotation.

5053. Clark, Ella E., ed. "Some Nez Perce Traditions Told by Chief Armstrong." *OHQ,* 53 (1952), 181–91.

Excerpt from a ms. written by Armstrong in 1930s contains data on ceremonialism, singing, and mythology. With text of a Coyote tale.

5054. ———. "Watkuese and Lewis and Clark." *WF,* 12 (1953), 175–78.

Describes a figure who aided the explorers and who is remembered in Nez Perce legendry.

5055. [Farrand, Livingston]. "Notes on the Nez Percé Indians." *AA,* 23 (1921), 244–46.

Random ethnographic data collected in 1902 include references to ceremonials.

5056. Howard, Helen Addison, and Dan L. McGrath. *War Chief Joseph.* Caldwell, Ida.: Caxton, 1958.

Biography includes description of storytelling situation with myth summary and description of the Smohalla Cult.

5057. Josephy, Alvin M., Jr. "The Last Stand of Chief Joseph." *AH,* 9, No. 2 (February 1958), 36–43, 78–81.

Historical account of Nez Perce retreat includes text of Joseph's surrender speech.

5058. Lyman, H. S. "Items from the Nez Perces Indians." *OHQ,* 2 (1901), 287–303.

Miscellany of customs and beliefs contains text of a Coyote tale.

5059. McBeth, Kate C. *The Nez Perces Since Lewis and Clark.* New York: Fleming H. Revell, 1908.

Historical account focuses on missionary work. Includes six myth texts.

5060. McWhorter, Lucullus Virgil. *Yellow Wolf: His Own Story.* Caldwell, Ida.: Caxton 1948.

Life history of a subject born in 1855 focuses on NA-EA relations.

5061. Packard, R. L. "Notes on the Mythology and Religion of the Nez Perce Indians." *JAF,* 4 (1891), 327–30.

Myth text and description of naming practices. Collected in 1880–1881.

5062. Phinney, Archie. *Nez Percé Texts. CUCA* No. 25 (1934).

Forty-one myth texts and abstracts collected in 1929–1930. With free and interlinear translations and linguistic and explanatory notes.

5063. Ramsey, Jarold. "From 'Mythic' to 'Fictive' in a Nez Perce Orpheus Myth." *WAL,* 13, No. 2 (August 1978), 119–31.

Analysis of a narrative collected in 1929 by Archie Phinney suggests that characters move beyond their mythic personalities to assume human dimensions.

5064. Skeels, Dell R. "A Classification of Humor in Nez Perce Mythology." *JAF,* 67 (1954), 57–63.

Typology of six categories of humor: tricks, pomposity coming to grief, sarcasm, the obscene, eccentric social behavior, stupidity.

5065. ———. "Eros and Thanatos in Nez Perce River Mythology." *AI,* 21, Nos. 3 and 4 (1964), 103–10.

Examination of the symbolism of water in Nez Perce Coyote myths. The river is a symbol of the womb and of the passivity of death.

5066. ———. "The Function of Humor in Three Nez Perce Indian Myths." *AI,* 11 (1954), 249–61.

Suggests that Coyote myths allow the discharge of psychic tension.

5067. Slickpoo, Allen P., Sr., Leroy L. Seth, and Deward E. Walker, Jr. *Nu Mee Poom Tit Wah Tit (Nez Perce Legends).* NP: NP, 1972.

Forty-six unannotated myth and folktale texts, including several Coyote tales. With commentary on content.

5068. Spinden, Herbert J. "Myths of the Nez Percé Indians." *JAF,* 21 (1908), 13–23, 149–58.

Eighteen myth texts collected in 1907. With explanatory notes and data on collecting situation.

5069. ———. "The Nez Percé Indians." *MAAA,* 2 (1907–1915), 165–274.

Ethnography based on fieldwork done in 1907–1908 includes data on shamanism, ceremonialism, mythology, and music.

5070. Stross, Brian. "Serial Order in Nez Percé Myths." *JAF,* 84 (1971), 104–13.

Treats the importance of sequential ordering of elements in myths. Reprinted in 149 (104–13).

5071. Walker, Deward E., Jr. "Nez Perce Sorcery." *Eth,* 6 (1967), 66–96.

Survey of aboriginal and contemporary sorcery complexes includes twenty legend texts and data on ceremonialism.

5072. ———. "The Nez Perce Sweat Bath Complex: An Acculturational Analysis." *SJA,* 22 (1966), 133–71.

Compares form and function of the ceremonial in traditional and contemporary life.

5073. Young, Joseph. "An Indian's View of Indian Affairs." *NAR,* 254, No. 1 (Spring 1969), 56–64.

Text of oration. Originally published in *NAR* for April 1879.

See also 458, 3234, 3366, 4980.

J. Okanagan

5074. Allison, Mrs. S. S. "Account of the Similkameen Indians of British Columbia." *JAIGBI,* 21 (1892), 305–18.

Culture survey includes data on religion and ceremonialism.

5075. Mourning Dove (Hu-mis'-hu-ma). *Coyote Stories.* Ed. Heister Dean Guie. With notes by L. V. McWhorter. Caldwell, Ida.: Caxton, 1934.

Twenty-seven Coyote stories. With data on storytelling traditions. No comparative notes.

5076. Hill-Tout, Charles. "Report on the Ethnology of the Okanákēn of British Columbia. An Interior Division of the Salish Stock." *JAIGBI,* 41 (1912–1913), 130–61.

Ethnography includes data on religion and ten unannotated myth texts (two in original with interlinear translations).

5077. Spier, Leslie, ed. *The Siknaietk or Southern Okanagan of Washington.* Menasha, Wis.: George Banta, 1938.

Ethnography based on fieldwork done by a team in 1930 includes data on ceremonialism and mythology.

5078. Watkins, Don. "A Boas Original." *IJAL,* 40 (1974), 29–43.

Folktale text collected by Franz Boas c. 1900. Includes linguistic analysis.

See also 4864, 4980, 4994.

K. Shuswap

5079. Dawson, George M. "Notes on the Shushwap People of British Columbia." *PTRSC,* 1st series, 9, section 2 (1891), 3–44.

Ethnography based on fieldwork done between 1877 and 1890 contains data on ceremonialism and unannotated myth and legend texts.

5080. Kuipers, Aert H. *The Shuswap Language. Grammar, Texts, Dictionary.* The Hague: Mouton, 1974.

Contains eight myth texts with free translations and linguistic analysis. Collected between 1968 and 1970.

5081. Smith, Harlan I. "An American Oberammergau.

The Passion-Play by American Indians." *Pu,* 5 (December 1908), 294–303.

Account of a Christian drama performed by NAs under direction of a missionary.

5082. Speare, Jean E., ed. *The Days of Augusta.* Seattle: Madronna, 1977.

Collection of stories and reminiscences of Mary Augusta Evans, 87, a Shuswap.

5083. Teit, James. "The Shuswap." Ed. Franz Boas. *MAMNH,* 4, Part 7 (1909), 443–789.

Ethnography includes data on religion and ceremonialism. With sixty-five myth texts and cycles with explanatory and comparative notes. From the Jesup North Pacific Expedition.

L. Thompson

5084. Teit, James. "European Tales from the Upper Thompson Indians." *JAF,* 29 (1916), 301–29.

Sixteen folktale texts with brief comparative notes. No commentary.

5085. ———. "More Thompson Indian Tales." *JAF,* 50 (1937), 173–90.

Six texts edited and annotated from Teit's mss. by Lucy Kramer.

5086. ———. "Mythology of the Thompson Indians." *MAMNH,* 12, No. 2 (1912), 199–416.

Ninety-five myths, fourteen folktales, and six legends with comparative notes. From the Jesup North Pacific Expedition.

5087. ———. "Story of Bear." *JAF,* 39 (1926), 450–59.

Unannotated myth text with some explanatory commentary.

5088. ———. "Tattooing and Face and Body Painting of the Thompson Indians, British Columbia." Ed. Franz Boas. *ARBAE,* 45 (1927–1928), 397–439.

Catalogue of processes and designs used in tattooing includes data on associated ceremonialism.

5089. ———. "The Thompson Indians of British Columbia." *MAMNH,* 2, Part 4 (1900), 163–392.

Ethnography includes data on religion, ceremonialism, and music. From the Jesup North Pacific Expedition.

5090. ———. *Traditions of the Thompson River Indians of British Columbia.* MAFS No. 6 (1898).

Thirty-eight myth and folktale texts with abstracts and extensive explanatory and comparative notes. Introduction by Franz Boas provides cultural background and surveys group's oral traditions. With two Lillooet texts.

See also 4980.

XI SUB-ARCTIC

A. General Works

5091. Arthur, Donald. "Song of the People." *IH,* 2, No. 1 (Spring 1969), 17–19, 48.

Song texts with data on their cultural significance.

5092. Bradley, Ian, and Patricia Bradley. *A Bibliography of Canadian Native Arts. Indian and Eskimo Arts, Crafts, Dance and Music.* Victoria, B. C.: GLC, 1977.

Unannotated list of 1495 books and articles dealing with arts of groups from Sub-Arctic, Arctic, Northwest Coast, Plains, Midwest, and Northeast.

5093. Chapman, John Wight. "Athapascan Traditions from the Lower Yukon." *JAF,* 16 (1903), 180–85.

Six myth texts from unspecified Sub-Arctic group. No commentary or annotations.

5094. ———. *A Camp on the Yukon.* Cornwall-on-Hudson, N. Y.: Idlewild, 1948.

Account of experiences of a missionary who went to Alaska in 1880s includes data on storytelling and ceremonialism for several Sub-Arctic groups.

5095. ———. "The Happy Hunting–Ground of the Ten'a." *JAF,* 25 (1912), 66–71.

Myth text collected in 1887. With data on collecting context.

5096. ———. "Notes on the Tinneh Tribe of Anvik, Alaska." *ICA,* 15, No. 2 (1906), 7–38.

Descriptions of ceremonials such as the potlatch and three translated myth texts.

5097. ———. "Tinneh Animism." *AA,* 23 (1921), 298–310.

Compares beliefs concerning the soul among NAs in Sub-Arctic to similar beliefs in India.

5098. Chapman, May Seely. *The Animalistic Beliefs of the Ten'a of the Lower Yukon Alaska.* Hartford, Conn.: Church Missions, 1939.

Pamphlet surveys Sub-Arctic supernaturalism.

5099. Clark, Ella E. *Indian Legends of Canada.* Toronto: McClelland and Stewart, 1960.

Eighty-eight myth, folktale, and legend texts from various groups in the Sub-Arctic, Midwest, Plains, Northeast, and Northwest Coast. No comparative notes, but explanatory comments accompany each text. All material has been previously published.

5100. Crowe, Keith J. *A History of the Original Peoples of Northern Canada.* Montreal: McGill-Queen's Univ. Press, 1974.

History and culture survey of groups in Sub-Arctic and Arctic includes myth summaries and data on singing.

5101. De Laguna, Frederica. "Indian Masks from the Lower Yukon." *AA,* 38 (1936), 569–85.

Description of masks includes data on associated ceremonialism and on the mythic figures represented by the masks.

5102. Fowke, Edith. *Folklore of Canada.* Toronto: McClelland and Stewart, 1976.

Includes data on Sub-Arctic, Plains, and Midwest groups. With narrative texts and ceremonial descriptions.

5103. Gibbs, George. "Notes on the Tinneh or Chepewyan [sic] Indians of British and Russian America." *ARSI for 1866,* pp. 303–27.

Contains three culture surveys with data on ceremonialism: "The Eastern Tinneh" (by Bernard R. Ross), "The Loucheux Indians" (by William L. Hardisty), and "The Kutchin Tribes" (by Strachan Jones).

5104. Helm, June. *The Indians of the Subarctic. A Critical Bibliography.* Bloomington: Indiana Univ. Press, 1976.

Unannotated list of 272 books and articles. Introductory essay includes a section, "Traditional Culture and Society," which deals with folklore materials.

5105. Hippler, Arthur E. "The Athabascans of Interior Alaska: A Culture and Personality Perspective." *AA,* 75 (1973), 1529–41.

Personality of Sub-Arctic NAs, shaped by socialization, is reflected in folklore, which emphasizes demons, aggression, and treachery.

5106. Jenness, Diamond. *The Corn Goddess and Other Tales from Indian Canada.* NMCB No. 141 (1956).

Twenty-five unannotated folktale texts from various groups: Iroquois, Ojibwa, Sarsi, Sekani, Carrier, Coast Salish, Eskimo. No commentary.

5107. Jetté, Julius. "On the Medicine-Men of the Ten'a." *JAIGBI,* 37 (1907), 157–88.

Description of shamanism includes data on ceremonialism and a legend text with free and interlinear translations.

5108. ———. "On the Superstitions of the Ten'a Indians (Middle Part of the Yukon Valley, Alaska)." *A,* 6 (1911), 95–108, 241–59, 602–15, 699–723.

Thorough survey of theology, ceremonialism, and supernaturalism. Contains song (words and music) and myth texts with interlinear translations.

5109. ———. "On Ten'a Folk-Lore." *JAIGBI,* 38 (1908), 298–367.

Ten myth and folktale texts with free and interlinear translations and extensive linguistic and explanatory notes. Includes general data on storytelling traditions.

5110. ———. "On Ten'a Folk-Lore (Part II)." *JAIGBI,* 39 (1909), 460–505.

Four myth and folktale texts with free and interlinear translations. Includes linguistic and explanatory notes.

5111. ———. "Riddles of the Ten'a Indians." *A,* 8 (1913), 181–201, 630–51.

Riddle texts (110) with translations and explanations. Prefaced by survey of riddling customs.

5112. Johnston, Thomas F. "Ancient Athabascan Ritual in Alaska." *IH,* 8, No. 3 (Summer 1975), 9–25, 46.

Description of Stick Dance. With photographs.

5113. Maclean, John. *Canadian Savage Folk. The Native Tribes of Canada.* Toronto: William Briggs, 1896.

Cross-cultural survey of groups in Sub-Arctic, Arctic, Plains, Plateau, Midwest, Northeast, and Northwest Coast includes data on religion and mythology.

5114. MacNeish, J. H., ed. "The Poole Field Letters." *An,* 4 (1957), 47–60.

Text of a letter written by a trapper-prospector in 1913 includes data on religious system and mortuary customs of NAs in northwestern Canada.

5115. Martin, Calvin. "The War Between Indians and Animals." *NH,* June-July 1978, pp. 92–96.

Describes mythic basis for slaughter of some animal species by various Sub-Arctic groups.

5116. McGuire, Joseph D. "Ethnology in the Jesuit Relations." *AA,* 3 (1901), 257–69.

Survey of ethnographic data in Jesuit records of mission in Canada between 1610 and 1791 includes references to verbal performances among Sub-Arctic, Northeast, and Midwest groups.

5117. Morice, A. G. "The Great Déné Race." *A,* 1 (1906), 229–78, 483–509, 695–730; 2 (1907), 1–34, 181–96; 4 (1909), 582–606; 5 (1910), 113–42, 419–43, 643–53, 969–90.

Cultural survey of Athapaskan-speaking groups in the Sub-Arctic, Southwest, and California includes data on verbal agility.

5118. Parsons, Elsie Clews. "A Narrative of the Ten'a of Anvik, Alaska." *A,* 16–17 (1921–1922), 51–71.

Myth text collected in 1920. With extensive explanatory and comparative notes.

5119. Ridington, Robin. "Wechuge and Windigo: A Comparison of Cannibal Belief Among Boreal Forest Athapaskans and Algonkians." *An,* n. s. 18 (1976), 107–29.

Compares beliefs in a cannibalistic monster among various Sub-Arctic and Midwest groups. With narrative texts.

5120. Schmitter, Ferdinand. "Upper Yukon Native Customs and Folk-Lore." *SMC,* 56, No. 4 (May 1910), 1–30.

Culture survey based on observations in 1906 includes data on ceremonialism and shamanism and fifteen unannotated myth texts.

5121. *Stories of Native Alaskans.* Fairbanks: Univ. of Alaska Press, 1977.

Fourteen myth and folktale texts with free translations from Sub-Arctic and Arctic groups. No annotations, but with some data on collecting methods. Prepared by Alaska Library Association.

5122. Sullivan, Robert J. *The Ten'a Food Quest.* CUAAS No. 11 (1942).

Survey of economic life contains data on ceremonialism.

5123. Teicher, Morton I. "Windigo Psychosis: A Study of a Relationship Between Belief and Behavior Among the Indians of Northeastern Canada," in 150, pp. 1–29.

Attempts to show influence of traditional beliefs of Sub-Arctic, Midwest, and Northeast groups on psychotic behavior. Includes texts of several myths and legends dealing with the Windigo figure.

5124. Wright, Arthur. "An Athabascan Tradition from Alaska." *JAF,* 21 (1908), 33–34.

Unannotated folktale text. No commentary.

See also 30, 172, 829, 848, 851, 857, 865, 1596, 1630, 1977, 4184, 4501, 4530, 4584, 4599, 4620, 4996, 5362, 5369.

B. Beaver

5125. Goddard, Pliny Earle. "The Beaver Indians." *APAMNH,* 10 (1917), 201–93.

Ethnographic notes include an extensive collection of myths, folktales, and legends. No commentary or annotations. Based on fieldwork done in 1913.

5126. ———. "Beaver Texts." *APAMNH,* 10 (1917), 295–397.

Texts with interlinear translations of narratives which appear in free translations in 5125. No commentary or annotations.

5127. Ridington, Robin. "Beaver Dreaming and Singing." *An,* n. s. 13 (1971), 115–28.

Describes role of dreams and songs in traditional religious system.

5128. ———. "The Medicine Fight: An Instrument of Political Process Among the Beaver Indians." *AA,* 70 (1968), 1152–60.

Describes contest in which individuals demonstrate their supernatural powers.

5129. ———, and Tonia Ridington. "The Inner Eye of Shamanism and Totemism." *HR,* 10, No. 1 (August 1970), 49–61.

Argues for parallelism between totemic thought and shamanistic cosmology. Uses examples from the Beaver.

C. Carrier

5130. Jenness, Diamond. "The Carrier Indians of the Bulkley River: Their Social and Religious Life." *BAEB* No. 133 (*AP* No. 25), 1943.

Ethnography based on fieldwork done in 1924–1925 includes data on religion and shamanism. With song texts (some with music).

5131. ———. "An Indian Method of Treating Hysteria." *PM,* 6 (1933), 13–20.

Ceremonial description with song texts (words only).

5132. ———. "Myths of the Carrier Indians of British Columbia." *JAF,* 47 (1934), 97–257.

Eighty-two myth, legend, and folktale texts collected in 1924–1925. No annotations or commentary.

5133. Morice, A. G. "Are the Carrier Sociology and Mythology Indigenous or Exotic?" *PTRSC,* 1st series, 10, section 2 (1892), 109–26.

Argues that Carrier culture, including mythology, has been greatly affected by external influences. With synopses of creation and etiological myths.

5134. ———. "Carrier Onomatology." *AA,* 35 (1933), 632–58.

Description of naming practices includes texts of narratives associated with particular names.

5135. ———. *The History of the Northern Interior of British Columbia (Formerly New Caledonia) [1660 to 1880].* Toronto: William Briggs, 1905.

Begins with NA history as preserved in hero legends recounted by Carrier storytellers.

See also 5106.

D. Chipewyan

5136. Bell, James Mackintosh. "The Fireside Stories of the Chippwyans." *JAF,* 16 (1903), 73–84.
Three folktale texts. No annotations, but with data on cultural background.
5137. Birket-Smith, Kaj. *Contributions to Chipewyan Ethnology.* Copenhagen: Gyldendal, 1930.
Ethnography based on fieldwork done in 1923 includes data on religion and ceremonialism and seventeen myth and legend texts. From Fifth Thule Expedition.
5138. Cohen, Ronald, and James W. Van Stone. "Dependency and Self-Sufficiency in Chipewyan Stories," in *Contributions to Anthropology 1961–62. Part II. NMCB* No. 194 (1964), 29–55.
Content analysis reveals attitude toward self-reliance in the value system of the culture.
5139. Goddard, Pliny Earle. "Chipewyan Texts." *APAMNH,* 10 (1917), 1–65.
Sixteen myth and folktale texts with free and interlinear translations. Collected in 1911. With occasional comparative notes.
5140. Jenness, Diamond, ed. "The Chipewyan Indians: An Account by an Early Explorer." *An,* 3 (1956), 15–33.
Ms. probably written by John Macdonell in the early 1800s deals with group's theology and ceremonialism.
5141. Li, Fang-Kuei. "A Chipewyan Ethnological Text." *IJAL,* 30 (1964), 132–36.
Contains personal narrative text with free translation and linguistic analysis. Collected in 1928.
5142. ———, and Ronald Scollon. *Chipewyan Texts.* Nankang, Taipei, Taiwan: Institute of History and Philology, 1976 (Academia Sinica Special Publication No. 71).
Nineteen myth and legend texts collected in 1928 and presented with free translations. With linguistic notes.
5143. Lowie, Robert H. "Chipewyan Tales." *APAMNH,* 10, Part 3 (1917), 171–200.
Eighteen myth texts collected in 1908. No commentary or annotations.
5144. Scollon, Ronald. "Two Discourse Markers in Chipewyan Narratives." *IJAL,* 43 (1977), 60–64.
Describes use of conjunctions and pronouns in listing narrative events in storytelling.
5145. Van Stone, James W. *The Changing Culture of the Snowdrift Chipewyan. NMCB* No. 209 (1965).
Acculturation study done in 1961 includes data on religious institutions and beliefs.
5146. Voudrach, Paul. "Good Hope Tales," in *Contributions to Ethnology V. NMCB* No. 204 (1967), 1–58.
Thirteen texts with summaries and analysis for self-reliance theme. No comparative notes.

See also 1853, 5103.

E. Coyukon

5147. Kroul, Mary V. "Definitional Domains of the Koyukon Athapaskan Potlatch." *ArA,* 9, Supplement (1974), 39–47.
Considers NA usage of the term "potlatch" and types of ceremonials designated by the term.
5148. Loyens, William J. "The Koyukon Feast for the Dead." *ArA,* 2, No. 2 (1964), 133–48.
Ritual description. With comparison to ceremonials of other groups.

F. Cree

5149. Ahenakew, Edward. "Cree Trickster Tales." *JAF,* 42 (1929), 309–53.
Twenty-five unannotated episodes from the Trickster cycle. No commentary.
5150. ———. *Voices of the Plains Cree.* Ed. Ruth M. Buck. Toronto: McClelland and Stewart, 1973.
Based on a ms. written in 1923. Primarily the life history and cultural descriptions of Chief Thundercloud (1849–1927) as collected by Ahenakew. With data on ceremonialism and extensive explanatory notes.
5151. Bauer, George W. "Cree Tales and Beliefs." *NF,* 12 (1971), 1–70.
Eight myth and legend texts with extensive data on informants and collecting situations. Introduction presents cultural background and information on storytelling traditions.
5152. Beardsley, Gretchen. "Notes on Cree Medicines, Based on a Collection Made by I. Cowie in 1892." *PMASAL,* 27 (1941), 483–96.
Primarily concerned with natural medicines, but deals with theory of illness involving supernatural forces.
5153. Bell, Robert. "The History of the Che-Che-Puy-Ew-Tis. A Legend of the Northern Crees." *JAF,* 10 (1897), 1–8.
Unannotated myth text with some data on cultural background.
5154. Bloomfield, Leonard. *Plains Cree Texts. PAES* No. 16 (1934).
Four myths, thirty-seven legends, three songs (words only), and descriptions of customs such as the Sun Dance collected in 1925. With free translations. No commentary or annotations.
5155. ———. *Sacred Stories of the Sweet Grass Cree. NMCB* No. 60 (1930).
Thirty-six myth texts collected in 1925. With free translations, linguistic notes, and informant data.
5156. Chamberlain, Alexander F. "Cree and Ojibwa Literary Terms." *JAF,* 19 (1906), 346–47.
List of terms used in reference to and performance of oral narratives.
5157. ———. "Notes of Cree Folk-Lore." *JAF,* 15 (1902), 60–62.
List of Cree terms dealing with supernaturalism and oral performance. From Fr. Lacombe's dictionary of Cree.

5158. Cooper, John M. "The Cree Witiko Psychosis." *PM,* 6 (1933), 20–24.

Presents folklore basis for psychotic craving for human flesh.

5159. ———. *The Northern Algonquian Supreme Being.* *CUAAS* No. 2 (1934).

Survey of the high god concept based on interviews conducted in early 1930s includes prayer texts and references to myths.

5160. Coze, Paul. "The Indian's Altar to His God." *T,* 74 (January 1940), 16–19, 45.

Description of the concept of *orenda* among the Cree. With comparisons to other NA traditions.

5161. Cresswell, J. R. "Folk-Tales of the Swampy Cree of Northern Manitoba." *JAF,* 36 (1923), 404–06.

Four unannotated folktale texts. No commentary.

5162. Darnell, Regna. "Correlates of Cree Narrative Performance," in 82, pp. 315–35.

Analysis of components of a creative performance by a Cree storyteller in 1971.

5163. Dusenberry, Verne. *The Montana Cree: A Study in Religious Persistence.* Stockholm: Almqvist & Wiksell, 1962.

Describes Cree religion which has survived despite inroads of Christianity. Includes texts of prayers, songs, and myths and detailed description of the Sun Dance.

5164. Flannery, Regina. "Gossip as a Clue to Attitudes." *PM,* 7 (1934), 8–12.

Studies functions of gossip in Cree culture.

5165. Hamilton, J. C. "Two Algonquin Legends." *JAF,* 7 (1894), 201–04.

Two unannotated myth texts from Cree storyteller. With data on informant.

5166. Honigmann, John J. "The Attawapiskat Swampy Cree: An Ethnographic Reconstruction." *APUAK,* 5, No. 1 (December 1956), 23–82.

Ethnographic notes compiled in 1947–1948 include data on singing, dancing, storytelling, and shamanism. With legend texts.

5167. ———. "European and Other Tales from the Western Woods Cree." *JAF,* 66 (1953), 309–31.

Eight folktale texts collected in British Columbia in 1943.

5168. LeBlanc, Thomas J. "The Cree." *AM,* 6 (1925), 343–48.

Culture survey includes data on religious attitudes and Christian ceremonialism.

5169. Linderman, Frank B. *Indian Old-Man Stories. More Sparks from War Eagle's Lodge-Fire.* New York: Scribner's, 1920.

Thirteen rewritten folktale texts, many of which deal with Trickster. No commentary or annotations. From the Cree and Ojibwa.

5170. Mandelbaum, David G. "The Plains Cree." *APAMNH,* 37, Part 2 (1940), 155–316.

Ethnography based on fieldwork done in 1934–1935 includes data on religious attitudes and ceremonialism. With personal narrative and song texts (words only).

5171. Newbery, J. W. E. "The Universe at Prayer," in 166, pp. 165–78.

Description of Sacred Pipe Ceremony among Cree and Ojibwa.

5172. Norman, Howard A. *The Wishing Bone Cycle. Narrative Poems from the Swampy Cree Indians.* Preface by Jerome Rothenberg. New York: Stonehill, 1976.

Poetic translations of Cree traditional narratives. With data on contexts.

5173. Oaks, Abel. "The Boy and the Buffalo." *IH,* 1, No. 4 (Fall 1968), 29.

Unannotated myth text. No commentary.

5174. Preston, Richard J. "Belief in the Context of Rapid Change: An Eastern Cree Example," in 126, pp. 117–29.

Describes transitions in beliefs and ceremonialism.

5175. Richardson, Boyce. *Strangers Devour the Land. A Chronicle of the Assault Upon the Last Coherent Hunting Culture in North America, the Cree of Northern Quebec, and Their Vast Primeval Homelands.* New York: Alfred A. Knopf, 1976.

Account of Cree resistance to construction of a series of dams in their homeland in the early 1970s. With data on joking and storytelling.

5176. Rogers, Edward S. "Natural Environment—Social Organization—Witchcraft: Cree Versus Ojibwa—A Test Case," in *Contributions to Anthropology: Ecological Essays. NMCB* No. 230 (1969), 24–39.

Relates witchcraft beliefs to social ecology.

5177. Rordam, Vita. "The Woman Who Spoke to a Dog. A Story of the Coast Crees Told by a Man of Winisk." *B,* 298 (Winter 1967), 54.

Rewritten myth text. No commentary.

5178. Rossignol, M. "Property Concepts Among the Cree of the Rocks." *PM,* 12 (1939), 61–70.

Considers group ownership of oral literature.

5179. ———. "The Religion of the Saskatchewan and Western Manitoba Cree." *PM,* 11 (1938), 67–71.

Survey of myth-based belief system.

5180. Saindon, J. Emile. "Two Cree Songs from James Bay." *PM,* 7 (1934), 6–7.

Song texts (words and music). With data on performance context.

5181. Simms, S. C. "The Metawin Society of the Bungees or Swampy Indians of Lake Winnipeg." *JAF,* 19 (1906), 330–33.

Ceremonial description. With two song texts.

5182. ———. "Myths of the Bungees or Swampy Indians of Lake Winnipeg." *JAF,* 19 (1906), 334–40.

Rewritten myth texts. Includes data on theology.

5183. Skinner, Alanson. "Notes on the Eastern Cree and Northern Saulteaux." *APAMNH,* 9, Part 1 (1911), 1–177.

Ethnographic sketches based on fieldwork done in 1908. For Cree, includes data on ceremonialism and shamanism with nineteen narrative texts and explanatory notes. For Saulteaux, includes data on ceremonialism and music with two unannotated myth texts.

5184. ———. "Notes on the Plains Cree." *AA,* 16 (1914), 68–87.

Ethnographic data includes ceremonial descriptions and a prayer text. Collected in 1913.

5185. ———. "Plains Cree Tales." *JAF,* 29 (1916), 341–67.

Eight myth and folktale texts and fourteen episodes from the hero cycle. Collected in 1913. No commentary or annotations.

5186. ———. "Some Remarks on the Culture of Eastern Near-Arctic Indians." *S,* n. s. 29 (1909), 150–52.

Survey of Cree culture includes data on shamanism. With comparison to Naskapi traditions.

5187. Stevens, James R. *Sacred Legends of the Sandy Lake Cree.* Toronto: McClelland and Stewart, 1971.
Seventy-six unannotated myth and legend texts. With data on cultural background.
5188. Swindlehurst, Fred. "Folk-Lore of the Cree Indians." *JAF,* 18 (1905), 139–43.
Seven unannotated myth and folktale texts. With data on storytelling context.
5189. Teit, James A. "Two Plains Cree Tales." *JAF,* 34 (1921), 320–21.
Unannotated myth texts. No commentary.
5190. Turner, D. H. "Windigo Mythology and the Analysis of Cree Social Structure." *An,* n. s. 19 (1977), 63–73.
Shows how oral narratives about cannibalistic monster relate to social organization.
5191. Wilkinson, Mentz. "The Making of a Chief." *Bl,* 195 (1914), 601–11.
Description of the installation ceremony for a Cree chief.
5192. Wolfart, H. Christoph. "Plains Cree: A Grammatical Study." *TAPS,* n. s. 63, Part 5 (1973), 3–90.
Contains a legend text collected in 1968. With free translation and linguistic analysis.
5193. Wuttunee, William I. C. "Peyote Ceremony." *B,* 299 (Summer 1968), 22–25.
Ritual description as observed in 1964.

See also 1236, 2077, 2078, 2169.

G. Dogrib

5194. Helm, June, and Nancy Oestreich Lurie. *The Dogrib Hand Game. NMCB* No. 205 (1966).
Thorough description of the game with song texts (words and music) and analysis. Includes data on dance and music by Gertrude Kurath.
5195. Helm, June, and Vital Thomas. "Tales of the Dogribs." *B,* 297, No. 2 (1966), 16–20.
Six unannotated myth and legend texts. With some data on collecting situation.
5196. ———. "Tales of the Dogribs." *B,* 297, No. 3 (1967), 52–54.
Three unannotated myth texts. No commentary.
5197. Richardson, John. "Habits and Character of the Dog-Rib Indians." *H,* 4 (1852), 690–92.
Negative culture survey includes data on singing, dancing, and supernaturalism.

H. Hare

5198. Hultkrantz, Åke. "The Hare Indians: Notes on Their Traditional Culture and Religion, Past and Present." *En,* 38 (1973), 113–52.
Ethnographic data derived from published materials and an interview conducted in 1972 contain extensive information on religion, mythology, ceremonialism, and the effect of acculturation. Harold Beyer Broch

challenged the interpretations of the interview data in *En,* 39 (1974), 159–69. Hultkrantz responded in *En,* 39 (1974), 170–78.

See also 4944.

I. Kaska

5199. Honigmann, John J. *Culture and Ethos of Kaska Society. YUPA* No. 40 (1949).
Ethnography based on fieldwork done in 1940s includes data on religion and world view. With five life history texts with psychological analysis.
5200. ———. *The Kaska Indians: An Ethnographic Reconstruction. YUPA* No. 51 (1954).
Ethnography based on fieldwork done in 1940s includes data on shamanism, cosmogony, theology, and ceremonialism.
5201. Taylor, P. "Tales from the Delta." *B,* June 1953, pp. 22–25.
Not available for examination.
5202. Teit, James A. "Kaska Tales." *JAF,* 30 (1917), 427–73.
Twenty-five myth and folktale texts collected in 1912 and 1915. With comparative annotations and data on cultural background.

See also 5226.

J. Kutchin

5203. Camsell, Charles. "Loucheux Myths." *JAF,* 28 (1915), 249–57.
Thirteen myth texts collected in 1905. With comparative and explanatory notes. Prepared for publication by C. M. Barbeau.
5204. Keim, Charles J., ed. "Kutchin Legends from Old Crow, Yukon Territory." *APUAK,* 11, No. 2 (January 1964), 97–108.
Eleven unannotated myth and legend texts. No commentary.
5205. Leechman, Douglas. "Loucheux Tales." *JAF,* 63 (1950), 158–62.
Five folktale texts collected in 1946.
5206. Osgood, Cornelius. *Contributions to the Ethnography of the Kutchin. YUPA* No. 14 (1936).
Based on fieldwork done in 1932. Includes data on singing, storytelling, religion, cosmogony, and shamanism. With six unannotated myth texts.
5207. Russell, Frank. "Athabascan Myths." *JAF,* 13 (1900), 11–18.
Three Loucheux and three Slave myths with explanatory notes.
5208. Slobodin, Richard. "Some Social Functions of Kutchin Anxiety." *AA,* 62 (1960), 122–33.
Argues that anxiety, much of which is manifested in stories about legendary "bush men," serves to reinforce group cohesion.

See also 5103, 5314.

K. Mountain

5209. Basso, Ellen B. "The Enemy of the Tribe: 'Bushman' Images in Northern Athapaskan Narratives." *AE*, 5 (1978), 690–709.

Ogre figures in oral narratives respond to cultural concerns about seasonality, social relationships, and technology. Data from Mountain.

L. Sarsi

5210. Christie, Robert. "Dance to the Sun." *SEP*, 224 (22 December 1951), 30–31, 64–65.

Description of the Sun Dance as observed in 1951.

5211. Dempsey, Hugh A. "Social Dances of the Blood Indians of Alberta, Canada." *JAF*, 69 (1956), 47–52.

Survey of ceremonialism.

5212. Goddard, Pliny Earle. "Sarsi Texts." *UCPAAE*, 11, No. 3 (1915), 189–277.

Ethnographic descriptions and narrative texts collected in 1905. With literal translations.

5213. Honigmann, John J. "Parallels in the Development of Shamanism Among Northern and Southern Athapaskans." *AA*, 51 (1949), 512–14.

Brief survey of ceremonial developments among the Sarsi. With comparison to Southwest cultures.

5214. Jenness, Diamond. *The Sarcee Indians of Alberta.* NMCB No. 90 ([1938]).

Ethnography based on fieldwork done in 1921 includes extensive commentaries from informants and data on the Sun Dance and other ceremonials.

5215. Simms, S. C. "Traditions of the Sarcee Indians." *JAF*, 17 (1904), 180–82.

Three myth and legend texts. No commentary or annotations.

See also 2077, 2078, 3023, 5106.

M. Sekani

5216. Jenness, Diamond. *The Sekani Indians of British Columbia.* NMCB, Anthropological Series No. 20 (1937).

Ethnography based on fieldwork done in 1924 includes data on ceremonialism and translated song texts (words only).

See also 5106.

N. Slave

5217. Asch, Michael I. "Social Context and the Musical Analysis of Slavey Drum Dance Songs." *Em*, 19 (1975), 245–57.

Shows that different musical events among the Slave are associated with different musical styles.

5218. Bell, Robert. "Legends of the Slavey Indians of the Mackenzie River." *JAF*, 14 (1901), 26–29.

Two unannotated myth texts. No commentary.

5219. Honigmann, John J. *Ethnography and Acculturation of the Fort Nelson Slave.* YUPA No. 33 (1946).

Based on fieldwork done in 1943. Includes data on ceremonials such as the Prophet Dance.

5220. MacNeish, June Helm. "Contemporary Folk Beliefs of a Slave Indian Band." *JAF*, 67 (1954), 185–98.

Includes descriptions of belief complexes and narrative texts.

5221. ———. "Folktales of the Slave Indians." *An*, 1 (1955), 37–44.

Five unannotated texts. No commentary.

5222. Mason, J. Alden. *Notes on the Indians of the Great Slave Lake Area.* YUPA No. 34 (1946).

Ethnography based on fieldwork done in 1943 includes data on music and ceremonialism.

5223. Williamson, Robert G. "Slave Indian Legends." *An*, 1 (1955), 119–43.

Eight unannotated texts dealing with the culture hero. With data on collecting situation.

5224. ———. "Slave Indian Legends." *An*, 2 (1956), 61–92.

Twelve unannotated texts, half of which deal with the culture hero.

See also 5207.

O. Tahltan

5225. MacLachlan, Bruce B. "Notes on Some Tahltan Oral Literature." *An*, 4 (1957), 1–9.

Five myth and legend texts collected in 1956. With good data on context.

5226. Teit, James A. "Field Notes on the Tahltan and Kaska Indians, 1912–15." Ed. J. H. MacNeish. *An*, 3 (1956), 39–171.

Ethnographic survey includes data on singing performances and text of a funerary song.

5227. ———. "Tahltan Tales." *JAF*, 32 (1919), 198–250.

Thirty myth and folktale texts (including thirty-five episodes from the Raven cycle). With occasional comparative and explanatory notes.

5228. ———. "Tahltan Tales." *JAF*, 34 (1921), 223–53, 335–56.

Forty-eight myth and folktale texts with occasional comparative and explanatory notes.

5229. ———. "Two Tahltan Traditions." *JAF*, 22 (1909), 314–18.

Two unannotated legend texts with brief commentary on cultural background.

P. Tanaina

5230.   Ackerman, Robert E. *The Kenaitze People.* Phoenix: Indian Tribal Series, 1975.
Tribal history includes summary of creation myth, description of the potlatch, and data on religious beliefs.

5231.   Johnston, Thomas F. "Music of the Tanaina Indians of South-Central Alaska." *TFSB,* 45 (1979), 12–16.
Musicological analysis on singing in various ritual and social contexts.

5232.   Osgood, Cornelius. "Tanaina Culture." *AA,* 35 (1933), 695–717.
Culture survey includes data on singing, storytelling, and ceremonials such as the potlatch.

5233.   Townsend, Joan B. "Ethnographic Notes on the Pedro Bay Tanaina." *An,* n. s. 5 (1963), 209–23.
Includes data on ceremonials and games, summaries of myths and legends, and outline of supernaturalism.

5234.   Vaudrin, Bill. *Tanaina Tales from Alaska.* Introduction by Joan B. Townsend. Norman: Univ. of Oklahoma Press, 1969.
Rewritten folktale and legend texts.

See also 416.

XII ARCTIC

5235. Agar, Lynn Price. "Storyknifing: An Alaskan Eskimo Girls' Game." *JFI,* 11 (1975), 187–98.

Describes the process of telling stories and using pointed objects to illustrate them in the mud or snow.

5236. Anderson, Eva Greenslit. *Dog-Team Doctor: The Story of Dr. Romig.* Caldwell, Ida.: Caxton, 1940.

Biography of a physician who served northwestern Alaska in late 1800s and early 1900s includes rewritten myth texts and accounts of healing ceremonials.

5237. Anderson, H. Dewey, and Walter Crosby Eells. *Alaska Natives: A Survey of Their Sociological and Educational Status.* Stanford, Cal.: Stanford Univ. Press, 1935.

Sociological survey done in 1930–1931 includes data on religion, ceremonialism, games, shamanism, singing, and storytelling.

5238. Arima, E. Y. "The Eskimo Drum Dance." *Arc,* 27 (1974), 68–69.

Description of a ceremonial among the Copper Eskimo.

5239. Arron, Walter Jack. "Aspects of the Epic in Eskimo Folklore." *APUAK,* 5, No. 2 (May 1957), 119–41.

Examination of folktales labeled "epic" by collector includes consideration of characterization of the hero, his relationship to cultural identity, and narrative style.

5240. Baldwin, Effie Faulkner. "An Eskimo Society Event." *WO,* 4 (May 1918), 13.

Ceremonial description.

5241. Balikci, Asem. *The Netsilik Eskimo.* Garden City, N. Y.: Natural History Press, 1970.

Culture survey based on fieldwork done between 1959 and 1965 includes data on ceremonialism and supernaturalism. With narrative excerpts.

5242. ———. "Shamanistic Behavior Among the Netsilik Eskimos." *SJA,* 19 (1963), 380–96.

Survey of shamanistic ceremonialism. Reprinted in 141 (pp. 191–209).

5243. Batty, Beatrice. *Forty-Two Years Amongst the Indians and Eskimo: Pictures from the Life of the Right Reverend John Horden, First Bishop of Moosonee.* London: Religious Tract Society, 1893.

Extracts from subject's letters include data on NA dancing and hymn-singing.

5244. Beaudry, Nicole. "Toward Transcription and Analysis of Inuit Throat-Games: Macro-Structure." *Em,* 22 (1978), 261–73.

Treats the several dimensions involved in transcribing the vocalizations exchanged during throat-games.

5245. Berg, Stephen. "Eskimo Versions." *N,* 216 (28 May 1973), 699.

Three poem texts based on material collected by Knud Rasmussen.

5246. Bergsland, Knut. "Aleut Dialects of Atka and Attu." *TAPS,* n. s. 49, Part 3 (1959), 5–128.

Includes song, legend, and folktale texts with literal translations and linguistic notes. Some collected in 1950s and some from nineteenth-century sources.

5247. Billman, Esther. "A Potlatch Feast at Sitka, Alaska." *APUAK,* 14, No. 2 (Spring 1969), 55–64.

Description of the ceremonial as reported by William Wells in 1877.

5248. Birket-Smith, Kaj. *Eskimos.* New York: Crown, 1971.

Profusely illustrated culture survey contains data on ceremonialism and mythology. With song texts. Focuses on Eskimo cultures in Greenland.

5249. ———, and Frederica de Laguna. *The Eyak Indians of the Copper River Delta, Alaska.* Copenhagen: Levin and Munksgaard, 1938.

Ethnography includes data on ceremonialism. With myth and folktale texts.

5250. Boas, Franz. "The Central Eskimo." *ARBAE,* 6 (1884–1885), 399–669.

Ethnography of various Eskimo groups includes twenty narrative and twenty song texts (words and music). With some comparative notes.

5251. ———. "Cumberland Sound and Its Eskimos." *PSM,* 26 (April 1885), 768–79.

Culture survey includes data on ceremonialism and storytelling.

5252. ———. "The Eskimo." *PTRSC,* 1st series, 5, section 2 (1887), 35–39.

Survey of themes and subjects in Eskimo mythology.

5253. ———. "The Eskimo of Baffin Land and Hudson Bay from Notes Collected by Captain George Comer, Captain James S. Mutch, and Rev. E. J. Peck." *BAMNH,* 15 (1907), 4–570.

Ethnography based on material collected in 1890s includes 151 translated myth and folktale texts and 12 myth and song texts with free and interlinear translations. With comparative and explanatory notes.

5254. ———. "Eskimo Tales and Songs." *JAF,* 7 (1894), 45–50.

Two folktale and six song texts (words only) with free and interlinear translations. With explanatory comments.

5255. ———. "Eskimo Tales and Songs." *JAF,* 10 (1897), 109–15.

Texts with free and interlinear translations collected in 1883–1884. With extensive explanatory and linguistic notes.

5256. ———. "The Folk-Lore of the Eskimo." *JAF,* 17 (1904), 1–13.

Survey of narrative folklore of Arctic groups with special attention to recurrent themes.

5257. ———. "Notes on the Eskimo of Port Clarence, Alaska." *JAF,* 7 (1894), 205–08.

Unannotated myth text. With data on cultural background and linguistic notes.

5258. ———. "Poetry and Music of Some North American Tribes." *S,* 9 (22 April 1887), 383–85.

Musicological and functional treatment of Eskimo singing. With four texts (words and music).

5259. ———. "Religious Beliefs of the Central Eskimo." *PSM,* 57 (October 1900), 624–31.

Describes mythic basis for beliefs and ceremonials.

5260. ———. "Two Eskimo Riddles from Labrador." *JAF,* 39 (1926), 486.

Texts with free translations collected in 1896. No commentary or annotations.

5261. Bogoras, W. B. "Elements of the Culture of the Circumpolar Zone." *AA,* 31 (1929), 579–601.

Survey of cultures throughout the Arctic regions of several continents includes data on how folklore relates to natural environment.

5262. Burch, Edward S., Jr. "The Nonempirical Environment of the Arctic Alaskan Eskimo." *SJA,* 27 (1971), 148–65.

Treats fusion of Christianity with NA beliefs in ghosts and other supernatural beings.

5263. Burrows, Elizabeth. "Eskimo Tales." *JAF,* 39 (1926), 79–81.

Abstracts of four folktales collected in the Yukon. No commentary or annotations.

5264. Butzin, Arthur F. "Alaskan Eskimos—Old and New." *MRW,* 60 (March 1937), 149–50.

Compares shamanism with Christianity. Reprinted from *The Moravian* for December 1935.

5265. Cameron, Agnes Deans. *The New North, Being Some Account of a Woman's Journey Through Canada to the Arctic.* New York: D. Appleton, 1910.

Travel narrative contains Eskimo song text and description of singing, summary of myths, and data on ceremonialism.

5266. *Canadian Eskimo Art.* NP: Minister on Northern Affairs and National Resources, 1954.

Contains four translated song texts.

5267. Carpenter, Edmund, ed. *Anerca.* Toronto: J. M. Dent, 1959.

Unannotated song texts. No commentary.

5268. ———. *Changes in the Sedna Myth Among the Aivilik.* APUAK, 3, No. 2 (May 1955).

Examines effects of Christianity on the supernatural system and mythology of the Aivilik.

5269. ———. "The Timeless Present in the Mythology of the Aivilik Eskimos." *An,* 3 (1956), 1–4.

Treats lack of chronological sense among the Aivilik and the immediacy of all events in their mythology.

5270. Cavanaugh, Beverly. "Annotated Bibliography: Eskimo Music." *Em,* 16 (1972), 479–87.

List of books and articles dealing with music from various Arctic groups.

5271. Charron, Claude. "Toward Transcription and Analysis of Inuit Throat-Games: Micro-Structure." *Em,* 22 (1978), 245–59.

Treats performance styles used in a game involving exchanges of guttural vocalizations.

5272. Colby, Benjamin N. "The Analysis of Culture Content and the Patterning of Narrative Concern in Texts." *AA,* 68 (1966), 374–88.

Uses Eskimo folktales to demonstrate computer analysis of narrative content.

5273. ———. "A Partial Grammar of Eskimo Folk-

tales." *AA,* 75 (1973), 645–62.

Describes the pattern of ideas in narratives from Alaska. Suggests that resulting grammar may apply to all Eskimo folktales.

5274. Collins, Henry B., Jr. "Culture Migrations and Contacts in the Bering Sea Region." *AA,* 39 (1937), 375–84.

Suggests that mythology was more likely than material culture to diffuse across the Bering Straits.

5275. Crantz, David. *The History of Greenland: Including an Account of the Mission Carried on by the United Brethren in That Country.* 2 volumes. London: Longman, Hurst, Rees, Orme, and Brown, 1820.

Book III treats NA inhabitants. Included are data on ceremonialism and mythology and a song text presented from the perspective of Christianity.

5276. Cumming, John R. "Metaphysical Implications of the Folktales of the Eskimos of Alaska." *APUAK,* 3, No. 1 (December 1954), 37–63.

Examines cosmological themes, considerations of human nature, and spiritual concepts in Eskimo folktales.

5277. Damas, David. "Nomads of the North," in 167, pp. 71–98.

Culture survey of Eskimo groups includes data on mythology and supernaturalism and a song text.

5278. Driggs, John B. *Short Sketches from Oldest America.* Philadelphia: George W. Jacobs, 1905.

Short vignettes of Arctic life include retellings of myths and legends and data on singing and ceremonialism.

5279. Duncan, Kenneth. "The Angnasheotik: An Account of the Invention of a Spiritual Entity Among the Ungava Eskimos." *Arc,* 15 (1962), 289–94.

Description of a demon figure developed in response to EA contact.

5280. Dyche, Lewis Lindsay. "The Curious Race of Arctic Highlanders." *Cos,* 21 (July 1896), 228–37.

Culture survey includes data on religion and theology.

5281. Eber, Dorothy, ed. *Pitseolak: Pictures Out of My Life.* Seattle: Univ. of Washington Press, 1978.

Life history of a woman. Free translation. Includes data on storytelling.

5282. Elliott, Henry W. *Our Arctic Province: Alaska and the Seal Islands.* New York: Scribner's, 1906.

Historical, geographical, and ethnographic survey includes data on ceremonial life and singing among Aleuts and other Arctic groups.

5283. Finnie, Richard. "Black Magic in the Arctic." *T,* 63 (May 1934), 18–21, 50.

Description of shamanistic rituals.

5284. ———. *Lure of the North.* Philadelphia: David McKay, 1940.

Includes a chapter on shamanism and excerpts from song texts.

5285. Forrest, Elizabeth Chabot. *Daylight Moon.* New York: Frederick A. Stokes, 1937.

Account of thirteen-years' residence in northern Alaska contains a description of the Whale Dance.

5286. Frederiksen, Svend. "Aspects of European Influence in West Greenlandic Poetry." *MWF,* 2 (1952), 251-61.

Treats EA traces in Eskimo songs.

5287. Fredson, John. "Wild Melodies from the Arctic." *Etu,* 47 (April 1929), 271.

Five song texts (music only) with commentary on cultural background and content of words.

5288. Gapp, S. H. "Among the Eskimos in Alaska." *MRW,* 56, No. 5 (May 1933), 239–44.
Culture survey includes data on religion and ceremonialism.

5289. Garber, Clark M. "Some Mortuary Customs of the Western Alaska Eskimos." *ScM,* 39 (September 1934), 203–20.
Sketchy data on ceremonialism.

5290. ———. *Stories and Legends of the Bering Strait Eskimos.* Boston: Christopher Publishing House, 1940.
Thirty-one unannotated myth, folktale, and legend texts. With data on storytelling contexts.

5291. Gearing, Frederick O. "Why Indians?" *SE,* 32 (1968), 128–31, 146.
Suggests reasons for studying NAs in social studies classes. With text of an Eskimo poem.

5292. Giffen, Naomi Musmaker. *The Roles of Men and Women in Eskimo Culture.* Chicago: Univ. of Chicago Press, 1930.
Discusses sex roles in singing, storytelling, shamanism, and ceremonialism.

5293. Gillham, C. E. *Medicine Men of Hooper Bay or The Eskimo's Arabian Nights.* London: Batchworth Press, 1955.
Retellings of myth and legend texts, especially those concerned with shamanism.

5294. Golder, F. A. "Aleutian Stories." *JAF,* 18 (1905), 215–22.
Six unannotated folktale texts. No commentary.

5295. ———. "Eskimo and Aleut Stories from Alaska." *JAF,* 22 (1909), 10–24.
Eleven unannotated myth and folktale texts. No commentary.

5296. ———. "A Kodiak Island Story: The White-Faced Bear." *JAF,* 20 (1907), 296–99.
Unannotated myth text. No commentary.

5297. ———. "Primitive Warfare Among the Natives of Western Alaska." *JAF,* 22 (1909), 336–39.
Three legend texts. With data on cultural background.

5298. ———. "The Songs and Stories of the Aleuts, with Translations from Veniaminov." *JAF,* 20 (1907), 132–42.
Four legend texts, one taken from the works of Fr. Venianimov. With data on singing and storytelling customs.

5299. ———. "Tales from Kodiak Island." *JAF,* 16 (1903), 16–31, 85–103.
Ten unannotated myth and folktale texts. With data on collecting situation.

5300. Hague, Eleanor. "Eskimo Songs." *JAF,* 28 (1915), 96–98.
Three song texts. With brief commentary on singing style.

5301. Hall, Edwin S., Jr. *The Eskimo Storyteller. Folktales from Noatak, Alaska.* Knoxville: Univ. of Tennessee Press, 1975.
Presents the narrative repertoires of two storytellers. With thorough data on informants, description of cultural significance of stories, and comparative notes.

5302. Harrington, Lyn. "Eskimo String Figures." *SAM,* 50 (May 1951), 319–21.
Description of play activity includes song texts (words only).

5303. Harrington, Richard. *The Face of the Arctic. A Cameraman's Story in Words and Pictures of Five Journeys into the*
Far North. New York: Henry Schuman, 1952.
Includes accounts of singing and dancing among Eskimo groups.

5304. Hauser, Michael. "Formal Structure in Polar Eskimo Drumsongs." *Em,* 21 (1977), 33–53.
Categorizes songs into three "form types."

5305. Hawkes, Ernest William. *The "Inviting-In" Feast of the Alaskan Eskimo. CGSMB,* Anthropological Series No. 3 (1913).
Description of the festival observed in 1912 includes song texts (words and music).

5306. ———. *The Labrador Eskimo. CGSMB,* Anthropological Series No. 14 (1916).
Ethnography based on fieldwork done in 1914 includes descriptions of religious beliefs, ceremonials, games, and music. With unannotated myth and song texts.

5307. Hayes, Isaac I. *An Arctic Boat Journey, in the Autumn of 1854.* Boston: Brown and Taggard, 1860.
Explorer's narrative includes data on Eskimo supernaturalism and a myth text.

5308. Hennigh, Lawrence. "Control of Incest in Eskimo Folktales." *JAF,* 79 (1966), 356–69.
Five folktale texts with data on role of incest theme in Eskimo oral literature.

5309. Holtved, Erik. "The Eskimo Legend of Navaranâq. An Analytical Study." *AArc,* 1 (1943), 1–42.
Historic-geographic study based on fourteen variants of a myth.

5310. Honigmann, John J. "Dance of the Ancient Ones." *B,* 299 (Autumn 1968), 44–47.
Description of the Drum Dance.

5311. ———. "Intercultural Relations at Great Whale River." *AA,* 54 (1952), 510–22.
Among the factors contributing to relations between NAs and EAs are games and dances.

5312. Horn, Patrice. "Eskimo Humor—More Than a Laughing Matter." *PT,* March 1974, pp. 14, 88.
Views Eskimo jokes as releases from tensions of harsh natural environment.

5313. Hosley, Edward H. "The McGrath Ingalik." *APUAK,* 9, No. 2 (May 1961), 93–113.
Ethnography based on fieldwork done in 1960 includes data on religious attitudes and ceremonials. With legend summaries.

5314. Hrdlička, Aleš. *Alaska Diary 1926–1931.* Lancaster, Penn.: Jaques Cattrell, 1943.
Diary of fieldwork experiences in the Arctic includes data on singing among the Eskimo and Kutchin.

5315. ———. *The Aleutian and Commander Islands and Their Inhabitants.* Philadelphia: Wistar Institute of Anatomy and Biology, 1945.
Ethnographic and archeological survey includes data on ceremonials, myths, and songs.

5316. ———. *The Anthropology of Kodiak Island.* Philadelphia: Wistar Institute of Anatomy and Biology, 1944.
Ethnographic and archeological survey contains data on religion, singing, and ceremonialism.

5317. Hughes, Charles Campbell. "Translation of I. K. Voblov's 'Eskimo Ceremonies.' " *APUAK,* 7, No. 2 (May 1959), 71–90.
Excerpts from descriptions of ceremonials observed in 1934–1936. Translated from Russian.

5318. ——, and Jane M. Hughes. *An Eskimo Village in the Modern World.* Ithaca: Cornell Univ. Press, 1960.
Ethnography based on fieldwork done in 1954–1955 focuses on acculturation. With data on ceremonialism and shamanism.

5319. Hutchinson, Ellen. "Order and Chaos in the Cosmology of the Baffin Island Eskimo." *Ant,* 1 (1977), 120–38.
Structural analysis of the Sedna myth and its associated ritual.

5320. "Ingalik Ceremony in Alaska, An" *JAF,* 26 (1913), 191–92.
Brief description of a dance.

5321. Ingstad, Helge. *Nunamiut: Among Alaska's Inland Eskimos.* New York: Norton, 1954.
Includes fairly good descriptions of storytelling and singing. With song texts (words and music).

5322. Jenness, Diamond. *Dawn in Arctic Alaska.* Minneapolis: Univ. of Minnesota Press, 1957.
Account of a winter in the Arctic in 1913 includes descriptions of singing, dancing, and other ceremonial behavior.

5323. ——. "Eskimo Folk-Lore. Part A: Myths and Traditions from Northern Alaska, the Mackenzie Delta and Coronation Gulf." *RCAP,* 13 (1924), 1–90.
Ninety-four unannotated myth and legend texts. Those collected in Eskimo have interlinear and free translations.

5324. ——. "Eskimo Folk-Lore. Part B: Eskimo String Figures." *RCAP,* 13 (1924), 1–192.
Describes over 150 string games. With related song texts and translations.

5325. ——. "Eskimo Music in Northern Alaska." *MQ,* 8 (1922), 377–83.
Describes singing contexts and styles. With four texts (music only).

5326. ——. "Eskimo String Figures." *JAF,* 36 (1923), 281–94.
Includes description of beliefs about string figures and texts of legends and personal narratives involving related supernaturalism.

5327. ——. "The Life of the Copper Eskimos." *RCAP,* 12 (1922), 1–277.
Ethnography includes data on religion, shamanism, singing, and games. With song texts.

5328. ——. "Stray Notes on the Eskimo of Arctic Alaska." *APUAK,* 1, No. 2 (May 1953), 5–13.
Data collected in 1913–1914 include narratives about shamans and song texts from children's games (words only).

5329. Jochelson, Waldemar. "People of the Foggy Seas: The Aleut and Their Islands." *NH,* 28 (1928), 413–24.
Culture survey includes data on religion. Compares Aleut folklore with that of other Arctic groups.

5330. Johnston, Thomas F. "Alaskan Eskimo and Indian Dance." *TFSB,* 41 (1975), 117–26.
Survey of song and dance styles from various parts of Alaska. With photographs.

5331. ——. "Eight North Alaskan Eskimo Dance-Songs." *TFSB,* 40 (1974), 122–36.
Texts (words and music) with free translations and musicological and contextual commentary.

5332. ——. "Eskimo Music: A Comparative Survey." *An,* n. s. 17 (1975), 217–32.
Overview of musical styles and of history of research.

5333. ——. "Eskimo Music from King Island, Alaska." *TFSB,* 42 (1976), 167–71.
Describes preservation of traditional music by organized dance teams.

5334. ——. "The Eskimo Songs of Northwestern Alaska." *Arc,* 29 (1976), 6–19.
Describes types, performances, and contexts of songs. Compared with music from southwestern Alaska.

5335. ——. "A Historical Perspective on Alaskan Eskimo Music." *IH,* 7, No. 4 (Fall 1974), 17–26.
Collection of photographs depicting musical performances. With musicological and contextual commentary.

5336. ——. "St. Lawrence Island Eskimo Music." *TFSB,* 42 (1976), 83–89.
Survey of aspects of musical performance. Illustrated with photographs.

5337. ——. "The Social Background of Eskimo Music in Northwest Alaska." *JAF,* 89 (1976), 438–48.
Catalogue of the aspects in the cultural environment which shape musical traditions.

5338. *Journal of a Second Voyage for the Discovery of a North-West Passage from the Atlantic to the Pacific; Performed in the Years 1821–22–23, in His Majesty's Ships Fury and Hecla, Under the Orders of Captain William Edward Parry.* New York: E. Duyckinck, 1824.
Travel narrative includes song texts (words and music).

5339. Kane, Elisha Kent. *Arctic Explorations in the Years 1853, '54, '55.* 2 volumes. Philadelphia: Childs and Peterson, 1856.
Explorer's narrative includes a song text (words and music) and data on ceremonialism.

5340. Kleivan, Inge. *The Swan Maiden Myth Among the Eskimo.* AArc No. 13 (1962).
Historic-geographic study based on forty-two variants of a myth. With some attention to cultural values in the myth.

5341. ——. *Why Is the Raven Black? An Analysis of an Eskimo Myth.* AArc No. 17 (1971).
Morphological and functional analysis of an etiological myth. Based on twenty-five variants.

5342. Koranda, Lorraine. "Eskimo Music." *MuA,* 82 (August 1962), 14–15.
Overview of singing traditions. With a song text (words only).

5343. ——. "Some Traditional Songs of the Alaskan Eskimos." *APUAK,* 12, No. 1 (Winter 1964), 17–32.
Seven song texts (words and music) collected in 1962. With contextual and musicological notes.

5344. ——. "Three Songs for the Bladder Festival, Hooper Bay." *APUAK,* 14, No. 1 (1968), 27–31.
Song texts (words and music) with context data.

5345. Kroeber, A. L. "Animal Tales of the Eskimo." *JAF,* 12 (1899), 17–23.
Survey of themes of Eskimo animal tales. With bibliography of published materials.

5346. ——. "The Eskimo of Smith Sound." *BAMNH,* 12 (1899), 265–327.
Ethnography based on fieldwork done in 1897–1898 includes data on religion, shamanism, and ceremonialism.

5347. ——. "Tales of the Smith Sound Eskimo." *JAF,* 12 (1899), 166–82.
Twenty-nine myth and folktale texts and six fragments collected in 1897–1898. With comparative and

explanatory notes.

5348. Lantis, Margaret. *Alaskan Eskimo Ceremonialism.* *MonAES* No. 11 (1947).

Survey of ceremonials and their distribution.

5349. ———. "The Alaskan Whale Cult and Its Affinities." *AA,* 40 (1938), 438–64.

Describes ritual dimensions of whale hunting. With a song text. Lantis added more data in *AA,* 42 (1940), 366–68.

5350. ———. *Eskimo Childhood and Interpersonal Relationships: Nunivak Biographies and Genealogies.* Seattle: Univ. of Washington Press, 1960.

Personality and culture study includes texts of eighteen life histories. With data on the role of personal narratives in Eskimo culture.

5351. ———. "The Mythology of Kodiak Island, Alaska." *JAF,* 51 (1938), 123–72.

Survey of myth traditions reveals affinities with other Arctic and Northwest Coast groups.

5352. ———. "Nunivak Eskimo Personality as Revealed in the Mythology." *APUAK,* 2, No. 1 (December 1953), 109–74.

Personality and culture study uses myths to reveal common conflict situations and personality traits.

5353. ———. "The Social Culture of the Nunivak Eskimo." *TAPS,* n. s. 35 (1946), 153–323.

Ethnography based on fieldwork begun in 1939 includes data on ceremonialism and myths.

5354. Lavrischeff, T. I. "Two Aleut Tales." *AA,* 30 (1928), 121–24.

Unannotated texts.

5355. Leden, Christian. "An Eskimo Feast." *LAg,* 321 (7 June 1924), 1110–11.

Describes singing and dancing. Reprinted from *Vossische Zeitung.*

5356. ———. "Napsangoak Gives a Dinner, Dance and Musicale." *WO,* 6 (May 1920), 42–43.

Ceremonial description.

5357. Leechman, Douglas. "Eskimo Music." *AM,* 18, No. 69 (September 1929), 67–69.

Survey of musical traditions among Arctic groups. With song texts.

5358. *Life with the Esquimaux. The Narrative of Captain Charles Francis Hall, of the Whaling Barque "George Henry," from the 29th May, 1860, to the 13th September, 1862. With the Results of a Long Intercourse with Innuits, and Full Description of Their Mode of Life, the Discovery of Actual Relics of the Expedition of Martin Frobisher of Three Centuries Ago, and Deductions in Favor of Yet Discovering Some of the Survivors of Sir John Franklin's Expedition.* 2 volumes. London: Sampson Low, Son, and Marston, 1864.

Includes data on Eskimo supernaturalism, ceremonialism, and storytelling. With legend summaries.

5359. Lucier, Charles. "Buckland Eskimo Myths." *APUAK,* 2, No. 2 (May 1954), 215–33.

Seventeen myth and legend texts collected in 1951. With comparative commentary.

5360. ———. "Noatagmiut Eskimo Myths." *APUAK,* 6, No. 2 (May 1958), 89–117.

Twenty-five unannotated myth and legend texts collected in 1952. With data on informants and collecting situation.

5361. Lutz, Maija M. *The Effects of Acculturation on Eskimo Music of Cumberland Peninsula.* Ottawa: National Museums of Canada, 1978.

Based on fieldwork done in 1973–1974. Contrasts contemporary music with that reported in the 1880s by Franz Boas. Emphasizes place of Christian hymnody in musical traditions.

5362. MacLeod, William Christie. "The Origin of Servile Labor Groups." *AA,* 31 (1929), 89–113.

Survey of classes of domestic laborers among Arctic, Sub-Arctic, and Northwest Coast groups includes texts of songs and legends which validate existence of such classes.

5363. Marsh, Donald B. "Canada's Caribou Eskimos." *NG,* 91, No. 1 (January 1947), 87–104.

Culture survey includes data on ceremonialism.

5364. Marsh, Gordon H. "A Comparative Survey of Eskimo-Aleut Religion." *APUAK,* 3, No. 1 (December 1954), 21–36.

Systematization of Arctic traditional religions includes data on supernaturalism and cosmology.

5365. Mason, Gregory. "Eskimo Marriage, Music, and Philosophy." *O,* 116 (23 May 1917), 141–42.

Treats affinities of Eskimo music with music of other NAs. Based on work of Christian Leden.

5366. Metayer, Maurice, ed. and trans. *Tales from the Igloo.* New York: St. Martin's Press, 1972.

Twenty-two unannotated myth and folktale texts from the Copper Eskimo. With historical data.

5367. Milan, Frederick A. "The Acculturation of the Contemporary Eskimo of Wainwright, Alaska." *APUAK,* 11, No. 2 (January 1964), 1–95.

Acculturation study based on fieldwork done in 1955 includes data on ceremonialism and supernaturalism.

5368. Moore, Riley D. "Social Life of the Eskimo of St. Lawrence Island." *AA,* 25 (1923), 339–75.

Ethnography based on fieldwork done in 1912 includes data on singing and storytelling.

5369. Morrow, Phyllis, and Toby Alice Volkman. "The Loon with the Ivory Eyes: A Study in Symbolic Archaeology." *JAF,* 88 (1975), 143–50.

Uses Arctic, Sub-Arctic, and Northwest Coast folklore to explain the significance of a decorated loon skull found in a human burial in Alaska.

5370. Murdoch, John. "Ethnological Results of the Point Barrow Expedition." *ARBAE,* 9 (1887–1888), 3–441.

Ethnography includes data on ceremonialism and song and chant texts.

5371. ———. "A Few Legendary Fragments from the Point Barrow Eskimos." *AmN,* 20 (July 1886), 593–99.

Myth and legend excerpts collected in 1881–1883. With data on cultural background.

5372. ———. "The Name of the Dog-Ancestor in Eskimo Folk-Lore." *AA,* o. s. 11 (1898), 223.

Response to an etymological comment by Signe Rink on an Eskimo folktale (5411, 5412).

5373. Murie, Olaus. "Winter Adventures on the Alaskan Trail." *AW,* 10, No. 1 (January 1973), 10–15, 59–60.

Memoir of life among Arctic groups in 1922 includes song texts.

5374. Nansen, Fridtjof. *Eskimo Life.* Trans. William Archer. London: Longmans, Green, 1893.

Culture survey includes data on ceremonialism, singing, and storytelling.

5375. Nelson, Edward William. "The Eskimo About Bering Strait." *ARBAE,* 18 (1896–1897), 3–518.

Ethnography includes data on ceremonialism and texts of narratives and songs (words and music).

5376. Nelson, Richard K. *Hunters of the Northern Ice.* Chicago: Univ. of Chicago Press, 1969.

Ethnography of Eskimo culture at Ft. Wainwright, Alaska, includes data on belief in sea creatures. Based on fieldwork done in 1964–1965.

5377. Neuman, Daniel S. "The Medicine Man of the Stone Age." *Esk,* 2, No. 6 (February 1918), 1–3.

Description of shamanistic myths and ceremonialism.

5378. ———. "Stone Age Religion." *Esk,* 1, No. 10 (June 1917), 1–3.

Survey of religious ideas of Arctic groups.

5379. Nørlund, Poul. *Viking Settlers in Greenland and Their Descendants During Five Hundred Years.* London: Cambridge Univ. Press, 1936.

Primarily archeological and historical. Contains data on Eskimo legends about Norsemen.

5380. Nourse, J. E., ed. *Narrative of the Second Arctic Expedition Made by Charles F. Hall: His Voyage to Repulse Bay, Sledge Journeys to the Straits of Fury and Hecla and to King William's Land, and Residence Among the Eskimos During the Years 1864–69.* Washington: Government Printing Office, 1879.

Includes legend texts and descriptions of ceremonials.

5381. Nungak, Zebedee, and Eugene Arima. *Unikkaatuat Sanaugarngnik Atyingualiit Puvirngniturngmit. Eskimo Stories from Povungnituk, Quebec, Illustrated in Soapstone Carvings.* NMCB No. 235 (1969).

Forty-six myth and folktale texts with free translations. With an extensive survey of the mythological system.

5382. Ookpik. "Kosga House Dancing." *Esk,* 1, No. 10 (June 1917), 4–5.

Condemnatory account of ceremonial dancing.

5383. Osgood, Cornelius. *Ingalik Mental Culture.* YUPA No. 56 (1959).

Ethnography based on fieldwork done in 1937 and 1956 includes data on music, cosmology, and supernaturalism. With twelve unannotated myth texts. Other narratives are included throughout the work.

5384. ———. *Ingalik Social Culture.* YUPA No. 53 (1958).

Ethnography includes data on shamanism and ceremonials such as the potlatch.

5385. Ostermann, H. *The Alaskan Eskimos as Described in the Posthumous Notes of Knud Rasmussen.* Ed. E. Holtved. Trans. W. E. Calvert. Copenhagen: Gyldendal, 1952.

Ethnographic notes include an extensive collection of myths and folktales.

5386. ———, ed. *Knud Rasmussen's Posthumous Notes on East Greenland Legends and Myths.* Copenhagen: C. A. Reitzel, 1939.

Translated myth and song texts.

5387. ———, ed. *Knud Rasmussen's Posthumous Notes on the Life and Doings of the East Greenlanders in Olden Times.* Copenhagen: C. A. Reitzel, 1938.

Ethnography includes data on ceremonialism and shamanism. With a life history text.

5388. ———, ed. *The Mackenzie Eskimos. After Knud Rasmussen's Posthumous Notes.* Copenhagen: Gyldendal, 1942.

Ethnography based on fieldwork done in 1924 includes data on ceremonialism and myth and folktale texts.

5389. Oswalt, Wendell H. *Alaskan Eskimos.* San Francisco: Chandler, 1967.

Culture survey includes data on shamanism, ceremonialism, and mythology.

5390. ———. *Mission of Change in Alaska: Eskimos and Moravians on the Kuskokwim.* San Marino, Cal.: Huntington Library, 1963.

Acculturation study includes thorough description of traditional shamanism and its response to Christianity.

5391. ———. "Traditional Storyknife Tales of Yuk Girls." *PAPS,* 108 (1964), 310–36.

Forty-one legend and folktale texts with thorough presentation of performance context.

5392. ———, and James W. Vanstone. *The Ethnoarcheology of Crow Village, Alaska.* BAEB No. 199 (1967).

Uses archeology and ethnography to reconstruct life at a site in Alaska. With data on ceremonialism.

5393. Peck, E. J. "The Eskimos of the Frozen North. An Account of Their Beliefs, Characteristics, and Needs." *MRW,* o. s. 37 (July 1914), 487–96.

Focuses on religious concepts: supernaturalism, theology, and eschatology.

5394. Pitseolak, Peter, and Dorothy Eber. *People from Our Side. An Eskimo Life Story in Words and Photographs.* Bloomington: Indiana Univ. Press, 1975.

Autobiography, translated from Pitseolak's syllabic ms., contains song texts and descriptions of ceremonials.

5395. *Private Journal of Captain G. F. Lyon, Of H. M. S. Hecla, During the Recent Voyage of Discovery Under Captain Parry, The.* London: John Murray, 1824.

Explorer's narrative of expedition in 1820s contains NA songs (words and music), ceremonial descriptions, and hunting narratives.

5396. Pryde, Duncan. *Nunaga. Ten Years of Eskimo Life.* New York: Walker, 1971.

Reminiscences of an employee of Hudson's Bay Company include description of the Drum Dance and anecdotes about shamans.

5397. Quimby, George I. *Aleutian Islanders. Eskimos of the North Pacific.* Chicago: Natural History Museum Press, 1944 (Anthropology Leaflet No. 35).

Culture survey includes data on games, ceremonials, and myths.

5398. Ransom, Jay Ellis. "Aleut Natural-Food Economy." *AA,* 48 (1946), 607–23.

Survey of foodways includes data on pre-hunting ceremonials.

5399. ———. "Aleut Religious Beliefs: Veniaminov's Account." *JAF,* 58 (1945), 346–49.

Presents translated excerpts from the Russian's account of Aleut religion in the early 1800s.

5400. ———. "Stories, Myths, and Superstitions of Fox Island Aleut Children." *JAF,* 60 (1947), 62–72.

Various folklore texts collected in 1936–1937 reflect traditional culture and the effects of acculturation.

5401. Rasmussen, Knud. "Five Eskimo Poems." Trans. Erik Haugaard. *ASR,* 44 (1956), 163–67.

Texts of songs collected between 1921 and 1924.

5402. ———. *Greenland by the Polar Sea. The Story of the Thule Expedition from Melville Bay to Cape Morris Jesup.* Trans. Asta and Rowland Kenney. London: William Heinemann, 1921.

Narrative of the Second Thule Expedition (1916–1918) includes data on NA mythology.

5403. ———. *The Netsilik Eskimos. Social Life and Spiritual Culture.* Trans. W. E. Calvert. Copenhagen: Gyldendal, 1931.

Ethnography based on fieldwork done in 1923 as part of the Fifth Thule Expedition includes data on shamanism, ceremonialism, and storytelling. With myth and folktale texts.

5404. Ray, Dorothy Jean. *Eskimo Masks: Art and Ceremony.* Seattle: Univ. of Washington Press, 1967.

Analyzes manufacture, functions, ceremonial uses, and mythic bases of masks.

5405. ———, ed. "H. M. W. Edmonds' Report on the Eskimos of St. Michael and Vicinity." *APUAK,* 13, No. 2 (December 1966), 1–143.

Ms. written in 1899 includes data on cosmology and ceremonials, especially the Feast of the Dead.

5406. Ray, P. H. *Report of the International Polar Expedition to Point Barrow, Alaska.* Washington: Government Printing Office, 1885.

Includes description of a storytelling session witnessed between 1881 and 1883.

5407. Richards, Eva Alvey. *Arctic Mood: A Narrative of Arctic Adventures.* Caldwell, Ida.: Caxton, 1949.

Account of residence in Alaska as a federal employee contains NA song and story texts and context data on storytelling for children.

5408. Rink, Henry. *The Eskimo Tribes. Their Distribution and Characteristics, Especially in Regard to Language, with a Comparative Vocabulary, and a Sketch Map.* London: Longmans, Green, 1887.

Extensive linguistic analysis with a short ethnography. Includes data on religion and narrative folklore.

5409. ———. *Tales and Traditions of the Eskimo with a Sketch of Their Habits, Religion, Language and Other Peculiarities.* Ed. Robert Brown. Edinburgh: William Blackwood & Sons, 1875.

Myth, legend, and folktale texts (150) with thorough data on Eskimo culture, including religion and storytelling. Early use of the "mirror of culture" concept. Translated from Danish.

5410. ———, and Franz Boas. "Eskimo Tales and Songs." *JAF,* 2 (1889), 123–31.

Four myths and two songs (words and music) with free and interlinear translations. Includes data on cultural background and translation problems.

5411. Rink, Signe. "The Girl and the Dogs—An Eskimo Folk-Tale with Comments." *AA,* o. s. 11 (1898), 181–87.

Thorough cultural and linguistic commentary on a narrative published in 5409. See also 5372.

5412. ———. "The Girl and the Dogs—Further Comments." *AA,* o.s. 11 (1898), 209–15.

Continuation of linguistic analysis in 5411.

5413. Roberts, Helen H., and Diamond Jenness. "Eskimo Songs: Songs of the Copper Eskimos." *RCAP,* 14 (1925), 1–506.

Texts and translations of 137 songs (words and music). With musicological commentary.

5414. Rooth, Anna Birgitta. *The Importance of Storytelling: A Study Based on Field Work in Northern Alaska.* Uppsala: Almqvist & Wiksell, 1976.

Thorough description of aspects of storytelling (style, time settings, rules and taboos, functions) as observed in 1966.

5415. Sekonik, Joe. "The Adventures of Ki-ya-yuk-tua-

look." *Esk,* 2, No. 5 (January 1918), 1–8.

Text of an episodic hero myth from northwestern Alaska.

5416. ———. "The Story of Apukeena. A Strange Tale of Point Hope." *Esk,* 2, No. 6 (February 1918), 4–6.

Rewritten myth text.

5417. Senungetuk, Joseph E. *Give or Take a Century. An Eskimo Chronicle.* San Francisco: Indian Historian Press, 1971.

Acculturation study includes data on singing and the traditional belief system.

5418. Shade, Charles I. "The Girls' Puberty Ceremony of Umnak, Aleutian Islands." *AA,* 53 (1951), 145–48.

Description of the ritual by an informant who had been an initiate in 1941.

5419. Silook, Paul. "The Creation of Sivookak (St. Lawrence Island)." *Esk,* 1, No. 10 (June 1917), 5.

Rewritten myth text.

5420. Smith, Harlan I. "Notes on Eskimo Traditions." *JAF,* 7 (1894), 209–16.

Two myth texts with comparative and explanatory notes. With a description of an initiation ritual.

5421. Smith, Middleton. "Superstitions of the Eskimo," in 130, pp. 113–30.

Includes data on ceremonial dancing and shamanism.

5422. Spencer, Robert F. *The North Alaskan Eskimo. A Study in Ecology and Society.* BAEB No. 171 (1959).

Ethnography based on fieldwork done in 1952–1953 includes data on ceremonialism and songs. With eighteen translated myth texts, three story texts with interlinear and free translations, and three children's stories.

5423. ———, and W. K. Carter. "The Blind Man and the Loon: Barrow Eskimo Variants." *JAF,* 67 (1954), 65–72.

Texts of a myth common throughout Arctic groups exhibit distinctive traits among the Barrow Eskimo.

5424. Stefánsson, Vilhjálmur. *The Friendly Arctic. The Story of Five Years in Polar Regions.* New York: Macmillan, 1921.

Explorer's narrative (1913–1918) includes data on Eskimo "superstitions" and narratives which validate them.

5425. ———. "The Home Life of the Eskimo." *H,* 117 (1908), 721–30.

Description of domestic pursuits of Mackenzie River Eskimo includes data on singing. With a song text.

5426. ———. "My Quest in the Arctic." *H,* 126 (1912–1913), 3–13, 176–87, 348–59, 512–22, 671–84, 888–900.

Account of visits to various Arctic groups between 1906 and 1912 includes summaries of intergroup stereotypes and of shamanistic legends.

5427. ———. "Religious Beliefs of the Eskimo." *H,* 127 (1913), 869–78.

Survey of belief system of Mackenzie River Eskimo includes description of shamanistic healing ritual, funeral ceremonials, and other ritual practices.

5428. ———. "The Stefánsson-Anderson Arctic Expedition of the American Museum: Preliminary Ethnological Report." *APAMNH,* 14, Part 1 (1914), 3–395.

Ethnographic notes collected between 1908 and 1912 include data on religion and rituals.

5429. Stein, Robert. "Eskimo Music," in 130, pp. 337–56.

Discussion of singing style includes song texts (words and music).

5430. Stokes, Frank Wilbert. "An Arctic Studio." *Cent,* n. s. 30 (1896), 408–14.

Artist's description of living among the Eskimo includes song texts (words and music).

5431. Thornton, Harrison Robertson. *Among the Eskimos of Wales, Alaska, 1890–93.* Ed. Neda S. Thornton and William M. Thornton, Jr. Baltimore: Johns Hopkins Press, 1931.

Ethnocentric account by a schoolteacher in Alaska includes data on ceremonialism, "fabulous tales," and singing.

5432. "Traditions of the Greenland Esquimaux." *ChJ,* 16 (1861), 216–18, 236–38, 282–83, 317–20, 365–66.

Four translated legends and folktales collected by Henry Rink. With data on historical background.

5433. Turner, Gordon P. "The Breath of Arctic Men: The Eskimo North in Poetry from Within and Without." *QQ,* 83 (1976), 13–35.

Compares Eskimo poetry with poetry by other Canadians which deals with the Arctic.

5434. Turner, J. Henry, and H. M. W. Edmonds. "St. Michael Eskimo Myths and Tales." *APUAK,* 14, No. 1 (1968), 43–83.

Eighteen unannotated myth and folktale texts from BAE archives. Probably collected in 1890s.

5435. Turner, Lucien M. "Ethnology of the Ungava District, Hudson Bay Territory." *ARBAE,* 11 (1889–1890), 159–350.

Ethnography of Eskimo and Montagnais-Naskapi includes data on ceremonialism and storytelling. With narrative texts.

5436. Turquetil, Arsène. "Have the Eskimo the Concept of a Supreme Being?" *PM,* 9 (1936), 33–38.

Considers evidence for belief in a high god.

5437. ———. "The Religion of the Central Eskimo." *PM,* 2 (1929), 57–64.

Surveys supernaturalism, ceremonialism, and storytelling.

5438. Tyrrell, J. W. "Three Years Among the Eskimos." *CaM,* 3 (June 1894), 119–35; (July 1894), 223–36.

Culture survey includes data on ceremonialism and a legend summary.

5439. Vallee, F. G. *Kabloona and Eskimo in the Central Keewatin.* Ottawa: Department of Northern Affairs and National Resources, 1962.

Study of EA influence on Eskimo culture in 1959–1960 includes data on religion, shamanism, mythical concepts, and ceremonialism.

5440. Van Dommelen, David B. "Folklore of the Greenland Eskimos." *ASR,* 50 (1962), 49–52.

Comments on richness of verbal art and the history of its collection in Greenland. With two previously published narrative texts.

5441. Vanstone, James W. *Point Hope, An Eskimo Village in Transition.* Seattle: Univ. of Washington Press, 1962.

Ethnography based on fieldwork done in 1955–1956 includes description of Christian worship and hymnody. With data on importance of hunting songs in the traditional culture.

5442. Wardle, H. Newell. "The Sedna Cycle: A Study in Myth Evolution." *AA,* 2 (1900), 568–80.

Interpretation of an etiological myth collected by Franz Boas.

5443. Weyer, Edward Moffat, Jr. *The Eskimos. Their Environment and Folkways.* New Haven: Yale Univ. Press, 1932.

Culture survey includes data on ceremonialism and mythology.

5444. Whittaker, C. E. *Arctic Eskimo. A Record of Fifty Years' Experience & Observation Among the Eskimo.* London: Seeley, Service, ND.

Culture survey includes myth summaries, song and folktale texts (provided by Diamond Jenness), and descriptions of games.

5445. Whymper, Frederick. *Travel and Adventure in the Territory of Alaska, Formerly Russian America—Now Ceded to the United States—and in Various Other Parts of the North Pacific.* New York: Harper & Brothers, 1869.

Travel narrative includes a rewritten myth, descriptions of ceremonials, and a song text (music only).

5446. Wickersham, James. "The Eskimo Dance House." *AAOJ,* 24 (1902), 221–23.

Ceremonial description.

5447. Wiget, Andrew O. "Form as Process in Folktale Narration: The Relationship Between Deep and Surface Structures," in 136, pp. 83–101.

Uses twenty-nine texts of an Eskimo folktale to elucidate complex relationships between its formalistic properties and the cultural structures it reflects.

5448. Zibell, Akugluk Wilfried, ed. *Unipchaat 1. Animal Stories of the Kobuk River Eskimos.* Fairbanks, Alas.: Summer Institute of Linguistics, 1974.

Pamphlet contains texts and free translations of four folktales. No commentary or annotations.

5449. ———. *Unipchaat 2. Animal Stories of the Kobuk River Eskimos.* Fairbanks, Alas.: Summer Institute of Linguistics, 1974.

Pamphlet contains texts and free translations of four folktales. No commentary or annotations.

5450. ———. *Unipchaat 3. Animal Stories of the Kobuk River Eskimos.* Fairbanks, Alas.: Summer Institute of Linguistics, 1974.

Pamphlet contains texts and free translations of five folktales. No commentary or annotations.

See also 3, 29, 172, 197, 202, 240, 245, 283, 470, 568, 800, 851, 1230, 1239, 1819, 4117, 4184, 4484, 4486, 4507, 4508, 4572, 4579, 4584–4586, 4589, 4601, 4620, 4625, 4734, 4917, 5092, 5100, 5106, 5113, 5121.

INDEX OF SUBJECTS

NOTE: Entries marked with a (g) are designations for tribal groups.

Beothuk (g), 1215, 1224
Berdache, 1951, 3288, 5039
Bible, 226, 646, 1005, 1669
Bibliography and reference, 1–77, 196, 227, 235, 241,
    251, 609, 618, 619, 664, 754, 785, 839, 856, 861, 870,
    872, 900, 942, 1305, 1382, 1385, 1514, 1634, 1742,
    1765, 1849, 2018, 2034, 2075, 2570, 2672, 2676, 2695,
    2791, 3024, 4139, 4140, 4171, 4200, 4556, 4596, 4863,
    4983, 5092, 5104, 5270, 5345
Bidai (g), 1348
Big Hoop ceremony, 3217
Big House ceremony, 924, 932
Big Star chant, 3233
Biloxi (g), 1341–43
Birch, 1234, 1279, 1749, 1754, 1828
Bird (see also specific birds), 712, 1467, 1599, 1669,
    1670, 2678, 2814, 3425, 3606
Black Elk, 573, 2517, 2522, 2568, 2599, 2612, 2613,
    2632, 2641
Blackfoot (g), 436, 1984, 2027, 2077, 2078, 2135–2216,
    2514
Black Hawk, 1310, 1918
Blanketry, 2913, 2932, 3027, 3154
Blessingway (Navajo), 2923, 3205
Blowsnake, Sam, 1953, 1955, 1959, 1961, 1964
Bluejay, 4987, 4995
Boas, Franz, 38, 284, 4632, 4769, 4972, 5361, 5442
Body Image, 4774, 4782
Bogey, 3352, 3838, 3916
Boudinot, Elias, 1387
Brant, Joseph, 1150
Bread dance, 1927
Brown, Joseph Epes, 573
Buffalo, 1982, 2040, 2057, 2068, 2093, 2118, 2122, 2171,
    2218, 2958
Buffalo dance, 1652, 1654, 1656, 3631
Bungling Host (folktale character), 641
Bureau of American Ethnology, 189, 1115, 5434
Buried treasure, 1462, 2764, 2837
Butterfly, 3507, 3588

C

Cabeza de Vaca, Alvar Nunez, 2679
Caddo (g), 1344–49, 2045
Cadman, Charles Wakefield, 1873
Cahuilla (g), 4176, 4177, 4182, 4196–4210
Calendar, 2361
California (culture area), 172, 192, 609, 721, 2919, 3152,
    3422, 3899, 3998, 4115–84, 4600, 4986, 5117
Calumet (see also Pipe Dance), 372, 502, 887, 1027,
    1473
Camping, 1998, 2002
Canada, 466, 822, 827, 828, 848, 851, 895, 899, 901,
    907, 908, 955, 961, 995, 1080, 1081, 1718, 1747, 1787,
    1788, 1822, 1824, 1832, 1991, 2026, 2145, 2168, 2654,
    2655, 4483, 4501, 4505, 4506, 4528, 4548, 4584, 4592,
    4608, 4666, 4681, 4697, 4700, 4703, 4707, 4715, 4721,
    4722, 4755, 4768, 4771, 4780, 4794, 4797, 4827, 4830,
    4848–53, 4946, 4956, 4957, 4965, 5047, 5074, 5076,
    5079, 5088–90, 5092, 5099, 5100, 5102, 5103, 5106,
    5113, 5114, 5123, 5132, 5135, 5161, 5167, 5175, 5179,
    5181, 5182, 5211, 5214, 5216, 5260, 5265, 5266, 5306,
    5363, 5381, 5433

Cannibalism, 902, 1277, 1561, 1709, 1818, 1820, 1863,
    4134, 4598, 4736, 4775, 5119, 5123, 5158, 5190
Cantometrics, 765, 1649
Canyon de Chelly, 2981, 3055, 3520
Captivity narrative, 2022, 2268, 4793
Carrier (g), 5106, 5130–35
Casa Grande, 3284
Cass, Lewis, 941
Catalineno (g), 4173
Catawba (g), 1319, 1350–59
Catch–Word, 609, 618, 619
Catlin, George, 2394
Catloltq (g), 4830
Cayuga (see Iroquois)
Cedar, 333
Chant, 173, 179, 242, 275, 276, 278, 372, 453, 462, 700,
    702, 766, 977, 982, 988, 1547, 1751, 1911, 2008, 2256,
    2445, 2687, 2688, 2705, 2745, 2924, 2980, 3000, 3030,
    3079, 3082, 3099, 3120, 3121, 3141, 3184, 3200, 3317,
    3459, 3460, 3682, 3691, 3802, 3806, 3906, 4083, 4241,
    4601, 5370
Charm, 1356, 1405, 1410–12
Chehalis (g), 4821, 4829
Chemehuevi (g), 4211, 4212
Cherokee (g), 396, 1026, 1064, 1311, 1319, 1357,
    1360–1470, 1503, 4043
Chetco (g), 4402, 4403
Cheyenne (g), 499, 1984, 1994, 2015, 2045, 2217–65,
    2276, 2459
Chicago, 1908, 1912
Chickasaw (g), 1471–77
Chicken pull, 3338
Chicoltin (g), 4644
Chieftainship, 1898
Childbirth, 330, 2149, 2808, 2868, 3058, 3062, 3626,
    3681, 3689, 3741, 4187, 4903, 5065
Children and childhood, 382, 396, 667, 672, 1344, 1487,
    1540, 1777, 1817, 1820, 1835, 1881, 2085, 2194, 2269,
    2310, 2419, 2439, 2752, 2798, 2839, 2867, 2911, 3057,
    3329, 3487, 3488, 3634, 3740, 3743, 3838, 3907, 3916,
    3935, 4063, 4536, 4978, 5048, 5328, 5400, 5407, 5422
Chilkat (g), 4894, 4911, 4932, 4939
Chilula (g), 4250
Chimariko (g), 4213, 4423
Chinook (g), 3, 417, 4645–74
Chinook (language), 3, 4531, 4552, 4583, 4661, 4667
Chipewyan (g), 1853, 5103, 5136–46
Chipmunk, 565
Chippewa (see Ojibwa)
Chiricahua (see Apache)
Chitimacha (g), 662, 1298, 1478–1480, 1533
Choctaw (g), 758, 1298, 1310, 1364, 1481–1501
Choptunk (g), 860
Christianity, 168, 226, 304, 338, 400, 410, 422, 465, 471,
    499, 505, 646, 716, 788, 852, 861, 863, 887, 890, 994,
    995, 1019, 1050, 1094, 1159, 1163, 1180, 1191, 1282,
    1289, 1291, 1301, 1310, 1354, 1359, 1378, 1391, 1425,
    1444, 1463, 1470, 1482, 1635, 1636, 1664, 1672, 1790,
    1800, 1807, 1872, 1874, 1907, 1996, 2158, 2343, 2401,
    2542, 2576, 2577, 2605, 2626, 2656, 2719, 3020, 3135,
    3158, 3243, 3250, 3283, 3307, 3334, 3335, 3347, 3378,
    3397, 3602, 3711, 3742, 3750, 3782, 3818, 3908, 3936,
    3959–62, 3964, 3968, 3975, 3979, 4008, 4025, 4216,
    4282, 4444, 4460, 4552, 4579, 4778, 4824, 4836, 4949,
    4955, 5004, 5059, 5081, 5094, 5163, 5168, 5243, 5262,
    5264, 5268, 5275, 5361, 5390, 5441

Christmas, 2605, 2721, 3366, 3374, 3413, 3427, 3428, 3733, 3755, 3908, 4225, 4778
Chumash (g), 4214–24
Cibola, 2857, 3542
Cinderella, 4607
Clairvoyance, 2874
Clan origin myth, 443, 521, 1533, 1962, 1967, 2773, 3125, 3627, 4573, 4620, 4683, 4750, 4771, 4913
Classifications of folklore, 1, 70, 548, 555, 651, 664, 676, 685, 708, 738, 748, 1032, 2303, 2372, 2686, 3040, 3169, 3227, 3278, 3644, 3774, 4162, 4256, 4520, 4584, 4711, 4871, 5304, 5334
Clayoquot (g), 4529, 4789
Cliffdwellers, 3399, 3400
Cloud, 539
Clown, 309, 327, 351, 573, 702, 2056, 2571, 2593, 2822, 3346, 3397, 3647, 3649, 3883, 3936
Cochise, 2691
Cochiti (g), 3332, 3333, 3338, 3444–51
Cocopa (g), 2838–43, 3990
Color, 767, 2967, 3257, 3658, 3945, 4158, 4240
Colorado, 4076, 4081, 4082
Colville (g), 4861, 4874, 5003
Comanche (g), 2045, 2266–80, 2363, 2704, 4062
Communal composition, 783
Communitas, 3883
Comox (g), 4800
Comparative analysis, 211, 213, 227, 388, 500, 503, 557, 568, 570, 575, 581, 630, 634, 668–71, 731, 764, 765, 854, 1030, 1389, 1394, 1416, 1422, 1539, 1691, 1964, 2075, 2107, 2307, 2308, 2370, 2374, 2537, 2635, 2797, 2915, 2919, 2920, 2962, 2978, 2982, 3017, 3023, 3033, 3130, 3248, 3275, 3292, 3395, 3397, 3464, 3508, 3510, 3709, 3759, 3784, 3858, 4125, 4229, 4393, 4399, 4420, 4437, 4472, 4523, 4567, 4774, 4943, 5309, 5329, 5334, 5433
Componential analysis, 3682
Composition, 778, 783, 4126, 4783
Computer analysis, 568, 5272
Condolence, 971, 988, 1042, 2115
Configurationalism, 380, 2800, 2825
Conjuration, 1768, 1769, 2341, 2581, 4989
Connecticut, 834, 1220
Conservatism, 1131
Contraception, 2808
Contrary (see also Berdache), 573, 2056, 2593
Coos (g), 3, 519, 4668, 4675–4680
Copper, 1585
Corn, 329, 549, 594, 595, 876, 905, 965, 1069, 1092, 1109, 1168, 1169, 1465, 1506, 1672, 2074, 2117, 2220, 2671, 2737, 2848, 3281, 3321, 3452, 3618, 3720
Corn dance, 372, 3753, 3757–59, 3762, 3765, 3769
The Cornplanter, 999, 1126, 1140
Cornplanter, Jesse, 987
Coronado, Francisco, 2669
Cosmogony (see Creation myth),
Cosmology, 491, 538, 918, 1056, 1138, 1191, 1444, 1526, 1696, 1769, 2118, 2561, 2607, 2621, 2654, 2750, 2775, 2824, 3163, 3188, 3337, 3696, 4058, 4085, 4220, 4418, 4424, 4426, 4472, 4843, 5033, 5129, 5276, 5319, 5364, 5383, 5405
Costano (g), 4148, 4222
Coeur d'Alene (g), 4980, 4994, 4999-5001, 5049
Coup, 2013
Courtship, 1403, 1415, 1602, 2318, 2425, 2472, 3621, 4691

Couvade, 3681
Cowichan (g), 4852
Cowlitz (g), 4731, 4821, 4856, 4857
Coyote, 192, 215, 414, 504, 546, 604, 2024, 2119, 2151, 2267, 2286, 2685, 2697, 2731, 2763, 2815–17, 2864, 3017, 3049, 3053, 3169, 3170, 3198, 3251, 3607, 3730, 3770, 3958, 4039, 4051, 4133, 4318, 4405, 4469, 4515, 4659, 4680, 4731, 4865, 4883, 4985, 5003, 5006, 5031, 5053, 5058, 5065–67, 5075
Coyoteway (Navajo), 3068, 3197, 3233
Coyukon (g), 5147, 5148
Crater Lake, 4277
Crawfish, 2502
Crazy Horse, 2523
Creation myth, 180, 195, 442, 446, 534, 538, 570, 576, 608, 626, 637, 651, 676, 929, 948, 951, 1015, 1036, 1072, 1115, 1124, 1151, 1254, 1349, 1385, 1416, 1498, 1500, 1527, 1578, 1665, 1769, 1790, 1839, 1912, 2110, 2116, 2132, 2406, 2468, 2475, 2561, 2584, 2607, 2654, 2691, 2750, 2775, 2792, 2824, 2838, 2846, 2856, 2859, 2904, 2930, 2934, 2938, 2957, 2967, 2972, 2977, 2997, 3003, 3007, 3034, 3066, 3077, 3085, 3161, 3163, 3180, 3234, 3245, 3275, 3293, 3314, 3395, 3397, 3423, 3440, 3481, 3582, 3593, 3639, 3727, 3746, 3833, 3848, 3852, 3858, 3867, 3897, 3900, 3910, 3932, 3953, 3988, 3994, 4095, 4113, 4129, 4135, 4160, 4167, 4182, 4194, 4211, 4241, 4243, 4298, 4300, 4301, 4307, 4310, 4323, 4328, 4362, 4372, 4373, 4381, 4420, 4459, 4471, 4531, 4622, 4696, 4706, 4707, 4768, 4776, 4850, 4909, 4956, 4958, 5133, 5200, 5206, 5230
Cree (g), 1236, 2077, 2078, 2169, 5149–93
Creek (g), 1311, 1324, 1325, 1329, 1364, 1427, 1490, 1502–28
Creek confederacy, 1325, 1527
Crime, 4927
Crow (g), 2027, 2077, 2078, 2281–2320, 2370, 3271, 3595, 4041, 4070
Cultural evolution, 480, 485, 583, 587
Culture change (see also Acculturation), 1145, 1685, 1772, 1775, 1931, 2145, 2316, 2481, 2621, 2928, 3005, 3014, 3158, 3627, 3960, 4674, 4690, 4712, 4714, 4777, 4781, 5174, 5441
Cupeno (g), 4177, 4225, 4226
Curse, 2288, 2298
Curtin, Jeremiah, 1014
Curtis, Edward S., 198, 265
Curtis, Natalie, 756, 757
Cushing, Frank Hamilton, 61, 3850, 3851, 3864, 3880
Custer, George A., 1981, 2124, 2251, 2612

D

Dance, 182, 218, 266, 308, 310, 318, 350, 377, 396, 429, 610, 699, 712, 746, 759, 760, 784, 823, 827, 887, 907, 955, 979, 1002, 1027, 1048, 1081, 1082, 1086, 1097, 1102, 1168, 1169, 1180, 1227, 1243, 1286, 1293, 1300, 1315, 1323, 1354, 1386, 1388, 1390, 1393, 1396, 1422, 1452, 1477, 1487, 1506, 1517, 1520, 1522, 1537, 1540, 1542, 1544, 1574, 1618, 1652, 1654, 1656, 1674, 1683, 1700, 1719, 1723, 1789, 1814, 1867, 1885, 1896, 1980, 2004, 2031, 2093, 2094, 2134, 2181, 2224, 2255, 2271, 2290, 2313, 2357, 2372, 2373, 2427, 2482, 2516, 2585, 2595, 2675, 2690, 2702, 2703, 2708, 2728, 2739, 2759, 2782, 2787, 2807, 2828, 2983, 2988, 2992, 3096, 3109,

U

Umbilicus, 330
Underhill, Ruth, 757
Uniped, 2709
Upward Reaching Way (Navajo), 2991, 3003, 3224
Utah, 4007, 4028, 4071
Ute (g), 2078, 2797, 2961, 4004, 4057, 4071–95

V

Vagina Dentata, 600
Variation, 519, 1934, 2308, 3709, 4289, 4589
Victorio (Apache leader), 2764
Victory dance, 2807
Viking, 4379
Vikita ceremony (Papago), 3236, 3238, 3256
Virginia, 1315, 1318, 1459
Vision, 360, 459, 468, 871, 1007, 1017, 1074, 1094, 1723, 1785, 1973, 1978, 2317, 2494, 2496, 2564, 2612, 2632, 2737, 2993, 5027
Vision quest, 1973, 1978, 2305, 2317, 2504, 2584
Volcano, 3247

W

Waco (g), 2670
Wailaki (g), 4159, 4160, 4401, 4409
Walam Olum, 914, 917, 926, 934, 940, 1457
Walapai (g), 2681, 2710, 2767, 2845, 3953–58
Wallace, Paul A. W., 962
Walton, Eda Lou, 756, 757
Wampanoag (g), 1280–83
Wampum, 867, 1153, 1251, 4380
Wappo (g), 4159, 4160, 4414–17
Warfare, 255, 277, 945, 1093, 1698, 1864, 1867, 1869, 1880, 1884, 1975, 2009, 2011, 2013, 2017, 2124, 2140, 2180, 2219, 2462, 2469, 2518, 2746, 2803, 2807, 2885, 2943, 2983, 2992, 3013, 3033, 3124, 3270, 3275, 3339, 4086, 4463, 4474, 4752, 4803, 5297
Wasco (g), 4655, 4667a, 4671
Washington (state), 4511, 4551, 4587, 4594, 4619, 4804, 4816, 4820, 4822, 4835, 4873, 4881, 4990, 5077
Washington, George, 1102
Washo (g), 2276, 4096–4114
Water, 2310, 3637
Water cult, 489
Water monster, 431, 1255, 1688, 2310, 4423, 4908, 4992
Waterway (Navajo), 3002, 3175
Weather, 901, 1197, 1779, 4456
Weaving, 3022, 3138, 3141, 3154
Whale, 4805, 4816, 5285, 5349
Whirlwind, 2660
White dog feast (Iroquois), 976, 982, 991, 1012, 1045, 1130, 1156
Whitman, Marcus, 5012
Wichita (g), 813, 2664–70
Wikchami (g), 4445
Wind, 1412
Windigo, 902, 1277, 1818, 1820, 1863, 5119, 5123, 5158, 5190
Windway (Navajo), 2942, 3036, 3047, 3219, 3223
Winnebago (g), 368, 408, 1584, 1609, 1628, 1937–72, 2003, 3964
Winter, 1589, 1994, 3547, 3813, 3915

Winter count, 2515
Wintun (g), 4126, 4158, 4169, 4179, 4418–35
Wisconsin, 299, 1587, 1590, 1592, 1786, 1833, 1834, 1909
Wish fulfillment, 1119
Wishosk (g), 4437
Wishram (g), 4169, 4670, 4671
Witchcraft, 877, 884, 888, 928, 974, 1136, 1137, 1269, 1270, 1444, 1639, 1702, 2730, 2747, 2799, 2888, 3042, 3109, 3140, 3322, 3395, 3674, 3781, 3800, 3905, 3949, 3950, 4178, 4965, 5176
Wiyot (g), 4149, 4436–40
Wolf, 3103, 4786, 4799
Women, 475, 517, 701, 880, 1083, 1085, 1094, 1152, 1650, 1778, 1804, 1929, 2006, 2095, 2167, 2252, 2273, 2287, 2329, 2332, 2524, 2744, 2748, 2756, 2761, 2762, 2793, 2796, 2830, 2831, 2835, 2836, 2850, 2891, 2962, 3031, 3043, 3129, 3221, 3297, 3605, 3645, 3827, 3914, 3970, 4172, 4311a, 4371, 4427, 4433, 4796, 4942, 5039, 5281, 5292, 5418
Woodworking, 1623
Wool, 3138
Word play, 1490, 1971, 2001, 2277
Work ethic, 4195
World view, 863, 890, 1766, 2290, 2358, 2546, 2631, 2632, 2777, 3046, 3067, 3135, 3167, 3200, 3357, 3361, 3383, 3384, 3835, 4137, 4248, 4363, 4431, 4471, 4659, 4774, 4912, 5002, 5199
World War I, 239
World War II, 1867, 2894
Wounded Knee, 272, 2045, 2602, 2639
Wovoka, 4002, 4029, 4038
WPA, 2048, 2449, 2610, 2611, 2622, 3258, 4982
Wuwuchim (Hopi), 3635, 3660
Wyandot (see also Huron), 946–48, 1284–91, 2458
Wynoochee (g), 4821
Wyoming, 4053, 4981, 4992

Y

Yakima (g), 3366, 4485, 4529, 4832, 4976–78
Yamasee (g), 1397
Yana (g), 4377, 4420, 4441–43
Yankton (see Sioux)
Yaqui (g), 3397, 3959–81, 3990
Yavapai (g), 2681, 3954, 3982–86, 3995
Yebatchai (Navajo), 2935, 3035, 3038, 3187
Yellowstone, 4984, 4997
Yokuts (g), 4148, 4169, 4444–59
Yosemite, 4013, 4339, 4353, 4354
Ysleta (g), 3812, 3815
Yuchi (g), 1311, 1523, 1576–80
Yuki (g), 4149, 4159, 4160, 4169, 4460–64
Yukon, 5093, 5094, 5098, 5101, 5108, 5120, 5204, 5263
Yuma (g), 2681, 2720, 2758, 3333, 3987–97
Yurok (g), 2874, 2875, 4149, 4158, 4169, 4465–80
Yuwipi (Sioux), 2553, 2563, 2580, 2581, 2586, 2587

Z

Zuni (g), 61, 202, 327, 340, 406, 2688, 2689, 2691, 2742, 2894, 2934, 3275, 3332, 3352, 3383, 3388, 3435, 3542, 3574, 3593, 3630, 3637, 3683, 3848–3952

INDEX OF AUTHORS, EDITORS AND TRANSLATORS

234 *Native American Folklore, 1879–1979*

Corser, H. P., 4517
Coston, Ruth C., 3474
Count, Earl W., 570
Courlander, Harold, 3475, 3476, 3846
Cowan, John L., 2690, 3318
Coze, Paul, 3319, 5160
Cozzens, Samuel Woodworth, 2691
Craig, Charles A., 4034
Craig, Leo, 3477
Crane, Edward, 703
Crane, Leo, 3320, 3478, 3479
Cranston, J. Herbert, 949
Crantz, David, 5275
Crapanzano, Vincent, 2931
Crawford, Isabel, 2343
Crawford, James M., 2839
Crawford, Roselle Williams, 2692
Cremony, John C., 2760
Cresswell, J. R., 5161
Critcher, Marge, 2455
Cronyn, George W., 236
Crosby, Thomas, 4836
Crow Dog, Leonard, 2007
Crow-Wing, 3636
Crowe, Keith J., 5100
Crowell, Samuel, 1012
Crumrine, Lynne S., 3963
Crumrine, N. Ross, 98, 4754
Cuero, Delfina, 4238
Culbertson, Anne Virginia, 1376
Culbertson, Thaddeus A., 1992
Culin, Stewart, 281, 282
Cummin, Hazel E., 2932
Cumming, John R., 5276
Cummings, Byron, 2682, 2761, 2762, 2933–35, 3194
Cummings, Emma, 2936
Cunningham, Caroline, 197
Curletti, Rosario, 4221
Current-Garcia, Eugene, 1515
Currier, Charles Warren, 405
Curtin, Jeremiah, 1013, 1014, 4185, 4355, 4420, 4671
Curtin, L. S. M., 3321, 3322, 3445
Curtis, Edward S., 172, 198, 2693, 2694, 3323, 4837
Curtis, Martha E., 1680, 1681
Curtis, Natalie, 173, 237, 406, 704, 705, 3324, 3480, 3731, 3802, 3988, 4518
Curtis, William E., 3864
Cushing, Frank Hamilton, 2844, 3481, 3482, 3865–72, 3880, 3923
Cushman, H. B., 407
Cusick, David, 1015
Custer, Augusta H., 3873

D

Daggett, Pierre M., 1297
Daklugie, Asa, 2763
Dall, William Healey, 283
Dam, Cornelia, 408
Damas, David, 5277

Dangberg, Grace, 4098, 4099
Dangel, R., 4125
Danker, Kathleen, 1940
Danziger, Edmund Jefferson, Jr., 1746
Darlington, William M., 1016
Darnell, Regna, 99, 284, 5162
D'Artaguette, Diron, 1876
Dauenhauer, Richard, 4900
Daughtery, Richard D., 4975
Davidson, D. S., 899, 1276
Davidson, John F., 1747
Davidson, Levette J., 12, 199
Davis, Edward H., 3238, 4227, 4293
Davis, George T. B., 4955
Davis, H. L., 285
Davis, Irvine, 3750
Davis, John B., 1377
Davis, Lawrence M., 3484
Davis, Robert Tyler, 4519
Davis, Rose M., 833
Davis, Stephen A., 138
Davis, Theodore R., 1993, 1994
Dawson, George M., 4692, 4755, 5041, 5079
Dawson, Principal, 571
Day, A. Grove, 238, 706
Day, Donald, 91, 92
Day, Gordon M., 409, 881
d'Azevedo, Warren L., 100, 4111
Deane, Reubena, 3989
de Angulo, Jaime, 4188, 4190–93, 4260, 4340, 4341, 4372–74, 4724
Deans, James, 4520–27, 4693–4704, 4901, 4956, 4957
de Anza, Juan Bautista, 3997
Deardorff, Merle H., 1017
de Baillou, Clemens, 1378
de Beauchamps, 1494
De Brebeuf, Jean, 950
de Courcy, Geraldine, 1510
Deetz, James J. F., 148
De Forest, John W., 834
Dégh, Linda, 101
De Huff, Elizabeth Willis, 2938, 3325–31, 3485, 3767, 3776–81, 3803, 3804
de Johly, Hastéen, 2939
de Laguna, Frederica, 4902–04, 5101, 5249
Deland, Charles E., 2390, 2456
de Lemos, Pedro, 3874
Dellenbaugh, F. S., 3486
Deloria, Ella Clara, 2528–31
Deloria, P. J., 2615
Deloria, Vine, Jr., 181, 410, 411, 806
De Mallie, Raymond J., 2532
Demetracopoulou, Dorothy, 4126, 4421, 4422, 4425
De Milford, Louis Le Clerc, 1510
Dempsey, Hugh A., 5211
Denig, Edwin Thompson, 2125, 2281
Dennis, Wayne, 3487, 3488
Dennison, Gene, 3199
Denny, Melcena Burns, 4469

Densmore, Frances, 13, 239, 412, 707–35, 1298, 1332, 1478, 1489, 1539, 1540, 1682, 1748–53, 1941, 2225, 2226, 2391, 2403, 2457, 2533–37, 3239, 3240, 3332, 3333, 3754, 3964, 3990, 4073, 4313, 4314, 4528, 4529, 4782–84
Desbarats, Peter, 1226
de Smet, Pierre Jean, 1988, 1995, 1996
Devereux, George, 2860–71
De Voe, Carrie, 2458
Dewdney, Selwyn, 1754, 1815
Dewey, Edward H., 836
Dewhirst, John, 4838
de Zavala, Adina, 1556
Dial, Adolph L., 413
Diamond, Stanley, 102
Dickason, Olive Patricia, 4530
Dickerson, Philip J., 1868
Dillingham, Peter, 14
Dimock, A. W., 2940
Dixon, Roland B., 3, 286, 514, 572, 1598, 4127, 4185–87, 4213, 4315–19, 4327, 4394–95, 4423, 4905
Dobie, J. Frank, 103–11, 414, 2695, 2764
Dobkins de Rios, Marlene, 736
Dobyns, Henry F., 2845, 3953
Dockstader, Alice W., 16
Dockstader, Frederick J., 15, 16, 470, 3489, 3490, 4906
Dodge, Ernest S., 1018, 1147
Dodge, Richard Irving, 1997
Dolores, Juan, 3257
Donaldson, Thomas, 3491
Donohoe, Thomas, 1019
Dooling, D. M., 573
Dorman, Rushton M., 415
Dorn, Edward, 4045
Dorris, Michael, 416
Dorsey, George A., 1344, 1345, 1869, 1870, 2083, 2084, 2112, 2113, 2227, 2228, 2459–68, 2500, 2538, 2664–68, 2696, 3492–94, 4958
Dorsey, J. Owen, 17, 200, 417, 807, 1341, 1342, 1864, 1871, 1913, 1942, 1998–2003, 2334–36, 2404–15, 2451, 2501–03, 2525, 2539–41, 2623, 4531
Dorson, Richard M., 418, 1755
Dory, William, 2941
Dougan, Marcia, 4215, 4294
Dougan, Rose, 3805
Dougherty, John, 3755
Douglas, Mary, 574
Dovington, L. A., 4038
Downey, Robert Angus, 18
Downing, Orlando Cuadra, 2697
Downs, James F., 4100
Dozier, Edward P., 3334–35, 3495–97, 3806–08
Drake, Benjamin, 1921

Holthoff, Cyd McMullen, 4051
Holtved, Erik, 5309, 5385
Holtz, R. D., 2707
Holy Dance, Robert, 2569
Honigmann, John J., 1230, 3023, 5166, 5167, 5199, 5200, 5213, 5219, 5310, 5311
Hooke, Hilda Mary, 848
Hooper, Lucile, 4199
Hoover, Herbert T., 1479, 2570
Horn, Patrice, 5312
Hosley, Edward H., 5313
Hough, Walter, 1065, 3572–74
Houghton, Frederick, 1066
Houghton, Louise Seymour, 1607
Howard, Helen Addison, 756, 757, 1068, 5056
Howard, James H., 300, 922, 1069, 1397, 1398, 1784, 1903, 2019–21, 2122, 2123, 2440, 2505, 2571–75, 2581
Howe, M. A. DeWolfe, 2576, 2577
Howland, Llewellyn, 1280
Hrdlička, Aleš, 2781, 3289, 3736, 5314–16
Hubbard, J. Niles, 1070
Hudson, Arthur Palmer, 201
Hudson, Charles, 1307, 1351, 1399
Hudson, John W., 4349, 4380
Hudson, Roy F., 4204
Hudson, Travis, 4219–21
Hudson, Wilson M., 93, 94
Huebener, G., 3759
Huff, Patti, 2455
Huggins, Captain E. L., 2578
Hughes, Charles Campbell, 5317, 5318
Hughes, J. C., 4575
Hughes, J. Donald, 2849
Hughes, Jane M., 5318
Huguenin, Charles A., 1071
Hultkrantz, Åke, 301, 445, 446, 597, 598, 1608, 2086, 4052–56, 4984, 5198
Hume, Christopher, 1785
Humfreville, J. Lee, 2579
Humphrey, Norman B., 255
Humphrey, Seth K., 256
Hungry Wolf, Adolf, 206, 3575
Hunt, George, 4739, 4763, 4764
Hunt, Irvin, 3366
Hunter, Charles E., 923
Hunter, J. Marvin, 2272
Hunter, John D., 2022
Huntington, Mary, 2441
Hurdy, John Major, 302
Hurt, Wesley R., 2023, 2580, 2581
Hutchinson, Ellen, 5319
Hyde, George E., 2074, 2479, 2582
Hymes, Dell, 127, 128, 4651–56, 4765, 4883

I

Ibish, Yusuf, 391

Ickes, Anna Wilmarth, 2708
Iliff, Flora Gregg, 3955
Ingenthron, Elmo, 1875
Ingersoll, Ernest, 4576
Ingstad, Helge, 5321
Inshtatheamba, 2510
Insley, Bernice, 208
Inverarity, Robert Bruce, 4577
Iron Teeth, 2250
Irvin, Terry T., 4578
Irvine, Albert, 4787
Irvine, Mrs. Alicia, 1400
Irving, John T., Jr., 2480
Ish-Ti-Opi, 758
Iverson, Peter, 3024
Ives, Edward D., 1176
Ives, Ronald L., 2709, 3247, 3248, 4076

J

J., 849
Jablow, Alta, 599
Jack, Edward, 1177
Jackson, Bruce, 600
Jackson, Donald, 1918
Jackson, Helen Hunt, 258
Jackson, Sheldon, 4579
Jacobi, Frederick, 3368
Jacobs, Elizabeth Derr, 4402, 4403, 4892
Jacobs, Melville, 38, 4580–83, 4657–65, 4677, 4678, 4724a–28, 4730–31, 4856, 4857, 4892
Jacobson, Claire, 455
Jacobson, Doranne, 3025
Jaeger, Ellsworth, 303
Jahner, Elaine, 2584
Jahoda, Gloria, 1309
James, Ahlee, 3825, 3826
James, E. O., 447, 601
James, George Wharton, 448, 2710, 3026, 3027, 3576–78, 3886, 4107, 4200, 4299–4300
James, Harry C., 3579, 3580
James, John, 1310
Jamieson, S. M., 4570
Janson, Donald, 2846
Jares, Edward E., 2711
Jarrell, Myrtis, 2017
Jarvis, Samuel Farmer, 304
Jeancon, Jean Allard, 3784
Jenkins, Linda Walsh, 305
Jenkins, William H., 1278
Jenks, Albert Ernest, 602, 1610, 1786
Jenness, Diamond, 449, 1787, 4584, 5106, 5130–32, 5140, 5214, 5216, 5322–28, 5413, 5444
Jensen, Joan M., 4236
Jensen, Marguerite, 3967
Jernigan, E. W., 2746
Jesser, Clinton J., 2598
Jett, Stephen C., 2712
Jette, Julius, 5107–11
Jewitt, John R., 4793

Jiskogo, 850
Jochelson, Waldemar, 5329
Joe, Eugene Baatsoslanii, 3028
Johnson, Barbara, 3249, 3968
Johnson, E. Pauline, 4666
Johnson, Elias, 1072
Johnson, Elizabeth Bishop, 209
Johnson, F. Roy, 1401, 1568
Johnson, Frederick, 1198, 1788
Johnson, Ludwell H., III, 603
Johnson, Mary Elizabeth, 4142
Johnson, Pauline, 1073
Johnson, W. Fletcher, 2585
Johnston, Basil, 1789
Johnston, Bernice Eastman, 4244
Johnston, Thomas F., 4585, 4917, 4918, 5112, 5231, 5330–37
Jonaitis, Aldona, 4919
Jones, David E., 2273
Jones, Elma, 1569
Jones, Hester, 3581, 3887, 3888
Jones, Hettie, 2024
Jones, J. A., 4077
Jones, J. Robert, 3720
Jones, James Athearn, 210
Jones, Livingston F., 4920
Jones, Louis Thomas, 211, 306, 811, 812
Jones, Peter [Kahkewaquonaby], 1790
Jones, Strachan, 5103
Jones, William, 3, 1611, 1642–46, 1673, 1791, 1792
Jorgensen, Joseph G., 4057
Joseph, Alice, 3250, 3668, 3669
Josephy, Alvin M., Jr., 3582, 5057
Josselin de Jong, Jan P., 2163
Judd, Mary Catharine, 212
Judd, Neil M., 3889
Judkins, Russell A., 1074
Judson, Katharine Berry, 851, 1612, 2025, 4143, 4586, 4587
Jung, C. G., 1964

K

Kaczkurkin, Mini Valenzuela, 3969
Kahlenberg, Mary Hunt, 2913
Kahnweiler, W. S., 4818
Kaiper, Dan, 4921
Kaiper, Nan, 4921
Kallmann, Helmut, 39
Kalm, Peter, 827, 859
Kane, Elisha Kent, 5339
Kane, Grace Franks, 1613
Kane, Henry, 2782
Kantner, Jo Ann, 4015
Kaplan, Bert, 3890
Karam, A. H., 3029
Kaschube, Dorothea V., 2284
Katz, Fred, 736
Katz, Jane B., 178
Kaufmann, Carole N., 4708
Kaut, Charles, 2776, 2783, 2784
Kaywaykla, James, 2743
Keech, Roy A., 3721, 3722, 3769

Oaks, Orville A., 332, 333
Ober, Sarah Endicott, 4603
Oberg, Kalervo, 4927, 4928
O'Brien, Lynne Woods, 2052a
O'Bryan, Aileen, 3120
O'Donnell, James H., III, 1105
Oglesby, Catharine, 3121
Oinas, Felix J., 101
O'Kane, Walter Collins, 3623, 3624
Olbrechts, Frans M., 1407, 1438, 1441
Olden, Sarah Emilia, 2615, 4267
O'Leary, Timothy J., 49
Oleodoska, 1114
Oliver, Marion L., 3625
Olofson, Harold, 4025
Olson, Paul A., 2446, 2455, 2557
Olson, Ronald L., 4604, 4640, 4770, 4771, 4819, 4929
O'Neale, Lila M., 3257
O'Neil, Michael R., 4475
Ookpik, 5382
Opler, Marvin K., 4081–85
Opler, Morris Edward, 53, 80, 1562, 2381, 2779, 2794–2826
Opsahl, Josephine, 4277
Orcutt, Samuel, 903
Orrick, Allan H., 146
Ortiz, Alfonso, 147, 477, 3383–84, 3833–35
Ortiz, Simon J., 781
Ortiz y Silva, Marga, 3385
Ósanai, Iva, 3230
Osborn, G., 1790
Osgood, Cornelius, 5206, 5232, 5383, 5384
Ostermann, H., 5385–88
Oswalt, Robert L., 4387
Oswalt, Wendell H., 5389–92
Ottaway, Harold N., 2253
Overholt, Mary Elisabeth, 3122
Overholt, Thomas W., 2053
Owen, Mary Alice, 1665, 1666
Owen, Narcissa, 1443
Owen, Roger C., 148
Owens, John G., 3548, 3552, 3626, 3902

P

Pach, Walter, 3386
Packard, R. L., 5061
Packeneau, Joseph, 2396
Page, James K., Jr., 3627
Paige, Darcy, 2616
Paige, Harry W., 2617, 2618
Painter, Muriel Thayer, 3975
Palmer, Rose A., 633
Palmer, William R., 4026, 4027
Paloheimo, Leonora Curtin, 3387
Pancoast, Chalmers Lowell, 3744
Pandey, Triloki Nath, 3903
Paredes, Americo, 149
Paredes, J. Anthony, 1518, 1818
Pargellis, Stanley, 1318
Park, Hugh, 1444

Park, Willard Z., 4005, 4040, 4040a
Parker, Arthur C., 182, 1009, 1106–13
Parker, Donald Dean, 2619
Parker, Everett, 1114
Parker, Seymour, 1819, 1820, 1973, 4772
Parker, William Thornton, 478, 1821
Parkhill, Forbes, 4086
Parmentier, Richard J., 3383
Parsons, Elsie Clews, 1204, 1205, 1347, 2365, 2723, 3123–25, 3292, 3342, 3388–97, 3446, 3481, 3482, 3568, 3628–37, 3656, 3709, 3713–15, 3724, 3738–40, 3745, 3748, 3751, 3788, 3789, 3836–39, 3904–22, 5118
Partridge, Emelyn Newcomb, 1206
Patencio, Chief Francisco, 4204, 4205
Patterson, John B., 1918
Paul, William, 4601
Payne, John Howard, 1445
Peale, Arthur L., 1218
Pearce, T. M., 2724
Pearson, Charles, 3638
Peck, Rev. E. J., 5253, 5393
Pedro, Joe A., 3398
Peek, Walter W., 183
Peet, Stephen D., 334, 480, 481, 483–89, 634–39, 1952, 2725, 3399, 3400, 3639
Peithmann, Irvin M., 1553, 1619
Pendergast, David M., 4028
Peniska, Edna, 2557
Pepper, George H., 2325, 3126
Perry, Samuel D., 1446
Petersen, Karen Daniels, 2224, 2254, 2255
Peterson, Bonnie J., 4352
Peterson, Frederick A., 1676
Peterson, George W., 1115
Petrullo, Vincenzo, 927
Petter, Rodolphe, 2256
Pettitt, George A., 640, 4811
Phillips, Alice, 4278, 4279
Phillips, W. S., 4605
Phinney, Archie, 5062
Phister, Nat P., 4029
Pichette, Pierre, 4985
Piddocke, Stuart, 4773
Pidgeon, William, 2620
Pierce, Joe B., 1620
Pierce, Harry Willard, 4166
Pierson, Mrs. Delavan L., 336
Pietroforte, Alfred, 4455
Pinkley, Edna Townsley, 3259
Pinkley-Call, Cora, 1890
Piomingo [John Robinson], 1519
Pitchlynn, Peter, 1496
Pitseolak, Peter, 5394
Podolsky, Edward, 782
Poirier, Genevieve Y., 4015
Pokagan, Simon, 1907, 1908
Pope, Polly, 641
Porter, C. Fayne, 252
Porter, Frank W., III, 860

Porter, Kenneth W., 1343
Posinsky, S. H., 4476
Postal, Susan Koessler, 568, 4774
Poteet, Chrystabel Berrong, 2257
Potts, William John, 1116, 2132, 4167
Pound, Louise, 783, 2054, 2055
Powell, John Wesley, 54, 490, 491, 642–44, 3871, 4001, 4087
Powell, Peter J., 2258, 2259
Powers, Louise K., 784, 785
Powers, Stephen, 4168–70
Powers, William K., 2621
Pradt, George H., 3401
Prescott, Philander, 2619
Preston, Richard J., 5174
Preston, W. D., 1117, 1118, 4727
Price, John A., 55, 4112
Prince, J. Dyneley, 928, 1207, 1218, 1248–52, 1257, 1258, 1267, 1268
Prithipaul, K. Dad, 166
Proctor, Edna Dean, 3923
Prucha, Francis Paul, 56
Pruitt, O. J., 1621
Pryde, Duncan, 5396
Purley, Anthony F., 3404
Putnam, G. R., 3996

Q

Qoyawayma, Polingaysi, 3640
Quaife, Milo Milton, 2386, 4649
Quam, Alvina, 3952
Quimby, George Irving, 1622, 5397

R

Rachlin, Carol K., 217, 464, 2037, 2038
Raczka, Paul, 2194
Radin, Paul, 337, 492, 493, 645, 1822–25, 1946, 1953–67, 4416, 4417
Raglan, Lord, 4030
Rain-in-the-Face, 1981
Ramsey, Jarold, 494, 646, 4606, 4667a, 4668, 4986, 5063
Rand, Silas, 1208–14
Randall, Betty Uchitelle, 4607
Randle, Martha Champion, 1119, 1120, 4060
Rands, Robert L., 1521
Ransom, Harry H., 109–11
Ransom, Jay Ellis, 5398–5400
Rasmussen, Knud, 5245, 5385–88, 5401–03
Ravenhill, Alice, 4608
Ray, Dorothy Jean, 5404, 5405
Ray, P. H., 5406
Ray, Verne F., 150, 2056, 4171, 4363, 4669, 4864, 4865, 4987–90
Rayfield, J. R., 647
Read, William E., 4325
Reade, John, 495, 786, 891
Reagan, Albert B., 1825–31, 2726, 2827, 3127, 3128, 3405, 3641,

Voblov, I. K., 5317
Voegelin, C. F., 675, 936, 940, 1118, 1929–34, 2322, 3681, 3682, 4410, 4411
Voegelin, Erminie W., 74, 75, 676, 937, 940, 1925, 1931, 1932, 1935, 2370, 4179, 4399, 4412, 4413
Vogel, Virgil J., 187, 356, 677
Voget, Fred, 1158, 1458, 2316, 4069–70
Vogt, Evon, 2894, 3742
Volkman, Toby Alice, 5369
Volney, C. F., 678
Von Berckefeldt, Susan, 3683
Von Schmidt-Pauli, Edgar, 357
Von Wrangell, Ferdinand Petrovich, 4625
Vorse, Mary Heaton, 3791
Voth, H. R., 2105, 3493–94, 3684–95
Voudrach, Paul, 5146

W

Waddell, William, 821
Wade, Edwin L., 3696, 4626, 4879
Wade, Forrest C., 1462
Wade, Lorraine Laurel, 4626
Wade, M. S., 4674
Wagner, Günter, 1578, 1579
Wagner, Roland M., 3179
Wake, C. Staniland, 526, 679, 911, 938, 2070–73, 2106, 2107, 3180
Waldron, Marion, 3428
Waldron, Webb, 3428
Walker, Deward E., Jr., 4627, 5067, 5071, 5072
Walker, Edwin F., 4180
Walker, F. R., 2653
Walker, J. R., 2607
Walker, Louise J., 1635, 1636, 1857–59
Walker, Robert Sparks, 1463
Walkup, Lucy, 2856
Wallace, Anthony F. C., 165, 939, 1159–62, 1570, 1571
Wallace, Ben J., 1677
Wallace, Ernest, 2280
Wallace, Paul A. W., 874, 1164, 1165
Wallace, William J., 2890, 4137, 4181, 4255–57, 4388
Walle, Alf H., 1972
Wallis, Ruth Sawtell, 1185, 1217
Wallis, Wilson D., 1185, 1217, 2078, 2654, 2655, 3697, 4939
Wallrich, William Jones, 2738
Walsh, Patrick, 3181
Walter, Paul A., 3429
Walters, Harry, 3032
Walters, L. V. W., 4817
Walton, Eda Lou, 797, 2208, 3182–85
Wapp, Ed, Jr., 305
Wardle, H. Newell, 5442
Warner, Louis H., 2739
Warren, David, 247

Warren, John C., 1266
Warren, William W., 1860, 1861
Washburn, Cephas, 1444
Washburn, Wilcomb E., 23, 263
Washington, George, 1102
Wassell, William H., 2656
Wasson, Will, 4680
Waterman, Thomas T., 131, 680, 797, 4182, 4240, 4241, 4480, 4628–30, 4805, 4880
Waters, Frank, 2080, 3186, 3187, 3698, 3699
Watkins, Don, 5078
Watkins, Frances E., 3188, 4723
Watkins, John A., 1501
Watson, Edith L., 2740
Watson, Lawrence W., 1186
Watt, Ellen, 2209
Wattles, Ruth Jocelyn, 3189
Waugh, Earle H., 166
Waugh, F. W., 1166
Wead, Charles K., 798
Webb, George, 3298
Webber, Alika, 1279
Webber, W. L., 4631
Webster, Helen L., 1213
Webster, Hutton, 358
Weeks, Thelma E., 4978
Weer, Paul, 940
Weightman, Doreen, 613, 614, 615
Weightman, John, 613, 614, 615
Weisel, George P., 5014
Weiser, Conrad, 1001
Weist, Katherine M., 2264
Weitlaner, R. J., 1167
Wells, William, 1717, 4896, 5247
Welsch, Roger L., 2449, 2450
Weltfish, Gene, 2493–96, 4183
Wengerd, Stephanie K., 3945
Weslager, C. A., 875, 941–43, 1275
Westez, Carlos, 897
Wetherill, Betty, 3946
Wetherill, Hilda Faunce, 3190, 3191
Wetherill, Louisa Wade, 2974, 3192, 3193, 3211
Wetherill, Lulu Wade, 2682, 3194
Wetherill, Mrs. Richard, 2937
Wey, Auguste, 4245
Weyer, Edward Moffat, Jr., 5443
Wharton, Clarence, 2371
Wheeler, Olin D., 1862
Wheeler-Jones, C. G., 3700
Wheelwright, Mary C., 2910, 2939, 3003, 3034–37, 3195–98, 3233
Wherry, Joseph H., 4184
Whipple, M. A., 124
Whitaker, Kathleen, 2835, 2836, 3947
White, Elizabeth C., 3640
White, Felix, Sr., 1940
White, Leslie A., 2046, 3430–31, 3441–43, 3675, 3749, 3752, 3766, 3771
White, Raymond C., 4306, 4307, 4308

Whiteford, Andrew Hunter, 1637
Whitehead, Alfred North, 3106
Whiteman, A. L., 2837
Whiting, Alfred F., 3701–03
Whitman, William, 2453, 2454, 2508, 3845
Whittaker, C. E., 5444
Whittlesey, Charles, 1863
Whorf, Benjamin Lee, 3666
Whymper, Frederick, 5445
Wickersham, James, 4881, 5446
Wielich, L., 758
Wiget, Andrew O., 5447
Wilburn, Hiram C., 1464
Wilder, Carleton Stafford, 3981
Wildschut, William, 2108, 2210, 2312, 2317–20
Wilkes, Florence E., 1168
Wilkinson, Mentz, 5191
Will, George F., 2074, 2328, 2398–2400
Williams, Alfred M., 1891
Williams, Emma, 4940
Williams, Frank, 4940
Williams, Jack R., 2741
Williams, Mentor L., 229
Williams, Texa Bowen, 4370
Williamson, Robert G., 5223, 5224
Willoughby, Charles C., 359, 4820
Willoya, William, 360
Wilson, Alan, 3199
Wilson, Charles B., Jr., 1169
Wilson, Daniel, 527, 528, 961
Wilson, E. F., 4974
Wilson, Eddie W., 361, 529–34, 2742
Wilson, Edmund, 1170, 3948
Wilson, Gilbert Livingstone, 2325, 2329–32
Wilson, R. N., 2211, 2212, 2213
Wilson, Thomas, 2657
Wingert, Paul S., 4882, 4961
Winship, George, 1223
Winslow, Charles S., 1912
Winter, Werner, 3957, 3958
Wissler, Clark, 362, 363, 535, 681, 2075–78, 2214–16, 2497, 2498, 2658–60
Witherspoon, Gary, 3200, 3201
Witt, Shirley Hill, 188
Wittfogel, Karl A., 3432
Witthoft, John, 659, 682, 876, 945, 1171, 1465–68
Wolf, Carolyn E., 76
Wolfart, H. Christoph, 5192
Wolff, Gerald W., 1893, 2388, 2499
Wolff, Hans, 1580
Wood, Charles Erskine Scott, 230
Wood, Edward Hubert, 3273
Wood, Nancy, 3792, 3793
Wood, W. Raymond, 2265
Woodruff, Charles E., 4258
Woodruff, Janette, 3271
Woods, Emma Edith, 1631
Woodward, Arthur, 3299, 3950
Woodward, Grace Steele, 1469